Con ...ny, 1–2030AD

Uni

Sub

h

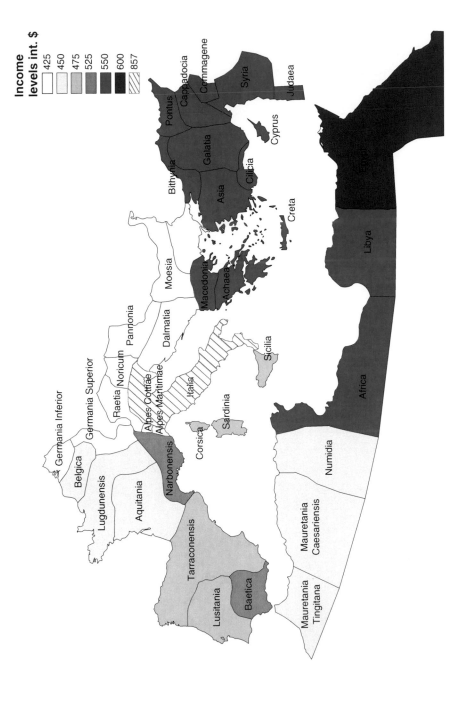

PER CAPITA INCOME IN THE PROVINCES OF THE ROMAN EMPIRE IN 14AD

**Income
levels int. $**

425
450
475
525
550
600
857

Contours of the World Economy, 1–2030AD

Essays in Macro-Economic History

Angus Maddison

OXFORD

UNIVERSITY PRESS

OXFORD

UNIVERSITY PRESS

Great Clarendon Street, Oxford ox2 6DP

Oxford University Press is a department of the University of Oxford.
It furthers the University's objective of excellence in research, scholarship,
and education by publishing worldwide in

Oxford New York

Auckland Cape Town Dar es Salaam Hong Kong Karachi
Kuala Lumpur Madrid Melbourne Mexico City Nairobi
New Delhi Shanghai Taipei Toronto

With offices in

Argentina Austria Brazil Chile Czech Republic France Greece
Guatemala Hungary Italy Japan Poland Portugal Singapore
South Korea Switzerland Thailand Turkey Ukraine Vietnam

Oxford is a registered trade mark of Oxford University Press
in the UK and in certain other countries

Published in the United States
by Oxford University Press Inc., New York

British Library Cataloguing in Publication Data
Data available

Library of Congress Cataloging in Publication Data
Data available

Typeset by SPI Publisher Services, Pondicherry, India
Printed in Great Britain
on acid-free paper by
Biddles Ltd., King's Lynn, Norfolk

ISBN 978–0–19–922721–1
ISBN 978–0–19–922720–4 (Pbk.)

10 9 8 7 6 5 4 3 2 1

☐ CONTENTS

☐ LIST OF FIGURES

☐ LIST OF TABLES

▢ LIST OF BOXES

⬜ ACKNOWLEDGEMENTS

I am grateful for comments on earlier drafts by Fatih Birol, Derek Blades, Alan Bowman, Henk-Jan Brinkman, Roger Brown, Ian Castles, John Coatsworth, Max Corden, Robert Cribb, François Crouzet, Pierre van der Eng, Stanley Engerman, Paul Frijters, Andre Hofman, Catrinus Jepma, Wim Jongman, Andrew Kamarck, Carol Kidwell, Tao Kong, Paul Lamartine Yates, David Landes, Debin Ma, Charles Maddison, John R. McNeill, Stanislav Menshikov, Jim Oeppen, Peter Oppenheimer, Guy Pfefferman, Leandro Prados de la Escosura, Prasada Rao, Dominic Rathbore, Osamu Saito, Simon Scott, Graeme Snooks, Kaoru Sugihara, Eddy Szirmai, Bart van Ark, and Harry X. Wu.

Elizabeth Maddison, Tom Kuipers, and Gerard Ypma gave me invaluable advice on the art of computing and Dirk Stelder was kind enough to construct the map of the Roman Empire for the frontispiece and Chapter 1.

I am particularly indebted to my friend Colin McEvedy (1930–2005), who shared my enthusiasm for quantitative exploration of the past, gave me invaluable guidance on historical demography, precious insights into the ancient world, and incisive answers to a welter of questions.

I benefited from discussions at meetings in which I presented parts of the analysis: the Kuznets Memorial lecture at Yale University in 1998, the Wendt lecture at the American Enterprise Institute, the Abramovitz lecture at Stanford University in 2001, a Harvard University Workshop organized by the Luxembourg Institute for European and International Studies in 2002, the Colin Clark lecture at the University of Queensland in 2003, the Ruggles lecture at the International Association for Research on Income and Wealth in Cork, the Figuerola Lecture at the Universidad Carlos III de Madrid in 2004, the Arndt lecture at the Australian National University in 2005, and seminars in Groningen and Queensland in 2006 on World Economic Performance, Past, Present, and Future, to mark my 80th birthday.

An earlier version of Chapter 2, *Growth and Interaction in the World Economy: The Roots of Modernity*, was published by the AEI Press, Washington, DC (2004); part of Chapter 3 appeared in *Australia Pacific Economic Literature* in 2006, and an earlier version of Chapter 6 in the *Review of Income and Wealth* in March 2005.

Introduction
and summary

The purpose of this book is to identify the forces which explain how and why some parts of the world have grown rich and others have lagged behind.

It is a companion study to earlier books of mine. *Monitoring the World Economy, 1820–1992* (1995) dealt with performance in the capitalist epoch, for which the evidence is incomparably richer than it was 60 years ago. There is still a need to fill gaps and crosscheck existing estimates, but the broad contours of development in this period are not under serious challenge. *The World Economy: A Millennial Perspective* (2001) and *The World Economy: Historical Statistics* (2003) had a much longer temporal perspective, back to the first century AD. Here growth was much slower, inter-country differences in income smaller, quantitative evidence weaker and harder to find, with greater reliance on clues and conjecture. There is also considerable disagreement amongst economic historians about the contours of development in these earlier centuries. However, recent research has made considerable advances in measuring economic progress and demographic change in western Europe and the major Asian countries back to 1500, and there is enough evidence to make tentative estimates for the Roman empire in the first century AD.

Scrutiny of distant horizons is a meaningful, useful, and necessary exercise because differences in the pace and pattern of change in major parts of the world economy have deep roots in the past. It is also useful to look into the future to see how the relative importance of the western and Asian economies is likely to change. I have therefore made projections for the world economy and its major components to 2030.

Quantification clarifies issues which qualitative analysis leaves fuzzy. It is more readily contestable and likely to be contested. It sharpens scholarly discussion, sparks off rival hypotheses, and contributes to the dynamics of the research process. It can only do this if the sources of the quantitative evidence and the nature of the conjectures and proxy procedures are described transparently so that a dissenting reader can augment or reject parts of the evidence, or introduce alternative hypotheses. Macro-economic quantification is not new. It started in the seventeenth century, as demonstrated in Chapter 5. It fell out of fashion until the 1950s when it became a major tool for policy analysis. I have tried here to promote its resurrection as a tool for historical analysis.

Although quantification is important, no sensible person would claim that it can tell the whole story. One needs to probe beyond quantifiable causes to deeper layers of explanation. This is a complex task because there are many interactive forces whose individual impact is difficult to specify. Countries have widely different institutions, traditions, and policies, which have a powerful impact on the operation of atomistic market forces. Hence the need to use a blend of evidence on proximate and deeper layers of causality.

There are three parts to the book. The first contains an analysis of the long-term performance of different parts of the world economy. The second analyses the development of techniques of macro-economic measurement since the seventeenth century. The third contains projections of world economic growth to 2030, and examines the possible impact of global warming.

THE CONTOURS OF WORLD DEVELOPMENT

Chapter 1 scrutinizes the process by which Rome established its hegemony in the Italian peninsula and created an empire of 3.3 million square km and a fifth of world population by 14AD. It included 84 per cent of the west European population, almost half of eastern Europe, more than half of Africa and all the west Asian countries bordering the Mediterranean. It was the most prosperous part of the world economy at that time. Based on the work of Beloch, Brunt, and Frier on Roman demography, and expanding Goldsmith's analysis of the income of the empire as a whole, I present new estimates of social structure, degree of urbanization, incidence of slavery, the hierarchy of incomes, and the average income level in individual provinces of the empire. It is clear that peninsular Italy and its ruling oligarchy were the main gainers. The eastern provinces gained little, but Romanization raised income levels in western Europe and north Africa. These areas began to savour the benefits of urban life, absorbed the technology of ancient civilizations in west Asia and benefited from new opportunities to trade and specialize. The Pax Romana created security. The legal system protected property rights. Roads, bridges, and harbours reduced transport costs. The elimination of piracy, creation of a common currency, and the spread of a common language greatly enlarged market size.

At the beginning of the fifth century, the western part of the empire collapsed and was repossessed by the barbarians. Urban civilization faded, central control collapsed, and standards of living declined. The eastern empire continued, but in the seventh century, most of west Asia, Egypt, and north Africa was incorporated into the Islamic world.

Chapter 2 examines the driving forces underlying the resurrection of western Europe and the transformation of the Americas. In the merchant capitalist epoch, 1500–1820, Europe made progress in science, maritime technology, business organization, and institutions, which had no parallel elsewhere. Contact with Europe transformed the Americas, where productive potential was augmented by ecological and technological transfers. Two-thirds of the indigenous population were wiped out by European and African diseases. They were replaced by European immigrants and slaves shipped from Africa.

There were big differences in the political and social structures the Iberians, the British, French, and Dutch colonialists created in Latin America, in the slave economies of the Caribbean, and in North America. They had a strong influence on economic performance in the colonial period and a powerful resonance in subsequent development. Between 1500 and 1820 per capita income rose faster in the Americas than in the rest of the world economy and North America caught up with west European income levels. By 1820 the greater part of the Americas had become politically independent and Europe had to look for colonial ventures elsewhere.

Chapter 3 analyses European interaction with Asia since 1500. It concentrates on the impact of the three main European colonialists, Portugal, the Netherlands, and Britain, on the four biggest Asian countries. China, India, Indonesia, and Japan represented 84 per cent of Asia's population, and GDP in 1500, 90 per cent in 1820, 56 per cent of population, and 72 per cent of GDP in 2003. It analyses how differences in their social structure, institutions, and intellectual horizons affected their divergent responses to the western challenge. It explains why Japan was different from the other three countries, why it caught up with the west and why its dynamism has faded. It reviews the process by which India and China have now embarked on very rapid growth and assesses their prospects for the next quarter-century. In 1500, Asia produced 65 per cent of world GDP, in 1820, 59 per cent. By 1950, its share had fallen to 19 per cent. By 2030 it is likely to be 53 per cent—much bigger than the share of the western world.

Chapter 4 reviews African development over the past two millennia. From the first until the seventh century, north Africa was a prosperous part of the Roman Empire. Its political and social structure was completely remoulded by the Muslim conquest. Links were severed with most of Europe, except Muslim Spain. Links with western Asia were strengthened, but there were serious conflicts between different parts of the Islamic world. The population of north Africa increased by a quarter from year 1 to 1820 and per capita income fell. In north Africa, plague seems to have been endemic from the sixth to the nineteenth century. It does not seem to have crossed the Sahara, where population grew eightfold in the same period.

There was negligible contact with black Africa until the Arab conquest when camel transport opened trade across the Sahara and initiated a flow of gold and slaves to the north. There was a gradual transition from hunter-gathering to an agricultural mode of production south of the Sahara. Soils were poor, there was shifting cultivation, with land left fallow for a decade or more after the first crops, but there was an ecological boost from the introduction of American plants (manioc, maize, and sweet potatoes). This led to increased density of settlement and substantial population growth, but had little impact on per capita income. Before contact with the Islamic world, there was universal illiteracy and absence of written languages (except in Ethiopia). This made it difficult to transmit knowledge across generations and between African societies. Contact with Islam brought obvious advantages. The

Arabs who came as traders had a written language and an evangelizing bent. They included sophisticated members of the Muslim intelligentsia, who were able to promote knowledge of property institutions, law, and techniques of governance as well cutting business deals.

European contact with Africa was renewed by Portugal in the fifteenth century, but was confined to coastal trading stations. The main commerce was the slave trade. Eleven million Africans were shipped to the Americas between 1500 and 1900. There was little scope for European settlement because of heavy mortality from African diseases. In 1820, there were less than 35,000 Europeans (30,000 in the Cape, and less than 5,000 elsewhere), compared to 13 million in the Americas.

When the transatlantic slave trade ended, European interest in tropical Africa waned. It revived when advances in medical technology reduced European mortality and intrepid explorers brought knowledge of Africa's potential to supply minerals and plantation crops. Steamboat, railway, and telegraphic communications made it feasible to penetrate beyond the coastal areas. European powers began to scramble for colonies in the 1880s. None of the indigenous peoples (except Ethiopians) managed to repel European firepower for very long, and face-offs between European powers were settled without serious conflict. Fifty-seven European colonies were established. The colonial impact is reviewed in detail for Algeria, Egypt, Ghana and South Africa.

From 1820 to 1980, African per capita income rose more than 3.7-fold. Colonialism introduced some dynamism, but there was a big difference in performance between black Africa and the white settler countries where average per capita income rose nearly fourfold. By the 1950s, population of European origin had risen to 6 million (1.7 in the Maghreb, 3.5 million in South Africa, about 800,000 elsewhere). There were about half a million people of Indian origin in East and South Africa.

Virtually all the European colonies were abandoned by 1963. White settler interests retarded the transition in Zimbabwe and Namibia, and in South Africa the indigenous population did not get political rights until 1994. Independence brought serious challenges. Very few countries, except Egypt, Morocco, and Ethiopia, had ever functioned as nation states. Most were multi-ethnic and political leadership had to create elements of national solidarity from scratch. There was a great scarcity of people with education or administrative experience. The new political elites frequently created one-party states or were involved in armed struggle. Cold war rivalry made donors less fastidious in allocating aid. As a result Africa accumulated large foreign debts which had a meagre developmental pay-off. It is the world's poorest region. Education and health standards are low, 40 per cent of the population is below 15 years of age compared to 16 per cent in western Europe. In 2005, average life expectation was 51 years, annual population growth 2.2 per cent—nine times faster than in western Europe. Between 1980 and 2003 African per capita income stagnated, whilst it rose by half in the rest of the world. In spite of the large increase in foreign aid which has recently been pledged, the outlook for significant increases in African income remains bleaker than in other parts of the world.

THE HISTORY OF MACRO-MEASUREMENT

Chapter 5 analyses the origins of macro-economic measurement and historical demography. Sophisticated techniques were first developed in the seventeenth century. The pioneers were William Petty (1623–87), John Graunt (1620–74), and Gregory King (1648–1712).

In 1665, Petty presented the first estimates of income, expenditure, stock of land, other physical assets, and human capital in an integrated set of accounts for the whole economy of England and Wales. His accounts were brilliantly original. They provided a quantitative framework for effective implementation of fiscal policy and mobilization of resources in time of war. They foreshadowed techniques of growth accounting developed by Edward Denison 300 years later.

Graunt was the first serious demographer. He derived vital statistics, survival tables, and the population of London by processing and analysing christenings and burials recorded in the bills of mortality from 1603 to 1662. His work inspired Halley (1693) to publish the first rigorous mathematical analysis of life tables, which provided an actuarial basis for life insurance. After a lengthy hiatus, historical demography has gained new vigour in the last half-century and provides important clues on per capita income development, particularly for distant periods where evidence on output is poor.

Gregory King built on the work of Petty and Graunt. He constructed much more accurate and consistent estimates of income and expenditure for England and Wales. He was able to improve population estimates by exploiting information from hearth and poll taxes, a new tax on births, marriages, and burials, and his own mini-censuses for a few towns. He estimated world population by major region. He quantified and compared the economic performance of England, France, and Holland, and their capacity to finance the war of the League of Augsburg in which most of western Europe was engaged from 1689 to 1697. His income account delineated the social hierarchy in a dramatic way, showing the income of 26 types of household from lords to vagrants. His quantitative depiction of the social panorama in 1688 had no precursors. His most valuable contribution was to provide detailed evidence to estimate GDP broken down by 43 categories of expenditure for 1688. This provides an invaluable inter-temporal link to the estimates for the Roman world and to modern national accounts.

Chapter 6 describes the macro-measurement tools available to modern economic historians. Official statisticians have now produced standardized estimates of annual growth of output back to 1950 for 163 countries representing more than 99 per cent of world output. Quantitative economic historians have carried such estimates back to 1820 for more than three-quarters of the world economy. These measures of economic growth over time are corrected to exclude the impact of inter-temporal price change.

For inter-country comparison and multi-country aggregation, it is also necessary to correct for inter-country differences in price level. These are not adequately reflected in exchange rates. Respectable purchasing power parity converters of national currencies are now available for countries representing 99 per cent of world output in our benchmark year, 1990. By merging the time series for economic growth with the crosscountry estimates of GDP levels now available we can make a coherent set of space–time comparisons.

For the capitalist epoch back to 1820, in which rapid technical change, structural transformation, and rising per capita incomes were the norm, quantitative historians have made great progress in measuring growth and interpreting its causes. Until recently, serious quantitative investigation of the 'merchant capitalist' epoch, 1500–1820, was neglected for three reasons: (i) growth then was much slower than it has been since 1820; (ii) the evidence is weaker and there is greater reliance on clues and conjecture; (iii) many (under the influence of Malthus) thought and think that it was a period of stagnation interrupted by catastrophe. Like Adam Smith, I take a much more positive view of what happened. I explain the derivation of my estimates of performance for 1500–1820 and my reasons for disagreeing with the pessimism of the real-wage pundits.

There is a school of thought which attributes modern economic growth to an 'industrial revolution' in Manchester, preceded by centuries of Malthusian stagnation. The metaphor was first popularized by Arnold Toynbee in 1884, and has continuing resonance, e.g., in Rostow's (1960) 'take-off', and Mokyr's (2002) history of technology. Nordhaus (1997) and DeLong (1998) have constructed fairytale scenarios which greatly exaggerate progress since 1800, before which they seem to believe that people lived like cavemen. These views are fundamentally wrong, and I present my evidence for believing that the roots of modern economic growth lie in advances achieved in a long apprenticeship during the merchant capitalist era.

THE SHAPE OF THINGS TO COME

Chapter 7 analyses the prospects for economic growth and likely changes in the structure of the world economy from 2003 to 2030. I assume faster advance than in 1973–2003, with some demographic slowdown and accelerated growth of per capita income. The latter is projected to rise by 80 per cent, i.e., an annual growth rate of 2.22 per cent. This is a good deal faster than at any time in world history, except in the golden age, 1950–73. I expect the most dynamic performance to come from the Asian economies, particularly China and India, with the Asian share of world GDP rising to 53 per cent, and that of western Europe, the US, and other western offshoots falling to 33 per cent. The average Asian income level would still be only a third of that in western Europe, so there would be reason to expect the 2003–30 changes in world economic structure to continue in the same direction thereafter.

Changes of this kind in economic leverage inevitably have political repercussions, making present membership of groups like the UN Security Council, or the G-8 summiteers obsolete. They will also reduce the capacity of the US to play a hegemonial role. Changes in these arrangements and ambitions would be necessary in order to maintain peaceful coexistence between the major powers, to reduce the size and spread of nuclear arsenals, and to mitigate the spread of various brands of religious fundamentalism. Major failures in these areas would probably make my relatively cautious economic projections seem euphoric. As these political problems are not susceptible to my quantitative kind of analysis, I have instead concentrated on the problem of global warming which is now widely seen a threat to planetary economic performance. Here I think my type of analysis is useful in deriving an objective perspective. I have examined the interaction between world economic growth and energy demand since 1820, and the outlook for the twenty-first century and made a critical assessment of the literature on this topic by the International Energy Agency, the Intergovernmental Panel on Climate Change, the House of Lords Committee, and the Stern Review of the Economics of Climate Change.

Part I

Contours of World Development, 1–2003AD

1 The Roman empire and its economy

INTRODUCTION

The Roman empire was the last of several civilizations to emerge in the Mediterranean in the first millennium BC.

The Etruscans: It is not clear whether they were indigenous or migrated from Asia minor. There is clear evidence that they were in western Italy at the beginning of the last millennium BC. At the time when Rome was still a small collection of villages, they had developed a sophisticated way of life with cities, domestic, and foreign commerce and political control of their Tuscan heartland. They also had a degree of political hegemony in the Po valley, Latium and Campania.

The Phoenicians/Carthaginians originated in Lebanon (Tyre, Sidon, and Byblos). They established a trading base in Carthage (in present-day Tunisia) around 800BC, with coastal settlements in Sicily, Sardinia, Corsica, southern Spain, the Balearics, and Cyprus. When Tyre was conquered by Babylon in 572BC, leadership fell to the Carthaginians. They were prosperous because of their large commercial empire. They relied heavily on foreign mercenary troops, and, as a coastal civilization, had a comparative advantage in building up their naval forces. Roman expansion involved three major wars with Carthage.

After conquering the Etruscans and Carthaginians, Rome obliterated their civilizations and Romanized the survivors.

The Greeks: From the eighth century BC, city states were created throughout the Greek peninsula, the Aegean islands, the Turkish coast, Crete, Cyprus, and the Black Sea coast. In Southern Italy, Taranto was founded by Sparta in 706BC. In Sicily, Syracuse was founded by Corinth in 733BC. There were Greek trading posts in southern France at Massilia (Marseilles), Naucratis in Egypt, and Cyrene in Libya.

The Greeks faced a major threat from the Persian empire, which conquered their cities in Asia Minor in 545BC. Xerxes invaded Greece in 480BC via Thrace. The Athenian Acropolis was stormed and its temples destroyed, but the Persians withdrew after their fleet was defeated at Salamis and their army at Platea.

Conflicts between Greek city states were endemic until Alexander, the ruler of Macedonia, established control over the peninsula and the Hellenized cities in western Turkey. In 332BC, he defeated the Persians, took Greater Syria and Egypt. In 331, he conquered Sogdiana and Bactria (in Uzbekistan and Afghanistan), penetrated the Punjab to Taxila in 326, returned via Baluchistan and died in Babylon aged 32.

After Alexander's death his empire was divided into monarchies by his generals. In all of these the Greek language was used by the ruling elite and Hellenic culture remained a powerful influence:

1. The Ptolemies took over as rulers of Egypt from 323 to 31BC.

2. In 312, Seleucus established an empire stretching from Asia Minor to Afghanistan. By the time the Romans became involved, the eastern part of the Seleucid empire had been lost. What was left was Asia Minor and Greater Syria.

3. The Attalid dynasty took control of Pergamum in 282BC after the death of Alexander's general Lysimachus.

4. In the fight for control of Macedon, Alexander's mother, wife, and son were murdered by his general, Cassander. Later, from 276 to 168BC, Macedonia came into the hands of the Antigonid dynasty.

The Romans conquered and Romanized the Greeks in southern Italy, Sicily, and Provence. They also took control of Greece, Asia Minor, greater Syria, Egypt, and Cyrenaica, but these areas retained their Hellenistic civilization and Greek language.

East of the Empire, Rome was involved in conflicts which kept the Parthians/Persians at bay, but it was basically a stand-off situation, with no significant or enduring Roman conquest.

The Barbarians: The other areas which became components of the Roman Empire were Spain, the Maghreb, Gaul, part of Germany, Switzerland, Austria, Hungary, Yugoslavia, Bulgaria, Romania, and Britain. All these were inhabited by people the Romans called barbarians. In most of them (and in the areas of Europe the Romans did not conquer) the inhabitants had no written language, no city life and their political organization was tribal. They had no clearly defined system of justice, property rights, or taxation. Their techniques of governance, capacity to mobilize resources for war, and to organize disciplined troops were much less effective than in the Roman world.

The technological gap between 'barbarians' and Romans was a good deal smaller than that between Europeans and the indigenous inhabitants of the Americas in the sixteenth century (where one side had horses and guns, and the other a stone-age technology). Most 'barbarians' were familiar with iron-age technology and had weapons which were quite effective by Roman standards. They were also able to use horses. Barbarians who had military training in Roman auxiliary forces were able to inflict great damage when they defected. This was the case with Arminius, whose troops slaughtered three Roman legions in Germany in 9AD and Tacfarinas who harried Roman forces in Numidia from 6 to 24AD.

Although barbarian lifestyles were simple, their basic nutritional levels were probably superior. Koepke and Baten (2005: 65 and 74) in their survey of human and mammal bones for the Roman period, concluded that the less densely settled areas had 'the highest per capita milk and beef consumption in Europe, since a high land ratio facilitates *ceteris paribus* a large number of cows and therefore a nutrition which is based on high quality proteins'. They were also taller than the inhabitants of Roman Italy, where 'a high share of pig bones was typical'.

Romanization was more important in transmitting literacy, urbanization, political organization, and economic development to the 'barbarian' provinces of the Empire than in the old civilizations of the eastern provinces and Egypt.

KEY CHARACTERISTICS ACCOUNTING FOR ROMAN SUCCESS IN EMPIRE BUILDING

1. Until 27BC, Rome was a constitutional republic, run by a propertied oligarchy. Political stability depended on checks and balances. Governance was divided between the magistrates (two consuls, the praetors, and the censors). The Senate and popular assemblies represented the citizen body. The power elite were the 300 senators (expanded to 600 by Sulla). They were a wealthy oligarchy, *de facto* elected for life. Augustus imposed a minimum property qualification of a million *sesterces*. He made them a hereditary order, with new men introduced by himself. Their status was marked by a broad purple band on their togas. They filled the leading offices of state on a rotating basis, being nominated from and by the senate for a period of one year. Early re-election to these offices was more or less forbidden.

   The Senate advised the magistrates on matters of domestic and foreign policy, public finance, justice, and religion, and made decisions on war and peace. In order to prevent too rapid an accession to power and influence, progression in a senatorial career was subject to constraints. A first ten years of military service was required before holding public office, and thereafter, graduated stages of ascension (as quaestor, then praetor) were required before becoming a consul.

   The Senate nominated military commanders (for one year, extendable if they were successful). They were nearly always chosen from the Senate itself. In times of war, generals had enormous powers of discretion and got a substantial share of the spoils of victory. They received public acclamation when they paraded their prisoners in official triumphal processions in Rome. As the empire grew, provincial governors were chosen from and by the Senate. Here too, they were able to enrich themselves by taking a cut from the provincial revenues. Governors had a small staff drawn from their own cronies. As a counterpart to their prerogatives of self-enrichment, the senatorial elite were expected to dispense public largesse. The senate also used public resources to curry favour with the citizen body by providing bread and circuses.

   The system was basically run by amateurs. There was no imperial bureaucracy. It was a highly competitive, though not quite meritocratic system. The normal career ladder (*cursus honorum*) provided a useful apprenticeship to a wide variety of official and military posts. Miscreants faced the possibility of prosecution for extremes of corruption or abuse of office.

In building up Roman control of the Italian peninsula and resisting the Hannibalic invasion the Senate had fairly coherent policy objectives, but in the first century BC, the frenzy of conquest led to a breakdown of the political system. There was a succession of civil wars because of rivalry between powerful generals—Marius and Sulla, Pompey and Caesar, Octavian and Mark Antony.

In 27BC, the political system changed fundamentally. The Republic became the 'Principate'. The effective and absolute ruler, Octavian, henceforth known as Augustus, called himself 'number one' (*princeps*) rather than king, but he promoted an imperial cult, proclaimed his godliness as the son of the divine Caesar and became chief priest (*pontifex maximus*). He had himself repeatedly elected to the republican office of consul, but his position as *princeps* did not require renewal, his discretionary power was virtually unlimited, and he nominated his successor. He smoothed the transition to a monarchical regime by sharing the spoils of office and the governance of the empire with the senatorial elite. He had a more coherent view of how to run an empire than was earlier the case. In the first century AD, an increasing proportion of the Senate were recruited from the provinces, first from southern Spain (Baetica), later from Gaul and Africa.

A second layer of elite citizens became increasingly important from the late second century BC. They were known as *equites*, a name originally reserved for cavalry officers. They were wealthy, and their status required a minimum property qualification, but they had greater freedom to engage in economic activity than senators, whose wealth was derived almost entirely from land ownership. Their role in governance was considerably enhanced by Augustus who made frequent use of them in administrative jobs which multiplied as the empire grew.

2. Rome had a pragmatic policy towards opponents. It was a mix of brutality and willingness to co-exist peacefully. Most of its enemies preferred coercive coexistence to extinction. In dealing with really recalcitrant enemies, Rome massacred or enslaved conquered populations, and confiscated all their property. If they cooperated they were treated as Roman clients, obliged to supply military help to Rome when needed, to cede control of external relations to Rome, but otherwise left autonomous in their internal governance. Some had to pay taxes to Rome, some not. In almost all cases, part of their property was forfeited to Rome and either sold back or allocated to Roman citizens. Their cities became *municipia*, with partial or full Roman citizenship, or *civitates foederatae*, technically independent but linked to Rome by treaties of alliance.

3. The Romans were pragmatic polytheists, generally willing to respect the gods and temples of the peoples they conquered, as well as introducing them to their own gods. Thus they minimized ideological conflict. They did not practice

ethnic discrimination. Race was never a barrier to Roman citizenship. Assimilation facilitated the process of Romanization.

4. A major factor of success in controlling conquered areas was the creation of a network of stone-paved all-weather roads radiating from Rome, with bridges and viaducts over rivers and gorges, cuttings and tunnels through mountains. Distance and date of construction were marked on stones at each Roman mile (1.485 km). They permitted swift passage of troops and official communications, and had a significant economic impact, increasing the size of markets and encouraging trade and regional specialization. The first was the via Appia which stretched from Rome to Capua and later to Brindisi. This helped guarantee the control of new Roman territory in the south. The via Aurelia–Aemilia linked Rome with Pisa and Genoa. The via Flaminia linked Rome to the Adriatic, and the via Pompillia went from there to Aquilea. Needham (1971: 28–29) estimated the length of the Roman paved road network to be about 78,000 km by the time of the emperor Trajan.

5. Roman conquest and capacity to retain conquered territory was due to the quality and relatively large size of its armed forces. In the Republic, all adult male citizens were liable to military service in the infantry for 16 years or for ten years in the cavalry. In addition, Rome drew on auxiliary forces supplied by its allies. The army was organized in legions of 4,000 to 5,000 men. Generals and senior officers were drawn from the ranks of the Senate, all of whom were required to have at least ten years of military service before acquiring public office. The top officials were the two consuls elected annually, each controlling two legions. There was a large turnover of senior commanders, but the degree of political experience of the militarized elite was also unusual, and it was not difficult to discard incompetent officers.

Within each legion, soldiers were divided into four age groups. The *velites* were the youngest and least experienced, next were the *hastati*. Those in the prime of life were *principes*, and the veterans were the *triarii*. The youngest had a sword, javelins, a light shield, and a helmet without a crest. The others had a much bigger and stronger shield, a sharp-pointed sword with cutting edges on both sides, and two throwing spears. They wore a breast plate, greaves on their legs, and a bronze helmet with three purple or black feathers about 45 cm high. The *triarii* had thrusting rather than throwing spears. Soldiers got a salary, a centurion getting twice as much as the infantry, and the cavalry three times as much. The infantry got a ration of 27 kg of wheat a month. The cavalry got more wheat and a large supply of barley for their horses. The quartermaster (*quaestor*) deducted the value of the food ration and clothing from their pay. The soldiery got a share of any booty taken in the campaigns and land allocations after their military service. For officers the potential extra income was a good deal larger, and successful generals were awarded lavish triumphal honours for their victories.

Military discipline was very severe. If a soldier neglected his picket duty on the night watch, his colleagues were compelled to beat him to death. If a group of soldiers deserted or showed cowardice in battle, a tenth were chosen by lot and the rest had to club them to death.

Legionary camps were always laid out on a standardized gridiron pattern with the general's tent in the centre. The six senior officers in each legion had tents at equidistant points, and the tents of centurions (in charge of 80 legionaires) were also distributed symmetrically. The soldiers' tents were in parallel lines on either side of the general's tent, facing the outer perimeter, with separate space for cavalry and infantry, for legionary and auxiliary troops. Space was reserved for horses, mules, baggage, and booty, with roadways running through the camp to avoid congestion when marching in and out, pitching, or breaking camp. Ramparts and ditches were constructed on all sides about 60 m from the tents, keeping the soldiers out of range of enemy missiles.

The clearest description of military organization is by Polybius (200–118BC), a Greek general detained in Rome for 18 years (168–150BC) where he became a friend of the Roman general Scipio Aemilianus. He accompanied him to Carthage in the third Punic war. He compared Roman procedure favourably to that of the Greeks who picked campsites because of their natural features and grudged the labour involved in trenching.

The Romans, on the other hand, prefer to undergo the fatique of digging and other defensive preparations for the sake of having a consistent and uniform plan. Every soldier invariably occupies the same position in the camp, so the process of pitching camp is remarkably like the return of an army to its native city (Polybius 1979: 339–40)

The army was also responsible for creating a large part of the military road network.

Polybius (1979: 508–13) also explained why the tight Greek phalanx formation, whose strength 'nothing can withstand ... or resist face to face' was vulnerable to greater Roman flexibility—in war the times and places for action are unlimited, whereas the phalanx required flat and level ground 'unencumbered by any obstacles such as ditches, gullies, depressions, ridges and water courses ... it is exceedingly rare to find a stretch of country of say two or three miles which contains no obstacles of this kind'.

The Roman navy was developed in the first war with Carthage. The biggest vessel, the *quinquereme*, was copied from a Carthaginian ship that had run aground. Each required 300 oarsmen, with five men to each oar. They managed to train the oarsmen (slaves or forced labour) quickly, constructed a fleet of ships using prefabricated parts, and invented a new device, the *corvus* (a gangway suspended at the prow of the ship), which could be hauled up and dropped on the deck of an enemy vessel, locking the ships together. Roman troops then swarmed aboard and engaged in hand-to-hand battle. The disadvantage was that its weight made ships vulnerable in storm conditions.

CONQUEST OF THE ITALIAN PENINSULA, 396–191BC

According to official chronology, Rome was founded in 753BC, but its early history is impregnated with legend and difficult to document.

Rome was originally a small settlement on the left bank of the Tiber, about 14 miles from the sea. By 500BC, the territory of the republic had expanded to the coast at Ostia and south to Alba Longa. It had become the biggest city in the relatively small Latin-speaking area known as Latium.

In the struggle to achieve hegemony in Italy, Rome had to tackle five adversaries: (1) its immediate neighbours in Latium; (2) the Etruscans immediately north of Rome; (3) non-Latin tribes—the Volsci and Aequi on the east being the nearest, the Oscan-speaking Samnites to the southeast the most significant; (4) the Celtic tribes between the Alps and the Appennines; (5) the Greek-speaking area in the south of the peninsula. Although it was known as Magna Graecia, it consisted of independent and quarrelsome city states. There was more solidarity between the Etruscan cities, but they too were not a coherent political entity.

The Romans were not alone as destroyers of Etruria. In 500BC, Etruscan territory stretched from the Alps to the bay of Naples. By 425BC they had lost everything south of Rome to the Greek city-states in the south. The Insubres (a Gallic tribe) took Melpum (Milan) and their other settlements in Lombardy in 396. In 384 a Greek fleet from Sicily plundered most of the Etruscan harbours, destroyed their settlements in Elba and Corsica, and ended their dominance of the Tyrrhenian sea. In 350 Gallic tribes took Felsina (Bologna) and established control of the Po valley.

The Romans captured the nearest Etruscan city, Veii, after a ten year siege in 396BC. This doubled their direct territorial control and established their suzerainty in what had been the Latin league. By 308 Rome had taken all that was left of Etruria.

Between 343 and 290BC, in three wars with the Samnites, Rome extended its control over a swathe of central Italy from the west coast to the Adriatic.

In 326 Rome made an alliance with the Greeks of Naples and Capua, in an attempt to conquer the other Greek cities in the south. The latter were supported by the Greek king, Pyrrhus of Epirus, who entered Italy in 280BC with 25,000 troops and 20 elephants. In 275, he was defeated and returned to Greece. Rome completed its control of the south in 272 by taking the biggest city, Tarantum (Taranto).

The barbarian Gauls migrated into northern Italy around 400BC. They put up the fiercest resistance to Roman conquest and occupied a very large area—116,000 square kilometres compared with 140,000 in the rest of peninsular Italy. In 390 they attacked and set fire to Rome. Eight hundred years later, tribes from the north sacked Rome in 410AD and played a major role in destroying the western Empire. They were skilled warriors with iron swords and shields, fighting without body armour and organized into kin-based tribal groups headed by kings. They came as nomadic herders, but took up agriculture in Italy. They were non-urban and illiterate, given to carousing.

Unlike Romans, they drank their wine neat. Their intellectuals were bards, seers, and druids. When Hannibal entered Italy in 218, many of these tribes sided with him. After he left, Rome conquered all the Celtic tribes south of the Alps and took control of Gallia Cisalpina in 191 BC. This completed its hegemony over the whole of peninsular Italy. In 49 BC, Caesar extended Roman citizenship to all the inhabitants of Cisalpine Gaul.

THE EMPIRE BUILDING PROCESS

The war started when Roman troops crossed to Sicily and took Messina to prevent Carthage from establishing a base too close to Italy. The Carthaginians held central and western Sicily. Most of the east coast was controlled by the Greek king, Hiero of Syracuse. He initially resisted the Roman intrusion, but became an ally in 263.

Rome gained some early victories against the Carthaginians, capturing Agrigento in 262. There was little further progress on land, but some success in naval engagements. In 257, Rome attacked the Carthaginian homeland in north Africa (about 200 km from Sicily). The invasion force had initial success, but was defeated in 255 by mercenary troops the Carthaginians hired from Greece. In retreating, more than 200 Roman ships were lost in a storm. A new Roman fleet captured Panormus (Palermo) on the northwest coast of Sicily in 254. The Carthaginians recaptured Agrigento in 251, but failed to dislodge the Romans from Palermo. In 250 the Roman fleet blockaded the port of Marsala on the western tip of Sicily, but the Carthaginian fleet broke the blockade and their land forces burnt the Roman siege engines.

After five years avoiding a naval confrontation, a new Roman fleet was victorious on the west coast of Sicily and Marsala was captured. The war ended with Carthage agreeing to evacuate the whole of Sicily and all the islands between Sicily and Italy, to surrender all Roman prisoners without ransom, and to pay an indemnity of 3,200 talents of silver (121 metric tons) over a ten-year period. The war had lasted without interruption for 24 years and Rome had lost 700 ships (half from shipwreck).

Hiero of Syracuse continued to rule a fifth of Sicily until his death in 215. His successor revolted, but was defeated in 212. The most prominent citizen of Syracuse, Archimedes the mathematician, was killed in the fighting. Most of its art treasures were taken to Rome.

In 241 BC, Sicily became the first Roman province overseas, with a governor appointed annually. It provided Rome with an annual wheat tribute. Scramuzza (1937: 262) gives a figure of 3 million modii (20,250 metric tons) for the Sicilian wheat tribute (tithe) in 71 BC. Corsica and Sardinia became provinces in 238.

Table 1.1. Acquisition of Provinces outside Peninsular Italy: 214BC–199AD

Sicily	Sicilia	241BC	Serbia	Moesia	29BC
Sardinia	Sardinia	238BC	Hungary	Pannonia	9AD
Corsica	Corsica	238BC	E. Adriatic coast	Dalmatia	9AD
Spain	Baetica	206BC	Bulgaria &		
	Tarraconensis	206BC	European Turkey	Thracia	46AD
	Cantabria	25BC	Romania	Dacia	105AD
Portugal	Lusitania	138BC			
Greece	Macedonia	148BC			
	Achaea	146BC	Tunisia	Africa	146BC
Crete	Creta	67BC	Libya	Cyrene	96BC
France	Narbonensis	121BC	Eastern Algeria	Numidia	46BC
	Aquitania	58–52BC	Egypt	Egypt	30BC
	Lugdunensis	58–52BC	Morocco & W. Alg	Mauretania*	40AD
	Alpes Poeninae	15BC			
	Alpes Maritimae	15BC	West Turkey	Asia	133BC
	Alpes Cottiae	15BC	South Turkey	Cilicia	102BC
Belgium	Belgica	58–52BC	North Turkey	Bithynia & Pontus	64BC
			Central Turkey	Galatia	25BC
Germany	Germania Inferior &	90AD	E. Turkey	Cappodocia	17AD
	Superior	90AD	Cyprus	Cyprus	58BC
	Agri Decumates	73–75AD	Syria & Lebanon	Syria	64BC
England & Wales	Britannia	43–84AD	Israel/Palestine	Judaea	4BC
Switzerland & Bavaria	Raetia	15BC	Jordan/W. Arabia	Nabatea	106AD
Austria	Noricum	15BC	NorthMesopotamia	Osrhoene	199AD

Note: Mauretania was a client state from 25BC.

Source: Cornell and Matthews (1982), and Cambridge Ancient History. Although the two provinces of Germania became provinces in 90AD, they were Roman military zones for more than a century before then.

The Second Carthaginian War, 218–201BC

The Carthaginians offset their losses in Sicily by carving out a new empire in Spain, where they had long-established trading posts with headquarters in Gades (Cadiz).

The Carthaginian general, Hamilcar, set out in 237, accompanied by his son-in-law Hasdrubal and his 9-year-old son Hannibal. Their troops established a territorial empire in south and southeast Spain, where there were possibilities for production of wheat, oil, wine, esparto-grass, and salt-fish. There were reserves of gold, copper, iron, and silver. They took the silver mining area of the Sierra Morena, the valley of the Guadalquivir in the south, and control of the eastern coast up to Alicante, from the indigenous tribes in these areas.

Hamilcar was drowned in 229. Hasdrubal took over and advanced further up the east coast to found a new headquarters at Carthago Nova (Cartagena). It had a magnificent harbour, easy communications with Africa, and rich silver deposits nearby. This was not a direct threat to Roman interests, but Rome had an amicable relationship with the Greek city of Massilia (Marseilles) which had trading posts on the northeastern coast of Spain. Rome warned the Carthaginians to stay south of Saguntum and they appeared to acquiesce.

After Hasdrubal's assassination by a Celt in 221, Hannibal took command in Spain. His father had inculcated a desire for vengeance against Rome. The resources available from the conquests in Spain and the quality and size of his military force made it seem feasible. In 219 he provoked Rome by besieging and capturing Saguntum. In 218, Rome sent an ultimatum, offering peace if he withdrew, or war if he didn't.

Rome expected the war to be fought in Spain and in Africa. Their army set out for Spain by sea. A fleet and another army were sent to Sicily with the intention of a direct attack on Carthage.

Hannibal's Invasion of Italy

Hannibal divided the Carthaginian force in Spain (90,000 infantry and 12,000) He set off with 50,000 infantry and 9,000 cavalry to attack Italy by land. For the defence of Spain, the rest of the troops were left under the control of his brother (another Hasdrubal). Hannibal's troops were highly trained multi-ethnic mercenaries— Libyan heavy infantry, Numidian cavalry, Balearic slingers, north African elephants, and their local mahouts. They marched 1,500 miles from Cartagena to the Alps in five months, crossed the Rhone near Arles, moved across the Alps in 15 days, and arrived in Cisalpine Gaul in December 218BC.

The area was full of tribes hostile to Rome. Hannibal was able to rally many to his side, but was disappointed in his hopes for significant defection further south. He won two battles, at the rivers Ticino and Trebbia in January 217, slaughtered a large Roman army at Lake Trasimene in Etruria in June, and had an even more resounding victory at Cannae on the southern Adriatic coast in 216.

After these losses the Roman general Fabius was chary of direct engagement and carried out a war of attrition. Hannibal captured some Greek cities in the south, Croton, Locri, Tarentum, and Capua, but a good deal of his energy was taken up with defence of these positions. Rome recaptured Capua in 211, tortured and executed its leaders, sold the rest of its population into slavery, and confiscated all their land and associated territories. In 209, they recaptured Tarentum and were similarly harsh with its inhabitants.

At this point, Hasdrubal moved to reinforce his brother, Hannibal. He made a wide sweep to the northwest of Spain, entering Gaul between San Sebastian and Biarritz. His troops crossed the Rhone near Lyons. They had small losses crossing the Alps in the spring of 207 and moved to the Adriatic coast hoping to join Hannibal in Umbria. But his messages were intercepted and his forces destroyed. Thereafter Hannibal was bottled up in Bruttium, in the toe of Italy.

Liquidation of Carthaginian Spain, 217–206BC

In 217, the Romans landed in north-east Spain, and moved down the Mediterranean coast plundering and burning coastal sites. The Carthaginian army withdrew to

Lusitania (Portugal) and a large number of northern Spanish tribes proclaimed their (opportunistic) allegiance to Rome.

There was an inconclusive struggle for several years over a wide swathe of territory in eastern Spain from the Guadalquivir to the Ebro. In 212, Rome's Celtiberian mercenaries defected and the leading Roman generals were killed.

Publius Scipio (236–183BC), the new Roman commander, made a swift and successful amphibious assault against Cartagena in 209BC. It had been considered impregnable, but in a brief interval when the tide was low, his soldiers waded waist-high through the water with their ladders, and the walls were scaled. Rome acquired the best defensive position in Spain, a large supply of military and naval equipment, 18 ships, stores of food, other essential supplies, and a large amount of silver and gold. The Carthaginian forces finally surrendered at Cadiz in 206BC.

In 204, Rome attacked Carthage from Sicily with a large army and fleet. Hannibal returned to Africa and was defeated at the battle of Zama in 202. The victor became known officially as Scipio Africanus.

In the peace treaty of 201 Carthage lost all her territory outside Africa, had to surrender the bulk of her fleet, and had to pay an indemnity of 10,000 talents of silver (378 metric tons) in instalments over 50 years.

Integration of Spain into the Empire, 197–14BC

Scipio founded the first Roman settlement at Italica, a few kilometres north of Seville. In 197BC, two Roman provinces were created, Hispania Ulterior in the south with its capital at Corduba (Cordoba), and Hispania Citerior in the northeast with its capital at Cartagena. The extension of the latter province to the Atlantic involved a long struggle with Celtiberian tribes. It ended with the destruction of Numantia, and enslavement of its population in 133BC. Lusitania (Portugal) was conquered in 138BC.

The indigenous tribes were fierce, unreliable, and rebellious. Effective Roman control was limited to the southern and eastern coast. It took two centuries to complete the conquest.

Augustus spent two years in Spain in 27–25BC, with six legions. His headquarters were at Tarragona which became the capital of Hispania Tarraconensis, replacing the old province of Hispania Citerior. He led expeditions into Cantabria and the Asturias to extend the boundaries of the province. The conquest was completed in 19BC by Augustus' trouble-shooter Agrippa.

Augustus returned in 15–14BC to complete administrative arrangements for the provinces. Baetica, corresponding roughly to Andalusia, replaced Hispania Ulterior. Merida became the capital of Lusitania (which included parts of Spain as well as Portugal). Roads were built to reinforce imperial power. The biggest was the via Augusta, which went from the Pyrenees, down the east coast to Tarragona, Valencia,

Cordoba, and Cadiz. There were also roads crisscrossing the country, from northwest to southeast and southwest to northeast.

Urbanization was a major instrument of Romanization. Roman settlers were installed in strategic locations. The cities had a degree of self-government and privileged status for a new elite including senators and equestrians. The emperors Trajan and Hadrian were both from Spain. Romanization reduced dependence on military control. Augustus left Spain with three legions. A few decades later, one was enough.

Romanization had important economic consequences. Agriculture expanded, particularly in the south. Baetica was an important producer and exporter of wine, olive oil, garum, other fish sauces, and olive oil (used for cooking, lighting, soap, and cosmetic purposes). Mineral production was greatly increased. Most of the mines were the property of the Emperor and were leased to private contractors using slave labour. There were large exports of ceramics, iron and metal products, gold, silver, copper, tin, and lead, which added to imperial revenue.

The Conquest of Greece, 148–63BC

The territorial expansion of Rome involved conflicts in Greece. During the second Punic war, Philip V of Macedon attacked Roman bases in Illyricum (on the Dalmatian coast) and made a treaty with Hannibal to harass Rome. He was also involved in conflicts with other states in Greece and the Greek islands (Chios and Rhodes) to extend his sphere of influence. Rome intervened as an ally of his Greek enemies, and defeated him decisively in 197BC. In the peace settlement he was confined to Macedon, paid a huge indemnity, and lost his fleet. Rome presented herself as a protector of Greek freedom with no territorial claims, aiming to be the patron of what it hoped would be client states.

At that time, the Greek mainland was divided politically into four parts. The largest, in the north, was Macedon. In central Greece, a congeries of mini-states established the Aetolian League to provide a common defence against Macedon and pool their military resources. In the south, the Achaean League was a defensive arrangement against Sparta.

In 172–168BC, Macedon again attempted to extend its area of control, but was defeated by Rome. Macedonia was split into four provinces. A thousand prominent Greeks, including Polybius, were exiled as hostages in Italy. Rome acquired effective suzerainty in Greece, but still made no territorial claims.

Finally, after putting down a revolt in Macedonia, Rome took it as a province in 148BC. Achaea became involved in a fight with Rome's ally Sparta. Rome demolished Corinth, massacred and enslaved its population, and made Achaea a province in 146BC.

Crete remained independent, and was a major haven for pirates. It was incorporated as a Roman province in 63BC with its capital at Gortyn. Until 298AD, the governance of Crete was linked with Cyrenaica.

Greece was treated favourably by Roman rulers, who generally held its civilization in great respect. For this reason its tax burden was lighter than that of many other provinces.

Acquisitions in North Africa, 146–30BC

Acquisitions in Africa began with the third Punic war, 149–146BC. The city of Carthage was demolished after a long siege and three-quarters of its population were slaughtered or committed suicide. The 50,000 survivors were sold into slavery together with the inhabitants of other Tunisian towns loyal to Carthage. A new Roman province, 'Africa', was established. Land was allotted to Italian settlers and to Carthaginians who had deserted to Rome. The Punic language was gradually superseded by Latin.

West of the new province was the kingdom of Numidia, a Roman ally since the second Carthaginian war. In 112BC, in the course of an internal conflict, some Roman citizens were killed. Rome eliminated King Jugurtha, and split the country between two of his relatives. In 46BC Caesar annexed the kingdom which became 'Africa Nova', twice the area of 'Africa', which was renamed 'Africa Vetus'.

In 25BC Augustus created a client state, Mauretania, stretching from mid-Algeria to northern Morocco. Juba was installed as king—he had grown up in Rome in Augustus' household. For practical purposes, Mauretania was an integral part of Roman Africa.

To the east the three autonomous Phoenician trading bases in Tripolitania (Sabratha, Oea, and Leptis Magna) became client states and were gradually integrated into the Roman empire. At the end of Augustus' reign a major road was built between Tripolitania and the Roman military base at Haidra in Tunisia (see Mattingly 1995: 51–3). The adjoining kingdom of Cyrenaica was bequeathed to Rome by its last Ptolemaic ruler in 96BC.

The north African provinces were important economically. Initially, Roman settlement was coastal except in Tunisia where large irrigated estates were worked mainly by tenant farmers. Exports of these provinces were heavily concentrated on grain shipped to Italy from Carthage and olive oil from Tripolitania. The bulk of the export shipments were tribute, financed by tax levies, though some represented repatriation of rental income by absentee Roman landlords. The population consisted of settlers or demobilized soldiers from Italy as well as descendants of the Carthaginians. The main city was Carthage, which was rebuilt and resettled by Augustus more than a century after its destruction. Garnsey (1983: 120 and 201), quotes an estimate by Whittaker that the annual grain tribute from north Africa under Augustus was about 16 million modii (108,000 metric tons).

There was substantial growth in the Maghreb in the subsequent centuries of Roman rule. The push to the southern pre-desert by Augustus and Tiberius 'more than doubled the arable area of Roman Africa' (Whittaker 1996: 618). A road network was developed and there was a substantial degree of urbanization as witnessed by the relics of city splendour which still exist. The Maghreb became an important intellectual centre. Its most brilliant writers were St Augustine of Hippo and Petronius, the satirist. Leptis Magna was the birthplace of Septimius Severus, Emperor from 193–211AD. He built a new harbour and adorned the city with a forum, a basilica and a colonnaded street leading to the harbour.

Acquisitions in West Asia, 133BC–199AD

Rome became involved in Asia Minor in the second century BC. After defeating the Seleucid king Antiochus III in 189BC, it acquired influence in the area, particularly with Pergamum, whose last ruler bequeathed his kingdom to Rome in 133BC. In 102BC, a Roman naval base was established on the southern coast, in Cilicia. Its aim was to suppress piracy in the eastern Mediterranean. In 58BC, Cyprus was annexed and attached to the province of Cilicia.

Mithridates, king of Bithynia (on the Black Sea coast) tried to block Roman expansion in the region, but was defeated by the Roman general, Pompey, who added Pontus and made it a Roman province in 64BC. He also annexed Syria and created an inner network of client states—'Bosporus, Colchis, Armenia Minor, Paphlagonia, Galatia, Cappadocia, Commagene, the Syrian and Cilician princedoms and Judea' (Seager 2002: 61). 'By this single campaign Pompey claimed to have raised the provincial revenues of the Roman state by 70 per cent.' (Cornell and Matthews 1982: 68).

Galatia was incorporated as a province in 25BC and Cappodocia in 17AD. Judaea reverted to Rome on the death of Herod in 4BC and the Nabatean kingdom (with its capital at Petra) became a Roman province in 106AD. The boundaries of the Asian provinces fluctuated a good deal during the period of Roman rule.

Rome was cautious in extending its formal control in Asia in case it provoked armed opposition from Parthia, whose empire stretched from the Euphrates to India. In 53BC, the Roman general, Crassus, was killed attacking Parthia, and in 36BC a similar venture by Mark Antony failed ignominiously. In 117AD, Trajan established a province east of the Euphrates, which was promptly abandoned by his successor, Hadrian. Eventually, in 199AD, part of upper Mesopotamia (Osrhoene) was made a province by Septimius Severus. Millar (1993) stresses the mutability of boundaries, and the 'uncertain profitability' of provinces which remitted substantial cash tribute but required a very large deployment of military force.

The Conquest of Gaul, 121–49BC

The Greek colony of Massilia (Marseilles) was established in 600BC as a base for merchants from Phocea in Asia Minor. They pursued their commerce up the Rhone

Valley and developed a string of trading posts along the Mediterranean coast, stretching from Nice to Asturias in northeast Spain. They introduced fruit orchards, wine, and olive oil production.

In 123BC, Massilia was threatened and appealed for Roman assistance. Rome destroyed the Celtic invaders and established a fortified camp at Aquae Sextiae (Aix-en-Provence).

The Roman province of Transalpine Gaul was established in 121BC, within which Massilia was an autonomous republic. The provincial capitals were Aix and Narbonne. Its territory stretched to Spain in the west and to Lake Geneva in the east.

In the spring of 59BC, Julius Caesar (100–44BC) was made governor of Transalpine Gaul, Cisalpine Gaul (northern Italy from the Alps down to Lucca and Ravenna), and the coastal bases in Illyricum (on the eastern Adriatic coast). His command was originally for five years. At that time, the political leadership in Rome was in the hands of a triumvirate consisting of Caesar, Pompey (106–48BC), who had eliminated pirates from the Mediterranean and won major victories in Asia, and Crassus (115–53BC), who led the army that put down the Spartacus slave revolt. Caesar was interested in bolstering his political leverage and wealth by military conquests. Pompey became governor of two Spanish provinces, but remained in Rome. Crassus became governor of Syria. In 56BC, Caesar's command in Gaul was extended to 50BC, in a power-sharing deal with Crassus and Pompey.

When Caesar arrived in Transalpine Gaul in March, 58BC, his first tasks were to repell a mass migration of Helvetii into the province, and expel the Germanic forces of Ariovistus.

He spent the next eight years conquering the 60 different tribal groups in the rest of Gaul, Belgium, southern Holland below the Rhine, and a long strip of Germany west of the Rhine. There were several million inhabitants, fierce warriors, familiar with the use and manufacture of iron weapons. Their headquarters were generally hilltop forts. They were used to fighting under tribal leaders, their religious needs were met by druids. They wore baggy trousers, had long hair, and were nearly all illiterate. Caesar had about 60,000 foot-soldiers, 4,000 cavalry, a few thousand mercenary German cavalrymen, an unknown number of auxiliary troops, and some Celtic allies. He was greatly outnumbered, but his army was better trained, better disciplined, and better equipped. He used his scouts efficiently, finding his way in a world without maps. He was a military genius, inspiring loyalty, imposing discipline, able to trick the enemy by great speed of movement, combined with patience and perseverance. Most of the time he was able to pick off his enemies piecemeal, as they were not at that time united in resisting conquest.

In the first year he defeated the Belgian tribes. Those in Normandy submitted without a fight. The Veneti (in present-day Brittany) were a greater problem, but he overcame their resistance, and was also successful in Aquitania. He found time for two expeditions to Britain in 55 and 54BC.

The greatest challenge came in 52BC, when Vercingetorix, an Auvergnat, whose father had briefly held suzerainty over all Gaul, raised an army of several hundred thousand from the tribes of central Gaul. The fighting ranged over a very wide area, in the course of which a substantial part of Caesar's allies defected. The final struggle occurred in Burgundy at Alesia, 50 km northwest of Dijon. Caesar mounted a siege. Vercingetorix managed to assemble a huge relief force. Caesar foresaw this possibility and surrounded the town with a double entrenchment, facing outwards as well as inwards, with pointed stakes in pits as a death trap for the relief force. They took flight and Vercingetorix surrendered.

The surviving Gauls were pacified by a degree of self-government and honours for their chiefs. Roman legions were distributed at strategic points within the conquered territory. It is not clear whether the tribute Rome received covered the costs of conquest and occupation in the first decades, but the booty certainly made Caesar very rich, and greatly reinforced his prestige and political leverage.

The area conquered by Caesar was known as Gallia Comata (long-haired Gaul). Augustus later divided it into three provinces, Aquitania, Lugdunensis, and Belgica, plus the military zone on the Rhine, populated by soldiers and their dependents.

The major push for Romanization, urbanization, and infrastructure investment took place in Provence (Narbonensis). A new town was created in the north at Vienne in 43BC and army veterans were settled there. In 30BC, Augustus created a naval base at Frejus and installed colonies of veterans at Orange and Nîmes. Other towns which flourished in the region in the early empire were Vaison-la-Romaine, Avignon, and Valence up the Rhone valley. They all got their quota of amphitheatres, aqueducts, baths, temples, basilicas, and fora. The via Aurelia ran from Rome to Arles, the via Domitia from Nimes to Spain, and the via Agrippa from Arles northwards to Lyon. There was also major investment in waterworks, the most spectacular being the Pont du Gard and its 50 km of canal supplying water to Nimes. Gaul was a major producer and exporter of wine, and red-glazed *terra sigillata* pottery. Graufesenque, near Millau in southern France, was the main centre of pottery production.

In the conflict between Caesar and Pompey in 49BC, Massilia sided with Pompey. As a punishment, it lost the autonomous status which had given her control of the coast from Montpellier to Nice.

Arelate (Arles) became the new capital of Provence. To feed its 12,000 population, a water-powered grain mill was constructed in the second century with a daily production of four to five tons of flour. It was built on a sharp slope with a 30 metre drop from the top of a hill. Acqueducted water was fed in at the top and diverted in two parallel channels, each of which had eight basalt grindstones. Below the mill, the outflow was used for irrigation. Another striking example of Roman technology of the same period was the pontoon bridge across the Rhone in Arles. It replaced a stone bridge which collapsed. The bridge stretched 280 metres across a river subject to violent floods. On each bank there were massive stone piers built on arches through which smaller ships could pass. For larger vessels, there was a drawbridge. The 192 metre mid-section was a wooden bridge supported by 20 boats with their prows pointed into the stream. They were tethered together and anchored to towers at the end of each pier. Their flexibility enabled them to resist the current, and they were easily reparable.

Acquisition of Egypt, 30BC

From 49 to 30BC, the contest for political leadership reverberated throughout the Empire. Caesar drove Pompey out of Italy, attacked and defeated the Pompeian forces in Spain, put down the rebellion in Massilia, and defeated Pompey in Greece in 48BC. Pompey took refuge in Egypt and was murdered. In 47BC, Caesar crossed to Egypt, defeated Ptolemy XIII, and established Cleopatra as sole ruler. He crushed a revolt in Asia Minor, and defeated the Pompeian loyalists in Africa. In 45BC, he went back to southern Spain and defeated Pompey's sons at Munda.

Caesar was assassinated in 44BC. This sparked another conflict for political hegemony, in which Mark Antony and Caesar's adopted son Octavian were the main protagonists. It involved fighting in Cisalpine Gaul, the Balkans, Greece, Asia Minor, and Egypt. Octavian defeated Antony at Actium in Greece in 31BC, pursued him to Egypt in 30BC, where he and his mistress, Queen Cleopatra, committed suicide. Octavian became master of the Roman world, and Egypt a Roman province.

Egypt was the most prosperous and densely settled province in the Empire and Alexandria was the main centre of learning in the Greek and Roman world. Egyptian output per hectare was much higher than in Italy because of the abundant and reliable flow of Nile water and the annual renewal of topsoil in the form of silt. Seed yields were ten to one—much higher than the Italian ratio of four to one (see Bowman 1996: 18 for Egypt, and Hopkins 2002: 198 for Italy), and there was no need for fallow. As a result, Egyptian agriculture produced a surplus which the Pharoahs and the Ptolomies used to support a brilliant civilization. Under its new status, as a Roman province, a substantial part of it's surplus was siphoned off. Large grain ships carried wheat from Alexandria to feed the population of Rome. Johnson (1936: 481) quotes the estimate of Aurelius Victor that the annual tribute from Egypt under Augustus was 20 million modii (135,000 metric tons). This would have covered 70 per cent of the consumption of the city of Rome.

Egyptian exports to Italy included flax and linen products, papyrus, glassware, jewellery, marble, porphyry, and other exotic building stones. Alexandria was also the main entrepot for merchandise coming up the Red Sea from India, Arabia, and East Africa.

Conquest of the Danubian Provinces as a Protective Shield, 16BC–AD

After the Egyptian conquest there were 44 years in which Augustus had supreme power, established a new kind of imperial rule and consolidated the empire.

This process was continued for another 23 years by his stepson and successor, Tiberius.

One of the first problems Augustus faced was the eastern border of Gaul, which Caesar had fixed on the Rhine. It was subject to attacks and migratory movements from Germany. Campaigns (16BC–16AD) to push the frontier further east were led by his two stepsons, Drusus and Tiberius, his grandson Germanicus, and Varus, Agrippa's son-in-law.

There was some success in annexing territory east of the Rhine, and Roman citizenship was given to sons of German chiefs who served as officers in the Roman army. One of these, Arminius, defected and exterminated Varus and three Roman legions (20,000 men) in 9AD. Germanicus was sent with large land forces and a fleet in an unsuccessful attempt at retaliation. As troops were needed urgently to put down a rebellion in Hungary, the attempt at conquest beyond the Rhine was abandoned.

Roman territory on the west bank of the Rhine remained a military area until 90AD, when it was split into two provinces. *Germania Inferior* stretched from the Dutch coast, south of Amsterdam, through Nijmegen, up to Bonn and Remagen. *Germania Superior* included Koblenz, Mainz, and from Strasbourg south to Lake Geneva.

Augustus and Tiberius created a defensive shield of provinces south of the Danube, stretching from Switzerland to the Black Sea.

Raetia was conquered in 15BC, with little resistance from the local tribes. It stretched from Konstanz in the west to Salzburg in the east, from the Brenner pass in the south to Regensburg. It remained under legionary occupation, together with the *Alpes Poeninae*, and was made a province later by the emperor Claudius. The *Alpes Cottiae* and *Alpes Maritimae* were conquered in 14BC. These three Alpine territories were sandwiched between Italy and Gaul.

Noricum, to the east of Raetia, contained most of present-day Austria except the Tirol and Vienna. It was incorporated peaceably into the empire at about the same time as Raetia.

Pannonia stretched along the Danube from Vindobona (Vienna) into Hungary, via Carnuntum, a major fort, Solva (Estergom) to Acquincum (Budapest). It then followed the sharp south bend of the Danube almost to Belgrade. There were Roman infiltrations into this area from 35BC until 9AD, when Tiberius established control.

Dalmatia stretched along the east Adriatic coast from Rijeka (50km south of Trieste) to the northern tip of Albania. It had been part of Illyricum, a former client state. It became an imperial province in 9AD, with its capital at Salona (Split). It was Diocletian's home town, and he retired there in 305AD, when he abdicated as emperor.

Moesia Superior, more or less equivalent to Serbia, stretched from Singidunum (Belgrade) to Scupi (Skopje). It was subdued and put under a Roman praefectus in 29BC. Later Tiberius added *Moesia Inferior* along the Danube to the Black Sea coast, where it became the headquarters of a Roman fleet (Classis Moesia). It occupied what is now northern Bulgaria and the Romanian Black Sea coast below the Danube.

Provinces Acquired after 14AD

Britannia. Julius Caesar made reconnaissance visits in 55 and 54BC. The emperor Claudius ordered the invasion about 90 years later in 43AD. It was not a very rational decision. The revenue it produced hardly covered the costs of occupation, and its exports were on a small scale compared with those of Spain and the Maghreb. Rome would have lost nothing strategically if it had never acquired Britain. The initial conquest required four legions. There was fierce resistance. The conquest of Ireland was never attempted. Wales was only partially controlled. Hadrian kept the Scots at bay by building a huge stone wall and ditch in 122–127AD which stretched nearly 120 km, from the coast near Carlisle to Newcastle. It had 17 forts and 160 signal towers. A second turf and earth wall was built further north between the Forth and Clyde by the next emperor, Antoninus Pius. From the end of the first century, the military headquarters was in York. From the end of the third century, Saxon invaders started to attack the northeast of Britain. Many Roman soldiers serving in Britain settled there after their discharge from the army, but otherwise Rome did not create settlements in Britain as it did in Spain, Gaul, or the Maghreb. Although there was some degree of Romanization, Collingwood (1937: 66) presented a rather gloomy picture of Roman cultural influence, 'in Britain wall-plaster is found everywhere, but *graffiti* on it are almost wholly lacking'. Rome abandoned Britain in 410AD.

Thracia became a client state in 148BC when Macedonia became a Roman province. It alternated between being a nuisance and an ally. Augustus partitioned the kingship in 12AD. Tiberius did the same in 19AD. It became a Roman province in 46AD. In the north and northwest it was bordered by Moesia, in the south by Macedon. The rest of its border was maritime, stretching from the Euxine (Black Sea), through the Propontis (Sea of Marmara), and the Aegean. It included part of modern Bulgaria (Sofia, and Plovdiv), and European Turkey.

Agri Decumates: In 74AD, Rome acquired a triangular strip of land in south-west Germany, including the Black Forest. This helped to shorten communications between the Rhine and Danubian armies. The territory was lost to a new tribal formation, the Alemanni, in 260.

Dacia was the only province north of the Danube, in the Transylvanian territory of modern Romania. It was conquered by Trajan and became a Roman province in 105AD. His campaign is illustrated in detail on Trajan's column in Rome. It was abandoned in 270AD.

Nabatea, with its capital at Petra, formerly a client state, was incorporated in the empire as the province of Arabia in 106AD.

Osrhoene in northwest Mesopotamia was a Parthian vassal with its capital at Edessa. For long a buffer state, it was annexed by Septimius Severus in 199AD. In 226, the Sassanians wiped out Parthia, revived the Persian empire and inflicted a series of military defeats on Rome between 240 and 260 in the process of reclaiming Mesopotamia. Osrhoene was recaptured by Diocletian in 296 and held by Rome until 336.

THE DISINTEGRATION OF THE EMPIRE

In the century and a half following the death of Augustus, the population of the empire rose by a third (see Table 1.4), including the six newly conquered provinces mentioned above. There seem to have been significant gains in per capita income in north Africa and some advance in the west European provinces. In Rome, there was very lavish public expenditure. Caligula built a 1,300 ton super-freighter to transport the obelisk now standing in front of St. Peter's from Egypt. Claudius created the new harbour of Portus at Ostia. Nero built his huge 'golden house'. The Flavian emperors built the Colosseum, Trajan's Forum, the Pantheon and Hadrian's villa at Tivoli. However, 164AD was probably the peak for income, urbanization, and population.

In 165–180, the Antonine plague (a smallpox pandemic) killed off a sixth of the population, including two emperors. In much of the third century, there was a chaotic political situation. There were 22 emperors between 235 and 284. All but two were murdered or killed in action. There was increasing pressure on the Rhine, Danube, and eastern frontiers. The Agri Decumates were lost to the Alemanni, Dacia to the Goths, and Osrhoene to the Sassanian-Persian empire. There was increasing strain on imperial finances and, as a consequence, a long period of currency debasement and price inflation. Between the first century and 270AD, the silver content of coins fell from 97 per cent to 4 per cent (Hopkins 1980: 123). In the third century population declined and it seems certain that there was some decline in per capita income.

At the end of the third century, the emperor Diocletian (284–305) made major changes in the imperial system to tighten control of the provinces and reinforce military effectiveness. He created a 'Dominate' to replace the 'Principate', taking the title of 'Dominus et Deus'. He doubled the number of provinces, increased the size of the bureaucracy and army. He made an unsuccessful attempt to stem inflation by issuing a maximum price decree. His persecutions were also unsuccessful in eliminating Christianity. Rome ceased to be the control centre of the empire. Diocletian nominated a co-emperor and two junior rulers (caesars) creating a tetrarchy (foursome) with authority over different areas. He took control of the eastern half of the empire with military headquarters in Sirmium on the Danube frontier, and residence in Nicomedia; his caesar was stationed at Antioch to deal with threats from the Sassanians; his co-emperor took care of the west, residing in Milan; with his caesar at Trier on the Rhine frontier.

The tetrarchic system broke down after Diocletian retired. The division of the empire into east and west was reinforced by Constantine (306–337), who built a new capital at Constantinople where a second imperial administration and senate were created. The wheat tribute from Egypt to Rome was redirected to Constantinople. He inaugurated a major change in the imperial ideology by deathbed conversion to Christianity. In 391, the emperor Theodosius banned paganism. Christianity became the state religion. A new hierarchy of bishops, priests, nuns, monks, and hermits was financed from public funds, and legacies from the faithful. This added another layer to the imperial bureaucracy, and religious schisms made it hard to control.

The new system increased the cost of imperial governance and the burden of taxes. It weakened the role of the local elites and city authorities who had played a major role in the governance and cohesion of the republic and the principate. 'Civic office became less popular in late antiquity than it had been in the early empire, when local aristocrats had competed fiercely and spent heavily in order to hold office'. In the early empire 'local aristocratic munificence ... paid for expensive amenities and entertainment ... to gain for the donors the applause of their fellow citizens'. Local elites lost interest in public office, and 'in Italy, and probably in most of the northern provinces, aristocratic munificence almost completely disappeared' (citations from Ward-Perkins 1998: 376–8).

In the fourth century the population of the empire declined, because the inflow of slaves was reduced, there was increasing incidence of endemic disease, and the Christian clergy were celibate. The manpower shortage led to increasing use of barbarian mercenaries in the military, and the eastern empire permitted settlement of barbarians in thinly populated areas.

In the course of time and through closer contact, barbarians became more sophisticated. The difference between their weaponry and that of Roman troops narrowed considerably and they were able to operate in bigger and better organized groups. By the third century, the main tribal groups were the Franks on the lower Rhine, Alemanni in southern Germany, Vandals in Hungary and Silesia, Visigoths and Ostrogoths further east. Even further east, the Huns were attacking and driving the other barbarians westward (see Starr 1965).

In 378, a Visigothic army inflicted a massive defeat on the eastern empire near Hadrianopolis, killing two-thirds of the Roman force and the emperor Valens. After this defeat the emperor Theodosius (379–395) recognized the Visigoths as allies and allowed a quarter million to settle within the empire.

In the fifth century, the bureaucracy and military of the western empire collapsed. In 406 Vandals, Alans, and Sueves crossed the Rhine and established themselves in different parts of Gaul. In 408, they crossed the Pyrenees and began the conquest of Roman Spain. Britain was abandoned to the barbarians in 410. In 429 the Vandals penetrated north Africa, captured Carthage ten years later and went on to establish bases in Sicily, Sardinia, Corsica, and the Balearic islands, cutting off major sources of Roman grain supply as well as tax and transfer income. In 455 they attacked and sacked Rome. The barbarian incursions were successful because of the inadequacy of the Roman military, and because civilian populations were often accommodating. Most of the barbarian invaders wanted to share the benefits of Roman civilization rather than destroy it. In time many of them became Christians.

In 408–410 Alaric the Goth besieged and sacked Rome. The emperor Honorius took refuge in Ravenna which became an enclave (exarchate) of the Byzantine empire until 751. The last Roman emperor was dismissed in 476 by Odoacer, a Goth who became king with the acquiescence of the Byzantine emperor. He was murdered and replaced in 493 by Theodoric, an Ostrogoth, who ruled until 526, again with Byzantine acquiescence.

In 533, the eastern emperor Justinian achieved a dramatic but temporary revival. His general, Belisarius, conquered Carthage, restored Roman rule in north Africa, drove the Vandals out of the Mediterranean, and defeated the Ostrogoths in Italy. The Byzantines ruled Italy from 535 to 568, then lost control to the Lombards. For the next thirteen centuries, sovereignty in Italy was fragmented.

At the end of the sixth century the Roman empire in the west was a mouldering corpse, though there were still some remnants of Romanization, and the process of demographic and economic decline was gradual. The final blow to most of the empire came in the seventh century when Muslim invaders took over in west Asia, Egypt, north Africa, and Spain. This was indeed a conquest and a change of civilizations. The greatly truncated Byzantine empire survived until 1453, when it too was conquered.

The Belgian historian Pirenne (1939: 242) provided a succinct description of the situation in western Europe in the ninth century:

If we consider that in the Carolingian epoch, the minting of gold had ceased, the lending of money at interest was prohibited, there was no longer a class of professional merchants, that Oriental products (papyrus, spices and silk) were no longer imported, that the circulation of money was reduced to a minimum, that laymen could neither read or write, that taxes were no longer organised, and that the towns were merely fortresses, we can say without hesitation that we are confronted by a civilisation that had retrogressed to the purely agricultural stage; which no longer needed commerce, credit and regular exchange for the maintenance of the social fabric.

ROMAN DEMOGRAPHY

Population of the Empire and Its Provinces

There have been three systematic attempts to estimate the population of component parts of the empire as shown in Table 1.2. The first was made by *Karl Julius Beloch* (1854–1929). He was born in Germany, wrote in German, had an American wife, and spent most of his life in Italy, teaching ancient history at the University of Rome from 1879 to 1929. He was a pioneer of quantitative economic history, and had a vast research output. His first article on population (of Sicily) appeared in 1874, and his last book on Italian population appeared posthumously in 1961! He was assiduous in his search for evidence, meticulous in documenting it, and very clear in explaining his detective work in crosschecking different sources and the conjectures he made to fill gaps in the evidence. His 1886 study is still the *magnum opus* of Roman demography. He stressed a point David Hume made in 1752: the need for scepticism about figures cited by classical authors.

Beloch made an accurate estimate of the area of different components of the empire, which was not available in ancient times. He used planimetric estimates by military cartographers: Behm 1866, Petermann 1872, and Strelbitzky 1882, making detailed adjustments for differences between ancient and modern boundaries (p. 28). All subsequent analysts of Roman demography have accepted Beloch's territorial estimates. By showing density of settlement, they provide an important crosscheck on the plausibility of his population estimates. Beloch was also careful in striving for chronological consistency in his crosscountry comparisons

He was very careful in describing changes in geographic coverage and administrative practice which have to be kept in mind when comparing census results (pp. 340–78). The last Republican census registered 910,000 citizens in 69BC. The third census of Augustus registered 4,937,000 in 14AD (see Augustus, *Res Gestae* in Brunt and Moore 1967: 22–3). The huge leap between the two was due in large part to administrative changes (see Beloch: 312–78). The Republican census did not include citizens living in northern Italy above the river Po, as Cisalpina was still a province. It also omitted citizens living in 60 towns and municipalities in the western provinces of the empire which the Augustan census included (see Beloch, p. 372 and 377).

The Republican censuses counted adult males. Those of Augustus included all citizens and their families, as well as widows and orphans. To make them comparable one needs to apply a multiplier of about 2.85 to the Republican figure (see p. 376). Some later analysts (Frank 1933: 315; Lo Cascio 1994, 2001:121; Morley 2001: 50–1) disregard or dispute the change in census coverage and apply the multiplier to the Augustan census results. As a result their estimates of the Italian population at the time of Augustus are highly inflated (twice as big as Beloch's), and they greatly exaggerate the rate of population growth.

In assessing the population of the Italian peninsula in 14AD, Beloch started with the census figure of 4.9 million; deducted citizens living in provinces outside peninsular Italy; added (p. 486) about 250,000 foreigners (*peregrini*) resident in Italy, and two million slaves. In his summary table (p. 507), he shows a total of six million (which was the mid-point of his range). On p. 437, he suggested that it might have been as high as seven million.

Egypt is the only other part of the empire for which census material has survived. Beloch's evidence was weaker and less detailed elsewhere, particularly for the Asian provinces (pp. 242–54) and the Maghreb where his discussion of sources (pp. 465–73) was rather fuzzy about the period covered.

In estimating the population of the city of Rome to have been 800,000 in 14AD, Beloch used three measures: (i) the area of the city within its walls to assess density of settlement; (ii) estimates of the number of people benefiting from free wheat distributions, with an upward adjustment (detailed by age and gender, males being 55.7% of the total) to include non-recipients; (iii) estimates (p. 406) of the housing stock—46,600 *insulae* and about 1,800 *domus*. He suggested (p. 475) that many of the *insulae* were multi-story blocks of apartments which could (with the help of Roman cement) reach a height of 60 feet (18 metres). The *domus* were elite residences with large retinues of slaves. Hence it would have been legitimate to assume 15 inhabitants per *insula* and 50 per *domus*. His three approaches were fairly concordant.

There are other analysts with very different estimates for the city of Rome. Gibbon (1776) assumed it had 1.2 million inhabitants, and it is still quite common to assume it had a round million. Russell (1958: 65 and 73), suggested a much smaller figure of 350,000 at the time of Augustus. He assumed that an *insula* was a single apartment, 'which can hardly have held, on the average, more than the simple man-wife-children unit which is usually 3.5'. He assumed that a patrician's residence, *domus*, had an average of ten inhabitants. This gave him a total of 173,000 inhabitants, but he augmented this low figure, because, 'Rome was known for its great apartment houses swarming with people'. Later, in Russell (1985: 12–19), he estimated the average height of *insulae* from surviving remnants of a large marble map of Rome (*Forma Urbis*), which apparently indicated the number of stories in each individual *insula*. He suggested that the average height was 1.84 stories, but did not use this coefficient to change his earlier assumption of 3.5 to 6.4 people per *insula*. He reverted to his low estimate of 173,000.

Peter Brunt (1971: 131 and 383) made a careful scrutiny of the evidence on Italian population, following closely in Beloch's footsteps. His estimates for peninsular Italy and Rome were seven million and 750,000 in 14AD. The main difference was that Brunt assumed a bigger slave ratio. He estimated the population of the peninsula to have risen from five million in 225BC to seven million in 14AD. For him the increase was mainly due to a rise in slave numbers from 12 to about 36 per cent of the total, with a stable or falling population of citizens. At one point (p. 124) Brunt suggested that there were three million slaves in a total population of 7.5 million, but, as he finally opted for a population of seven million (p. 131), this implies that he reduced his slave estimate to 2.5 million.

The massive inflow of slaves had a dramatic socioeconomic impact. Keith Hopkins (1978a: 61–8) agued that slaves could be worked twice as intensively as free labour, and had a much smaller ratio of female and child dependents. As a result farmland could be worked more intensively, there were economies of scale which led to creation of large estates and extra income for the elite, expulsion of free peasantry, many of whom became urban proletarians, surviving on food or cash handouts (*frumentationes, congiaria* and *alimenta*). The system was viable as long as the process of imperial expansion and enslavement continued. Thereafter slave recruitment became a major problem as slave fertility was inadequate to maintain their number.

Following Beloch and Brunt, the next systematic attempt to provide estimates for all parts of the empire was made by *Colin McEvedy and Richard Jones* (1978). They were more ambitious in temporal scope and country coverage than any other historical demographer, covering the development of world population at intervals of two centuries from 400BC to 1000AD, and at shorter intervals to 1975. Their estimates are shown in clear and easily digestible fashion with graphs and maps. The descriptive text is forthright and reader-friendly.

Their estimates for 1AD are shown in Table 1.2. McEvedy published six other historical-demographic atlases of which *New Penguin Atlas of the Ancient World* (2nd edn, 2002) is the most useful for our purpose.

The McEvedy and Jones total for the empire (40.25 million) is about three-quarters of Beloch's 54 million. For Europe their total is similar but their estimates are much smaller for Asia and the Maghreb. For the Asian provinces Beloch showed 19.5 million; McEvedy and Jones 11 million less. Beloch estimated 11.5 million for Roman Africa; McEvedy and Jones 3.3 million less. They commented in detail on the reasons for the divergence (p.115 for Cyprus; p. 136 for Asia Minor; p. 140 for Syria; p. 220 for the Maghreb; p. 224 for Libya; p. 228 for Egypt).

Bruce Frier (2000) provided the third major round of estimates for 14AD. His aggregate result is 16 per cent lower than Beloch's and 11 per cent higher than McEvedy and Jones, whose estimates he treats with respect. My compromise estimate in Table 1.2 is closest to that of Frier.

Table 1.2. Population of the Roman Empire at the Death of Augustus, 14AD

	Beloch (1886)		McEvedy & Jones (1978)	Frier (2000)	Maddison	Maddison
	Area 000 sq km	Population (000s)	Population (000s)	Population (000s)	Population (000s)	Density (pop/km)
Peninsular Italy	250	6,000	7,000*	7,000	7,000	28.0
Sicily	26	600			600	23.0
Sardinia & Corsica	33	500			500	15.2
Iberia	590	6,000	5,000	5,000	4,150	7.0
Narbonensis	*100*	*1,500*			*1,500*	15.0
*Tres Galliae***	*535*	*3,400*			4,300	8.0
Gaul	635	4,900	5,750	5,800	5,800	9.1
Greek peninsula	267	3,000	2,000	2,800	2,000	7.5
Danubian Lands***	430	2,000	3,050	2,700	3,050	7.1
Roman Europe	**2,231**	**23,000**	**22,800**	**24,400**	**23,100**	**10.4**
Asia Minor****	547	13,000	6,000	8,200	8,000	14.6
Greater Syria*****	109	6,000	3,050	4,300	4,000	36.7
Cyprus	9.5	500	200	200	200	21.1
Roman Asia	**665.5**	**19,500**	**9,250**	**12,700**	**12,200**	**18.3**
Egypt	28	5,000	4,000	4,500	4,500	160.7
Cyrenaica******	15	500	400	400	400	26.7
Maghreb	400	6,000	3,800	3,500	3,800	9.5
Roman Africa	**443**	**11,500**	**8,200**	**8,400**	**8,700**	**19.6**
Total Empire	**3,339.5**	**54,000**	**40,250**	**45,500**	**44,000**	**13.2**

Notes: *includes Sicily and Sardinia; ** includes Aquitania, Lugdunensis, Belgica (Belgium and half of Netherlands), and Germany west of the Rhine; ***includes Switzerland (Raetia), Austria (Noricum), Hungary (Pannonia), Yugoslavia, Albania, and half of Bulgaria (Dalmatia and Moesia); ****includes Greek islands; *****includes Lebanon and Palestine; ******includes Tripolitania.

Source: Columns 1 and 2 from Beloch, p. 507; column 3 from Frier, p. 812; column 4 from McEvedy and Jones (for 1AD), p. 59 for Gaul, p. 105 for Iberia, p. 107 for Italy, p. 113 for Greece, pp. 87, 89, 93, 113 for Danube lands; pp. 115, 135, 139 for Asia; and pp. 223, 225, 227 for Africa. McEvedy and Jones estimate that, in 1AD, 2.7 million people lived in areas which later became part of the empire; these were Britannia, 0.6; Dacia, 0.8; Thracia 0.26; Nabatea and Osrhroene about 1 million. The rest of Europe had about 6.3 million inhabitants in an area of 7 million square km, i.e., an average density of 0.9 per square km (0.4 in European Russia, 2.0 elsewhere).

I had the following detailed considerations in mind in arriving at the compromise estimate:

1. For peninsular Italy, Frier used Brunt's estimate. This seems reasonable, though it differs from Beloch and McEvedy.

2. There is no disagreement on Sicily, Sardinia and Corsica.

3. For Iberia, Frier used McEvedy's estimate which is lower than Beloch's. I used the detailed and well-documented estimate of Carreras Monfort (1996) which is even lower.

4. For Gaul, the estimates of McEvedy and Frier are virtually identical and agree with Beloch's 1899 revision.

5. For Greece, I used McEvedy. Frier includes Albania and European Turkey in Greece. Albania was part of Dalmatia—included in the Danube provinces. European Turkey was part of Thracia—not a Roman province until 46AD.

6. I used McEvedy's estimate for the Danubian lands.

7. McEvedy and Frier both consider Beloch's estimates for Asia Minor and Syria to be too big. Frier's estimate was derived from Russell (1958: 148). Frier's table shows a total of 12.5 million, but his text (p. 811) suggests 12 million, which I adopted.

8. McEvedy and Frier agree that Beloch's estimate for Cyprus was too big.

9. Frier differs from Beloch and McEvedy on Egypt, but his judgement must be taken as authoritative as he has scrutinized the evidence much more intensively (in *The Demography of Roman Egypt*, 1994, co-authored with Roger Bagnall).

10. McEvedy and Frier have lower estimates than Beloch for Cyrenaica and the Maghreb. There is not much difference between them and I adopted Frier's figures.

Population Change, 300BC–600AD

Beloch's comparative estimates were essentially synchronic. He concentrated almost exclusively on the level of population in 14AD. Tables 1.3 and 1.4 show estimates of McEvedy and Jones for 300BC to 600AD and Frier's estimates for 14 to 164AD.

McEvedy and Jones show an average growth rate of 0.1 per cent a year from 300BC to 1AD, a slowdown to 0.056 per cent for 1–200AD, and a drop thereafter, as the empire decayed. The level in 600AD was slightly lower than it was 900 years earlier.

Frier shows total population of the empire growing by 0.17 per cent a year for the 150 year period he covers. This is a good deal faster than the McEvedy and Jones estimate for 1–200AD. However, these growth rates are more compatible than they seem. Frier chose his terminal point because it immediately preceded the Antonine plague, a smallpox epidemic which killed off 10 to 20 per cent of the population in different parts of the empire and had lingering effects thereafter. If we assume 15

Table 1.3. McEvedy and Jones' Estimates of Population Change, 300BC–600AD (within 14AD boundaries) (000s)

	300BC	200BC	1AD	200AD	400AD	600AD
Italy	4,500	5,000	7,000	7,000	5,000	3,500
Iberia	3,900	4,500	5,000	5,500	5,000	4,000
Roman Gaul	3,750	4,400	5,750	7,500	5,750	4,500
Greece	2,750	2,500	2,000	2,000	1,500	800
Danubian lands	2,275	2,550	3,050	3,550	3,450	2,600
Roman Europe	**17,175**	**18,950**	**22,800**	**25,550**	**20,700**	**15,400**
Asia Minor	4,500	5,000	6,000	7,000	6,000	5,000
Greater Syria	2,250	2,600	3,025	2,750	2,200	1,900
Cyprus	200	200	200	200	200	200
Roman Asia	**6,950**	**7,800**	**9,250**	**9,950**	**8,400**	**7,100**
Egypt	3,500	4,000	4,000	5,000	4,000	3,000
Cyrenaica	250	300	400	500	300	200
Maghreb	2,000	2,200	3,800	4,000	3,600	3,600
Roman Africa	**5,750**	**6,500**	**8,200**	**9,500**	**7,900**	**6,800**
Total	**29,875**	**33,250**	**40,250**	**45,000**	**37,000**	**29,300**

Source: McEvedy and Jones (1978). They give figures at 200 year intervals, starting with 400BC. I interpolated their estimates for 400BC and 200BC to derive the estimates for 300BC. The figures exclude provinces acquired after 14AD.

per cent mortality, Frier's figure for 200AD would be 50 million, and his growth rate would be 0.05 per cent a year. Frier regards (p. 813) the 164AD level as a peak, not regained in the Mediterranean basin until the sixteenth century. In terms of growth the two approaches concur, though Frier's estimate of population level is about 13 per cent higher than that of McEvedy and Jones.

Table 1.4. Frier's Estimates of Population 14–164AD

	(000s)	
	14AD	164AD
Italy*	8,100	8,700
Iberia	5,000	7,500
Roman Gaul	5,800	9,000
Greece	2,800	3,000
Danubian Lands	2,700	4,000
Roman Europe	**24,400**	**32,200**
Asia Minor	8,200	9,200
Greater Syria	4,300	4,800
Cyprus	200	200
Roman Asia	**12,700**	**14,200**
Egypt	4,500	5,000
Cyrenaica	400	600
Maghreb	3,500	6,500
Roman Africa	**8,400**	**12,100**
Total	**45,500**	**58,500**
Territory Annexed after 14AD		**2,700**

Note: *includes Sicily, Sardinia and Corsica.

Source: Frier (2000: 812, 814).

Life Expectation

Frier used modern demographic modelling techniques to analyse forces affecting population growth (age and gender distribution, life expectation at birth, fertility, and migration). His conclusions on life expectation seem to be upwardly biased. On p. 791 he concluded that, 'empirical evidence generally supports the modern consensus that average life expectation of Romans at birth was normally about 25 years, or perhaps lower'. Here he seems to be endorsing the view of Hopkins (1966), who suggested a range from 20 to 30 years, without evidence to justify the proposition. In fact, the evidence Frier cites suggest an average nearer to 23 years. He cites four sources:

1. The third century AD table of Ulpian based on actuarial estimates of life expectation for calculating annuity payments. Frier (1982) analysed it in detail. Its implied average life expectation at birth for the two sexes combined was 21 years, with a range from 19 to 23.
2. Skeletal evidence from fourth century Pannonian cemeteries closely supported Ulpian's schedule.
3. North African tombstones suggested a life expectancy at birth of 22.5 years for both sexes combined.
4. Evidence from 300 Egyptian census returns in Bagnall and Frier (1994: 109) suggested the average for both sexes was between 22 and 25 years (p. 109).

Frier (2000) used Coale and Demeny's Model West, level 3 (where expectation of life at birth is 25 years for females and 22.8 for males) to illustrate the probabilities of survival for different age cohorts. Model West level 2 (22.5 years for females and 20.4 for males) seems more appropriate and was used in Bagnall and Frier (1994).

There was no Roman taboo or legal constraint on infanticide and exposure (child abandonment) and Frier acknowledged the 'not negligible' impact of these practices in reducing life expectancy.

He does not mention military mortality. Duncan-Jones (1994: 35) estimated that only 45 per cent of soldiers survived after 25 years of service, implying a life expectation at birth for this group under 20 years.

He did not discuss the life expectation of slaves which was likely to have been considerably lower than that of the free population. However, he assumed that slave reproduction would be inadequate to keep up their number. He estimated this would require an annual slave inflow of 20,000.

Frier stressed the adverse effect of poor sanitation and infectious diseases in large cities, but did not quantify their impact on life expectation. In England in 1700, life expectation at birth was 38—much higher than in Rome—but only 18.5 in London and 41.3 in rural areas (see Woods, p. 365, and Wrigley et al. p. 614). The urban–rural differential could well have been just as sharp in the Roman empire.

Slave Population, Reproduction, and Inflows into the Empire

Following Scheidel (1997: 158), I assume that slaves were 10 per cent of the Empire's population. Brunt estimated that there were 2.5 million slaves in peninsular Italy. I assume there were two million in the rest of the Empire, an average of 5.4 per cent of the population. For Egypt, Bagnall and Frier (1994: 48–49) found that slaves were less than 11 per cent of the population and mostly female domestic servants. Whittaker (1996: 611) argued that in Roman Africa: 'the continuity of dependent relations between the rich and poor... must explain why there is so little evidence of Roman-style imported slavery on the land.' For other parts of the empire it is not clear what the slave ratio was.

Between the middle of the third century until the death of Augustus, the slave population grew as a result of conquest. Grant (1960: 131) gave an indication of the scale and sources of the inflow as follows:

slaves flooded into Rome from all quarters as a result of victorious wars. For example, there were 75,000 enslaved prisoners from the First Punic War, 30,000 from a single city— Tarentum—in the second of those wars, many Asiatics after Rome's successes against the Seleucid king, Antiochus III (189–8BC), 15,000 slaves from Epirus in 167BC, a similar number after Marius' victory over the Germans (102–1BC), perhaps nearly half a million in Caesar's Gallic Wars. They were sold in the great slave markets such as Capua and Delos. The markets were also kept well provided by the pirate kidnapers who, with the collaboration of eminent Romans, infested the Mediterranean; as well as by the exposure and sale of children by the destitute rural population.

Scheidel (1997) and Harris (1980 and 1999) disagreed about the relative importance of slave reproduction in maintaining slave numbers once the conquest inflow had tapered off. Scheidel used a demographic model to detail the various forces needed to offset mortality and manumission of slaves. He examined three different scenarios and concluded that slave reproduction would have been adequate to cover more than 80 per cent of replacement needs. He suggested an annual import of '14,000 young barbarians' would have sufficed to maintain slave numbers. This was lower than Frier suggested. Harris (1980) assumed that an annual import of 5 per cent would have been needed to keep the slave population stable. With a population of 4.5 million slaves, as I assumed, this would have required an annual import of 225,000. Scheidel's estimate of import requirements seems too low and Harris' too high.

Replacement by reproduction prevailed in the slave economy of the ante-bellum US and this might have been the case in Rome if conditions had been similar. In some respects slave conditions were better in the Roman empire than in the Caribbean and Brazil. The climate was more favourable. Slaves who were educated and skilled were able to purchase manumission and become Roman citizens without the racial stigma that would have been operative in the Americas.

Table 1.5. Ratios of Slave and Non-Slave Survival in the Americas

		Arrivals 1500–1820 (000s)	1820 Population (000s)	Ratio col.2/col.1
Caribbean	Whites	450	554	1.2/1.0
Caribbean	Blacks	3,700	2,400	0.6/1.0
Brazil	Whites	500	1,500	3.0/1.0
Brazil	Blacks	2,600	2,500	1.0/1.0
USA	Whites	718	7,884	11.0/1.0
USA	Blacks	400	1,772	4.4/1.0

Note: The figures for blacks in 1820 include mulattos.

Source: Maddison, 2001, pp. 35–38, and Maddison, 2003, p. 115.

On the other hand, as Finley (1971) showed, a large proportion of Roman slaves did back-breaking work in agriculture and mining, many of them were fettered and flogged. They were 'denied the most elementary of social bonds, kinship', they could not marry, and if they had 'families' these could be dispersed through sale by their owner. After the slave revolt of Spartacus in 71BC, 6,000 slaves were crucified. Tacitus described a case in 61AD where a slave owner was murdered by one of his slaves, and all 400 of them, including women and children, were executed as a collective punishment by decision of the Senate (see Finley, pp. 75, 102). A substantial quota of slaves were killed in the arena in a grisly form of public entertainment. In all these respects, they were worse off than slaves in Brazil and the Caribbean. Replacement was therefore a serious problem when imperial conquest tapered off.

Table 1.5 gives a rough idea of the differences in the degree to which slaves and white settlers were able to reproduce themselves in the Caribbean, Brazil, and the US.

Urbanization

Urbanization was a major tool in assimilating conquered populations.

Rome consolidated its territorial control in conquered areas by establishing *coloniae*, fortified urban settlements in strategic locations. They were populated by Roman citizens and retired soldiers designated by the authorities. They were built on land seized by Rome and laid out in a standard gridiron pattern of straight streets. Two main roads, the *decumanus maximus* and the *cardo maximus*, intersected at the centre of town where the forum was located, with other public buildings (a basilica, tribunal, and temples) nearby, and city gates at the periphery. They were intended to be miniature reproductions of Rome. Cadastral surveys were carried out and standardized land allotments made by a procedure known as centuriation. The city-builders also ensured the water supply. Salmon (1969: 159–64) lists 136 '*coloniae*' in Italy and 272 elsewhere in the Empire.

Urbanization was also a major feature of the elite lifestyle. Urban facilities were financed from the public purse and funding by the wealthy elite from their own pockets. There was large scale investment in aqueducts, baths, fountains, public toilets, sewers, drains, warehouses, granaries, markets, cemeteries, and jails which made urban life viable. Roads, bridges, harbours, and canals made them accessible. There were fora, law courts, fortresses, and city walls to provide justice and defence. Circuses, gymnasia, hippodromes, theatres, libraries, amphitheatres, basilicas provided entertainment and edification. Ostentatious public buildings— imperial palaces, temples, capitols, triumphal arches, statues, colonnaded arcades, and mausolea—reinforced the status and authority of the ruling elite and catered to religious needs. All these elements were present in Rome on a colossal scale. 'The architectural elements and the activities they implied were strikingly similar wherever one went. All these things in an expense-be-damned fashion expressed the highest ambitions of imperial civilisation' (MacMullen 1980: 57).

The massive public structures were possible because of the sophistication of Roman technology and engineering. They were the first to develop waterproof cement using pozzolana (volcanic dust). This had amazing strength and could support huge vaults. The most impressive is the Pantheon built in 118–125AD. Its vault has a diameter and height of 43 metres and is still standing.

There are several sources on Roman urbanization, but it is difficult to distinguish clearly between urban and smaller aggregations.[1] Hopkins (1978a: 69–70) stressed that 'the distinction between large village and town is arbitrary and was sometimes unclear in the ancient world'. In fact the administration of the empire was devolved in large degree to more or less autonomous city authorities who were also responsible for surrounding rural areas.

For the purpose of comparison with later experience of urbanization, I prefer a cut-off point distinguishing towns with 10,000 and more inhabitants as urban.

The most detailed quantitative estimates of town size in the Roman empire are those of Russell (see Table 1.6). His estimates make it possible to separate cities with a population of 10,000 or more from smaller aggregations. Russell's total for this category of city was about 1.8 million, an urban ratio of only 4.1 per cent for an Empire with 44 million inhabitants. However, he clearly had a downward bias. His figure for the city of Rome was half of Brunt's, and for Alexandria half of the estimate of Bagnall and Frier.

Goldsmith (1983: 272, footnote 49) suggested that the city of Rome had a population of a million, the rest of peninsular Italy another 300,000 in 30 cities with more than 5,000 inhabitants, and a further 300,000 in 400 smaller 'cities'. He then rounded this down to 1.5 million—an urban ratio over 21 per cent of his seven million total. If we take Brunt's estimate of 750,000 for Rome and restrict the estimate for other towns to those with more than 10,000, it seems more likely that the total for peninsular Italy would have been about a million—an urban ratio of 14 percent (similar to the Italian level in 1800 (see Table 1.7).

For the rest of the empire, Goldsmith suggested an urban ratio of 11.5 per cent— 5.5 million in a total population he estimated to be 48 million. If we applied his overall ratio to our total population estimate of 37 million outside peninsular Italy, his total would drop to 4.2 million. He suggested there were three million people in

Table 1.6. Russell's Estimates of the Size of 51 Cities in the Empire

	(000s)			(000s)			(000s)
Italy			**Spain**			**Egypt**	
Rome	350		Cadiz	65		Alexandria	216
Capua	36		Tarragona	27		Oxyrhyncus	34
Pisa	20		Cordoba	20		Memphis	34
Catania	18		Merida	15		Hermopolis	24
Naples	15		Cartagena	10		Arsinoe	20
Bologna	10		Pamplona	10		Antinoe	16
						Heliopolis	14
Asia Minor			**Syria**			**North Africa**	
Smyrna	90		Antioch	90		Carthage*	50
Ephesus	51		Apamea	37		Rusicade	20
Nicomedia	34		Damascus	31		Cirta	20
Ancyra	34		Bostra	30		Hadrumetum	20
Pergamum	24		Tyre	20		Sicca V.	16
Cyzicus	24		Baalbek	13.5		Thugga	13
Mytilene	23		Sidon	12		Thysdrus	10
Nicaea	18		Jerusalem	10		Hippo Regis	10
Antiocheia	17		**Greece**			Lambraesis	10
Miletus	15		Corinth	50			
Isaura	12		Athens	28			
Trebizond	10						

Note: *Russell shows a range of 35–50 for Carthage, I have shown his upper limit.

Source: Russell (1958: 65–83). I have excluded all cities for which his estimate was below 10,000, or which refer to periods later than the first century AD.

nine cities having more than a 100,000 population. This may be a bit exaggerated, but is easier to accept than his suggestion that another 2.5 million people in 3,000 smaller cities with more than 1,000 inhabitants should be treated as urbanites. Using our cut-off criterion, most of the latter group would be excluded. It seems more likely that urban dwellers totalled three million in the provinces, or 8 per cent of our 37 million.

Within the provinces, Egypt was the most urbanized and the best documented. Bagnall and Frier (1994: 54–55) estimated the population of Alexandria to have been about half a million in the period they cover (first to third century AD) and cite Rathbone's estimates for district capitals (*metropoleis*). Of these Hermopolis had a population of about 37,000, and there were four or possibly five others which were bigger. I infer from their work that there were around 800,000 urban dwellers in Egypt—about 18 per cent of the population. This leaves 2.2 million in the other provinces—about 7 per cent of their population. This would make an imperial total of 4 million—an average urban ratio of 9 per cent in the empire as a whole.

It is interesting to compare this with the standardized estimates shown in Table 1.7 for western Europe, China, and Japan.

The Roman Empire ratio was similar to that of western Europe in 1700. This was a high level of urbanization for an empire whose per capita GDP (as shown below) was around $570 compared with about $1,000 in western Europe in 1700.

However, inter-country differentials between urbanization ratios are not uniquely related to differences in per capita income. In 1800, per capita income in China was

Table 1.7. Urbanization Ratios in Europe and Asia, 1500–1890 (population in cities 10,000 and over as percent of total population)

	1500	1600	1700	1800	1890
Belgium	21.1	8.8	23.9	18.9	34.5
France	4.2	5.9	9.2	8.8	25.9
Germany	3.2	4.1	4.8	5.5	28.2
Italy	12.4	15.1	13.2	14.6	21.2
Netherlands	15.8	24.3	33.6	28.8	33.4
Portugal	3.0	14.1	11.5	8.7	12.7
Scandinavia	0.9	1.4	4.0	4.6	13.2
Spain	6.1	11.4	9.0	11.1	26.8
Switzerland	1.5	2.5	3.3	3.7	16.0
England & Wales	3.1	5.8	13.3	20.3	61.9
Scotland	1.6	3.0	5.3	17.3	50.3
Ireland	0.0	0.0	3.4	7.0	17.6
Western Europe	**5.8**	**7.9**	**9.5**	**10.2**	**29.6**
China	3.8	4.0a	n.a.	3.8	4.4
Japan	2.9	4.4	n.a.	12.3	16.0

Notes and Sources: (a) 1650 European countries from de Vries (1984: 30, 36, 46). The total for Western Europe is a weighted average. China and Japan from Rozman (1973) adjusted to refer to cities 10,000 and over, see Maddison (1998: 33–36). The great virtue of de Vries' work was the establishment of symmetric lower limit for all countries, i.e., 10,000 inhabitants or more. Unfortunately, it is difficult to update his estimates beyond 1890. In the regular UN surveys the lowest comparable unit is cities of 500,000 and over, below that the lower limit distinguishing urban from rural agglomerations is not clear: (a) because it reflects administrative and legal considerations which preclude quantification or (b) where there are explicit quantitative cut-offs, they are not standardized—varying from 200 in Denmark, Norway, and Sweden; 1,000 in Australia and Canada; 1,500 in Ireland; 2,000 in France, Germany, and the Netherlands; 2,500 in China and the US; 4,000 in Japan; 5,000 in Belgium and India; to 10,000 in Italy, Portugal, Spain and Switzerland. See UN Population Division (2004), *World Urbanization Prospects*, 2003 (ed) New York, pp. 111–28.

about $600 and the urbanization ratio was 3.8 per cent. In Japan, per capita income was about $650 and the urbanization ratio 12.3 per cent (see Table 1.7 for these ratios, and Maddison 2003: 262 for per capita income). The China/Japan dichotomy was due to differences in regime. China was run by an imperial bureaucracy which raised income from taxes on the peasantry and fostered rural development. In Japan the military regime of the shogun forced the daimyo and their samurai to live in a single castle town in each of their 280 domains, and abandon their previous managerial role in agriculture. Daimyo were required to spend part of the year in the capital, Edo, and to keep their families there permanently as hostages for good behaviour. The shadow emperor and his court were confined to Kyoto. In 1800, Japan had a population of 30 million: the capital, Edo had a million inhabitants, Osaka and Kyoto about 300,000 each; Kanazawa and Nagoya more than a 100,000 (see Chapter 3).

ROMAN INCOME

Measuring the Income of the Empire in 14AD

There are two estimates worthy of note. The first was made by Keith Hopkins (1934–2000), a distinguished sociologist and professor of ancient history. Hopkins (1980) presented an impressionistic overview of the economics of empire which included a rough estimate (pp. 118–20) of the per capita subsistence level in terms of food, clothing, heat, and housing. He expressed the total of these items in wheat units (250 kg per person per year). Actual wheat consumption was assumed to be 220 kg, with 15 kg worth of wheat units for clothing and another 15 kg worth for heating and housing. He added a third (he said it was a quarter) for seed and then multiplied it by Beloch's 54 million estimate of population of the empire in 14AD. Hopkins should not have treated seed as consumption as it is an intermediate rather than a final product. In any case, he allowed too much for seed. If the seed ratio was a quarter, it should have been 55 kg (25 per cent of per capita wheat consumption of 220 kg). Hopkins (2002: 198) allowed a third of 250 kg (83.3 kg) per person year for seed. Production of clothing and housing did not require seed input.

Hopkins (1980) suggested rather casually that the gross product of the empire would average out at less than twice his minimum subsistence level. He revised his estimates in 1995/96, this time assuming a population of 60 million, and guessing the actual product to have been 50 per cent higher than his minimum. He made a disdainful acknowledgement of Goldsmith's (1984) article, suggesting it was 'error prone' because it was 'based on the average of all previous scholarly guesses'.

The second estimate was made by Raymond Goldsmith (1904–88) a quantitative historian-economist, polyglot, and bibliophile, who made major contributions to comparative analysis of national income, financial structure, capital formation, and capital stock. He pushed his comparative analysis very far back in time. Goldsmith (1984) on the size and structure of the Roman empire was a first instalment of his wider survey (1987) of financial systems in Periclean Athens, Augustan Rome, the Abbasid caliphate, the Ottoman and Moghul empires, Tokugawa Japan, Medici Florence, Elizabethan England, and the Dutch Republic. Goldsmith's estimates were for actual GDP (gross domestic product), not minimum income. His approach was more coherent in terms of national accounting conventions and arithmetic than Hopkins'.

Goldsmith estimated national income from the expenditure side and presented a reconciliation from the income side, as shown in Table 1.8.

He assumed that the population of the empire was 55 million. For most purposes, the population figure is unimportant as Goldsmith's basic estimate was for per capita income. In Table 1.9 I adjusted his figures and used my population estimate of 44 million.

Goldsmith, like Hopkins, gave no country or regional breakdown of his estimates. This is a pity, as it seems clear that per capita GDP in peninsular Italy was significantly higher than in other provinces. It had a higher labour input per head of population as it made proportionately greater use of slave labour. Labour productivity was probably higher because of the better infrastructure of roads and harbours, and greater specialization of agriculture, in a country with large imports of cereals.

The GNP (gross national product) and NDI (national disposable income) of peninsular Italy were higher than GDP because the state received a large flow of various types of tribute and tax income from the provinces, and the elite group received substantial rents on property they had acquired in the provinces. Senators also had a large income from official emoluments, perquisites, and other spoils of office (e.g., Cicero was governor in Cilicia; Pliny in Bithynia and Pontus, Sallust in Africa Nova; and Tacitus proconsul in Asia). Equestrian entrepreneurs benefited as contractors for public works or as tax-farmers. Because of the burden of these transfers, the disposable income of the rest of the empire was lower than its GDP.

In the official terminology of modern national accounts, Gross domestic product (GDP) equals expenditure, value added in production, or income generated within the territory of a country. Gross national product (GNP) is GDP plus or minus net receipts from transfers of property or labour income from the rest of the world. National disposable income (NDI) is GNP plus or minus net current transfers received in money or in kind from the rest of the world (these would include taxes and tribute grain). See *System of National Accounts 1993*, Eurostat, IMF, OECD, UN, and World Bank.

Although I accepted Goldsmith's estimate of total GDP: (i) I modified his estimate of elite income which was much too low, and differentiated between income of free and slave labour (Table 1.9); (ii) His estimate is for the Empire as a whole. I made separate estimates for the GDP of peninsular Italy (the metropole) and the rest of the empire. I found per capita GDP in peninsular Italy to be more than 50 per cent higher than in the rest of the empire (Table 1.10); (iii) I made a rough quantification of tax and transfers from the rest of the empire to peninsular Italy to measure their respective levels of NDI (national disposable income). I found average per capita NDI two-thirds higher in the metropole; (iv) Goldsmith (1984: 280) tried to get an inter-temporal perspective on the per capita income level in the Roman empire by comparing it with that in England in 1688 as estimated by Gregory King. I pursued this lead further, linking the Roman estimate with my analysis of King's work in Chapter 5 below. In this way I was able to estimate Roman per capita levels in 1990 Geary-Khamis dollars; (v) finally, I made stylized conjectures of levels of per capita income in different provinces of the empire (see Tables 1.11 and 1.12).

Goldsmith's Expenditure Account and Maddison's Modifications

1. Goldsmith took annual per capita wheat consumption of adult males to be 50 *modii* = 337.5kg, and assumed an average 253 kg per capita for the whole population, including women and children.

2. The price of wheat was taken to be 3HS (*sestercii*) per modius, i.e., 0.441HS per kilo.

3. Therefore the annual cost of wheat per person was 112HS. He assumed total grain consumption, including an unspecified quantity of barley, would have cost 130HS per person per annum.

4. Grain was taken to be 65 per cent of food consumption. His rationale for this ratio was that it was close to that in India in 1951–61.

5. Thus he assumed that total per capita food consumption cost 200HS. He then added 75 per cent, 150HS, for non-food items, arguing that this was approximately equal to the proportion in England and Wales in 1688. Hence total consumption expenditure per capita was 350HS.

6. He suggested that government consumption was about 5 per cent of GDP and allowed less than 3 per cent for investment (pp. 283–4). His estimates for both items seem too low.

I modified Goldsmith's estimate for 'government and investment' which seemed too low. My estimate for this item is 13 per cent of GDP compared to Goldsmith's 8 per cent. I reduced his estimate for 'other consumption' accordingly.

I derived my estimate of government consumption from Hopkins and Rathbone. Hopkins (2002: 199–200) suggested that government expenditure on the military was about 450–500 million HS in the middle of the first century. Rathbone (1996: 312) suggests that the military accounted for less than half of all imperial spending in this period, At that time, therefore government expenditure would have been about 1.1 billion.[2]

For gross investment expenditure, there is little firm evidence. But in an economy with such a large commitment to urban splendour, roads, shipping, harbours, granaries, aqueducts, etc. the investment/GDP ratio could not have been significantly lower than in England in 1688. Thus I estimated gross investment to have been 6.5 per cent of GDP.

I made much bigger modifications to Goldsmith's income estimates, adjusting his labour income estimate downwards and raising the estimate of elite income.

Table 1.8. Goldsmith's Estimates of GDP (Expenditure and Income) in the Empire as a Whole in 14AD

	Expenditure			Income	
	HS per capita	Total GDP million HS		% of total income	GDP million HS
Wheat	112	6,160	Labour income	83	17,380
Other cereals	18	990	Non-labour income	17	3,520
Other food	70	3,850	**Total income**	**100**	**20,900**
Other consumption	150	8,250			
Total private consumption	**350**	**19,250**			
Government & Investment	30	1,650	**Employment** (000s)	22 million	
Total GDP (Expenditure)	**380**	**20,900**	**Population** (000s)	55 million	

Notes: The Roman coinage system consisted of the sestertius, which was the equivalent of 2.5 asses (hence the abbreviation HS, which means two and a half). Four sesterces were equal to one denarius. There were 100 sestercii (25 denarii) in the aureus, which was worth 8 grammes of gold.

Source: Goldsmith (1984: 273).

Table 1.9. Maddison's Modified Version of Goldsmith's GDP Estimates for the Empire as a Whole in 14AD

	Expenditure			Income	
	HS per capita	Total GDP million HS		% of total income	GDP million HS
Wheat	112	4,928	Labour income	74	12,314
Other cereals	18	792	Elite income	26	4,406
Other food	70	3,080	**Total Income**	**100**	**16,720**
Other consumption	130	5,720	**Employment** (000s)	17.8 million	
Total private consumption	**330**	**14,520**	Slaves & subsistence	3.6 million	1,080
Government & Investment	50	2,200	Free labour & income	14.2million	11,284
Total GDP (Expenditure)	**380**	**16,720**	**Population** (000s)	44 million	

Notes: First 3 items of per capita expenditure from Table 1.8 multiplied by 44 million instead of 55 million. I assumed government expenditure and investment to be substantially higher than Goldsmith, and reduced 'other consumption' correspondingly. Total income was assumed to equal total expenditure for me as for Goldsmith, but my treatment of income distribution is more detailed and different from his.

Goldsmith did not differentiate between free and slave labour. He assumed all those employed received 3.5HS per day and worked 225 days a year, yielding an average annual income of 790HS. He assumed that all those employed had an average of 1.5 dependants, yielding an average annual per capita income of 315HS. He assumed that all workers had 140 non-working days a year. It seems likely that slaves had much lower incomes, fewer dependants, and more working days a year. I assumed that the employment ratio for the free population was 36 per cent, implying 1.8 dependants per worker. I assumed, following Scheidel, that about 10 per cent of the empire's population were slaves (4.5 million) and that four-fifths (3.6 million) of them were working, with a low dependancy ratio of 0.25. He assumed 40 per cent (22 million) of his 55 million population were employed. I assumed a similar ratio,[3] but differentiated between the intensity of slave and non-slave labour input. I assumed that the average subsistence cost of a slave (with 0.25 of a dependant) was 300HS.

The rationale for Goldsmith's estimate of elite income (about 17 per cent of the total) was not explained. It was simply a residual derived by deducting labour income from the total (see Goldsmith 1984: 273). His total of 3,520 million HS (in Table 1.8) was not compatible with his 4,305 million HS on pp. 276–9. My estimate of elite income is 26 per cent of the total.

Measuring the Difference between Income Levels in Peninsular Italy and the Rest of the Empire

My amendments to Goldsmith's income account have important implications because they permit a breakdown between peninsular Italy and the rest of the empire. Goldsmith's income account was very simple. He estimated labour income without differentiating between the free and the slaves, and took property income as a residual. Labour compensation was taken to be 3.5HS a day, and he assumed 225 working days per year. Thus average annual per capita labour compensation was taken to be 790HS. He assumed 1.5 dependents per worker, thus his average annual per capita income from labour was 315HS.

Labour Income

Slaves constituted a tenth of the Empire's population and provided nearly a fifth of its labour input. The slave ratio was biggest in peninsular Italy where they were more than a third of the population and about half of the labour input. The difference between these two ratios in my reckoning is due to the fact that slaves had a very much smaller ratio of female and child dependents than free labour.

The average subsistence cost of a working slave (including the cost of slave dependents) was assumed to be 300HS a year. The total cost of maintaining 3.6 million working slaves would have been 1,080 million HS.

I assumed that the free labour force was 36 per cent of the free population (14.2 million) with an average annual wage of 790HS (as in Goldsmith) and a total income of 11,234 million HS. Thus total labour income (slave and non-slave) was 12,314 million HS (see Table 1.9).

Elite Income

Goldsmith estimated (pp. 277–8) the income and wealth of the elite. Both were proportionately higher in Italy than in the 36 provinces which constituted the rest of the Empire. He classified the elite by four levels of social status. Roman social rank and status were more closely and explicitly related to property qualifications than in most other societies. The bulk of elite income was derived from property, including slave ownership. Some part of it was derived from professional earnings and office-holding, but I have not classed this as labour income.

Goldsmith assumed that the elite derived a 6 per cent return on capital assets. The Emperor had an annual income of at least 15 million HS. The minimum property qualification for senators was one million HS. Goldsmith assumed that their average wealth was 2.5 million, yielding an average income of 150,000. Thus total income for the 600 senators was 90 million HS. He assumed there were 40,000 knights (*equites*), with an average fortune of half a million and an average income of 30,000, for a total of 1,200 million HS. Sixty per cent of this equestrian order were taken to be Italian residents. He estimated that there were 360,000 *decuriones* (municipal councillors) residing in 3,000 cities of the Empire, with a total income of three billion (implying 8,333HS per capita).

I accepted his estimates for the first three groups but reduced the number of decurions to 240,000 because my estimate of the Empire's population was lower than

THE ROMAN EMPIRE AND ITS ECONOMY

his and he exaggerated the degree of urbanization. For him elite income was 17 per cent of GDP. For me it was 26 per cent.

I assumed that all the income of the emperor and senators, 60 per cent of equestrian income, a third of decurion income and property income not allocable by status originated in peninsular Italy. This makes a total of 1,858 million HS for the elite in peninsular Italy and 2,548 million in the rest of the empire. Labour income was 1,880 million in peninsular Italy, and 10,434 million in the rest of the empire. Dividing by the respective populations, 7 million and 37 million, we arrive at an estimate of per capita income of *534HS per head* originating in peninsular Italy, *351HS* in the rest of the empire, and 380*HS* for the empire as a whole (see bottom panel of Table 1.10, which also makes the comparison in terms of 1990 Geary-Khamis dollars). These estimates refer to income generated, but peninsular Italy also benefited from income transfers from the rest of the Empire, as shown below.

The Impact of Tax and Tribute Payments

The allocation of income between peninsular Italy and the provinces in Table 1.10 does not take account of the net flow of transfers and tribute to the state.

In the Republican period, the net inflow of tribute from the provinces to the metropole was largely in the form of booty, war indemnities, and roughly assessed 'taxes' collected by Roman tax-farmers. Jones (1974: 114–15), lists 114 million HS in ten instalments under the peace treaty after the first Carthaginian war; 240 million in 50 instalments after the second; 280 million in booty from Spain in 206–196BC; 360 million in 12 instalments from Syria in 189BC; 160 million from Cyprus in 58BC, 40 million from Caesar's conquest of Gaul. He cites Pompey's claim that his conquests raised the annual flow of tribute from Asia to 340 million. It was because of these inflows that land and other direct taxes were abolished in peninsular Italy in 167BC. This tax immunity was not infringed until Caracalla extended citizenship in 212AD to all free inhabitants of the empire, and it did not disappear completely until the time of Diocletian.

By the end of Augustus' reign the process of conquest was largely complete, and military casualties were much smaller. The flow of booty and war indemnities was replaced by a more regular flow of tax income to the metropole from land and capitation taxes. Taxable capacity was assessed with the help of censuses, which provided information on the number of inhabitants in each province, the amount and sources of their wealth. It was collected more efficiently by the state authorities than by tax farmers.

In some provinces metropolitan military expenditure was probably bigger than taxes and tribute received by the state. In 14AD there were 25 legions stationed in the provinces, a total of about 150,000 troops. Most of the cost was borne by the imperial authorities. About the same number of troops served in auxiliary forces whose cost was borne almost entirely by the provinces.

Table 1.10. Regional Breakdown of Labour and Elite Income in, 14AD

	(I) Labour Income				
	population (000s)	activity ratio	employment (000s)	income per worker HS	total income Mill. HS
Peninsular Italy					
Free	4,500	0.36	1,620	790	1,280
Slave	2,500	0.80	2,000	300	600
Total	7,000	0.52	3,620	519	1,880
Rest of Empire					
Free	35,000	0.36	12,600	790	9,954
Slave	2,000	0.80	1,600	300	480
Total	37,000	0.38	14,200	735	10,434
Total Empire					
Free	39,500	0.36	14,220	790	11,234
Slave	4,500	0.80	3,600	300	1,080
Total	44,000	0.405	17,820	691	12,314

(II) Elite Income (million HS)

	Total Empire		Peninsular Italy		Rest of Empire	
	persons	income	persons	income	persons	income
Emperor	1	15	1	15	0	0
Senators	600	90	600	90	0	0
Knights	40,000	1,200	24,000	720	16,000	480
Decurions	240,000	2,000	80,000	667	160,000	1,333
Other	50,000	1,101	17,000	366	33,000	734
Total elite	330,601	4,406	121,601	1,858	209,000	2,548

(III) Total GDP (million HS)

	Total Empire	Peninsular Italy	Rest of Empire
Labour	12,314	1,880	10,434
Elite	4,406	1,858	2,548
Total	16,720	3,738	12,982

(IV) Average Per Capita GDP

	Total Empire	Peninsular Italy	Rest of Empire
14AD HS	380	534	351

(V) Average Per Capita Disposable Income

	Total Empire	Peninsular Italy	Rest of Empire
14AD HS	380	571	344
1990 Geary-Khamis dollars	570	857	516

Eight legions were stationed in Gaul to guard the frontier on the Rhine from barbarian incursions. Seven legions guarded the long frontier of the Danubian provinces (see Keppie 1996). It seems probable that these provinces were a net drain on the metropole. The main net contributors were Egypt, north Africa, Sicily, Spain, southern Gaul, and west Asia (see Hopkins 1980: 101). The most easily quantifiable contributions were the flows of tribute grain from Egypt, north Africa, and Sicily. From the sources cited above, we know that there was an annual flow of about 135,000 metric tons from Egypt, 108,000 from north Africa, and 20,250 tons from Sicily; a total of 263,250 tons a year. At Goldsmith's price of 0.441HS per kilo, their total value would have been 116 million HS. This would have added 3.1 per cent to the disposable income of peninsular Italy. There was also a large flow of olive oil as tribute from north Africa and Spain. The Asian provinces provided a substantial net flow of tribute in cash, and Duncan-Jones (1994: 53) suggests that this was also the case for Egypt. There was imperial income from Spanish mines, which were the largest producers of precious metals. Total net flows of tribute in cash and kind would have raised the disposable income of peninsular Italy to 4,000 million HS—about 7 per cent above its GDP. Per capita disposable income would have been about HS571. Disposable income of the provinces would have fallen 2 per cent—lowering their average per capita income to 344HS. Thus per capita disposable income in peninsular Italy was two-thirds higher than in the rest of the empire

Inter-Temporal Comparison of Roman Income

Goldsmith (pp. 280–1) compared the level of Roman per capita income in 14AD with that of England and Wales in 1688, using gold and wheat as alternative numeraires. I followed a similar procedure, using the 1688 link to express Roman performance in 14AD in 1990 Geary-Khamis dollars.

1. *Comparing Rome in 14AD with England in 1688 in gold units.* In Rome, 100HS equalled 1 aureus which was worth 8 grammes of gold. Thus the average per capita income of 380HS in the Empire as a whole equalled 30.4 grammes. For a population of 44 million, GDP was equal to 1,338 metric tons of gold. For England and Wales in 1688 Goldsmith quoted a per capita income equivalent to 70 grammes. Gregory King had esti-mated English expenditure to be £41.6 million, but Goldsmith was citing an upwardly adjusted figure of £48 million by Phyllis Deane. In Chapter 5 (Tables 5.6 and 5.11), I adjusted King's estimate upwards to £54 million and per capita income to £9.958. Isaac Newton, as master of the mint, fixed the value of £1 = 7.988 grams of gold in 1702. Assuming this to have been valid for 1688, English per capita income equalled 79.5 grammes, and total income 432 metric tons of gold. Thus per capita income in the Roman empire would have been 38 per cent of that in England and Wales in 1688 (i.e., 30.4/79.5 grammes of gold).

In Maddison (2001, 2003), I used 1990 dollars (with PPP conversion) as my numeraire to compare per capita income in England and Wales in 1688 with performance in modern times. My per capita estimate for England and Wales in 1688 was $1,411 (in 1990 dollars). Applying the 38 per cent gold ratio, implies an average per capita GDP in the Roman empire of $540.

2. *Comparing Rome in 14AD with England in 1688 in cereal units.* We can also get an inter-temporal link using cereal units. Per capita GDP can be converted into cereal units by multiplying cereal consumption by the ratio of total expenditure to cereal expenditure, i.e., a Roman multiplier of 2.92 (380/130HS). In Rome per capita wheat consumption was 253kg per capita plus 40kg wheat equivalent of other cereals. Thus total per capita income would have been around 855 cereal units (293 multiplied by 2.92). Applying the same procedure to England in 1688 yields a multiplier of 7.95 (£9.958/£1.253). Thus with English cereal consumption of 254kg per capita, total per capita income in England would have been equivalent to 2,019 cereal units.[4] Using cereal units as the numeraire, Roman per capita income would have been 42.3 per cent of that in England and Wales, i.e., a higher relative standing for Rome than in gold units.

3. *Average of gold and cereal units.* I took an average of the gold and the wheat ratios, assuming that average per capita income in the Roman empire was about 40 per cent of the $1,411 in England and Wales in 1688, i.e., $570 using the same numeraire (1990 Geary-Khamis dollars, see bottom line of Table 1.10).

Tentative Estimates of Disposable Income in Each Province

After allowance for transfers of tax and tribute to the metropole, per capita disposable income rises to 571HS in peninsular Italy and falls to an average of 344HS in the provinces. In terms of 1990 Geary-Khamis dollars this means $857 per capita in peninsular Italy and an average of $516 in the rest of the Empire.

There is no direct way of quantifying levels of income in each province, but there are some clues. We know that Egypt, Greece, Carthage, and the west Asian provinces were ancient civilizations, with settled agriculture, urban life, some degree of literacy, a legal system to protect property rights, and a fairly elaborate social hierarchy before Roman conquest, whereas most provinces in western, central, and eastern Europe operated with 'barbarian' levels of technology and institutions before they were conquered. There were western areas, such as Baetica, Narbonensis, and Tunisia, where there had been some economic development before Roman conquest, and where Rome, subsequent to conquest, invested in urban and economic development, and encouraged migration by settlers from peninsular Italy. There were some recently incorporated provinces, like Algeria or the newly acquired parts of Gaul, where Rome was interested in promoting development, but had had little time to do so by 14AD. Other recently incorporated provinces (on the German frontier, Switzerland, Austria,

Table 1.11. Hierarchy of Per Capita Income Levels Outside Peninsular Italy, 14AD

1990 G-K $	
600	Egypt: most prosperous because of Nile water supply and transport
550	Greece, Tunisia, Libya, Asia Minor, Greater Syria, and Cyprus
525	Baetica and Narbonensis: most prosperous parts of Spain and France
475	Sicily, Sardinia, Corsica, Iberia, excluding Baetica
450	Other Gaul, Algeria, and Morocco
425	Danubian provinces—recently barbarian
	Income Levels in Neighbouring Areas Outside the Empire
500	Iran, Iraq, Jordan, heritage of ancient civilization
400	Neighbouring Africa and Europe, at barbarian level of development

and the Balkans) were acquired for defensive rather than developmental purposes and operated not much above 'barbarian' levels of technology.

I kept these differences in mind in making stylized estimates of per capita disposable income by province. Table 1.11 shows a six-step hierarchy ranging from $425 in the least prosperous provinces to $550 in provinces with a heritage of ancient civilization, and $600 in Egypt. The estimates were constrained by the need to arrive at an average per capita level of $516 for the group as a whole. They are highly tentative and obviously open to challenge. I venture to present them in the hope that they may spark further research.

Table 1.12 shows the stylized per capita levels, population, and total income within the individual provinces of the empire, ordered by date of acquisition. (See also Figure 1.1.) It should be remembered that the income levels refer to national disposable income rather than GDP.

Table 1.13 reallocates the Table 1.12 results for European countries, within present boundaries.

Economic Growth Performance of Component Parts of the Empire, 300BC–14AD

Table 1.14 gives a rough indication of growth performance in different parts of the empire from 300BC, when Rome had yet to establish its hegemony in the Italian peninsula, to 14AD, when the process of empire building was largely complete.

In terms of population and per capita disposable income, the gains were much greater in the metropole than in the provinces. In the Italian peninsula, population grew by nearly 80 per cent, and per capita income doubled. Population grew by more than 40 per cent in both the eastern and the western provinces. Per capita income rose much less—about 16 per cent in the western and 7 per cent in the eastern provinces.

Italian Peninsula. In 300BC, Rome had extended its area of control over the neighbouring tribes of Latium, and what was left of Etruria. It had girded itself for further

Table 1.12. Provincial Population, Per Capita and Total Income in 14AD (Highly Provisional Estimates)

	Population (000s)	per capita NDI: (1990 G-K dollars)	Total NDI (million 1990G-K dollars)
Peninsular Italy	**7,000**	**857**	**6,000**
Sicily, Sardinia & Corsica	1,100	475	523
Baetica	1,500	525	788
Other Iberia	2,650	475	1,259
Narbonensis	1,500	525	788
Other Gaul	4,300	450	1,935
Greek peninsula	2,000	550	1,100
Danubian Provinces	3,050*	425	1,296
European Provinces	**16,100**	**478**	**7,689**
Roman Europe	**23,100**	**593**	**13,689**
Tunisia & Libya	1,200**	550	660
Algeria	2,000	450	900
Morocco	1,000	450	450
Egypt	4,500	600	2,700
Roman Africa	**8,700**	**541**	**4,710**
Roman Asia	**12,200***	**550**	**6,710**
Total Provinces	**37,000**	**516**	**19,109**
Total Roman Empire	**44,000**	**570**	**25,109**
Non-Roman W. Asia	5,400****	500	2,700
Non-Roman Africa	8,300	400	3,320
Non-Rom. W. Europe	4,000*****	400	1,600
Non-Rom. E. Europe	2,500******	400	1,000

Notes: *Austria (500), Switzerland (300), Albania (200), half Bulgaria (250), Hungary (300), Yugoslavia (1,500); **Tunisia (800), Libya (400); ***Asia Minor (8,000), Greater Syria (4,000) & Cyprus (200); ****Iran (4,000), Iraq (1,000), Jordan (400); *****Britain (800), Germany (2,500), half Netherlands (100), Scandinavia (500), other (100); ******half Bulgaria (250), Czech lands (1,000), Poland (450), Romania (800), excludes European Russia (2,000).

Sources: Population as in Table 1.2. Per capita income as in Table 1.11.

conquest, had an army of four legions and had started to build strategic roads, the via Appia from Rome to Capua and the via Valeria from Rome to the Adriatic coast, but it had yet to conquer the tribes of central Italy, the Celtic barbarians in north, and the Greek city states in the south. The barbarian region had a third of the population with a per capita income of $400; the Greek city states another third with an income level of $450. The rest including Rome were in between with an income level of $425, which was also the average for the whole peninsula. At that time the city of Rome had a population of 60,000 (see Cornell 1995: 385) and none of the ostentatious public buildings and amenities which it acquired later.

The conquest of Italy enriched the Roman heartland and its elite, by seizure of landed property and enslavement of Rome's enemies, but there was also a boost to productivity in the peninsula as a whole from the ending of regional conflicts, gradual spread of Latin as a common language, establishment of a road network, investment in public works, the creation of a common currency and legal system.

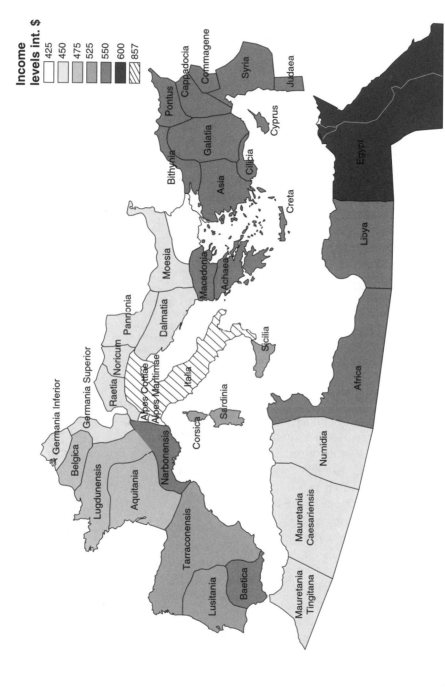

Figure 1.1. Per capita income in the provinces of the Roman Empire in 14AD.

Table 1.13. European Population, Per Capita and National Disposable Income in 14AD, Within Present-Day Boundaries

	Population (000s)	Per capita income 1990 GK $	Total NDI million 1990 GK $
Austria	500	425	213
Belgium	300	450	135
Denmark	180	400	72
Finland	20	400	8
France*	5,000	473	2,366
Germany**	3,000	408	1,225
Greece	2,000	550	1,100
Italy***	8,000	809	6,475
Netherlands****	200	425	85
Norway	100	400	40
Portugal*****	400	450	180
Spain******	3,750	498	1,867
Sweden	200	400	80
Switzerland	300	425	128
UK	800	400	320
Other W.E.*******	300	466	140
Total W.E.	25,050	576	14,433
E. Europe********	4,750	412	1,956

Note: *area of modern France, including Corsica and excluding Belgian, German and Dutch components of Roman Gaul; **area of modern Germany: population 500,000 in the Roman and 2.5 million in the non-Roman area; ***includes Sardinia and Sicily; ****includes 100,000 in Roman and 100,000 in non-Roman Netherlands; *****Roman Lusitania; ******Baetica and Tarraconensis; *******includes Cyprus; ********excludes European Russia.

Much bigger gains came from acquisition of provinces outside the peninsula. This led to an inflow of booty and slaves on a very large scale and allowed the elite to acquire large property holdings and rental income outside the peninsula. It provided opportunities for Italians to settle as colonists on favourable terms in Spain, Africa, and southern France. These acquisitions involved very heavy costs, particularly the first two Carthaginian wars, and the civil wars which arose from conflicting ambitions of the leading empire builders (Marius and Sulla, Caesar and Pompey, Antony and Octavian). The net advantages of Roman imperialism became very obvious in the reign of Augustus, when peace was generally established, and the military effort was directed to security rather than conquest.

The inflow of slaves meant that labour input per head of population in peninsular Italy was proportionately much higher than in the provinces. A more intensive use of agricultural land with slave labour and the large inflow of tribute wheat made it possible to increase specialization of agricultural output. Peninsular Italy also had a better infrastructure of roads and ports than the rest of the empire. The main beneficiaries of this transformation and growth were the elite group.

Table 1.14. Economic Performance of Three Components of the Empire in 300BC and 14AD

	300BC			14AD		
	Population (000s)	Per Capita Income 1990 GK $	Total Income million 1990 GK $	Population (000s)	Per Capita Income 1990 GK $	Total Income million 1990 GK $
Peninsular Italy	**3,900**	**425**	**1,658**	**7,000**	**857**	**6,000**
Greece	2,750	500	1,375	2,000	550	1,100
West Asia	6,950	500	3,475	12,200	550	6,710
Egypt	3,500	600	2,100	4,500	600	2,700
Hellenic Provinces	**13,200**	**527**	**6,950**	**18,700**	**562**	**10,510**
Sicily, Sardinia, Corsica	600	425	255	1,100	475	523
Massilia/Narbonensis	750	425	319	1,500	525	788
Other Gaul	3,000	400	1,200	4,300	450	1,935
Iberia	3,900	400	1,560	4,150	493	2,047
Danubian Provinces	2,275	400	910	3,050	425	1,296
Tunisia & Libya	750	450	338	1,200	550	660
Other Maghreb	1,500	400	600	3,000	450	1,350
Western Provinces	**12,775**	**406**	**5,182**	**18,300**	**470**	**8,599**
Grand Total	**29,875**	**462**	**13,790**	**44,000**	**570**	**25,109**

Source: McEvedy and Jones population in 300BC from Table 1.3, Maddison population in 14AD from Table 1.2. Stylized estimates of the hierarchy of per capita income levels as in Table 1.12.

Hellenic Provinces. In 300BC, the eastern kingdoms had been Hellenized and to some extent homogenized by Alexander's conquests a generation earlier and the subsequent large flow of migrants from Greece to western Asia and Egypt (where Alexandria, Naucratis, and Ptolemais were Greek cities). These eastern kingdoms benefited from the 3,000-year heritage of ancient civilization. They had a settled agriculture, major urban settlements (Pergamon, Ephesus, Antioch, Alexandria), alphabets, writing, an educated elite, coinage, legal and administrative systems. When they became provinces they were able to supply Rome with luxury goods (silk, linen, pepper, spices, incense, perfumes, papyrus, parchment, jewellery, and precious stones), which they produced or imported from China, India, East Africa, southern Arabia, and the Black Sea. They discovered the art of glassblowing in the first century BC which spread rapidly throughout the empire.

The Ptolemaic regime in Egypt founded the library of Alexandria about 300BC. Its policy was to acquire everything written in Greek and to make translations of important works in other languages. It built up a collection of half a million manuscript rolls; the biggest in the ancient world. The Ptolemies also created the Museum, a think-tank and research institute which funded the activities of mathematicians, astronomers, geographers, engineers, and doctors, such as Euclid, Eratosthenes, Ptolemy, Ctesibius, Hipparchus, and, for a time, Archimedes.

Rome had nothing to teach the eastern provinces in terms of technology and social institutions, and accepted the fact that Greek was their lingua franca. Roman settlement in these provinces was modest compared to that in the west. In fact there was a bigger flow from this area to Rome than movement in the opposite direction. After the Roman conquest, there was 'extensive' growth in the Hellenic provinces—accommodating an increased population, with no significant improvement in per capita income.

Western Provinces. In 300BC, some of the areas which became provinces had benefited from ancient civilization. Sicily was a Greek offshoot and the city of Massilia (Marseilles) was an important centre for Greek traders. The city and port of Carthage in northern Tunisia was the headquarters of a Mediterranean trading empire, and had a prosperous agricultural hinterland. Otherwise, Gaul, the Rhine–Danube provinces, Spain and the Maghreb were barbarian territory. Most of the inhabitants had no written language or city life and their political organization was tribal. They had no clearly defined system of justice, property rights and taxation. Their techniques of governance and capacity to mobilize resources for war and organize disciplined troops were much less effective than in peninsular Italy. Their per capita incomes and density of settlement were lower and technology more primitive. There were tracks rather than roads, huts rather than houses, fords rather than bridges. Agriculture was based to a substantial degree on migratory transhumance and pastoralism. There were still hunter-gatherers in the forests.

When Rome acquired these provinces, it played a developmental role by establishing law and order and a degree of literacy; introducing Roman settlers, new agricultural products such as vines and olives, new industries making household utensils and pottery; developing the mining industry; creating urban centres; building bridges and road networks. It created a common currency and helped to monetize these economies. Their international trade was greatly enhanced by improvement in harbours and shipping, and elimination of piracy. Increasing specialization helped the economic growth of Gaul, Spain, and the Maghreb up to 14AD.

The Disintegration of the Empire

My quantification of the Roman economy ends in 14AD. I have not tried to quantify the stages of decline. However, I can venture an impressionistic assessment of what happened between 14AD and the Muslim conquests of the seventh and eighth centuries, which can be summarized as follows:

1. For a century and a half after the death of Augustus the empire grew and flourished , and six further provinces were added. The peak in terms of income and population was probably 164AD.

2. This was followed by a century in which plague, civil wars, military weakness, and loss of some provinces led to a decline in population and per capita income.

3. There was an administrative and military overhaul by Diocletian and Constantine at the end of the third and beginning of the fourth century which shifted the locus of governance to the east and propped up the empire for another century. Nevertheless, population continued to decline and per capita income did not grow.

4. In the fifth century, barbarian invaders occupied Italy, Gaul, Iberia, and the Maghreb. They changed the regime, but did not intend to destroy the economy. However, the change enfeebled it and there was a gradual process of decline.

5. In the sixth century, there was a brief reprise when the army of the eastern empire managed temporarily to recapture Italy and north Africa, without doing anything to stop economic erosion.

6. In the seventh and eighth centuries, Muslim invaders conquered Egypt, north Africa, Iberia, and a large chunk of west Asia. All was left was the Byzantine rump. The Mediterranean had been a free trade area, but was now divided into hostile halves. The Islamic invaders did not set out to destroy the economy they conquered. They built their own significantly integrated empire, enriched their heartland by use of tribute Egyptian wheat and fostered some degree of prosperity in the oecumene they created.

Table 1.15 compares the situation in the year 1000 in what had been the Roman world with that in 14AD.

Table 1.15. Changes in Performance of Major Countries in the Roman Empire, 14–1000AD

	Per capita income 1990 G-K $		Population 000s		NDI million 1990 G-K $	GDP
	14AD	1000AD	14AD	1000AD	14AD	1000AD
France	473	425	5,000	6,500	2,366	2,763
Greece	550	400	2,000	1,100	1,100	400
Italy*	809	450	8,000	5,000	6,475	2,250
Portugal	475	425	400	600	190	255
Spain	495	450	3,750	4,000	1,857	1,800
Danubian provinces	425	410	3,050	3,850	1,296	1,561
Other**	450	425	900	1,133	405	482
Roman Europe	**593**	**431**	**23,100**	**22,183**	**13,689**	**9,511**
Egypt	600	550	4,500	5,000	2,700	2,750
N. Africa	479	430	4,200	5,500	2,012	2,365
Roman Africa	**542**	**487**	**8,700**	**10,500**	**4,712**	**5,115**
Asia Minor	550	600	8,000	7,000	4,400	4,200
Greater Syria	550	600	4,000	2,000	2,200	1,200
Cyprus	550	600	200	150	110	90
Roman Asia	**550**	**600**	**12,200**	**9,150**	**6,710**	**5,490**

Notes: *includes Sicily and Sardinia; **includes Belgian, Dutch and German components of Gaul.

Source: See Tables 1.12 and 1.13 for 14AD, and www.ggdc.net/Maddison for 1000AD.

It is clear that there was a significant decline in per capita income in all the west European provinces, with the biggest drop in Italy where population fell by a third and per capita income by nearly half. However, the income level was higher than it had been in 300BC, before the empire was created. The fall was relatively mild in Islamic Iberia and very sharp in Greece, where population fell most, and per capita income fell to the barbarian level. In Egypt and north Africa, population rose somewhat and the per capita income drop was milder than in Europe. In the Asian provinces, population fell but per capita income grew substantially.

Improvability of the Goldsmith–Maddison Income Estimates

A great deal can probably be done to improve the expenditure estimates in Tables 1.9 and 1.10 and the inter-temporal comparison between the Roman empire and seventeenth century England. Gregory King managed to specify 43 categories of expenditure for England, but Goldsmith provided a quantitative estimate for only one commodity—wheat. Other expenditures were derived by coefficients, some of which were drawn from a non-classical context. It should be possible to squeeze more evidence from existing sources on consumption of wine, beer, meat, fish, fruit, and oil (see Hitchner in Scheidel and von Reden). It should also be possible to get a rough idea of consumption of clothing and footwear (see Jongman 2006 for a move in this direction). With more detail of this kind it should be possible to make a much firmer inter-temporal link with Gregory King, whose estimates are much better than anything else we have back to the seventeenth century.

⬚ ENDNOTES

1. Beloch (1886: 472–490) explored the evidence for city size from the fifth century BC in Greece to Ausonius' catalogue of Roman cities in 400AD. The biggest cities at the time of Augustus were Rome which he estimated to have 800,000, Alexandria half a million, and Ephesus 200,000. He suggested there were quite a few ('eine ganze Reihe') towns in the Hellenic Orient with 100,000, but did not specify them. For the Italian peninsula at the time of Augustus, outside the capital, he mentions Ostia, Puteoli, and Pompeii as noteworthy. Other towns he considered rather unimportant. He stressed the big fall in population in Syracuse, Carthage, and Capua which at the time of Augustus were still depopulated as a result of war. He presented (pp. 486–7) evidence on the area of 48 towns. For Greece, Sicily, and Asia Minor he listed 21 cities having more than 30 hectares and 16 in peninsular Italy. Pompeii, with a population of 20,000, had 65 hectares. Towns with an area below 30 hectares presumably had a population less than 10,000.

   Jones (1966: 237–9) found evidence for 122 cities in Gaul, 75 in the Balkan provinces, and 650 in Africa. However, the vast majority were 'little country towns with quite small territories'. In Jones (1974: 4) he made clear how easy it is to exaggerate the degree of urbanization in the Roman world: 'the term city (*civitas*, πόλις) did not in antiquity denote a town. Juridically a rural canton whose inhabitants lived scattered in villages, was a *civitas*'.

2. There was no consolidated Roman budget. The main public expenditure commitments were: (a) Military—pay and occasional bonuses for 150,000 soldiers in the 28 legions, for auxiliary forces of the same size, for sailors in the fleets, and the Praetorian guard in Rome; fodder for the cavalry; maintenance of equipment, forts, ships, roads, bridges, and other land transport facilities; payment of military retirement benefits (lump sums of cash on discharge or attributions of land); subsidies to client states on the frontiers to encourage peaceful coexistence: (b) Provision of free or subsidized food (*frumentationes*), or cash handouts (*congiara* and *alimenta*); maintenance of harbour facilities and public warehouses, payment of private shippers bringing wheat from Egypt, north Africa, and Sicily to safeguard the food supply: (c) Provision of water via aqueducts for fountains, public baths and sewerage in the cities: (d) Provision of public entertainment— gladiatorial fights, chariot races, performances of wild animals, victory parades, banquets, etc. (e) Construction and maintenance of public buildings. (f) Costs of administering the empire— remuneration of governors, legates, proconsuls, procurators and their entourage: (g) Costs of the imperial household. There are details of various categories of public expenditure and income in Frank (1940: 4–18).

On public revenue no comprehensive figures are available. There was a wide variety of state revenues, allocations from the emperor, profits from conquest—booty and slaves, seigniorage from issuing coinage and 'voluntary' contributions from the power-elite, who were expected to justify their elevated social status by making ostentatious contributions to public welfare, e.g., by construction of public buildings and provision of public entertainment.

Table 1.16. Demographic Characteristics Influencing Labour Force Participation

	% of population aged			Life expectancy at birth	Birth rate per 1000 population	Employment as percent of population
	0–14	15–64	65+			
Roman Egypt	35.1	61.7	3.2	21.5	44.1	40.4
Mexico 1950	42.0	53.2	4.4	50.6	45.3	30.8
Brazil 1950	42.5	54.5	3.0	50.9	44.0	33.0
China 1950	33.6	61.9	4.5	40.8	43.8	33.8
India 1950	38.9	57.8	3.3	38.7	45.4	39.1
Indonesia 1950	39.1	56.9	4.0	37.5	42.7	39.0
Japan 1950	35.6	59.6	4.9	63.9	23.7	42.7
France 1950	22.7	65.9	11.4	66.5	19.5	47.0
Germany 1950	23.2	67.1	9.7	67.5	16.0	42.0
Italy 1950	26.3	65.4	8.3	66.0	18.3	40.0
UK 1950	22.5	66.8	10.7	69.2	15.9	44.5
USA 1950	27.0	64.7	8.3	68.9	24.3	40.5

Sources: Egypt from Bagnall and Frier, pp. 104–5 for first three items and birth rate; life expectancy from pp. 32–3, 22.5 for females 20.5 for males (model west). Employment ratios as assumed in text, with slave population 11 per cent of population, p. 48. Other countries, first five columns from *World Population Prospects 2000* Revision, vol. 1, UN, New York, 2001. Employment ratios from Maddison (2001 Appendices A and E), except India which is from Sivasubramonian (2000: 63).

3. Goldsmith assumed that the working population would have been 'approximately two-fifths of the total', (p. 271), and refers to a World Bank table which shows the proportion aged 15–64 in a large array of countries, but not the proportion employed. The most detailed demographic analysis of the Roman world is Bagnall and Frier (1994) for Roman Egypt. Table 1.16 compares demographic characteristics affecting the employment ratio in eleven countries in 1950, when they were closer

to the Egyptian situation than they are now. This table suggests that Goldsmith's assumption of a 40 per cent ratio is plausible, as it is not too different from that in India and Indonesia in 1950. The main difference was that Roman Egypt had a higher infant mortality rate (330 per 1,000, compared with 201 in Indonesia, and 190 in India), lower life expectation and the presence of slave labour. Indian and Indonesian per capita income in 1950 was not much higher than that in Roman Egypt.

4. King's estimates of English grain production are shown in Table 1.17. Wheat was only 24 per cent of the total by weight and 31 per cent by value. The total value of cereal production was £6.8 million, 12.6 per cent of GDP. Cereals were cheaper in Rome than in England in terms of gold. A metric ton of wheat cost 441HS = 35.28 grams of gold in Rome, and the weighted average price per metric ton of cereals in England was £4.93 = 39.38 grams of gold.

Table 1.17. King's Estimate of English Cereal Production in 1688

	Output metric tons	Price £/ton	Value £million
Wheat	326,585	6.43	2.1
Rye	203,208	4.92	1.0
Barley	566,988	4.74	2.5
Oats	283,040	4.23	1.2
Total/Average	1,379,821	*4.93*	6.8

Source: *King, Natural and Political Observations and Conclusions on the State and Condition of England*, manuscript of 1696, in Barnett (1936: 36). King shows quantities in bushels, prices in fractions of a pound. His output excludes production for seed, and the yield/seed ratio was similar to that in Roman Italy: 'in some sorts of grain being near a 4th of the Produce in others, a 5th'. Bushel/kg conversion coefficients for different cereals are from FAO (1948: 573–4).

☐ BIBLIOGRAPHY

Abrams, P. and E. A. Wrigley (eds) (1978), *Towns in Societies: Essays in Economic History and Historical Sociology*, Cambridge University Press.

Acemoglu, D., S. Johnson and J. Robinson (2002), 'Reversals of Fortune: Geography and Institutions in the Making of the Modern World', *Quarterly Journal of Economics* 117, 1231–94.

Alföldi, A. (1965), *Early Rome and the Latins*, University of Michigan Press, Ann Arbor.

Andreau, J. (1999), *Banking and Business in the Roman World*, Cambridge University Press.

Appian (1982), *Roman History*, Loeb Classical Library, Harvard University Press (translated from Greek of circa 150AD).

Astin, A. E., F. W. Walbank, M. Frederiksen and R. M. Ogilvie (eds) (1989), *Rome and the Mediterranean to 133BC*, Cambridge Ancient History, vol. VIII, Cambridge University Press.

Augustus (14), *Res Gestae*, see Brunt and Moore (1967).

Badian, E. (1968), *Roman Imperialism in the Late Republic*, Oxford University Press.

Bagnall, R. S. (1993), *Egypt in Late Antiquity*, Princeton University Press.

Bagnall, R. S. and B. W. Frier (1993), *The Demography of Roman Egypt*, Cambridge University Press.

Bairoch, P. (1988), *Cities and Economic Development*, University of Chicago Press.

Barnett, G. E. (1936), *Two Tracts by Gregory King*, Johns Hopkins Press, Baltimore.

Beloch, J. (1880), *Der italische Bund unter Roms Hegemonie*, Leipzig.

Beloch, J. (1886), *Die Bevölkerung der Griechisch-Römischen*, Welt, Duncker and Humblot, Leipzig.

Beloch, J. (1890), *Campanien: Geschichte und Topographie des antiken Neapel und seiner Umgebung*, Breslau.

Beloch J. (1898), 'Antike und moderne Grossstädte', *Zeitschrift der Socialwissenschaft*, 1, pp. 413–23 and 500–8.

Beloch, J. (1899a), 'Die Bevölkerung Galliens zur Zeit Caesars', *Rheinisches Museum*, 54, pp. 414–38.

Beloch, J. (1899b), 'Die Bevölkerung im Altertum', *Zeitschrift der Socialwissenschaft*, 2, pp. 500–620.

Beloch, J. (1937–61), *Bevölkerungsgeschichte Italiens*, 3 vols, I in 1937, II in 1939, III in 1961, De Gruyter, Berlin.

'Julius Beloch', see Momigliano (1994), pp. 97–120.

Blazquez, J. M. (1978), *Economia de la Hispania Romana*, Ediciones 'Najera', Bilbao.

Boak, A. E. R. (1955), *Manpower Shortage and the Fall of the Roman Empire in the West*, University of Michigan Press, Ann Arbor.

Bowman, A. K. (1996), *Egypt after the Pharaohs, 332BC–AD642, from Alexander to the Arab Conquest*, British Museum Press, London.

Bowman, A. K., E. Champlin and A. Lintott (eds) (1996), *The Augustan Empire, 43BC–AD69*, *The Cambridge Ancient History*, vol. X, Cambridge University Press.

Bowman, A. K., P. Garnsey and D. Rathbone (eds) (2000), *The High Empire, AD70–192*, *The Cambridge Ancient History*, vol. XI, Cambridge University Press.

Bowman A. K. and E. Rogan (eds.) (1999), *Agriculture in Egypt from Pharaonic to Modern Times*, Oxford University Press.

Bromwich, J. (1993), *The Roman Remains of Southern France: A Guidebook*, Routledge, London.

Brunt, P. A. (1971), *Italian Manpower, 225BC– AD14*, Clarendon Press, Oxford.

Brunt, P. A. and J. M. Moore (eds) (1967), *Res Gestae Divi Augusti*, Oxford University Press.

Butcher. K. (2003), *Roman Syria and the Near East*, British Museum Press, London.

Caesar (1972), *The Conquest of Gaul*, Penguin, Harmondsworth (translation from the Latin of about 50BC).

Caesar (1972, *The Civil War*, Penguin, Harmondsworth (translation from the Latin of about 50BC).

Cameron, A. and P. Garnsey (eds) (1998), *The Late Empire, AD337–425*, *The Cambridge Ancient History*, vol. XIII, Cambridge University Press.

Carreras Monfort, C. (1995–96), 'A New Perspective for the Demographic Study of Roman Spain', *Revista de Historia da Arte e Arqueologia*, 2, pp. 59–82.

Cassius Dio (1987), *The Roman History: The Reign of Augustus*, Penguin, London (translation from the Latin of about 220AD).

Casson, L. (1971), *Ships and Seamanship in the Ancient World*, Johns Hopkins University Press, Baltimore.

Chilver, G. E. F. (1941), *Cisalpine Gaul*, Clarendon Press, Oxford.

Churchin, L. A. (1991), *Roman Spain: Conquest and Assimilation*, Routledge, London.

Churchin, L. A. (2004), *The Romanization of Central Spain*, Routledge, London and New York.

Coale, A. J. and P. Demeny (1983), *Regional Model Life Tables and Stable Populations*, 2nd edn, Academic Press, New York.

Collingwood, R. G. (1937), '*Roman Britain*', in Frank, vol. III.

Cornell, T. J. (1995), *The Beginnings of Rome*, Routledge, London and New York.

Cornell, T. J. and J. Matthews (1982), *Atlas of the Roman World*, Phaidon, Oxford.

D'Arms, J. H. and E. C. Kopff (eds) (1980), *The Seaborne Commerce of Ancient Rome,* Memoirs of the American Academy in Rome, 36.

Duby, G. (ed) (1987), *Atlas Historique Mondial*, Larousse, Paris.

Duncan-Jones, R. (1982), *The Economy of the Roman Empire*, Cambridge University Press.

Duncan-Jones, R. (1990), *Scale and Structure in the Roman Economy*, Cambridge University Press.

Duncan-Jones, R. (1994), *Money and Government in the Roman Empire*, Cambridge University Press.

Duncan-Jones, R. (1996), 'The Impact of the Antonine Plague' *Journal of Roman Archaeology*, pp. 108–36.

Edwards, C. and G. Woolf (eds) (2003), *Rome the Cosmopolis*, Cambridge University Press.

FAO (1948), *Les Grands produits agricoles: compendium international de statistiques,* Failli, Rome.

Finley, M. (1973), *The Ancient Economy*, Chatto & Windus, London (1999 edition, with introduction by Morris).

Finley, M. (ed) (1977), *Atlas of Classical Archaeology*, Chatto & Windus, London.

Finley, M. (1980), *Ancient Slavery and Modern Ideology*, Chatto & Windus, London.

Frank, T. (1924), 'Roman Census Statistics from 225 to 28BC', *Classical Philology*, pp. 329–41, University of California.

Frank, T. (1930), 'Roman Census Statistics from 508 to 225BC', *American Journal of Philology*, 51, pp. 313–24.

Frank, T. (ed) (1933 onwards), *An Economic Survey of Ancient Rome*, 6 vols, Patterson, N.J.

Frank, T. (1940), *Rome and Italy of the Empire*, Johns Hopkins University Press, vol.V of his 6 volume survey

Frier, B. W. (1982), 'Roman Life Expectancy: Ulpian's Evidence', *Harvard Studies in Classical Philology,* 86, pp. 213–51.

Frier, B. W. (2000), 'Demography', in Bowman, Garnsey and Rathbone, pp. 787–816.

Garnsey, P. (1998), *Cities, Peasants and Food in Classical Antiquity*, Cambridge University Press.

Garnsey, P. (1988), *Famine and Food Supply in the Graeco-Roman World*, Cambridge University Press.

Garnsey, P. (1983), 'Grain for Rome', in Garnsey et al. pp. 118–30.

Garnsey, P., K. Hopkins and C.R. Whittaker (eds) (1983), *Trade in the Ancient Economy*, Chatto, London.

Garnsey, P. and R. Saller (1987), *The Roman Empire: Economy, Society and Culture*, Duckworth, London.

Gibbon, E. (1776–88), *The History of the Decline and Fall of the Roman Empire*, 6 vols, Strahan & Cadell, London.

Goitein, S. D. F. (1967–93), *A Mediterranean Society: The Jewish Communities of the Arab World as Portrayed in the Documents of the Cairo Geniza*, 6 vols, University of California Press.

Goldsmith, R. W. (1984), 'An Estimate of the Size and Structure of the National Product of the Early Roman Empire', *Review of Income and Wealth*, September.

Goldsmith, R. W. (1987), *Pre-Modern Financial Systems: A Historical Comparative Study*, Cambridge University Press.

Goody, J. (1971), *Technology, Tradition and the State in Africa*, Oxford University Press.

Grant, M. (1961), *The World of Rome*, Mentor Books, New York.

Greene, K. (1986), *The Archaeology of the Roman Economy*, Batsford, London.

Greene, K. (2000), 'Technological Innovation and Economic Progress in the Ancient World: M. I. Finley Reconsidered', *Economic History Review*, February, pp. 29–59.

Gunderson, G. (1976), 'Economic Change and the Demise of the Roman Empire', *Explorations in Economic History*, 13, pp. 43–68.

Haley, E. W. (2003), *Baetica Felix*, University of Texas Press, Austin.

Harris, W. V. (1980), '*Towards a Study of the Roman Slave Trade*', in D'Arms and Kopff.

Harris, W. V. (1985), *War and Imperialism in Republican Rome 327–70BC*, Clarendon Paperbacks, Oxford.

Harris, W. V. (1999), 'Demography, Geography and the Sources of Roman Slaves', *Journal of Roman Studies*, 89, pp. 62–75.

Harvey, P. (1969), *The Oxford Companion to Classical Literature*, Clarendon Press, Oxford.

Heather, P. (2005), *The Fall of the Roman Empire*, Macmillan, London.

Hopkins, K. (1965), 'Elite Mobility in the Roman Empire', *Past and Present*, 32, December.

Hopkins, K. (1966), 'On the Probable Age Structure of the Roman Population', *Population Studies,* November, pp. 245–64.

Hopkins, K. (1978a), '*Economic Growth and Towns in Classical Antiquity*', in Abrams and Wrigley, pp. 35–77.

Hopkins, K. (1978b), *Conquerors and Slaves*, Cambridge University Press.

Hopkins, K. (1980), 'Taxes and Trade in the Roman Empire (200BC–400AD)', *Journal of Roman Studies*, LXX, pp. 101–25.

Hopkins, K. (1983), 'Introduction', in Garnsey et al.

Hopkins, K. (1999), *A World Full of Gods: The Strange Triumph of Christianity*, Weidenfeld & Nicolson, London.

Hopkins, K. (2002), 'Rome, Taxes, Rent and Trade', in Scheidel and von Reden.

Hume, D. (1742), 'On the Populousness of Ancient Nations', in *Essays, Literary, Moral and Political*, Ward Lock, London (n.d.).

Ibn Khaldun (1958), *The Muqqadimah: An Introduction to History*, 3 vols (translated by Franz Rosenthal), Routledge & Kegan Paul, London.

Johnson, A. C. (1936), *Roman Egypt to the Reign of Diocletian*, Johns Hopkins Press, Baltimore.

Johnson, A. C. and L. C. West (1949), *Byzantine Egypt: Economic Studies,* Princeton University Press.

Jones, A. H. M. (1955), 'The Decline and Fall of the Roman Empire', *History*, October, pp. 209–26.

Jones, A. H. M. (1966), *The Decline of the Ancient World*, Longman, London and New York.

Jones, A. H. M. (1971), *Cities of the Eastern Roman Provinces*, Oxford University Press.

Jones, A. H. M. (1974), *The Roman Economy: Studies in Ancient Economic and Administrative History*, Blackwell, Oxford.

Jongman, W. M. (1988), *The Economy and Society of Pompeii*, Amsterdam.

Jongman, W. M. (2002), '*Beneficial Symbols: Alimenta and the Infantilisation of the Roman Citizen*', in Jongman and Kleijwegt.

Jongman, W. M. (2003a), 'Rome: The Political Economy of a World-Empire', *Medieval History Journal*, 6, 2, pp. 303–26.

Jongman, W. M. (2003b), '*Slavery and the Growth of Rome: the Transformation of Italy in the First and Second Century BCE*', in Edwards and Woolf.

Jongman, W. M. (2006), '*Consumption in the Early Roman Empire*', in Saller et al.

Jongman, W. M and M. Kleijwegt (2002), *After the Past: Essays in Ancient History in Honour of H. W. Pleket*, Brill, Leiden.

Kahrstedt, R. (1944), *Kulturgeschichte der römischen Kaiserzeit*, Bruckmann, München.

Kahrstedt, U. (1960), *Die wirtschsaftlichen Lage Grossgriechenlands in der Kaiserzeit*, Historia Einzelschriften, Franz Steiner Verlag, Wiesbaden.

Keay, S. J. (1988), *Roman Spain*, British Museum Publications, London.

Keller, W. (1974), *The Etruscans*, Knopf, New York.

Keppie, L. (1984), *The Making of the Roman Army: From Republic to Empire*, Batsford, London.

Keppie, L. (1996), 'The Army and the Navy', in Bowman et al., pp. 371–96.

Koepke, N. and J. Baten (2005), 'The Biological Standard of Living in Europe during the last two Millennia', *European Review of Economic History*, 9, pp. 61–95.

Lazenby, J. F. (1996), *The First Punic War*, UCL Press, London.

Lévy, J-P. (1967), *The Economic Life of the Ancient World*, University of Chicago Press.

Ligt, L. de (1993), *Fairs and Markets in the Roman Empire*, Gieben, Amsterdam.

Livy (1960), *The Early History of Rome*, Penguin, Harmondsworth (original Latin circa 15BC translated by de Selincourt).

Livy (1965), *The War with Hannibal*, Penguin, Harmondsworth (original Latin circa 15BC translated by de Selincourt).

Lo Cascio, E. (1994), 'The Size of the Roman Population: Beloch and the Meaning of the Augustan Census Figures', *Journal of Roman Studies*, 84, 53–40.

Lo Cascio, E. (2001), '*Recruitment and the Size of the Roman Population from the Third to the First Century BCE*', in Scheidel.

Lo Cascio, E. and P. Malanima (2005), 'Cycles and Stability: Italian Population before the Demographic Transition, 225BC–AD 1900', December, pp. 5–40.

Lomas, K. (1996), *Roman Italy: 338BC–AD200*, UCL Press, London.

Luttwak, E. N. (1976), *The Grand Strategy of the Roman Empire from the First Century AD to the Third*, Johns Hopkins University Press, Baltimore and London.

McEvedy, C. (1995), *The Penguin Atlas of African History*, 2nd edn., Penguin, London.

McEvedy, C. (2002), *The New Penguin Atlas of Ancient History*, Penguin, London.

McEvedy, C. and R. Jones (1978), *Atlas of World Population History*, Penguin, London.

MacMullen, R. (1980), *Roman Social Relations, 50 BC to AD284*, Yale University Press, New Haven.

MacMullen, R. (1984), 'The Roman Emperor's Army Costs', *Latomus Revue d'etudes latines*, XLIII, pp. 571–80.

McNeill, J. R. and W. H. (2003) *The Human Web: A Bird's-Eye View of World History*, Norton, New York.

Maddison A. (1982), *Phases of Capitalist Development*, Oxford University Press.

Maddison A. (1998), *Chinese Economic Performance in the Long Run*, OECD, Paris.

Maddison A. (2001), *The World Economy: A Millennial Perspective*, OECD, Paris.

Maddison A. (2003), *The World Economy: Historical Statistics*, OECD, Paris.

Mattingly, D. J. (1995), *Tripolitania*, Batsford, London.

Milanovic, B. (2006), 'An Estimate of Average Income and Inequality in Byzantium around Year 1000', *Review of Income and Wealth*, September, pp. 449–570.

Millar, F. (1993), *The Roman Near East, 31BC–AD337*, Harvard University Press, Cambridge, MA.

Millar, F. et al. (1981), *The Roman Empire and its Neighbours*, 2nd edn., Duckworth, London.

Momigliano, A. D. (1994), 'Julius Beloch', in *Studies on Modern Scholarship*, University of California Press, Berkeley.

Mommsen, T. (1912), *The History of Rome* (translation by W. P. Dickson), Dutton, London.

Mommsen, T. (1996), *A History of Rome under the Emperors*, Routledge, London and New York.

Moritz, L. A. (1958), *Grain Mills and Flour in Classical Antiquity*, Oxford University Press.

Morley, N. (2001), 'The Transformation of Italy, 225–28BC', *Journal of Roman Studies*, 91, pp. 50–62.

Morris, I., R. P. Saller, and W. Scheidel (eds) (2006), *The Cambridge Economic History of the Greco-Roman World*, Cambridge University Press.

Moscati, S. (1988), *The Phoenicians*, Bompiani, Milan.

Needham, J. (1971), *Science and Civilisation in China*, vol. IV, 3, Cambridge University Press.

Newell, C. (1988), *Methods and Models in Demography*, Guilford, New York.

Pallottino, M. (1955), *The Etruscans*, Penguin, Harmondsworth.

Pauly-Wissowa (1894–), *Realencyclpädie der classischen Altertumswissenschaft*, 100 volumes.

Pirenne, H. (1939), *Mohammed and Charlemagne*, Allen & Unwin, London.

Pleket, H. W. (1990), '*Wirtschaft*', in Vittinghoff.

Polybius (1979), *The Rise of the Roman Empire*, Penguin, Harmondsworth (original Greek circa 140BC translated by Scott-Kilvert).

Potter, D. S. and D. J, Mattingly (eds) (1997), *Life, Death and Entertainment in the Roman Empire*, University of Michigan Press.

Rankin, H. D. (1987), *The Celts and the Classical World*.

Rathbone, D. W. (1990), 'Villages, Land and Population in Graeco-Roman Egypt', *Proceedings of the Cambridge Philological Society*, 216, 36, pp. 13–142.

Rathbone, D. W. (1996), '*The Imperial Finances*', in Bowman et al.

Rathbone, D. W. (1997), 'Prices and price formation in Roman Egypt', *Economie antique: prix et formation des prix dans les economies antiques*, Saint-Bertrand-de-Comminges, pp. 183–244.

Raven, S. (1993), *Rome in Africa*, 3rd edn. Routledge, London.

Rich, J. and G. Shipley (eds) (1993), *War and Society in the Roman World*, Routledge, London.

Richardson, J. S. (1986), *Hispaniae: Spain and the Development of Roman Imperialism, 219–82BC*, Cambridge University Press.

Rickman, G. E. (1971), *Roman Granaries and Store Buildings*, Cambridge University Press.

Rickman, G. E. (1980), *The Corn Supply of Ancient Rome*, Clarendon Press, Oxford.

Robinson, J. S. (1996), *The Romans in Spain*, Blackwell, Oxford.

Rostovtzeff, M. (1926), *The Social and Economic History of the Roman Empire*, 2 vols, Oxford University Press (2nd edn, 1957).

Rostovtzeff, M. (1941), *The Social and Economic History of the Hellenistic World*, 3 vols, Oxford University Press (reprinted 1953).

Rozman, G. (1973), *Urban Networks in Ch'ing China and Japan*, Princeton University Press.

Russell, J. C. (1958), *Late Ancient and Medieval Population*, American Philosphical Society, Philadelphia.

Russell, J. C. (1985), *The Control of Late Ancient and Medieval Population*, American Philosphical Society, Philadelphia.

Salmon, E. T. (1969), *Roman Colonization Under the Republic*, Thames & Hudson, London.

Scheidel, W. (1997), 'Quantifying the Source of Slaves in the Early Roman Empire', *Journal of Roman Studies*, 87, pp. 157–69.

Scheidel, W. (ed) (2001), *Debating Roman Demography*, Brill, Leiden.

Scheidel, W. (2002), 'A Model of Demographic and Economic Change in Roman Egypt after the Antonine Plague', *Journal of Roman Archaeology*, 15, pp. 97–114.

Scheidel, W. and S. von Reden (2002), *The Ancient Economy*, Edinburgh University Press.

Scramuzza, V. M. (1937), '*Roman Sicily*', in Frank, vol. III.

Seager, R. (2002), *Pompey the Great*, Blackwell, Oxford.

Sivasubramonian, S. (2000), *The National Income of India in the Twentieth Century*, Oxford University Press, New Delhi.

Snooks, G. D. (1997), *The Ephemeral Civilization*, Routledge, London and New York.

Starr, C. G. (1965), *A History of the Ancient World*, Oxford University Press.

Suetonius (1980), *The Twelve Caesars*, Penguin, Harmondsworth (original Latin circa 100AD, translated by Robert Graves).

Tacitus (1956), *Annals of Imperial Rome*, Penguin, Harmondsworth (original Latin circa 100AD, translated by Grant).

Tainter, J. A. (1988), *The Collapse of Complex Societies*, Cambridge University Press.

Talbert, R. J. A. (ed) (1985), *Atlas of Classical History*, Routledge, London and New York.

Temin, P. (2001). 'A Market Economy in the Early Roman Empire', *Journal of Roman Studies,* 91, pp. 169–81.

Temin, P. (2002), 'Price Behavior in Ancient Babylon', *Explorations in Economic History* 39, pp. 46–60.

Temin, P. (2003), '*Estimating GDP in the Early Roman Empire*', paper for conference Innovazione tecnica e progresso economico nel mondo romano, organized by Elio Lo Cascio, 13–16 April.

Temin, P. (2004), 'Financial Intermediation in the Early Roman Empire', *Journal of Economic History*, September, pp. 705–33.

Toynbee, A. J. (1965), *Hannibal's Legacy: The Hannibalic War's Effect on Roman Life*, 2 vols, Oxford University Press.

Vittinghoff, F. (ed) (1990), *Europäische Wirtschafts und Sozialgeschichte in der Römischen Kaiserzeit*, Klett-Cotta, Stuttgart.

Ward-Perkins, B. (1998), '*The Cities*', in Cameron and Garnsey, pp. 71–410.

Ward-Perkins, B.(2005), *The Fall of Rome and the End of Civilisation*, Oxford University Press.

White, K. D. (1984), *Greek and Roman Technology*, Thames & Hudson, London.

White Jr, L. (ed) (1966), *The Transformation of the Roman World*, Univerity of California Press, Berkeley.

Whittaker, C. R. (1994), *Frontiers of the Roman Empire: A Social and Economic Study*, Johns Hopkins University Press, Baltimore.

Whittaker, C. R. (1996), '*Roman Africa: Augustus to Vespasian*', in Bowman et al.

Whittaker, C. R. (2004), *Rome and its Frontiers: The Dynamics of Empire*, Routledge, London.

Woods, R. (2000), *The Demography of Victorian England and Wales*, Cambridge University Press.

Wrigley, E. A., R. S. Davies, J. E. Oeppen and R. S. Schofield (1997), *English Population History from Family Reconstitution, 1580–1837*, Cambridge University Press.

2 The resurrection of western Europe and the transformation of the Americas

WHY AND WHEN DID THE WEST GET RICH?

Changes in the Momentum of Growth over the Long Term

Over the past millennium, world population rose nearly 24-fold, per capita income 14-fold, GDP 338-fold. This contrasts sharply with the preceding millennium, when world population grew by only a sixth, and per capita income fell. From the year 1000 to 1820, growth was predominantly extensive. Most of the GDP increase went to accommodate a four-fold increase in population. The advance in per capita income was a slow crawl—the world average increased only by half over a period of eight centuries.

In the year 1000, the average infant could expect to live about 24 years. A third died in the first year of life. Hunger and epidemic disease ravaged the survivors. By 1820, life expectation had risen to 36 years in the west, with only marginal improvement elsewhere.

After 1820, world development became much more dynamic. By 2003, income per head had risen nearly ten-fold, population six-fold. Per capita income rose by 1.2 per cent a year: 24 times as fast as in 1000–1820. Population grew about 1 per cent a year: six times as fast as in 1000–1820. Life expectation increased to 76 years in the west and 63 in the rest of the world.

Within the capitalist epoch (i.e., the period from 1820 onwards), the pace of advance has been uneven. One can distinguish five distinct phases. The 'golden age', 1950–73, when world per capita income grew nearly 3 per cent a year, was by far the best. Our age, from 1973 onwards (henceforth characterized as the 'neo-liberal' order), is second best, with a growth rate half of that in the golden age. The old 'liberal order' (1870–1913) was third-best, only marginally slower in terms of per capita income growth. In 1913–50, growth was well below potential because of two world wars and the intervening collapse of world trade, capital markets, and migration. The slowest growth was registered in the initial phase of capitalist development (1820–70)

Table 2.1. Levels of Per Capita GDP, Population, and GDP: World and Major Regions, 1–2003AD

	1	1000	1500	1820	1870	1913	1950	1973	2003
Levels of per Capita GDP (1990 international dollars)									
Western Europe	576	427	771	1,202	1,960	3,457	4,578	11,417	19,912
Western Offshoots	400	400	400	1,202	2,419	5,233	9,268	16,179	28,039
West	**569**	**426**	**753**	**1,202**	**2,050**	**3,988**	**6,297**	**13,379**	**23,710**
Asia	456	465	568	581	556	696	717	1,718	4,434
Latin America	400	400	416	691	676	1,494	2,503	4,513	5,786
E. Europe & f. USSR	406	400	498	686	941	1,558	2,602	5,731	5,705
Africa	472	428	416	421	500	637	890	1,410	1,549
Rest	**453**	**451**	**538**	**580**	**609**	**880**	**1,126**	**2,379**	**4,217**
World	**467**	**450**	**567**	**667**	**873**	**1,526**	**2,113**	**4,091**	**6,516**
Interregional Spread	1.4:1	1.2:1	1.9:1	2.9:1	4.8:1	8.2:1	13.0:1	11.5:1	18.1:1
West/Rest Spread	1.3:1	0.9:1	1.4:1	2.1:1	2.3:1	4.5:1	5.6:1	5.6:1	5.7:1
Population (million)									
Western Europe	25	26	57	133	188	261	305	359	395
Western Offshoots	1	1	3	11	46	111	176	251	346
West	**26**	**27**	**60**	**144**	**234**	**372**	**481**	**610**	**741**
Asia	168	183	284	710	765	978	1,383	2,249	3,734
Latin America	6	11	18	22	40	81	166	308	541
E. Europe & f. USSR	9	14	30	91	142	236	267	360	409
Africa	17	32	47	74	90	125	228	390	853
Rest	**200**	**241**	**378**	**898**	**1,038**	**1,419**	**2,045**	**3,307**	**5,537**
World	**226**	**267**	**438**	**1,042**	**1,272**	**1,791**	**2,526**	**3,916**	**6,279**
% West/World	11.5	10.1	13.7	13.8	18.4	20.8	19.1	15.6	11.8
Levels of GDP (billion 1990 international dollars)									
Western Europe	14.4	10.9	44.2	159.9	367.5	902.2	1,396	4,097	7,857
Western Offshoots	0.4	0.7	1.1	13.5	111.5	582.9	1,635	4,058	9,708
West	**14.9**	**11.7**	**45.3**	**173.4**	**479.0**	**1,485.2**	**3,032**	**8,155**	**17,565**
Asia	76.7	84.9	161.3	412.5	425.6	680.7	991	3,864	16,555
Latin America	2.2	4.6	7.3	14.9	27.3	120.8	416	1,389	3,132
E. Europe & f. USSR	3.5	5.4	15.2	62.6	133.8	367.1	695	2,064	2,339
Africa	8.0	13.8	19.4	31.3	45.2	79.5	203	550	1,322
Rest	**90.5**	**108.7**	**203.2**	**521.3**	**632.0**	**1,248.1**	**2,303**	**7,868**	**23,348**
World	**105.4**	**120.4**	**248.4**	**694.6**	**1,111.2**	**2,733.3**	**5,337**	**16,022**	**40,913**
% West/World	14.1	9.7	18.2	25.0	43.1	54.3	56.8	50.9	42.9

Source: Maddison (2003: 256–62), updated and revised. For further detail, see Statistical Appendix A, this volume, and www.ggdc.net/Maddison.

when significant growth momentum was largely confined to European countries, western offshoots and Latin America.

The Divergence Between the West and the Rest

Table 2.1 shows the evolution of per capita income in six major regions from year 1 to 2003AD. In the year 1000 the inter-regional spread was very narrow indeed. By 2003 all regions had increased their incomes, but there was an 18:1 gap between the richest and the poorest region, and a much wider inter-country spread.

One can also see the divergence between the 'west' (western Europe, US, Canada, Australia, New Zealand) and the rest of the world economy. Real per capita income in

Table 2.2. Growth Rates of Per Capita GDP, Population, and GDP, 1–2003AD (annual average compound growth rates)

	1–1000	1000–1500	1500–1820	1820–70	1870–1913	1913–50	1950–73	1973–2003
Per capita GDP								
Western Europe	−0.03	0.12	0.14	0.98	1.33	0.76	4.05	1.87
Western Offshoots	0.00	0.00	0.34	1.41	1.81	1.56	2.45	1.85
West	**−0.03**	**0.11**	**0.15**	**1.07**	**1.56**	**1.24**	**3.33**	**1.93**
Asia	0.00	0.04	0.01	−0.09	0.52	0.08	3.87	3.21
Latin America	0.00	0.01	0.16	−0.03	1.86	1.40	2.60	0.83
E. Europe & f. USSR	−0.00	0.04	0.10	0.63	1.18	1.40	3.49	−0.02
Africa	−0.01	−0.01	0.00	0.35	0.57	0.91	2.02	0.32
Rest	**0.00**	**0.04**	**0.02**	**0.10**	**0.86**	**0.67**	**3.31**	**1.93**
World	**0.00**	**0.05**	**0.05**	**0.54**	**1.30**	**0.88**	**2.91**	**1.56**
Population								
Western Europe	0.00	0.16	0.26	0.69	0.77	0.42	0.71	0.32
Western Offshoots	0.05	0.08	0.44	2.86	2.07	1.25	1.54	1.08
West	**0.00**	**0.16**	**0.27**	**0.98**	**1.08**	**0.70**	**1.04**	**0.65**
Asia	0.01	0.09	0.29	0.15	0.57	0.94	2.14	1.70
Latin America	0.07	0.09	0.07	1.26	1.63	1.96	2.72	1.90
E. Europe & f. USSR	0.05	0.15	0.35	0.89	1.19	0.33	1.31	0.43
Africa	0.06	0.07	0.15	0.40	0.75	1.65	2.36	2.64
Rest	**0.02**	**0.09**	**0.27**	**0.29**	**0.73**	**0.99**	**2.11**	**1.73**
World	**0.02**	**0.10**	**0.27**	**0.40**	**0.80**	**0.93**	**1.93**	**1.59**
GDP								
Western Europe	−0.03	0.28	0.40	1.68	2.11	1.19	4.79	2.19
Western Offshoots	0.05	0.08	0.78	4.31	3.92	2.83	4.03	2.95
West	**−0.02**	**0.27**	**0.42**	**2.05**	**2.67**	**1.95**	**4.40**	**2.59**
Asia	0.01	0.13	0.29	0.06	1.10	1.02	6.09	4.97
Latin America	0.07	0.09	0.22	1.23	3.52	3.40	5.38	2.75
E. Europe & f. USSR	0.04	0.21	0.44	1.53	2.37	1.74	4.85	0.42
Africa	0.05	0.07	0.15	0.75	1.32	2.57	4.43	2.97
Rest	**0.02**	**0.13**	**0.29**	**0.39**	**1.60**	**1.67**	**5.49**	**3.69**
World	**0.01**	**0.15**	**0.32**	**0.94**	**2.12**	**1.82**	**4.90**	**3.17**

Source: Derived from Table 2.1.

the west increased 2.8-fold between the year 1000 and 1820, and 20-fold from 1820 to 2003. In the rest of the world income rose much more slowly—slightly more than a quarter from 1000 to 1820 and seven-fold since then. The west had 43 per cent of world GDP in 2003, but only 12 per cent of world population. Average income was $23,710 (in 1990 purchasing power). The rest, by contrast, with 88 per cent of world population, had an average income of $4,172 (see Tables 2.1 and 2.2).

Experience of Growth, Divergence and Convergence Since 1950

In the past half-century, there have been major changes in the pace and pattern of growth in different parts of the world.

The years 1950 to 1973 were a golden age of unparalleled prosperity. World per capita GDP rose at an annual rate near 3 per cent, world GDP about 5 per cent

Table 2.3. Life Expectation, 1000–2003AD
(years at birth for both sexes combined)

	World	West	Rest
1000	24	24	24
1820	26	36	24
1900	31	46	26
1950	49	66	44
2003	64	76	63

Source: Maddison (2003: 31), updated from Population Division, US Bureau of the Census.

and exports almost 8 per cent. Performance was better in all regions than in any earlier phase. There was a significant degree of convergence in per capita income and productivity, with most regions growing faster than the US (the lead economy).

After 1973, there was a marked slowdown. Global GDP growth was cut by half. There was substantial divergence between different regions and performance in many of them was below potential.

In the advanced capitalist countries, per capita GDP growth slowed substantially. To a significant degree this was due to a deceleration of technical progress in the US, the country operating closest to the frontier of technology. There was less scope for rapid catch-up in productivity in western Europe and Japan as these 'follower' countries had eroded the once-for-all opportunities they had exploited in the golden age. Some slowdown in these economies was warranted, but policy failings made it bigger than it need have been (see Maddison 2001: 131–41 for a detailed analysis).

By far the best performance in 1973–2003 came from economies of east Asia (except Japan) which produce a quarter of world GDP and have half the world's population. The success of resurgent Asia has been extraordinary. Per capita growth was faster after 1973 than in the golden age and more than ten times as fast as in the old liberal order (1870–1913). There has been significant catch-up on the advanced capitalist group and a replication (in various degrees of intensity) of the big leap forward achieved by Japan in the golden age.

If the world consisted only of the advanced capitalist countries and resurgent Asia, the pattern of development since 1973 could be interpreted as a clear demonstration of the possibilities for conditional convergence suggested by neo-classic growth theory. This supposes that countries with low incomes have 'opportunities of backwardness', and should be able to grow faster than more prosperous economies operating near the technological frontier. This potential can only be realized if the lower income countries are successful in mobilizing and allocating resources efficiently, improving their human and physical capital to assimilate and adapt appropriate technologies. The resurgent Asian countries were successful in seizing these opportunities.

In all other regions of the world, performance deteriorated in 1973–2003. The loss of momentum was very sharp in Africa and Latin America. These economies suffered major shocks as the result of slowdown in the advanced capitalist countries. The shocks crippled their growth momentum and left their economic policy in disarray. Their economic performance in the golden age had not been due to any great virtues of domestic policy, but was dependent on the diffusion effects of high growth momentum in the advanced countries. The sharp slowdown in the capitalist core sparked off debt crises, inflation, fiscal, and monetary problems in Latin America and Africa. The biggest of these system shocks was the political and economic collapse that accompanied the disintegration of the USSR into 15 independent states. This shock also led to political change in east European countries and to the collapse of their command economies. They had major problems in adjusting their policies and institutions in order to function successfully as new members of a capitalist world economy which offered new opportunities for trade and access to foreign capital, but also involved new dangers of instability and new rules of behaviour.

THE DRIVING FORCES THAT EXPLAIN THE ACCELERATION IN WESTERN GROWTH SINCE 1820

In analysing growth causality, it is useful to distinguish between proximate and measurable influences and deeper, non-quantifiable features which help explain the unique dynamism of west European performance over several centuries.

For the period since 1820, it is possible to quantify the proximate causes which explain the performance of major capitalist economies (see the detailed accounts for the UK, US, and Japan in Chapter 6, Tables 6.4 and 6.5).

The UK was the lead country in terms of labour productivity in the nineteenth century and played a strongly diffusionist role in world development through export of capital and its policy of free trade. The US overtook the UK as the productivity leader in the 1890s, and had faster productivity growth thereafter. Japan was the archetype catch-up country, overtaking Chinese levels of performance in the Tokugawa period, catching up with western Europe in terms of per capita GDP (but not productivity) by the 1990s. The Japanese catch-up effort involved high rates of investment in human and physical capital (which is also characteristic of other Asian economies—Korea, Taiwan, China, Hong Kong, and Singapore—where there has been substantial catch-up in the past half century). Instead of overtaking the US, as was once predicted, the Japanese economy has stagnated in the past decade.

The most dynamic feature was the explosive growth in the stock of machinery and equipment per head. It rose by a multiple of 155 in the UK and 372 in the US between 1820 and 2003, 332 in Japan after 1890. The stock of non-residential structures rose much less, 21-fold in the UK, 33-fold in the US and 89-fold in Japan.

Most machinery is power-driven, but energy consumption rose much more slowly than the stock of machinery. In the US, where there was an abundance of easily available timber in 1820, per capita consumption of primary energy rose three-fold, against six- in the UK and twenty-fold in Japan. Thus there has been enormous progress in the efficiency of energy conversion due to improvements in machines. Growth has also been underpinned by technical progress in locating and extracting energy from minerals. These now supply more than four-fifths of the world's energy. In 1820, the ratio was less than 6 per cent, and 94 per cent was derived from biomass.

In the course of the nineteenth century, great increases in the efficiency of steam engines were achieved by development of compound and turbine technology. Landes (1965: 504–9) illustrated this by comparing the 60 horsepower engine of a P&O paddle-wheeler of 1829 with twin-turbines generating 136,000 horsepower for the Cunard liner Mauretania in 1907. Thereafter, ships shifted increasingly to oil and diesel engines, which produced much more power than the same weight of coal, and eliminated the need for stokers.

Steam engines also revolutionized passenger and freight transport by land in the nineteenth century. Starting from scratch in 1826, almost a million kilometres of rail track had been built by 1913. The internal combustion engine reinforced the momentum of change, added greatly to individual freedom of movement, and enlarged choice in location of industrial and commercial activity. In 1913, the fleet of passenger cars was about 1.5 million vehicles. In 2002, it was 530 million. In the second half of the twentieth century, air passenger miles rose from 28 billion in 1950 to 2.6 trillion in 1998. Development of electricity had at least as big an impact. It provided a multi-purpose, efficient, and convenient source of heat, light, and power, whose availability transformed household operation, office work, the nature and locus of industrial activity, and the potential for scientific research.[1]

Human capital, i.e., the average number of years of education per person employed (weighted by level attained) rose by a factor of 12 in the US, 11 in Japan, and 8 in the UK. It was profitable to invest in this rapid expansion of physical and human capital because the rhythm of technical progress was much faster in the nineteenth and twentieth centuries than ever before.

International trade increased rapidly after 1820. The volume of exports per head of population rose 103-fold in the UK, 114-fold in the US, and by a much higher proportion in Japan (whose economy was closed to foreign trade until 1855). It was important in enabling countries to specialize in the types of product at which they were most efficient. It eliminated the handicap of countries with limited natural resources. It was also important in diffusing new products and new technology.

CHANGES IN THE STRUCTURE OF DEMAND AND EMPLOYMENT

Increases in per capita income and productivity bring big changes in economic and social structure. Changes in the pattern of consumer demand, the role of government, the rate of investment, share of foreign trade, and the direction of technical progress all have a major impact on the nature of economic activity.

These structural changes are interesting in themselves and the statistical record of such change provides corroborative evidence of the pace and pattern of growth. For instance, if we see growing urbanization, a fall in the proportion employed in agriculture, or a fall in the proportion of consumer expenditure on food, we can infer that there have been advances in productivity in agriculture and growth in GDP per capita.

As per capita income rises, spending priorities change. At low levels of income, food absorbs a high proportion of consumer budgets.[2] As nutrition improves, priority switches to clothing. At higher levels, expenditure on health, education, entertainment, and transport increases dramatically. Changes in the pattern of demand have a powerful influence on the direction of inventive activity which leads to creation of new goods.

Table 2.4 shows the change in the pattern of demand over the past three centuries in Britain (the country for which such changes are best documented). In 1688, traditional necessities (the first six items) constituted three-quarters of total expenditure and nearly 90 per cent of personal consumption. In the course of the eighteenth century, the quality and variety of food, clothing, household utensils, and furnishings was greatly improved by imports from Asia and the Americas and the import substitution which they sometimes induced. By 2001, these six items were less

Table 2.4. Structure of British Expenditure, 1688 and 2001 (per cent of total)

	1688 England & Wales	2001 UK
Food	25.7	5.2
Beverages and tobacco	13.6	3.2
Clothing and footwear	19.2	3.6
Light, fuel, and power	3.7	1.9
Furniture, furnishings, and household equipment	9.3	3.8
Personal services	3.0	1.4
Total: Items 1–6	74.5	19.1
Rent and imputed rent	4.1	9.1
Education and health	2.1	13.2
Recreation and entertainment	0.9	8.3
Transport and communication	0.8	10.6
Other	1.9	13.2
Total: Items 7–12	9.8	54.4
Total private consumption (Total items 1–12)	84.2	73.5
Government consumption*	9.0	9.8
Gross capital formation	6.8	16.7
Total gross domestic expenditure	100.0	100.0
Level of per capita GDP (1990 international $)	1,411	20,554

Note: *excluding education and health.

Source: Maddison (2003: 18), updated to 2001 from OECD, *National Accounts of OECD, Countries*, 1991–2002, vol. IIb, Paris, 2004: 772 and 793.

Table 2.5. Structure of Employment in the Netherlands, UK, and USA, 1700–2003 (percentage of total employment)

		Netherlands	United Kingdom	United States
1700	Agriculture	40	56	n.a.
	Industry	33	22	n.a.
	Services	27	22	n.a.
1820	Agriculture	42	37	70
	Industry	28	33	15
	Services	30	30	15
1890	Agriculture	36	16	38
	Industry	32	43	24
	Services	32	41	38
1950	Agriculture	14	5	13
	Industry	40	47	33
	Services	46	48	54
2003	Agriculture	3	1	2
	Industry	20	24	20
	Services	77	75	78

Notes and Sources: Maddison (1991: 32) for 1700; Maddison (1995a: 253) for the United Kingdom and the United States 1820–90; Netherlands 1820 and 1890 from Smits, et al. (2000: 115–16); Maddison (1991: 248) for 1950; OECD, *Labour Force Statistics, 1983–2003* for 2003. Agriculture includes forestry and fishing; industry includes mining, manufacturing, electricity, gas, water, and construction; services is a residual including all other activity, private and governmental (including military).

than a fifth of the total, and there had been big proportionate increases in expenditure on services and investment goods.

Government in most countries is now responsible for the bulk of expenditure on education and health, and influences the pattern of spending through very large transfer expenditures. In the course of the twentieth century, government responsibilities increased everywhere, but much more in western Europe than in the US.

Table 2.5 shows changes in the structure of employment over the past three centuries in the three successive lead countries. In 1700 Dutch per capita income was the highest in Europe, the economy already had relatively a high level of international specialization, a highly productive agriculture, and large imports of grain. By the standards of the time, the proportion employed in agriculture (40 per cent) was very low (a good deal lower than the British ratio). In the eighteenth century, Dutch exports fell, industry contracted, and dependence on domestic agriculture rose. The UK became the most dynamic economy. British farm productivity rose rapidly and the proportion employed in agriculture declined to 37 per cent in 1820. In the nineteenth century British imports of food rose dramatically because of the policy of free trade.

Over the long run, the relative importance of agricultural employment has fallen more dramatically than expenditure on food. British farm employment fell from 56 per cent of the work force in 1700 to 1 per cent in 2003, and food fell from

26 to 7 per cent of consumer expenditure. A large part of food expenditure now goes to meet processing and packaging, transport and distributive costs for a heavily urbanized population. In the seventeenth century a majority of the population produced their own food, milked their own cows, made their own butter and cheese, and baked their own bread. Another reason is that modern farmers use large inputs of fertiliser, pesticide, machinery, and fuel, and their value added is substantially smaller than their gross output.[3]

Fundamental Features Underlying Western Europe's Ascension 1000–1820

The main changes between the first and tenth centuries in western Europe were: (a) the collapse of the Roman empire—a large scale cohesive political unit which was never resurrected, and its replacement by a fragmented, fragile, and unstable polity; (b) a fall in per capita income, disappearance of urban civilization, and predominance of self-sufficient, relatively isolated, and ignorant rural communities where a feudal elite extracted an income in kind from a servile peasantry; the virtual disappearance of trading links between western Europe, north Africa and Asia.

The years between 1000 and 1500 were a period of resurrection in which western Europe's population grew faster than that in any other part of the world. Northern countries grew significantly faster than those bordering the Mediterranean. The urban proportion (in terms of towns with more than 10,000 population) rose from 0 to 6 per cent, a clear indicator of expansion in manufacturing and commercial activity. Factors making it possible to feed the increased population were an increase in the area of rural settlement, particularly in the Netherlands, Northern Germany, and the Baltic coast and the gradual incorporation of technological changes which raised land productivity. The classic analysis of these rural changes is by Lynn White (in Cipolla 1972: 153):

…the heavy plough, open fields, the new integration of agriculture and herding, three field rotation, modern horse harness, nailed horseshoes and whipple tree had combined into a total system of agrarian exploitation by the year 1100 to provide a zone of peasant prosperity stretching across Northern Europe from the Atlantic to the Dnieper.

White probably exaggerated the precocity of their impact and the degree of prosperity, but these technical improvements were clearly of fundamental importance. The switch from a two field to a three field system also increased food security and reduced the incidence of famine. A growing proportion of agricultural output went as inputs into clothing production (wool), wine and beer (cereals and vines), and fodder crops for an increased horse population. There was a degree of regional specialization in food production with growing international trade in cereals, live cattle, cheese, fish, and wine. Increased trade in salt and the reintroduction of spice imports helped improve the palatability and conservation of meat and fish.

Increased use of water and windmills augmented the power available for industrial processes, particularly in new industries such as sugar production and paper making. There was international specialization in the woollen industry. English wool was exported to Flanders for production of cloth which was traded throughout Europe. The silk industry was introduced in the twelfth century and had grown impressively in southern Europe by 1500. There were big improvements in the quality of textiles and the varieties of colour and design available. Genoa introduced regular shipments of alum from Chios to Bruges in the thirteenth century. There were improvements in mining and metallurgy which helped transform and expand European weapons production (see Nef 1987; Cipolla 1970). Improvements in shipping and navigation techniques from the eleventh to the fifteenth century underpinned the increase in trade in the Mediterranean, the Baltic, the Atlantic islands, and the northwest coast of Africa.

There were big advances in banking, accountancy, marine insurance, improvements in the quality of intellectual life with the development and spread of universities, the growth of humanist scholarship, and, at the end of the fifteenth century, the introduction of printing.

There were important changes in the political order. Scandinavian raiders who had made attacks on England, the low countries, Normandy, and deep into Russia had become civilized traders and established effective systems of governance in Scandinavia itself, in England, Normandy, and Sicily. The beginnings of a nation-state system had emerged, with a reduction in the fragmentation of political power that had characterized the middle ages. The 100 years war (1337–1453) was not the last of the conflicts between England and France, but the national identity of the two countries was much more clearly defined after it was over. At the end of the fifteenth century, the *reconquista* had established Spanish identity in its modern form.

It is not possible to quantify the proximate causes of western growth before 1820 in the same detail as one can from 1820 onwards, but it is not difficult to identify the fundamental changes in west European intellectual horizons and institutions which were a prerequisite for the modest economic progress in this period and for the acceleration thereafter. From 1000 to 1820, investment in machinery, equipment, and human capital was also modest, but its quality was transformed by the invention of printing, advances in science, and the spread of secular university education for the elites. Technical progress was slower than now, and much less capital-intensive. Some of it derived from trial-and-error, but institutional support for scientific research had a very direct impact on technology, particularly in shipping and navigation. I have spelled out the changes in this domain in considerable detail below, and explained how they were diffused between the major merchant capitalist empires. Technical progress in this period was not energy-intensive. It relied on more effective wind power, improvements in the efficacy of horsepower, and an increase in hours worked per capita. There was very modest use of mineral fuels and heavy reliance on biomass. In proportionate terms, globalization was much more important from 1500 to 1870 than it has been since. A great part of the increase in productivity was due gains from increased specialization and increases in the scale of production—gains of the type which were stressed by Adam Smith in his analysis of the causes of economic progress up to 1776.

Four Major Intellectual and Institutional Changes in the West Before 1820

There were four major intellectual and institutional changes in the west before 1820 which had a profound impact on economic performance and had no counterpart in other parts of the world in this period.

1. A fundamental change was the recognition of human capacity to transform the forces of nature through rational investigation and experiment. The first European university was created in Bologna in 1080. By 1500 there were 70 such centres of secular learning in western Europe (see Goodman and Russell 1991: 25). Until the mid-fifteenth century, most of the instruction was oral, and the learning process was similar to that in ancient Greece. Things changed after Gutenberg printed his first book in Mainz in 1455. By 1500, 220 printing presses were in operation throughout western Europe and had produced eight million books (see Eisenstein 1993: 13–17). The productivity of universities and their openness to new ideas were greatly enlarged.

   The main centre of European publishing was Venice where printed books were first produced in 1469. Before then, scribes, bookbinders, and specialists in ornamental calligraphy and illustration produced sacred books or translations of Greek and Latin classics for city archives or wealthy private collectors. Productivity in book production was revolutionized and costs had fallen dramatically by the 1470s. In 1483 the Ripoli press produced 1,025 copies of Plato's *Dialogues*. A scribe would have taken a year to produce one volume. Assuming that the Ripoli Press had higher capital outlays on equipment than institutions employing scribes, and needed one man-year of skilled labour input to produce its 1,025 copies, one can infer that productivity in book production increased at least 200-fold. By the middle of the sixteenth century, the Venetian presses had produced some 20,000 titles, including music scores, maps, books on medical matters, and a flood of new secular learning.

   The latter point is of great significance. Before printing, books were cherished for their artistic or iconic value, and their content mainly reflected the wisdom and dogma of the past. Printing made books much cheaper. Publishers were much more willing to risk dissemination of new ideas and to provide an outlet for new authors. The proportion of the population with access to books was greatly increased, and there was a much greater incentive to aspire to literacy. It should also be stressed that, with the exception of China, the European printing revolution had no counterpart in most other parts of the world until the beginning of the nineteenth century. The major difference between Europe and China was the competitive character of European publishing, and the international trade in books. This frustrated the attempts of the Papacy to achieve thought control through the Inquisition and censorship. China was a centralized state, with vestigial foreign contacts. The education of its bureaucracy was devoted to ancient classics, and they were able to exercise thought control by more subtle and effective methods than the papacy in Europe.

Further changes in intellectual horizons occurred between the sixteenth and seventeenth centuries, when medieval notions of an earth-centred universe were abandoned. Thanks to the Renaissance, the seventeenth century scientific revolution, and the eighteenth century enlightenment, western elites abandoned superstition, magic, and submission to religious authority. The scientific approach gradually impregnated the educational system. Circumscribed intellectual horizons were abandoned. A Promethean quest for progress was unleashed. The impact of science was reinforced by the creation of academies and observatories which inaugurated empirical research and experiment. Systematic recording of experimental results and their diffusion in written form were a key element in their success.

2. The emergence of important urban trading centres in Bruges, Venice, and other cities in Flanders and northern Italy in the eleventh and twelfth centuries was accompanied by changes which fostered entrepreneurship and abrogated feudal constraints on the purchase and sale of property. Nondiscretionary legal systems protected property rights. The development of accountancy helped further in making contracts enforceable. State fiscal levies became more predictable and less arbitrary. The growth of trustworthy financial institutions and instruments provided access to credit and insurance, made it easier to assess risk and organize business rationally on a large scale over a wide area.

3. The adoption of Christianity as a state religion in 380AD led to basic changes in the nature of European marriage, inheritance, and kinship. The papacy imposed a pattern that differed substantially from what had prevailed earlier in Greece, Rome, and Egypt and differed dramatically from that which was to characterize the Islamic world. Marriage was to be strictly monogamous, with a ban on concubinage, adoption, divorce, and remarriage of widows or widowers. There was a prohibition on consanguineous marriage with siblings, ascendants, descendants, including first, second, and third cousins, or relatives of siblings by marriage. A papal decision in AD385 imposed priestly celibacy.

The main purpose of these rules was to limit inheritance entitlements to close family members and to channel large amounts to the church which became a property owner on a huge scale. At the same time they broke down previous loyalties to clan, tribe, and caste, promoted individualism and accumulation, and reinforced the sense of belonging to a nation-state (see Goody 1983; Lal 2001).

4. A fourth distinctive feature was the emergence of a system of nation-states in close propinquity, which had significant trading relations and relatively easy intellectual interchange in spite of their linguistic differences. In many respects this was a benign fragmentation. It stimulated competition and innovation. Migration to or refuge in a different culture and environment were options open to adventurous and innovative minds.[4] However, the mercantilist commercial policies of the leading European countries were mutually discriminatory and restrictive. Beggar-your-neighbour policies were buttressed by wars. Between 1700 and 1820 the UK was involved five major wars (for a total of 55 years) due in large degree to its pursuit of worldwide commercial supremacy.

The Locus of Technical Change, 1000–1820

Advances in ship design and navigation were the most dynamic form of technical progress in western Europe from 1000 to 1820.[5] Without them, western Europe would not have achieved its dominant role in world trade. It would not have strengthened its internal linkages via Mediterranean and Baltic trade, gone on to discover and appropriate huge areas of land, precious metals, and biological resources in the Americas, and capture a major share of Asian trade by circumnavigating Africa.

For the benefit of those who consider the period 1000 to 1820 to have been an era of technological stagnation, it is useful to examine the evolution of shipping and navigational technology in some detail and demonstrate the close interaction between science and technology from the sixteenth century onwards.

Table 2.6 compares the growth of world trade and GDP since 1500. The ratio between the two rates of growth is shown in the third column. The ratio was higher between 1500 and 1870 than it has been since.

Table 2.6. Globalization: Growth in Volume of World Trade and GDP, 1500–2003 (annual average compound growth rates)

	World Trade	World GDP	col.1/2
1500–1820	0.96	0.32	3.0
1820–70	4.18	0.94	4.4
1870–1913	3.40	2.12	1.6
1913–50	0.90	1.82	0.5
1950–73	7.88	4.90	1.6
1973–2003	5.38	3.17	1.7
1820–2003	3.97	2.25	1.8

Notes and Sources: World trade volume 1500–1820 derived from growth in tonnage of the world merchant fleet (Maddison 2001: 95) with a 50 per cent upward adjustment for technical improvements which augmented effective carrying capacity; 1820–70 from Maddison (1982: 254); 1870–1990 from Maddison (2001: 362), updated to 2003 from IMF *International Financial Statistics*. World GDP from www.ggdc.net/Maddison. See O'Rourke and Williamson (2002), for a similar estimate of the growth in intercontinental trade volume for 1500–1800, obtained by a totally different approach.

Between 1470 and 1820, western Europe's merchant fleet increased about 17-fold. Per head of population, the rise was more than six-fold. Its effective carrying capacity rose more than this because of technical progress in design of ships, sails, and rigging, improvements in instruments and techniques of navigation, in cartography, and in knowledge of geography, winds, and currents. Voyages became less dangerous for ships and their crews. Travel time became more predictable and regular, ships became bigger, and crew requirements per ton of cargo were reduced. European domination of the world's oceans was reinforced by advances in naval armament, and the capacity to organize business on a large scale in ventures that required significant capital outlays over a relatively long period.

In the year 1000, Mediterranean ships were no better than a thousand years earlier. Ships were rigged with square sails which were efficient only when the wind was astern. Voyages against the wind could be extremely lengthy and uncertain.[6] Harbour facilities were inferior to those constructed by the emperor Claudius at Portus (near Ostia) for the food supply of Rome, and Alexandria's great port and lighthouse had disappeared. Some navigational aids were the same as in Roman times—lead lines for sounding depth of water and a windrose which helped identify the direction of winds. The stars and the sun provided guidance on position and time of day. However, there were no charts or sailing instructions (*periploi*) showing depths, anchorages, and tides—of the kind the Greeks and Romans had.

In the thirteenth century there were significant improvements. The most important was the magnetic compass showing 32 directional points, somewhat like a windrose, but with a pointer directed continuously to the north. A stern-post rudder replaced trailing oars as a more effective means of steering. The power of rudders was strengthened by use of cranks and pulleys, making it much easier to maintain course in bad weather. There were improvements in Mediterranean sails, notably the use of the Arab lateen rig set at an angle to the mast, instead of a rectangular sail set square to the mast. This made it possible to sail in a wider range of wind conditions, and reduced the time spent idling in port or at anchor. The Venetian sandglass made it possible to measure the lapse of time accurately over a given interval, and the wooden traverse board allowed mariners to plot the course of a voyage. The board had a face like a compass with eight holes at each compass point, and eight pegs attached in the centre. At each half-hour of the four hour watch, a peg was placed in the appropriate hole to indicate the course of the ship in that interval. Traverse tables provided trigonometrical guidance in estimating daily progress and calculation was made easier by the adoption of Arabic numerals. About the same time, *portolans* (charts with an indication of ports, anchorages, tides, depths, and winds) began to appear. They provided sailing instructions derived from the experience of earlier mariners. They showed coastal outlines and distances between ports, with an array of alternative courses (rhumb lines). If none of the lines were appropriate for the intended voyage, they nevertheless helped the mariner design and pursue his own trajectory, using a ruler and dividers. Portolans were made of vellum (a single sheepskin up to 5 feet long and half as wide) with directions inscribed in black and red ink.

These changes increased the productivity of Venetian ships, which previously had not ventured the trip to Egypt between October and April when the sky was frequently overcast. With these instruments, a ship could make two return journeys a year from Venice to Alexandria instead of one.

Innovations in shipbuilding reduced costs and improved efficiency. In Roman times the hull had been constructed first. Ships were held together by watertight cabinetwork of mortice and tenon. The second stage was the insertion of ribs and braces. From the eleventh century, the keel and ribs were built first, and a hull of nailed planks was added, using fibre and pitch to make it watertight.

In the fifteenth century, the locus of maritime progress switched to Portugal, which was exploring the Atlantic islands and the African coast. Major changes in rigging harnessed wind energy more efficiently than in earlier Mediterranean vessels. With more masts and a complex array of sails, ships became more manoeuvrable and faster. They could tack into the wind with much greater ease. The Venetian galley, whose motive power depended on oarsmen, became obsolete. A new type of vessel, the caravel, was more robust and able to operate successfully in the stormier seas and stronger currents of the Atlantic.

The Portuguese made major progress in navigation, developing new instruments and much better charts. In the Northern hemisphere, the pole star provided a more or less constant bearing and altitude. On a north–south passage, navigators could observe the pole star each day at dawn and dusk (when they could see both the star and the horizon). By noting changes in altitude they could get some idea of changes in their position. In sailing east–west, they could keep a steady course by maintaining a constant polar altitude. All this had been done very crudely, using finger spreads or other rough means of measuring altitude. In the fifteenth century, the Portuguese developed the quadrant, which made judgement of latitudes and distance sailed more accurate. They also devised techniques to correct for the slight rotation of the polar star. In the southern hemisphere which Portuguese ships had now begun to enter, there was no star with the same properties and the sun was used instead. The sun's altitude could not be measured with a quadrant, as its light was too bright for the naked eye, so a variant of the astronomer's astrolabe was developed for mariners. Because of the earth's movement, the altitude of the sun was different every day, so altitude readings had to be adjusted for daily changes in the sun's declination. These tables were constructed by the astronomer Zacuto in the 1470s. After practical tests of the instruments and tables on trial voyages, a naval almanac, *Regimento do Astrolabio et do Quadrante* was compiled and was used by da Gama when he sailed to India in 1497.

In the fifteenth century, there were improvements in measuring speed and distance travelled at sea. The nautical mile became the standard unit of distance and the log-line that trailed from the stern was marked by knots spaced uniformly to mark fractions of a mile. The running time of the sandglass was adjusted to match.

European knowledge of world geography was revolutionized by the establishment of the new routes in the southern hemisphere, the discovery of the Americas, and

Magellan's circumnavigation of the globe. New maps were needed, charts were improved, atlases began to appear, and the invention of printing greatly facilitated their diffusion. Globes were produced to give a more accurate idea of world geography on long routes. In 1569, the Flemish mapmaker, Gerard Mercator, developed a projection technique to represent the world's sphericity on a flat surface. On his charts, parallels of latitude and meridians of longitude cut each other at right angles. Meridians were spread apart as they approached the poles. As a counterbalance, the spacing of latitude degrees was increased progressively toward the poles. As a result, the line of a constant compass bearing was straight. This was of great potential use for navigators but not widely adopted until the seventeenth century. Calculation of a ship's course was greatly simplified by Napier's 1614 invention of logarithms, which became available to mariners in the form of decimal tables (invented by Briggs in 1631). Logarithmic slide-rules were available to mariners from the middle of the seventeenth century along with other trigonometric shortcuts. In 1594, the English navigator, John Davis, invented a simple backstaff that could be used to measure solar altitude, without sighting the sun directly. By the end of the seventeenth century it had replaced the seaman's quadrant and astrolabe. It was superseded by a much more precise reflecting octant invented by the English mathematician, Halley, in 1731 as a by-product of his work on reflecting telescopes. This was further improved in 1757 by a sextant developed by the British navy. This permitted a quick and accurate reading of any celestial object against the horizon.

The search for accurate measurement of longitude had been under way for a long time. Philip III of Spain offered large financial rewards in 1598 and similar incentives had been offered in France and Holland. In 1714 the British government created a Board of Longitude which offered a £20,000 prize for an invention accurate within narrow specifications. The prize was won by John Harrison, who after 25 years of effort, made a chronometer in 1760 (about twice the size of a pocket watch), which was unaffected by the movement of a ship and changes in the weather. This was successfully tested in trials to the West Indies in 1762–4. Captain Cook, who had used the new *Nautical Almanac* and lunar method of estimating longitude in his first Pacific voyage in 1768–71, used a copy of Harrison's watch on his 1772–5 trip round the world. When he returned to Plymouth three years later, the cumulative error in longitude was less than eight miles.

By the end of the eighteenth century, great progress had been made in ships and rigging, in gunnery, meteorological and astronomical knowledge, and the precision of navigational instruments. Maps had been enormously improved and were supplemented by detailed coastal surveys. Sailing had become safer, the duration of voyages more predictable, and the incidence of shipwreck had fallen significantly. There was also progress in reducing disease mortality on long voyages.

In his voyage round the world in 1740–4, Anson successfully harried the Spanish in the Pacific and captured a huge treasure ship with loss of only four men by enemy action, but 1,300 died from disease, mainly scurvy. This experience led the British naval physician James Lind to carry out dietary experiments. In 1753 he published his results and recommended orange and lemon juice as a preventive measure. Captain Cook, in his voyage of 1768–71, experimented with a number of anti-scorbutic items, including oranges, lemons, and sauerkraut. He had only one case of scurvy, but it was not until 1795 that regular issue of lemon juice was adopted by the Royal Navy.

European naval weaponry and modes of warfare had changed completely by the sixteenth century. The oared galley, which was used for close combat, ramming, and boarding, was last used at the battle of Lepanto in 1571. It was replaced by ships manoeuvrable enough to engage the enemy at a distance with broadsides from heavy artillery pieces. Bronze guns had been replaced by much improved and cheaper iron weaponry.

At first naval guns were fired from the superstructure and the size of ships was enlarged to maximize firepower. Very large ships of this kind (the English *Harry Grace à Dieu* 1514, the French *Grand François* 1534, the Portuguese *São Jão* 1552, and the Swedish *Elefanten* 1559, were unstable and sank very quickly. The British developed a more successful design around 1550—the galleon—a medium-sized ship, fast and manoeuvrable with guns on the main deck, firing cannon through ports cut in the hull. They proved successful in 1588 against bigger ships in the Spanish Armada. The Dutch also found them effective against the large carracks used by the Portuguese in their Asian trade.

The Scientific Revolution

From the middle of the sixteenth century to the end of the seventeenth there was fundamental progress in western science that had important consequences for navigation and brought revolutionary changes in European perceptions of the universe, the interaction between the earth, the other planets, the sun, and the stars. The revolution started in 1543 with the publication of Copernicus' heliocentric theory rejecting the scholastic notion that the earth was the centre of the universe. This was followed by detailed observation of the movement of celestial bodies and the nature and mutability of their orbits by Kepler and Galileo, estimates of celestial distance and new conclusions about the laws of motion. From 1610, Galileo made his own refractor telescopes and used them to observe the mountains and craters of the moon, the spots on the sun, the satellites of Jupiter, the phases of Venus, and the stars of the Milky Way. His quarter century of observation greatly enriched the empirical evidence for the Copernican hypothesis. In 1632 he published his *Dialogue on the Two Chief Systems of the World* (Ptolemaic and Copernican). As a result he was detained by the Church authorities, and under threat of torture was forced to recant. He remained sequestered and his works were banned by papal decree until 1757. The counter-reformation papacy was militant in its persecution of heresy and heretical books. The Jesuit order and the Inquisition were major instruments of this policy, and intellectual freedom in Italy was further weakened by Spanish control of Lombardy and the kingdom of Naples.

In the mid-seventeenth century, the locus of the scientific revolution moved to northern Europe, notably England, France, and Holland. The climax was Newton's publication of his *Principia* in 1687, which showed that the whole universe was subject to the same laws of motion and gravitation. Newton's conclusions, like those of Galileo were carefully tested against empirical evidence of celestial phenomena. He constructed a new type of reflecting telescope for his own observations and followed closely the research results of the Royal Society founded in 1662. Newton was President from 1703 to 1727. The French Académie des Sciences was created more or less simultaneously and the astronomical research of both institutions was buttressed by astronomical observatories. The Paris Observatoire was established in 1672 and the Greenwich Observatory in 1675. Interaction between the two academies was close. Newton was influenced by the research at the French Academy by the Dutch scientist Huygens and the precise measurements of celestial distance by Picard and Cassini at the Paris Observatory.

Progress in astronomy and physics was accompanied by major advances in mathematics and design of new instruments (telescopes, micrometers, microscopes, thermometers, barometers, air-pumps, clocks and watches, and the steam engine) that had important implications, short and long term, for the progress of navigation. Their practical implications for seamanship were the particular domain of the British Navy and the Greenwich Observatory. They were also part of Colbert's efforts to reconstruct the French navy from 1669 onwards.[7]

The link between scientific research and practical matters of navigation is clear from the work of Edmond Halley (1656–1742). He wrote his first paper for the Royal Society in 1676 when he was 19. It dealt with irregularities he had observed in the orbits of the planets Jupiter and Saturn which were then believed to be uniformly elliptic. Over the next 65 years he wrote another 80 scientific papers (see MacPike 1932). He encouraged Newton to finish his *Principia*, financed its publication and checked the proofs. He served as Secretary of the Royal Society in 1685–93, Professor of Geometry at Oxford from 1704, Astronomer Royal from 1720, and honorary member of the French Académie des Sciences from 1729.

In 1677 he went to St. Helena for 18 months to make the first catalogue of stars observable in the southern hemisphere. He used a telescope with a micrometer to measure their position and coordinates. In 1679 the Royal Society sent him to Danzig for two months to check the accuracy of Hevelius' catalogue of stars visible in the northern hemisphere. From 1680 to 1705 he made a comparative analysis of the orbits of 24 comets, explained the reasons for their apparently erratic variation and predicted correctly the return of Halley's comet in 1758. He studied the orbits of the planets Mercury and Venus, which are nearer the sun than the earth is. He had used his 1677 observation of the transit of Mercury to make a crude measure of the sun's distance from the earth. In 1691 he predicted transits of Venus for 1761 and 1769 and suggested that they be observed at extreme points of the earth in order to measure the dimensions of the solar system. His suggestions were implemented, the 1769 transit being observed by Cook during his expedition to Tahiti.

Halley made three important contributions of great practical significance for mariners. Between 1683 and 1715 he measured the earth's atmosphere, the causes of variation in air pressure, the origins of trade winds and monsoons. He produced the first meteorological chart of wind patterns in the Atlantic, Indian, and Pacific oceans in 1686. He followed this by studies of rates of evaporation and replenishment of water. He estimated the daily evaporation of water in the Mediterranean to be 5.3 billion tons, and analysed the ways this was replaced by rainfall, river flows, etc.

In 1683 he started collecting observations of variance in terrestrial magnetism (which caused puzzling effects on compass readings). He speculated on their origin at different levels below the earth's surface and the effect of the earth's rotation. In 1698–1700 he directed a naval expedition in the Atlantic to measure magnetic variation systematically, and in 1701 published the first chart showing isogonic lines of equal magnetic variation distributed over the earth's surface. Thereafter charts of this kind became an essential part of a navigator's equipment.

Halley's third major contribution was painstaking daily lunar observation over a period of two decades in order to provide tables for accurate measurement of longitude. The results were incorporated in the annual *Nautical Almanac* published at Greenwich from 1767 onwards.

The scientific revolution had a very direct influence on European navigation and capacity to penetrate distant oceans. It was of fundamental long term importance in virtually all areas of activity. Advances in knowledge were closely linked with empirical investigation and the production of precision instruments (telescopes, microscopes, clocks, and watches). The revolution in cosmology stirred the European imagination and promoted Promethean ambitions.

These developments in Europe were an essential prelude to the much faster economic development that occurred in the nineteenth and twentieth centuries. They had no counterpart in other parts of the world.

THE EUROPEAN TRANSFORMATION OF THE AMERICAS, 1500–1820

The European Encounter and its Impact

When contact was first established, the Americas were thinly settled. The population was a third of the European and land area 11 times as large. The technological level was greatly inferior. There were no wheeled vehicles, draught animals, sailing ships, metal tools, weapons, or ploughs. There were no cattle, sheep, pigs, or hens. The most densely populated areas (Mexico and Peru) had significant urban centres and a sophisticated vegetarian agriculture. Elsewhere, most of the inhabitants were hunter-gatherers.

Table 2.7. The Economies of the Americas' Five Regions, 1500–2003 (population in 000s; per capita GDP in 1990 int.$; GDP in million 1990 int.$)

	1500	1600	1700	1820	2003
Mexico					
Population	7,500	2,500	4,500	6,587	103,718
Per capita GDP	425	454	568	759	7,137
GDP	3,188	1,134	2,558	5,000	740,226
15 Other Spanish America (ex. Caribbean)					
Population	8,500	5,100	5,800	7,571	215,918
Per capita GDP	412	432	498	680	5,575
GDP	3,500	2,201	2,889	5,152	1,203,697
30 Caribbean Countries					
Population	500	200	500	2,926	39,691
Per capita GDP	400	430	650	635	4,421
GDP	200	86	325	1,857	175,489
Brazil					
Population	1,000	800	1,250	4,507	182,033
Per capita GDP	400	428	459	646	5,563
GDP	400	342	574	2,912	1,012,733
Total Latin America					
Population	17,500	8,600	12,050	21,591	541,359
Per capita GDP	416	438	527	691	5,786
GDP	7,288	3,763	6,346	14,921	3,132,145
USA and Canada					
Population	2,250	1,750	1,200	10,797	322,550
Per capita GDP	400	400	511	1,231	28,458
GDP	900	700	613	13,286	9,179,125

Notes and Source: Maddison (2003: 114), updated. 2003 population from *International Data Base*, International Programs Center, Population Division, US Bureau of the Census (update of 26 April, 2005). GDP movement in Latin America, 2000–3, at constant prices from ECLAC database supplied by Andre Hofman (an update of the estimates in *Statistical Yearbook of Latin America and the Caribbean*, 2004: 195), Puerto Rico from CIA, *World Factbook*, Canada and US from OECD, *National Accounts*, vol. 1, 2006.

American populations had no resistance to diseases which Europeans brought (smallpox, measles, influenza, and typhus) or to African diseases (yellow fever and malaria) which arrived shortly afterwards. By the middle of the sixteenth century two-thirds were wiped out by mortality twice that of Europe during the Black Death of the fourteenth century.[8]

The two advanced civilizations (Aztec in Mexico and Inca in Peru) were destroyed. Their populations were reduced to anomie and serfdom. Hunter-gatherer populations elsewhere were marginalized or exterminated. The conquest of the Americas was unequivocal. The economy of these relatively empty lands was completely revamped. The continent was repopulated by the arrival of nearly eight million African slaves between 1500 and 1820 and about two million European settlers. In 1820, 41 per cent were white, 26 per cent indigenous, 22 per cent black or mulatto, and 11 per cent *mestizo* (see Table 2.8a). The high proportion of whites in 1820 indicates who benefited from the transformation of the Americas. European settlers

Table 2.8a. Ethnic Composition of the Americas in 1820 (000s of inhabitants)

	Indigenous	Mestizo	Black and Mulatto	White	Total
Mexico	3,570	1,777	10	1,230	6,587
Brazil	500		2,500	1,507	4,507
Caribbean			2,366	554	2,920
Other Latin America	4,000	1,800	400	1,485	7,685
US	325		1,772	7,884	9,981
Canada	75			741	816
Total	8,470	3,577	7,048	13,401	32,496

Sources: Mexico from Maddison (1995b: 315–16). Brazil from Maddison (2001: 235). Caribbean as below. US from Maddison (2001: 250). Canada from Maddison (2001: 180). Other Latin America from Maddison (2001: 235), excluding the Caribbean.

had higher fertility, longer life expectation, and much higher average incomes than African slaves and the indigenous population.

Although the initial impact of conquest and colonization was massively destructive, the long term economic potential was greatly enhanced. Capacity to support a bigger population was augmented by the introduction of new crops and animals (see Crosby 1972). The new items were wheat, rice, sugar cane, vines, cabbages, lettuce, olives, bananas, yams, and coffee. The new animals for food were cattle, pigs, chickens, sheep, and goats. The introduction of transport and traction animals— horses, oxen, asses, and mules—along with wheeled vehicles and ploughs (which replaced digging sticks) were a major contribution to productive capacity. There was a reciprocal transfer of New World crops to Europe, Asia, and Africa—maize, potatoes, sweet potatoes, manioc, chilis, tomatoes, groundnuts, haricot, lima, and string beans, pineapples, cocoa, and tobacco—which enhanced the rest of the world's production and capacity to sustain population growth.

Population and output recovered somewhat in the seventeenth century, but in 1700 were still well below 1500 levels. Growth accelerated rapidly in the eighteenth

Table 2.8b. Ethnic Composition Within the Caribbean, 1820 (000s of inhabitants)

	Black and Mulatto	White	Total
Cuba and Puerto Rico (Spanish colonies)	453	400	853
Haiti and Dominican Rep. (independent)	742	70	812
British colonies	827	53	880
French colonies	230	20	250
Dutch colonies	74	6	80
Danish and Swedish colonies	40	5	45
Total	2,366	554	2,920

Sources: Cuba and Puerto Rico from Shepherd and Beckles (2000: 274, 285); Haiti and Dominican Republic (independent in 1804 and 1821 respectively), French, Dutch, Danish, and Swedish colonies derived from Engerman and Higman (1997); British colonies from Higman (1984). Caribbean includes British Guiana and Surinam.

century. Aggregate population, per capita income and total GDP rose much faster than anywhere else in the world. The 1820 level of GDP was more than three times that of 1500, and average per capita income well above the world average. The economy, technology, and economic institutions of the Americas had been transformed. Large parts were relatively empty, still pushing out the frontier of settlement, but most of the continent had achieved political independence in nation states still recognisable today.

The Americas continued to grow faster than the rest of the world economy. In 1820, they accounted for less than 4 per cent of world GDP, by 2003 nearly a third. Between 1820 and 2003, there was net immigration of 80 million people.

There was significant variance in the per capita growth trajectory of different parts of the Americas. A good deal was due differences in the nature of the colonial regimes and the institutions and social structures they created:

1. Spain concentrated its main activity on Mexico and Peru, which were the most densely populated at the time of conquest. Docile indigenous populations were compelled to supply labour to mining and agriculture. Slave imports were comparatively modest (about 1.5 million over the whole period of Spanish rule). The main aims were to transfer a fiscal tribute (in precious metals) to Spain and to hispanicize and catholicize the indigenous population.

2. Portuguese objectives were much more commercial, developing plantation agriculture for export. As the indigenous population were hunter-gatherers and hard to capture, the colonial labour force was composed largely of African slaves. Between 1500 and 1870, 3.8 million were transported to Brazil.

3. The Dutch, British, and French introduced plantation agriculture in Caribbean islands seized from Spain in the seventeenth century. The indigenous populations had been virtually exterminated before they arrived, 3.8 million slaves were imported in the colonial period, and production became highly specialized. A large part of the food supply was imported, and per capita exports were much higher than elsewhere in the Americas. The number of white settlers was relatively small and they were occupied mainly in supervising slave labour. Plantation owners were a wealthy absentee elite, living mainly in their respective metropoles.

4. North America had a substantial neo-European economy, where abundant land and natural resources were exploited by European labour. Virginia, Maryland, and the Carolinas relied on slave labour for their tobacco and cotton plantations, but the slave proportion was smaller, the climate healthier, and the work-load lighter than in Caribbean sugar production. As a consequence, life expectation of slaves was longer and slave imports much smaller (about 400 thousand). The socio-political order of the northern colonies permitted much freer access to land and education than in Spanish America, Brazil, and the Caribbean, with a smaller drain of tribute and profit to the metropole.

European Gains from the Americas

There were seven main types of economic gain to Europe:

1. A new supply of precious metals (about 1,700 tons of gold and 73,000 tons of silver). About a third of this was destined to finance European imports from Asia.

2. Imports of exotic products—sugar, tobacco, cotton, coffee, and cocoa from the slave colonies.

3. Imports from the northern colonies of fish, furs, ships, timber, and other materials required for shipbuilding.

4. Export markets for European manufactures.

5. Profits from the slave trade.

6. Opportunities for European migration to a continent with much greater per capita land availability.

7. Windfall ecological gains from the transfer of indigenous American plants. For Europe the most important were maize and potatoes. Maize and manioc went to raise Africa's capacity to sustain population growth. Sweet potatoes, peanuts, and maize served the same purpose in China.

Spanish Policy and Institutions

Spain followed a policy of conquest imperialism, exterminated the Aztec and Inca elites and their priesthood, and seized their property. Large estates (*encomiendas*) were allocated to a privileged elite of Spaniards, giving them control of the labour of a traumatized Indian population.[9] Churches and convents were built on the ruins of Aztec and Inca temples. The main agents of social control were the religious orders. The old gods, calendars, records, relics, and institutions disappeared in the process of catholicization.

A major reason for this approach was long experience in re-conquest of territory from the Moors. Spain had the military know-how and organization for conquest, and a church experienced in evangelizing, converting, and indoctrinating a con-quered population. Islam and Judaism were proscribed in Spain, just as the Inca and Aztec religions were extirpated in Mexico. Furthermore, the church in Spain was firmly under national control; the king was free to appoint bishops under a sixteenth century treaty with the papacy. Centuries of militant struggle had concentrated power and legitimacy on the Spanish monarchy as the ultimate arbiter, against which rebellion even in very distant colonies was seldom imagined.

In the sixteenth century, the bulk of European trade with the Americas was Span-ish. Initially, it was concentrated on the Caribbean islands, where gold was available from alluvial deposits and there were experiments with plantation agriculture. The main locus of activity shifted after the discovery of rich silver deposits at Potosí in the Viceroyalty of Peru in 1545, at Zacatecas (1546) and Guanajuato (1548) in the Viceroyalty of New Spain.[10] The economic value of these mines was greatly enhanced by application of the new mercury amalgamation process. This cold procedure permitted high rates of extraction from low-grade ores at much lower cost than earlier fuel-intensive techniques.

Development of the mines required huge investment, transport over large distances, and massive inputs of Indian labour. The industry was developed and financed by private interests (including foreign bankers), who made substantial remittances to Europe. A 20 per cent tax (*quinto real*) was levied on the value of silver. Proceeds of the *quinto* and other levies permitted large state transfers to Spain. From the second half of the seventeenth century, there were also large illicit shipments to destinations other than Spain (see Morineau 1985).

The logistics of silver production were most complex in the Viceroyalty of Peru. The Potosí mine (in present-day Bolivia) was 13,000 feet above sea level. Mercury was discovered and developed at Huancavelica, but had to be moved 1,600 kilometres to the mines in skin bags (a two-month journey on the back of llamas or mules). Silver was moved by pack animal from the mines to Callao (the port of Lima) or Arica to be shipped up the Pacific coast. It was then transported by pack animal to the port of Nombre de Dios (later Portobello) on the Caribbean side of the isthmus of Panama for shipment to Seville. In Mexico, mercury was shipped to the mines from Almadén in Spain and the silver transported to Veracruz on the Atlantic coast.

Shipments to Spain were made in annual convoys, with armed escort vessels. In addition to silver, exports included hides and leather, dyestuffs, sugar, and tobacco. All traffic was funnelled into and out of Spain via Seville (replaced by Cádiz in the eighteenth century), and virtually all traffic from or to the Americas went via Veracruz in Mexico, Portobello in Panama, and Cartagena in present-day Colombia. Trade on all these routes was reserved to Spanish ships. The organization of convoys was closely supervised and controlled by the *Casa de Contratación* in Seville. Exports via Seville consisted of Spanish wine, olive oil, furniture, cloth, paper, and iron wares, but re-exports of French textiles and manufactures of other European countries were usually much bigger. There were restrictions on manufactures in the colonies; production of wine and oil was permitted in Peru but not in New Spain. Spain itself shipped very few slaves until late in the eighteenth century. When slaves were wanted, the trade was subcontracted initially to Portugal (Treaty of Tordesillas, 1494), and later to the British (Treaty of Utrecht, 1713). Trade with Asia was limited to the annual galleon which left Acapulco for Manila, loaded with silver. The return cargo consisted mainly of Chinese silks. Trade between Manila and China was done mainly by Chinese merchants.

The inflow of silver had a limited impact in strengthening the Spanish economy. Some of it financed the construction of baroque churches and palaces. Much more went to finance Spain's hegemonial commitments in Europe. The government waged an eighty-year war trying to reconquer the Netherlands. It launched a huge Armada in 1588 in an attempt to invade England. It had to defend its territorial possessions in Italy (Naples, Sicily, and the Duchy of Milan), parts of northern France, Franche Comté and the southern Netherlands (Belgium). From 1580 to 1640 it ruled Portugal. It was a major protagonist in wars to restrain the expansion of the Ottoman Empire. The government was the most zealous agent of the counter-reformation, using the inquisition to ban books, burn heretics, expel Jews and Muslims and, at a later stage, Moriscos (Muslim converts to Christianity) from Spain. These policies weakened intellectual development, commercial life, and agriculture.

Twice in the sixteenth century the government defaulted on public debt. On several occasions it confiscated private shipments of bullion, compensating the owners with worthless government bonds. This induced large-scale smuggling by merchants and traders in the colonies who understated their shipments of silver to Spain, or shipped it elsewhere in Europe to avoid taxes and seizures by British, Dutch, and French corsairs.

In the sixteenth century, the number of ships leaving Spain for the Americas averaged 58 a year (see Usher 1932: 206). By the mid-seventeenth century, the fleet system 'was a shell of its former self, sailing late in the season, unable to sail for years at a time, composed of ageing and unsafe ships, many of them built abroad' (Macleod 1984: 372). In the seventeenth century, Spain's economy stagnated. Population growth was checked by attacks of plague and hunger. It suffered defeats in land and sea battles whilst defending its European Empire. Administrative control in Spain and the colonies was costly and inefficient. The reign of Charles II (1664–1700), a near imbecile, was 'an unmitigated disaster, a bleak chronicle of military defeat, royal bankruptcy, intellectual regression and widespread famine' (Brading 1984: 389).

On the death of this last Spanish Habsburg, France installed a Bourbon monarch, Philip V. After the long war of Spanish Succession (1701–13) he was eventually recognized by other European powers, but the peace treaty forced Spain to cede Milan, Sardinia, Naples, and the Spanish Netherlands (Belgium) to Austria; Sicily to the kingdom of Savoy. Gibraltar and Minorca were ceded to Britain which also acquired commodity and slave trading rights in the Americas.

The seventeenth-century decline of Spanish power and income did little damage to the colonies. Silver output continued and the colonial elite retained a larger part of the profit. As Spanish control weakened, local industries developed, trade between the colonies and contraband trade with other European countries and their colonies became significant.

Expanded use of European crops and livestock and the abundance of land facilitated the growth of agriculture and the area of settlement. Wheeled transport, commercial activity and urbanization increased. Creoles (whites born in the Americas) and *mestizos* (offspring or descendants of unions between whites and the indigenous population), were a rapidly increasing proportion of the population and became local oligarchies, buying administrative and judicial offices. Spanish district officials (*corregidores*) depended on bribes for most of their income. Regulations were bent and tax burdens were softened to accommodate the interests of the creole population. They had lower incomes than the much smaller elite group of *peninsulares* (Spanish civil servants, judiciary, military, and clergy), but they were more prosperous than most of the population in Spain. The indigenous population was an underclass, with the legal status of minors. Most were rural. Some provided cheap labour for haciendas or mines. Most lived in isolated villages, engaged in subsistence agriculture.

In the eighteenth century, the Bourbon regime increased the efficiency of administration and resource allocation in Spain. The population increased considerably and there was some growth in per capita income. It also revamped its administration and improved resource allocation in the Americas. Trade and government revenue from the Americas increased. In 1748–78 ship sailings to the Americas averaged 74 a year compared with 33 between 1718 and 1747. In 1739 a new Viceroyalty of New Granada (the area which is now Venezuela, Colombia, and Ecuador) was carved out of the old Viceroyalty of Peru. In 1776, Peru was further truncated to create a new Viceroyalty of La Plata with its capital at Buenos Aires (including present-day Argentina, Bolivia, Chile, Paraguay, and Uruguay), and Venezuela was given greater autonomy within New Granada. These changes led to a significant reorientation of trade to the benefit of the expanding economies of Buenos Aires and Venezuela, and to the detriment of Lima. Taxation of mining was changed to increase production incentives, and Mexican silver production rose substantially. Sales taxes were collected directly, rather than by tax-farmers, and their incidence was raised. Government control of tobacco taxes was strengthened. There were important moves to free trade. The clumsy and expensive fleet system was abolished in 1778. Trade was permitted between all Spanish and colonial ports. In 1789, restrictions on the slave trade were ended.

Between 1763 and 1795, there were major changes in the mode of colonial governance to tighten Spain's control and increase its revenues. *Intendants*, a new type of paid official, replaced the *corregidores*. These posts were filled by peninsular Spaniards. There was closer control of town councils (*cabildos*) and a major shake-up of the higher judiciary. Most of the judgeships in the *audiencias* had been sold to wealthy creole lawyers, who were replaced by a career service of peninsular Spaniards. The role of local militias was reduced in favour of the regular army. In 1767, all Jesuit priests were expelled from Spain and the Americas. The government seized and sold the colossal assets of their order and took over the administration of Paraguay, which the Jesuits had controlled for two centuries. As they had provided cheap mortgages and other financial services, this was not a popular move in the colonies. Subsequently, the privileges and immunities of the other clergy were substantially reduced.

The Bourbon reforms alienated the local *creole* elite and independence became more readily conceivable than in earlier centuries. The British colonies of North America had achieved independence and the *ancien régime* had collapsed in France. However, there was more creole reluctance to revolt than that of colonists in British North America because the very unequal social structure increased the risk of takeover by mestizos or the indigenous population. This apprehension was greatest in Peru where there had been an indigenous revolt (Tupac Amaru) in 1780, and in Mexico where there was an Indian insurrection in 1810.

The move to independence was reinforced by events in Spain. In 1793, after the execution of Louis XVI, Spain joined an international coalition against France. After its defeat in 1795, it switched sides, became a subservient ally of France and declared war on England. Britain mounted a very successful blockade of trade with the Americas, sank the Spanish fleet at Trafalgar, and briefly occupied Buenos Aires. In 1808, Ferdinand VII forced his father, Charles IV, to abdicate in his favour. Almost immediately, he himself was forced to abdicate in favour of Napoleon's brother, Joseph, who was sustained in power until 1813 by French occupation troops. Ferdinand was kept captive in France. The French takeover was contested by popular uprisings and creation of municipal juntas as centres of resistance. By 1810, the effectively functioning resistance forces were confined to the city of Cádiz where a council of regency convoked a parliament (Cortés) to draft a liberal constitution in 1812. This held out the promise of a constitutional monarchy in Spain, but proposed to retain a subservient status for the colonies.

The French regime was not regarded as legitimate in Latin America and control by the metropole had effectively collapsed. Creole elites in Caracas, Bogota, Buenos Aires, and Santiago stepped into the vacuum. They converted their municipal councils (*cabildos*) into juntas and took over their administration from the local representatives of the imperial power, without renouncing their theoretical allegiance to Spain. They faced opposition from the old officialdom and military to a degree which varied in different parts of the continent. The imperial authorities in Peru and Venezuela were their most ferocious opponents.

In 1814 Ferdinand VII returned from exile, repudiated the liberal constitution and acted as an absolute monarch, dispatching 10,000 troops to repress the opposition forces in Venezuela. He would have been better advised to try conciliation. His efforts provoked intensified resistance and the emergence of effective republican armies led by San Martin in the south and Bolivar in the north. Ferdinand tried to send reinforcements from Spain in 1820, but his troops rebelled instead of embarking.

By 1826, the last Spanish forces surrendered, the American empire had disappeared and more than 14 million people were no longer Spanish. In 1790, the Empire covered 16.1 million square kilometres. Cuba and Puerto Rico were all that was left (123 thousand square km, and less than 700,000 people). Nine new nations emerged in the south with a population of 6.6 million. In the north, newly independent Mexico had 6.5 million. The five small countries of Central America formed a temporary union. Louisiana was ceded to Napoleon in 1800, and he sold it to the US in 1803. Florida was ceded to the US in 1819.

With independence the old bureaucracy and military disappeared, along with the Inquisition and the remittance of fiscal tribute to Spain. The creoles took over political power, but the struggle for independence had damaged the economies, exacerbated social tension and led to decades of economic instability. Bolivar had hoped to create a Latin American federation and was deeply disappointed by the mutual hostility between the new states. Unstable governments relied on military force as a sanction for power. More than half the population remained an indigenous underclass with no legal rights, or access to education and property. The independence of Latin America was recognized by the UK and the US in 1823. The papacy delayed until 1835. Spain began to acknowledge it in 1836 but took several decades to finalize the process.

As a result of political chaos, Mexico had 71 rulers (elected and unelected) in 1821–76 and more than 200 Ministers of Finance. In the same period the US had 14 presidents and 26 secretaries of the treasury and took over half of Mexico's territory. Mexican per capita income was lower in 1877 than in 1820 (see Figure 2.1a for a comparison of the development of per capita income in Mexico and the US, 1700–2001).

Portuguese Policy and Institutions

When the Portuguese arrived in Brazil in 1500, they did not find an advanced civilization with hoards of precious metals for plunder, or a social discipline and organization geared to provide steady tribute that they could appropriate. Brazilian Indians were mainly hunter-gatherers, though some were moving towards agriculture using slash-and-burn techniques to cultivate manioc. Their technology and resources meant that they were thin on the ground. They had no towns, no domestic animals. They were stone-age men and women, hunting game and fish, naked, illiterate, and innumerate.

In the first century of settlement, it became clear that it was difficult to use Indians as slave labour. They were not docile, had high mortality when exposed to western diseases, could run away and hide rather easily. Portugal imported African slaves for manual labour. The ultimate fate of the indigenous population was rather like that in North America. They were pushed beyond the fringe of colonial society.

In the sixteenth and seventeenth centuries Portuguese gains from Brazil came from plantation agriculture, commodity exports, and commercial profit. A small settler population controlled highly profitable export-oriented sugar plantations in the Northeast. Their techniques, using slave labour, followed the pattern the Portuguese had developed at São Tomé in Africa. Cattle ranchers in the dry backlands area (*sertão*) provided food for workers in sugar production. Official revenue from Brazil was rather small, about 3 per cent of Portuguese public revenue in 1588 and 5 per cent in 1619; at that time, Asia provided ten times as much (see Bethell 1984, Vol.1: 286).

Portuguese trade with Brazil was much less rigidly organized than that of Spain with its colonies. There was less state interference and greater scope for participation by other European countries. There was a significant Brazilian owned merchant marine engaged in coastal shipping and the slave trade with Africa (see Klein 1999: 36). The governance of the colony was less tightly controlled, and the ecclesiastical regime more tolerant. In 1640 when Portugal regained independence from Spain, it allied itself closely with the United Kingdom. The British were allowed to have merchants in Brazil and Portugal, and to engage in the carrying trade. In return the British propped up the Portuguese empire with military guarantees.

Brazilian sugar exports peaked in the 1650s. Earnings fell thereafter because of lower prices and competition from the rapidly growing output in the Caribbean. The setback in sugar caused large parts of the northeast to lapse into a subsistence economy. In the 1690s, the discovery of gold, and, in the 1720s, diamonds in Minas Gerais, opened new opportunities. During the eighteenth century, there was considerable immigration from Europe, and internal migration from the northeast to Minas, to engage in gold and diamond development. Eighteenth century prosperity in Minas is obvious even today from the number of elaborate buildings and churches in Ouro Preto, the centre of mining activity. As Minas is very barren, food and transport needs of the mining area stimulated food production in neighbouring provinces to the south and in the northeast, and mule-breeding in Rio Grande do Sul. The gold industry was at its peak around 1750, with production around 15 tons a year, but as the best deposits were exhausted, output and exports declined. In the first half of the eighteenth century, identifiable royal revenues from the gold trade were around 18 per cent of Portuguese government revenue. Total Brazilian gold shipments over the whole of the eighteenth century were between 800 and 850 tons.

In the second half of the eighteenth century, Portuguese finances were in desperate straits. Revenues from Brazil were squeezed by the decline in gold production. Income from Asia had collapsed and Portugal had to bear the costs of reconstructing Lisbon after the 1755 earthquake. To meet this problem, Pombal, the Portuguese prime minister, expelled the Jesuits from Brazil (1759), confiscated their vast properties, and sold them to wealthy landowners and merchants for the benefit of the crown. Most of the property of other religious orders was taken over a few years later.

When gold production collapsed, Brazil turned back to agricultural exports. At independence in 1822, the three main exports were cotton, sugar, and coffee.

At the end of the colonial period, half the population were slaves. They were fed on a crude diet of beans and jerked beef, and worked to death after a few years of service. A privileged fraction of the white population enjoyed high incomes but the rest of the population (indigenous, free blacks, mulattos, and large numbers of whites) were poor. Land-ownership was concentrated on slave owners, thus a very unequal distribution of property buttressed a highly unequal distribution of income. There was also substantial regional inequality. The poorest area was the northeast, and Minas had passed its peak. The most prosperous area was around the new capital, Rio de Janeiro.

Independence came to Brazil very smoothly by Latin American standards. In 1808, the Portuguese Queen and the Regent fled to Rio to escape the French invasion of the motherland. They brought 10,000 of the mainland establishment with them—the aristocracy, bureaucracy, and some of the military. They set up their government and court in Rio and Petropolis, intending to run Brazil and Portugal as a joint kingdom (both parts by then being about equal in terms of population). However, the two countries split without too much enmity in 1822. Brazil became independent with an emperor who was the son of the Portuguese monarch. This regime changed in 1888–89 with the abolition of slavery and establishment of a republic (see Figure 2.1b on the comparative economic performance of Brazil and the US, 1700–2001).

Characteristics of Dutch, British, and French Colonialism in the Caribbean

The Caribbean was the initial locus of Spanish activity in the Americas, but was neglected after the discovery of silver in Peru and Mexico and the virtual extinction of the indigenous population. For two centuries thereafter, Spain used the Caribbean mainly as a base for its treasure fleets.

The Caribbean became a centre of activity for Dutch, British, and French corsairs (officially sanctioned raiders and pirates). The French destroyed Havana in 1538 and again in 1554. In 1595 Drake sacked Portobello. The Dutch Admiral Piet Heyn captured the whole Spanish treasure fleet off Cuba in 1628 acting as an agent for the Dutch West India Company. The British Admiral Blake pursued and captured the fleet off Cadiz in 1655. Corsairs sacked Maracaibo, Portobello, Trinidad, and Veracruz between 1666 and 1683. It was because of this piracy that Spain adopted a convoy system for its trade with the Americas.

The British took the uninhabited island of Barbados in 1627 with a view to production of foodstuffs and tobacco with indentured white immigrants. A little later the French took Guadeloupe, Martinique, and six other islands with similar intentions. In the 1620s, the Dutch occupied the northeast of Brazil (during the period when Spain had taken over Portugal). They were expelled in 1654, and moved to Barbados, Guadeloupe, and Martinique, demonstrating the profitability of sugar production, providing technical assistance, machinery, shipping, marketing facilities, and slaves. The British and French colonies were quickly transformed. Henceforth they concentrated almost exclusively on sugar and relied on imports for most of their food supply. Tobacco cultivation and white immigration dwindled rapidly. After the Dutch had served their purpose, they were expelled.[11]

The French and British ran their colonies on a mutually exclusive basis. They could sell only to their respective metropoles and their colonies (though there were substantial re-exports from England and France to foreign markets). A similar pattern of exclusivity applied to imports. The food imports of the British colonies came mainly from England; timber and other supplies from New England. The French and British took over most of the slave trade to the Caribbean. Sugar refining was done mainly in the metropoles.

Sugar proved so profitable that the British seized Jamaica from Spain in 1655. The French gained a footing in the western part of Hispaniola, which became their colony of St. Domingue in 1697. These two large islands became the biggest producers in the Caribbean. The Spanish were left with Cuba, Puerto Rico, the eastern half of Hispaniola (lost to France in 1795), and Trinidad (lost to Britain in 1803). Until the second half of the eighteenth century, Spanish sugar production was quite small.

It started to expand rapidly after the British occupation of Havana in 1762–3. By 1787, Cuba was exporting 56 kg per head of population. During the war of American independence, Cuban exports replaced the sugar and rum that the British colonies had shipped to North America.

Caribbean sugar production rose about ten-fold between the 1660s and the 1780s. By 1787, sugar exports of the 19 British West Indian colonies averaged 195 kgs per head; exports of French colonies 240 kgs.

Sugar plantations were large business enterprises requiring substantial capital investment. As the labour force were slaves, there was extreme income inequality in the islands. The profits were siphoned off to absentee owners who preferred the healthier climate of their home country.

The Caribbean lobby of sugar planters and slave traders was very powerful socially and politically in the UK. In 1661, Charles II created 13 baronets with interests in Barbados. Planters and slavers were also well represented in the House of Commons. Absentee owners educated their children in England. There was only one secondary school in Barbados, another in Jamaica, and no provision for higher education. Codrington, a planter on the Leeward islands, gave his books to the library he financed in All Souls College, Oxford. The Lascelles family from Barbados later married into British royalty. William Beckford had an imposing country seat in Wiltshire, became Lord Mayor of London, and, in 1763, after the war with France, persuaded his friend the prime minister (Chatham) to give Guadeloupe back to France, as its acquisition would have established an unwelcome competitor in the protected British sugar market (see Williams 1970: 114, 132).

During the Napoleonic wars, French interests in the Caribbean suffered greatly from interruptions in trade, and the slave revolt in Haiti which gained its independence in 1804. French sugar shipments from the Caribbean were 70 per cent lower in 1815 than in 1787, and never recovered their previous level again, partly because of the development and protection of beet sugar production in France.

Britain abolished the slave trade in 1807, and slavery in 1833, with £20 million compensation for the slave owners and nothing for the slaves. Abolition was due in substantial part to the success of humanitarian reformers in convincing public opinion to end a repugnant form of exploitation. The loss of privileged export markets in North America after 1776 and the successful slave revolt in Haiti persuaded the planting lobby that their days were numbered and that it was in their interest to settle for compensation. France abolished the slave trade in 1817 and slavery in 1848. The Dutch abolished slavery in 1863.

The ending of slavery raised costs and weakened the competitive position of most Caribbean producers (in spite of the introduction of 700,000 indentured Asian workers between 1838 and 1913). In 1787 the Caribbean had accounted for 90 per cent of world sugar exports. By 1913 its share had fallen to a sixth. There was diversification in favour of coffee and cotton, but the main impact was stagnant or falling income. Eisner (1961: 119, 153) estimated per capita real income in Jamaica fell by a quarter between 1832 and 1870, and exports from 41 to 15 per cent of GDP; by 1930, the per capita GDP level was about the same as in 1832! For the British and French islands, this experience was probably fairly typical. However, Spain retained slavery in Cuba and Puerto Rico until 1886 and was successful in expanding and modernizing sugar production; exports rose from 30,000 tons in 1787 to 2.8 million in 1913.

In the nineteenth century there was a precipitate fall in the relative importance of Caribbean trade. In 1774, the Caribbean provided 29 per cent of total British imports. By 1913, less than 1 per cent. The collapse in French imports was equally dramatic. By contrast, British imports from North America rose from 12.5 per cent of the total in 1774 to 22.6 per cent in 1913.

In the eighteenth century, the Caribbean was the most profitable area of European colonisation in the Americas. By 1870, it was an impoverished backwater.

British North America

The economy and social structure of North America was very different from that in the Caribbean, Brazil, or the Spanish Viceroyalties.

In the northern colonies, slaves were less than 5 per cent of the population. A large part of the predominantly white labour force were farmers working their own land. The average family farm in New England, the mid-Atlantic States, and Pennsylvania in 1807 had well over 100 acres (Lebergott 1984: 17). Per capita income was about the same as in the United Kingdom and more evenly distributed.

Most of the northern colonies had been formed by Protestants of various denominations who were keen on education. There were eight universities in the north (Harvard, founded in 1636; Yale, 1701; University of Pennsylvania 1740; Princeton, 1746; Columbia, 1754; Brown, 1764; Rutgers, 1766; Dartmouth, 1769) and one (William and Mary, 1693) in the south. The level of education in the northern colonies was above that in the United Kingdom.

In 1820, the states that relied most heavily on slave labour (Maryland, Virginia, the Carolinas, and Georgia) contained about 30 per cent of the US population. About 40 per cent were slaves, compared with 85 per cent in the Caribbean. Whites (indentured servants and others) were a significant part of the labour force. The main plantation crops were tobacco, rice, and indigo, where work intensity was less than in sugar. The climate was healthier than in the Caribbean. Life expectation and possibilities for natural growth of the black population were greater. Growth of the labour force depended much less on the slave trade.

Although the British Navigation Acts made the colonies route most of their trade with Europe through Britain they provided favoured access to markets within the empire. These were particularly important for exports of foodstuffs, shipping services, and ships. On the eve of the war of independence, the merchant marine of the colonies was over 450,000 tons, all of which (coastal craft, West Indies schooners, fishing and whaling boats, and ships for trade with England) were built in New England shipyards with easy access to cheap timber, pitch and tar. American yards built an increasing proportion of the British merchant fleet in the course of the eighteenth century. In 1774, 30 per cent was American built.

The North American colonies had a significant urban population in Boston, New York, and Philadelphia. They had a politically sophisticated elite familiar with the ideas and ideals of the French enlightenment. Their incentive to break the colonial tie was reinforced in 1763, after the Seven Years War, in which the British ended French rule in Canada and French claims to territory west of the 13 colonies. Hitherto, the most likely alternative to British rule had been French rule. Thereafter it was independence.

A striking characteristic of US economic growth after independence was its much greater dynamism than that of its neighbour Mexico, which was a Spanish colony until 1825. It is therefore useful to compare the different institutional, societal, and policy influences transmitted by Spain and the United Kingdom.

The main reasons for Mexican backwardness compared with the ex-British colonies in North America were probably as follows:

1. The Spanish colony was subject to a bigger drain of resources. A considerable part of domestic income went into the pockets of peninsular Spaniards who took their savings back home. Official tribute took another 2.7 per cent of GDP (see Maddison 1995b: 316–17).

2. The British colonial regime imposed mercantilist restrictions on foreign trade, but they were much lighter than in New Spain. Thomas (1965) suggested that the net cost of British trade restrictions was about 42 cents per head in the American colonies in 1770 (about 0.6 per cent of GDP).

3. The British colonists had better education, greater intellectual freedom, and social mobility. Education was secular with emphasis on pragmatic skills and Yankee ingenuity of which Ben Franklin was the prototype. New Spain had only two universities in Mexico City and Guadalajara, which concentrated on theology and law. Throughout the colonial period the Inquisition maintained a tight censorship and suppressed heterodox thinking.

4. In New Spain, the best land was controlled by hacienda owners. In North America the white population had much easier access to land, and in New England family farming enterprise was typical. Restricted access to land in Spanish colonies was recognized as a hindrance to economic growth both by Adam Smith and the Viceroy of New Spain. Rosenzweig (1963) quotes the latter as follows (my translation):

   Maldistribution of land is a major obstacle to the progress of agriculture and commerce, particularly with regard to entails with absentee or negligent owners. We have subjects of his majesty here who possess hundreds of square leagues—enough to form a small kingdom—but who produce little of value

5. New Spain had a privileged upper class, with a sumptuary lifestyle. Differences in status—a hereditary aristocracy, privileged groups of clergy and military with tax exemptions and legal immunities—meant that there was much less

entrepreneurial vigour than in the British colonies. The elite in New Spain were rent-seekers with a low propensity to productive investment.

6. In the government of New Spain, power was highly concentrated, whereas in British North America there were 13 separate colonies. Political power was fragmented, so there was much greater freedom for individuals to pursue their own economic interests.

7. Another source of advantage for North America was the vigour of its population growth because of the rapid inflow of migrants. Population of the 13 colonies rose tenfold from 1700 to 1820, and by less than half in Mexico. Economic enterprise was much more dynamic when the market was expanding so rapidly.

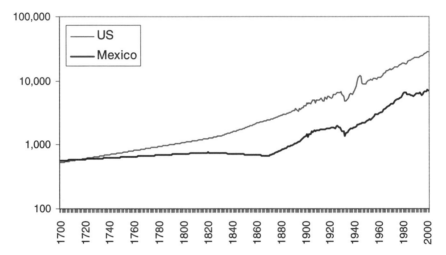

Figure 2.1a. Comparative levels of Mexico/US GDP per capita, 1700–2100

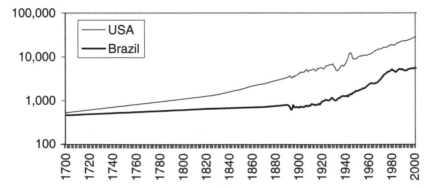

Figure 2.1b. Comparative levels of Brazil/USA GDP per capita, 1700–2100

Source: Maddison (2003), vertical axis shows levels in 1990 international (PPP) dollars.

⬚ APPENDIX

Table 2.9a. New World Population, 1820–2003 (000s at mid-year)

	1820	1870	1913	1950	1973	1990	2003
Argentina	534	1,796	7,653	17,150	25,210	33,022	38,741
Brazil	4,507	9,797	23,660	53,443	103,469	151,084	182,033
Chile	771	1,945	3,431	6,091	9,897	13,128	15,663
Colombia	1,206	2,392	5,195	11,592	23,069	32,859	41,662
Mexico	6,587	9,219	14,970	28,485	57,557	84,914	103,718
Peru	1,317	2,606	4,295	7,633	14,350	21,511	27,159
Uruguay	55	343	1,177	2,194	2,834	3,106	3,382
Venezuela	718	1,653	2,874	5,009	11,893	19,325	24,655
Total 8 L. American countries	**15,695**	**29,751**	**63,255**	**131,597**	**248,280**	**358,948**	**437,011**
Bolivia	1,100	1,495	1,881	2,766	4,680	6,574	8,586
Costa Rica	63	137	372	867	1,886	3,027	3,896
Cuba	605	1,331	2,431	5,785	9,001	10,545	11,269
Dominican Republic	89	242	750	2,353	4,796	7,078	8,783
Ecuador	500	1,013	1,689	3,370	6,485	10,318	13,074
El Salvador	248	492	1,008	1,940	3,878	5,100	6,470
Guatemala	595	1,080	1,486	2,969	5,254	8,001	11,456
Haïti	723	1,150	1,891	3,097	4,743	6,126	7,771
Honduras	135	404	660	1,431	3,078	4,792	6,843
Jamaica	401	499	837	1,385	2,036	2,348	2,689
Nicaragua	186	337	578	1,098	2,247	3,684	5,254
Panama	0	176	348	893	1,659	2,390	3,040
Paraguay	143	384	594	1,476	2,692	4,236	6,037
Puerto Rico	248	645	1,181	2,218	2,863	3,537	3,878
Trinidad and Tobago	60	124	352	632	985	1,198	1,093
Total 15 L. American countries	**5,096**	**9,509**	**16,058**	**32,279**	**56,285**	**78,954**	**100,139**
Total 24 small Caribbean	800	1,141	1,518	2,062	3,308	3,735	4,208
Total Latin America	**21,591**	**40,401**	**80,831**	**165,938**	**307,873**	**441,638**	**541,359**
US	9,981	40,241	97,606	152,271	211,909	250,132	290,343
Canada	816	3,781	7,852	14,011	22,560	27,791	32,207
Australia	334	1,775	7,821	8,267	13,380	17,022	19,732
New Zealand	100	291	1,122	1,908	2,992	3,360	3,951
Total western offshoots	**11,231**	**46,088**	**111,401**	**176,458**	**250,841**	**298,304**	**346,233**

Table 2.9b. New World Per Capita GDP, 1820–2003 (1990 Geary–Khamis $)

	1820	1870	1913	1950	1973	1990	2003
Argentina		1,311	3,797	4,987	7,962	6,436	7,666
Brazil	646	713	811	1,672	3,882	4,923	5,563
Chile	694	1,290	2,988	3,670	5,034	6,402	10,951
Colombia			1,236	2,153	3,499	4,840	5,228
Mexico	759	674	1,732	2,365	4,853	6,085	7,137
Peru			1,032	2,308	4,023	3,021	4,007
Uruguay		2,181	3,310	4,659	4,974	6,474	6,805
Venezuela	460	569	1,104	7,462	10,625	8,313	6,988
Average 8 countries	**712**	**742**	**1,618**	**2,696**	**4,875**	**5,465**	**6,278**
Bolivia				1,919	2,357	2,197	2,617
Costa Rica				1,963	4,319	4,747	6,516
Cuba				2,046	2,245	2,948	2,569
Dominican Republic				1,027	2,005	2,473	3,700
Ecuador				1,863	3,290	3,903	3,419
El Salvador				1,489	2,342	2,119	2,720
Guatemala				2,085	3,539	3,631	4,060
Haïti				1,051	1,014	1,032	740
Honduras				1,313	1,581	1,857	1,934
Jamaica	700	535	608	1,327	4,130	3,786	3,680
Nicaragua				1,616	2,921	1,438	1,514
Panama				1,916	4,250	4,471	5,787
Paraguay				1,584	2,038	3,287	2,953
Puerto Rico				2,144	7,302	10,539	14,485
Trinidad and Tobago				3,674	8,685	9,272	16,984
Average 15 countries	**636**	**486**	**1,038**	**1,750**	**2,926**	**3,292**	**3,646**
Total 24 small Caribbean	636	549	1,174	1,980	4,350	4,844	5,623
Average Latin America	**691**	**676**	**1,494**	**2,503**	**4,513**	**5,072**	**5,786**
US	1,257	2,445	5,301	9,561	16,689	23,201	29,037
Canada	904	1,695	4,447	7,291	13,838	18,872	23,236
Australia	518	3,273	5,157	7,412	12,424	17,106	23,287
New Zealand	400	3,100	5,152	8,456	12,878	13,909	17,565
Average western offshoots	**1,202**	**2,419**	**5,233**	**9,268**	**16,179**	**22,345**	**28,039**

Table 2.9c. New World GDP Levels, 1820–2003 (million 1990 Geary–Khamis $)

	1820	1870	1913	1950	1973	1990	2003
Argentina		2,354	29,060	85,524	200,720	212,518	296,991
Brazil	2,912	6,985	19,188	89,342	401,643	743,765	1,012,733
Chile	535	2,509	10,252	22,352	49,816	84,038	171,514
Colombia			6,420	24,955	80,728	159,042	217,791
Mexico	5,000	6,214	25,921	67,368	279,302	516,692	740,226
Peru			4,434	17,613	57,729	64,979	108,829
Uruguay		748	3,896	10,224	14,098	20,105	23,012
Venezuela	330	941	3,172	37,377	126,364	160,648	172,282
Total 8 countries	**11,172**	**22,065**	**102,344**	**354,755**	**1,210,400**	**1,961,787**	**2,743,378**
Bolivia				5,309	11,030	14,446	22,473
Costa Rica				1,702	8,145	14,370	25,388
Cuba				11,837	20,209	31,087	28,948
Dominican Republic				2,416	9,617	17,503	32,496
Ecuador				6,278	21,337	40,267	44,702
El Salvador				2,888	9,084	10,805	17,600
Guatemala				6,190	18,593	29,050	46,512
Haïti				3,254	4,810	6,323	5,752
Honduras				1,880	4,866	8,898	13,234
Jamaica	281	267	509	1,837	8,411	8,890	9,895
Nicaragua				1,774	6,566	5,297	7,952
Panama				1,710	7,052	10,688	17,590
Paraguay				2,338	5,487	13,923	17,827
Puerto Rico				4,755	20,908	37,277	56,170
Trinidad and Tobago				2,322	8,553	11,110	18,566
Total 15 countries	**3,240**	**4,620**	**16,670**	**56,490**	**164,668**	**259,934**	**365,105**
Total 24 small Caribbean	509	626	1,782	4,083	14,392	18,094	23,662
Total Latin America	**14,921**	**27,311**	**120,796**	**415,328**	**1,389,460**	**2,239,815**	**3,132,145**
US	12,548	98,374	517,383	1,455,916	3,536,622	5,803,200	8,430,762
Canada	738	6,407	34,916	102,164	312,176	524,475	748,363
Australia	173	5,810	24,861	61,274	172,314	291,180	459,504
New Zealand	40	902	5,781	16,136	37,177	46,729	69,400
Total western offshoots	**13,499**	**111,493**	**582,941**	**1,635,490**	**4,058,289**	**6,665,584**	**9,708,029**

☐ ENDNOTES

1. See Landes (1966: 504–21) for a masterly survey of technical change in the use of energy and power. For development of rail and automobile transport, see Maddison (1995a: 64 and 72). For 1998 passenger miles by air and the 1999 passenger car fleet, see Worldwatch Institute, *Vital Signs*, 1999 and 2001 editions.

2. Ernst Engel (1821–96), Director of the Prussian statistical office, was the first economist to make international comparisons of the structure of consumer demand. In his budget studies, he found that the share of food expenditure varied inversely with income. As food is the main product of agriculture, he concluded that, in the course of economic development, agriculture would decline relative to other sectors of the economy, see Houthakker (1987) in the *Palgrave Dictionary of Economics*, vol. 2, Macmillan, London, pp. 142–4.

3. See Kuznets (1966: 274–6) for a discussion and illustration of the importance of changes in the PTD (processing, transport, and distribution) component of food expenditure. This rose from 29

to 56 per cent of US food expenditure between 1869 and 1949–57. Within the farm sector there has also been a growing dependence on outside inputs. In 1975, these represented 33 per cent of farm input (net of feed and seed) in the UK (see Maddison 1995b: 212–13). In the seventeenth century they would have been close to zero.

4. Inter-country exchange of ideas was an important aspect of Europe's benign fragmentation, which is illustrated by the experience of leading intellectuals. Thus René Descartes could escape French thought control under Louis XIV by living in the Netherlands from 1628 to 1649, and Pierre Bayle did the same in 1681–93. Voltaire moved to England in 1726–9, Berlin 1750–3, and Switzerland in 1755–78 to escape thought control under Louis XV. Hobbes took refuge in France from England's Cromwellian regime in 1640–52. William Petty went to France and the Netherlands to further his education. Others, like Edward Gibbon, David Hume, John Locke, Adam Smith, Arthur Young, and Horace Walpole went abroad for significant periods to exchange ideas. Christiaan Huygens went to London and Paris to interact with colleagues in their academies. Goethe and Winckelman went to Italy to seek inspiration from the relics of Roman civilization. Young milords went on the grand tour for a variety of reasons. Religious dissidents like the Huguenots could find exile in other countries. This type of international interaction was much more rare in Asian countries.

5. This is an assertion which I cannot prove rigorously. I am certain that the economic significance of European technical advance between 1000 and 1820 was much greater in maritime and other forms of water transport than in movement of people and freight overland. There were of course improvements in the traction power of horses because of the introduction of better harness, shoulder-collars, nailed horseshoes, stirrups, etc. in the tenth and eleventh centuries (see White 1962), and in the suspension and wheels of road passenger vehicles from the sixteenth century onwards. By the eighteenth century there were better quality and longer road networks in England and France (see Parry 1967: 215–18 and Girard 1966). Harrison (1992) suggests that long-term improvement in bridges was modest in England. Improvements in inland waterways and barge traffic were significant in the Netherlands at an early stage (see de Vries 1978) and somewhat later in France and England. The introduction of the camel in the Maghreb revolutionized trans-Saharan trade from the sixth century onwards, but the role of camel transport in caravan trade between Europe and China and Europe—India was adversely affected by the advent of Europe–Asia maritime transport from 1500 onwards (see Steensgaard 1974).

6. See Nordenskjiold (1897: 4) on the uncertainties. He cites the experience of St Paul, who was sent as a prisoner from Caesarea (in Syria) to Rome. The vessel, with 276 people aboard, skirted the coast northward, intending to winter in Crete, but hit a storm and was driven for two weeks in damaged condition, and was shipwrecked in Malta (see *Acts of the Apostles*, chap. 27). In 533, the emperor Justinian sent his general, Belisarius, with 15,000 soldiers and 20,000 sailors from Constantinople to attack Carthage in a large fleet of ships. Their journey took three months, rowing through the Aegean to Sicily, Malta, then blown by a storm to Tunis.

7. See Marquet (1931) and Haudrere (1993) for an account of French scientific research on navigational problems.

8. There is considerable disagreement on the size of the pre-conquest population of the Americas. The two extreme protagonists are Rosenblat and Borah. Angel Rosenblat (1945) suggested a total of 13.4 million, relying to a considerable extent on literary evidence at the time of the conquest. Woodrow Borah (1976: 17) suggested a total 'upwards of 100 million'. This aggregate estimate was derived mainly by extrapolation, 'admittedly hasty and general', of his results for central Mexico where he compared his estimate of the pre-conquest population (25 million) with the figure of one million recorded by the Spanish census of 1605. From these he assumed a depopulation rate of 95 per cent. The evidence for his 25 million figure is flimsy. If such a level had been attained by 1500,

it is highly unlikely that it would have taken 400 years for Mexico to recover. In Europe, it took only 150 years to regain the population level before the black death, with much less technical advance than occurred in Mexico. My estimate for the population of all the Americas in 1500 is about 20 million (see Maddison 2001: 231, and 233–6 for the derivation of this figure and Maddison (1995b) for a much more detailed analysis of Mexico).

9. *Encomienda, repartimiento, mita,* and debt peonage were variant ways of mobilizing indigenous labour in Spanish colonies, some of which had roots in pre-colonial practice. In the Viceroyalty of Peru, the *mita* system involved compulsory labour—virtually all labour in the silver mines was of this kind. In Mexico, the Aztec tax system involved levies in kind which could be commuted by supplying labour. The initial Spanish practice was to allot these levies in a given area to Spaniards who had helped in the conquest or otherwise gained official favour. Some of these *encomiendas* were hereditary, but many were not. Over time, most of these claims were forfeited, and with the growing monetization of the economy, taxes were levied in silver or commuted in the form of labour. Thus there was a growth of 'free' labour in Mexico, but those who could not meet the tax obligation were ensnared in various forms of debt peonage. As the indigenous population had the legal status of children, there was obviously a large element of coercion. In this situation, it is not surprising that slavery remained unimportant in Mexico. The northern parts of the Viceroyalty of New Spain were inhabited by Chichimecs and other hunter-gatherer groups who could not be tamed, and found it easy to avoid capture once they acquired horses. See Macleod (1984) for a detailed analysis of these variants.

10. Initially Spain (or rather the kingdom of Castile) divided the Americas into two administrative units: the Viceroyalties of New Spain and Peru, with their capitals in Mexico City and Lima respectively. The former included or came to include present day Mexico, the Caribbean, Central America (Costa Rica, Guatemala, Honduras, Belize, Nicaragua, and El Salvador), and part of what is now the USA (California, Colorado, Florida, Louisiana, Nevada, New Mexico, Texas, and Utah). The Viceroyalty of Peru included the rest of the Americas from Panama to the south, with the exception of Brazil, whose western boundary was fixed by the Treaty of Tordesillas in 1494. The Viceroyalties were divided into 35 governorships at one time or another in the sixteenth and seventeenth centuries. The Philippines, whose conquest was begun in 1567, was a governorship dependent on New Spain. A separate Viceroyalty of New Granada was created in 1739, with its capital at Bogota. It included present-day Colombia, Ecuador, Panama, and Venezuela. In 1776, another Viceroyalty, Rio de la Plata, was created with its capital at Buenos Aires. It included Argentina, Bolivia, Chile, Paraguay, and Uruguay. In 1750, the Treaty of Madrid modified the Tordesillas boundary of Brazil, enlarging threefold the area recognized as Portuguese (see Brading (1984) on the nature and impact of the eighteenth century administrative changes).

11. The Dutch made early and ambitious attempts to create an empire in the Americas. Their first ventures occurred during the Spanish occupation of Portugal which cut off access to their traditional salt supply in Setubal. From 1599 to the 1620s they developed an alternative source in salt pans at Punta de Araya on the coast of Venezuela. They created the Dutch West India Company (WIC) to harass Spanish shipping, participate in the slave trade and engage in sugar production. Between 1630 and 1654 they occupied the northeast coast of Brazil (Recife and Paraiba), where sugar plantations and export trade were developed by sephardic Jewish settlers from Amsterdam (mainly of Portuguese origin). Access to the slave trade was opened by the Dutch seizure of Elmina, Luanda, and 20 other Portuguese outposts on the African coast. The profitability of slavery and sugar was buttressed by rapid expansion of sugar refining in Amsterdam. In 1654, the Dutch were expelled from Brazil, and moved their sugar activity further north. Plantations were developed in Suriname and the area that became British Guiana in 1803 (Demerara, Essequibo,

and Bernice). They also initiated and financed sugar production in Barbados and Martinique, but in the 1660s were expelled by the British and French. They continued to operate as slave traders and merchants from island bases in Curaçao (which they acquired in 1637), St. Eustatius and St. Martin and remained as relatively marginal sugar producers in Suriname. The Dutch colony of New Netherlands, with its capital New Amsterdam had been taken over by the British in 1664. In 1674 it was formally ceded (as New York) in exchange for a free hand in Suriname.

⬚ REFERENCES

Acemoglu, D., S. Johnson and J. Robinson (2005), 'The Rise of Europe: Atlantic Trade, Institutional Change, and Economic Growth', *American Economic Review*, June, pp. 546–80.

Barrett, W. (1990), 'World Bullion Flows, 1450–1800', in Tracy (1993).

Bethell, L. (ed) (1984–92), *The Cambridge History of Latin America*, 10 vols, Cambridge University Press.

Borah, W. C. and S. F. Cook (1963), *The Aboriginal Population of Central Mexico on the Eve of the Spanish Conquest*, University of California, Berkeley.

Borah, W. C. (1976), 'The Historical Demography of Aboriginal and Colonial America: An Attempt at Perspective', in Denevan, pp. 13–34.

Bordo, M. D. and R. Cortés-Conde (2001), *Transferring Wealth and Power from the Old to the New World*, Cambridge University Press.

Brading, D. A. (1984), '*Bourbon Spain and its American Empire*', in Bethell, 1, pp. 389–439.

Braudel, F. (1984), *The Perspective of the World*, Fontana, London.

Cipolla, C. M. (1970), *European Culture and Overseas Expansion*, Pelican, London.

Cipolla, C. M. (ed.) (1972), *The Fontana Economic History of Europe*, 6 vols, Collins/Fontana Books, London.

Crosby, A. W. (1972), *The Columbian Exchange: Biological and Cultural Consequences of 1492*, Greenwood Press, Westport.

Denevan, W. M. (ed) (1976), *The Native Population of the Americas in 1492*, University of Wisconsin.

Eisenstein, E. L. (1993), *The Printing Revolution in Early Modern Europe*, Cambridge University Press.

Eisner, G. (1961), *Jamaica, 1830–1930: A Study in Economic Growth*, Manchester University Press.

Engerman, S. L. and B. W. Higman (1997), '*The Demographic Structure of the Caribbean Slave Societies in the Eighteenth and Nineteenth Centuries*', in Knight, pp. 45–104.

Flyn, D. and A. Giraldez (2004), 'Path Dependence, Time Lags and the Birth of Globalisation: a Critique of O'Rourke and Williamson', *European Review of Economic History*, 8, pp. 81–108.

Flyn, D., A. Giraldez, and R. von Glahn (eds) (2003), *Global Connections and Monetary History, 1470–1800*, Ashgate.

Galileo, G. ([1632] 1953), *Dialogue on the Great World Systems* (with annotations and introduction by G. de Santillana), University of Chicago Press.

Goodman, D. and C. A. Russell (1991), *The Rise of Scientific Europe, 1500–1800*, Hodder & Stoughton, London.

Goody, J. (1983), *The Development of the Family and Marriage in Europe*, Cambridge University Press.

Grassman, S. and E. Lundberg (eds) (1981), *The World Economic Order: Past and Prospects*, Macmillan, London.

Habakkuk, H.J. and M. Postan (eds) (1965), *The Cambridge Economic History of Europe*, Cambridge University Press.

Higman, B. W. (1984), *Slave Populations of the British Caribbean, 1807–1834*, Johns Hopkins University Press, Baltimore.

Hofman, A. A. (2000), *The Economic Development of Latin America in the Twentieth Century*, Elgar, Cheltenham.

Klein, H. S. (1999), *The Atlantic Slave Trade*, Cambridge University Press.

Knight, F. W. (ed.) (1997), *General History of the Caribbean*, vol. III, UNESCO, London.

Kuznets, S. (1966), *Modern Economic Growth*, Yale University Press, New Haven.

Lal, D. (2001), *Unintended Consequences*, MIT Press, Boston.

Landes, D. S. (1965), 'Technological Change and Development in Western Europe, 1750–1914', in Habakkuk and Postan, vol. VI, Part II.

Landes, D. S. (1969), *The Unbound Prometheus*, Cambridge University Press.

Landes, D. S. (1998), *The Wealth and Poverty of Nations*, Little Brown, London.

Lebergott, S. (1984), *The Americans: An Economic Record*, Norton, New York.

Lewis, W. A. (1981), 'The Rate of Growth of World Trade, 1830–1973', in Grassman and Lundberg.

Lovejoy, P. E. (2000), *Transformations in Slavery*, Cambridge University Press.

McEvedy, C. and R. Jones (1978), *Atlas of World Population History*, Penguin, Middlesex.

Macleod, M. J. (1984), 'Aspects of the Internal Economy of Colonial Spanish America: Labour; Taxation; Distribution and Exchange', in Bethell, vol. 2.

McNeill, W. H. (1963), *The Rise of the West*, University of Chicago Press.

McNeill, W. H. (1977), *Plagues and Peoples*, Anchor Books, Doubleday, New York.

McNeill, W. H. (1990), 'The Rise of the West after Twenty-Five Years', *Journal of World History*, vol. 1/1.

McNeill, J. R. and W. M. (2003), *The Human Web: A Bird's-Eye View of World History*, Norton, New York.

MacPike, E. F. (1932), *Correspondence and Papers of Edmond Halley*, Oxford University Press.

Maddison, A. (1982), *Phases of Capitalist Development*, Oxford University Press.

Maddison, A. (1987), 'Growth and Slowdown in Advanced Capitalist Countries: Techniques of Quantitative Assessment', *Journal of Economic Literature*, June, pp. 649–98.

Maddison, A. (1995a), *Monitoring the World Economy, 1820–1992*, OECD, Paris.

Maddison, A. (1995b), *Explaining the Economic Performance of Nations: Essays in Time and Space*, Elgar, Aldershot.

Maddison, A. (2001), *The World Economy: A Millennial Perspective*, OECD, Paris.

Maddison, A. (2003), *The World Economy: Historical Statistics*, OECD, Paris.

Maddison, A. (2005) website http://www.ggdc.net/Maddison/

Maddison, A. and B. van Ark (2000), 'The International Comparison of Real Product and Productivity', in Maddison, Prasada Rao and Shepherd.

Morineau, M. (1985), *Incroyables gazettes et fabuleux metaux*, Cambridge University Press.

Nef, J. U. (1987), 'Mining and Metallurgy in Medieval Civilisation', in Postan et al. (eds), vol. II, pp. 693–762.

O'Rourke, K. H. and J. G. Williamson, (2002), 'After Columbus: Explaining Europe's Overseas Trade Boom, 1500–1800', *Journal of Economic History*, June, pp. 417–56.

Postan, M. M. et al. (eds) (1963–87), *The Cambridge Economic History of Europe*, vol. I (1966), vol. II (1987), and vol. III (1963), Cambridge University Press.

Ridgway, R. H. (1929), *Summarised Data of Gold Production*, Economic Paper No. 6, Bureau of Mines, US Dept of Commerce, Washington, DC.

Rosenblat, A. (1945), *La Población Indígena de América desde 1492 hasta la Actualidad*, ICE, Buenos Aires.

Rozenzweig, F. (1963), 'La economia Novo-Hispaña al comenzar del siglo XIX', *Revista de Sciencias Politicas y Sociales*, UNAM, July–September.

Schäfer, D. (ed) (1915), *Forschungen und Versuche zur Geschichte des Mittelalters und der Neuzeit*, Fischer, Jena.

Smith, A. ([1776], 1976), *An Inquiry into the Nature and Causes of the Wealth of Nations*, University of Chicago.

Solow, B. L. (ed) (1991), *Slavery and the Rise of the Atlantic System*, Cambridge University Press.

Thomas, R. P. (1965), 'A Quantitative Approach to the Study of the Effects of British Imperial Policy upon Colonial Welfare: Some Preliminary Findings', *Journal of Economic History*, December.

Tracy, J. D. (1993), *The Rise of Merchant Empires: Long Distance Trade in the Early Modern World, 1350–1750*, Cambridge University Press.

Usher, A. P. (1932), 'Spanish Ships and Shipping in the Sixteenth and Seventeenth Century', *Facts and Figures in Economic History, Festschrift for E.F. Gay*, Harvard University Press.

Vogel, W. (1915), '*Zur Grösse der europaischen Handelsflotten im 15., 16. und 17. Jahrhundert*', in Schäfer.

Vries, J. de (1984), *European Urbanization, 1500–1800*, Methuen, London.

Vries, J. de (2003), 'Connecting Europe and Asia: A Quantitative Analysis of the Cape Trade Route, 1497–1795', in Flynn et al.

Williams, E. (1970), *From Columbus to Castro: The History of the Caribbean, 1492–1969*, Deutsch, London.

3 The interaction between Asia and the West, 1500–2003

Direct maritime contact between western Europe and Asia was initiated by Vasco da Gama in 1497. The European impact on Asia was important but much more modest than what happened in the Americas in the centuries following 1492. Asia's population was five times that of western Europe and 14 times as big as the Americas in 1500. The technological level in Asia was much more sophisticated than in the Americas, and its major states—the Ottoman Empire, Safavid Persia, the Moghul Empire, China, and Japan—were infinitely better equipped to resist conquest than the Aztecs, Incas, and tribes of the Americas. Asian destinations were much more remote, with a sailing time measured in months rather than weeks. In 1820 there were more than 13 million people of European origin in the Americas. In Asia there were less than 100,000.

There were three major reasons which underlay the European initiative:

1. Developments in European ship design, navigation, and naval weaponry opened the way for ventures which would have been impossible 50 years earlier.

2. In the UK and the Netherlands, the legal system protected commercial property rights and ensured the enforceability of contracts. State levies were predictable and not arbitrary, and credit for long term ventures was available. As a result groups of capitalists in these countries were able to establish corporations like the Dutch Far East Company (VOC), and the British East India Company (EIC) which could organize risky ventures over huge distances.

3. In Asia there was limited scope for seizure of land and turning indigenous peoples into serfs or slaves, so dealings with Asians had to be done in most cases on a commercial basis. Asians were not very interested in acquiring European commodities, so it was very convenient that Europe was flush with precious metals acquired from the Americas. China and India were particularly keen to accept these in return for trade goods.

In the merchant capitalist period, from 1500 to 1800, European countries were fierce rivals. They sought exclusive rights when making arrangements with Asian countries and they practiced beggar-you-neighbour policies or outright warfare with each other. After 20 years of mutual slaughter in the revolutionary and Napoleonic wars, things changed. After 1820 there was a gradual switch to collusive policies. The main imperialist power, the UK, practiced free trade and most-favoured-nation treatment. This was a major feature of multi-country imperialism in China.

The old monopoly companies (VOC and EIC) disappeared in favour of a wider variety of western enterprise and investment, and governments aimed at territorial conquest and control. The disparity in military and naval power between Asia and Europe had grown much larger. By 1820 the British and Dutch had already established territorial hegemony in India and Indonesia. They were interested in extending this type of imperialism, and were to be joined by France, Russia, the United States, and others with similar ambitions. A striking aspect of this new type of imperialism was the extremely active participation of Japan, the only Asian country which made a serious effort to catch up with the west. Its imperialism was only one facet of its radical institutional changes to mimic the west.

EUROPEAN–ASIAN INTERACTION FROM 1500 TO 1820

The initiative for Portuguese penetration of Asia came from the crown. Unlike the other Europeans except the Spanish, they had evangelical as well as commercial aspirations. Their trading empire consisted of armed ships and a string of fortified bases: Elmina and Mozambique on the African coast; Hormuz at the entry to the Persian Gulf; Goa on the northwest coast of India (headquarters of Asian trading operations and the Jesuit order); Malacca controlled trade and shipping between India and Indonesia; Macao was the main locus of trade with China. There were also important trading posts at Jaffna in Ceylon, Nagasaki in Japan, Ternate and Timor in Indonesia. They held Goa from 1510 to 1961, Timor from 1613 to 1975, and Macao from 1557 to 1999.

Portuguese imports from Asia were heavily concentrated on pepper and spices. Initially they were financed by bullion shipments as Asians had little interest in European goods. An increasing proportion was financed from fees levied on Asian

Table 3.1. Number of Ships Sailing to Asia from Seven European Countries, 1500–1800

	1500–99	1600–1700	1701–1800
Portugal	705	371	196
Netherlands	65[a]	1,770	2,950
England		811	1,865
France		155	1,300
Other		54	350
Total	770	3,161	6,661

Notes: 'Other' refers to ships of the Danish, Swedish, and Ostend companies, but excludes the Pacific trade of Spanish ships operating from Acapulco; *a* = 1590s.

Source: Bruijn and Gaastra (1993: 7, 17, 178, 183).

Table 3.2a. Gold and Silver Shipments from the Americas to Europe, 1500–1800 (metric tons)

	Gold	Silver
1500–1600	150	7,500
1601–1700	158	26,168
1701–1800	1,400	39,157
Total (1500–1800)	1,708	72,825

Source: Morineau (1985: 570).

traders using ports controlled by Portugal, and their own earnings in intra-Asian trade. The most lucrative of the latter were their sales of Chinese silks for three thousand tons of Japanese silver between the 1550s and 1638.

Portuguese penetration of the Asian oceans was facilitated by the withdrawal of China and Japan from international trade. At the beginning of the fifteenth century, Chinese naval technology was superior to that of Europe. Chinese fleets were deployed in spectacular voyages throughout the Indian Ocean and down the East African coast from 1405 to 1433.

Thereafter, China concentrated on internal trade via the reconstructed Grand Canal, and more or less abandoned international trade and construction of sophisticated ships. From 1639 to the middle of the nineteenth century, European trade with Japan was restricted by the Tokugawa regime to a small Dutch trading settlement at Deshima, near Nagasaki.

When the Portuguese arrived in the Indian Ocean, there was no powerful naval force to oppose them. They were attacked by an Egyptian fleet in 1509, but it was decisively defeated at Diu off the coast of Gujarat. The Asian traders with whom the Portuguese competed belonged to merchant communities (with varying ethnic, religious, family, or linguistic ties) operating without armed vessels or significant interference from governments. Although southern India, where Portugal started its

Table 3.2b. Exports of Silver and Gold from Western Europe, 1601–1780 (metric tons of 'silver equivalent')

	To the Baltic	To west Asia	Dutch (VOC) to Asia	British (EIC) to Asia	Total to Asia
1601–50	2,475	2,500	425	250	3,175
1651–1700	2,800	2,500	775	1,050	4,325
1701–50	2,800	2,500	2,200	2,450	7,150
1751–80	1,980	1,500	1,445	1,450	4,395
1601–1780	10,055	9,000	4,845	5,200	19,049

Notes and Source: Barrett, in Tracy (1990: 251). His silver/gold conversion ratio was about 14.5/1 (see p. 228). If we apply this conversion ratio, the total inflow in Table 3.2a would have been about 97,600 tons of silver equivalent. The total outflow shown here would have been 30 per cent of this.

Asian trade, was ruled by the empire of Vijayanagar, conditions in coastal trade were set by rulers of smaller political units, who derived income by offering protection and marketing opportunities.

The income of the rulers of Vijayanagar and the Moghul empire was derived from land taxes, and they had no significant financial interest in foreign trade. In Indonesia, political power was fragmented, the Hindu state of Majapahit was in decline and uninterested in foreign trade. In China and Japan the situation was different and the Portuguese had to negotiate a limited entry, cap in hand.

Portuguese trade with Asia declined in the seventeenth century. They lost their bases in Hormuz in 1622 and Muscat in 1650. The Dutch took over the trade monopoly with Japan in 1639 and captured Malacca in 1641. They drove the Portuguese out of Sri Lanka between 1638 and 1658, when they finally took Jaffna. Dutch competition weakened Portuguese interests in Bengal and on the west coast of India. Nevertheless Goa and Macao were retained for more than 400 years and Portugal compensated for its Asian losses by developing an empire in Brazil.

The total volume of European shipping in Asian waters was four times as big in the seventeenth century and nine times as big in the eighteenth as it had been in the sixteenth. Portugal became a marginal participant, with about 12 per cent of the trade in the seventeenth and 3 per cent in the eighteenth century. The Dutch accounted for half of the expanded trade, the British about a quarter. French and three small European companies (Danish, Swedish, and Ostend) accounted for the rest.

The European market for traditional exports of pepper and spices was limited. The bulk of the new export items were raw silk, a huge variety of cotton textiles from India, coffee from Arabia and Indonesia, and tea from China.

The Dutch Company (VOC) accounted for 45 per cent of the European voyages to Asia from 1500 to 1800 and a higher proportion of the tonnage. It was given a monopoly charter (in 1602), which it needed in order to organize trade with heavy capital outlays over extended periods. Each 30,000 mile return voyage to its Asian headquarters in Java (Batavia) took at least 18 months. Dutch ships were armed and the company had the power to wage war, make treaties with Asian rulers, establish fortified ports, enlist soldiers and administrators.

The company had six shipyards in the Netherlands and maintained a fleet of about 100 vessels. The average vessel was replaced after ten years during which it would have made four return trips to Asia. Over the lifetime of the company, 1,500 ships were constructed for Asian trade. At the end of the sixteenth century the Portuguese were using large carracks with an average size well over 1,000 tons. The Dutch started with ships below 500 tons. By the 1770s the average carrying capacity was about 1,000 tons, which was bigger than vessels used by the English and French companies. Dutch losses from shipwreck and seizure were below 3 per cent over the whole period 1600–1800, which was very much smaller than Portuguese experience.[1]

By 1750, the company employed more than 12,000 sailors and 17,000 soldiers as well as administrative personnel in Asia. Over the whole period 1600–1800, the VOC sent nearly a million sailors, soldiers, and administrators to its 30 Asian trading posts. This was about the same as the combined total for other European companies (British, French, Portuguese, Danish, Swedish, and Austria's Ostend Company). The proportion of the Dutch Company's servants who returned to Europe (about a third) was a good deal lower than that of other companies. This was due to the greater role of intra-Asian trade in the VOC's operations and the bigger proportion of VOC personnel who stayed in Asia permanently, but it seems likely that the mortality rate was higher. In the course of the eighteenth century, the incidence of malaria rose dramatically in Batavia as the area of swamp-land around the city increased.

After the British took over the governance of Bengal in 1757, they discriminated against the Dutch and reduced their trade with India. The Dutch position in China trade was also greatly inferior to the British who used opium shipments from India to finance tea purchases in Canton, whereas the Dutch had to pay in bullion for tea delivered by Chinese traders to Batavia. The outbreak of the Napoleonic wars led to a British takeover of Dutch settlements in India, Malacca, Ceylon, South Africa, and temporarily in Indonesia.

In the second half of the eighteenth century, the VOC had ceased to be a profitable organization. It was dissolved in 1800, after several decades distributing dividends bigger than its profits. The profit decline had several causes. The company had very high overheads in hiring military, naval, and administrative personnel to run what had become a territorial empire. Its officers conducted an increasingly large private trade of their own in the company's ships. There was a good deal of corruption which benefited the servants, but not the shareholders of the company. Given the changing commodity structure of trade and the locus of operation, Batavia was no longer the ideal headquarters it had been initially, when the spice trade was predominant.

THE IMPACT OF ASIAN TRADE ON EUROPE, 1500–1820

Asian trade stimulated expansion of the European shipping industry and improvement of navigation techniques. It created new employment opportunities and provided new consumer goods for which demand was highly elastic. Tea and coffee improved social life. To the degree that they replaced gin and beer, they increased life expectation. Asian textiles and porcelain created new fashions in clothing, domestic utensils, decorative fabrics, and wallpaper. Familiarity with these new goods eventually sparked European import—substitution particularly in textiles, pottery, and porcelain.[2]

The most striking thing about the operation of European companies from 1500 to 1800 was not their exploitation of Asia, but their enmity to each other. This was most extreme in relations between the Portuguese and the Dutch, but it was also visible in British–Dutch and British–French action and attitudes. Apart from the cost of armed struggle there were heavy military commitments to deter conflict, monopolistic

Table 3.3. Population of Asian Countries, 1500–2003 (000s)

	1500	1700	1820	1950	2003
China	103,000	138,000	381,000	546,815	1,288,400
Japan	15,400	27,000	31,000	83,805	127,214
India	110,000	165,000	209,000	359,000	1,049,700
Bang & Pak				85,094	294,575
Indonesia	10,700	13,100	17,927	79,043	214,497
South Korea	5,470	8,342	9,395	20,846	48,202
North Korea	2,530	3,858	4,345	9,471	22,466
Philippines	500	1,250	2,176	21,131	84,620
Sri Lanka	1,000	1,200	1,213	7,533	19,742
Thailand	2,000	2,500	4,665	20,042	63,271
Taiwan	200	1,000	2,000	7,981	22,603
Hong Kong	neg.	neg.	20	2,237	6,810
Singapore	neg.	neg.	5	1,022	4,277
Other east Asia	15,200	19,450	22,482	78,910	237,782
Total east Asia	**266,000**	**380,700**	**685,228**	**1,322,930**	**3,484,159**
Arabia	4,500	4,500	5,202	9,483	53,466
Iran	4,000	5,000	6,560	16,357	67,148
Iraq	1,000	1,000	1,093	5,163	24,683
Turkey	6,300	8,400	10,074	21,122	68,109
Other west Asia	2,000	1,900	2,218	7,722	36,403
Total west Asia	**17,800**	**20,800**	**25,147**	**59,847**	**249,808**
Total Asia	**283,800**	**401,500**	**710,375**	**1,382,777**	**3,733,967**
Western Europe	**57,332**	**81,460**	**133,040**	**304,941**	**394,604**

Notes and Source: Maddison (2001: 238) and McEvedy and Jones (1978) for 1500–1700, Maddison (2003: 152–7 and 160–9 for 1820–1950). Thereafter from US Bureau of the Census; neg. = negligible; Arabia includes Bahrain, Kuwait, Oman, Qatar, Saudi Arabia, United Arab Emirates, and Yemen.

interdiction of European markets to competitors, and creation of separate networks of trading posts. All of this raised the costs and reduced the benefits of trade to Europeans as well as Asians. It contrasted unfavourably with conditions in the trading world of Asia before European entrance, and the widespread acceptance of free trade in Asia between the 1840s and 1920s.

THE IMPACT OF EUROPE ON ASIA, 1500–1820

European trading posts in Asia were nearly all on the coastal periphery, and until the eighteenth century, infringements of Asian sovereignty were generally limited. In the second half of the century a major change occurred when Britain took over the administration and revenues of part of the collapsing Moghul Empire. In Indonesia, the Dutch achieved monopoly control of the spice islands early in the seventeenth century by slaughtering the inhabitants, and installing new plantations operated by slave labour. Elsewhere in Indonesia there was a lesser degree of coercion and control until after the Napoleonic wars. Europeans posed no challenge to Chinese or Japanese sovereignty until the nineteenth century.

Table 3.4a. Per capita GDP in Asian Countries, 1500–2003 (1990 international $)

	1500	1700	1820	1950	2003
China	600	600	600	448	4,803
Japan	500	570	669	1,921	21,218
India	550	550	533	619	2,160
Bangladesh				540	939
Pakistan				643	1,881
Indonesia	565	580	612	840	3,555
South Korea	600	600	600	854	15,732
North Korea	600	600	600	854	1,127
Other east Asia	**544**	**548**	**557**	**826**	**4,458**
Average east Asia	**567**	**571**	**580**	**669**	**4,329**
Arabia	550	550	550	2,065	6,313
Iran	600	600	588	1,720	5,539
Iraq	550	550	588	1,364	1,023
Turkey	600	600	643	1,623	6,731
Other west Asia	645	645	645	2,234	7,707
Average west Asia	**590**	**591**	**607**	**1,776**	**5,899**
Asian average	**568**	**572**	**581**	**717**	**4,434**
Western Europe	**771**	**997**	**1,202**	**4,578**	**19,912**

Notes and Source: Maddison (2001), Appendix B and Maddison (2003), pp. 154–7 and 180–8, updated. I assumed that the average per capita movement 1500–1820 for China, Japan, India, Indonesia and Korea combined was valid for all the other countries of east Asia.

Table 3.4b. GDP of Asian Countries, 1500–2003 (million 1990 international $)

	1500	1700	1820	1950	2003
China	61,800	82,800	228,600	244,985	6,187,984
Japan	7,700	15,390	20,739	160,966	2,699,261
India	60,500	90,750	111,417	222,222	2,267,136
Bangladesh & Pakistan				49,994	423,679
Indonesia	6,046	7,598	10,970	66,358	762,545
South Korea	3,282	5,005	5,637	17,800	758,297
North Korea	1,518	2,315	2,607	8,087	25,310
Other east Asia	10,142	13,721	17,237	114,699	1,957,225
Total east Asia	**150,822**	**217,380**	**397,207**	**885,111**	**15,081,356**
Arabia	2,475	2,475	2,861	19,583	337,528
Iran	2,400	3,000	3,857	28,128	371,952
Iraq	550	550	643	7,041	25,256
Turkey	3,780	5,040	6,478	34,279	458,454
Other west Asia	1,290	1,226	1,430	17,252	280,549
Total west Asia	**10,495**	**12,291**	**15,269**	**106,283**	**1,473,739**
Total Asia	**161,317**	**229,671**	**412,476**	**991,393**	**16,555,095**
W. Europe	**44,183**	**81,213**	**159,851**	**1,396,078**	**7,857,394**
US	**800**	**527**	**12,548**	**1,455,916**	**8,430,762**

Sources: As for Table 3.4a.

The companies created new markets in Europe for Asian products. Prakash (1998: 317), estimates that British and Dutch purchases of textiles accounted for about 11 per cent of textile employment in Bengal in the period 1678–1718. The EIC also created new cities as centres of commerce (Bombay, Calcutta, and Madras). There was relatively little demand for European goods in Asia. European purchases were financed by transfer of precious metals or earnings from intra-Asian trade. However, the export of silver to India and China did help to monetize their economies. The most obvious adverse economic impact of the European companies on Asia was to displace the shipping and marketing activities of Asian traders.

Four Country Confrontation: The Experience of India, Indonesia, Japan, and China

To understand the European impact and the long run divergence of development within Asia it is useful to compare the experience of India, Indonesia, China, and Japan which accounted for 84 per cent of Asian population in 1500.

The British Impact on India

The British connection with India started in 1600 with the creation of the East India Company's (EIC) monopoly in Asian trade. For the first century and a half, it operated around the Indian coast and created new towns—Madras (1639), Bombay (1668), and Calcutta (1690)—as trading bases. By the middle of the eighteenth century the main exports were textiles and raw silk from India, and tea from China. Purchases of Indian products were financed mainly by exports of bullion, and from China by export of Bengali opium and raw cotton. After 1757, when the EIC took over the governance of Bengal, the British relationship with India became exploitative. Exports to Britain and opium exports to China were financed from Bengal tax revenue.

Until the eighteenth century the British generally maintained peaceful relations with the Moghul empire whose authority and military power was too great to be challenged. After the death of Aurangzeb in 1707, Moghul control disintegrated. The later Moghul emperors were token suzerains. Provincial governors became *de facto* rulers as *nawabs* of successor states.

At the height of its power, under the Emperors Akbar (1556–1605), Jehangir (1605–27) and Shah Jehan (1627–58), the Moghuls practiced religious toleration. This is one of the reasons they were more successful than the earlier Muslim sultanates of Delhi in establishing an extensive domain in a country with great racial, linguistic and religious complexity and a bigger population than Europe. Aurangzeb (1658–1707) abandoned the policy of religious tolerance, destroyed Hindu temples, re-imposed the *jizya* (a capitation tax on non-Muslims) and confiscated some non-Muslim princely states when titles lapsed. After his death, there was a series of wars for the spoils of empire. In western India, the Mahrattas established an independent

Hindu state with their capital at Poona. The *Nizam-ul-Mulk*, a high Moghul official who foresaw the collapse of the empire, installed himself as the autonomous ruler of Hyderabad in 1724. In 1739, the Persian emperor Nadir Shah invaded India, massacred the population of Delhi and took away so much booty (including Shah Jehan's peacock throne and the Kohinoor diamond) that he was able to remit Persian taxes for three years. He also annexed Punjab and set up an independent kingdom in Lahore. The Punjab was later captured by the Sikhs. In other areas which nominally remained in the Empire, e.g. Bengal, Mysore, and Oudh, the power of the Moghul emperor declined, as did his revenue. Continuous internal warfare weakened the economy and trade of the country.

It was because of these internal political and religious conflicts that the EIC was able to gain control of India. It exploited the differences skilfully by making temporary alliances and picking off local potentates one at a time. Most of its troops were local recruits who were well disciplined and paid regularly. They conquered the Moghul province of Bengal in 1757, took over the provinces of Madras and Bombay in 1803, and seized the Punjab from the Sikhs in 1848. They also succeeded in marginalizing their French and Dutch commercial rivals. However, the British government did not establish direct rule until after the Indian mutiny in 1857 when the East India Company was dissolved.

After its military victory at Plassey in 1757, the EIC operated a dual system in Bengal. It had effective control and the *nawab* was its puppet figurehead. The main objectives of the Company were to enrich its officials and finance its exports from the tax revenues of Bengal instead of shipping bullion to India, but territorial conquest changed its role from trading to governance. Its operations were subjected to British parliamentary surveillance in 1773, and the *nawab* was replaced by a Governor General (Warren Hastings) in direct charge of administration, but with Indian officials. The Company's trade monopoly was revoked in 1813 in India and in 1833 in China.

Hastings was dismissed in 1782, and his successor, Cornwallis, created a new system of governance closer in sprit to the meritocratic bureaucracy of China than to anything that existed in the UK at that time. All high level posts were reserved for the British, and Indians were excluded. A well-paid civil administration was created which was more or less incorruptible, cheaper, and much more effective in maintaining law and order than that of the Moghuls. From 1806 the Company trained its recruits at Haileybury College near London. From 1833 nominees were selected by competitive examination. After 1853, selection was entirely on merit. In 1829, the system was strengthened by establishing districts throughout British India small enough to be controlled by an individual British official who exercised autocratic power as revenue collector, judge, and chief of police.

The British raj was operated by remarkably few people. There were only 31,000 British in India in 1805 (of which 22,000 in the army, and 2,000 in civil government). In 1931, there were 168,000 (60,000 in the army and police; 4,000 in civil government; 26,000 in the private sector, and 78,000 family dependents). They were never more than 0.05 per cent of the population—a much thinner layer than the Muslim rulers had been.

There was a strong streak of Benthamite radicalism in the EIC administration. James Mill became a senior Company official in 1819 after writing a monumental history of India which showed strong contempt for its institutions.[3] The historian Macaulay was a very influential Company official, and Malthus was the Professor of Economics at Haileybury. Bentham himself was consulted on the reform of Indian institutions. The Utilitarians used India to try experiments and ideas (e.g., competitive entry to the civil service) which they would have liked to apply in England. After the Indian mutiny in 1857, when the British government took over direct control, these radical westernizing approaches were dropped and policy became more conservative. There was no attempt at further extension of direct rule over 'native states' ruled by Indian princes, but they were subject to 'guidance' from official British 'residents'. There were several hundred native states with about a fifth of India's population, the biggest being Hyderabad, Jammu and Kashmir, and Mysore. The Portuguese retained Goa with 0.15 per cent of India's population and the French had an even smaller toehold at Pondicherry.

The Moghul empire was finally liquidated. As Muslims had played the leading role in the mutiny, the British ceased using them in the Indian army or in government jobs.

The changes which the British made in the system of governance had major socioeconomic consequences. Tables 3.8 and 3.9 contrast the Indian social structure at the peak of the Moghul empire and at the end of British rule. The British took over a Moghul tax system which provided the elite with land revenue equal to 15 per cent of national income. By the end of the colonial period, land tax was only 1 per cent and the total tax burden, 6 per cent. The main gains from tax reduction and associated changes in property rights went to upper castes in the village economy, to *zamindars* who became landlords, and to village moneylenders. The wasteful warlord aristocracy of the Moghuls was eliminated, and replaced by a small westernized elite with a smaller share of national income. A residual group of cooperative princelings and maharajahs remained in the 'native states'. Until the 1920s, the new elite was almost entirely British, with British consumption patterns. This reduced the demand for the luxury products of India's traditional handicrafts. The damage to India's main industry was reinforced in the nineteenth century from duty-free imports of British cotton textiles.

In the first century of British rule, there was a continuation of the fall in per capita income which had started at the beginning of the eighteenth century as the Moghul state disintegrated. From 1857 to independence in 1947, there was a slow rise in per capita income, and accelerated population growth. Table 3.5 shows changes in income and population in India and Britain from 1600 to the end of colonial rule in 1947. In this period, British per capita income rose nearly seven-fold, with a meagre 12 per cent rise in India. From 1947 to 2003, the proportionate increase was similar in both countries, but, since 1990, the Indian growth rate has been much more rapid.

The 'drain' of resources to the United Kingdom as a consequence of foreign rule was a major target of criticism by Indian nationalists from the end of the nineteenth

Table 3.5. Comparative Macro-economic Performance of India and Britain, 1600–2003 (per capita GDP, 1990 international dollars)

	1600	1757	1857	1947	2003
India	550	540	520	618	2,160
UK	974	1,432	2,757	6,604	21,310
Population (000)					
India	135,000	185,000	227,000	414,000	1,049,700
UK	6,170	12,157	28,186	49,519	60,271
GDP (million 1990 int. dollars)					
India	74,250	99,900	118,040	255,852	2,267,136
UK	6,007	17,407	77,717	327,044	1,280,625

Source: Maddison (2001 and 2003) and www.ggdc.net/Maddison

century. It was measured by the size of the Indian export surplus which was about 1 per cent of Indian national income from 1868 to the 1930s. This meant a transfer of about a fifth of India's net savings which might otherwise have been used to import capital goods, and it did indeed disappear after independence. Even more important was the fact that 5 per cent of the national income went to British personnel in India. Most of this would have gone to an Indian elite if the British had left India 50 years earlier and been replaced by an Indian elite pursuing policies.

However, if the British had not ruled India from the mid-eighteenth to late nineteenth century, it seems unlikely that a modernizing elite or the legal and institutional

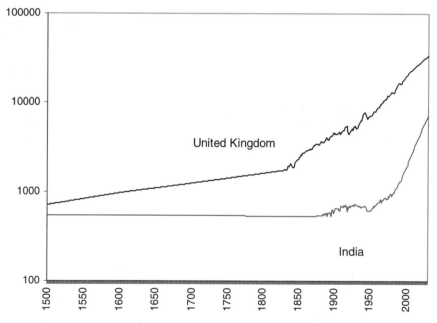

Figure 3.1. Comparative levels of India/UK GDP per capita, 1500–2030 (1990 international dollars)

Table 3.6. India's Balance on Merchandise and Bullion, 1835–1967

	Balance in current prices (annual average)	Balance in 1948–9 prices (£ million)	Per capita balance at 1948–9 prices (£)
1835–54	4.5	n.a.	*n.a.*
1855–74	7.3	50.0	0.21
1875–94	13.4	80.0	0.30
1895–1913	16.8	77.6	0.26
1914–34	22.5	59.2	0.19
1935–46	27.9	66.1	0.17
1948–57*	−99.9	−97.6	−0.21
1958–67*	−472.7	−384.7	−0.67

Notes and Source: *Figures refer to India, Pakistan, and Bangladesh.

Constant price figures for 1948 onwards deflated by the national income deflator, earlier years by the price index of Mukherjee (1969). Imports are recorded c.i.f. and exports f.o.b.

framework for its operation would have emerged from the ruins of the Moghul empire.

The consequences of British rule can be seen by examining the socioeconomic structure inherited from Moghul India and noting the changes which arose from innovations in the mode of governance, property rights, and the structure of demand and output.

The Moghul Social Structure. Muslims were the ruling elite in India from the thirteenth century until the British takeover. The Moghuls had the military power to squeeze a large surplus from a passive village society. The ruling class had an extravagant lifestyle whose luxuries were supplied by urban artisans producing high quality cotton textiles, silks, jewellery, decorative swords, and weapons.

Members of the Moghul aristocracy derived their income from the land. They were not hereditary landlords. Their income from *jagirs* (allocations of tax revenue from a collection of villages) and their estates were liable to royal forfeit on death. Part of this income was for their own sustenance, the rest was paid to the central treasury in cash or in the form of troop support. Moghul practice derived from the traditions

Table 3.7. The British 'Drain' on India, 1868–1930

	Commodity exports as per cent of Indian net domestic product	Indian export surplus as per cent of Indian net domestic product	Indian export surplus as per cent of British net domestic product
1868–72	5.2	1.0	1.1
1911–15	9.0	1.3	0.9
1926–30	9.6	0.9	0.5

Notes and Source: Maddison (1986b), pp. 646–8. The 'drain' (i.e., the colonial burden as measured by the trade surplus of the colony) figures prominently in the literature of Indian nationalism (see Naoroji, 1901).

of the nomadic societies which had created Islam. Nobles were regularly posted from one *jagir* to another. This system of warlord predation led a wasteful use of resources and negligible levels of productive investment. There was little motive to improve landed property. The nobility lived in walled castles with harems, gardens, and fountains. They maintained polygamous households with large retinues of servants and slaves. They had huge wardrobes of splendid garments in fine cottons and silk. The emperors built magnificent palaces and mosques at Agra, Delhi, Fatehpur Sikri and Lahore.

Jagirdars had an incentive to squeeze village society close to subsistence, spend as much as possible on consumption, and die in debt to the state. However, there were also Hindu nobles (*zamindars*) who retained hereditary control over village revenues, and Hindu princes who continued to rule and collect revenues in autonomous states within the empire, whose incentives were different.

The income which the Moghul elite, native princes, and *zamindars* managed to squeeze from the rural population was proportionately quite large. It amounted to about 15 per cent of the national income (see Table 3.8). But, by the end of British rule, the successors of the old elite got only 3 per cent.

The reason why the Moghuls could raise so much in tax revenue, without a ruling class directly supervising the production process, was that the rural population

Table 3.8. Social Structure of the Moghul Empire around 1600

Percentage of labour force		Per cent of national income after tax
18	**NON-VILLAGE ECONOMY**	52
1	Moghul Emperor and Court Mansabdars Jagirdars Native princes Appointed zamindars Hereditary zamindars	15
17	Merchants and bankers Traditional professions Petty traders & entrepreneurs Soldiers & petty bureaucracy Urban artisans & construction workers Servants Sweepers Scavengers	37
72	**VILLAGE ECONOMY** Dominant castes Cultivators and rural artisans Landless labourers Servants Sweepers Scavengers	45
10	**TRIBAL ECONOMY**	3

Source: Maddison (1971: 33).

Table 3.9. Social Structure of India at the End of British Rule

Percentage of labour force		Per cent of national income after tax
18	**NON-VILLAGE ECONOMY**	44
0.06	British officials and military / British business, plantation owners, traders, bankers	5
0.94	Native princes / Big zamindars and jagirdars	3
	Indian capitalists, merchants and managers / The new Indian professional class	6
17	Petty traders, small entrepreneurs, traditional professions, clerical and manual workers in government, soldiers, railway and industrial workers, urban artisans, servants, sweepers & scavengers	30
75	**VILLAGE ECONOMY**	54
9	Village rentiers, rural moneylenders small zamindars, tenants-in-chief	20
20	Working proprietors, protected tenants	18
29	Tenants-at-will, sharecroppers, village artisans and servants	12
7	**TRIBAL ECONOMY**	2

Source: Maddison (1971: 69).

(mostly Hindus) were very docile. Villages were defensive, self-contained units designed for survival in periods of war and alien domination. They paid taxes collectively to whoever held state power. Conquerors of India had a readymade source of income and no incentive to change the system.

The chief characteristic of Indian society which differentiated it from others was the institution of caste. It segregated the population into mutually exclusive groups whose economic and social functions were clearly defined and hereditary. Old religious texts classified Hindus into four main groups. *Brahmins*, a caste of priests, were at the top of the social scale whose purity was not to be polluted by manual labour. Next in rank came warriors (*kshatriyas*), traders (*vaishyas*) and farmers (*sudras*). Below this there were outcastes (*melechas*) to perform menial and unclean tasks. Members of different castes did not intermarry or eat together, and kept apart in social life. This system had an adverse effect on productivity because it pushed village living standards to a level that reduced physical working capacity; allocated jobs on a rigid basis of heredity rather than aptitude; prompted a ritualistic rather than a functional attitude to work; and maintained tabus on animal slaughter (see Lal 2005, on the origins and impact of caste).

In relations with the state, the village usually acted as a unit. Land taxes were generally paid collectively and the internal allocation of the burden was left to the village headman or accountant. The top group in the villages were allies of the state, co-beneficiaries in the system of exploitation. In every village the bottom

Table 3.10. Intensity of Land Use in Japan, China, India, Indonesia, and Australia, 1993

	Total land area (000 ha.)	Arable land & permanent crop area (000 ha.)	Proportion cultivated (per cent)	Population (000s)	Arable land per head of population (ha.)
Japan	37,780	4,463	11.8	124,753	0.04
China	959,696	95,975	10.0	1,178,440	0.08
Indonesia	181,157	30,987	17.1	188,359	0.16
India	328,759	169,650	51.6	899,000	0.19
Australia	771,336	4,486	6.0	17,769	2.62

Source: FAO Yearbook (1994).

layer were untouchables squeezed tight against the margin of subsistence. Without caste sanctions, village society would probably have been more egalitarian. A more homogeneous peasantry might have been less willing to put up with such heavy fiscal levies.

Below village society, about 10 per cent of the population lived in a large number of tribal communities. Aboriginal tribes led an independent pagan existence as hunters or forest dwellers, completely outside Hindu society and paying no taxes to the Moghuls.

As a result of the social system, the Indian economy was characterized by long term stagnation and negligible levels of productive investment. The irrigated area was about 5 per cent of the total compared with a third in China. Animal dung was rarely used as manure, and a largely vegetarian population got little benefit from large numbers of sacred cows. There were no agricultural handbooks or governmental attempts to bolster agricultural productivity. Crop yields seem to have been stagnant over the long run.

Availability of land was an important characteristic of India which had an impact on its social structure and caste system. The cultivable area was much greater in relation to population in India than in China and Japan. An economy with relatively abundant land is more likely to use coercive institutions (the caste system, feudalism, slavery, serfdom, or apartheid), than in countries such as China and Japan where land was much scarcer, and rural property relationships relied much more on market incentives. Domar (1989: 225–38) provided an insightful analysis of the impact of land abundance/scarcity on social institutions and Boserup (1965) analysed the incentives to increase per capita labour input in response to land shortage.

The British Impact on Indian Agriculture. The colonial government modified traditional institutional arrangements in agriculture by creating property rights whose character was much closer to those of western capitalism. Except in the autonomous princely states, the old warlord aristocracy was dispossessed. Their previous income from *jagirs*, and that of the Moghul state, was appropriated by the British. In the Bengal presidency (i.e., modern Bengal, Bihar, Orissa, and part of Madras), the second layer of Moghul property rights belonging to tax collectors (*zamindars*) was reinforced. They acquired hereditary status, so long as they paid their land taxes, and their tax liabilities were frozen at the 1793 level. In the Madras and Bombay presidencies the British dispossessed most of the old Moghul and Mahratta nobility and big zamindars, and vested property rights and tax obligations in the traditionally dominant castes in villages. Lower caste cultivators became their tenants.

Because of the emergence of clearer titles, it became possible to mortgage land. The status of moneylenders was improved by the change from Muslim to British law. There had been moneylenders in the Moghul period, but their importance grew substantially under British rule, and a considerable amount of land changed hands through foreclosures.

Over time, two forces raised the income of landowners. One of these was the increasing scarcity of land as population expanded. This raised land values and rents. The second was the decline in the incidence of land tax. As a result, there was a widening of inequality within villages. The village squirearchy received higher incomes because of the reduced burden of land tax and the increase in rents; the income of tenants and agricultural labourers declined because their traditional rights were curtailed and their bargaining power reduced by greater land scarcity. The class of landless agricultural labourers grew in size under British rule.

The colonial government increased the irrigated area about eight-fold. Eventually more than a quarter of the land of British India was irrigated, compared with 5 per cent in Moghul India. Irrigation was extended both as a source of revenue and as a measure to mitigate famines. A good deal of the irrigation work was in the Punjab and Sind. The motive here was to provide land for retired Indian army personnel, many of whom came from the Punjab, and to increase settlement in an area near the disputed frontier with Afghanistan. These areas, which had formerly been desert, became the biggest irrigated area in the world and major producers of wheat and cotton, both for export and for sale in other parts of India.

Improvements in transport facilities (railways, steamships, and the Suez canal) helped agriculture by permitting some degree of specialization on cash crops. This increased yields somewhat, but the bulk of the country stuck to subsistence farming. Plantations were developed for indigo, sugar, jute, and tea. These items made a significant contribution to exports, but in the context of Indian agriculture as a whole, were not very important. In 1946, the two primary export items, tea and jute, were less than 3.5 per cent of gross value of Indian crop output. Thus the enlargement of markets through international trade was less of a stimulus in India than in other Asian countries such as Burma, Ceylon, Indonesia, or Thailand.

There was some transfer of crops from the Americas to India. Tobacco arrived after 1600. Its cultivation developed rather quickly and extensively. Maize was introduced in the seventeenth century, but was not widely diffused. There was more enthusiasm for pineapples, which arrived at the same time.

Under British rule, the India remained subject to recurrent famines and epidemic disease. In 1876–8 and 1899–1900 famine killed millions of people. In the 1890s there was a widespread outbreak of bubonic plague and in 1919 a great influenza epidemic.

In the 1920s and 1930s there were no famines, and the 1944 famine in Bengal was due to war conditions and transport difficulties rather than crop failure. However, the greater stability after 1920 may have been partly due to a lucky break in the weather.

The British Impact on Indian Industry.   Although European contact with India was quite extensive from 1500, there was little transfer of European technology before the nineteenth century. European companies in India were not directly involved in productive activity in the pre-colonial period. Their orders for Indian goods went through Indian merchants and brokers, so they had little influence on techniques of production (see Habib 1978–9 and Qaisar 1982). Education in India was confined to a narrow group. It was religious, not secular, for both Muslims and Hindus, so there was little chance of acquiring new technical knowledge through reading.

The Jesuits brought a printing press to Goa and started operating it in 1556. They presented a polyglot bible to the emperor Akbar in 1580, but did not succeed in arousing much curiosity. The English East India Company brought a printer to Surat in 1675, but he was not able to cast type in Indian scripts, so the venture failed. Printing was not considered seriously by the aristocratic patrons of Indian scribes and manuscript illuminators.

There was an interest in European handguns, muskets, and artillery. Indian rulers employed European technicians in this field, and Indian artisans were quite adept in copying and developing many items. However, Indian troops seldom acquired weaponry equivalent to the European. Their gunsmiths did not succeed in casting iron suitable for artillery pieces, which continued to be cast in bronze.

The Portuguese built ships of European design in India for sale to local merchants. The British built ships in Surat for use by the East India Company, and English ship's carpenters seem to have transmitted their knowledge to Indian artisans. However, they had little serious impact on traditional Indian ship design. India already had astrolabes and other navigational devices, and made little attempt to copy European instruments.

Land transport was unaffected by European technology before the introduction of railways. Bullocks remained the basic draught animal. Horses were not used for carts and carriages. India did not replicate the horse harness developed in Europe in the tenth century, and, in China, much earlier. The wheelbarrow had been invented in China in the third century and in the twelfth in Europe, but long after the contact with Europe, India continued to move loads by head or hod. The Indian glass industry seems to have been immune to European technology. India made no attempt to replicate European clocks. Lanterns, mirrors, telescopes, and eyeglasses were 'foreign curiosities and rarities', not produced in India.

Moghul India had a bigger industry than any other country which became a European colony, and was unique in being an industrial exporter in pre-colonial times. A large part of this industry was destroyed as a consequence of British rule.

Between 1757 and 1857 the British wiped out the Moghul court, and eliminated three-quarters of the aristocracy (except those in princely states). They also eliminated more than half of the local zamindars and in their place established a bureaucracy with European tastes. The new rulers wore European clothes and shoes, drank imported beer, wines and spirits, and used European weapons. Their tastes were mimicked by the male members of the new Indian 'middle class' who acted as their clerks and intermediaries. As a result of these political and social changes, about three-quarters of the domestic demand for luxury handicrafts was destroyed. This was a shattering blow to manufacturers of fine muslins, jewellery, luxury clothing and footwear, decorative swords, and weapons. My own guess is that the home market for these goods was about 5 per cent of Moghul national income.

The second blow came from massive imports of cheap textiles from England after the Napoleonic wars. Home spinning, which was a part-time activity of village women, was greatly reduced. A significant proportion of demand for village hand loom weavers must also have been displaced, though many switched to using factory instead of home spun yarn.

Modern cotton mills were started in Bombay in 1851, preceding those in Japan by 20 years and China by 40. Production was concentrated on coarse yarns which were sold domestically and to China and Japan. Exports were half of output. India began to suffer from Japanese competition in the 1890s. Exports to Japan were practically eliminated by 1898. Shortly after, Japanese factories in China began to reduce India's market there. By the end of the 1930s, Indian exports of yarn to China and Japan had disappeared, piece goods exports had fallen off, and India imported both yarn and piece goods from China and Japan.

If the British had been willing to give tariff protection, India could have copied Lancashire's textile technology more quickly. Instead British imports entered India duty free. By the 1920s when Indian textile imports were coming mainly from Japan, British policy changed. By 1934 the tariff on cotton cloth had been raised to 50 per cent with a margin of preference for British products. As a result there was a considerable substitution of local textiles for imports. In 1896 Indian mills supplied only 8 per cent of Indian cloth consumption, 20 per cent in 1913 and 76 per cent in 1945. By the latter date there were no imports of piece goods.

Modern jute manufacturing started in 1854 and the industry expanded rapidly in the vicinity of Calcutta. It was largely in the hands of foreigners (mainly Scots). Between 1879 and 1913 the number of jute spindles rose ten-fold—much faster than growth in the cotton textile industry. Most of the jute output was for export.

Coal mining, mainly in Bengal, was another industry which achieved significance. Its output, which by 1914 had reached 15.7 million tons, largely met the demands of the Indian railways.

In 1911 the first Indian steel mill was built by the Tata Company at Jamshedpur in Bihar. The Indian industry started 15 years later than in China, where the first mill was built at Hangyang in 1896. The first Japanese mill was built in 1898. In both

China and Japan the first steel mills (and the first textile mills) were government enterprises.

Indian firms in industry, insurance, and banking were given a boost from 1905 onwards by the *swadeshi* movement, which was a nationalist boycott of British goods in favour of Indian enterprise. During the First World War, lack of British imports strengthened the hold of Indian firms on the home markets for textiles and steel. After the war, under nationalist pressure, the government started to favour Indian enterprise in its purchase of stores and it agreed to create a tariff commission in 1921 which started raising tariffs for protective reasons.

Many of the most lucrative commercial, financial, business, and plantation jobs in the modern sector were occupied by foreigners. Long after the East India Company's legally enforced monopoly privileges were ended, the British continued to exercise effective dominance through their control of the banking sector. In 1913, foreign banks held over three-quarters of total deposits, Indian Joint Stock Banks less than one-fourth. In the eighteenth century there had been very powerful Indian banking houses (dominated by the Jagath Seths) which handled revenue remittances and advances for the Moghul empire, the Nawab of Bengal, the East India Company, other foreign companies, and Indian traders, and which also carried out arbitrage between Indian currency of different areas and vintages. These indigenous banking houses were largely pushed out by the British.

The system of 'managing agencies', originally set up by former employees of the East India Company, was used to manage industrial enterprises and to handle most international trade. They were closely linked to British banks, insurance and shipping companies. Managing agencies had a quasi-monopoly in access to capital, and they had interlocking directorships which gave them control over supplies and markets. They dominated the foreign markets in Asia. They had better access to government officials than did Indians. The agencies were in many ways able to take decisions favourable to their own interests rather than those of shareholders. They were paid commissions based on gross profits or total sales and were often agents for the raw materials used by the companies they managed. Thus the Indian capitalists who did emerge were highly dependent on British commercial capital and many sectors of industry were dominated by British firms, e.g., shipping, banking, insurance, coal, plantation crops, and jute.

Indian industrial efficiency was hampered by the British administration's neglect of technical education, and the reluctance of British firms and managing agencies to provide training or managerial experience to Indians. Even in the Bombay textile industry, where most of the capital was Indian, 28 per cent of the managerial and supervisory staff were British in 1925 and the British component was even bigger in more complex industries. This raised production costs. At lower levels there was widespread use of jobbers for hiring workers and maintaining discipline. Workers were generally unskilled and had to bribe the jobbers to get and retain their jobs. There were also problems of race, language, and caste distinctions between management, supervisors, and workers. The small size and very diversified output of the enterprises hindered efficiency. It is partly for these reasons (and the overvaluation of the currency) that Indian exports had difficulty in competing with Japan.

It is interesting to speculate on India's fate if it had not had two centuries of British rule. There are three major alternatives which can be seriously considered. One would have been the maintenance of indigenous rule with a few foreign enclaves, as in China. Given the fissiparous forces in Indian society, it is likely that there would have been major civil wars and the country would probably have split up. Without direct foreign interference with its educational system, India would probably not have developed a modernizing intelligentsia because Indian society was deeply conservative, and it did not have a homogeneous civilization around which to build its reactive nationalism. If this situation had prevailed, population would certainly have grown less but the average standard of living might possibly have been a little higher because of the bigger upper class, and the smaller drain of resources abroad. Another alternative to British rule would have been conquest and maintenance of power by another west European country such as France or Holland. This probably would not have produced results very different in economic terms from British rule. The third hypothesis is perhaps the most intriguing, i.e., conquest by a European power, with earlier accession to independence. If India had had self-government from the 1880s, after a century and a quarter of British rule, it is likely that both income and population growth would have been accelerated. There would have been a smaller drain of funds abroad, greater tariff protection, more state enterprise, and favours to local industry, more technical training—the sort of things which happened after 1947. However, India would probably not have fared as well as Meiji Japan, because the fiscal leverage of government would have been smaller, zeal for mass education less, and religious and caste barriers would have remained as important constraints on productivity.[4]

Independent India. British colonialism in India came to an end in 1947. In spite of partition and the splitting off of Pakistan, the transition to independence was relatively smooth and amicable. The whole period since 1947 has been one of political stability, by the standards of other Asian countries. The nationalist movement was an alliance of three elements: (a) a well-organized bourgeois nationalist group which had been preparing for independence since 1885. Its members accepted western values and many of the changes in the social system brought by colonialism; (b) Nehru brought a mild version of socialism into the movement and exaggerated hopes for economic planning and state industry; (c) the indigenist element was captured by the saint politician Mahatma Gandhi, who emphasized the virtues of handloom weaving and the holy attributes of self-sufficiency He was willing to cooperate with the westernizers and the socialists in the congress party and persuaded them to adopt non-violent political action.

The combination of Nehru's planned economy and Gandhian pressures in favour of self-sufficiency dampened economic growth for a long period, broken in 1991 by the emergence of Manmohan Singh as finance minister. The subsequent freeing up of the economy accelerated economic growth, and has helped to make India one of the most dynamic economies in Asia.

Manmohan Singh is now prime minister of India and gave a favourable appreciation of the long term political and cultural consequences of interaction with the UK:

Today, with the balance and perspective offered by the passage of time and the benefit of hindsight, it is possible for an Indian Prime Minister to assert that India's experience with Britain had its beneficial consequences too. Our notions of the rule of law, of a Constitutional government, of a free press, of a professional civil service, of modern universities and research laboratories have all been fashioned in the crucible where an age old civilization met the dominant Empire of the day. These are all elements which we still value and cherish. Our judiciary, our legal system, our bureaucracy and our police are all great institutions, derived from British-Indian administration and they have served the country well. Of all the legacies of the Raj, none is more important than the English language and the modern school system. (Singh 2005)

The Dutch Impact in Indonesia

The Portuguese were the first Europeans to make direct contact with Indonesia. Albuquerque captured the strategic port of Malacca on the west coast of Malaya facing Sumatra in 1511. It dominated the narrow straits which linked the trading worlds of the Indian Ocean and the China seas and was the main emporium for trade between them.

At that time there was no central power in Indonesia. Sumatra had once been the seat of the Srivijaya empire, which had long disappeared. It was now divided into a number of petty islamicised states. The Hindu kingdom of Majapahit was on its last legs in eastern Java and most of the Javanese coastal trading areas were controlled by Muslim rulers.

The spices of the Moluccas (Ternate, Tidore, Makian, Moti, and Bacan), the Banda islands, Ceram, and Ambon. were the main commercial attraction. Most of these were small volcanic islands and had a world monopoly of cloves, nutmeg, and mace. Their high-value products were sold in Asia and exported in small but growing quantity to Europe from 1400 by Arab traders via Egypt. Reid (1993: 14) suggests that spice exports to Europe increased about fourfold between 1400 and 1500, fell sharply around 1500 due to Ottoman restrictions on trade via Egypt, then rose to about five times their previous peak around 1600.

The Portuguese established a fortified base in Ternate in 1522 and in 1529 bought out the Spanish, who had an outpost in Tidore. They were able to restore and enlarge the flow of spices to Europe, but were forced out of Ternate in 1575 by a native revolt.

The first four Dutch ships arrived at Bantam on the western tip of Java in June 1596. They invited the local merchants aboard—'a multitude of Javanese and other nations as Turks, Chinese, Bengali, Arabs, Persians, Gujarati, and others—each

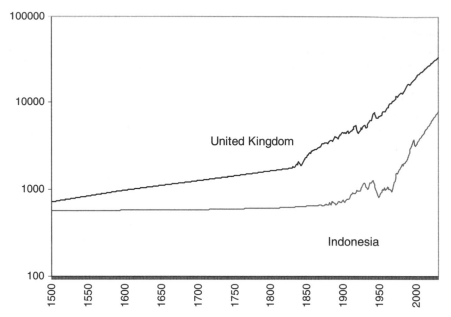

Figure 3.2. Comparative levels of Indonesia/UK GDP per capita, 1500–2030 (1990 international dollars)

nation took a spot on the ships where they displayed their goods, the same as if it were on a market' (van Leur 1955: 3).

The Dutch were sufficiently impressed by the potential for Asian trade that they set up a joint stock company, the VOC in 1602, with a monopoly in Asian markets. At that time Portugal had been annexed by Spain. The Dutch were at war with Spain in Europe and particularly eager to end the Iberian presence in Indonesia. They were able to do this rather quickly, though they did not capture Malacca until 1641. They established their Asian headquarters at Batavia near Bantam in 1619.[5] Then they took aggressive action against indigenous traders and their Portuguese, Spanish, and English competitors. In 1621, they killed or enslaved almost all the nutmeg producers of the Banda islands and replaced them by Dutch planters and slave workers who delivered their whole crop to the VOC. In 1623, the chief factor of the English East India Company at Ambon and 20 of his associates were beheaded.

At the beginning of the seventeenth century, three-quarters of Dutch exports from Asia consisted of spices and pepper. Here the profit margin was particularly high because they had cornered the market. They expanded pepper production in Java and Sumatra in competition with India. In the peak year, 1670, they shipped more than 4,000 tons of black pepper, and 60 tons of white pepper to the Netherlands (Glamann 1981: 83). By the end of the seventeenth century, the relative importance of spices and pepper had fallen.[6] The biggest items exported to Europe were silk and cotton goods from China and India for which demand was more elastic. Dutch earnings from intra-Asian trade had become important because of their privileged position in

Japan. The Dutch introduced sugar production to Java in 1637. They found it difficult to compete with producers in Brazil and the Caribbean but found a limited market in Asia. They introduced coffee production at the end of the seventeenth century.

When the Dutch arrived in Java there were important sultanates in Bantam and Cheribon. The central Javan kingdom of Mataram had emerged, but none of these had the anything like the authority of the rulers of China, India, or Japan. Their administrative and military organization was weaker, inland communications were poorer, and the institutional arrangements by which the ruling class squeezed a surplus from the population were more feeble. However, there was a variety of debt-bondage and other forms of dependency which local rulers were able to impose. The economy was much less urbanized and monetized than that of India, China, or Japan. Fiscal levies were in kind or labour service rather than land tax. Within villages, the control mechanisms for extracting tribute were weaker than in the caste-bound Indian villages with their clearer hierarchy and more powerful religious sanctions. The volcanic soil was very fertile in Java and at that time land was relatively abundant. As a consequence, peasants probably worked less than in India. They found it easier to migrate within Indonesia or to overthrow rulers who imposed too great a squeeze.

In the seventeenth and eighteenth centuries the Dutch had a fairly marginal impact on the Indonesian economy and its native rulers. Their income was derived by capturing the income from trade previously enjoyed by the Portuguese and Asian trading communities. When they arrived, slavery existed on a limited scale. It was legalized by a Dutch ordinance issued in 1622 and not abolished until 1860. In 1673, about half the population of their headquarters in Batavia were slaves. Later it seems that the incidence of slavery declined in favour of other types of forced labour (see Reid 1983).

The VOC was dissolved in 1800. In 1801 the Indies became a Dutch colony, and there were significant moves towards the creation of a territorial empire. Control from Batavia was reinforced, the separate governorships in Semarang and the sultanates of Bantam and Cheribon were abolished. The status of Dutch representatives at the successor states to Mataram (Jogjakarta and Soerakarta) was strengthened. In 1810, the Netherlands was occupied by France, and the Indies came under British administration. The British appointed Raffles as Lieutenant-Governor. He continued to westernize the administration and introduced legislation for land taxation. In 1817, he published his two volume *History of Java*, a remarkable statistical survey and guide to its economic potential:

The soil of Java is remarkable for the abundance and variety of its production. With very little care or exertion on the part of the cultivator it produces all the fruits of a tropical climate: while in many districts, its mountains and eminences make up for the difference of latitude, and give it all the advantages of temperate regions. Rice, the great staple of subsistence gives a return of thirty, forty, or fifty fold. Such is the fertility of the soil, that in some places after yielding two, and sometimes three crops in the year, it is not even necessary to change the culture. Water, which is so much wanted, and which is seldom found in requisite abundance in tropical regions, here flows with the greatest plenty (pp. 107–8).

Table 3.11a. Indonesian Population and Real Income by Ethnic Group, 1700–1929 (per capita income in 1928 guilders)

	Indigenous		Chinese & other Asian		Europeans*		Total	
	pop. (000s)	per cap income	pop. (000s)	per cap income	pop. (000s)	per cap income	pop. (000s)	per cap income
1700	13,015	47	80	156	7.5	1,245	13,103	48.4
1820	17,829	49	90	193	8.3	2,339	17,927	50.8
1870	28,594	50	279	187	49.0	2,163	28,922	54.9
1913	49,066	64	739	240	129.0	3,389	49,934	76.2
1929	58,297	78	1,334	301	232.0	4,017	59,863	98.2

Note: *includes Eurasians.

Source: Maddison (2001: 87). Real income refers to net domestic product.

The Java war (1825–30) was the last resistance of the Javanese aristocracy to Dutch rule. The revolt was led by Diponegoro, the eldest son of the sultan of Yogyakarta. It involved bitter guerrilla fighting in which 200,000 Javanese perished directly or indirectly. After this, the Dutch abandoned the westernization of property rights and land taxation which Raffles had envisaged. They adopted a policy of dual administration, retaining traditional rulers, law and custom as major instruments of their rule. There were two phases of Dutch policy after 1830. Both involved intensive development of tropical crops for export.

Phase 1: the Cultivation System, 1830–70. The first phase, from 1830 to 1870, was the so-called 'Cultivation System' (*cultuurstelsel*) where claims on indigenous income were exercised by forced deliveries of crops or compulsory labour service. To prevent evasion or flight, the movement and residence of the indigenous and Chinese populations were controlled. From 1816 onwards, pass-laws were imposed to maintain labour discipline and enforce ethnic *apartheid*. The Dutch maintained a government export monopoly, fearing that most of the profits would have gone to British or other foreign merchants under an open-trade regime. Export prices for sugar and coffee rose after the abolition of the African slave trade in the 1830s which ruined their competitors in the Caribbean. Indonesian GDP per capita rose very little

Table 3.11b. Indonesian Real Income and Shares of Each Ethnic Group, 1700–1929

	Total income (mill. 1928 guilders)	Indigenous share (%)	Share of Chinese & other Asiatics	European Share
1700	633.5	96.7	1.9	1.4
1820	910.4	96.0	1.9	2.1
1870	1,587.9	90.0	3.3	6.7
1913	3,806.9	82.5	6.0	11.5
1929	5,880.6	77.4	6.8	15.8

Source: Maddison (2001: 87).

Table 3.12. Indonesian Commodity Exports at Constant (1928) Prices, 1830–1937 (000 guilders)

	1830	1870	1913	1928	1937
Sugar	995	21,747	217,848	375,796	167,372
Tea		3,140	37,430	98,210	94,062
Cinchona		2	5,561	4,866	128,235
Rubber		0	8,497	278,050	522,605
Palmoil		0	15	9,197	62,725
Coffee	13,824	61,121	20,450	80,935	69,862
Tobacco	359	11,930	119,383	95,823	66,689
Copra		n.a.	49,776	106,490	117,003
Pepper		n.a.	27,618	42,870	54,957
Maize		n.a.	3,962	12,950	17,241
Cassava		n.a.	3,563	33,775	85,670
Petroleum		0	24,720	108,482	187,625
Tin		17,688	74,088	96,555	108,440
Other	11,949	53,813	102,795	233,027	291,719
Total	**27,127**	**169,441**	**695,706**	**1,577,026**	**1,974,205**

Source: Maddison (1989: 666–7), derived from Creuzberg (1976).

from 1820 to 1870, but the Dutch share of GDP rose from 2 to nearly 7 per cent and the number of resident Dutch nationals rose nearly six-fold. Half of government revenue in Indonesia was remitted to the Netherlands and the Dutch King received income from his monopoly in shipping export crops. The government dominated production of sugar and coffee and sold monopoly franchises to opium-dealers, but most of the tobacco crop was in private hands. Favoured individuals were subsidized to create sugar processing factories.

There were ample opportunities for corruption amongst the 76 local regents and heads of the 34,000 villages of Java. This was not part of the drain from Indonesia, but strengthened class differentiation within the indigenous population. Traditional levies of tribute on village society were reinforced by more efficient Dutch bureaucratic techniques.

Phase 2: The Plantation Economy, 1870–1929. From 1848, when the Netherlands acquired a more democratic political system, there was growing criticism of exploitative practices and bureaucratic cronyism in Indonesia. In 1870, the opening of the Suez Canal and the development of steam shipping made it clear that Indonesian potential was not being fully used, and the Dutch authorities decided to open the colony to private enterprise and investment. Thereafter there was a considerable acceleration of economic growth, with extension of political control and economic development to Sumatra, Borneo, the Celebes, and the lesser Sundas.

From 1870, as private enterprise established itself in plantation agriculture on a commercial basis, costs and benefits were assessed more rationally and agronomic research helped to raise yields, particularly for sugar. Europeans were allowed to acquire heritable leaseholds for plantations for a 75-year period, and the size of the

Table 3.13. Indonesian Export Growth and Export Surpluses, 1698–1930

	Commodity exports as per cent of Indonesian net domestic product	Indonesian export surplus as per cent of Indonesian net domestic product	Indonesian export surplus as per cent of Dutch net domestic product
1698–1700	1.8	0.7	1.1
1778–80	1.7	0.9	1.7
1868–72	18.4	7.4	5.5
1911–15	21.9	7.6	8.7
1926–30	29.4	10.3	8.9

Source: Maddison (1989: 646–7).

Dutch community grew very fast. In 1870, the government had been responsible for 55 per cent of export crop production; by the early 1890s this had dropped to zero. From the turn of the century, there was a rapid development of new export commodities (petroleum, rubber, and tin) from Sumatra. By then, it had been fully incorporated into the Dutch East Indies. The British ceded their claims in Sumatra against those of the Dutch in the Gold Coast (Ghana) and the costly 30-year war between the Dutch and the Acehnese was ended. There was substantial foreign investment (mainly Dutch) in Indonesia. It was higher on a per capita basis than in other Asian countries, except Malaya and Korea (see Table 3.14).

From 1870 to 1937, Indonesian per capita product rose more than three-quarters and per capita exports grew five-fold. Per capita income of the indigenous population rose by about half, due in part to more intensive labour input. The average per capita income of the Chinese community (whose contribution to small-scale

Table 3.14. The Net Foreign Capital Position of Asian Countries in 1938

	Million US $	Per capita US $
Burma	187	12
Ceylon	104	21
China	1,787	3
India	3,441	11
Indochina	391	17
Indonesia	2,371	35
Japan (1932)	637	10
Korea (1941)	1,718	73
Malaya	695	164
Philippines	279	18
Taiwan	201	31
Thailand	200	14

Notes and Source: Maddison (1990: 369). Japan from Allen and Don-nithorne (1954: 264), converted from yen to dollars. China includes Manchuria. See also van der Eng (1998: 309), who shows that capital invested in Indonesia was about half of Dutch foreign assets in 1938.

Table 3.15. The Dimensions of Foreign Presence in Asia, 1929–41

	Number of persons	Percent of population
Dutch colony		
Indonesia (1930)	240,162	0.40
British colonies		
Burma (1931)	34,000	0.23
Ceylon (1929)	7,500	0.15
India (1931)	168,134	0.05
Malaya (1931)	33,811	0.77
French colony		
Indochina (1937)	42,345	0.18
Japanese colonies		
Korea (1930–35)	573,000	2.62
Taiwan (1930)	228,000	4.96
Manchukuo (1941)	1,200,000	2.80
US colony		
Philippines (1939)	36,000	0.15
China	267,000	0.06

Notes and Sources: Maddison (1990: 363), and Maddison (1998: 52). Includes Eurasians in Indonesia (134,000); Malaya (16,043); and Indochina (approx. 14,000). The Philippine figure includes 10,500 Japanese, but excludes US military personnel and 200,000 Hispano-Filipino mestizos. There were 9,700 foreigners resident in Japan in 1935.

entrepreneurship was an important component of growth) rose about 60 per cent. The biggest gains were made by the resident Dutch community whose average per capita income doubled to a level 50 times that of the indigenous population. Their share of domestic product rose from around 7 to nearly 16 per cent.

There was also a growth in remittances to the Netherlands. These represented profits from foreign investment and efficiency in production and marketing. In the *cultuurstelsel* period they had represented plunder.

At the end of the colonial period the Dutch presence in Indonesia was proportionately higher than in any of the European colonies in Asia, except Malaya (see Table 3.15). It was eight times bigger relative to population than the British presence in India. The number of European army personnel was about the same proportionately, but the number of Europeans in the civil administration was nearly 15 times higher than in India. The Dutch presence in the private sector (particularly in mining and plantations) was also much bigger. They also had a higher tendency to settle as families, with a higher proportion born in Indonesia.

The 'Ethical' Policy. At the end of the nineteenth century there was extensive discussion in the Netherlands of the exploitative character of the colonial regime and the government embarked on a so-called 'ethical' policy in 1900 which in theory was intended to raise native welfare. The authorities were all the more willing to increase their spending and tighten surveillance of their allies in the native administration, as there had just been a major colonial war in Sumatra and there was an increasing need to deal with nationalist political activity.

The main impact of the policy was to increase the size and pay scales of the existing bureaucracy, to add new specialist technical services, and to raise government investment. A good deal of this investment went on irrigation works whose benefits flowed mainly to western sugar plantations. Until 1932 the government maintained a 'coolie' ordinance which bolstered the supply of cheap labour to plantations (mainly in Sumatra) and enforced penal sanctions on runaway workers. Levels of spending on social services and education for the indigenous inhabitants remained abysmally low. In 1930, according to the census, only 6.4 per cent of the indigenous population were literate, and only 0.32 per cent in the Dutch language.

The Dutch managed to integrate the enfeebled remnant of the native ruling class into their bureaucratic system by running a dual administration with European officials in the '*Europees bestuur*' and a parallel native administration '*Inlands bestuur*' composed almost exclusively of indigenous aristocrats and their cronies lower down the scale. Control was exercised by the thick layer of European officials who spent a good deal of time as watchdogs over a native administration whose ostensible dignity and regalia camouflaged their basic role as Dutch puppets. Native states had 20.6 per cent of the population in 1930 compared with 24.2 per cent in the Indian native states. They had more autonomy, their rulers had bigger incomes and maintained separate armed forces.

Independent Indonesia.   The Indonesian transition to independence was much less smooth than that in India and had very adverse economic consequences. The Japanese invaded in March 1942. Dutch forces capitulated quickly, and all Dutch nationals were interned. Japan took over and took steps to encourage collaboration. The indigenous nobility and officials who had been auxiliaries of the Dutch were given authority to take over Dutch administrative tasks. However, their prestige and political influence were greatly reduced by Japanese support for two other groups which had no role in the Dutch mode of governance. A new body, the Masjumi, was created to reconcile the Muslim population and give them some share in decision-making. Soekarno (1901–70) and Hatta (1902–80) leaders of the nationalist party (PNI, founded in 1927) imprisoned by the Dutch, were released to create a mass movement endorsing the Japanese take-over. The latter group were the biggest gainers. After the Japanese surrender in August 1945, Soekarno declared independence, with himself as president and Hatta as vice president. Until 1959, the political regime was a parliamentary democracy, with three major parties participating in the political process.

The Dutch intervened militarily to try to re-establish colonial rule, met with strong resistance and withdrew in December 1949, reluctantly acknowledging Indonesian independence. In 1959 Soekarno abolished the parliamentary system in favour of 'guided democracy'. He became the supreme leader, with support from the army and from the communist party. He devoted most of his energies to an assertive foreign policy to raise the international status of the country. He was a leading figure, together with Nehru, Nasser, Tito, and Chou en-lai, in creating the non-aligned movement and hosted the preparatory meeting in Bandung in 1955. The movement was intended to keep the third world neutral in the east-west conflict, but Soekarno took a position against many western interests, and drifted into dependence on the USSR for military supplies.

In 1957, the government confiscated all Dutch property in Indonesia. In 1962, the remaining Dutch colony in western New Guinea was seized and incorporated as Irian Jaya. In 1963, Soekarno made a strong stance against the creation of Malaysia as a new state, and withdrew from the United Nations in protest. He was also vociferous in condemning US intervention in Vietnam. Finally, Soekarno was deposed by the army in 1967.

Soekarno paid no serious attention to the economy. His 'policies' harmed private enterprise within Indonesia and repelled foreign investment. In 1966, the budget deficit was 50 per cent of expenditure. Between 1957 and 1965, the cost of living index rose by more than 70 per cent a year. In 1967, per capita income was one quarter below the level in 1941. At that time about 16 per cent had gone to Dutch residents who had since departed. Nevertheless, ordinary Indonesians were worse off than they had been 26 years earlier.

General Suharto took over as president in 1967, and at least 40,000 of Soekarno's communist allies were massacred. Suharto's foreign minister, Adam Malik, took a pro-western stance and quickly reversed Soekarno's foreign policy. The Sultan of Yogyakarta (the most eminent aristocrat to have supported the independence movement) became minister of economics. He promoted private enterprise and foreign investment, compensated foreign enterprises whose assets had been seized, tried to balance the budget, reduce the inflation rate, and integrate the country into the world economy. As a result, foreign creditors agreed to a massive write-down of Indonesian foreign debt, followed by large inflows of foreign capital, particularly into the oil industry. Between 1967 and 1997, Indonesian per capita income almost quadrupled—rising by 4.7 per cent a year.

The Suharto regime came under severe pressure in mid-year 1997 as a consequence of the east Asian financial crisis which led to massive withdrawals of foreign short term capital. The crisis was most severe in Indonesia, where the exchange rate depreciated 55 per cent by December and output fell. The regime was further weakened by Suharto's health problems, discontent with his probable successor, and the dubious financial dealings of his family. He resigned in May 1998 and there have since been four presidents. By 2004 per capita income was barely one per cent higher than in 1997, but there were some signs of economic recovery.

Japan's Response to the West

The Japanese reaction to western contact was different from that of other Asian countries. It was more carefully monitored, controlled, and manipulated, and the

Table 3.16. Chinese Imports of Silver from Japan and the Philippines, 1550–1700 (metric tons)

	Shipments from Japan	Portuguese shipments via Macao	Shipments of Mexican silver via the Philippines	Total
1550–1600	1,280	380	584	2,244
1601–40	1,968	148	719	2,835
1641–85	1,586	0	108	1,694
1685–1700	41	0	137	178
Total 1550–1700	4,875	428	1,548	6,951

Notes and Source: von Glahn (1996: 140 and 232). From 1571, when the Spanish installed themselves in the Philippines, Mexican silver was shipped from Acapulco to Manila, but Spaniards played little part in the Manila–China trade. The overseas Chinese population of Manila acted as intermediaries for Chinese ships.

Japanese were much more interested in borrowing western technology. Japan remodelled its society and economy in 1868 in an attempt to catch up with the west economically and militarily. It had already demonstrated a capacity to remodel its society drastically at the end of the sixteenth century, and there was another drastic change after the second world war.

The first western contact occurred in 1543, when Portuguese sailors were shipwrecked on Tanegashima island, below the southernmost tip of Kyushu. They had firearms unknown in Japan. The potential of this new weaponry was quickly appreciated by the military who managed to copy the guns and manufacture them in Japan. They had an important effect in deciding the outcome of the Japanese civil wars which began in 1467 and ended in 1573. Japanese were also interested in Portuguese ships, maps, and navigation techniques. The technology and behaviour of these 'southern barbarians' were displayed most clearly on very large multi-panelled lacqueur screens, which were the major artistic innovation of the Momoyama period (1568–1603).

At this time, opportunities for Portuguese traders as intermediaries in Chinese–Japanese commerce were particularly favourable. The Chinese had severed trade relations with Japan, whose ships could only trade indirectly with China via Korea, the Ryukyu islands, and Vietnam. Enmity between the two countries was heightened by political changes in Japan. By the middle of the sixteenth century the Ashigawa shogunate—which had accepted tributary status in trade with China—was on its last legs. It was succeeded by three ruthless military dictators, Nobunaga (1573–82), Hideyoshi (1582–98), and then by Tokugawa Ieyasu who ruled Japan from 1598 to 1616, wiped out his potential enemies, and created a powerful new system of government.

These political developments occurred at the time Japan became a major silver producer. Rich deposits were discovered in the 1530s, and a new technology for extracting metal from low grade ores was widely diffused shortly after (see Innes 1980). By the end of the fifteenth century, China had abandoned its hugely inflated paper currency in favour of silver. The gold/silver price ratio was much more favourable there than in Japan. As China would not allow Japanese ships to enter its harbours, silver was shipped by Chinese smugglers and the Portuguese. Portuguese ships were able to bring Indonesian spices from Malacca to Macao, sell them in China, buy Chinese silks and gold, go from Macao to harbours in the south of Japan (first Hirado and then Nagasaki), sell these Chinese products, buy Japanese silver, sell it in Macao, and buy silk again for shipment to Japan.

Portuguese traders were soon followed by Jesuit missionaries. Francis Xavier was the first to arrive in 1549–51. They were very successful in making converts. Eventually, the number of Japanese Christians rose to about 300,000 (many more than the Jesuits converted in India or in China). In 1596, the Spanish authorities in Manila sent a mission of Franciscans to proselytize. The Japanese got the impression that Spain might want to take over Japan as it had the Philippines, and, on Hideyoshi's order, the Spanish missionaries and 19 of their Japanese converts were crucified at Nagasaki. From that point on, Japan became increasingly hostile to Portuguese missionary activity, and made contact with English and Dutch traders who were less intrusive and had no religious ambitions. Eventually Christianity became illegal. The Jesuits and Portuguese were expelled in 1638. The English had pulled out in 1623. Henceforth trade with the Japanese mainland was confined to Chinese and Dutch traders. Japanese were forbidden to build ocean-going vessels or to travel abroad. However, trade with Korea continued via the Japanese island of Tsushima, and trade with the Ryukyu islands (Okinawa) was organized by the Satsuma domain in southern Kyushu.

The Dutch were the only Europeans allowed to trade in Japan between 1639 and 1853. From 1641 they were confined to a small artificial island (Deshima) in the harbour of Nagasaki. The profitability of this trade faded at the end of the seventeenth century because rising costs led to a fall in silver production, and demand for Chinese silk and porcelain fell because of the growth of import-substituting industries in Japan. Although the importance of foreign trade fell, the small Dutch outpost was useful to Japan. In the course of their long stay in Japan, the Dutch stationed three very distinguished doctors in Deshima-Engelbert Kaempfer (1690–92), an adventurous German savant and scientist, C.P. Thunberg (1775–76), a distinguished Swedish botanist and Franz Philipp von Siebold (1823–29 and 1859–62), a German physician and naturalist. These scholars wrote books which were important sources of western knowledge about Japan, but the Dutch also had a significant impact in transmitting knowledge of European science and technology to Japan.

The Japanese did not have the cultural inhibitions against things foreign which existed in China and India. They had already adopted many things Chinese, and when they found anything better, they were willing to consider it seriously.

In the seventh century, Japan modelled its society, religion, literature, and institutions on those of Tang China. It created a national capital at Nara, on the model of the Tang capital, Chang-an. It adopted Chinese style Buddhism, and allowed its religious orders to acquire very substantial properties and income. It adopted Chinese ideograms, the kanji script, Chinese literary style, Chinese clothing fashions, the Chinese calendar, methods of measuring age and hours. There was already a substantial similarity in the crop-mix and food consumption, with a prevalence of rice agriculture, and much smaller consumption of meat and meat products than in Europe. There was greater land scarcity in Japan and China than in Europe or India, so the agriculture of both countries was very labour intensive.

However, Japanese economic performance remained inferior to Chinese until the end of the eighteenth century. Unlike China, Japan did not create a meritocratic bureaucracy and had no educated secular elite. Knowledge of printing was available almost as early as in China, but there was little printed matter except for Buddhist tallies and talismans. From 1185, the emperor was shunted aside, and effective governance of the country fell into the hands of a hereditary shogun and a decentralized military elite. As a result, property relations in agriculture had a closer resemblance to those of feudal Europe rather than China. The division of Japan into particularistic and competing feudal jurisdictions meant that farming and irrigation tended to develop defensively on hillsides. The manorial system also inhibited agricultural specialization and development of cash crops.

Japan also lagged in industry. Whilst the Chinese had switched from hemp to cotton clothing in the fourteenth century, the change did not come in Japan until the seventeenth. Japanese production of silk was small, and consumption depended on imports from China until the end of the seventeenth century. Shipping and mining technology remained inferior to that in China until the seventeenth century. Rural by-employments were slower to develop.

The old regime collapsed in 1598 after a century of civil war. The old capital, Kyoto was largely destroyed, a new order emerged from the wreckage, with a new capital in Edo (Tokyo). Ieyasu established the Togugawa shogunate in 1603, after serving Nobunaga, and Hideyoshi, who had developed some of the techniques of governance which he adopted. Hideyoshi carried out two cadastral surveys between 1582 and 1590. They assessed the productive capacity of land in terms of *koku* of rice equivalent (150kg, enough to provide subsistence for one person for a year). This *kokudaka* assessment was the basis on which shoguns subsequently allocated income to daimyo. The income initially represented about 40 per cent of the harvest.

Hideyoshi's cadastral survey also had an important impact on social organization and property rights. It marked a sharp departure from feudalism.

Under the new system, fields were recorded in the name of free cultivators (*hyakusho*) who tilled the land. Hyakusho families, furthermore, were grouped into villages (*mura*) which now became the standard fiscal and administrative units in the countryside…A line was drawn within Japanese society between the farming and non-farming populace…the basis was laid for the eventual perfection of a four-class social system wherein samurai, peasants, artisans and merchants were given separate legal identities (Hall 1971: 154–5).

The Togugawa Shogunate, 1603–1867. The effective ruler was a new type of Shogun, with much tighter control over a unified country. He and his leading retainers (*hatamoto*) occupied land which generated about a quarter of the country's rice revenue. The puppet emperor, the imperial household, and aristocracy in Kyoto had only

0.5 per cent. The Shinto and Buddhist temple authorities shared 1.5 per cent—a great deal less than they had previously enjoyed.[7] The rest of Japan was ruled by 270 hereditary lords (*daimyo*), whose administration was carried out by their warrior vassals (*samurai*) from castle towns. About a third of the rice revenue was allocated to relatively small (*fudai*) daimyo, and the rest to more powerful and more distant (*tozama*) lords—leading members of the military elite who had survived the civil war (see Hall and McClain 1991: 150–6). Some of the *tozama* daimyo had opposed Ieyasu in the decisive battle at Sekigahara in 1600. The biggest of these were Choshu in southern Honshu and the Satsuma in southern Kyushu. Ieyasu reduced the size of their holdings, rather than risking further conflict with domains which could muster a large force of samurai. They accepted the situation as they were autonomous within their own domains. However, under the *sankin-kotai* system, all daimyo were required to build residences (*yashiki*) in Edo where they kept their wives and children permanently as hostages for good behaviour. They themselves had to leave their domains every alternate year to reside with their retainers and family in Edo.

This system was an onerous obligation. Roberts (1998: 18) described its impact on the Tosa domain in southern Shikoku in the 1690s:

Tosa annually moved from 1.5 to 3 thousand people and their baggage the 500-mile trek over mountain, sea and coastal highway between home and great metropolis of Edo. In the spring of 1694, a time of Edo residence, the domain population statistics recorded 4,556 Tosa people in Edo. It can be said without exaggeration that well over half of Tosa's expenses were related to the costs of the alternate residence system.

Daimyo domains varied greatly in size. The Shogun's income was seven million *koku* (over a million tons). The minimum income of the smaller *daimyo* was 10,000 *koku* (1,500 metric tons) of rice, but 28 daimyo had annual incomes ranging from 100,000 to over a million *koku*. At the end of the Togugawa period, the largest were Kanazawa, Sendai, Satsuma, and Choshu (Craig 1961: 11; Reischauer and Fairbank 1958: 605). The daimyo sold part of their rice stipends to merchants for cash. Over time they became increasingly indebted to merchants and bankers who were concentrated in Osaka.

It was a system of checks and balances. It established a more-or-less secular state, where Confucian values were important, and internal peace was maintained on a lasting basis. Rural areas were completely demilitarized. Hideyoshi carried out a sword hunt in 1588, which disarmed all but the samurai, and after a period of gradual suppression of their production, the use of firearms was banned in 1615. The shogun held unchallenged hegemonial power after 1615 when he killed Hideyoshi's surviving relatives and destroyed their castle in Osaka. The daimyo and their *samurai* were compelled to live in a single castle town in each domain, destroy their smaller fortified settlements, and abandon their previous managerial role in agriculture. As compensation they received stipends in kind (rice) supplied by the peasantry in their domain. Daimyo had no fixed property rights in land and could not buy or sell it. The shogun could move them from one part of the country to another, confiscate, truncate, or augment their rice stipends in view of their behaviour (or intentions as determined by shogunal surveillance and espionage). Between 1601 and 1705, 'some 200 daimyo had been destroyed; 172 had been newly created, 200 had received increases in holdings; and 280 had their domains transferred' (Hall and McClain 1991: 150–1). The shogun's magistrates directly administered the biggest cities (Edo, Kyoto, Osaka, and some others), controlled foreign relations and the revenue from gold and silver mines.

The Impact on Agriculture. Under the new regime, the farm population were no longer servile households subjected to arbitrary claims to support feudal notables and military. Rice levies were large but more or less fixed and fell proportionately over time as output expanded. The ending of local warfare meant that it was safer to develop agricultural land in open plains. There was greater scope for land reclamation and increases in area under cultivation. This was particularly true in the previously underdeveloped Kanto plain surrounding the new capital Edo.

The dominant cultivation unit was about one hectare per family, but there was considerable inequality in villages with dominance of the local headman and his lieutenants. Only people on the land registers paid the land tax and could participate in the village assembly. Tenantry was significant, but tenants were social inferiors to landowners. Land tax was levied on the village as a whole, and the burden was distributed by the village assembly.

The termination of feudalism brought substantial social changes which led to accelerated population growth in the seventeenth century:

family formation became common, a population explosion was kindled, and the seventeenth century saw a baby boom in villages. Servants who spent their lifetimes unmarried gradually disappeared and the proportion married increased. A single household came to be composed of a single married couple and their lineal relations, and, as a result, mean household size decreased significantly. This phenomenon is clearly evident in village population registers from 1670. During the Tokugawa period, almost all of the arable land was cultivated, and only a few areas of level pasture and forest remained [Population growth also] sent large numbers of men and women into the abruptly created cities. (Hayami 1986: 3)

Printed handbooks of best practice agriculture started to appear on Chinese lines *Nogyo Zensho* (*Encyclopaedia of Farming*, 1697) was the earliest commercial publication, and by the early eighteenth century there were hundreds of such books (see Robertson 1984). Quick-ripening seeds and double cropping were introduced. There was increased use of commercial fertilizer (soybean meal, seaweed, etc.), and improvement in tools for threshing. There was a major expansion of commercial crops—cotton, tobacco, oil seeds, sugar (in south Kyushu and the Ryukyu islands), and a very substantial increase in silkworm cultivation. These changes in agricultural practice brought a significant increase in per capita labour input, and a substantial growth of rural industrial by-employment.

Some idea of the progress of agricultural production in Tokugawa Japan can be derived from the cadastral surveys. In 1598, total output was estimated to be 18.5 million *koku*. At the beginning of the eighteenth century, the total had risen to 26.1 million, more or less equivalent to the increase in population (see Hall 1991: 152). Nakamura (1968) made an estimate of cereal production for 1600 to 1872 which showed that cereal output per capita increased by a quarter over the Tokugawa period as a whole. In 1874, rice and other cereals were 72 per cent of the value of gross farm output. Other traditional products were 10.7 per cent, and relatively new crops (cotton, sugar, tobacco, oil seeds, silk cocoons, and potatoes) 17.2 per cent. Most of the latter were absent in 1600 and escaped taxation, so their production grew faster than cereals. If one assumes that these other items were about 5 per cent of output in 1600, this would imply a growth of total farm output per capita of about 40 per cent for the Tokugawa period as a whole. For the period before 1600 there is no real quantitative evidence, but it seems likely that there was little growth in agricultural output per head in the sixteenth century which was so severely plagued by civil war.

Interpreting the Eighteenth Century Demographic Slowdown. In the eighteenth century, there was a significant deceleration in Japanese population growth-less than 15 per cent from 1700 to 1820, after a 46 per cent increase from 1600 to 1700.[8] The older interpretation of this change was Malthusian and attributed the slowdown to increased mortality from famine and disease as a result of land scarcity.

The modern interpretation, based on village studies of fertility, mortality, and life expectation is very different. There were famines in the eighteenth and early nineteenth century, but the demographic slowdown seems to have been due to vol- untaristic checks—greater incidence of celibacy, birth control within marriage, and later marriage. There is evidence that the 1720s to the 1840s were characterized by low birth rates, death rates that fluctuated around the birth rate, and a life expectation (about 34 years at birth) near that in western Europe at that time (36 years) and much higher than in China and India (24 and 21 years—see Maddison 2001: 29–30). As a result the age structure was favourable to high labour inputs—60 per cent or more of the population were in the age group 15 to 64, two-thirds of the population were active, only one-third were dependents. The counterpart was an increased standard of living for the mass of the population—attributable to increases in cultivated area, yields, fertilizers, and tools, increased activity in industrial and service by- employment, increased commercialization, and specialization of the economy.

Urbanization. In 1600, 4.4 percent of Japanese lived in towns of 10,000 population or more. By 1800 more than 12.3 per cent lived in such cities. This change contrasted sharply with the situation in China where the ratio remained more or less stable at 4 per cent between 1500 and 1800.[9] The change in Japan was due in large part to Toku- gawa policy. Edo, which had been a village, became a city of a million inhabitants. About a quarter of these were daimyo relatives and dependents who were compelled to live there (see Smith 1986: 350). More than 200 castle towns were created, half of whose population were *samurai*. Most of these had not been cities before 1600. Kanazawa and Nagoya were the biggest castle towns, with a population over 100,000. Kyoto and Osaka both had populations over 300,000 in the mid-eighteenth century. Kyoto was the seat of the emperor and his court and the centre of a prosperous agricultural area. Osaka had become a large commercial metropolis. The three-fold increase in the urban proportion was due in part to the concentration of samurai in castle towns, and to the obligation on daimyo to maintain a second residence in Edo. But it also reflected an improvement in the standard of living.

The urban centres created a market for the surrounding agricultural areas. They also created a demand for servants, the service trades, entertainment, and theatres. Merchants ceased to be mere quartermasters for the military, and acted as commodity brokers, bankers, and moneylenders. They were active in promoting significant expansion of coastal trade, and shipping in the inland sea (see Crawcour 1963). Thus there was a large increase in many types of service activity per head of population.

Education and Interest in Western Knowledge. There was a substantial increase in levels of education, with an emphasis on secular neo-Confucian values rather than Buddhism. There was a huge increase in book production and circulation of woodblock prints. Between the eighth century and the beginning of the seventeenth century fewer than 100 illustrated books appeared in Japan but by the eighteenth century there were large editions of books with polychrome illustrations and 40 per cent literacy of the male population.

The Japanese had depended on Chinese books for knowledge of the west (e.g., Chinese translations of works by Matteo Ricci and other Jesuits in Peking), but in 1720 the shogun, Yoshimune, lifted the ban on European books. An important turning point occurred in 1771 when two Japanese doctors observed the dissection of a corpse and compared the body parts (lungs, kidneys, and intestines) with those described in a Chinese book and a Dutch anatomy text. The Dutch text corresponded to what they found. The Chinese text was inaccurate. As a result translations of Dutch learning (*rangaku*) became an important cultural influence. Although they were limited in quantity, they helped destroy Japanese respect for 'things Chinese', and accentuate curiosity about 'things western'. The Dutch window on the western world was influential in preparing the ground intellectually for the Meiji Restoration of 1868. Dutch learning (painfully acquired) was the major vehicle of enlightenment for Japan's greatest westernizer, Yukichi Fukuzawa (1832–1901), whose books sold millions of copies, and who founded Keio University on western lines.

Although the Tokugawa regime had a positive impact on growth, and helped Japan catch up and pull ahead of Chinese per capita GDP, it had serious drawbacks.

It involved the maintenance of a large elite (about 6 per cent of the population) whose effective military potential was very feeble in meeting the challenges which came in the nineteenth century, and whose lifestyle involved extremely lavish expenditure. Their consumption represented about a quarter of GDP. The Meiji regime was able to capture substantial resources for economic development and military modernization by dismantling these Tokugawa arrangements.

The system of hereditary privilege and big status differentials with virtually no meritocratic element, meant a large waste of potential talent. The frustrations involved are clearly illustrated in Fukuzawa's autobiography. The Tokugawa system was inefficient in its reliance on a clumsy collection of fiscal revenue in kind and over-detailed surveillance of economic activity. It also imposed restrictions on the diffusion of technology. The most important was the ban on wheeled vehicles on Japanese roads and the virtual absence of bridges. These restrictions were imposed for security reasons, but made journeys very costly and time consuming. There were restrictions on the size of boats which inhibited coastal shipping and naval preparedness. There were restrictions on property rights (buying and selling of land), arbitrary levies by the shogun, and debt defaults by daimyo and samurai which could push bankers and merchants into bankruptcy. The policy of seclusion, rebuffing all direct or diplomatic contact with the west, was due to security considerations, but was a serious constraint on the potential for economic growth.

The First Western Shock, 1853–69. The Tokugawa regime's policy of seclusion broke down as a result of western intrusion. In June 1853, Commander Perry of the US navy entered Tokyo Bay with four warships and a request from President Filmore to negotiate a treaty of amity and commerce. The regime hoped to shake off the Americans as it had done with earlier western attempts to penetrate Japanese ports. However, the presence of foreign warships was new and the Japanese knew that China had been opened up to trade by military and naval aggression in the opium war of 1842. The shogun's advisers realized that they must be cautious as their weaponry was no match against the westerners. They tried to procrastinate, but in March 1854 Perry returned with nine ships. The Shogunate agreed to a treaty which opened two ports to foreign ships for supplies and repairs. It made no provision for trade, but authorized the presence of an American consul general. Harris, the consul, arrived in 1856, and pushed for a more ambitious treaty. He pointed to the British and French attack on China (1858–60) as a further warning against non-compliance. A new treaty was signed in July 1858 which opened six ports to foreign trade, admitted American consuls to all the ports with extraterritorial privileges, and allowed only moderate import and export duties. Within a few weeks Japan was pressured to sign similar treaties with France, the Netherlands, Russia and the UK. They were on the same lines as the treaty the British had forced on China except that they made no provision for opium imports.

These treaties created major political problems for the Shogunate. There was loss of face for abandoning the policy of seclusion under foreign pressure. The Shogun's chief councillor circulated a copy of the 1853 American proposals to all daimyo and solicited their views on the nature of the Japanese response. In doing this he undermined the shogun's prerogative of determining foreign policy unilaterally. The answers showed there was a strong feeling in favour of continuing the exclusionist policy. Nevertheless, this first treaty was signed. When the more ambitious 1858 treaties came up, the new chief councillor, Ii Naosuke, sought the approval of the emperor. Normally, this would have been a formality, but the emperor, under pressure from the exclusionist faction, refused. Nevertheless, these treaties were also signed. In 1860, Ii was the victim of a well-organized assassination and the anti-Tokugawa movement gathered momentum. It was reinforced by the fact that the shogun had died in 1858, and was replaced by a 12-year-old.

In an attempt at conciliation, the Shogunate abandoned the *sankin kotai* requirement of dual residence in 1862, and the number of daimyo residing in Edo dropped precipitously. The two large *tozama* domains of Satsuma and Choshu encouraged the imperial court to restore the emperor as effective ruler. After a short struggle, the last Tokugawa Shogun Yoshinobu (who succeeded in 1866 and had already offered to resign) was overthrown in November 1867. The regime change was accomplished relatively smoothly without a civil war. The victors made no attempt to repudiate the 'unequal treaties'.

The new Emperor Meiji succeeded his father in February 1867 at the age of 14. He became head of state from January 1868. He was a symbol of Japanese tradition stretching back two thousand years. His family line was thought to be of divine origin. His legitimacy was never challenged, and he became the focus of a new kind of Japanese nationalism.

The Nature of the Meiji Reforms.　Japan responded to the western challenge with sweeping reforms which provided up-to-date western capitalist institutions, set it firmly on a path of accelerated economic growth and military strength. The change was drastic and effective.

The Meiji reforms abolished the Shogunate and the 270 daimyo domains. The emperor moved from Kyoto to Edo (renamed Tokyo) as head of a centralized state divided in 1871 into 46 prefectures. The samurai were replaced by a conscript army. The legal equality of different social classes was established and the old distinctions in dress and rights of samurai, peasants, artisans, and merchants were abolished. Westernization in dress and social habits was promoted and the pigtail hairstyle vanished. People were free to choose their trade or occupation, and could produce any crop or commodity. Private property was established in land which could now be sold freely. State taxes in cash replaced the old rice levies, and their incidence was equalized throughout the country. Internal tolls on the movement of goods and passport checkpoints for movement of people were abolished. Prohibitions on the export of rice, wheat, copper, and raw silk were jettisoned.

The stipends of the daimyo and samurai were commuted into state pensions and government bonds. The functions of the warrior class were replaced by modern armed forces conscripted on the basis of universal military service. The calendar was changed, mass vaccination was introduced, Buddhism was disestablished. A national monetary and banking system was set up. Agricultural and industrial development were promoted.

The leaders in this revolution and the most influential in the new government and military were from Choshu and Satsuma and the other southern domains (Tosa and Saga) most hostile to the Shogun. The new elite were backed financially by rich merchants and particularly by the House of Mitsui.

In general, the daimyo did not resist change. They no longer had the expense of maintaining a dual residence. They were released from liability for their huge debts, and received pensions for loss of office. In 1884, 507 members of daimyo families were admitted to a newly established peerage, along with 137 *kuge* families-members of the pre-Tokugawa aristocracy previously attached to the court in Kyoto (see Jansen and Rozman 1986: 85). Their pensions were commuted into bonds in 1876. The annual interest was only a third of the value of their rice stipends in 1867. Between 1876 and the end of the Meiji period, the price level doubled, which further reduced the real income from these bonds.

The samurai had to find jobs and the new state apparatus was their primary source of employment. The imperial, prefectural, and municipal governments were full of them, as were the police and armed forces. The government also tried to provide samurai with jobs in industry, but many were embittered and rallied to the brief Satsuma Rebellion of 1877.

Yamamura (1974: 119–20) described the problems of estimating samurai numbers in 1872 when commutation bonds were issued in lieu of their stipends which were then abolished. The total number of samurai and quasi-samurai considered for compensation was 426,000. Including family members, the total was 1.94 million—5.6 per cent of the population.[10]

The switch to fixed money taxes forced many small peasants to sell their land. The proportion of tenanted land rose from 31 per cent at the beginning of the Meiji period to 46 per cent at the end.

The role of government in the economy was much bigger than that in most European countries and the US. Its expenditure on goods and services rose to about 10 per cent of GNP in the 1880s. The administration carried out about 40 per cent of the capital formation in the economy, as well as providing large transfer payments to ex-samurai and daimyo and maintaining a high level of military expenditure.

A major priority was to build up human capital. The educational system was redesigned to produce modern skills. The alphabet was simplified to foster literacy. In 1886 four years of schooling were made compulsory, and in 1907 this was extended to six years. By the end of the Meiji period almost two-thirds of children were getting elementary schooling, and a fifth went to secondary schools. Modern universities were created. Higher technical schools were established for medicine, military science, navigation, commerce, and fisheries. Tokyo Imperial University was established to train civil servants and research institutions were set up. The government sent people to study in Europe and brought in foreigners to help set up a modern army, navy, legal system, public health service, police, and administration, as well as to modernize agriculture and industry. Official translations of foreign books and technical literature were sponsored.

The government developed advisory services to improve techniques of crop production and promoted consumption of meat, milk, milk products, and wool. In Tokugawa times, horses and cattle had been used only for transport and military purposes. The government imported foreign strains of cattle, horses, sheep, pigs, and poultry. They helped to diversify the Japanese diet and made an important contribution to traction power and manure. The government also sponsored literature on livestock farming and trained veterinarians.

At the beginning of the Meiji period, merchants had no experience in managing modern industrial establishments and were shy of becoming entrepreneurs. The government itself therefore started enterprises in a number of fields. It built some of the railway lines and guaranteed a financial return on others. It set up a cotton spinning mill, a silk reeling mill, an agricultural machinery plant, a cement works, a glass factory, a brick factory, and modern mines. Many were sold off to private business from the early 1880s onwards, though the government remained active in heavy industries connected with armaments.

Mitsubishi shipping interests were built up with continuous government help, so that by 1913 Japan had the world's sixth largest merchant marine. The increased earnings from shipping helped finance rapidly expanding imports. The steam tonnage of the mercantile marine rose from 26 thousand in 1873 to 1.5 million in 1913. The merchant fleet carried 57 per cent of her trade in 1914 and 80 per cent by 1919, when a surplus on invisible trade was achieved.

The government provided medium and long term finance to industry via a variety of specialized institutions. This was very important in a country without a capital market which deliberately avoided foreign direct investment. The Japan Industrial Bank (1902) provided credit to industry. A network of local Banks for Industry and Agriculture was created in the 46 prefectures. Savings banks, post office savings, and insurance companies were fostered, and the Yokohama Specie Bank (founded 1880) provided short term credits to finance Japanese exports.

In the modern sector of the economy, industrial activity was increasingly concentrated in the hands of a few large holding companies (*zaibatsu*), which had close political links with the government and combined industrial and banking activities. Many of the higher personnel of the zaibatsu had previously been civil servants.

The Japanese textile industry grew because of its comparative advantage in cheap female labour. The silk industry was the first to prosper from the opening up of the economy, as European production was badly hurt by silkworm disease in the 1860s. Raw silk was the biggest export of the Meiji period. At first, the cotton industry was badly hit by imports. From the 1890s onwards the position changed, the number of cotton spindles rose from 77,000 in 1887 to 2.4 million in 1913, imports of yarn and piece goods disappeared and Japan became an important exporter.

By 1868 Japan had moved to almost complete free trade. Some of the immediate consequences were disturbing. Her monetary system and the parity between gold and silver were different from those abroad, and she lost on this account. Foreign goods damaged several Japanese handicraft industries. However, she benefited greatly from foreign technology and capital goods. With good sea communications and very limited natural resources, Japan had more to gain from international specialization than most countries. Until the 1930s, it benefited from the fact that the vast markets of India and China were unprotected by significant tariff barriers or other trade restrictions. It was in these countries and her colonies that she first built up markets for manufactured exports.

In the early days, foreign traders with extra-territorial rights in Japan enjoyed monopoly profits. Many were British 'managing agencies' originally created in India. The Japanese copied this type of company. By the end of the Meiji period, their *zaibatsu* had built up powerful specialized trading houses with agents abroad who handled foreign sales and purchased imports. Thereafter, most Japanese firms concentrated on production, and left foreign marketing to specialized trading companies.

Japanese Imperialism. A major objective of military modernization was to increase Japan's international standing so that the unequal treaties would be abrogated and her national sovereignty respected. Her military successes did have the desired effect. In 1899 extraterritorial rights for foreign traders were terminated and in 1911 she regained full freedom to modify import duties. Having achieved this, Japan felt free to expand her colonial empire without western interference.

A major concern was Russian expansionism. In 1860, Russia had acquired 82 million hectares of former Chinese territory in eastern Siberia, including a large stretch of Pacific coast, and a frontier with Korea. Japan felt vulnerable to Russian penetration of its northern island Ezo (renamed Hokkaido by the Meiji regime), which was thinly inhabited. More than half of the 120,000 population in 1870 were indigenous Ainu, whose lifestyle resembled that of Eskimos in Alaska. Thanks to Japanese migration and resettlement of samurai, the population rose to 800,000 by 1900. A deal was made in 1875 to recognize Russian sovereignty in Sakhalin island in return for Russian recognition of Japanese sovereignty in the Kurile islands which stretched up to the Kamchatka peninsula.

The sovereignty of the Ryukyu islands (halfway between Japan and Taiwan) was ambiguous. They had been an important base for trading activity of the Satsuma domain in southern Kyushu for more than two centuries, and were considered a Satsuma tributary. China considered they were Chinese, but had little contact with them. In 1879, Japan made a formal claim of sovereignty which China rejected, but in 1882 they became the prefecture of Okinawa. In 1876, Japan made an uncontested claim to the Bonin (Ogasawara) and Kazan islands (Iwojima) about 1,300km east of Okinawa.

Japan's ambition was to make Korea a tributary state and open it to Japanese trade. This was not a new idea. Hideyoshi had tried to do it at the end of the sixteenth century. An 1869 attempt to establish diplomatic relations was unsuccessful, but in 1876, a large naval force succeeded in imposing a treaty opening the ports of Pusan, Inchon, and Wonsan to foreign trade. However, Korea remained a Chinese tributary and was increasingly subject to Russian influence. In 1894, the Japanese army invaded Korea, drove out the Chinese and crossed the Yalu river into China. They seized Port Arthur and Dairen on the northern Liaotung (Kwantung) coast of the Yellow Sea, and occupied Weihaiweh on the southern Shantung coast. At the same time the Japanese navy occupied the Pescadores islands between the Chinese mainland and Taiwan.

In the Treaty of Shimonoseki (1895) China was forced to recognize that its suzerainty over Korea had lapsed. Taiwan, the Pescadores, and the Liaotung peninsula were ceded to Japan. Chungking, Soochow, Hangchow, and Shasi were opened to Japan with treaty port status. Japanese citizens (and hence other foreigners) were now permitted to open factories and manufacture in China. Japan received an indemnity of 200 million taels, raised to 230 million when it agreed (under French, German, and Russian pressure) to withdraw from Liaotung. This was the biggest indemnity China had ever paid. It amounted to a third of Japanese GDP.

The Japanese victory sparked off an avalanche of foreign claims on China. In 1896, Russia got a narrow strip of land (1,700 km long) across Manchuria to build a new 'Chinese Eastern Railway' to Vladivostok (a shortcut that completed its Trans-Siberian railway). In 1897 it occupied Port Arthur and Dairen and obtained the right to build a 1,100 km. 'South Manchurian Railway' from Harbin to Port Arthur. In the same year, Germany got a naval base in Shantung. In 1898 Britain got a 99-year lease on 'new territories' to enlarge its base in Hong Kong, a lease on a port in Shantung and acknowledgement of its sphere of influence in the Yangtse area. The French got a lease on Kwangchow, opposite Hainan island, and a sphere of influence in the south China. The Japanese were granted a sphere of influence in Fukien opposite Taiwan.

In 1904–5, anxious for a free hand in Korea and southern Manchuria, Japan attacked Russia. Its army drove Russian troops out of Dairen, Port Arthur, southern Manchuria, and southern Sakhalin. The navy destroyed the Russian Pacific fleet in August 1904. Russia sent its larger Baltic fleet which arrived in August 1905. Most of its vessels were destroyed off Tsushima at the end of the month. The peace treaty of Portsmouth (New Hampshire) in September ceded south Sakhalin (Karafuto) to Japan, recognized its paramount political, military, and economic role in Korea, transferred ownership of the South Manchurian Railway to Japan, and, with the assent of China, ceded its lease of Port Arthur, Dairen, and the Kwantung peninsula to Japan. Korea became a Japanese colony in 1910.

In 1914, Japan sided with the allied powers, but was not involved actively in hostilities, suffered no physical damage or manpower losses. At no cost to itself it seized the German colony of Tsingtao in Shantung and the Micronesian islands (Marianas except Guam, the Caroline, and the Marshall islands). After the war, it received a League of Nations mandate to continue its rule in Micronesia, but was obliged to return Tsingtao to China.

The First World War was a great stimulus to produce industrial import substitutes for herself and for other Asian markets where goods were not available from the belligerent powers. Japan greatly increased her share of the textile market in China and India at Britain's expense. Shipping earnings prospered in a world where demand was high and normal supply lines greatly restricted. Japan paid off her foreign debt and its large payments surpluses led to accumulation of large exchange reserves.

In the early 1930s when world trade collapsed and discriminatory protectionist blocs emerged, Japan reacted by creating its own 'co-prosperity sphere' which incorporated Manchuria.

Manchuria slipped from Chinese control after the Ch'ing regime collapsed in 1911. In the 1920s it was ruled by the warlord Chang Tso-lin, a Japanese crony. After his assassination in 1928, Japan's Kwantung army occupied the capital at Mukden, and took control of Manchuria. Japan opened a second front in 1932, by attacking Shanghai, and as the price of withdrawal, obliged China to turn the area around Peking and Tientsin into a demilitarized zone, which left the north defenceless. In 1932 Japan set up a puppet state in Manchuria, adding the Inner Mongolian province of Jehol in 1933. In 1934 the former Chinese emperor, Pu-yi, was installed as emperor of Manchukuo, but the real power was exercised by the commander of the Kwantung army (300,000 strong). The Chinese government persuaded the League of Nations to condemn this action. Japan left the League, but no sanctions were imposed. In 1935, the USSR (which since 1916 had an alternative rail link to Vladivostok north of the Amur river) sold its Chinese Eastern Railway to Japan, and moved out of Manchukuo.

Japan made major investments in Manchurian coal, metalliferous mining, and manufacturing in the 1930s. Value added in modern manufacturing more than quadrupled between 1929 and 1941: in mining it trebled. By 1945, Manchuria was producing about half of modern manufacturing in China. Its GDP growth averaged 4.1 per cent a year from 1924 to 1941. Agriculture, forestry and fishery represented only about a third of GDP. In 1945 there were more than a million Japanese civilians in Manchukuo. This group consisted mainly of bureaucrats, technicians, administrative, managerial, and supervisory personnel. 10 per cent were in agriculture, about 45 per cent in industry, commerce and transport, and 26 per cent in public service.

Manchukuo was larger than Japan's other colonies. In 1941, it had a population of 45 million (area 1.3 million sq. km), compared with a Korean population of 24 million (area 221,000sq. km.), and Taiwan's 6 million (area 36,000 sq. km.). Karafuto was as big as Taiwan, but only 400,000 Japanese lived there. The Pacific mandated islands were tiny (2,000 sq. km) with an indigenous population of 40,000 and about 100,000 Japanese. The area of the Kwantung leased territory was 3,500 sq. km. Japan itself had a population of 74 million (area 382,000 sq. km).

Japanese colonialism was different from that of the western powers in Asia. There was a much bigger settlement of Japanese civilians, a much larger military and police control, bigger investment in industry (especially in Korea and Manchukuo). About 40 per cent of Japanese trade was with the empire and colonial development was closely linked to Japanese production plans. The impact of these investments was important for subsequent post-colonial development (see Table 3.17).

From 1913 to 1941, Japanese GDP grew by 4 per cent a year, and the *per capita* gap with the advanced capitalist countries was substantially narrowed. As can be seen

Table 3.17. Comparative Economic Performance of Japan and its Former Colonies, 1820–2003 (annual average compound growth of real GDP)

	1820–70	1870–1913	1913–41	1941–55	1955–90	1990–2003
Japan	0.4	2.4	4.0	1.1	6.6	1.1
Korea	0.1	1.0	3.7	0.0	8.0	5.6
Manchukuo	n.a.	n.a.	3.8a	n.a.	n.a.	n.a.
Taiwan	0.3	1.6	4.5	2.1	8.4	5.1
China	−0.4	0.6	0.7b	1.2c	5.3	8.6
India	0.4	0.8	0.4	1.3	4.1	5.7
Indonesia	1.1	2.0	2.5	−0.3	4.9	4.1
UK	2.1	1.9	1.7	0.8	2.8	2.3

Notes: a = 1924–41; b = 1913–38; c = 1938–55.

Sources: Manchukuo from Chao (1979: 258); other countries from Maddison (2003), updated.

from Table 3.17, its colonies also grew much faster than the Asian and world average in this period.

Expanded Imperial Ambitions, 1937–45. In July 1937, Japan attacked north China and took Peking and Tientsin. Nanking resisted, was taken in December and 100,000 Chinese civilians were massacred. Chinese government forces retreated to the deep southwest in Chungking. Japan occupied most of the big cities and most prosperous parts of the economy in east China. In 1940, it set up a puppet government in Nanking under Wang Ching-wei, a prominent Chinese defector. The situation in China remained like this until 1945.

Japan made a treaty of alliance with Germany in 1940 and soon after embarked on a whirlwind drive to expand its Asian empire at the expense of the European colonialists and the United States. Vietnam was occupied in September 1940. A pre-emptive strike in December 1941 destroyed part of the US Pacific fleet, airports, and port facilities in Pearl Harbor and temporarily crippled US naval power for two months. This enabled Japan to occupy Hong Kong, Malaya, Singapore, Burma, Indonesia, the Philippines, New Guinea, and the Solomon islands at very little cost to itself.

Defeat and Occupation, 1945–52. After a series of bitterly fought sea and air engagements, American forces started to push Japan out of the Solomons in August 1943. By mid-1945 they had retaken the Philippines, Okinawa, and the Marianas. They had the option of launching a conventional attack on Japan from Okinawa and losing perhaps half a million men, or striking with atomic weapons from the Marianas. They dropped atomic bombs on Hiroshima on 6 August and Nagasaki on the 9 August. Japan surrendered unconditionally on the 15 August. American troops occupied Japan peacefully, and General MacArthur assumed dictatorial powers until 1949.

The Peace Treaty was not signed until 1952. Japan lost all of its colonies, and did not recover Okinawa and the Marianas until 1968. Five million refugees came back from overseas. The armed forces were abolished. An American organized reform redistributed a third of the land. The big business groups (*zaibatsu*) were broken up (a move which was reversed after the occupation). There was a new constitution which reduced the status of the emperor and abolished the peerage.

The outbreak of the Korean war changed the situation in Japan's favour. The war itself was a stimulus to the economy. The US became interested in providing for the defence of Japan, and promoting its economic recovery. It became the most important ally of the US in Asia.

Japan was able to launch a process of unprecedentedly rapid economic growth in the 1950s. It was able to exploit opportunities of backwardness of two kinds: (a) recuperation from war and redeployment of resources for peaceful purposes; and (b) renewal of the effort to catch-up with the advanced capitalist countries which it had started in 1868.

Reasons for Japanese Super-Growth 1950–70s.

1. *Social and Political Stability:* The Japanese population was relatively very homogeneous ethnically and linguistically, without religious discord or immigration. It had a much higher and more equally distributed level of education than was normal in Asia. Company unions and a general practice of lifetime employment promoted harmony in the labour market. There has effectively been one-party rule for the past 50 years.

2. *Complete demilitarization*: released a large economic surplus (bigger than the Meiji benefits from dismantlement of the fossilized Tokugawa military structure). It reduced military spending from 25 per cent of GDP to practically zero. Millions of demobilized military personnel, people released from manufacture of military supplies, aircraft, and ships, and people who had previously worked in the colonies, provided a skilled and disciplined work force, and a huge reserve of technical, managerial, and administrative talent. It took several years to make these changes and recover pre-war levels of per capita income (the 1941 level was not surpassed until 1956). Thereafter came the real miracle of catch-up, with per capita income growth of 8.3 per cent a year until 1973.

3. *Quantity and quality of labour input*: like most countries with several centuries experience of intensive multi-cropping in rice agriculture, there was a tradition of hard work, long working hours, and virtually no holidays. Thanks to modest demographic momentum, the age structure favoured a high ratio of employment to population. In 1950 the average level of education was similar to that in western Europe (9.1 years, compared with 10.8 in the UK, 10.4 in Germany, and 9.6 in France) and very much higher than in Asia (1.4 in India, 2.2 in China, 3.4 in Korea, and 3.6 in Taiwan).[11] Education was also increasing at a substantial rate, to an average level of 16.6 years in 2001 compared with 15.5 in the UK. This had an enormous impact in facilitating economic catch-up. I visited Japan for a month in 1961—the year of Jimmu prosperity when GDP rose 1 per cent a month. I visited the Sony factory founded by Akio Morita

and Masaru Ibuka (ex-naval engineers). It produced simple transistor radios, the foremen had PhDs in physics and all the operatives working and living in the factory had high school education. I had the same impression of efficiency in the Ishikawajima Harima shipyards, in riding the bullet train from Tokyo to Kyoto, and in the Bank of Japan, the Economic Planning Agency, the Ministries of Education and Agriculture, where one could find ten economists in a room all fresh and eager to talk after their morning callisthenics.

4. *Frugal traditions and a high propensity to save*: the Japanese non-residential fixed capital stock grew 8 per cent a year per capita in 1950–73. This was facilitated by the high rate of personal savings and the unusually large capacity of the government to finance investment.

5. *Favourable opportunities for entering the world market*: as an ally of the United States, Japan enjoyed favourable access to US, west European, and world markets, joining the GATT at an early stage and becoming a founder member of OECD in 1961. It maintained a very competitive exchange rate until the mid-1970s. As a result its exports grew by more than 15 per cent a year in 1950–73, faster than all other countries except Korea and Taiwan.

The Sharp Deceleration in Japanese Growth since 1973. Between 1973 and 1990, the momentum of Japanese growth slowed dramatically. Per capita GDP grew 3 per cent a year compared with 8.1 per cent in the previous phase of super-growth. This deceleration was not surprising as Japan had reached a level of per capita income comparable with that of other advanced capitalist countries. The important catch-up bonus underlying earlier growth had largely been exhausted. However, 3 per cent was faster than average for the advanced group of economies. The slowdown was greatly accentuated after 1990. GDP growth 1990–2003 was a slow crawl—less than 0.9 per cent a year. Export growth was also much weaker in this period than in 1973–1990.

Unfortunately, there were exaggerated expectations of the potential for growth and profit. High investment rates continued in the late 1980s. There was a stock-market bubble, a boom in land and housing prices. After its peak in 1989, the stock market index fell by half by 1992, and is still well below its peak. The collapse was just as severe for residential land and housing. The fall in the net worth of families and in business profits created a very deflationary situation. The Bank of Japan's discount rate was reduced to 0.5 per cent in 1995 and remained there until very recently, but consumers remained extremely cautious in their spending and borrowing. Many businesses became insolvent or bankrupt and banks found themselves with massive non-performing assets.

The government responded to this situation of very weak demand and depressed expectations by a massive increase in spending on public works, and large budget deficits.[12] It gave financial aid to institutions which should have been allowed to go bankrupt. Some idea of the extent of Japanese overinvestment can be derived by

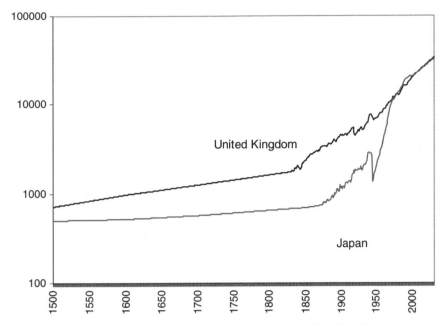

Figure 3.3. Comparative levels of Japan/UK GDP per capita, 1500–2030 (1990 international dollars)

comparison of the 2003 non-residential capital—output ratios in Japan (3.95), the US (2.34) and the UK (1.75) in Table 6.5 of Chapter 6.

After 15 years of stagnation, there are now signs of improvement. The government made the banks write off half of their bad debts and will privatize the post office bank. Efficiency has been increased by foreign investors. Nissan faced bankruptcy until Renault invested in it, took over the management and marketing and turned it into one of the best performers in the automobile industry. Many firms have abandoned their traditional policies of lifetime job security, and have become vigorous in cost-cutting and technological development. As profits improved, the stock market rose significantly in 2005. Nevertheless , it seems likely that Japanese growth will continue to be slower than in western Europe, as shown in Figure 3.3.

The Transformation of China

In world perspective China's performance has been exceptional. In 1300, it was the world's leading economy in terms of per capita income. It outperformed Europe in levels of technology, the intensity with which it used its natural resources, and capacity for administering a huge territorial empire. By 1500, western Europe had overtaken China in per capita real income, technological, and scientific capacity. From the 1840s to the middle of the twentieth century, China's performance actually declined in a world where economic progress elsewhere was very substantial. In the

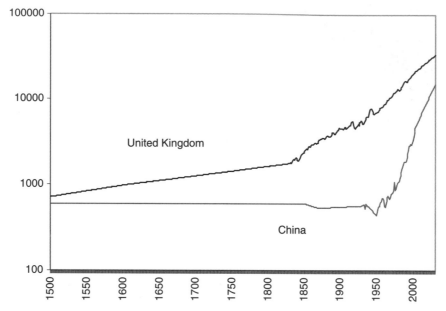

Figure 3.4. Comparative levels of China/UK GDP per capita, 1500–2030 (1990 international dollars)

past half-century, China has been transformed in a catch-up process which seems likely to continue in the next quarter century. By 2030 Chinese per capita income seems likely to be well above the world average. In terms of GDP, it will very probably have overtaken the US as the world's biggest economy (see Figure 3.5).

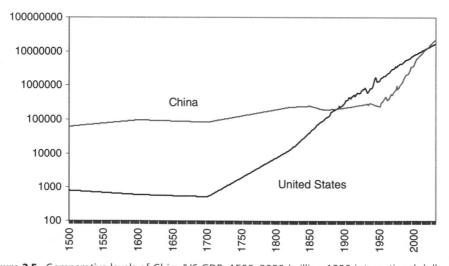

Figure 3.5. Comparative levels of China/US GDP, 1500–2030 (million 1990 international dollars)

China was a pioneer in bureaucratic governance. In the tenth century, it was already administered by professionally trained public servants, recruited by examination on a meritocratic basis. The bureaucracy, schooled in the Confucian classics, was the main instrument for imposing social and political order in a unitary state over a huge area. It had no challenge from a landed aristocracy, an established church, a judiciary, dissident intellectuals, or an urban bourgeoisie, and only rarely from the military. They used a written language common to all of China, and the official Confucian ideology was deeply ingrained in the education system. This system was relatively efficient and cheap to operate compared with the multi-layered structure of governance in feudal Europe and Japan. In Tokugawa Japan, the shogunal, daimyo and samurai households were about 6 per cent of the population compared with 3 per cent for the imperial household, bureaucracy, military, and degree-holding gentry who composed the ruling elite in China. Fiscal levies accounted for 5 per cent of GDP in China compared with 25 per cent in Japan. However, the Chinese bureaucracy augmented their official income several-fold by 'customary charges' and non-fiscal exactions and the gentry had rental incomes. Altogether, the income of the Chinese elite was probably about 15 per cent of GDP.

In the west, recruitment of professionally trained public servants on a meritocratic basis was initiated by Napoleon, more than a millennium later, but European bureaucrats never had the social status and power of the Chinese literati. Within each European country power was fragmented between a much greater variety of countervailing forces. Europe had a system of nation-states in close propinquity. They were outward looking, had significant trading relations and relatively easy intellectual interchange. This benign fragmentation stimulated competition and innovation to a degree not possible in China.

The economic impact of the Chinese bureaucracy was very positive for agriculture. Like the Physiocrats, they thought it was the key sector from which they could squeeze a surplus in the form of taxes and compulsory levies. They nurtured it with hydraulic works. Thanks to the precocious development of printing (500 years before Europe) they were able to diffuse best practice techniques by widespread distribution of illustrated agricultural handbooks. They settled farmers in promising new regions. They developed a public granary system to mitigate famines. They fostered innovation by introducing early ripening seeds which eventually permitted double or triple cropping. They promoted the introduction of new crops—tea in the Tang dynasty, cotton in the Sung, sorghum in the Yuan, new world crops such as maize, potatoes, sweet potatoes, peanuts and tobacco in the Ming.

Land shortage was compensated by intensive use of labour, irrigation, and natural fertilisers. Land was under continuous cultivation, without fallow. The need for fodder crops and grazing land was minimal. Livestock was concentrated on scavengers (pigs and poultry). Beef, milk, and wool consumption were rare. The protein supply was augmented by widespread production of fish and ducks in small scale aquaculture. Higher land productivity permitted denser settlement, reduced the cost of transport, raised the proportion of farm output which could be marketed, released labour for rural handicraft activity, particularly the spinning and weaving of cotton, which provided more comfortable, more easily washable, and healthier clothing.

Between the eighth and the thirteenth centuries there was a major shift in the centre of gravity of the economy. In the eighth century three-quarters of the population lived in north China, where the main crops were wheat and millet. By the end of the thirteenth, three-quarters lived south of the Yangtse. This area had been swampy and lightly settled, but with irrigation and early ripening seeds, it provided an ideal opportunity for massive development of rice cultivation, and an increase in per capita income by a third. Thereafter, from the thirteenth to the beginning of the nineteenth century, China was able to accommodate a four-fold increase in population whilst maintaining average per capita income more or less stable. Its capacity for *extensive* growth was most clearly demonstrated in the eighteenth century. Its GDP grew faster than that of western Europe, even though European per capita income grew by a fifth.

Outside agriculture the bureaucratic system had negative effects. The bureaucracy and the associated gentry were quintessential rent-seekers. They prevented the emergence of an independent commercial and industrial bourgeoisie on the European pattern. Entrepreneurial activity was insecure in a framework where legal protection for private activity was exiguous. Any activity that promised to be lucrative was subject to bureaucratic squeeze. Larger undertakings were limited to state or publicly licensed monopolies.

China's Exposure to the World Economy. The most striking example of the adverse effect of bureaucratic regulation was the virtual closure of China to international trade early in the fifteenth century, and the subsequent disappearance of its sophisticated shipbuilding industry.

In view of the historic importance of this withdrawal, it is worth retracing Chinese experience from the thirteenth to the early fifteenth century when China was the most dynamic force in Asian trade.

China's exposure to world trade was greatly enhanced when the Sung were driven out of north China and relocated their capital at Hangchow, south of the Yangtse. It was a prosperous and densely populated region of rice cultivation. It was not necessary to bring food supplies from distant areas, and the Sung had deliberately sabotaged the dykes of the Grand Canal. They relied more heavily on commercial taxes than most Chinese dynasties and fostered the development of ports and foreign trade. Their major port was Ch'üan-chou, about 600 km north of Canton. They fostered large scale production techniques for the ceramics industry and new products for the export market. As a result the kilns of Ching-te-chen (in Kiangsi) prospered greatly.

In order to defend the Yangtse and coastal areas against Mongol attacks the first Chinese professional navy was created in 1232. The ships included treadmill operated paddle-wheelers with protective armour plates, for service on the Yangtse. These were armed with powerful catapults to fling heavy stones or other missiles at enemy ships.

After the Sung were defeated, the Yuan dynasty (1279–1368) enlarged shipbuilding for grain transport to Peking, for maritime commerce with Asia and for naval operations. They reopened overland commerce to Europe and the Middle East on the silk route. They also launched two unsuccessful maritime invasions of Japan in 1274 and 1281. The first attempt involved a fleet of 900 ships. The second was much larger and carried an invasion force of a quarter of a million.

As in the Sung, a large proportion of the trading community in the Yuan dynasty were immigrants from all parts of the Muslim world. This is clear from the observations of Marco Polo, the Venetian who came to China in the last quarter of the thirteenth century, and Ibn Battuta from Morocco more than 50 years later. Both left striking testimony to the vigour of the international trade of China at that time.

Early in the Ming dynasty (1368–1644), China embarked on a series of naval expeditions into the 'eastern' and 'western oceans'. They were initiated by the Yung-lo emperor, the third ruler of the Ming dynasty (1402–24). He was a usurper, who had deposed his nephew in a successful military rebellion. The naval ventures were intended to display China's power and wealth and enhance his own legitimacy. They were also intended to extend Chinese suzerainty over a much wider area. Korea was a permanent member of the Chinese system of tributary relationships and Yung-lo persuaded Japan to accept a similar status in 1404 (which lasted with a brief interruption until 1549). In the tribute system, there was an initial exchange of 'gifts' (consisting on the Chinese side of specialties such as silk, gold lacqueur, and porcelain) and the other side were permitted to reciprocate with goods of lower value.

These tributary relations were conceived as a vehicle for assertion of China's moral and cultural superiority, to act as a civilizing force on barbarians at the frontiers, and thereby enhance China's security. For this reason the government expected to play a leading role in developing and supervising the exchange relationships, and private trade was prohibited. The underlying idea was not to create a colonial empire, but to assert China's benign hegemony. This traditional view of Chinese relations with the outside world was very different from that of the Mongol dynasty whose objective was world conquest, and the Yung-lo emperor probably felt the need to re-establish a more attractive image of Chinese civilization.

Seven expeditions between 1405 and 1433 penetrated very deep into the 'western oceans'. They were commanded by Admiral Cheng-ho, a member of the emperor's household since he was 15 years old who had become a comrade in arms. Cheng-ho was a eunuch. There were thousands of eunuchs in the Ming imperial household and emperors of this dynasty used them as a trusted and loyal counterweight to the power of the bureaucracy. Most of the latter regarded the expeditions as a waste of money, at a time when there were very large commitments in moving the Ming capital from Nanking to Peking and in rebuilding the Grand Canal. These involved very heavy fiscal burdens, and special levies on the coastal provinces. Yung-lo augmented his revenues by printing massive quantities of paper money. The resulting inflation led to a disappearance of paper money transactions in the private economy. From

Table 3.18. Exchange Rates between Ming Paper Currency and Silver, 1376–1540

	Official	Market
1376	1.00	1.00
1397	0.07	
1413	0.05	
1426	0.0025	
1540	0.0003	0.0001

Source: Atwell in Twitchett and Mote (1998: 382).

the 1430s, silver became the predominant instrument of exchange in the private economy, and was accepted by government for tax payments.

Under the Yung-lo emperor, the Ming navy consisted of 2,700 patrol vessels and combat ships attached to guard stations or island bases, 400 large warships stationed near Nanking and 400 grain transport freighters (see Needham 1971: 484). Another 317 ships were built for the Cheng-ho expeditions at the Longjiang shipyards near Nanking which had seven very large dry-docks. The biggest vessels in the maritime expeditions to the western oceans were 'treasure ships'. Cheng-ho's flagship was one of these and had a much bigger capacity than Columbus' ship the Santa Maria. It is estimated to have been 120–5 metres long, about 50 metres wide and 12 meters deep; the Santa Maria appears to have been 34 meters long, 7.9 metres wide and 4 metres deep (see Xi and Chalmers 2004).

Chinese ships differed substantially from those in Europe or Asian vessels in the Indian ocean. The treasure ships had nine masts, and smaller ships also had multiple masts. Transverse laths of bamboo attached to the sail fabric permitted precise stepwise reefing. When sails were furled, they fell immediately into pleats. When sails were torn, the area affected was restricted by the lathing. Big ships had 15 or more watertight compartments, so a partially damaged ship would not sink and could be repaired at sea. They also had up to 60 cabins so the crew quarters were much more comfortable than in European ships. Watertight compartments were first introduced into the British navy in 1795 (see Xi and Chalmers 2004).

Table 3.19 shows the characteristics of the six naval expeditions of the Yung-lo emperor, and the seventh which sailed after his death. The first three had India and its spices as their destination. The last three explored the east coast of Africa, the Red Sea, and the Persian Gulf. The fleets were very large and the big ships were intended to overawe the rulers of the countries which were visited. The intentions were peaceful but the military force was big enough to deal effectively with attacks on the fleet, which occurred on only three occasions.

A major purpose of these voyages was to establish good relations by presentation of gifts and to escort ambassadors or rulers to or from China. There was no attempt to establish bases for trade or for military objectives. There was a search for new plants for medical purposes, and one of the missions was accompanied by 180 medical personnel. There was also an interest in types of African livestock which

Table 3.19. Chinese Naval Diplomacy: Voyages to the 'Western' and 'Eastern' Oceans, 1405–33

Date	Number of Ships	Number of Naval Military & Other Personnel	Places Visited in Western Oceans	Places Visited in Eastern Oceans
1405–07	62 large, 255 small	27,000	Calicut	Champa, Java, Sumatra
1407–09	small number	n.a.	Calicut & Cochin	Siam, Sumatra, Java
1409–11	48	30,000	Malacca, Quilon	Sumatra
1413–15	63	29,000	Hormuz, Red Sea, Maldives, Bengal	Champa, Java,Sumatra
1417–19	n.a.	n.a.	Hormuz, Aden, Mogadishu, Malindi	Java, the Ryukyu islands, Brunei
1421–22	41	˙n.a.	Aden, East Africa	Sumatra
1431–33	100	27,500	Ceylon, Calicut, Aden, Hormuz, Jedda, Malindi	Vietnam, Sumatra, Java, Malacca

Notes and Source: Needham (1971) and Levathes (1994). The detailed official records of these trips were destroyed by the bureaucracy who were opposed to renewal of such expeditions. The evidence is based on the writings of participants and later imperial histories.

were unknown in China. The expeditions brought back ostriches, giraffes, zebras, elephant tusks, and rhinoceros horns. However, these were exotica. The international interchange of flora and fauna was negligible compared to what occurred after the European encounter with the Americas.

Cheng-ho died at sea on the seventh voyage and support for distant diplomacy evaporated. The broadening of China's tributary relations with countries of the 'western oceans' had not enhanced China's security and the naval expeditions had exacerbated a situation of fiscal and monetary crisis. The meritocratic bureaucracy had always opposed a venture which promoted the eunuch interest. They terminated these ventures and destroyed the official records of the expeditions. There was increasing concern to defend the new northern capital against potential invasion from Mongolia or Manchuria. The new capital's food supply was guaranteed by the Grand Canal which had been reopened in its full length in 1415 (2,300 km—equivalent to the distance from Paris to Istanbul). It functioned better than ever before because of new locks which made it operational on a full-time basis. Grain shipments by sea to the capital had already ceased, sea-going grain ships were replaced by canal barges, and naval commitments to coastal defence could be relaxed.

As oceanic diplomacy was ended, there was no longer a need for treasure ships. Coastal defences were reduced and by 1474 the fleet of large warships had been cut from 400 to 140. Most of the shipyards were closed, and naval manpower was reduced by retrenchment and desertions. Tributary arrangements for countries within the Eastern Ocean (Burma, Nepal, Siam, Indochina, Korea, and the Ryukyus) continued, but the ban on private trade continued, and sea-going junks with more than two masts were prohibited.

China turned its back on the world economy when its maritime technology was superior to that of Europe. During large parts of the Ming and Ch'ing dynasties, it virtually cut itself off from foreign commerce. As a result, there was large scale development of illicit private trade and piracy. The main beneficiaries were Chinese and Japanese pirates, and the Portuguese who were allowed to establish a base in Macao in 1557, which they kept until 1999. In the seventeenth century the Dutch tried unsuccessfully to dislodge the Portuguese from Macao, and were expelled from Taiwan in 1661.

Chinese Disdain of the West and Its Consequences. China failed to react adequately to the western technological challenge until the middle of the twentieth century, mainly because the ideology, mindset, and education system of the bureaucracy promoted an ethnocentric outlook, indifferent to developments outside China. There were Jesuit scholars in Peking for nearly two centuries; some of them like Ricci, Schall, and Verbiest had intimate contact with ruling circles, but there was little curiosity amongst the Chinese elite about intellectual or scientific development in the west. In 1792–3, Lord Macartney spent a year carting 600 cases of presents from George III. They included a planetarium, globes, mathematical instruments, chronometers, telescopes, measuring instruments, plate glass, copperware, and other miscellaneous items. After he presented them to the Ch'ien-lung emperor, the official response was: 'there is nothing we lack . . . We have never set much store on strange or ingenious objects, nor do we need any more of your country's manufactures.' These deeply ingrained mental attitudes helped prevent China from emulating the west's protocapitalist development from 1500 to 1800, and from participation in much more dynamic processes of economic growth thereafter. It did not start establishing embassies or legations abroad until 1877.

Between 1820 and 1950, the world economy made enormous progress by any previous yardstick. World product rose eight-fold, and world per capita income 2.6-fold. US per capita income rose eight-fold, European income four-fold and Japanese three-fold. In other Asian countries except Japan, economic progress was very modest but in China per capita product actually fell. China's share of world GDP fell from a third to one-twentieth. Its real per capita income fell from 90 to 20 per cent of the world average. Most Asian countries had problems similar to those of China, i.e., indigenous institutions which hindered modernization and foreign colonial intrusion. But these problems were worse in China, and help to explain why its performance was exceptionally disappointing.

Internal Forces Undermining the Manchu Regime. Chinese development was interrupted by internal causes and by foreign intrusion. Internal disorder took a heavy toll on population and economic welfare (see Table 3.20). The Taiping rebellion (1850–64) affected more than half of China's provinces and did extensive damage to its richest areas. In the five provinces most affected, population in the early 1890s was 50 million lower than it had been 70 years earlier. Parts of the same area bore the main brunt of the Yellow River floods in 1855. Due to governmental neglect of irrigation works it burst its banks and caused widespread devastation in Anhwei and Kiangsu. It had previously flowed to the sea through the lower course of the Huai River, but after 1855, it flowed from Kaifeng to the Shantung peninsula, more than 400 km

Table 3.20. China's Population by Province, 1819–1953 (million)

	1819	1893	1953
Provinces most affected by Taiping rebellion[a]	153.9	101.8	145.3
Provinces affected by Muslim rebellions[b]	41.3	26.8	43.1
Ten other provinces of China proper[c]	175.6	240.9	338.6
Three Manchurian provinces[d]	2.0	5.4	41.7
Sinkiang, Mongolia, Tibet, Ningsia, Tsinghai	6.4	11.8	14.0
Total	379.4	386.7	582.7

Notes: (a) Anhwei, Chekiang, Hupei, Kiangsi, Kiangsu; (b) Kansu, Shensi, Shansi; (c) Fukien, Honan, Hopei, Hunan, Kwangsi, Kwangtung, Kweichow, Shantung, Szechwan, Yunnan; (d) Heilungkiang, Kirin, Liaoning.

Source: Maddison (1998: 47).

north of its previous channel. There were Muslim rebellions in Shensi, Kansu, and Sinkiang, where population fell due to brutal repression in the 1860s and 1870s. In the republican era there were two decades (1927–49) of civil war between the Kuo Ming Tang (KMT) forces of Chiang Kai Shek and the communists led by Mao Tse Tung.

The Impact of Colonial Intrusions.   Colonial penetration began with the capture of Hong Kong by British gunboats in 1842. The immediate motive was to guarantee free access to Canton to exchange Indian opium for Chinese tea. A second Anglo-French attack in 1858–60 destroyed the summer palace of the emperor in Peking. The subsequent treaty opened access to the interior of China via the Yangtse and the huge network of internal waterways which debouched at Shanghai.

This was the era of free trade imperialism. Western traders were individual firms, not monopoly companies. In sharp contrast to their hostile and mutually exclusive trade regimes in the merchant capitalist epoch, the British and French had made their Cobden–Chevalier Treaty to open European commerce on a most-favoured-nation basis. European countries acted collusively in applying the same principle in treaties imposed on China. Hence twelve other European countries, Japan, the US, and three Latin American countries acquired the same trading privileges before the First World War.

The treaties forced China to maintain low tariffs. They legalized the opium trade and gave foreigners extra-territorial rights and consular jurisdiction in 92 'treaty ports' opened between 1842 and 1917. Some of these 'ports' were far inland, e.g., Harbin in the middle of Manchuria, and Chungking 1,400km up the Yangtse. Six territories were 'leased' to Britain, France, Germany, Japan, and Russia. To monitor the Chinese commitment to low tariffs, a maritime customs inspectorate was created (with Sir Robert Hart as Inspector General from 1861 to 1908) to collect tariff revenue for the Chinese government. A large part of this was earmarked to pay the 'indemnities' which the colonialists demanded to defray the costs of their attacks on China. The treaty port system was not terminated until 1943.

In addition to these 'port' arrangements, China also suffered large territorial losses and the dismantlement of its network of tributary states. In 1860, 82 million hectares of land and a huge stretch of Pacific coast were ceded to Russia, where it constructed its new port, Vladivostok. In the 1860s, the khanates of Tashkent, Bokhara, Samarkand, Khiva, and Khokand became part of the Russian empire. In 1882, the Ryukyus were lost to Japan. In 1885, Indochina was ceded to French suzerainty and in 1886 Burma to British. In 1895, Taiwan was lost to Japan which also got suzerainty over Korea. In 1911, Tibet proclaimed its independence and expelled its Chinese population. In 1915, Russia gained suzerainty over Outer Mongolia. In 1931–3, Japan took over China's Manchurian provinces and Jehol to create its puppet state of Manchukuo. The Manchu reaction to these intrusions was feeble and ineffective, and serious Chinese resistance did not start until the Japanese attack in 1937.

The centre of this multi-lateral colonial regime was the international settlement in Shanghai. The British picked the first site in 1843 north of the 'native city'. The French, Germans, Italians, Japanese, and Americans had neighbouring sites along the Whangpoo River opposite Pudong, with extensive grounds for company head-quarters, the cricket club, country clubs, tennis clubs, swimming pools, the race course, the golf club, movie theatres, churches, schools, hotels, hospitals, cabarets, brothels, bars, consulates, and police stations of the colonial powers. There were similar facilities, on a smaller scale, in Tientsin and Hankow. Most of the Chinese allowed into these segregated settlements were servants.

Foreigners were the main beneficiaries of this brand of free trade imperialism and extra-territorial privilege. The treaty ports were glittering islands of modernity, but the character of other Chinese cities did not improve, and those which had been damaged by the massive Taiping rebellion of 1850–64 had deteriorated. Chinese agriculture was not significantly affected by the opening of the economy.

The continued expansion in treaty port facilities and the freedom which foreigners obtained in 1895 to manufacture in China contributed substantially to the growth of the modern sector, including railways, banking, commerce, industrial production, and mining. There was also an associated growth of Chinese capitalist activity, which had its origins mainly in the *compradore* middlemen of the Treaty ports. There was an inflow of capital from overseas Chinese who had emigrated in substantial numbers to other parts of Asia.

The share of exports in Chinese GDP was small (0.7 per cent of GDP in 1870, 1.2 per cent in 1913)—much smaller than in India, Indonesia, and Japan. China regained its tariff autonomy in 1928 and there was some relaxation of other constraints on its sovereignty in the treaty ports. In the first half of the twentieth century, China ran a significant trade deficit, quite unlike the situation in India and Indonesia which had large surpluses. Remittance from some of the 9 million overseas Chinese to their families covered part of the deficit and there was a large outflow of silver in the 1930s following the US devaluation in 1932 and China's switch from a silver to a paper currency in 1935.

From the 1860s onwards, the most dynamic areas in the Chinese economy were Shanghai and Manchuria. Manchuria had been closed to ethnic Chinese settlement by the Manchu dynasty until 1860. They became interested in promoting Han Chinese settlement after they had been forced to cede the very thinly settled territory north of the Amur River to Russia. Between 1860 and 1930 the Manchurian population grew tenfold-from 3.3 to 31.3 million (see the discussion of Manchurian experience in the above section on Japan).

Shanghai rose to prominence because of its location at the mouth of a huge system of waterways.

The total of inland waterways navigable by junks in nearly all seasons was nearly 30,000 miles. To this must be added an estimated half million miles of canals or artificial waterways in the delta area. It is not surprising therefore that between 1865 and 1936, Shanghai handled 45 to 65 per cent of China's foreign trade (Eckstein et al. 1968: 60–1).

It was already an important coastal port in the Ch'ing dynasty with a population of 230,000 in the 1840s. By 1938 this had risen to 3.6 million and Shanghai was the biggest city in China. It now has a population of 16 million.

The Ch'ing regime collapsed in 1911, after seven decades of major internal rebellion, and humiliating foreign intrusions. The bureaucratic gentry elite were incapable of achieving serious reform or modernization, because of a deeply conservative attachment to a thousand year old polity on which their privileges and status depended. After its collapse there were nearly four decades in which political power was taken over by the military. They too were preoccupied with major civil wars, and faced more serious foreign aggression than the Ch'ing. They did little to provide a new impetus for economic change and the five-tier political structure of the KMT government was far from democratic. The treaty-port form of colonialism was not ended until 1943.[13] The limited modernization of the economy came mainly in the treaty ports and in Manchuria, where foreign capitalist enterprise penetrated and the sprouts of Chinese capitalism burgeoned.

Economic Performance in the Maoist Period, 1949–78. The establishment of the People's Republic marked a sharp change in China's political elite and mode of governance. The degree of central control was much greater than under the Ch'ing dynasty or the KMT. It reached to the lowest levels of government, to the workplace, to farms, and to households. The party was highly disciplined and maintained detailed oversight of the regular bureaucratic apparatus. The military were tightly integrated into the system. Propaganda for government policy and ideology was diffused through mass movements under party control. Landlords, national, and foreign capitalist interests were eliminated by expropriation of private property. China became a command economy on the Soviet pattern

After a century of surrender or submission to foreign incursions and aggression, the new regime was a ferocious and successful defender of China's national integrity, willing to operate with minimal links to the world economy. For most of the Maoist period there was little contact with the outside world. From 1952 to 1973 the United States applied a comprehensive embargo on trade, travel and financial transactions, and from 1960 onwards the USSR did the same.

BOX 3.1. China's Emergence from International Isolation, 1949--2001

1949 Oct.	People's Republic of China created. Diplomatic recognition by Burma, India and communist countries in 1949, by Afghanistan, Denmark, Finland, Israel, Norway, Pakistan, and the United Kingdom in 1950.
1950 Feb.	USSR agreed to provide financial and technical assistance—eventually $1.4 billion in loans and 10,000 technicians. China acknowledged the independence of Outer Mongolia, agreed to joint Soviet–Chinese operation of Manchurian railways, Soviet military bases in Port Arthur and Dairen, and Soviet mining enterprises in Sinkiang.
1950, 25 June	North Korea invaded south, penetrating deeply to Pusan.
1950, 27 June	US changed its neutral line on Taiwan, sent in 7th Fleet.
1950 Oct.	China sent 'volunteers' (eventually 700,000) to N. Korea to push back UN forces advancing towards the Chinese border on Yalu River.
1950–1	China took over Tibet.
1953 July	Korean armistice.
1954	India ceded former British extraterritorial claims to Tibet.
1958	China menaced Taiwan in Quemoy and Matsu incidents. Khrushchev retracted offer of nuclear aid.
1959	Revolt in Tibet, Dalai Lama fled to India.
1960	USSR withdrew Soviet experts, abandoned unfinished projects.
1962	Border clash with India over Aksai-chin road from Sinkiang to Tibet.
1964	First Chinese atom bomb test, 1969 first hydrogen bomb test.
1963–9	Border clashes with USSR in Manchuria. China questioned legitimacy of Soviet/Chinese boundaries in Manchuria and Sinkiang.
1971 April	US lifted trade embargo on China.
1971 Oct.	China entered the United Nations, Taiwan ousted.
1972 Feb.	President Nixon visited China.
1972 Sep.	Visit of Prime Minister Tanaka normalised diplomatic relations with Japan.
1973	US and China established *de facto* diplomatic relations.
1978 Dec.	US established formal diplomatic relations, derecognised Taiwan.
1979 Feb.–Mar.	Border war with Vietnam after expulsion of ethnic Chinese and Vietnamese destruction of Khmer Rouge regime in Cambodia.
1980	China became a member of the World Bank and IMF, 1986 entered Asian Development Bank.
1997	Hong Kong restored to China; 1999, Macao restored to China
2001	China admitted to the World Trade Organization

Source: MacFarquhar and Fairbank (1987 and 1991).

In the Maoist era, these political changes had substantial costs which reduced the returns on China's development effort. Its version of communism involved risky experimentation on a grand scale. Self-inflicted wounds brought the economic and political system close to collapse during the Great Leap Forward (1958–60), and again in the Cultural Revolution (1966–76) when education and the political system were deeply shaken. Allocation of resources was extremely inefficient. China grew more slowly than other communist economies and somewhat less than the world average. Nevertheless, economic performance was a great improvement over the past. GDP trebled, per capita real product rose by more than 80 per cent and labour productivity by 60 per cent from 1952 to 1978. The economic structure was transformed. In 1952, industry's share of GDP was one-sixth of that in agriculture. By 1978, it was bigger than the agricultural. China achieved this in spite of its political and economic isolation, hostile relations with both the United States and the Soviet Union, and wars with South Korea and India.

The Reform Period since 1978. After 1978, there was a major political shift to pragmatic reformism which relaxed central political control and modified the economic system profoundly. These changes brought a more stable path of development and a great acceleration of economic growth. From 1978 to 2003 GDP rose 7.9 per cent a year, population growth decelerated and per capita real income rose 6.6 per cent a year. Growth was faster than in any Asian country. A major reason was the exceptionally high rate and accelerating growth of investment (see Table 3.21).

The other main reason for growth acceleration was increased efficiency in resource allocation. Collective agriculture was abandoned and production decisions reverted to individual peasant households. Small scale industrial and service activities were freed from government control and their performance greatly outpaced that of the state sector. Exposure to foreign trade and investment were greatly enhanced. These

Table 3.21. Ratio of Gross Fixed Investment to GDP at Current Prices (percentages)

	1978–89	1990–9	2000–3
China	29.0	33.3	38.5
India	20.2	22.2	22.7
Indonesia	23.4	26.4	19.4
Japan	29.4	29.5	25.0
Hong Kong	26.9	29.3	26.3
Malaysia	29.6	36.1	24.0
Singapore	39.5	35.4	27.3
South Korea	29.5	35.6	29.9
Taiwan	23.4	22.9	19.4
Thailand	28.0	36.8	23.0
USSR/Russia	28.7	18.0*	18.0
US	19.3	17.5	18.8

Note: *1995–9.

Source: China from *China Statistical Yearbook 2005*, China Statistics Press, Beijing, pp. 63–4. Japan, Korea and US from *National Accounts for OECD Countries*, Vol. 1, *Main Aggregates, 1993–2004*, Paris, 2006, and 1978–92 from the 1999 edition. Indonesia supplied by Pierre van der Eng from Indonesian national accounts. Other Asian countries from Asian Development Bank, *Key Indicators of Developing Asian and Pacific Countries*, 1999 and 2005 editions. USSR, 1978–89 from Maddison (1998), Russia from Goskomstat.

changes strengthened market forces and introduced consumers to a wide variety of new goods.

The new Chinese policies were indigenously generated and quite out of keeping with the prescriptions for 'transition' which were proffered and pursued by the USSR. The contrast between Chinese and Soviet performance in the reform period is particularly striking. As China prospered, the Soviet economy collapsed and the USSR disintegrated. In 1978 Chinese per capita income was 15 per cent of that of the former Soviet Union. In 2003 it was 89 per cent of its level.

The reform period was one of much reduced international tension. China's geopolitical standing, stature, and leverage were greatly increased. China became the world's second largest economy, overtaking Japan by a respectable margin and the former USSR by a very large margin. China took back Hong Kong and Macao peacefully, and inaugurated a 'two systems' policy designed to attract Taiwan back into the national fold.

The rigid monopoly of foreign trade and the policy of autarkic self-reliance were abandoned after 1978. Foreign trade decisions were decentralized. The yuan was devalued and China became highly competitive. Special enterprise zones were created as free trade areas. In response to the greater role for market forces, competition emerged, resource allocation improved, and consumer satisfaction increased. There was a massive increase in interaction with the world economy through trade (see Table 3.22), inflows of direct investment, and a very large increase in opportunities for study and travel abroad, and for foreigners to visit China. By 1998, the stock of foreign direct investment was bigger than that of any other country except the US and

Table 3.22. Asian and Western Merchandise Exports at Constant Prices, 1870–2003 (million 1990 dollars)

	1870	1913	1929	1950	1973	2003
Japan	51	1,684	4,343	3,538	95,105	402,861
China	1,398	4,197	6,262	6,339	11,679	453,734
India	3,466	9,480	8,209	5,489	9,679	86,097
Indonesia	172	989	2,609	2,254	9,605	70,320
S. Korea	6	171	1,292	112	7,894	299,578
Philippines	55	180	678	697	2,608	27,892
Taiwan	7	70	261	180	5,761	134,884
Thailand	88	495	640	1,148	3,081	72,233
Total 8 Asia	**5,243**	**17,266**	**24,294**	**19,757**	**145,412**	**1,547,589**
France	3,512	11,292	16,600	16,848	104,161	404,077
Germany	6,761	38,200	35,068	13,179	194,171	785,035
UK	12,237	39,348	31,990	39,348	94,670	321,021
US	2,495	19,196	30,368	43,114	174,548	801,784
4 countries	**25,005**	**108,036**	**114,026**	**112,489**	**567,550**	**2,311,917**

Notes and Source: Maddison (2001: 361) for 1870–1973, Japan and western countries updated from OECD *Economic Outlook* (2002) to (2001), thereafter from IMF, *International Financial Statistics*, other Asian countries from ADB, *Key Indicators* (2005). Taiwan 1870–1913 from Ho (1978: 379–80); Korea 1900–13 from Maddison (1989: 140), 1870–1900 volume movement assumed to be the same as for Japan. Hong Kong exports in 1990 dollars were $10,379 million in 1973 and $240,813 million in 2003.

Table 3.23. Comparative Dynamics of Income and Export Performance, Asia and the West, 1950–2003 (annual average compound growth rates)

	Per capita GDP			Export Volume		
	1950–73	1973–90	1990–2003	1950–73	1973–90	1990–2003
Japan	8.1	3.0	0.9	15.3	6.7	2.6
China	**2.8**	**4.8**	**7.5**	**2.7**	**10.3**	**16.5**
India	1.4	2.6	3.9	2.5	3.7	12.8
Indonesia	2.6	3.1	2.6	6.5	6.0	8.1
S. Korea	5.8	6.8	4.7	20.3	13.2	12.5
Philippines	2.7	0.7	1.0	5.9	6.9	10.0
Thailand	3.7	5.5	3.4	4.9	11.5	5.5
Taiwan	6.7	5.3	4.3	16.3	12.6	9.2
Hong Kong	5.2	5.5	2.1	0.6	5.5	2.1
France	4.0	1.9	1.3	8.2	4.2	5.2
Germany	5.0	1.7	1.2	12.4	4.5	5.1
UK	2.4	1.9	2.0	3.9	4.0	4.3
USA	2.5	2.0	1.7	6.3	4.9	5.6

UK. At the same time, China was prudent in retaining control over the more volatile types of international capital movement. Although it had to wait 15 years to be admitted to the World Trade Organisation, it is now the world's third largest exporter.

China still has important problems to solve. The degree of regional inequality is very large, with average household income nearly eight times as high in Shanghai as in Guizhou, the poorest province. The big rural–urban differentials in income, education, health, and employment opportunity are a major cause of discontent.

There are still large state industrial enterprises which are a hangover from the Maoist period. Most of them make substantial losses. They are kept in operation by government subsidy and default on loans which the state banks are constrained to give them, though their relative importance has declined significantly. In 1992, the state industrial sector employed 45 million people, by 2005 this had fallen to 10 million.

Another major problem is the large volume of non-performing loans in the banking sector. This is largely controlled by the state, which does not make efficient allocation of the funds it captures from savers.

However, it is difficult to be pessimistic about the prospects for an economy which has shown such dynamism in the last quarter century and where foreign investment and foreign trade have done so much to improve efficiency in resource allocation. China is still a low-income, low-productivity country and there are opportunities for rapid catch-up which are not open to advanced economies operating nearer to the frontier of technology. Follower countries can draw upon the lead countries' fund of technology by building up their stock of human and physical capital, opening their economies to international trade, developing institutions which nurture absorptive capacity and maintaining political stability. When the catch-up countries draw closer to the lead countries their growth rate is likely to decelerate.

Table 3.24. Comparative Performance of China, India, Japan, Russia, and the USA, 1990–2003

	(GDP levels in billion 1990 PPP dollars)					(Chinese GDP as per cent of)			
	Russia	Japan	China	USA	India	Russia	Japan	USA	India
1990	1,151	2,321	2,124	5,803	1,098	185	92	37	199
1991	1,093	2,399	2,264	5,792	1,112	207	94	39	204
1992	935	2,422	2,484	5,985	1,169	266	103	42	212
1993	854	2,428	2,724	6,146	1,238	319	112	44	220
1994	745	2,455	2,997	6,396	1,328	402	122	47	226
1995	715	2,504	3,450	6,558	1,426	483	138	53	242
1996	689	2,590	3,521	6,804	1,537	511	136	52	229
1997	699	2,636	3,707	7,110	1,611	530	141	52	230
1998	662	2,609	3,717	7,407	1,716	561	142	50	217
1999	704	2,605	3,961	7,736	1,820	563	152	51	218
2000	774	2,667	4,319	8,019	1,900	558	162	54	227
2001	814	2,673	4,781	8,079	2,009	587	179	59	238
2002	852	2,664	5,374	8,209	2,080	631	202	65	258
2003	914	2,699	6,188	8,431	2,267	677	229	73	273

Source: Available at: www.ggdc.net/Maddison.

Why China Did Better Than Russia in Moving Towards a Market Economy. China has had very much greater success than Russia since it abandoned the communist command economy. Table 3.24 compares its GDP growth performance since 1990 with that of Russia, India, Japan, and the USA. It has grown more rapidly than all these countries, but the contrast with Russia is by far the most striking. In 1990, Chinese GDP was less than twice as big as Russian, but by 2003 it was six and a half times as large. It is therefore worth summarizing the reasons for the difference in China's performance:

1. Chinese reformers gave first priority to agriculture. They ended Mao's collectivist follies and offered individual peasant households the opportunity to raise their income by their own efforts. Russian reformers more or less ignored agriculture, and the potential for individual peasant household enterprise had been killed off by Stalin in the 1920s. The Chinese government encouraged small-scale manufacturing production in township and village enterprises. Local officials and party elite got legal opportunities for greatly increasing their income if they ran the enterprises successfully.

2. The Chinese state did not disintegrate as the USSR did. The proportion of ethnic minorities was very small by comparison with the USSR, and the political system did not collapse. By patient diplomacy and creating capitalist enclaves it reintegrated Hong Kong and Macao as special administrative regions.

3. In the reform era, China benefited substantially from the great number of overseas Chinese. A large part of foreign investment and foreign entrepreneurship

has come from Hong Kong, Singapore, Taiwan, and the Chinese in other parts of the world

4. China started from a very low level of productivity and income. In 1978, when the reform era began, per capita income was less than 15 per cent of that in the USSR and its degree of industrialization was much smaller. If the right policies are pursued, backwardness is a favourable position for a nation which wants to achieve rapid catch-up. The very fact that the Chinese income level was so much lower than that of Hong Kong, Japan, Malaysia, South Korea, Singapore, and Taiwan made it easier to capture the advantages of backwardness, and make big structural changes. It meant that its period of super-growth could stretch further into the future than theirs.

5. The leadership was very sensitive to the dangers of hyper-inflation which China had experienced when the KMT were in charge. Instead of destroying private savings as in Russia, they were encouraged and have increased enormously. They are the main reason that it has been feasible to raise investment to such high levels. In Russia, the reform process involved a period of hyper-inflation, large-scale capital flight, currency collapse and default on foreign debt. The Chinese government has been internationally creditworthy with negligible capital flight.

6. The state sector was not privatized, but has waned by attrition. There are now many wealthy entrepreneurs in China and some have enjoyed official favours, but China has not created oligarchs in the way that Russia did.

7. China gave high priority to promotion of manufactured exports , setting up tax-free special enterprise zones near the coast. Exports were also facilitated by maintaining an undervalued currency. The rebound in the Russian economy since 1998 has been largely driven by the rise in the price of its exports of oil and natural gas.

8. Chinese family planning policy reduced the birth rate and changed the population structure in a way that promoted economic growth. In 1978–2003 the proportion of working age rose from 54 to 70 per cent. In China, life expectation has risen. In Russia it has fallen.

The Outlook. Table 3.24 provides a comparative perspective on China's growth prospects over the next quarter century. For capita GDP growth, I assume a sizeable slowdown—from 7.3 per cent a year in 1990–2003 to 4.5 per cent in 2003–30. Some slowdown is warranted for several reasons. In the reform period, changes in age structure made it possible to raise the activity rate to a degree that cannot be repeated. Because of the low starting point, the average educational level of the labour force was multiplied by a factor of five from 1952 to 1995. China has suffered environmental deterioration in its push for rapid growth. In future it will have to devote greater resources to mitigate this damage.

Table 3.25. China in the World Economy, 1500–2030AD

	China	Japan	India	W Eur.	US	World	China/World Ratio
Population (million)							
1500	103.0	15.4	110.0	57.3	2.0	438.4	0.23
1820	381.0	31.0	209.0	133.0	10.0	1,041.8	0.37
1913	437.1	51.7	303.7	261.0	97.6	1,791.1	0.24
1950	546.8	83.8	359.0	304.9	152.3	2,524.3	0.22
1973	881.9	108.7	580.0	358.8	211.9	3,916.5	0.23
2003	1,288.4	127.2	1,049.7	394.6	290.3	6,278.6	0.21
2030	1,458.0	121.0	1,421.0	400.0	364.0	8,175.0	0.18
Per Capita GDP (1990 int $)							
1500	600	500	550	771	400	566	1.06
1820	600	669	533	1,204	1,257	667	0.90
1913	552	1,387	673	3,458	5,301	1,526	0.36
1950	448	1,921	619	4,579	9,561	2,113	0.21
1973	838	11,434	852	11,416	16,689	4,091	0.20
2003	4,803	21,218	2,160	19,912	29,037	6,516	0.74
2030	15,763	30,072	7,089	31,389	45,774	11,814	1.33
GDP (billion 1990 int $)							
1500	61.8	7.7	60.5	44.2	0.8	248.3	0.25
1820	228.6	20.7	111.4	160.1	12.5	694.6	0.33
1913	241.4	71.7	204.2	902.3	517.4	2,733.3	0.09
1950	245.0	161.0	222.2	1,396.2	1,455.9	5,336.7	0.05
1973	739.4	1,242.9	494.8	4,096.5	3,536.6	16,022.9	0.05
2003	6,187.9	2,699.0	2,267.1	7,857.4	8,430.8	40,913.0	0.15
2030	22,982.8	3,488.0	10,074.0	12,556.0	16,662.0	96,580.0	0.24

Notes and Source: 1500–2003 Maddison (2003), updated, 2030 from Chapter 7. The projections are not the result of an econometric exercise, but are based on an analysis of changes in the momentum of growth in different parts of the world economy, and the likelihood of their continuation or change. Estimates of GDP levels are adjusted to reflect purchasing power parities in the benchmark year 1990 (see Maddison 1998, pp.149–166). In China the purchasing power of the yuan is much higher than the exchange rate. There is often significant error in comparative economic analysis because ignorance of the pitfalls of exchange rate conversion leads to serious understatement of the level of Chinese GDP. This is true in journalism, political discourse, and amongst some economists. Thus newspapers frequently refer to Japan as the world's second largest economy, though its GDP is less than half the Chinese. It should also be noted that official Chinese statistics exaggerate GDP growth for reasons explained in Maddison (1998), which contained a detailed re-estimation of performance. With the help of Professor Harry X Wu, I have revised and updated the estimates for 1952–2003, making the same type of downward adjustment to the official estimates of growth in real value added in industry and in 'non-material' services.

There has been a relative decline of income in rural areas and a neglect of rural educational and health facilities. Bigger resources will be needed to compensate for this. Some slowdown can also be expected as the average technological level gets closer to the frontier in the advanced countries. Technical advance will be more costly as imitation is replaced by innovation. Even on my rather conservative assumptions, China would again become the world's biggest economy by 2018, and the US would take second place. The average per capita level would still be a good deal lower than in the US, western Europe, and Japan, but it would be well above the world average.

☐ APPENDIX

Table 3.26a. Asian Population, 1820–2003 (000 at mid-year)

	1820	1870	1913	1950	1973	1990	2003
China	381,000	358,000	437,140	546,815	881,940	1,135,185	1,288,400
India	209,000	253,000	303,700	359,000	580,000	839,000	1,049,700
Indonesia	17,927	28,922	49,934	79,043	124,271	178,500	214,497
Japan	31,000	34,437	51,672	83,805	108,707	123,537	127,214
Philippines	2,176	5,063	9,384	21,131	41,998	64,318	84,620
South Korea	9,395	9,753	10,589	20,846	34,073	42,869	48,202
Thailand	4,665	5,775	8,689	20,042	40,302	55,197	63,271
Taiwan	2,000	2,345	3,469	7,981	15,526	20,279	22,603
Bangladesh				45,646	72,471	109,897	138,448
Burma	3,506	4,245	12,326	19,488	29,227	39,655	46,030
Hong Kong	20	123	487	2,237	4,213	5,688	6,810
Malaysia	287	800	3,084	6,434	11,712	17,504	23,093
Nepal	3,881	4,698	5,639	8,990	12,685	19,325	26,470
Pakistan				39,448	71,121	114,578	156,127
Singapore	5	84	323	1,022	2,193	3,047	4,277
Sri Lanka	1,213	2,786	4,811	7,533	13,246	17,193	19,742
Total 16 Asian countries	**666,075**	**710,031**	**901,247**	**1,269,461**	**2,043,683**	**2,785,773**	**3,319,505**
Afghanistan	3,280	4,207	5,730	8,150	13,421	14,669	27,060
Cambodia	2,090	2,340	3,070	4,471	7,534	9,355	13,160
Laos	470	755	1,387	1,886	3,027	4,210	5,922
Mongolia	619	668	725	779	1,360	2,216	2,712
North Korea	4,345	4,511	4,897	9,471	15,161	20,019	22,466
Vietnam	6,551	10,528	19,339	25,348	45,736	67,283	81,791
23 Small Asian Countries	1,798	1,903	2,237	3,364	5,781	8,625	11,542
Total 29 east Asian countries	**19,153**	**24,912**	**37,385**	**53,469**	**92,020**	**126,378**	**164,654**
Total 45 east Asian countries	**685,228**	**734,943**	**938,632**	**1,322,930**	**2,135,703**	**2,912,151**	**3,484,159**
Bahrain				115	239	500	667
Iran	6,560	8,415	10,994	16,357	31,491	57,036	67,148
Iraq	1,093	1,580	2,613	5,163	10,402	18,135	24,683
Israel				1,286	3,197	4,512	6,117
Jordan	217	266	348	561	1,674	3,262	5,460
Kuwait				145	894	2,142	2,183
Lebanon	332	476	649	1,364	2,825	3,147	3,728
Oman				489	857	1,773	2,807
Qatar				25	142	481	817
Arabia/S. Arabia*	5,202	5,749	6,658	3,860	6,667	16,061	25,157
Syria	1,337	1,582	1,994	3,495	6,931	12,436	17,586
Turkey	10,074	11,793	15,000	21,122	38,503	56,085	68,109
United Arab Emirates				72	391	1,951	2,485
Yemen				4,777	7,580	12,416	19,350
Palestine	332	429	700	1,017	1,124	1,897	3,512
Total 15 west Asian countries	**25,147**	**30,290**	**38,956**	**59,847**	**112,918**	**191,834**	**249,808**
Total Asia	**710,375**	**765,233**	**977,588**	**1,382,777**	**2,248,621**	**3,103,985**	**3,733,967**

Notes: Figures from 1820 to 1913 include Bahrain, Kuwait, Oman, Qatar, UAE, Yemen, and Saudi Arabia.

Source: Maddison (2003) for 1820–1949, updated from US Bureau of the Census, April 2005 version, except China and India (from national sources) and Indonesia (supplied by Pierre van der Eng).

Table 3.26b. Asian Per Capita GDP, 1820–2003 (1990 Geary–Khamis $)

	1820	1870	1913	1950	1973	1990	2003
China	600	530	552	448	838	1,871	4,803
India	533	533	673	619	853	1,309	2,160
Indonesia	612	654	904	840	1,504	2,526	3,555
Japan	669	737	1,387	1,921	11,434	18,789	21,218
Philippines	584	624	988	1,070	1,964	2,224	2,536
South Korea	600	604	869	854	2,824	8,704	15,732
Thailand	570	608	841	817	1,874	4,633	7,195
Taiwan	550	550	747	924	4,091	9,886	17,284
Bangladesh				540	497	640	939
Burma	504	504	685	396	628	778	1,896
Hong Kong	600	683	1,279	2,218	7,105	17,541	24,098
Malaysia	603	663	900	1,559	2,560	5,132	8,468
Nepal	397	397	539	496	622	808	1,007
Pakistan				643	954	1,589	1,881
Singapore	500	682	1,279	2,219	5,977	14,220	21,530
Sri Lanka	550	851	1,234	1,253	1,504	2,448	3,839
Total 16 Asian countries	**580**	**549**	**679**	**668**	**1,568**	**2,707**	**4,459**
Afghanistan				645	684	604	668
Cambodia				482	778	880	1,268
Laos				613	770	929	1,322
Mongolia				435	860	1,333	1,040
North Korea	600	604	869	854	2,824	2,841	1,127
Vietnam	527	505	727	658	836	1,025	2,147
23 Small Asian countries	556	535	752	1,151	2,080	2,254	2,966
Total 29 east Asian countries	**556**	**535**	**752**	**702**	**1,213**	**1,339**	**1,704**
Total 45 east Asian countries	**580**	**549**	**682**	**669**	**1,553**	**2,647**	**4,329**
Bahrain				2,104	4,376	4,104	5,589
Iran	588	719	1,000	1,720	5,445	3,503	5,539
Iraq	588	719	1,000	1,364	3,753	2,458	1,023
Israel				2,817	9,645	12,968	16,360
Jordan	590	718	1,000	1,663	2,388	3,792	4,220
Kuwait				28,878	26,689	6,121	10,145
Lebanon	657	845	1,350	2,429	3,155	1,938	3,507
Oman				623	3,279	6,479	6,896
Qatar				30,387	43,806	6,804	8,915
Arabia/S. Arabia*	550	575	600	2,231	11,040	8,993	7,555
Syria	658	844	1,350	2,409	4,017	5,701	7,698
Turkey	643	825	1,213	1,623	3,477	5,445	6,731
United Arab Emirates				15,798	24,887	13,070	17,818
Yemen				911	1,640	2,272	2,619
Palestine	614	751	1,250	949	2,184	3,806	2,563
Total 15 west Asian countries	**607**	**742**	**1,042**	**1,776**	**4,854**	**4,863**	**5,899**
Total Asia	**581**	**556**	**696**	**717**	**1,719**	**2,784**	**4,434**

Notes: *Figures from 1820 to 1913 include Bahrain, Kuwait, Oman, Qatar, UAE, Yemen, and Saudi Arabia.

Source: Derived from Tables 3.27a and 3.27c.

Table 3.26c. Asian GDP, 1820–2003 (million 1990 Geary–Khamis $)

	1820	1870	1913	1950	1973	1990	2003
China	228,600	189,740	241,431	244,985	739,414	2,123,852	6,187,984
India	111,417	134,882	204,242	222,222	494,832	1,098,100	2,267,136
Indonesia	10,970	18,929	45,152	66,358	186,900	450,901	762,545
Japan	20,739	25,393	71,653	160,966	1,242,932	2,321,153	2,699,261
Philippines	1,271	3,159	9,272	22,616	82,464	143,025	214,595
South Korea	5,637	5,891	9,206	17,800	96,231	373,150	758,297
Thailand	2,659	3,511	7,304	16,375	75,511	255,732	455,204
Taiwan	1,100	1,290	2,591	7,378	63,519	200,477	390,671
Bangladesh				24,628	35,997	70,320	130,013
Burma	1,767	2,139	8,445	7,711	18,352	30,834	87,269
Hong Kong	12	84	623	4,962	29,931	99,770	164,103
Malaysia	173	530	2,776	10,032	29,982	89,823	195,543
Nepal	1,541	1,865	3,039	4,462	7,894	15,609	26,660
Pakistan				25,366	67,828	182,014	293,666
Singapore	3	57	413	2,268	13,108	43,330	92,079
Sri Lanka	667	2,372	5,938	9,438	19,922	42,089	75,786
Total 16 Asian countries	**386,556**	**389,842**	**612,085**	**847,567**	**3,204,817**	**7,540,179**	**14,800,812**
Afghanistan				5,255	9,181	8,861	18,088
Cambodia				2,155	5,858	8,235	16,687
Laos				1,156	2,331	3,912	7,830
Mongolia				339	1,170	2,954	2,821
North Korea	2,607	2,725	4,257	8,087	42,819	56,874	25,310
Vietnam	3,453	5,321	14,062	16,681	38,238	68,959	175,569
23 Small Asian Countries	1,000	1,018	1,682	3,871	12,022	19,439	34,239
Total 29 east Asian countries	**10,651**	**13,328**	**28,115**	**37,544**	**111,619**	**169,234**	**280,544**
Total 45 east Asian countries	**397,207**	**403,170**	**640,200**	**885,111**	**3,316,436**	**7,709,413**	**15,081,356**
Bahrain				242	1,046	2,054	3,729
Iran	3,857	6,050	10,994	28,128	171,466	199,819	371,952
Iraq	643	1,136	2,613	7,041	39,042	44,583	25,256
Israel				3,623	30,839	58,511	100,065
Jordan	128	191	348	933	3,999	12,371	23,040
Kuwait				4,181	23,847	13,111	22,149
Lebanon	218	402	876	3,313	8,915	6,099	13,072
Oman				304	2,809	11,487	19,358
Qatar				763	6,228	3,276	7,284
Arabia/S. Arabia*	2,861	3,303	3,995	8,610	73,601	144,438	190,056
Syria	880	1,335	2,692	8,418	27,846	70,894	135,372
Turkey	6,478	9,729	18,195	34,279	133,858	305,395	458,454
United Arab Emirates				1,130	9,739	25,496	44,274
Yemen				4,353	12,431	28,212	50,678
Palestine	204	322	875	965	2,455	7,222	9,000
Total 15 west Asian countries	**15,269**	**22,468**	**40,588**	**106,283**	**548,120**	**932,968**	**1,473,739**
Total Asia	**412,476**	**425,638**	**680,788**	**991,393**	**3,864,556**	**8,642,381**	**16,555,095**

Notes: *Figures from 1820 to 1913 include Bahrain, Kuwait, Oman, Qatar, UAE, Yemen, and Saudi Arabia.

Source: Maddison (2003: 154–7 and 180–8), updated (except for China) from ADB, *Key Indicators 2005*; Japan and South Korea 2003 from OECD, *National Accounts, vol., 2006*. China 1950 onwards revised with new estimates for the industrial sector supplied by Harry X. Wu. South and North Korea (1911–74) amended to correct an error in Maddison (2003). Philippines, 1902–1940, amended in line with Hooley (2005). 1820 estimates amended for Hong Kong, the Philippines, Singapore, Sri Lanka, Taiwan, and Thailand.

⬜ ENDNOTES

1. Curtin (1984: 142), suggests that Portugal lost 28 per cent of its ships sailing to India between 1500 and 1634.

2. See O'Brien et al. (1991) on the effect of imports in creating a market for cotton textiles in England.

3. See Stokes (1959: 53):

   James Mill's *History of British India* was principally an attempt to make a philosophic analysis of Indian society and assess its place in the 'scale of civilization'. Undoubtedly one of his main aims was to dispel what he considered the silly sentimental admiration of oriental despotism which had marked the earlier thinkers of the Enlightenment. Even such a 'keen-eyed and skeptical judge' as Voltaire had succumbed, and the conservative tendencies of the Enlightenment had been mischievously strengthened. Mill's indictment of so-called Hindu and Muslim civilization is a *tour de force*... In India there was a 'hideous state of society', much inferior in acquirements to Europe even in its darkest feudal age. So far from any diffidence on account of his entire lack of personal experience of India, Mill prided himself that the severity of his judgement was all the more justified by its very disinterestedness.

4. It is interesting to recall Marx's expectation of the impact of British rule, written before the mutiny, when the westernization policy of the Benthamites was still operative: 'England has to fulfil a double mission in India: one destructive, the other regenerating—the annihilation of old Asiatic society, and the laying of the material foundations of Western society in India', *New York Daily Tribune*, 8 August 1853 (reprinted in Avineri 1969). In his articles on India, Marx stressed the fact that the British were breaking up the village community, uprooting handicraft industry, and establishing private property in land—'the great desideratum of Indian society'. He also expected irrigation and railways to have a significant effect on economic growth, and that industrialisation would destroy the caste system: 'Modern industry, resulting from the railway system, will dissolve the hereditary divisions of labour, upon which rest the Indian castes, those decisive impediments to Indian progress and Indian power.'

5. Batavia was the headquarters of VOC operations throughout Asia. It was 13 miles from Bantam, 38 from Cheribon, 82 from Palembang, 96 from Surabaya, 160 from Malacca, 300 from Ambon, 325 from Banda, 350 from Ternate, 328 from Thailand, 430 from Colombo, 496 from Cochin, 600 from Bengal, 738 from Japan, 900 from Mocha, 1483 from the Cape of Good Hope, and 3500 from the Netherlands (see Glamann 1981: 26)

6. The spice islands lost their monopoly in the last quarter of the eighteenth century when a French diplomat smuggled out some seedlings. Today they are grown in Grenada, Madagascar, Sri Lanka, and Tanzania.

7. Buddhist power and property in Japan were drastically reduced by Nobunaga who destroyed thousands of monastic buildings and slaughtered an even larger number of monks in the 1570s (see Hall 1971: 144).

8. There was a sharp contrast between Chinese and Japanese demographic experience from 1700 to 1820. In Japan, population grew 15 per cent, or 0.12 per cent a year. In China population rose by 2.75, i.e., by 0.85 per cent a year.

9. See Table 1.7, for Chinese and Japanese urbanization ratios, i.e., people living in all towns with population of 10,000—derived from Rozman (1973).

10. In 1870, the Japanese population was 34.4 million and the samurai 426,000. At the same time, the Chinese population was more than ten times as large—381 million, but its armed forces (Manchu bannermen and the Green standard troops) were about a million. This gives some idea of the unusually heavy military burden of the Tokugawa regime.

11. For the comparison of years of education of the population aged 15 and over (both sexes, weighted in equivalent years of primary education), see Maddison (1989a: 78).

12. *The Economist*, 8 October (2005: 11) commented as follows:

> The slow growth of productivity that makes OECD forecasters gloomy about Japan's potential was a consequence of the country's astonishing waste of capital during the 1990s, combined with a reluctance to cut jobs. Money was misallocated during the great stock and property bubble of the 1980s, but then even more was wasted in the next decade, as banks kept 'zombie' companies alive and politicians raided the biggest pork barrel in history.

13. The *China Handbook, 1937–1943*, Chinese Ministry of Information (1943: 178–9), gives details of the winding up of foreign concessions. Before the First World War, '19 countries enjoyed extraterritoriality and consular jurisdiction in China under the terms of unequal treaties'. They were Austro-Hungary, Belgium, Brazil, Denmark, France, Germany, Great Britain, Italy, Japan, Mexico, the Netherlands, Norway, Peru, Portugal, Russia, Spain, Sweden, Switzerland, and the United States. Austro-Hungary and Germany lost their rights in the First World War, Russian rights were suspended by the Chinese in 1920, and the USSR accepted this in 1924. The 1919 Versailles Peace Conference refused to consider abolition of extraterritoriality, and when the Chinese tried to terminate the system in 1921 and 1929, most of the treaty powers dragged their feet. By the end of 1930 Mexican, Finnish, Persian, Greek, Bolivian, Czech, and Polish nationals became amenable to Chinese jurisdiction. After the outbreak of war in 1937 China ended extraterritorial privileges for Italians, Japanese, Rumanian, Danish, and Spanish nationals. In 1943, the United Kingdom and the United States gave up their extraterritorial privileges in a treaty with China, and the system was thus ended.

☐ REFERENCES

ADB (Asian Development Bank), (2005), *Key Indicators*, Manila.

Allen, G. C. and A. W. Donnithorne (1954), *Western Enterprise and Far Eastern Economic Development*, Allen & Unwin, London.

Avineri, S. (1969), *Karl Marx on Colonialism and Modernization*, Anchor Books, Doubleday, New York.

Barrett, W. (1990), '*World Bullion Flows, 1450–1800*', in Tracy.

Boomgaard, P. (1993), '*Economic Growth in Indonesia, 500–1990*', in Szirmai et al.

Boserup, E. (1965), *The Conditions of Agricultural Growth*, Allen & Unwin, London.

Bray, F. (1984), *Agriculture*, vol.VI:2 of Needham (1954–94).

Bruijn, J. R. and F. Gaastra (eds) (1993), *Ships, Sailors and Spices*, NEHA, Amsterdam.

Chao, K. (1979), '*The Sources of Economic Growth in Manchuria, 1920–1941*', in C. Hou and T. Yu (eds), *Modern Chinese Economic History*, Academia Sinica, Taipei.

Craig, A. M. (1961), *Chōshū in the Meiji Restoration*, Harvard University Press.

Cranmer-Byng, J. L. (1962), *An Embassy to China: being the Journal kept by Lord Macartney during his Embassy to the Emperor Ch'ien Lung, 1793–1794,* Longmans, London.

Crawcour, E. S (1963), 'Changes in Japanese Commerce in the Tokugawa Period', *Journal of Asian Studies*, pp. 387–400.

Creutzberg, P. (1975), *Indonesian Export Crops, 1816–1940*, vol. 1, *Changing Economy in Indonesia*, Nijhoff, The Hague.

Cullen, L. M. (2003), *A History of Japan, 1582–1941*, Cambridge University Press.

Domar, E. D. (1989), *Capitalism, Socialism and Serfdom*, Cambridge University Press.

Eckstein, A., W. Galenson, and T. C. Liu (eds) (1968), *Economic Trends in Communist China*, Aldine, Chicago.

Eckstein, A., K. Chao and J. Chang (1974), 'The Economic Development of Manchuria: The Rise of a Frontier Economy', *Journal of Economic History*, pp. 235–64.

Flyn, D., A. Giraldez, and R. von Glahn (eds) (2003), *Global Connections and Monetary History, 1470–1800*, Ashgate.

Frank, A. G. (1998), *Reorient: Global Economy in the Asian Age*, University of California, Berkeley.

Fukuzawa, Y. (1972), *An Autobiography of Yukichi Fukuzawa* (revised translation by Eiichi Kiyooka), Schocken Books, New York.

Furber, H. (1976), *Rival Empires of Trade in the Orient, 1600–1800*, Oxford University Press.

Glamann, K. (1981), *Dutch–Asiatic Trade, 1620–1740*, Nijhoff, the Hague.

Grassman, S. and E. Lundberg (eds) (1981), *The World Economic Order: Past and Prospects*, Macmillan, London.

Habib, I. (1963), *The Agrarian System of Moghul India, 1556–1707*, Asia Publishing House, London.

Habib, I. (1978–9), 'The Technology and Economy of Moghul India', *Indian Economic and Social History Review*, XVII, No. 1, pp. 1–34.

Hall, J. W. (1971), *Japan from Prehistory to Modern Times*, Tuttle, Tokyo.

Hall, J. W. and M. B. Jansen (eds) (1968), *Studies in the Institutional History of Early Modern Japan*, Princeton University Press.

Hall, J. W. and J. P. Mass (eds) (1974), *Medieval Japan—Essays in Institutional History*, Yale.

Hall, J. W. and T. Toyoda (eds) (1977), *Japan in the Muromachi Age*, Berkeley.

Hall, J. W, K. Nagahara, and K. Yamamura (eds) (1981), *Japan Before Tokugawa: Political Consolidation and Economic Growth, 1500–1650*, Princeton University Press.

Hall, J. W. and J. J. McClain (eds) (1991), *Early Modern Japan, Cambridge History of Japan*, vol. 4, Cambridge.

Hanley, S. B. and K. Yamamura (1977), *Economic and Demographic Change in Preindustrial Japan*, Princeton University Press.

Hayami, A. (1986), 'Population Trends in Tokugawa Japan, 1600–1868', paper presented at the 46th session of the International Statistical Institute Congress.

Ho, P. T. (1959), *Studies on the Population of China, 1368–1953*, Harvard University Press.

Ho, S. P. S. (1978), *Economic Development of Taiwan*, Yale University Press.

Hooley, R. (2005), 'American Economic Policy in the Philippines, 1902–1940', *Journal of Asian Economics*, 16, pp. 464–88.

Innes, R. L. (1980), *The Door Ajar: Japan's Foreign Trade in the Seventeenth Century*, PhD thesis, University of Michigan, microfilm.

Jansen, M. B. and G. Rozman (1986), *Japan in Transition: From Tokugawa to Meiji*, Princeton University Press.

Kodansha Encyclopedia of Japan (1983), 6 vols., Tokyo University Press.

Lal, D. (2005), *The Hindu Equilibrium*, Oxford University Press.

Legge, J. D. (1980), *Indonesia*, 3rd edn, Prentice Hall of Australia, Sydney.

Levathes, L. (1994), *When China Ruled the Seas: The Treasure Fleet of the Dragon Throne, 1405–1433*, Simon & Schuster, New York.

Li, B. (1998), *Agricultural Development in Jiangnan, 1620–1850*, Macmillan, London.

Lin, J. Y. (1995), 'The Needham Puzzle', *Economic Development and Cultural Change*, January, pp. 269–92.

Liu, G. W. (2005), *Westling for Power: The State and the Economy in Late Imperial China, 1000–1770*, PhD thesis, Harvard University.

McEvedy, C. and R. Jones (1978), *Atlas of World Population History*, Penguin, Middlesex.

McEvedy, C. (1998), *Historical Atlas of the Pacific*, Penguin, London.

MacFarquhar, R. and J. K. Fairbank (eds) (1987 and 1991), *The Cambridge History of China*, vols. 14 and 15, Cambridge University Press.

Maddison (1969), *Economic Growth in Japan and the USSR*, Norton, New York.

Maddison (1971), *Class Structure and Economic Growth: India and Pakistan Since the Moghuls*, Allen & Unwin, London; Norton, New York.

Maddison, A. (1989), 'Dutch Income in and from Indonesia 1700–1938', *Modern Asian Studies*, 23, 4, pp. 645–70 (reprinted in Maddison 1995b).

Maddison, A. (1989a), *The World Economy in the Twentieth Century*, OECD, Paris.

Maddison, A. (1990), 'The Colonial Burden: A Comparative Perspective', in Scott and Lal, pp. 361–75.

Maddison, A. (1995a), *Monitoring the World Economy, 1820–1992*, OECD, Paris.

Maddison, A. (1995b), *Explaining the Economic Performance of Nations: Essays in Time and Space*, Elgar, Aldershot.

Maddison, A. (1998), *Chinese Economic Performance in the Long Run*, OECD, Paris.

Maddison, A. (2001), *The World Economy: A Millennial Perspective*, OECD, Paris.

Maddison, A. (2003), *The World Economy: Historical Statistics*, OECD, Paris.

Maddison, A. (2006), 'Do Official Statistics Exaggerate China's GDP Growth? A Reply to Carsten Holz', *Review of Income and Wealth*, March, pp. 121–6.

Maddison, A. (2006) Available at: www.ggdc.net/Maddison/

Maddison, A. and G. Prince (eds) (1989), *Economic Growth in Indonesia*, Foris, Dordrecht.

Maddison, A., D. S. Prasada Rao, and W. Shepherd (eds) (2000), *The Asian Economies in the Twentieth Century*, Elgar, Aldershot.

Moosvi, S. (1987), *The Economy of the Moghul Empire c.1595: A Statistical Study*, Oxford University Press, Delhi.

Morineau, M. (1985), *Incroyable garettes et fabuleux metaux*, Cambridge University Press.

Mukherjee, M. (1969), *National Income of India*, Statistical Publishing Society, Calcutta.

Myers, R. H. and M. R. Peattie (1984), *The Japanese Colonial Empire, 1895–1945*, Princeton University Press.

Nakamura, J. I. (1966), *Agricultural Production and the Economic Development of Japan, 1873–1922*, Princeton.

Nakamura, S. (1968), *Meiji Ishin no Kiso Kozo*.

Naoroji, D. (1901), *Poverty and Un-British Rule in India*, London (Government of India Reprint, Delhi, 1962).

Needham, J. (1970), *Clerks and Craftsmen in China and the West*, Cambridge University Press.

Needham, J. (1971), *Science and Civilisation in China*, vol. 4, part III, *Civil Engineering and Nautical Technology*, Cambridge University Press.

Needham (1981), *Science in Traditional China: A Comparative Perspective*, Harvard University Press.

Perkins, D. W. (1969), *Agricultural Development in China, 1368–1968*, Aldine, Chicago.

Pomeranz, K. (2000), *The Great Divergence: China, Europe and the Making of the Modern World Economy*, Princeton University Press.

Prakash, O. (1998), *European Commercial Enterprise in Pre-colonial India*, Cambridge University Press.

Qaisar, A. J. (1982), *The Indian Response to European Technology and Culture*, Oxford University Press, Bombay.

Raffles, T. S. (1978), *The History of Java*, 2 vols., Oxford University Press, Kuala Lumpur (reprint of 1817 edition).

Reid, A. (ed) (1983), *Slavery, Bondage and Dependency in Southeast Asia*, University of Queensland Press.

Reid, A. (1993),*Southeast Asia in the Age of Commerce, 1450–1680*, Yale University Press.

Ren, R. (1997), *China's Economic Performance in International Perspective*, OECD, Paris.

Ridgway, R. H. (1929), *Summarised Data of Gold Production*, Economic Paper No. 6, Bureau of Mines, US Dept of Commerce, Washington, D.C.

Roberts, L. S. (1998), *Mercantilism in a Japanese Domain*, Cambridge University Press.

Robertson, J. (1984), 'Japanese Farm Manuals: A Literature of Discovery', *Peasant Studies*, 11, Spring, pp. 169–94.

Rozman, G. (1973), *Urban Networks in Ch'ing China and Tokugawa Japan*, Princeton University Press.

Scott, M. and D. Lal (eds) (1990), *Public Policy and Economic Development: Essays in Honour of Ian Little*, Oxford University Press.

Shinohara, M. (1962), *Growth and Cycles in the Japanese Economy*, Kinokuniya, Tokyo.

Singh, M. (2005), '*Address by Prime Minister Manmohan Singh at Oxford University*', in acceptance of an honorary degree on 8 July.

Smith, H. D. (1986), '*The Edo-Tokyo Transition: In search of Common Ground*', in Jansen and Rozman.

Stokes, E. (1959), *The English Utilitarians and India*, Oxford University Press.

Szirmai, A., B. van Ark, and D. Pilat (eds) (1993), *Explaining Economic Growth: Essays in Honour of Angus Maddison*, North Holland, Amsterdam, London and New York.

Teng, S. Y., J. K. Fairbank et al. (eds) (1954), *China's Response to the West: A Documentary Survey*, Harvard University Press, Cambridge, MA.

Tracy, D. (ed) (1990), *The Rise of Merchant Empires: Long Distance Trade in the Early Modern World, 1350–1750*, Cambridge University Press.

Tracy, D. (ed) (1991), *The Political Economy of Merchant Empires*, Cambridge University Press.

Turnbull, C. M. (1997), *A History of Singapore, 1819–1975*, Oxford University Press, Kuala Lumpur.

Twitchett, D. and F. W. Mote (1998), *The Cambridge History of China, 1368–1644*, Part 2, Cambridge University Press.

Van der Eng, P. (1998), 'Exploring Exploitation: The Netherlands and Colonial Indonesia, 1870–1940', *Revista de Historia Econmica*, XVI, No. 1, pp. 291–321.

Van Leur, J. C. (1955), *Indonesian Trade and Society*, van Hoeve, The Hague.

Von Glahn, R. (1996), *Fountain of Fortune: Money and Monetary Policy in China, 1000–1700*, University of California Press.

Vries, J. de (2003), 'Connecting Europe and Asia: A Quantitative Analysis of the Cape Trade Route, 1497–1795', in Flyn et al.

Xi, L. and D. W. Chalmers (2004), 'The Rise and Decline of Chinese Shipbuilding in the Middle Ages', *International Journal of Maritime Engineering*, Royal Institute of Naval Architects.

Yamamura, K. (1974), *A Study of Samurai Income and Entrepreneurship*, Harvard University Press.

4 The impact of Islam and Europe on African development: 1–2003AD

INTRODUCTION

The long-term economic development of Africa is difficult to quantify with any precision. However, it is possible to discern the broad contours of population growth and there are some clues on the development of per capita income.

There is a marked difference between experience north of the Sahara and in the rest of the continent. For most of the past two millennia, income and urbanization levels were higher, economic and political institutions more sophisticated in the north than in the south. North African history is reasonably well documented because there are substantial written records. Knowledge of the south is based on archaeological or linguistic evidence until the ninth century when written evidence of northern visitors becomes available.

Over the long run, population growth was much more dynamic south of the Sahara. Two thousand years ago, about half of all Africans lived in the north; by 1820, four-fifths were in the south. Between the first century AD and 1820, the population of the north increased by a third (with many intervening setbacks). In the south it increased nearly eight-fold (see Table 4.1). In terms of *extensive* growth (i.e., capacity to accommodate population increase without a fall in per capita income), the south clearly had the edge. It seems likely that northern per capita income was lower in 1820 than in the first century. South of the Sahara, it probably increased modestly (See Table 4.2).

The greater demographic dynamism of the south is surprising, given its substantial losses from the slave trade. There are two reasons for this: (a) in north Africa, plague seems to have been endemic from the sixth to the nineteenth century. It does not seem to have crossed the Sahara; (b) the changes in agricultural technology were much greater in the south.

Two thousand years ago, much of black Africa was inhabited by hunter-gatherers using stone age technology. By 1820, they had been pushed aside and were a fraction of the population. The proportion of agriculturalists and pastoralists with iron age tools and weapons increased dramatically. Land productivity was also helped by the

Table 4.1. African Population, 1–2003AD (000s)

	1	1000	1500	1600	1700	1820	2003
Egypt	4,500	5,000	4,000	5,000	4,500	4,194	74,719
Morocco	1,000	2,000	1,500	2,250	1,750	2,689	31,689
Algeria	2,000	2,000	1,500	2,250	1,750	2,689	31,714
Tunisia	800	1,000	800	1,000	800	875	9,873
Libya	400	500	500	500	500	538	5,499
Total N. Africa	**8,700**	**10,500**	**8,300**	**11,000**	**9,300**	**10,985**	**153,494**
Sahel	1,000	2,000	3,000	3,500	4,000	4,887	34,335
Other W. Africa	3,000	7,000	11,000	14,000	18,00	20,777	217,536
Total W. Africa	**4,000**	**9,000**	**14,000**	**17,500**	**22,000**	**25,664**	**251,870**
Ethiopia and Eritrea	500	1,000	2,000	2,250	2,500	3,154	74,098
Sudan	2,000	3,000	4,000	4,200	4,400	5,156	38,114
Somalia	200	400	800	800	950	1,000	8,025
Other east Africa	300	3,000	6,000	7,000	8,000	10,389	108,841
Total east Africa	**3,000**	**7,400**	**12,800**	**14,250**	**15,850**	**19,699**	**229,078**
Angola, Zaire, Equatoria	**1,000**	**4,000**	**8,000**	**8,500**	**9,000**	**10,757**	**94,136**
Malawi, Zambia, Zimbabwe	75	500	1,000	1,100	1,200	1,345	34,917
Mozambique	50	300	1,000	1,250	1,500	2,096	18,801
South Africa, Swaziland, and Lesotho	100	300	600	700	1,000	1,550	47,659
Namibia and Botswana	75	100	200	200	200	219	3,629
Madagascar	0	200	700	800	1,000	1,683	16,980
Indian Ocean	0	0	10	20	30	238	2,856
Total southern Africa	**300**	**1,400**	**3,510**	**4,070**	**4,930**	**7,131**	**125,246**
Total Africa	**17,000**	**32,300**	**46,610**	**55,320**	**61,080**	**74,236**	**853,422**

Notes: Sahel includes Chad, Mauritania, Mali, Niger. *Other West Africa* includes Benin, Burkina Faso, Cape Verde, Cote d'Ivoire, Gambia, Ghana, Guinea, Guinea Bissau, Liberia, Nigeria, Senegal, Sierra Leone, Togo & W. Sahara. *Other East Africa* includes, Burundi, Djibouti, Kenya, Rwanda, Tanzania, Uganda *Equatoria* includes Cameroon, Central African Rep, Congo, Equatorial Guinea, Gabon, São Tomé & Principe. *Indian Ocean* includes Comoros, Mauritius, Mayotte, Reunion, Seychelles.

Source: 1–1820AD from McEvedy and Jones (1978), except Egypt in 1AD, which is from Frier (2000). 2003 from International Programs Center, US Bureau of the Census, www.census.gov/ipc, 26/4/05.

introduction and gradual diffusion of maize, cassava, and sweet potatoes from the Americas from 1500 onwards.

Possibilities for trade across the Sahara were revolutionized by the introduction of camels between the fifth and eighth centuries. A camel could carry about a third of a ton of freight, go without food for several days, and without water for up to 15 days, this was due to

its prodigious capacity—twenty-five gallons in ten minutes drinking time—its retention of the water it takes in, and its memory for water holes. Compared to other animals, the camel loses less water by perspiration, skin evaporation and urination. Camels can subsist on thorny plants and dry grasses that other animals cannot digest (Goldschmidt 1979: 21)

In Roman Africa there was virtually no contact with the lands south of the Sahara and, except for Egypt, the most advanced part of the economy was within 200 km of the Mediterranean coast. By the eleventh century, Muslim traders with caravans of more than 1,000 camels were a common feature of trade with black Africa. The

Table 4.2. African GDP per Capita, 1–2003AD (1990 international dollars)

	1	1000	1500	1600	1700	1820	2003
Egypt	600	550	500	500	500	500	3,034
Other N. Africa	479	430	430	430	430	430	3,227
Sahel and W. Afr.	400	415	415	415	415	415	1,176
Rest of Africa	400	400	400	415	415	415	1,245
Average	472	428	416	424	422	421	1,549

Notes and Sources: Chapter 1, Table 1.15 for first column. 1000–1820 are stylized conjectures.1820–2001 from Maddison (2003: 197–201) updated to 2003 from IMF, *World Economic Outlook*, April 2005. The rationale for the conjectures derives from the analysis of the main currents in African history. In the first century AD, north Africa belonged to the Roman Empire. Egypt was the richest part because of the special character of its agriculture, which had yielded a large surplus for governance and monuments in Pharaonic times, and was generally siphoned off as tribute by Roman and Arab rulers. Most of the Maghreb had a prosperous and urbanized coastal fringe, with Berber tribes between them and the Sahara.There was no contact then with black Africa which I assume had an average income only slightly above subsistence ($400 in my *numeraire*). After the Arab conquest of north Africa in the seventh century, camel transport opened trade across the Sahara, permitting a rise in per capita income in Morocco, the Sahel, and west Africa. I assume that the gradual transition within black Africa from a hunter-gatherer to an agricultural mode of production led to greatly increased density of settlement with higher per capita labour inputs, but had little impact on per capita income.

Arab conquest changed the civilization and institutions of north Africa and had a powerful Islamizing influence in the sahel and savannah lands south of the Sahara which stretched for 6,000 km between the Atlantic and the Red Sea. By the fourteenth century, the area of Muslim culture and influence stretched more than 3,000 km further south than the Roman domain. The degree of Islamization varied south of the Sahara, but the only area, above the equator, clearly outside its range was the Christian kingdom of Ethiopia.

THE EUROPEAN IMPACT ON NORTH AFRICA BEFORE THE SEVENTH CENTURY

Until the seventh century AD, and for the preceding millennium, a good part of the Mediterranean coastlands to the west were controlled by a hegemonial elite of Carthaginians and Romans. Egypt was ruled by a Greek dynasty (the Ptolemies) from 323 to 30BC when they came under Roman control. Rome took Carthage and its prosperous agricultural hinterland in Tunisia in 146BC. Cyrenaica became a Roman province in 96BC, the Berber kingdoms in Numidia in 46BC, and the northern fringe of Morocco in 44AD. In Egypt and Cyrenaica, the administrative language remained Greek. In the rest of Roman Africa, it was Latin.

From 30BC, all of North Africa was effectively under Roman rule. The Mediterranean was a Roman lake with magnificent ports in Italy and Alexandria and substantial flows of trade between Africa, Europe, and the Middle East. Hopkins (1980), using information on 545 dated shipwrecks, concluded that in the period

200BC–200AD 'there was more seaborne trade in the Mediterranean than ever before and more than there was for the next thousand years'. Egyptian agricultural productivity was much higher than in Italy because of the abundant and reliable flow of Nile water and the annual renewal of topsoil in the form of silt. Fertility was very high with seed yields of ten to one—much higher than the Italian ratio of four to one.[1] As a result, Egypt produced a surplus which the Pharoahs and the Ptolomies used to support a brilliant civilization. Under the new dispensation, as a Roman colony, a substantial part (approaching 10 per cent of Egyptian GDP) was siphoned off.[2] Large grain ships carried wheat from Alexandria to feed the population of Rome. There were exports of Egyptian flax and linen products, papyrus, glassware, and jewellry. Alexandria was also the main entrepot for merchandise coming up the Red Sea from India, Arabia, and east Africa.

The Romans had little interest in speculative and logical investigation, but Alexandria remained the intellectual centre of the ancient world for three centuries after the Roman conquest. Amongst the luminaries of this era were Claudius Ptolemy the astronomer and geographer, and Pappus the mathematician. Its library suffered serious damage during the Roman takeover in 30BC, but its final destruction did not occur until 270AD (see Casson 2001: 47).

The Roman Empire was divided at the end of the third century by Diocletian. Egypt came under the control of the eastern Empire and the grain exports of Alexandria were redirected to Constantinople in 330AD. The quality of intellectual life in Alexandria declined sharply after the establishment of Christianity as a state religion by the emperor Constantine in 323. Thereafter, the educated class in Egypt conversed increasingly in Coptic rather than Greek, and a good deal of the economic surplus went to sustain large monastic communities whose main cerebral activity was to defend their monophysite doctrine against the orthodoxy of the patriarch in Constantinople.

Tunisia and the provinces to the west were seized by Vandal invaders in 429. They were recaptured by forces of the emperor Justinian in 533, but it was clear that the economy of the Roman empire in Africa was in decline and that political control was weakening. Hopkins (1980) suggests that Mediterranean trade in 400–650 had fallen to about a fifth of the level in the first and second centuries.

Overland trade between the western provinces of Africa and the lands to the south was negligible. Roman settlement was initially fairly close to the coast except in Tunisia where large irrigated estates were worked mainly by tenant farmers. The cultivated area was extended under Roman rule: 'Augustus' and Tiberius' push to the southern pre-desert more than doubled the arable area of Roman Africa' (Whittaker 1996: 618). Exports of the African provinces were heavily concentrated on grain shipped to Italy from Carthage and olive oil from Tripolitania. Most of the export shipments were tribute, financed by tax levies; but some represented repatriation of rental income by absentee landlords. The population consisted mainly of settlers or demobilized soldiers from Italy as well as descendants of their Carthaginian or Hellenized predecessors. The main city was Carthage, which was rebuilt more than a century after its destruction by the Romans in 146BC. On the southern periphery, a string of forts constituted the frontier (*limes*). Within the frontier, private property prevailed and cadastral surveys were used to assess land tax liability. Between the Sahara and this frontier there were a large variety of tribes. Many were nomads or pastoralists, with little notion of property rights or boundaries. The Romans called them barbarians (*barbari*), from which the name Berber is derived.[3] They were generally hostile or recalcitrant towards the Roman regime and frequently engaged in hit-and-run raids. There was a small amount of trans-Saharan trade, via the oases of Fezzan in the Libyan desert. Herodotus (writing about 450BC) suggested that the Carthaginians had some access to sub-Saharan gold south of Morocco, but there is no record of Roman trade of this kind (see Mauny 1961; Bovill 1995), and little significant trade in slaves. Rome imported circus animals from Morocco, where the fauna were more varied than now.

In west Africa, Roman ships did not venture beyond Cape Bojador (just south of the Canary Islands), because the prevailing winds made a return journey impossible.

The boundary of Roman Egypt was fixed about 80 km south of the first Nile cataract at Aswan. There was only limited overland contact with the Nilotic Sudan (Meroe) and Ethiopia to the south, but both kingdoms became Christian in Byzantine times.

There was a large maritime trade with east Africa, Arabia, and India. Direct trade with India started in the second century BC, when Greek sailors from Ptolemaic Egypt discovered how to navigate in monsoon winds. By the time of Augustus, Strabo the geographer reported that 120 ships a year were sailing from Egypt to India. Wine, bronze, tin, gold, and various manufactured articles were shipped up the Nile to Coptos and moved overland to Red Sea ports at Myos Hormos or Berenice. Manned by Egyptian Greeks, they sailed through the Gulf of Aden to India by two major routes—to the north around Gujarat and to the southwest coast at Kerala or further south to Ceylon (see Casson 1989). They brought back spices, pepper, jewellery, and cotton goods. They were able to buy Chinese silks, mirrors, and other goods which had come overland to India. The Indian trade was financed in substantial part by export of silver and gold. The volume and dating of Roman coins found in India provide an indication of the locus and changing intensity of commerce. Trade with east Africa stretched along the Eritrean and Somali coast, round the horn down to a point slightly south of Zanzibar. The main east African exports were gold, ivory, cinnamon, slaves, hides, and elephants. Within the Red Sea there was trade with Axum (northeast Ethiopia) via its port of Adulis, and imports of aromatics (frankincense and myrrh) from the Arabian coastal ports.

Arab, Asian, and 'Roman' traders seem to have co-existed peacefully in the Indian Ocean. Indeed the former were there well before and after the Romans. Along the east African coast, there had been very lengthy contact with Asian trade. A significant part of the food supply of tropical east Africa was derived from bananas and plantains—introduced from Indonesia via Madagascar.

By the end of the fourth century, Egyptian shipping to India had declined sharply. Much of the European market had disappeared with the collapse of the western Empire, and Asian goods for the new imperial capital came to Constantinople via the Persian Gulf. What remained of the seaborne traffic to Egypt was serviced mainly by Arab or Axumite intermediaries (see Warmington 1928: 136–40).

THE ISLAMIC CONQUEST AND ITS IMPLICATIONS

In the seventh century, the Roman empire in Egypt and the rest of north Africa was destroyed by a new civilization whose hegemony lasted longer and extended much further south. It had very little contact with European countries across the Mediterranean until the twelfth century, but quickly developed trading and cultural links deep into the heart of Africa.

The Muslim conquest of Egypt started in 639 and ended in 642. The attack on the rest of north Africa, which the invaders called the *Maghreb*, started in 647 and was completed 60 years later. Spain was taken from its Visigothic rulers between 711 and 713. In western Asia, the Muslim conquest of Palestine and Syria (634), Iraq (637), and Iran (643) was breathtakingly quick.

The Muslim conquest derived its force from a new, uncompromisingly monotheistic, religion created in 622 with the exodus (*hijra*) of the prophet Muhammad and his adherents from hostile Mecca to friendly Medina. The fervour of the faithful was reinforced by their conviction that the surest path to paradise was martyrdom in war against infidels and the assurance that enemies would rot in hell. Conquest was facilitated by the presence of sizeable Arab populations in Syria, Iraq, and Iran, and the weakness of the two huge empires they attacked. The Byzantine was tottering and the Sassanian in Iraq and Persia already in a state of collapse. They were enfeebled by decades of mutual conflict and internal dissension.

Following the prophet's death in 632, the mantle of political leadership was vested in four successors (*caliphs*) from his immediate entourage and relatives. The first was one of his fathers-in-law and the fourth his only son-in-law. The succession was not in principle hereditary, and Muhammad left no male offspring, but in the long run the caliphate was either occupied or contested by his descendants or claimants who fabricated their ancestry.

The first caliph, Abubakar, consolidated the Muslim power base in Arabia. His successors, Umar and Uthman, continued to exercise control from Medina and commissioned the first written version of the prophet's revelations (the *Koran*). It was they who sent generals to attack the Byzantine and Persian empires, and appointed governors of conquered provinces. Their mobile cavalry—mounted on camels and horses—was incredibly successful. They seized hoards of gold and treasure from the Persian empire. They gained control of the fertile agricultural lands of Iraq and Egypt, from which they were able to squeeze large tax revenues. They captured Syria, which was strategically located for trade and for keeping the rump of the Byzantine empire in check. They also took Palestine, the heartland of monotheistic religion.

In 656 Uthman was murdered. His successor, Ali, moved his capital to Iraq, and was killed at Najaf in the ensuing civil war. He was defeated by a rival claimant to the caliphate, Muawiya, a relative of Uthman, brilliant general and creator of an Arab navy which had captured Cyprus and Rhodes. He had a secure power base in Syria, where he was governor. In 661 he established an Ummayad family dynasty in Damascus. The new regime was challenged in 680 by Husayn, the grandson of the prophet, but he and his family were massacred at Karbala.

In 750, the last Ummayad caliph and most of his family were killed by a new caliph, Abbas, a descendant of the prophet's uncle. He created a dynasty which lasted for five centuries. The Abbasids built a new, more cosmopolitan capital in Baghdad (adjacent to Ctesiphon, the old Sassanian metropolis). Their lifestyle and mode of governance were closer to the Persian model than to Arabian tradition. They kept the title of caliph, but effective political power passed to military rulers (sultans) from 945 until 1258 when the dynasty was destroyed by Mongol invaders.

By the tenth century, it was clear that the Muslim world was not a political monolith and that the strength of its rulers was based on secular force. The caliphate was politically impotent and unable to prevent schismatic tendencies in the domain of religion.

Although political diversity and fragmentation were much greater in the Muslim than in the Roman world, there were, nevertheless, powerful forces which gave it an oecumenical character and coherence:

1. There was the regular recital of a simple prayer in Arabic five times a day and religious education which involved close scrutiny and memorization of the Koran, Arabic became the *lingua franca* of the Muslim world. The introduction of religious schools (*madrasas*) in the tenth century helped the male population to acquire some degree of literacy. Communication was helped by the manufacture of paper which was introduced from China via Samarkand in the eighth century. This made it possible to replace papyrus scrolls by leaved books. However, the Muslim world was slow to adopt printing. The first press was authorized by the Ottoman empire in 1729 (see Lewis 1989: 49–50).

2. The prophet himself had been a merchant, so freedom of commercial transit was given high priority in Muslim territories which stretched from Spain to northern India, through central Asia to China, and from the Mediterranean coastlands deep into black Africa. The unity of the Muslim world was powerfully reinforced by the obligation on all believers who could afford it to make at least one pilgrimage (*hajj*) to Mecca. All Muslim rulers were required to facilitate their passage and security.

3. Islam was more tolerant in its attitude towards Jewish and Christian communities within its domain than Christian Europe was to non-Christians. However,

they were more heavily taxed than Muslims and many eventually converted to Islam.

4. The Muslim world demonstrated considerable assimilative and absorptive power. The Roman world had made a sharp distinction between civilization and barbarism. Conversion to Islam was a simpler process than acquisition of Roman citizenship. Thus the new religion managed to bring the Berbers of the Maghreb into its fold, assimilated a large portion of black Africa, and absorbed barbarian invaders from east Asia (Seljuk Turks and Mongols).

5. The Islamic legal system was not codified like the Roman, but provided an element of commonality which was present throughout the Muslim world. The Koran itself contained a good deal of guidance on practical matters. Thereafter, more detailed jurisprudence, precedents, rules of family and property law, codes of social behaviour and religious practice were incorporated in *hadiths*— records of tradition whose authority derived ultimately from sayings ascribed to the prophet. The written form of the hadith indicated the chain of learned commentators who had transmitted their wisdom between generations. Rulers in different parts of the Muslim world appointed judges (*qadis*) who were relatively autonomous in dealing with cases which involved no challenge to the political order. They used the authority of the hadiths to adjudicate, mediate, or arbitrate in family or property matters. The sytem resembled Jewish law, where rabbis used the wisdom of the Talmud to settle disputes between members of the community, without intercession of the political power. There were four schools of orthodox Sunni jurisprudence (Maliki, Hanafi, Shafii, and Hanbali). The Shia had three (Ismaili, Zaydi, and Twelver Shiites). There was also the Ibadi school of the Kharijites (see Udovitch 1981: 438; Schacht 1964).

Qadis were drawn from the *ulama*, the scholarly Muslim intelligentsia. Hadith literature and traditions varied between different parts of the Muslim world, but it is clear from the experience of ibn Batutta and ibn Khaldun that a distinguished scholar could become a qadi in widely separated locations.

6. The Muslim world displayed great intellectual vigour at a time when Europe was comatose and amnesiac. The early Abbasid caliphs (particularly Harun al-Rashid and Mamun) played a pioneering role in sponsoring secular learning. They created libraries, observatories, and a house of wisdom (*bayt al-hikwah*) in Baghdad. They invited scholars from Syria, Mesopotamia, Persia, and Transoxiana. They financed translations of Greek and Indian works on philosophy, astronomy, mathematics, and medicine, and encouraged the study of Persian literature. They hired calligraphers and copyists who disseminated this work in book form. In mathematics, al-Kharizmi (780–850), al-Biruni (973–1050), and Omar al-Khayyam (1038–1124, born in Khorassan) made advances in astronomy, algebra, and trigonometry, introduced Indian numerals and the essentials of decimal reckoning. Avicenna (ibn Sina, 973–1037, born in Bukhara) was a distinguished contributor to and codifier of medical knowledge.

The authorities also promoted the development of navigational instruments (astrolabes, quadrants, globes, and the magnetic compass).

Scholarly activity in Baghdad faded in the course of the twelfth century and disappeared with the Mongol invasion. Intellectual leadership had already passed to Muslim Spain whose links with Africa were close. Its highly cosmopolitan luminaries included al-Bakri, the eleventh century geographer; Averroes (ibn-Rushd, 1126–98), rationalist philosopher, judge in Seville and court-physician in Marrakesh; Moses Maimonides (ibn-Maymun, 1135–1204), a philosopher who tried to reconcile reason and religion, was born in Cordoba, moved to Morocco and then became physician to Saladin and head of the Jewish community in Cairo. The library of Cordoba and the University of Granada offered important support to intellectual life in Spain. In north Africa, universities in Fez, Kairouan, and al-Azhar in Cairo performed a similar function. In the thirteenth century Spanish territory under Muslim control contracted drastically and intellectual activity faded.

However, in the Maghreb, three writers provided brilliant insights into the history, geography, and institutions of Africa. The world traveller, ibn Battuta (1304–77), born in Tangier, presented a comparative socio-political picture of all parts of the Muslim world (Middle East, China, India, Islamic and black Africa) in his day and also threw light on the high status and universal acceptance which members of the *ulama* enjoyed throughout the Muslim world.

Ibn Khaldun (1332–1407), born in Tunis, provided a more scholarly diachronic perspective of the Berber dynasties of the Magreb, their interaction with the Arabs and with al-Andalus, as well as a fascinating and deeply pessimistic assessment of long term patterns in Muslim history in his *Muqaddimah*. Leo Africanus (al-Fazi), born in and expelled from Granada in 1493, educated in Fez, captured off Tunisia in 1518, taken to the Vatican as a protégé of the Medici Pope, Leo X, wrote a pedestrian but useful description of conditions in Africa in his day;

7. Watson (1983) argued that there was an agricultural 'revolution' in the Islamic world between 700 and 1100AD, followed by a decline due to nomadic intrusions and salinization. The 'revolution' derived from a systematic effort by the Abbasid caliphate to collect and diffuse knowledge about botany, agriculture, and pharmacology in books and translations which were made available in libraries in major cities of the empire, and from experiments in botanical gardens in Basra, Damascus, al-Fustat, the Maghreb, Seville, Cordoba, and Valencia. Diffusion of new knowledge was all the more effective because of the use of Arabic as a *lingua franca*, interaction through migratory movement, travel for commercial purposes and pilgrimage to Mecca. New crops diffused westwards were sugar cane, cotton, rice, hard wheat, sorghum, taro, indigo, oranges, and eggplants. More intense land use was possible, replacing fallow by summer crops in desert areas, because of improved irrigation and water storage, cisterns, underground canals (*qanats*), and improvements in

Table 4.3.

	1	1000	1500	1700	1820	2003
(a) West Asian Population, 1–2003AD (000s)						
Arabia*	2,000	4,500	4,500	4,500	5,202	53,466
Iran	4,000	4,500	4,000	5,000	6,560	67,148
Iraq	1,000	2,000	1,000	1,000	1,093	24,683
Turkey**	8,000	7,000	6,300	8,400	10,074	68,109
Other***	4,400	2,000	2,000	1,900	2,218	36,403
Total	19,400	20,000	17,800	20,800	25,147	249,809
(b) West Asian Per Capita GDP, 1–2003AD (1990 international dollars)						
Arabia*	400	600	550	550	550	6,313
Iran	500	650	600	600	588	5,539
Iraq	500	650	550	550	588	1,023
Turkey**	550	600	600	600	643	6,731
Other***	550	645	645	645	645	7,707
Total	521	620	590	591	607	5,899
(c) West Asian GDP, 1–2003AD (million 1990 international dollars)						
Arabia*	800	2,700	2,475	2,475	2,861	337,528
Iran	2,000	2,925	2,400	3,000	3,857	371,952
Iraq	500	1,300	550	550	643	25,256
Turkey**	4,400	4,200	3,780	5,040	6,478	458,454
Other***	2,420	1,290	1,290	1,226	1,431	280,549
Total	10,120	12,415	10,495	12,291	15,270	1,473,739

Notes: *includes Bahrain, Kuwait, Oman, Qatar, Saudi Arabia, United Arab Emirates, and Yemen; **1–1000AD excludes European Turkey; ***Syria, Lebanon, Palestine, and Jordan

Source: www.ggdc.net/Maddison

water-lifting technology. Watson argued that these developments permitted faster population growth:

the agricultural revolution was bound up with an ill-documented but none the less real demographic revolution which seems to have touched most parts of the Islamic world from roughly the beginning of the eighth till the end of the tenth century (p. 129)

Watson is right to stress the importance of crop diffusion in raising productivity and per capita income, but exaggerates population growth. The estimates of McEvedy and Jones (1978) show a rise of 12.5 per cent in the the Islamic world from 700 to 1000AD (when the total was about 30 million), i.e., a rate of growth of 0.04 per cent a year. Watson also advances improbably high estimates of urbanization (p. 133). He suggests that three new cities in Iraq (Baghdad, Basra, and Samarra) had over half a million inhabitants, and that Kufa could have had up to 400,000. He credits Fustat-Cairo, Kairouan, and Cordoba with half a million each, with two large cities (Isfahan and Nishapur) near that level in Iran.

8. Slavery was an institution common to both the Muslim and Roman worlds. Slaves were chattels who could be bought and sold, and their status was hereditary. A large proportion were enemies captured in war, some were seized

for sale by dealers or their intermediaries. Long serving Roman slaves were not infrequently freed. Muslims, in principle, enfranchized slaves who converted to Islam. Most slaves in the Roman empire were Europeans. A larger proportion were black in the Islamic world. In both systems, they were used as household servants or for manual labour in agriculture and mining, but in polygamous households, there was a large demand for concubines and eunuchs. There was extensive use of slaves in Muslim armies particularly in those of the Seljuk Turks, Mamluk Egypt, and the Ottoman empire. In Africa, the incidence of slavery was modest in Roman times (by comparison with that in the Muslim period or, indeed, with Roman Italy). Bagnall and Frier (1994: 48), estimate that under 11 per cent of their sample of the Egyptian population were slaves in the second century AD. In the rest of the Roman provinces of north Africa, there was 'little evidence of Roman-style imported slavery on the land' (see Bowman et al. 1996: 611). By the seventh century, under Byzantine rule, the incidence of slavery had declined further (see Ostrogorsky 1968: 76);

9. Muslim marriage and family institutions were very different from those which prevailed in western Europe. Polygamy was permitted up to a limit of four wives, divorce was easy, and the conjugal circle could be readily enlarged by concubinage. The ruling elites usually maintained very large housholds, retinues of slaves and eunuchs. These arrangements encouraged conspicuous consumption, fratricidal disputes about inheritance and political instability. They also inhibited accumulation of capital. Widows were advised to remarry, whereas in the west they were expected to leave their assets to the church. There was no religious hierarchy, no ordained or celibate priesthood, so there was not the huge increase in ecclesiastical assets of the kind which was experienced in western Europe.

EGYPT AS AN ISLAMIC STATE

Tributary of the Ummayad and Abbasid Caliphates, 642–969

Egypt was the most prosperous part of Africa, with a relatively large urban population, a sedentary agriculture, a substantially monetized economy, a significant industrial and commercial sector, and a very long history as an organized state. Its agriculture was fertile enough to feed the urban population and to provide tribute grain for shipment to Constantinople. Its natural waterways lowered the cost of transporting freight and passengers through the middle of a densely populated country. The prevailing winds blew from the north, so that one could sail upstream and float downstream. On both sides and to the south it was surrounded by desert which gave it some protection against invasion. The level of economic prosperity and the population declined from the third century. The Justinian (bubonic) plague of 542–3 took a devastating toll and recovery was hindered by subsequent outbreaks of disease and recurrent poor harvests in a period when the Nile waters were at a low level.

The collapse of the Roman empire in the west had ended virtually all trade with Europe. Trade down the Red Sea disappeared when Constantinople became the Imperial capital. Byzantine commerce with Asia was conducted via the Persian Gulf or by overland caravan. The entrepot trade and manufactured exports of Alexandria, the capital city, declined substantially. The orthodox Greek patriarch played a major role in governance, but the majority of Egyptian Christians were monophysite Copts. Thus the community was split by doctrinal discord and disputes about ecclesiastical property.

In 619, Sassanid Persia captured Egypt, Syria, and Palestine, and maintained its occupation until 627, when the Byzantine emperor Heraclius destroyed their army at Nineveh. The Sassanid dynasty collapsed and the Byzantines regained all their former territories, but the strain of this and simultaneous campaigns against enemies in the Balkans exhausted their capacity to face further conflict, and reduced Heraclius to a physical and mental wreck.

The Muslim conquest of Egypt was quick and relatively smooth. It was greatly eased by the docility or active cooperation of a large part of the population. In the first phase, Arab forces moved from Palestine to the junction of the Nile valley and the delta at Babylon, which was surrendered in 641 by Cyrus, the orthodox patriarch and governor of Egypt. The invaders established their camp nearby at al-Fustat, which became the new capital of Egypt. Alexandria was attacked without success, but in 642, it too was surrendered by Cyrus. The Egyptian fleet was handed over in return for favourable treatment of the Coptic church. At this stage, the Coptic Patriarch, Benjamin, came out of hiding and was given full possession of all ecclesiastical property (see Brett, 1978).

There was a large exodus of the Greek elite from Alexandria. Domain land belonging to the Byzantine state and aristocracy was taken over by the new Arab elite. Taxes on other land continued to be collected by the former district administration (the *pagarchy*) who were also responsible for hydraulic works (dikes, canals, walls, and ditches) at village and district level. The grain tribute which had previously gone to Constantinople was redirected, first to Arabia, and later to Damascus and Baghdad.

With the income from their large estates, the new Arab aristocracy were able to create lavish households with retinues of slaves and to provide support for associates and attendants lower down the ladder of power. Fustat was no longer a garrison town, but a centre of court life embellished with large mosques and palaces. However, Egypt was essentially an Ummayad colony, with a governor appointed by Damascus. After 700, there were censuses to assess fiscal potential and a financial controller (*wali*) as an independent crosscheck on the administration.

When the Umayyad caliphate was destroyed, Egypt's elite were displaced by new governors and their entourages from Baghdad, but the provincial administration seems to have been more or less unchanged. In the ninth century, governors of Turkish origin were appointed in Egypt with greater autonomy and additional administrative responsibilities in western Arabia.

Over the long run, an increasing proportion of Egypt's Coptic population converted to Islam. There was a gradual Arabisation of speech and local administration. Eventually, Coptic became a liturgical rather than a spoken language. As taxes were lighter on Muslims, their increased proportionate importance reduced government revenues and created fiscal problems.

Nomadic Arab immigrants were largely confined by government policy to peripheral desert areas on either side of the Nile and its delta or filtered South, to the border area with Nubia.

Trade with Europe and down the Red Sea was negligible in the colonial period, but trade with Muslim lands to the east increased, and new routes were opened in the southwest via Lake Chad for trade in gold and slaves with black Africa.

The political regime changed radically in 969, when Egypt became independent after a thousand year lapse. It remained independent until 1517.

Independent Egypt 969–1517

Fatimids, 969–1171

At the end of the ninth century, a new Shi'ite dynasty, the Fatimids (so named as they claimed descent from Muhammad's dughter Fatima), took power in Tunisia. In 909, they set up a rival caliphate in their new capital at Mahdia and gained control of the whole Maghreb. In 969, their general, Jawhar, captured Egypt, built a new city, Cairo, and a new mosque-university, al-Azhar. In 973, the Fatimids moved their capital from Mahdia to Cairo. They brought a substantial naval force from Tunisia and created shipyards in Egypt using timber imported from Lebanon. The new elite took over the property of the ousted Abbasid administration, stopped tribute to Baghdad, and acquired their own tribute income from their control of western Arabia, Syria, and Palestine. With the resources available they were able to create mosques and palaces, and establish a luxurious lifestyle in Cairo. They hoped to build a new pan-Islamic empire and destroy the Abbasid caliphate. To this end they established a centre of Shi'ite religious study (*Dar al-Hikma*) in Cairo, and attacked the mainstream Sunni version of Islam in their religious propaganda. They had little success as evangelists. Even in Egypt a large proportion of the Muslim population were unimpressed.

There was an important expansion of Egypt's role in international trade under the Fatimids. They gained control of the African and Asian shores of the Red Sea and reopened trade with India at the expense of Abbasid trade via the Persian gulf. After several centuries of vestigial contact, Italian traders from Genoa, Pisa, and Venice reopened European trade with Egypt (and with the Maghreb). The first two vizirs of the Fatimids were Jewish and Christian, and their economic policies were tolerant and liberal. They did not interfere with private trading activity in Egypt where a major role was played by Jewish and Coptic Christian merchants. Although state income from customs duties rose, the levies were 'reasonable'—according to Goitein (1967: vol. 1, chap. 1).

After its first century of power, the Fatimid empire started to unravel. Within Egypt they had trouble with nomadic Arabs. They expelled the Hilal and Sulaym tribes who moved west and created havoc in the Maghreb where the Fatimids lost control. The Normans seized Sicily in 1072 and occupied the Tunisian coast from 1134 to 1159. At the end of the eleventh century, Syria and Palestine were taken over by European Crusaders (see the Appendix to this chapter).

The Fatimid army consisted initially of Berber tribesmen. In Egypt they used slave soldiers (*mamluks*) of Turkish origin as their cavalry, and Nubian slaves as infantry. In 1065, there was a military revolt, which caused major damage to dams and canals and provoked a famine. Although control over the military was reestablished, they were not effective against the Crusaders (known in the Arab world as Franks).

In 1153, Egypt lost its last foothold in Palestine and in 1168 Cairo was besieged. The Crusader forces were driven out of Egypt with the help of troops sent by Nur al-Din, ruler of Damascus. Their general was Salah al-Din al-Ayyubi (a Kurdish aristocrat, born in Takrit in 1138; died in Damascus in 1193), better known to the Franks as Saladin. In 1169, he established himself as *vizir* (chief minister) of the Fatimids. In 1171, he abolished the Fatimid caliphate and established a new Sunni dynasty in Cairo which was recognized by the Abbasid caliphate. Saladin became the second Ayyubid sultan in 1174, on the death of Nur.

Ayyubids, 1171–1250

Saladin confiscated the lands and revenues of the Fatimid elite and redistributed them to his Kurdish soldiery and his own family. He made major institutional changes in the property system and the regulation of foreign trade.

He tried to establish a *modus vivendi* with the Franks, as they had opened up profitable possibilities for trade with Europe on a scale which paralleled the situation a thousand years earlier when the Mediterranean was a Roman lake. Unfortunately, the Franks (as the Crusaders were called) were too ambitious and overplayed their hand. They wanted hegemony over Egypt and control of trade with Asia. In Saladin's lifetime, they were kept at bay. In 1182, when their fleet came down the gulf of Aqaba and attacked his forts on both sides of the Red Sea, his navy captured all their ships and executed their crews. In 1187, he recaptured Jerusalem. The Franks then organized their third and largest crusade. Saladin lost some ground to them, but they did not get Jerusalem and their leaders withdrew in 1192.

In allocating land, Saladin changed from Fatimid tax farming to a form of military feudalism not unlike that subsequently adopted in the Moghul and Ottoman empires. Fiefs allotted to the military provided the equivalent of a salary and covered the expense of maintaining troops. In principle, these grants were not hereditary, and were frequently reallocated, but, in practice, some became family properties.

Trade relations with foreigners became closely regulated and protectionist. Non-Muslims could operate only in Alexandria, where they were allowed to maintain *fun-duqs*. These served as warehouses for their goods and provided residential and office accomodation on the same lines as *fondaca* for foreign traders in Venice. Contract arrangements were generally secure as they were registered with the government which collected taxes on all transactions. Foreigners could not unload their goods until they had been checked by customs officials. Venetians and Genoese were prominent amongst these merchants. Egypt retained a monopoly on Red Sea trade with Asia. Foreigners had to buy Egyptian goods and imported Asian spices, aromatics, dyes, textiles, porcelain, and other products from Egyptian wholesale merchants. They also had to sell their wares to these *Karimi* traders. Coptic and Jewish traders within Egypt lost the favoured position they had enjoyed under the Fatimids. The Karimi had a base at Aden where Indian ships unloaded, as well as trading posts in Arabia, India, Indonesia, and China and some participation in overland caravan trade. At this time there was little Egyptian trade with east Africa and not much south of the Sahara.

The major Egyptian export industries were flax and cotton textiles; carpets and cushions; glass and crystal products; paper; ceramic ware; refined sugar; decorative swords; and metal items. In agriculture, the product-mix had widened under Arab rule and there were new kinds of crop rotation. The main new crops were cotton, rice, and sugar-cane. The introduction of sugar stimulated production of a wide variety of confectionary products.

Saladin's successors continued to be be involved in conflict with the Franks, who invaded Egypt unsuccesfully in 1218 and again in 1249. On both occasions, the intruders captured the port of Damietta, but were defeated in battle at Mansura in the delta. In 1250, the Egyptian Mamluk troops captured the French king Louis IX, destroyed his army, then killed the last of the Ayyubid sultans and took over as rulers in Egypt (see Appendix to this chapter).

Mamluks, 1250–1517

The change of regime involved a smaller property transfer than earlier takeovers, as Mamluks were already an important part of the Ayyubid establishment, but it did change the mode of governance. The Mamluk elite was recruited by import of Turkish and Tartar boys from the Russian steppes and the Caucasus. They were shipped as slaves from the Black Sea through the Bosphorus with the acquiescence of the Byzantine authorities.[4] After intensive military training, they were freed and inducted into the cavalry. They were the ruling elite from which Egyptian sultans were henceforth selected, but in principle, their children were not eligible for top positions. They were given landed fiefs, which were regularly reallocated, and could not be sold.

They continued to speak Turkish and were never really Arabized. They did little for Muslim culture, but were an effective military force. They installed a puppet caliphate in Cairo, which gave them added legitimacy as the paramount power in the Middle East, with control of western Arabia, Syria, and Palestine. In 1258, Mongol invaders destroyed the empire of the Seljuk sultans and took control of Anatolia, Persia, and Iraq. In 1260, they invaded Syria, but were defeated by the Mamluks. By 1291, the last Crusader toeholds in Palestine were eliminated. At a later stage, the Mamluks were lucky in keeping Timur (Tamerlane) out of Egypt. Between 1387 and 1400, this nominal Muslim ravaged and conquered Persia, Iraq, and Syria, wreaking great damage on their economies. Fortunately, after cross-examining Ibn Khaldun in Damascus in January and February 1401 on the geography and politics of Egypt and the Maghreb, Timur gave up the idea of pushing his conquests further west, and departed for China in 1401 (see Rosenthal 1967: vol. 1, pp. lxiii–lxv).

Trade relations with Europe thrived after the Crusaders disappeared. Egypt made commercial treaties with Florence, Genoa, Venice, Sicily, Catalonia, and Marseilles, more or less on the lines laid down by Saladin. Its Karimi merchants traded down the Red Sea to India, Indonesia, and China. Customs duties provided the government with a large revenue from this trade. Cairo also organised annual convoys of African pilgrims on *hajj* to Mecca and Medina. These pilgrims had commercial as well as religious interests. Cairo was the major entrepot for trade with the Maghreb and Muslim Spain (*al-Andalus*).

There was substantial trade with the gold-rich states which had emerged in west Africa. The big stretch of savannah land between Senegal and east Africa was known in Arabic as the *Bilad al-Sudan* (land of the blacks). In 1324, the potential for profitable trade with these countries was dramatised by the spectacular pilgrimage of the king of Mali, Mansa Musa. At that time his country was the biggest and most prosperous in the western Sudan, and had been Islamized in the twelfth century. The king came to Cairo with a large retinue of slaves and soldiers, and a camel caravan carrying more than 10 tons of gold.[5] The Sultan lent him a palace where he stayed for three months before leaving for Mecca. He also stopped on his way back. By this time, he had spent all his money on lavish presents, alms, donations to religious charities, purchases of slaves, and other items, and had incurred debts which he honoured in gold on his return. This memorable visit was very effective in demonstrating the potential of trans-Saharan trade. It was of particular interest to Egypt, whose traditional gold supply (from the al-Allaqi mines, in the desert southeast of Egypt) was exhausted.

In 1272 the Mamluks defeated the army of Nubia at Dongola and Egypt acquired significant influence in this formerly independent kingdom on its southern border. In 1315 it installed a Muslim prince as king, and two years later the cathedral of Dongola became a Mosque. Islamization opened the country to a large inflow of nomadic Arabs who also moved further south and into the Sahara southwest of Egypt. These political, religious, and ethnic changes facilitated Egyptian trade with this region. However, there was little contact with east Africa (see Hrbek 1977).

In 1348–50, Egypt was one of the areas most severely affected by the black death. The pneumonic plague epidemic ravaged its densely settled population. It seems likely that its incidence was similar to that in western Europe. If so, Egypt probably lost about a third of its population.

In fact, plague remained endemic in Egypt and the Maghreb until the end of the eighteenth century with recurrent attacks in urban areas (see Iliffe 1995: 161–2). Its virulence, persistence, and impact seem to have been more serious than in Europe. It was probably the major reason for the prolonged demographic stagnation of north Africa, where population in 1820 was not much different from its level 800 years earlier (see Table 4.1).

The impact of plague was greater in Egypt than elsewhere in north Africa, because it was more urbanized. After the first plague attack, the Mamluk regime had severe fiscal problems as government revenue fell. In 1400 official income from Syria disappeared because of the destruction wrought by Timur's invasion. Revenue was adversely affected by the large proportion of fiefs (*iqta*) which had been converted into religious charities (*waqf*) which were not subject to land tax.

To offset the fall in land taxes, the government started to debase the currency in 1424. At the same time, it confiscated private sugar plantations and refineries and raised prices to increase the profit margin, but domestic consumption and exports fell. Venetian merchants began to develop competitive sugar production in Crete and Cyprus. In 1429, the government banned Egyptian traders from selling imported spices to foreigners. Here again it raised prices and damaged the income of Karimi merchants who moved a significant amount of capital elsewhere. European merchants were enraged, explored ways of getting spices by contraband or piracy and began to contemplate alternative routes to Asia. By the end of the century, the Portuguese had circumnavigated Africa and destroyed the Egyptian spice monopoly. They attacked Egyptian trading bases and shipping in Asia, and harassed shipping in the Red Sea. In 1509, the Portuguese destroyed an Egyptian fleet off Diu in Northwest India.

Egypt as a Province of the Ottoman Empire, 1517–1798

A new Turkish nation emerged in Anatolia around 1300 from the wreckage of the Seljuk empire. The Ottoman ascension was rapid. Their first empire in the Balkans and Anatolia collapsed in 1402 under onslaught from Timur's forces, but recovered within three decades. Their main target was the moribund Byzantine empire. In 1453, they captured Constantinople, whose population had dwindled to 50,000. Many churches were converted into mosques, but Jews and Christians were tolerated and the Orthodox patriarch remained. The Ottomans had ambitions for paramountcy of the Islamic world. Their forces engaged the Mamluks in Syria in 1516, and in Cairo in 1517. Equipped with quilted body armour, bows and arrows, sabres, and lances, the Mamluks were easily defeated by Ottoman gunpowder and artillery. Egypt lost control of Syria and western Arabia and became a provincial backwater under a Turkish viceroy, paying an annual tribute to the Ottoman sultan.

In 1529 the Ottomans added Hungary to their empire and, in 1534, took Kurdistan and Mesopotamia from Safavid Persia. By 1551, their domain included the whole of the Maghreb except Morocco. Their empire was comparable in size to the Byzantine under Justinian.

The Ottoman takeover in Egypt was rendered easier by the defection of the Mamluk governor of Aleppo, who became their first viceroy (*pasha*) of Egypt. Thereafter the pashalik was occupied by high officials from Istanbul. The Ottomans increased the proportion of land held by the crown, but Mamluks and their descendants retained much of their property and had an important share of political power. They established a prescriptive right to command the annual pilgrimage caravan to Mecca, the annual tribute convoy to Istanbul, to act as treasurers of Egypt and as interim viceroys when the pashalik was vacant. They were also important as provincial governors (see Holt 1975: 14–39).

In course of time Ottoman control over Egypt was eroded by local notables who were frequently able to reject or eliminate pashas sent from Istanbul. The decline in political control weakened tax revenue. As a result, there was substantial inflation, neglect of irrigation works, and the same tendency to squeeze merchant income that there had been under the Mamluk regime.

By the end of the eighteenth century, the population and per capita product of Egypt were well below their level in the eleventh century. In the same period, western Europe had almost trebled its per capita income and increased its population more than five-fold.

The Napoleonic Invasion and its Impact, 1798–1805

The political and socioeconomic order in Egypt was transformed by the French invasion and occupation of 1798–1801. It shattered the corrupt and incompetent Mamluk elite, destroyed their military, and demolished their property rights. It demonstrated the value of western education and organization. It revolutionized the study of Egyptian history in a way which reinforced national consciousness. Within four years of the French departure, Egypt had acquired a new political leadership which modernized the country, reformed its economy, and changed the mode of governance.

The French invasion was conceived and organized by Napoleon. In 1796–7 he had conducted a lightning campaign which transformed the political landscape of Italy, creating the Cisalpine republic which stretched from the Alps to Tuscany and

Bologna, displacing the Genoese oligarchy by a Ligurian republic. A Roman republic replaced the Papal states, and the Pope was exiled to France. Napoleon advanced close to Vienna and dictated peace terms, reconciling Austria to its losses by handing over the Venetian republic. When he returned to Paris in December 1797, the directory asked the 28-year-old general to organize an invasion of England. In February 1798, he visited Dunkirk and the Flemish coast to examine the troops and ships assembled there. He decided the resources were inadequate, and concluded that he could damage British interests more effectively and with much less risk by making Egypt a French colony, constructing a canal through the isthmus of Suez and threatening British access to India. The directory agreed and gave him command of a force financed from the large indemnities extorted from Italy and Switzerland.

His expedition departed from Toulon and Italian ports in mid-May 1798. The army consisted of 35,000 troops, 26 handpicked generals, 300 laundresses and seamstresses, 700 horses, siege artillery, guns, and ammunition. The naval force included 13 ships of the line, seven frigates, eight gunboats, more than 200 troop transports and 15,000 sailors. In addition there was a scientific contingent of 150 scholars to survey Egypt's resources and reconstruct its history. These *savants* included mathematicians, geographers, surveyors, engineers, chemists, medical personnel, archaeologists, a botanist, a zoologist, a mineralogist, an authority on balloon warfare, a flower painter, a musician, and a poet. There were also translators and a printing press equipped with Arabic characters. Vivant Denon was a key figure—a draughtsman and engraver who had organized the selection and transfer of captured works of art in the Italian campaign and helped cataloque the antiquities and buildings which were identified in the 24 volume *Description de l'Egypte* (1810–22).

On 9 June, the journey was broken for ten days to capture Malta. The knightly order of St John was dissolved, the administration was re-ordered, a garrison was left behind, and Napoleon sailed off with their treasure.

Alexandria was captured easily at the end of June. Mamluk forces (10,000 cavalry and 16,000 infantry) tried to block entry to Cairo but were defeated with small French casualties three weeks later. The remnants fled to Palestine and Upper Egypt.

Established in Cairo, Napoleon set out to create a new colonial adminstration and tax system. The landholdings of Mamluk tax-farmers were confiscated (about two-thirds of the cultivated area), a register of landed property was created and a cadastral survey was initiated. His savants held seminars every five days at the new Institut d'Egypte to report on their work. Consultative councils (*diwans*) were created at national and provincial level in cooperation with local legal and religious authorites and non-Mamluk dignitaries. They were asked for advice on administration, justice, and tax collection. Napoleon declared his respect for Islam and pointed to his humiliation of its enemies—the pope and the knights of St John. He hoped his quick military success would persuade the Ottoman sultan to accept the French takeover without resistance.

This hope was frustrated by British naval action. Admiral Nelson destroyed a large part of the French fleet anchored at Aboukir bay, near Alexandria, on 2 August 1798.

The sultan was promised further aid by Britain and Russia, and declared war on France. To preempt an Ottoman attack, Napoleon took 13,000 troops in January 1799 to attack enemy forces in Palestine and Syria. After a difficult march through the Sinai desert, he made quick progress through Gaza, captured Jaffa, and executed 3,000 prisoners in early March. He hoped to capture the naval base and coastal fortress at Acre which had been constructed by Crusaders six centuries earlier. Here again, he was thwarted by British naval action. Before the siege began, Sidney Smith, British commander in the eastern Mediterranean, captured the gunships Napoleon had sent ahead with his siege artillery and ammunition. Smith was able to defend Acre with his 800 sailors, the firepower of his own ships and those he had captured. The French destroyed a large Turkish relief force, but abandoned the siege after nine weeks after losing 5,000 killed, wounded, or plague victims.

Napoleon managed to get his troops back to Egypt and defeated a force the Turkish fleet had put ashore at Aboukir. In spite of the failure at Acre, the French position in Egypt was reasonably secure. Mamluk and Ottoman forces had been defeated in several major battles, the French had established a colonial administration, and made significant progress in their scientific work. Lack of contact with France reinforced Napoleon's autonomy as ruler of Egypt, a role he greatly enjoyed.

Shortly after the battle of Aboukir, he received French newspapers revealing a catastrophic situation back home. A new anti-French coalition had been created, an Austro-Russian army had undone his work in Italy, enemy forces had moved into Holland and Switzerland, and a Bourbon restoration seemed likely in Paris. On 23 August, he departed with some of his staff and savants in two frigates, leaving general Kléber in charge of Egypt. He arrived in Paris on 16 October. By the 19 of November, the directory had been overthrown. Napoleon became ruler of France, as first consul, in December 1799.

In January 1800, Kléber began negotiations for evacuation, in return for safe conduct and transport of his army to France. Ottoman forces advanced into Egypt, but Kléber annihilated them at Heliopolis, and the French were evacuated in August 1801, as originally agreed.

Muhammad Ali and Modernization 1805–48

A British expeditionary force remained in Egypt in 1801–3, intending to restore the pre-war political order, but in fact left a political vacuum. Muhammad Ali, a Turk from Kavalla in Macedonia (1769–1849), emerged as the new ruler of Egypt, establishing a modernizing regime similar to the Napoleonic model and to that of Meiji Japan after 1867. He arrived as commander of an Albanian contingent in the Ottoman army. He had the same energy, ambition, military, and administrative skills as Napoleon. He eliminated a succession of Ottoman nominees, before being appointed governor in 1805. Although he acknowledged the suzerainty of Istanbul and paid annual tribute, he remained fully in charge of Egypt until 1848, and his family were acknowledged as hereditary rulers in 1841.

He created a new Turkish-speaking elite from his own family and friends. He killed the remaining Mamluks and confiscated the income which they and the religious authorities had derived from agriculture. He completed the cadaster which Napoleon had initiated. Farm productivity was raised by irrigation works (built with the aid of French engineers). He introduced mechanical pumps and a regular supply of water was provided throughout the year, increasing the cultivable area, and permitting multicropping. Long-staple cotton was introduced from the Sudan as the major export product. Production and export of rice, indigo, and sugarcane was expanded. Official income from agriculture was augmented by monopolies in the sale of farm products. The increased revenue was used to modernize the administration, to promote industrial development and build the strength of the armed forces. Conscription was used to turn large numbers of peasants into soldiers. The troops were drilled by French instructors. A staff college and cavalry school trained the officer corps, and a naval arsenal was established under the direction of French officers. He and his sons Tusun, Ismail, and Ibrahim were very able generals.

There were major improvements in public provision for health. From 1827, modern military and civilian hospitals were built in Cairo, the new board of health created a quarantine service to check the incidence of plague and cholera, new clinics provided widespread vaccination against smallpox. A school for midwives reduced the heavy incidence of stillbirths. More than 400 doctors received modern professional training, a substantial part of it in France. These health measures had a significant effect on population growth. In 1800, the population was lower than in 1000. By 1850, it had increased by nearly 60 per cent.

There were major improvements in education. The Bulaq press was created in 1820, school textbooks were translated and published in Turkish and Arabic. The government circulated an official gazette and news-sheet. Modern secular schools were established with a western curriculum. In higher education a medical and an engineering school were created. By the mid-nineteenth century Egypt had acquired the nucleus of a westernized professional class whose influence outweighed that of the old religious elite (*ulama*). The competence of traditional Islamic courts and *qadis* was restricted by the introduction of new codes of criminal, commercial, and administrative procedure.

There was a major effort to promote industrial development, with foreign advisors and imported machinery. Government factories were set up to produce cotton, silk, jute, and wool textiles, uniforms, weaponry, military equipment, glass, sugar, and leather goods. Many of these plants required large subsidies. Tariffs, other trade barriers and government monopolies were created to promote import substitution. An Anglo-Ottoman agreement required a lowering of these barriers in 1838. Its impact would have been severely damaging to the markets for government enterprises, but it was delayed under various pretexts so long as Ali was alive.

Military commitments absorbed a large part of Egypt's resources. In order to reconcile the sultan to his autonomy in Egypt, Muhammad Ali agreed to provide military assistance in Arabia (1811–18) and Greece (1824–27).

In Arabia the problem was Muslim fundamentalism. The religious leader, Abd al-Wahab (1703–92) denounced the laxity of Turkish rule. He was particularly offended by Sufi mysticism which thrived in Turkey. He advocated a return to pure and unadulterated Islam as practised by the *Rashidun* (the first four 'rightly-guided' caliphs in Arabia). He regarded the Ottomans as heretics and advocated a jihad against their rule. His main supporter was Muhammad ibn Saud, emir of Daraiyya. By the end of the century he had created a Saudi-Wahhabi state which dominated the whole of central Arabia. In 1802, the Wahhabis pillaged Karbala and destroyed the tomb of Husayn, a place of pilgrimage for Shia Muslims. By 1807, they occupied Mecca and Medina, and closed Hijaz to all pilgrim caravans. The Wahhabis were a menace to British interests in the Red Sea and Persian Gulf, and their ideas were an obvious threat to Muhammud Ali's secular and westernizing style of governance. Egyptian forces drove them out of Mecca and Medina, captured the Saudi capital in 1818, killed the Wahhabi *ulama*, and sent the Saudi ruler to Istanbul for execution. In return for these services Egypt was given a protectorate over Hijaz and was able to occupy Yemen until the British took it over in 1839. Meantime, the Saudi-Wahhabi state was reconstituted on a smaller scale.

In 1824–7, there was a second expedition in aid of the sultan. 17,000 troops were sent under the command of Muhammad Ali's son, Ibrahim, to fight the Greeks in their war of independence. The Egyptian troops were successful on land and occupied Athens, but their fleet was demolished by a combined British–French–Russian force at Navarino in 1827. The sultan wanted to continue the struggle, but Muhammad Ali refused and negotiated the withdrawal of his army with the western powers.

Muhammad Ali conducted a third military venture in Syria in 1831–41. He wanted the province to add to his revenues, and as a buffer against future Ottoman attack. He had expected to get the governorship as a reward for his efforts in Arabia and Greece. The invasion followed the same path as Napoleon, with a passage through the Sinai and Gaza, capture of Jaffa and a six month siege of Acre. After Acre was captured the army advanced through Syria into Anatolia, taking Adana and defeating the Ottoman army at Konya. In 1833, the sultan agreed to make Ibrahim governor of major Syrian cities (Acre, Aleppo, Damascus, and Tripoli) on an annual basis. Ali agreed to this modest settlement, knowing that if he pressed for independence, he would provoke British, French, and Russian intervention. Eventually in 1840, the British landed troops in Beirut and forced an Egyptian withdrawal from Syria. In the 1841 settlement, the sultan made Ali's family hereditary rulers of Egypt and in return he agreed to make a large reduction in the size of his army.

The fourth military venture was the creation of an empire south of Egypt. The frontier was at the first cataract of the Nile, just above Aswan. Lower Nubia lay between the first and the third cataract, and was theoretically part of the Ottoman empire. Further south was the moribund Funj sultanate, from Dongola in the north to Sennar on the banks of the blue Nile. Further west was the sultanate of Darfur which had taken Kordofan from the Funj. Muhammad Ali's aim was to unify these three areas into an Egyptian colony, which would also include the Red Sea ports of Suakin and Massawa and extend to the borderlands of Ethiopia. In 1820–1, his forces conquered the Funj sultanate, and detached Kordofan from Darfur. The main economic objectives were to gain control of the slave trade to Egypt, the gold which was reputed to lie in these regions, and to squeeze revenue from Sudanese agriculture by the same tactics used in Egypt. In 1821, a strategic military camp was created at Khartoum (at the junction of the White and the Blue Nile) which became the capital of the new state. A modern administration was established, with provincial authorities and a governor-general. Agricultural advisors, vets, and irrigation experts were sent to enlarge the cultivated area, improve crops and the quality of livestock. Steps were also taken to reduce losses from locusts and other insect pests.

Muhammad Ali's Successors and the British Takeover

The successors of Muhammad Ali continued the modernization of Egypt, notably by providing a modern infrastructure. Between 1851 and 1858 a railway was built from Cairo to Alexandria and extended to Suez. Bridges were built, harbours were improved. Between 1854 and 1869 the Suez canal was built and a 9,500 mile telegraph network was created. The government's capacity to sqeeze revenue from agriculture was diluted as members of the elite and foreigners acquired land and peasant property rights were improved. Government control over trade and exports was reduced by the abolition of official monopolies. From the 1860s there was a large influx of foreigners who enjoyed immunity from Egyptian justice and taxation under Ottoman 'capitulations' extorted by the European powers. There were very few Europeans in Egypt in 1798. By 1840 there were 6,000, by 1907, 140,000 (Daly 1998: 254 and 274).

There was a sharp increase in foreign borrowing by Egypt. It was organized by European banks which sold bonds at large discounts. The terms of the arrangement for constructing the Suez canal were particularly onerous. Sultan Said had to subscribe a large part of the initial capital, provide labour for the construction, and hand over a large strip of land bordering the canal.

In 1875 there was a debt crisis, which required the sale of 44 per cent of the Suez Canal capital to the British government and loss of sovereignty to agents of the foreign bondholders who set up a *Caisse de la Dette* in 1876 to consolidate Egypt's foreign liabilities and earmark tax revenues for debt service. British nominees took over as minister of finance and director of customs, and the French were given responsibility for public works. Khedive Ismail was deposed in 1879, when he proposed reduction of interest payments. In 1882, colonel Urabi led a movement against foreign interference and as minister of war Egyptianized the officer corps by forcing nearly 600 Turkish-speaking officers to retire. The British sent an invasion force to Alexandria, defeated Urabi, and created a new Egyptian army under British officers. From 1883 onwards, effective control of the country passed to Britain's 'consul-general' who had power to nominate and dismiss ministers, including the prime minister. Egypt had become a British colony even though there was no formal annexation and Mohammad Ali's family contined to hold the office of Khedive under the theoretical suzerainty of the Ottoman empire.

After an initial period of indifference to Egypt's colonial empire, the British took over the Sudan in 1898, calling it the Anglo-Egyptian Sudan, but controlling it more tightly than Egypt.

Khedive Ismail had followed an activist policy in the Sudan, establishing steam navigation on the upper Nile and creating a telegraph network to expand the area of control. In the southwest, Darfur was taken and the local sultan killed in 1874. In the south, Samuel Baker, a British explorer, was appointed governor of Equatoria in 1869, followed in 1874–6 by General Gordon. Their instructions were to establish a chain of forts as far as Uganda.

There was strong resisistance to Egyptian expansion in these areas by the population which was non-Muslim and did not speak Arabic. There was a good deal of violence and an influx of slave traders. In the far south, king Mutesa of Buganda repulsed the Egyptians, but the Shilluk (whose capital was at Fashoda), the Azande, Dinka, and Nuer tribes were incorporated unwillingly in the empire. Amongst the Muslim population there was also discontent, not only because of Egyptian exactions, but at the displacement of their Sufi religious leaders. They also resented the appointment of Gordon as governor-general of the Sudan in 1877–9. In 1881, there was a successful revolt led by Muhammad Ahmad, a Sufi religious leader, who proclaimed himself the Mahdi (divinely guided leader) and denounced the occupiers as unbelievers. He succeeded in establishing his puritanical rule in the southwest, defeated a force led by colonel Hicks and surrounded Khartoum. Mahdist rule lasted till 1896, setting up a new administration, judiciary, and tax regime. By this time the British had taken over Egypt and did not want to be involved. In 1884 they sent General Gordon to Khartoum to arrange withdrawal of the Egyptian troops and administration. Within a few months he was captured and beheaded by Mahdist troops. In 1896, the British sent an invasion force, and destroyed the Mahdist regime. In 1898, they created the Anglo-Egyptian Sudan which lasted until Sudanese independence in 1956, with borders similar to those of today. It is the biggest country in Africa with a surface area of 2.5 million square km.

THE MAGHREB AND THE INITIATION OF TRANS-SAHARAN TRADE IN GOLD AND SLAVES

The Muslim conquest of north Africa started in 642–5 with the successful takeover of Cyrenaica and Libya (the three coastal cities: Leptis Magna, Oea, and Sabratha known as Tripolitania). The Byzantine army was defeated at Sbeitla in Tunisia in 647, but its navy was able to protect Carthage until 698. After several decades of conflict with Berber tribes, control over the Maghreb was achieved by 710. Byzantine civilization had been obliterated, the coastal cities were in ruin, the Christian community was a tiny fraction of what it had been and eventually disappeared. Most of the sedentary Berber population had been driven into the mountains and the fringes of the desert. The remnants of the irrigated and export-oriented agriculture of Roman times had been largely destroyed. Arab forces took a substantial part of the Berber population as slaves, and the Berber sense of alienation remained a persistent source of political instability. The conquest of Spain in 711 was much smoother than that of the Maghreb. As in Egypt, a large part of the population welcomed the invaders and the economic damage was minimal.

The main Arab garrison and administrative headquarters in north Africa was established in Ifriqiya (Tunisia) at Kairouan, 150 km south of Carthage. There were also important bases at Tlemcen in Algeria and Tangier in Morocco. The process of Islamicizing the Berbers was complicated. They were a miscellany of tribes fairly hostile to each other, without the consolidating force of a written language, and had never been bonded together in an organized state. Once converted, they tended to divide opportunistically into different sects which reinforced existing enmities. The situation became more complicated when Muslim leadership passed to the Abbasid caliphate in Baghdad in 750. The Muslim rulers of Spain (*al-Andalus*) remained loyal to the Ummayads and developed links with Berber tribes in the western Maghreb (Morocco).

At the beginning of the ninth century, the Abbasids delegated power to an autonomous (Aglabid) dynasty in Kairouan. The Aglabids were vigorous and enterprising. By 832 they had conquered Sicily and included it in their domain. After a century of power, they were displaced by the Fatimids, a more powerful, independent, and ambitious dynasty. The Fatimids claimed descent from the prophet, set up a new Shi'ite caliphate in rivalry with Baghdad, created a new capital at Mahdia, and established control of most of the Maghreb. From then until 1517, the political destiny of north Africa was independent of the world east of Libya. However there was strong rivalry between the Shia Fatimids in Tunisia and the Sunni Muslims in Spain (al-Andalus) who established their own Ummayad caliphate in 929. The main locus of rivalry was in Morocco, where both sides had Berber allies and zones of influence—the Sanhaja in the south sided with the Fatimids and the Zanata, in the northeast, with al-Andalus.

By the eleventh century, the influence of these rival caliphates had eroded. The Fatimids had moved their headquarters to Cairo and lost control of the Maghreb. The Ummayad caliphate collapsed in 1031 and al-Andalus fragmented into 23 petty kingdoms. The time was therefore propitious for the emergence of greater autonomy in the Maghreb. Morocco, which had once been a tribal backwater, became an independent Berber state in 1055. It became significantly more prosperous as its geography favoured trade with Black Africa and Spain.

When the Arabs conquered the Maghreb they severed the Mediterranean trading links which had previously existed and explored new opportunities across the desert. They established camel caravan routes from Tunisia and Libya deep into the Sahara to places where it was possible to trade horses for black slaves supplied by traders from the south. Bigger profits could be derived from the gold trade with ancient Ghana (about 800 km northwest of modern Ghana, between the Senegal and Niger rivers, just inside the southern boundary of modern Mauretania), which had a lengthy history as state before the Arabs established contact in the early eighth century. The most direct route was through Morocco. Muslim merchants on these new routes were active in making converts to Islam. Early in the eleventh century, ancient Ghana was the first of the black African states to convert to Islam.

The most important traded item in Muslim Africa was gold from western Sudan. Production increased steadily from the eighth century onwards. By the fourteenth century, Levtzion (1973: 132), suggests that it represented two-thirds of world gold output.[6] Until the twelfth century most of it circulated within the Muslim world, but from then onwards there was increasing demand from Europe, mainly from Genoa, Venice, Pisa, Florence, and Marseilles. European traders conducted their operations in Muslim ports on the Mediterranean coast. They had only vestigial contact with African gold producing areas until the second half of the fifteenth century when Portugal gained access to the west African coast.

From the eighth to the twelfth century, the main source of supply for Muslim traders was Awdaghast in ancient Ghana. The goldfield was at Bambuk, somewhat further south, but its exact whereabouts was kept secret. Most exports were in the form of gold dust which was melted and moulded into ingots. Gold nuggets were reserved for African chiefs or kings who used them as insignia of rank. The king of Ghana had a 15 kg gold nugget to which he is said to have tethered his horse. In the thirteenth century Walata in Mali became the main centre for trade, and production was concentrated on the Bure goldfield. Levtzion (1973: 156) suggests that output was eight times as big as in the Bambuk field. In the fourteenth century, pressure of demand was such that production was started further south at the Akan mines (in present-day Ghana). In the fifteenth and sixteenth centuries the main trading centre for gold was Timbuktu in the empire of Songhay. Mining wealth was the main reason why Ghana, Mali, and Songhay were able to emerge as powerful states in an area where technology was relatively backward. Income from gold produced an economic surplus which allowed the rulers to maintain the attributes of power. It made it possible for them to import horses and weapons, and maintain cavalry forces.

The main barter transactions were gold for salt. In the Sahel region, salt was very scarce, but was a necessity for people doing heavy work. Some of the salt came from maritime sources on the Atlantic coast. But it was much easier to transport rock salt. From the eleventh to the sixteenth century, the main source was in the Sahara at Taghaza, where it was mined by slave labour, cut into large blocks, and transported south by camel. Levtzion (1973: 173) gives an idea of the salt/gold exchange ratio, which was roughly 16/1. Of 400 camels carrying salt to Timbuktu, only 25 went back north with gold, the other camels being sold in the Sahel. Salt was not the only trade item in this north–south trade. There was also a lively exchange between trading centres within the Sudan, particularly in kola nuts—an African stimulant equivalent to coffee or tobacco. Further east, in the central Sudan, Kanem was the main centre of the slave trade.

There were several alternative routes for trans-Saharan trade. From the eighth to the tenth century the gold trade was dominated by Ibadi traders who originated in Iraq and belonged to the Kharijite sect.[7] In the eleventh and first half of the twelfth century, it was more or less monopolized by the Alvoravids, whose main trading base was in southern Morocco at Sijilmasa, about 20 days by camel from Awaghast in Ghana. At a later stage there was a diversity of gold routes to Morocco, Algeria, Tunisia, and Egypt, and from Mediterranean ports to European customers. In the the eleventh and twelfth centuries, the Muslim countries were the only ones to mint gold coins. Marseilles first issued them in 1227, Florence in 1252, and Venice in 1284.

THE CHANGING CHARACTER OF MOROCCAN DYNASTIES AND THEIR INTERACTION WITH EUROPE AND BLACK AFRICA

In the long run, four Arab states emerged in the Maghreb: Morocco, Algeria, Tunisia, and Libya. The least developed in the seventh century was the area of present-day Morocco. At that time its social organization was tribal, the economy mainly nomadic, and there was no written language. Tangier and Ceuta were the only towns. By 1820, the population was two and a half times as large as at the time of Arab conquest. Growth was faster than elsewhere in the Maghreb (see Table 4.1). It was the most successful in creating some semblance of nationhood, in raising per capita income and urbanization. Its interaction with Europe and black Africa was closer and had a greater impact on its development than was the case elsewhere in the Maghreb. Moroccan forces played a significant role in prolonging a Muslim presence in Spain. Morocco successfully resisted attacks on its independence from Portugal, Spain, and the Ottoman empire. It was the last of the north African states to become a European colony (1912 compared with 1830 for Algeria). The following analysis concentrates on Moroccan experience and neglects developments elsewhere in the Maghreb.

Almoravids, 1055–1147

The Almoravids established the first Berber empire in Morocco in 1055, and extended their hegemony from Ghana to northeast Spain. They were led by nomadic Sanhaja tribesmen from the southern edge of the Sahara. Their most striking physical feature was that men wore veils and women did not. They started with the conquest and

Islamization of ancient Ghana in 1055, then took southern Morocco where they founded Marrakesh as their capital in 1070. They conquered Fez in 1075, and completed their African empire in 1083 by capturing Ceuta.

The Almoravids were Muslim fundamentalists. Their spiritual leader, ibn-Yasin, favoured a narrow interpretation of the Koran and strict application of religious law (*shari'a*). He regarded looser interpretations as corrupt, decadent, and heretical. Ibn-Yasin gave the Almoravids their name, which is a Spanish version of al-Morabitun (people of the ribat). A *ribat* was originally an isolated frontier fort, but its connotation changed to mean a retreat or monastery for a holy man.

However, their success did not depend only on ideology. They guaranteed the security of the Saharan gold trade, demonstrated the economic advantages of a unified and powerful state, increased the size of the urban population, helped monetize the economy by introducing a gold coinage, recruited scholars and administrators from Spain, and, for a time, transformed nomad tribesmen into a successful national army.

Shortly after the Almoravids completed their African empire, they extended their rule to Europe. The 23 small Muslim kingdoms in al-Andalus (the Muslim area of Spain) which had emerged after the disintegration of the caliphate of Cordoba in 1031, were in very feeble condition and asked the Almoravids for help. Alfonso VI of Castile had captured a large chunk of their territory between the Duero and Tagus rivers and established his capital in Toledo in 1085. The Almoravids stopped the Christian advance, abolished the 23 petty Muslim kingdoms, and established their authority over the whole of al-Andalus from 1094 to 1147. Their bigotry towards Christians, Jews, and those Muslims they considered to be heretics made them unpopular in al-Andalus and sharpened religious antagonism between Islam and Christianity in Spain, where there had previously been a large degree of tolerance on both sides.

The contemporaneous confrontation of Crusaders and Muslims in Palestine found an echo in Spain. Three Christian military orders were created—the Castilian order of Calatrava (in 1158), the Leonese order of Alcantara (1166), and the order of Santiago (1170). They consisted of knights dedicated to the fight against Islam and eager for the spoils of conquest. Thereafter they played a powerful role in the governance and resettlement of Spain and the ethnic cleansing which led to a massive outflow of Muslim and Jewish refugees, many of whom settled in Morocco.

Almohads, 1147–1250

Almoravid rule in Morocco and al-Andalus was ended in 1147 by a rival Berber group, the Masmuda. They were sedentary agriculturalists from the southern mountains of the Anti-Atlas. The religious ideas of their leader, ibn-Tumart, differed greatly from those of the Almoravids. He asserted the right to personal freedom in interpreting the Koran, and allowed scope for mystical revelation and sainthood. He claimed to be a descendant of the prophet and was regarded as the *mahdi*, an inspired leader sent to re-establish the true faith. His followers were known as *al-muwahhidun* (unitarians), or Almohads.

The Almohad empire did not extend as far south as the Almoravid, but reached further east, establishing a somewhat shaky control of the whole Maghreb. The major drawback of the eastern extension was a large inflow of nomadic Arabs into the plains of Morocco, where their depredations did significant damage to sedentary agriculture.

In 1172, the Almohads took over the Almoravid empire in al-Andalus, but suffered a crushing defeat in the battle of Las Navas de Tolosa in 1212. Thereafter al-Andalus disintegrated. Portugal became independent in 1249. Between 1235 and 1250 Castile gained control of Cordoba, Seville, and Cadiz. The Catalans captured the Balearic islands in 1229 and Valencia in 1238, Sicily in 1282, Sardinia and Corsica in 1327. However, the Muslim kingdom of Granada continued as a tributary of Castile until 1492.

In 1291 the Genoese defeated a Moroccan fleet controlling the straits of Gibraltar. This made it possible for European traders to open up sea routes between the Mediterranean, the Atlantic and the North Sea for the first time in centuries. However, the western Mediterranean was infested with Barbary pirates until the early nineteenth century.

Merinids, 1250–1472

In 1248, the Almohads lost control of northern Morocco, western Algeria and al-Andalus. The Merinids destroyed the Almohad army as it retreated from Spain and established their capital in Fez in 1250. Their political base was an alliance of Zanata Berbers and Arabs. Their official language was Arabic, their empire was confined to Morocco, and they had no distinctive doctrinal message. The urban population practiced orthodox Islam, but rural Berbers had developed an attachment to Sufi mysticism and a cult of hermit saints. During their lifetime these holy men (*marabouts*) were religious leaders in villages.

From 1275 to 1334 the Merinids had sufficient income from the gold trade to sustain military adventures in Spain, but they were more of a nuisance than a threat. They were defeated by Christian forces and retreated. The Merinid regime collapsed in 1472. Their former viziers, the Watassids, took control of Fez and the surrounding region until a new dynasty, the Saadis, emerged in 1517. Meanwhile, in 1492, Morocco absorbed a large inflow of Muslim and Jewish refugees from Spain.

Saadis, 1517–1660s

The Saadis were the most impressive of the Moroccan dynasties. They faced threats from Portugal and Spain in the north and west and the Ottoman Turks in the east, but their military and diplomatic response was brilliant. They created a modern army on Ottoman lines, with renegade Turkish advisers. Military equipment and naval stores were imported from England in exchange for sugar and saltpetre.

Between 1415 and 1521, the Portuguese had established 13 coastal bases in Morocco, including Agadir (where they built a new port in 1505). Their motive was to guarantee their new sea routes round Africa and to control the overland trade in gold. When the Spanish reconquista was completed, Spain also started to acquire African bases, taking Melilla in 1497 as well as ports in Algeria and Tunisia.

In 1541 the Saadis drove the Portuguese from all the Moroccan ports except Ceuta, Tangier, and Mazaghan. In 1578, the Portuguese king, Sebastian, invaded Morocco, hoping to instal a puppet regime. He and his puppet were killed and their army annihilated by the Saadis at the battle of Alcazar. Portugal was incorporated into Spain in 1580, but the Spanish were too busy fighting the Dutch and building their empire in the Americas to pose a threat in Africa. The Saadi response to outside challenges was impressive enough to deter European assaults on the sovereignty of Morocco until the early twentieth century.

The Saadi ruler, al-Mansur, felt secure enough to extend his empire to the south and gain as tight a control of the gold trade as the Almoravids had enjoyed. In 1586 his troops took control of the salt mines of Taghaza in the Sahara, and, in 1591–3, destroyed the Songhay empire. A Moroccan governor was installed in Timbuktu, and a large hoard of gold was sent as tribute to Marrakesh. This venture deep into Africa reinforced the influence of Islam in that region, and inhibited inland penetration by the European powers.

The gamble was risky and costly. Moroccan troops had to cover 2,500 km to get to Songhay; more than 25,000 died in the desert crossing. The booty and the favoured access to gold brought a period of great prosperity to Morocco's rulers and some of it went to strengthen military defences. Muslim pashas continued in Timbuktu until 1770, but from the middle of the seventeenth century they were no longer controlled by Morocco, whose monopoly of the gold trade disappeared.

Alawids 1660s Onwards

After the death of sultan al-Mansur in 1603, the kingdom of Morocco split into two, with Marrakesh and Fez as rival capitals controlled by his two sons. Continuous warfare led to anarchy and insecurity, and Morocco had to absorb most of the 300,000 Morisco refugees expelled from Spain in 1609–10. Some of these set themselves up as pirates in Salé and Rabat.

Morocco was reunified by a new dynasty, the Alawids from the eastern oasis of Tafilelt. Like the Saadis, the Alawids were *Sharifs*, i.e., descendents of the prophet, whose religious charisma was important in holding their fragile empire together.

Their performance was much less impressive than that of the Saadis. Their main achievement was their durability as an independent state.

The new ruler, Moulay al-Rashid, was proclaimed sultan of the new dynasty in Fez in 1666. In 1669 he took Marrakesh. His authority was recognized by the orthodox religious leadership (*ulama*), by provincial governors (*ca'ids*), and by judges (*qadis*) in the *bled el makhzen*, i.e., the Arabized area of settled farmers and city-dwellers in the plains—the triangle Fez–Meknes–Rabat, the north coast to Tangier, and a southward triangle Rabat–Marrakesh–Mogador. He had little control of the *bled es sida*, inhabited by Berber tribes in the mountains and deserts. They were about half the population and occupied two-thirds of the country as pastoralists, nomads, or semi-nomads in tribal or lineage groups with local leaders and local holy men, the *marabouts*. Many of these areas were impenetrable by representatives of the makzhen, and in virtually all of them it was impossible to collect taxes.

The second sultan, Moulay Ismael (1672–1727) spent much of his long reign suppressing revolts and attempting to gain control over the whole country. In the south, he established nominal control of the whole western Sahara (the area that later became Spanish Sahara, Mauretania, southern Algeria, and northern Mali), and was recognized as caliph in Timbuktu. He made slave raids in this area, but was not able to extract tribute in gold as al-Mansur did in the sixteenth century.

He bolstered the central power by building up a royal guard of black slaves (*abid*) with no roots in the local population. He recruited slaves by raids and purchase in the southern Sahara. They were provided with slave wives, their children were kept in breeding nurseries, taken into the king's palace at Meknes at age 10 for a period of training and became soldiers at age 18. At his death he had 150,000 of these soldiers, concentrated in Mahalla and Meknes, and also serving as frontier guards (see Levtzion 1975: 145–60). During his reign and for long afterwards, Moroccan pirates, based in Salé and Rabat, attacked European ships in the north Atlantic and made coastal raids on England, France, Iceland, Ireland, Italy, Portugal, Spain, and the Americas, to take Christian prisoners they sold as slaves. Moulay Ismael resisted persistent British diplomacy which attempted to stop these activities (see Milton 2004).

As Ismael had about 500 sons, the succession was not clear. During the 30 years after his death, the royal guard installed or deposed 11 puppet sultans before Mohammed II took over and reasserted control in a long reign from 1757 to 1790 (see Abun-Nasr 1987). He and subsequent sultans reduced the size of the royal guard drastically and relied more on soldiers provided by Arab tribes in return for tax exemption. Mohammed II suppressed the Salé pirates and concluded accords with European countries and the US to open the country to legitimate trade.

The authority and effective control of succeeding sultans varied a good deal. Sultan Moulay Hassan (1873–94) was one of the most successful in strengthening his authority through military and administrative reforms. His military resources were too weak to prevent a takeover by a colonial power, but his diplomacy was effective in exploiting the disagreements and conflicts of interest between France, Spain, and

Table 4.4. World Gold Output by Region, 1493–1925 (million fine ounces)

	1493–1600	1601–1700	1701–1800	1801–50	1851–1900	1901–25
Africa	8.153	6.430	5.466	2.025	23.810	202.210
Americas	8.976	19.043	52.014	22.623	140.047	152.463
Europe	4.758	3.215	3.480	6.034	17.379	8.296
Asia			0.085	6.855	49.150	51.900
Australasia					104.859	62.658
Other	1.080	0.161	0.161	0.498	0.986	
World	22.968	28.849	61.206	38.036	336.231	477.527

Source: Ridgway (1929: 6).

the UK. These kept Morocco independent when most of the rest of Africa had been colonized. When the colonial takeover finally occurred in 1912, 'the international treaties and horse-dealing that allowed French entry into Morocco obliged the French to treat it as a protectorate' (Gellner 1981: 183). This implied a very different regime from that in Algeria where the French dismantled the indigenous central authority. In Morocco, France preserved the dynasty and the *makzhen* officialdom. It kept the sultan and his palaces, the pashas, caids, and councils of village notables, but a new settler population was installed. By 1956 there were 555,000 Europeans, more than ten times as many as in 1912. This compared with 255,000 in Tunisia and about a million in Algeria in 1956. The Jewish population of Morocco was 170,000 in 1956, much larger than in Algeria and Tunisia. There had been Jewish communities in the Maghreb before the Arab conquest. They had been augmented disproportionately in Morocco because the exodus from Spain had been concentrated there (Amin 1966: 25).

BLACK AFRICA AND THE IMPACT OF ISLAM

Agricultural conditions in black Africa contrasted sharply with those prevailing in Egypt. There was an abundance of land in relation to population, but soils were poor and were not regenerated by manure, crop rotation, natural or human provision of irrigation. As a consequence, there was an extensive, shifting cultivation, with land being left fallow for a decade or more after the first crops. Nomadic pastoralists were generally transhumant over wide areas for the same reason—poor soils. The main agricultural implements were digging sticks, iron hoes for tillage, axes and machetes for clearing trees and bush. There were no ploughs (except in Ethiopia) and virtually no use of traction animals in agriculture. There were no wheeled vehicles, no watermills, windmills, or other instruments of water management (see Goody 1971).

There were no individual property rights in land. Tribes, kin-groups or other communities had customary rights to farm or graze in the areas where they lived, but collective property rights and boundaries were vague. Chiefs and rulers did not collect rents or land taxes, or squeeze their agriculturalists with feudal levies. The main instrument of exploitation was slavery. Slaves were generally acquired by raids on neighbouring groups. Hence there was a substantial beggar-your-neighbour element in intergroup relations.

Slavery was endemic in Africa before western contact. There was a flow of more than four million from black Africa across the Sahara in the eight centuries before 1500, an average of somewhat more than 5,000 a year (see Table 4.5a). The traffic was organized by Muslim traders from the north. The flow from north to south was negligible.

Lovejoy (2000: 25) describes the main routes as follows:

One went north from ancient Ghana to Morocco; a second stretched north from Timbuktu to Tuwat in southern Algeria; a third passed from the Niger Valley and the Hausa towns through the Air Massif to Ghat and Ghadames; a fourth travelled north from Lake Chad to Murzuk in Libya; a fifth reached north from Dar Fur in the eastern Sudan to the Nile Valley at Assiout; and a sixth passed north of the confluence of the Blue and the White Nile to Egypt

Slaves usually walked through the desert with a caravan of camels carrying food, water, slave drivers, and other passengers.

Ibn Battuta (pp. 337–8) describes how he joined such a caravan in September 1353 on the edge of the desert at Tagadda in northern Mali. He bought two camels with provisions for 70 days for the journey to Sigilmasa in southeast Morocco. The caravan included 600 female slaves. The trip was largely through uninhabited territory, but there were occasional waterholes, a village where the main items of diet were dates and dried locusts, and a hold-up by veiled Berbers who demanded pieces of cloth as the price for free passage. In Tuwat, he joined another convoy heading west. The distance from Tagadda to Sijilmasa was more than 2,000 km. The guides who escorted caravans across the desert relied mainly on the stars for navigation.

Transport facilities in black Africa were poor. Camels thrived in the dry heat of the desert but could not function further south. Muslim Africa had ships which could navigate and trade in the Mediterranean, and in Egypt there was substantial and relatively safe travel on the sailing boats of the Nile. In the western Sudan, the rivers were only partially navigable, particularly the Niger, Senegal, and Gambia. Ibn Battuta in the fourteenth century and Leo Africanus 160 years later both described the vessels on these rivers as primitive paddle-boats made of hollowed-out tree trunks. The frequency of cataracts and rapids meant that merchandise had frequently to be trans-shipped by head porterage. Ibn Battuta records the hazardous presence of crocodiles and hippos. Donkeys seem to have been available in black Africa as transport animals, but horses were very expensive and had a short life expectation because of the climate and the fact that they were highly sensitive to tsetse flies (see Law 1980). They were were a major import item from north Africa, but did not breed easily south of the Sahara, and, in any case, Arab traders were reluctant to supply breeding mares. Horses were used almost exclusively for military and prestige puposes by the ruling groups and their lightly armed cavalry (horses and riders wore padded armour as a defence against arrows). This was the case in ancient Ghana, Mali, Songhay, and Kanem, and for later elite groups (Ashanti in Ghana, Hausa and Fulani in northern Nigeria).

A striking feature of black Africa before contact with the Islamic world, was universal illiteracy and absence of written languages (except in Ethiopia). This made it difficult to transmit knowledge across generations and between African societies. Contact with Islam brought obvious advantages. The Arabs who came as traders had a written language, and an evangelizing bent. They included sophisticated members of the Muslim intelligentsia (*ulama*), who were able to promote knowledge of property institutions, law, and techniques of governance as well cutting business deals. Before the Moroccan conquest of Songhay in 1591, Muslim visitors were generally peaceful and posed no threat to African chiefs and rulers. The latter saw clear advantages in Islamization which helped them build bigger empires and acquire stronger instruments of coercion. They were able to exchange gold and slaves for horses and weapons (steel sword blades and tips for spears, and, at a later stage, guns and gunpowder). Black African traders also saw the advantages of conversion. As converts (*dyulas*) they became members of an oecumene with free access to markets well beyond their previous horizons. Thus there was a gradual spread of hybrid Islam in black Africa from the eleventh century onwards. Conversion had its main effect on the ruling groups whose insignia and sanctions of power were a mix of Islam and tradition, whilst their subjects continued to be animists. The rulers gained significant income from levies on trade transactions and *dyulas* profited directly from these business deals.[8] Visiting traders from the north were offered legal protection and property rights. This point was stressed by Ibn Battuta and Leo Africanus, though both were disdainful of traditional elements in court life and ritual.

In the first few generations, black African Muslims were orthodox Sunni, uninterested in the Shia or Sufi variants which prevailed in the Maghreb. Over centuries of contact, participation in the *hajj* to Mecca, and creation of a sophisticated centre of learning in the Great Friday mosque of Timbuktu, Islamization gradually became more profound. Governance and economic institutions in a large part of black Africa were profoundly influenced by these centuries of interaction with Islam.

In the eighteenth and nineteenth centuries, *jihads* reinforced Islamization by use of force and penetrated more deeply in rural areas. These movements had their origin in Senegal and Guinea which by then had developed their own Sufi zealots and marabouts, many of whom belonged to Qadariya brotherhoods. They succeeded in creating Sufi states in Futa Toro and Futa Jallon in the eighteenth century. In the nineteenth century a new caliphate was created in the Niger delta at Hamdallahi which controlled Timbuktu and Jenne. The most successful was the jihad of 1804 which created a new and powerful state in northern Nigeria, grouping former Fulbe pastoralists and Hausa agriculturalists. Sokoto was created in 1819 as the new capital. The caliph exercised authority over 30 emirs of component units of agriculturists growing sorghum and millet. They traded in kola nuts, salt, and cloth, but their prosperity was based on the slave trade. Their horsemen set out every dry season to capture slaves from non-Muslim peoples. The slaves were used for farming and porterage, in harems and for sale across the Sahara (see Iliffe 1995).

Analysts of state formation in black Africa make a distinction between complex and acephalous groups (Goody 1971), state and stateless societies (Levtzion, Lovejoy, and others). There was a great variety of polities by the time that European contact was established and the differentiation grew wider as a result of the varying degree of contact with Islam. Slave traders were generally the most Islamized. Slaves tended to be taken from the acephalous, stateless, and least Islamized groups. There were two reasons for this. The Muslim states tended to have the most powerful armed forces, and they generally avoided enslaving Muslims.

THE EUROPEAN ENCOUNTER WITH AFRICA

Between the eleventh and the fourteenth centuries, European contact with Africa took place in the Mediterranean. One of the motives for the Crusades was to restore direct trade with Asia, but Saladin evicted the Franks from Jerusalem after destroying their fleet in the Red Sea in 1182. His successors repulsed their attacks on Alexandria and eliminated their last toehold in Palestine in 1291. Christian merchants were able to trade in their *fonduqs* in Alexandria until 1517 when the Ottomans captured Egypt and the rest of north Africa (except Morocco). In 1571 they took Cyprus, which for three centuries had been the last remnant of the Crusader empire.

In the western Mediterranean, the situation was quite different. The Muslims were driven out of Portugal by 1249. By the end of the thirteenth century, the Spanish reconquista was largely completed. The only part of al-Andalus which remained was the kingdom of Granada. Sicily was captured by the Normans at the end of the eleventh century. The Balearic islands were captured by the Catalans in the course of the thirteenth; Sardinia and Corsica in 1327. The Genoese defeated a Moroccan fleet controlling the straits of Gibraltar in 1291. After that it was possible for European traders to open sea routes between the Mediterranean, the Atlantic, and the North Sea, though they were subject to harassment by Barbary pirates until their destruction by the British fleet in 1816.

There were several Iberian incursions into north Africa as the reconquista drew to a close. The motives were mixed. The reconquista had generated religious zealotry in both Portugal and Spain. The Muslim world was regarded as an enemy to be destroyed. There was substantial rhetoric and a serious intention to mount new Crusades. There was also a desire to get direct access to the gold trade. From the eleventh century European traders (from Genoa, Pisa, Florence, Venice, Marseilles, and Catalonia) bought gold in Ceuta, Tangier, Tunis, and other Mediterranean ports where Muslim authorities permitted the establishment of *fonduqs* and guaranteed security of commercial transactions. The Iberians were not able to make a significant dent on Muslim sovereignty or to establish Christianity in north Africa. All they gained, at very substantial cost, were some coastal bases whose economic value was no greater than the commercial facilities which the Muslim authorities had been willing to negotiate.

The Pioneering Role of Portugal in Contact with Black Africa

The most ambitious of the European interventions were those of Portugal in Morocco. In 1415, Ceuta was captured, but a first attempt to take Tangier in 1437 was an ignominious failure. Several bases were established on the Atlantic coast of Morocco by 1521, but Moroccan forces recaptured these in 1541 and in 1578 they annihilated a Portuguese invasion force (as described above). In view of the Moroccan successes and the fact that the Ottoman empire was then in control of the rest of north Africa, there were no other serious European incursions before Napoleon's invasion of Egypt in 1798, and the French conquest of Algeria in 1830.

Direct European contact with black Africa was made possible by Portuguese innovations in the design of ships and rigging, techniques of navigation, navigational instruments and cartography. These advances made it possible to circumnavigate Africa and trade directly with India and other Asian destinations from 1497 onwards. The motivation for these developments was mixed. There was an evangelical commitment to convert heathens and to establish contact with existing Christian communities in Africa (Ethiopia) and Asia. The project was financed by the Order of Christ, of which Prince Henrique was the master. A papal bull, *Romanus Pontifex*, of 1455, gave Portugal a monopoly in African trade. The main economic considerations were to develop sugar production on the Atlantic islands, get direct access to west African gold, and to the Asian spice trade. A further, more important, economic incentive was created by the discovery of the Americas in 1492. The Treaty of Tordesillas gave part of the new continent to Portugal. This provided an incentive to export slaves to the Americas.

The Portuguese set up a trading base at Arquim on the coast of Mauretania in 1445, and created an island settlement at Cabo Verde (opposite Senegal) in 1460. It was possible to buy gold in this region in return for cloth, horses, trinkets, and salt. There were also profitable opportunities for intermediary trade, buying slaves in one African market and selling them in another. In 1482, a strongly fortified base was created at Elmina, on the coast of present day Ghana, which gave more direct access to the Ashanti gold mines. Between 1471 and 1500, Portuguese traders exported about 17 tons of African gold.

Their activities diverted some gold from the old routes across the Sahara. Levtzion (1975: 144) describes the Portuguese impact as follows:

The trans-Saharan trade declined but did not stop. Saharan salt continued to attract much of the gold of the upper Niger and the upper Senegal. It seems that only a fraction of the gold from these regions reached the Europeans in the Senegambia, who were more successful in obtaining slaves. But, from the Akan forest of the south much of the gold ceased to flow north and reached the Europeans on the Gold Coast

In the case of both the gold and slave trades, the Portuguese presence caused an extension of African trading networks to the coast. The Portuguese did not penetrate far inland and plunder was not a feasible option. When they tried to seize slaves directly, they took substantial casualties. When they tried to penetrate inland to find the gold mines, they suffered even bigger losses from yellow fever, malaria, and sleeping sickness. Portuguese policy therefore relied on coastal trading posts and market transactions.

The most significant Portuguese effort at missionary activity was in the kingdom of Kongo, located in what is now northern Angola. King Nzinga Nvemba (ruled 1506–43) was converted and became Dom Afonso I. A Congolese prince was sent to Lisbon to be educated, and, in 1518, a reluctant pope was persuaded to consecrate him as the first black African bishop. However, the experiment was not a lasting success and faded after Afonso's death. Many of the missionaries died quickly from tropical diseases. The Christian kingdom was attacked in 1568–73 by Jaga cannibals who devastated several regions before being expelled by a Portuguese expeditionary force. A group of four Jesuits were held prisoner for several years and one of the survivors reported that the country could only be converted by force of arms. In the 1480s new island bases were establisheded in São Tomé and Principe (in the Bight of Biafra to the northwest of Congo) and sugar plantations were created with slave labour. These islands also provided a convenient staging post for later slave exports to the Americas. By the 1530s Portuguese traders were exporting up to 5,000 slaves a year from the Congo–Angola region. From then on Portugal gave greater priority to slaving than to saving souls. Until the nineteenth century, its activity in Angola was restricted to the two ports of Luanda and Benguela, and their hinterland (see Birmingham 1976).

On the east coast, the situation the Portuguese encountered was quite different. Economic life was much more sophisticated and the population much more cosmopolitan. There was a long string of Islamized coastal settlements stretching from Somalia to Mozambique. Each was more or less independent, with little attempt to dominate the others politically. They had already had extensive trading contact with southern Arabia, the Persian Gulf, and Asia in Roman times. The local population were an Afro-Arab mix, with a coastal *lingua franca*, Swahili. This is a Bantu language influenced by long contact with Arabs; the name derives from the Arabic *as-Sawahil*, meaning 'the coastal lands'. The coastal ports—Kilwa, Malindi, Mombasa, Mozambique, and Sofala—were frequented by merchants from Arabia,

Persia, Gujarat, and Malabar. They imported silk and cotton textiles, spices, Chinese porcelain, and cowrie shells (which were used as a form of currency). They exported cotton, timber, ivory, gold, and slaves. They had professional pilots familiar with monsoon conditions in the Indian Ocean. Their ships were sturdy, but very vulnerable to Portuguese guns, as their timbers were not nailed but stitched together with cords made of coir fibre.

The Portuguese had three main objectives in the area: (a) to establish a secure staging post for their ships in the Asian trade; (b) to gain access to east African gold; (c) to do as much damage as they could to the Muslim traders on the coast.

Their main base for the India trade was the island of Mozambique. This was convenient for ships, but proved unheathy for sailors. Between 1528 and 1558, 30,000 Portuguese died there from tropical diseases and the aftermath of scurvy (see Boxer 1991: 218).

The first gold consignments reached Lisbon in 1506, but the quantity exported was lower than from west Africa. The gold came from inland mines and reached the coast at Sofala, where the Portuguese built a fortified post. Later they moved further north, to Quelimane and used the Zambezi river valley as the main artery for shipments to the coast, using canoes and head porterage where there were rapids. Gold came from an area stretching from modern Bulawayo to Salisbury. Great Zimbabwe, in the south, had been the centre of gold production from the eleventh to the fourteenth century, but the site was abandoned (leaving monumental stone-terraced buildings) before the Portuguese arrived. They got their gold from the Mutapa tribal confederacy in northern Rhodesia. A number of Portuguese adventurers established landed estates in the Zambezi river valley. Some of these *prazeros* made fortunes trading in gold, slaves, and ivory, but most of them died from tropical diseases.

The Portuguese did their best to drive Arab traders out of Indian Ocean trade. They captured the main Omani port of Muscat in 1508, and blockaded Arab trade in the Persian Gulf after taking Hormuz in 1515. They mounted a series of expeditions against east African coastal settlements to impede their trade with Arabia, the Persian Gulf, and India. They succeeded in doing this for a period of nearly two centuries until 1622, when the Safavid empire of Persia recaptured Hormuz with help from ships of the British East India Company. In 1650 the Arabs recaptured Muscat and a number of Portuguese ships in the harbour. With these as a model, they were remarkably successful in building well armed vessels able to face the Portuguese on even terms. 'By the end of the seventeeth century they had expelled the Portuguese from Mombasa and from all the Swahili island-or city-states along the East African coast (Pate, Pemba, Zanzibar, Malindi, etc.) over which they claimed suzerainty, north of Cape Delgado' (Boxer 1991: 134). A residual Portuguese presence was maintained on Mozambique island and the adjoining coast.

The Omanis maintained a loose suzerainty of the east African coast and its slave trade until the end of the eighteenth century. In the nineteenth they strengthened their position. The Omani ruler moved his capital to Zanzibar in 1840 and developed plantation agriculture there and on the island of Pemba. By the 1860s these islands were the major world producer of cloves.

There was some Portuguese contact with the Christian kingdom of Abyssinia from 1520, with military intervention in 1541–3 to prevent the country from being taken over by the Ottoman empire. However, differences between Ethiopian and Roman Catholic doctrine and ritual created disharmony and the Jesuit mission was expelled in 1633.

One important result of Portuguese contact with black Africa was the introduction of crops from the Americas. The most important for the African food supply and capacity to expand population were roots and tubers. Cassava (manioc) was brought from Brazil to the Kongo kingdom, the Niger delta, and the Bight of Benin early in the sixteenth century. It had high yields, was rich in starch, calcium, iron, and vitamin C. It was a perennial plant, tolerant of a wide variety of soils, invulnerable to locusts, drought resistant, and easy to cultivate. It provides its own storage. It can be left in reserve, unharvested, for long periods in good condition after ripening. Cassava flour can be made into cakes for long distance travel and was a staple food for slave transport across the Atlantic (see Jones 1959). Sweet potatoes were another significant addition to Africa's food supply.

Maize was an American crop which the Portuguese introduced on the west and east African coasts. By the seventeenth century it was present in Senegal, the Congo basin, South Africa, and Zanzibar.

Over the centuries these crops have been widely diffused. In the mid-1960s, three-quarters (43 million tons) of African output of roots and tubers came from cassava and sweet potatoes (see FAO, *Production Yearbook*, 1966). Maize (15 million tons) represented a third of black Africa's cereal output, the traditional millet and sorghum, 47 per cent, rice, 12 per cent, and other cereals, 8 per cent.

Other significant American plants which were important in the long term were beans, peanuts, tobacco, and cocoa. Bananas and plantains were Asian crops widely diffused in east Africa before the Portuguese arrived; coffee, tea, rubber, and cloves were later introductions from Asia.

The Atlantic Slave Trade and the Context of Slavery in Africa

The Netherlands, UK, and France entered African trade as rivals to Portugal (and to each other) in the seventeenth century. Their operations were concentrated on the west coast above the Equator and their main interest was the slave trade. The exceptions were the Dutch settlement in south Africa (founded in 1652), and French plantation agriculture which started early in the eighteenth century in Ile de France (Mauritius) and Ile de Bourbon (Reunion). These Dutch and French settlements relied heavily on slave labour.

Table 4.5a shows Lovejoy's summary of recent research on African slavery. His major contribution is to put the Atlantic trade in the overall context of African slavery and slave trading. Slavery was a major characteristic of the Muslim world. In the eight and a half centuries of Islamic rule in north Africa between 650 and 1500, 4.3 million slaves were shipped from black Africa across the Sahara, i.e., an average of 5,000 a year; a further 2.2 million were shipped from east African ports to Arabia, the Persian Gulf, and India, i.e., an average of 2,600 a year, or 7,600 a year for all of these Muslim destinations. Austen (1979: 66), estimates 20 per cent mortality in the course of shipments across the desert. If this ratio is also valid for east African shipments, the total demographic drain would have been 9,500 a year.

In 1100, which is roughly the mid-point in this period, the total population of black Africa was probably around 25 million. From 1500 to 1900, the slave flow to these Islamic destinations increased to an average of 12,700 a year, or an annual drain of 15,800, if we assume the same rate of mortality in transit. The population of black Africa in 1700 (the mid-point in this period) was about 52 million, so the proportionate drain was lower than in 650–1500. However, shipments to the Americas after 1500 were a new and subtantially bigger burden. Lovejoy's total is 11 million for 1500–1900, an average of about 28,000 a year. The grand total was over 40,000 a year, including the drain to Muslim destinations. Curtin's total is 9.4 million, but would be 10.7 if we apply Klein's coefficient for mortality losses in transit—an average 12 per cent on the transatlantic crossing between 1590 and 1867 (Klein 1999: 140). Table 4.5b shows Klein's breakdown of the regions from which slaves were taken.

The age–sex composition of the Atlantic trade was different from that to Islamic destinations. Two-thirds of the Atlantic flow consisted of young males of working age, who were destined for hard labour in plantation agriculture, with low life expectation and little hope of manumission. The proportions were reversed in shipments to Muslim destinations. Two-thirds were women and children. The women were destined to be concubines or domestic servants. Male children were often taken to be trained as soldiers. Some were castrated before the trip to be sold as eunuchs. The range of occupations to which male slaves could aspire was much wider than in the Americas and the prospects of manumission for them or their eventual offspring were much greater.

The British exported more than 2.5 million Africans to the Americas; most came from Sierra Leone and the Guinea coast. The French brought 1.2 million from the Senegal–Gambia region and the Dutch about half a million, mainly from the Gold Coast. The Portuguese were driven out of these regions and concentrated on shipments from Angola to Brazil and Spanish America. Their total shipments from 1500 to 1870 were about 4.5 million.

In the overwhelming majority of cases it was the Africans who controlled the slaves until the moment of sale. African slave traders came down the coast or the riverbanks in a relatively steady and predictable stream to well-known trading places. European traders tended to spend several months on the coast or travelling upriver gathering their slaves a few at a time (Klein 1999: 90–1).

Table 4.5a. Slave Exports from Black Africa, 650–1900, by Destination (000s)

	650–1500	1500–1800	1800–1900	650–1900
Americas	81	7,766	3,314	11,159
Trans-Sahara	4,270	1,950	1,200	7,420
Asia	2,200	1,000	934	4,134
Total	6,551	10,716	5,448	22,713

Notes and Sources: Lovejoy (2000: 19, 26, 47, 142, and 147). Lovejoy refers to exports from 'Africa', but treats Africa north of the Sahara as an 'external market' (p. 24), so, in fact, he covers exports from Africa south of the Sahara. His figures for the Americas are similar to those of Curtin (1969) for 1500–1800, but substantially larger for 1800–1900 (see Maddison 2003: 115). Part of the difference is that Curtin shows arrivals whereas Lovejoy does not appear to allow for deaths in transit. The difference is also due to Lovejoy's use of the Du Bois archive. So far, this appears to be available only as a CD ROM, without the meticulously documented description of the source material which Curtin provided. For trans-Saharan exports, Lovejoy uses 1979 estimates of R.A. Austen; for Asia he cites 14 different sources (p. 142). For the two latter areas the evidence is much weaker than for the Americas, and the possible range of error correspondingly higher. In addition to the slave exports shown in this table, there was also a huge slave economy within black Africa This had always existed, but grew very rapidly in the nineteenth century as Atlantic exports were blocked.

Table 4.5b. Regional Origin of African Slaves Exported to the Americas, 1662–1867 (000s)

Senegambia	600	Bight of Biafra	1,658
Sierra Leone	756	West Central Africa	3,928
Gold Coast	710	South East Africa	392
Bight of Benin	1,871	Total	9,915

Source: Klein (1999: 209).

Within Africa, slaves were acquired in several ways. Some were the offspring of slaves. A large proportion were captured in wars or were supplied as tribute by subject or dependent tribes. In the sixteenth century the wars between the Kongo kingdom and the Jaga invaders produced a surge in the supply from Angola. The same was true during the west African jihads in the eighteenth and nineteenth centuries. Criminals of various kinds were a steady source. There was large scale raiding of poorly armed tribes without strong central authorities, and kidnapping of individual victims.

Klein (1999: 208–9) shows the rate of flow across the Atlantic from 1662 to 1867. It rose steadily from an average of 9,000 a year in 1662–80 to a peak of 76,000 in 1760–89, fell to 61,000 in 1816–30, 51,000 in 1831–50, and 10,500 in 1851–65. Lovejoy shows the average price per slave in constant (1601) prices for 1663–1775. In 1663–82, the average price was £2.9, £10 in 1703–32, and £15.4 in 1733–75. African income from slavery therefore appears to have risen more than 40-fold from the end of the seventeenth to the end of the eighteenth century. In fact the exchange was usually a barter of trade goods for slaves. The main import item was textiles which the original Portuguese traders bought in Morocco. By the eighteenth century, they were mainly Indian fabrics specially made for the west African market. Other important trade goods were tobacco and alcohol, jewellery, bar iron, weapons, gunpowder, and cowrie shells from the Maldives. At their peak, in the late eighteenth century, Klein (1999: 125), suggests that these imports 'only reached £2.1 million sterling of goods per annum, which probably represented less than 5 percent of the total West African income for the 25 million or so resident population'.

Slavery within black Africa rose substantially after the abolition movement reduced the Atlantic flow and the price of slaves dropped. The momentum of enslavement continued, and a much larger proportion of the captives were absorbed within Africa. Lovejoy (2000: 191–210) estimates that, at the end of the nineteenth century, 30–50 per cent of the population of the western, central, and Nilotic Sudan were slaves. In the 1850s, half the people in the caliphate of Sokoto in northern Nigeria were slaves. In Zanzibar, the slave population rose from 15,000 in 1818 to 100,000 in the 1860s. There was a large increase of slave employment in peasant and plantation agriculture producing palm oil products, peanuts, cloves, and cotton for export. In the Belgian Congo, southeast and southern Africa there was a rapid expansion of mining activity at the end of the century, with a servile labour force, whose *de facto* situation was equivalent to slavery. Eltis (1991: 101) shows a very large increase in commodity exports from Africa in the course of the nineteenth century.

Conclusions on the European–African Interaction, 1500–1820

The costs and benefits of the transatlantic slave trade were felt very unevenly. The biggest losers were the 1.5 million who died in transit, the 11 million who were enslaved had their life expectation shortened by hard labour, meagre rations, and brutal treatment. Normal family life was destroyed and there was virtually no hope of manumission. The gainers were the slave traders and the European settlers in the Americas who exploited slave labour. Within Africa, the demographic losses were concentrated on tribes and people least able to protect themselves. Demographic growth was certainly reduced. Between 1500 and 1820, the African population grew about 0.16 per cent a year compared with 0.26 in western Europe and 0.29 in Asia. The disruption caused by slavery reduced per capita income in the areas from which slaves were seized. The imports which slave exporters gained in exchange raised consumption but not production potential.

European countries did nothing to transmit technical knowledge to Africa, nor did they attempt to promote education, printing, or development of alphabets. China had printing in the ninth century, western Europe from 1453, Mexico in 1539, Peru 1584, and the north American colonies from the beginning of the seventeenth century. The first printing press in Africa came to Cairo in 1820. There was a significant transfer of plants from the Americas to Africa (mainly cassava, sweet potatoes, and maize), but the impact was not so great or rapid as the ecological exchange between Europe and the Americas, which involved a huge transfer of European animals for food, transport, and textile fibres. In Africa there was much less interaction with

Europeans than in the Americas. In 1820, there were less than 35,000 Europeans in Africa, compared to 13 million in the Americas.

Settlement in Africa was much less attractive to Europeans than movement to the Americas. Africa had diseases which caused very high rates of mortality to Europeans, but Africans were not particularly susceptible to European diseases. Africans had much better weapons to defend themselves than the indigenous population of the Americas. European interest in Africa was mainly the trade in slaves and gold. Europeans acquired slaves through African intermediaries. If slaves had had to be seized by conquest and capture, the cost would have been much higher and the development of the Americas slower.

We should note some African institutions which hindered development, but were not due to European influence. One of these, on which Ibn Khaldun (1982) commented at length, was the fragility of the states which emerged in the Muslim world (a point which applies *a fortiori* to black Africa). Ibn Khaldun stressed the persistence of tribal affiliations and lineages, and the continuence of nomadic traditions destructive of attempts to develop sedentary agriculture and urban civilization. For this reason he saw no measure of progress from the seventh to the fourteenth century in which he lived. He stressed the cyclical rise and fall of Muslim regimes, and deeply regretted the decay of al-Andalus, where his ancestors had lived for centuries. Gellner's (1969, 1973, and 1981) analysis echoed that of ibn Khaldun. He stressed the fragility of Muslim states in the Maghreb, where a weak central authority co-existed with strong tribes, particularly in Morocco, where 'rulers were simultaneously utilising native institutions at quite different levels—a theocratic, nominally absolutist but effectively enfeebled sultanate, and anarchic but militarily effective tribesmen, with petty local tyrants emerging in between' (Gellner 1981: 182).

A significant hindrance to progress in Islamized Africa was the disappearance of the commitment to secular knowledge and learning which had prevailed in Baghdad in the heyday of the Abbasid caliphate and had been so brilliantly pursued in the caliphate of Cordoba. It was replaced by reliance on revealed religion, and reduced tolerance for non-Muslim communities. Within black Africa, there was universal illiteracy (except in Ethiopia), before Islamic penetration. Contact with Islam mitigated this situation, but illiteracy remained a major hindrance to progress.

African societies failed to secure property rights. The power elite were autocratic and predatory, which inhibited accumulation of capital and willingness to take business risks. This was very obvious in the Mamluk regime in Egypt. There were few countervailing forces in African societies. Goitein's detailed scrutiny of the Cairo Geniza archive led him to be very upbeat about the emergence of a commercial business class in Fatimid Egypt, but freedom of enterprise was snuffed out in later dynasties. The most striking example of deficient property rights was slavery itself, which was closely linked with the polgygamous family structure and limitation on the rights of women. These two institutions were probably the major impediment to physical and human capital formation.

BOX 4.1. European Enclaves and Colonies in Africa, 1415--1919

Portugal

Ceuta, 1415–1580; Arquim, 1445; Cabo Verde, 1460; Tangier, 1471–1662; Elmina, 1482–1637; Angola, 1484; Fernando Po (Equatorial Guinea), 1493–1778; São Tomé and Principe, 1493; Mozambique, 1505; Agadir 1505–49; Guinea-Bissau (separated from Cabo Verde), 1879.

Spain

Melilla, 1497; Ceuta, 1580; Equatorial Guinea, 1778; Rio de Oro (western Sahara), 1884; Spanish Morocco, 1912.

Netherlands

Mauritius, 1600–1712; Elmina, 1637–1872; Cape Colony, 1652–1797.

France

Reunion (Ile de Bourbon), 1649; Mauritius, 1715–1810; Seychelles, 1742–1814; Egypt, 1798–1800; Algeria, 1830; Mayotte, 1841; Gabon, 1843; Comoros, 1843; Senegal, 1854; Tunisia, 1882; Cote d'Ivoire, 1883; French Somaliland (Djibouti), 1884; Congo (Brazzaville), 1885; Comoros, 1885; Guinea, 1889; Dahomey (Benin), 1892; Upper Volta (Burkina Faso) 1892; Central African Republic (Oubangui-Chari), 1894, Madagascar, 1895; Mali, 1898; Chad, 1900; Mauretania, 1903; Niger, 1908; Morocco, 1912; Togo, 1919; Cameroon, 1919. Federation of French West Africa (eight colonies), 1895, capital at Dakar in Senegal; Federation of French Equatorial Africa (four colonies), 1910, capital Brazzaville.

Britain

Tangier, 1662–84; Cape Colony, 1797; Sierra Leone, 1808; Mauritius, 1810; Seychelles, 1814; Natal, 1845; Basutoland (Lesotho), 1868; Gold Coast, 1874, and Ashanti, 1896 (Ghana); Egypt, 1882; Somaliland (Somalia), 1884; Bechuanaland (Botswana), 1884–8, Nigeria, 1884–90; Kenya, 1886; Zululand, 1887: Gambia, 1888; Uganda, 1888; Southern Rhodesia (Zimbabwe), 1890; Northern Rhodesia (Zambia), 1891; Nyasaland (Malawi), 1891; Swaziland, 1894; Zanzibar, 1895; Sudan, 1898; Transvaal, 1902; Orange Free State, 1902; Union of South Africa (Cape, Natal, Orange Free State, and Transvaal), 1910; German Cameroon, 1919; Namibia, 1919; Tanganyika, 1919; German Zanzibar, 1919.

Belgium

King Leopold, proprietor of Congo Free State, 1885, taken over by Belgian government as Belgian Congo, 1908; Burundi, 1919; Rwanda, 1919.

Germany

Kamerun, 1884; Togo, 1884; German West Africa (Namibia), 1884–5; German East Africa (Tanganyika); Burundi and Rwanda, 1890; part of Zanzibar, 1895. Lost in 1919.

Italy

Somaliland, 1886; Eritrea, 1889; Libya, 1912; Ethiopia, 1936. Lost in 1941.

AFRICA FROM 1820 TO 1960

In 1820, Algeria, Tunisia, Libya, and Egypt were part of the Ottoman Empire; Spain had toeholds in Morocco; Portugal, in Angola and Mozambique; and the British had taken over the Dutch settlement at the Cape. The rest of the continent was unknown and unexplored, occupied by hunter-gatherers, pastoralists, or practitioners of subsistence agriculture. Levels of technology were primitive. The only territorial units which resembled those of today were Egypt, Ethiopia, and Morocco. Slaves were the main export.

When the transatlantic slave trade ended, European involvement in tropical Africa waned, but a series of changes renewed their interest. New medical technology greatly reduced European mortality. 'Before the 1850s, the annual mortality of newly arrived Europeans varied between 250 and 500 per thousand' Curtin (1995). The discovery that quinine could counter the parasites transferred by mosquito bites caused European death rates to fall to 50 per 1,000 in the second half of the nineteenth century. Later discoveries and development of drugs helped reduce mortality from yellow fever and sleeping sickness.

From 1800 to the 1870s, there was a spectacular increase in European knowledge of tropical Africa. Exploration by intrepid explorers like James Brooke, Mungo Park, Heinrich Bart, Richard Burton, John Hanning Speke, David Livingstone, and Henry Morton Stanley revealed its geography and potential to supply minerals and plantation crops.

The development of steamboat, railway, and telegraphic communication technology, construction of roads and ports, and the opening of the the Suez Canal in 1869 made it feasible to penetrate beyond the coastal areas.

The invention of the machine-gun increased the European advantage in armed conflict with Africans. The growth of the international capital market after 1870, and the development of European banking within Africa greatly facilitated the possibilities for financing investment.

European powers began to scramble for colonies in Africa in the 1880s. France and Britain were the most successful. Twenty-two countries eventually emerged from French colonization, 21 from British, five from Portuguese, three from Belgian, two from Spanish. Germany lost its colonies after the First World War, Italy after the Second. In 1820, there were less than 35,000 Europeans in Africa (30,000 in the Cape, and less than 5,000 elsewhere). By the 1950s, this had risen to 6 million (1.7 in the Maghreb, 3.5 million in South Africa, about 800,000 elsewhere). There were also about half a million Indians in east and South Africa.

Territorial conquest was relatively cheap. None of the indigenous peoples (except Ethiopians) managed to repel European firepower for very long, and the risky face-offs between the European powers were settled without serious conflict.

The new rulers created boundaries to suit their mutual convenience, with little regard to local traditions or ethnicity. English, French, and Portuguese became the official linguistic vehicles. European law and property rights protected the interests of colonists who got the best land, but African incomes were kept low by forced labour and discrimination enforced by apartheid and cognate practices. In economic and social matters the approach was generally minimalist. Little was done to cater for popular education.

African per capita income was not significantly different in 1820 from what it was in 1500, and probably somewhat lower than it was 1,000 years before that. In the colonial period from 1820 to 1960, it rose more than 2.5-fold. This was a good deal less than the nearly six-fold increase in western Europe and the 4.5-fold increase in Latin America, but it was better than Asian experience, and the African level was somewhat higher than the Asian in 1960.

It is clear that colonialism introduced some dynamism into the African economies, but there was a big difference in performance between black Africa, where incomes doubled, and the white settler countries, where average per capita income rose nearly four-fold and where the white population benefited from big increases in white–black inequality. It is not easy to quantify performance in the colonial period for many African countries back to 1820, but for six countries acceptable studies are available.

South Africa

It is clear from Table 4.6 on the expansion of the railway network and Table 4.7 on population and per capita GDP growth that the South African economy was the most dynamic. The chief beneficiaries were white settlers. Ross (1975: 221) estimated that there were nearly 15,000 of them in 1795. Their number had grown rapidly since 1701 because of early marriage, high fertility, and immigration. Assuming that this growth rate was the same for the next 25 years, there would have been 27,000 in 1820,

Table 4.6. Length of Railway Line in Service, 1870–1913 (kilometres per million population)

	1870	1913
Algeria	70	632
Egypt	168	359
Ghana	0	165
Morocco	0	84
Tunisia	0	1,105
South Africa	0	2,300
Argentina	408	4,374
Australia	861	6,944
India	38	184
UK	685	715
USA	2,117	9,989

Source: Mitchell (1982) and Maddison (1995: 64).

Table 4.7. African Population, GDP, and Per Capita GDP, 1820–2003

	1820	1913	1960	1980	2003
Population (000s)					
Algeria	2,689	5,497	10,909	18,806	31,714
Egypt	4,194	12,144	26,847	42,634	74,719
Ghana	1,374	2,043	6,958	11,016	21,020
Morocco	2,689	5,111	12,423	19,487	31,689
Tunisia	875	1,870	4,149	6,443	9,873
South Africa	1,550	6,153	17,417	29,252	44,482
6 country total	13,371	32,818	78,703	127,638	213,497
51 other countries	60,865	91,879	205,116	344,285	639,925
African Total	74,236	124,697	283,819	471,923	853,422
GDP (million 1990 international Geary–Khamis $)					
Algeria	*1,157*	6,395	22,780	59,273	99,362
Egypt	*1,992*	10,950	26,617	88,223	226,683
Ghana	*570*	1,595	9,591	12,747	28,595
Morocco	*1,156*	*3,630*	16,507	44,278	92,385
Tunisia	*376*	1,651	5,571	18,966	49,048
South Africa	*643*	9,857	52,972	128,416	191,742
6 country total	*5,894*	34,078	134,038	351,903	687,815
51 other countries	*25,267*	*45,408*	167,540	374,002	634,272
African Total	*31,161*	*79,486*	301,578	725,905	1,322,087
GDP per capita (international Geary–Khamis $)					
Algeria	*430*	1,163	2,088	3,152	3,133
Egypt	*475*	902	991	2,069	3,034
Ghana	*415*	781	1,378	1,157	1,360
Morocco	*430*	*710*	1,329	2,272	2,915
Tunisia	*430*	883	1,343	2,944	4,968
South Africa	*415*	1,602	3,041	4,390	4,311
6 country average	*441*	1,038	1,703	2,757	3,222
51 other countries	*415*	*494*	817	1,086	991
African Average	*420*	*637*	1,063	1,538	1,549

Notes and Source: Maddison (2003: 200), updated to 2003, as in Tables 4.1 and 4.2. Estimates of GDP growth for African countries are of poorer quality than for other parts of the world. Conjectures are shown in italics.

but British immigration would have raised this to something in the region of 30,000 (i.e., 2 per cent of the total population).

The white expansion displaced the relatively weak and thinly settled indigenous herdsmen and hunters (Khoisan) in the Cape colony which had mainly been a staging post for trade with Asia. By 1870 a quarter of a million whites had fanned out east and north into Natal, the Orange Free State, and Transvaal. They seized the best land and water supplies from Xhosa, Zulu, and other indigenous groups, and then exploited them in various forms of semi-servile labour. In the next 20 years the discovery of diamonds and gold created a boom in investment and immigration in South Africa and the Rhodesias. By 1913, there were 1.3 million whites in South Africa (22 per cent of the population), with an elaborate system of social segregation to buttress their privileged position. By the 1950s they were about 3.5 million (about a quarter of the population).

Algeria

Algeria was the first French conquest in the Maghreb. It had been a province of the Ottoman empire since the sixteenth century. It was ruled by a 'dey', selected from and by the Turkish janissary garrison. His control was limited to Algiers and its surrounding area. Under him there were beys in Constantine in the east, Titteri in the centre, and Oran in the west. Nomadic Berber and Arab tribes controlled the desert fringes in the south. The mountainous area of Kabylie, between Algiers and Constantine to the east was an independent Berber enclave. The Sahara, 85 per cent of Algerian territory, was a desert virtually uninhabited except for Tuareg tribes. In the cities the *ulama* represented Muslim orthodoxy; in the tribal areas, the marabouts held sway.

Until the 1820s, a major source of the dey's income came from piracy. There was no regular merchant fleet as Muslim ships could not enter European ports. The corsairs captured European vessels, seized their cargoes, and enslaved their crews on behalf of the dey who received a large part of their profits. This income fell sharply after the British sank the corsair fleet and bombarded Algiers in 1816. The deys had difficulty paying their troops; six were asassinated between 1805 and 1815, and the regime started to crumble.

The dey quarrelled with France over money he was owed for grain supplied during the Napoleonic wars. French recalcitrance led the dey to flick the French consul with his fly-swatter. In 1830, in the last months of the Bourbon monarchy, the French fleet was sent to make a retaliatory show of force in Algiers. This escalated into a military takeover and the dey fled into Neapolitan exile. The new regime of Louis Philippe was not enthusiastic about this venture, but annexed Algeria as a colony in 1834. In 1848, Algeria was proclaimed to be French territory with three coastal departments, Oran, Algiers, and Constantine. The south was controlled by the French army and its generals, who initiated a huge land-grab.

The landed property of the dey and the beys was confiscated and sold to French settlers and speculators at an early stage. In 1844, *habus* land (property of religious foundations) was seized and in 1846 a substantial area of tribal land held in usufruct was declared vacant and taken over by the French authorities. There were major revolts against French rule in the 1840s by Abd al-Qadir in the west and Ahmed Bey in the East, and another by al-Mokri and the Berbers in Kabylie in 1871. After these were suppressed, there were further massive land seizures in these areas. By 1955, French colons occupied 2.7 million hectares, (40 per cent of the cultivated area). Almost 90 per cent of this was in large holdings with hired Muslim labour. There was a rapid growth of cereal production before the first world war. Europeans introduced cultivation of vines and there was a large growth in wine production. They developed specialized production of fruits and vegetables for domestic consumption and export.

Most of the European population was in urban areas. In the mid-1950s, Europeans were 10 per cent of the total population, but a third of the urban population. Amin

(1966) estimated the average non-Muslim income in 1955 to be nearly eight times as high as that of the Muslim population.

Ghana

Ghana was one of the most successful countries in black Africa. The traditional sector appears to have expanded in line with population from 1891 to 1911 and rose about half in per capita terms from 1911 to 1960. Its new cocoa economy rose very rapidly indeed. Exports rose from 80 lbs in 1891 to 89 million in 1911, when 600,000 acres and 185,000 man-years were absorbed in its production. To a large degree the cocoa boom was sustained by more intensive use of land and previously underemployed rural labour. The main beneficiaries were peasant farmers (see Szereszewski 1965).

Clark and Haswell (1970: 193 and 203) stressed the role of modern transport in moving from a subsistence economy to bulk exports of cotton, oilseeds, groundnuts, cocoa, coffee, bananas, tobacco, rubber, and minerals. In mid-nineteenth century Ghana, there was no possibility of exporting maize though its domestic price was only one-fifteenth of that in the world market. They estimated the impact of successive reductions in the cost of moving grain by head porterage, boat, steamboat, railway, and motor vehicle. In typical tropical African conditions, the cost of a ton/km by steamboat or railway was less than 6 per cent of the cost by head porterage. The leap from ancient to modern transport was made more abruptly in Africa than elsewhere. Horse-drawn transport had never been an option because of the vulnerability of horses to tropical disease. Thus there had been no incentive to build roads.

A second dynamic element in Ghana was gold. It had been exported for centuries, but in the 1870s there was a beginning of modern operations. The discovery of huge reserves in South Africa in 1886 sparked an analogous euphoria and investment boom in Ghana. By 1901, 42 companies were operating, and by 1911, a railway connection had been built from the coast to Kumasi through the gold mining areas. There were also improvements in transport facilities from Accra to its cocoa-growing hinterland, investment in modern port facilities in Secondi and Accra, and development of internal river transport by steam launches. The export ratio rose from 8 to 19 per cent of GDP between 1891 and 1911. A good deal of the benefits of growth were felt by the locals. In 1911 there were 2,245 Europeans (about 0.1 per cent of the population). In Algeria at that time there were three-quarters of a million European settlers (about 14 per cent of the total).

POST-COLONIAL AFRICA, 1960 ONWARDS

The post-war situation in western Europe was one of rapid economic growth. It was clear that possession of colonies did not contribute to its prosperity, and all the European colonies were eventually abandoned. The British colonial bond was broken in Egypt in 1956, in Ghana in 1957, Nigeria in 1960, Tanzania in 1961, and Kenya in 1963. White settler interests retarded the process in Zimbabwe and Namibia, and in South Africa the indigenous population did not get political rights until 1994. French de-colonization started with Morocco in 1956, ended in black Africa in 1960, and was more or less completed with the exodus from Algeria in 1962. Belgium abandoned the Congo in 1960. Portugal and Spain made their exit in 1975. Independence brought many serious challenges. One was the newness of the nation-states. Their political leadership had to create elements of national solidarity and stability from scratch. Twelve of the French colonies had belonged to two large federations whose administrative and transport network was centred on Dakar and Brazzaville. These networks had to be revamped. In several cases, the new political elites sought to achieve political stability and reinforce their legitimacy by creating one-party states with incumbent presidents keeping their position for life. In the absence of countervailing power from peasants or the urban poor, regimes became patrimonial, favouring their ethnicity, clan, region, or religious group. This facilitated corruption and reduced pressures to change mistaken policies. In some cases, this form of despotism was fairly enlightened, in others, well-intentioned utopians led their countries into disastrous experiments, and in a few, venal and repressive rulers produced even worse results.

The process of state creation involved armed struggle in many cases. In Algeria, Angola, Mozambique, Sudan, Zaire, and Zimbabwe, the struggle for independence involved war with the colonial power or the white settler population. A few years later, Nigeria, Uganda, and Ethiopia suffered from civil wars and bloody dictators. More recently Burundi, Cote d'Ivoire, Liberia, Rwanda, Sierra Leone, Somalia, Sudan, Uganda, and Zaire have all had the same problem. These wars had a heavy cost, both human and economic, and were a major impediment to development.

There was a great scarcity of people with education or administrative experience. Suddenly, these countries had to create a political elite, staff a national bureaucracy, establish a judiciary, create a police force and armed forces, send out dozens of diplomats, find school teachers, and build up health services. The first big wave of job opportunities strengthened the role of patronage and rent-seeking, and reduced the attractions of entrepreneurship. The existing stock of graduates was too small to meet the new demands and there was heavy dependence on foreign personnel.

Many countries overburdened their weak state apparatus with new economic tasks. 'Planning' was à la mode. It was encouraged by many foreign advisers and appealed to the social engineering aspirations of some of the new leaders. The late colonial practice of rigging prices and exchange rates was reinforced rather than weakened. Dependence on foreign aid was taken to be axiomatic.

African independence came when the cold war was at its height, and the continent again became the focus of a different kind of international rivalry. China, the USSR, Cuba, and east European countries supplied economic and military aid to countries viewed as proxies in a worldwide conflict of interest. Western countries were strongly influenced by this competitive situation. They were less fastidious in allocating aid than they might otherwise have been. As a result Africa accumulated large foreign debts which had a meagre developmental pay-off.

Africa has over 13 per cent of world population, but only 3 per cent of world GDP. It is the world's poorest region, with a per capita income only 5 per cent of that in the richest region. Average life expectation at birth in 2005 was 51 years—49 in the sub-Sahara (where the incidence of AIDS is particularly severe) and 72 in north Africa. This compares with 67 in Asia, 72 in Latin America and 79 in western Europe. It has the most rapid demographic expansion. In 2005, annual population growth rate was 2.25 per cent in the African continent—nine times faster than the 0.25 per cent in western Europe in that year.

As a result of rapid population growth, age structure is very different from that in western Europe. In Africa, 56 per cent are of working age compared with 67 per cent in western Europe; 41 per cent of Africans are below 15 years old and 3 per cent, 65 or over. In western Europe 16 per cent are under 15 and 17 per cent, 65 or older. More than 40 per cent of the adult population of Africa are illiterate. They have a high incidence of infectious and parasitic disease (malaria, sleeping sickness, hookworm, river blindness, yellow fever). Over two-thirds of HIV infected people live in Africa. As a result the quantity and quality of labour input per head of population is much lower than in other parts of the world.

Poverty and economic stagnation or decline are predominant characteristics of Africa, but there are important variations in levels of income and growth performance. Table 4.8 distinguishes between the 15 countries where average per capita income is above $2,000 (with PPP, rather than exchange rate, conversion) and the 42 countries below this level. In the first group, per capita income averaged $3,468 in 2003, and the rest only $923. Countries in the first group had an average income near that of western Europe in 1913, in the rest it is well below the west European level in 1700.

The first group consists of five countries on the Mediterranean littoral (Algeria, Egypt, Libya, Morocco, and Tunisia). Of these Egypt, Morocco, and Tunisia had reasonable growth performance in 1973–2003, but the 2003 level of per capita income in Algeria was 8 per cent below its 1985 peak, and in Libya a quarter of the 1970 peak.

The second group, at the southern tip of the continent, consists of Botswana, Namibia, South Africa, and Swaziland. Botswana has been one of the world's fastest growing economies (6 per cent per capita from 1960 to 2003), largely based on exploitation of its diamond resources. South Africa's per capita income in 2003 was 4 per cent below its 1981 peak, and Namibia's 9 per cent below.

The third group of six small countries consists of special cases. Equatorial Guinea, Gabon, and the Congo have relatively high and expanding levels of petroleum production and export. The three others are islands in the Indian Ocean with population growth rates well below the African average. Reunion is a French overseas department with a high degree of subsidy from the metropole. In the Seychelles and Mauritius

Table 4.8. Variations of Income Level Within Africa, 2003

	GDP per capita (1990 int. $)	GDP (million 1990 int. $)	Population (000)
Algeria	3,133	99,362	31,714
Egypt	3,034	226,683	74,719
Libya	2,427	13,348	5,499
Morocco	2,915	92,385	31,689
Tunisia	4,968	49,048	9,873
5 Mediterranean countries	**3,133**	**480,826**	**153,494**
Botswana	4,938	8,078	1,636
Namibia	3,778	7,529	1,993
South Africa	4,311	191,742	44,482
Swaziland	2,751	3,125	1,136
4 South African countries	**4,274**	**210,474**	**49,247**
Congo	2,006	6,847	3,413
Equatorial Guinea	13,556	6,873	507
Gabon	3,737	4,974	1,331
Mauritius	11,839	14,330	1,210
Reunion	4,926	3,719	755
Seychelles	5,850	468	80
6 special cases	**5,100**	**37,211**	**7,296**
Total for 15 countries	**3,468**	**728,511**	**210,037**
Total for 42 other countries	**923**	**593,576**	**643,385**
Total Africa	**1,549**	**1,322,087**	**853,422**

Source: www.ggdc.net/Maddison

the majority of the population are of Indian origin, bilingual in English and French. Seychelles has a high tourist income. Mauritius has been successful in developing exports of manufactures, and, more recently, services.

More than three-quarters of Africa's population belongs to the fourth group whose per capita income is lowest. Their income peaked in 1980. This group of countries is the hard core of African poverty.

Many recent attempts to explain Africa's weak economic performance echo the earlier judgements of Ibn Khaldun and Ernest Gellner about the fragility of African states. Bloom and Sachs (1998), Collier and Gunning (1999), and Ndulu and O'Connell (1999) all give major emphasis to problems of *'institutional quality'* or *'governance'*. Ndulu and O'Connell found that in 1988 only five countries 'had multi-party systems allowing meaningful political competition at the national level'. They categorized 11 as military oligarchies, 16 as plebiscitary one-party states, 13 as competitive one-party, and two as settler oligarchies (Namibia and South Africa, where the situation has now changed). In most of the one-party states, the incumbent rulers sought to keep their position for life. In most states, rulers relied for support on a narrow group who shared the spoils of office. Corruption became widespread, property rights insecure, business decisions risky. Collier and Gunning (p. 93) suggested that in 1999 nearly two-fifths of African private wealth consisted of assets held abroad (compared with 10 per cent in Latin America and 6 per cent in East Asia). Such

Table 4.9. Total External Debt of African Countries, 1980–2003 ($ million)

	1980	1990	1998	2003
Algeria	19,365	27,877	30,678	23,573
Angola	n.a.	8,594	10,786	9,316
Cameroon	2,588	6,679	9,66	9,414
Côte d'Ivoire	7,462	17,251	14,852	12,187
Egypt	19,131	32,947	32,440	31,383
Ethiopia	824	8,634	10,347	7,151
Ghana	1,398	3,881	6,933	7,551
Kenya	3,387	7,058	6,824	6,860
Morocco	9,258	24,458	23,739	18,910
Mozambique	n.a.	4,653	8,289	4,543
Nigeria	8,921	33,440	30,295	34,963
South Africa	n.a.	n.a.	24,753	27,807
Sudan	5,177	14,762	16,843	18,389
Tanzania	5,322	6,438	7,670	6.990
Tunisia	3,527	7,691	10,845	16,736
Zaire	4,770	10,270	13,203	11,254
Zimbabwe	786	3,247	4,581	4,483
Total 17 countries	91,916	217,879	263,044	251,510
Other Countries	20,217	52,171	63,572	70,668
Total Africa	**112,133**	**270,051**	**326,616**	**322,178**

Sources: 1980 and 1990 from Maddison (2001: 166); 1998 and 2003 from the Statistical Annexes of OECD (2005 and 2006).

estimates are necessarily rough, but with presidents like Mobutu in Zaire or Abacha in Nigeria, it is not difficult to believe that the proportion was high.

A major factor in the slowdown since 1980 has been external debt (see Table 4.9). As the cold war faded from the mid-1980s, foreign aid levelled off, and net lending to Africa fell. Although the flow of foreign direct investment has risen in the past few years, it is low ($18 per head in 2003) compared with the flow to Asia, Latin America, and eastern Europe. The official aid flow has also risen, but is low compared to the debt overhang. In 2003, net official development assistance flows (grants and loans, bilateral and multilateral) to Africa totalled $26.3 billion, an average of $31 per head of population.[9]

The African debt burden is the heaviest relative to per capita income. Capacity to finance investment from domestic saving is lower than in other continents (see Sachs et al. 2004: 144). African countries have benefited from debt relief in the past decade from initiatives of the World Bank, IMF, and Paris Club, but in 2003 total foreign debt was $321 billion ($337 per head of population).

African economies are volatile because export earnings are concentrated on a few primary commodities. Extremes of weather (droughts and floods) are more severe and have a heavy impact.

The outlook for the future is depressing unless the are significant changes within Africa. Levels of education and health are poor. Population growth is still explosive. Problems of political stability, armed conflict, institutional adjustment, and integration into the world economy continue to be formidable obstacles to growth. Most of these problems require changes within Africa, but their course could obviously be influenced by further financial help, and abolition of agricultural protectionism in the EU, Japan, and the US.

In the past few years there has been increasing recognition of the extreme poverty of Africa, with significant initiatives to address the problem. In 2000, the United Nations adopted Millennium Development Goals (MDGs) aimed at cutting world poverty by half by 2015, and improving education and health. In 2001, a 'New Partnership for Africa's Development' (NEPAD) was created by African states. Under the leadership of President Obansanjo of Nigeria, it adopted a 'Strategic Framework' to foster progress towards democracy and good governance, peace, and security. It established a mechanism for regional cooperation to promote economic development in partnership with the developed world. In 2002, the United Nations established its Millennium Development Project, under the leadership of Jeffrey Sach, to implement the MDGs.

The momentum for changes of this kind was reinforced by the British government's Commission for Africa (with 18 members—half African, half European). It included Gordon Brown, the chancellor of the exchequer, and Hilary Benn, the minister of development, as very active participants, and the prime minister as chairman. Their report, *Our Common Interest* was published early in 2005. It was less apocalyptic in tone, but more ambitious in its proposals and time horizon than those of the UN project. It recommended a doubling of aid to Africa, mainly in grants, within a shorter period of three to five years, a programme of 100 per cent debt cancellation by 2015, and the creation of a $4 billion fund to help cushion the disruptive effect of natural disasters or volatility in export prices. The report was outspoken about the need to end agricultural protectionism in developed countries. Abolition of these subsidies would have a bigger impact than the aid proposals: 'Rich countries spend about US$350 billion a year on agricultural protection and subsidies, the European Union is responsible for 35 per cent of this, the United States 27 per cent and Japan for 22 per cent' (see p. 54).

Effective implementation of such an ambitious programme requires a matching effort by African countries to reduce institutional barriers to effective resource allocation, reinforce arrangements for peaceful resolution of conflicts, and devote a large part of the development effort to improving education and health. On p. 114, it suggests that capital flight from Africa is running at about $15 billion a year, and urges African governments to persuade savers that their investments 'will not be stolen, confiscated, or subjected to arbitrary taxation'. The report is fairly comprehensive and realistic about the difficulties of implementation, but here as in NEPAD and MDGs, there is no mention of the need to promote knowledge and availability of contraceptive techniques. If reductions in mortality are balanced by reductions in fertility, Africa could experience a pronged surge in its productive capacity, with a rise in the proportion of the population of working age. A surge of this kind was an important ingredient in China's successful strategy for accelerated growth.

The British report and the UN MDGs had a significant resonance. In May 2005, 15 countries of the European Union agreed to raise their foreign aid to 0.51 per cent of their GDP by 2010, raising the total to $125 billion from $79 billion in 2004. The July 2005 G-8 summit at Gleneagles agreed to double development assistance to Africa to a total of $50 billion in 2010, and to make a start with debt cancellation for 18 countries. It agreed in principle to phasing out agricultural subsidies, without specifying the dimension and timing of such action. However, the outlook for significant reduction of agricultural protection and export subsidies looks bleak.

APPENDIX: THE CRUSADES, 1096–1270

There were six main crusades. The first, in 1096–9, was the most successful. It was organized in response to a complex situation in the Muslim world. Palestine was controlled by Fatimid Egypt; Christians could not bear arms or ride horses and had to pay a head tax from which Muslims were exempt, but all Christian sects and jews enjoyed religious freedom, their shrines were respected, and European pilgrims had access. However, the Fatimids, who were Shi'a, were regarded as heretics by their Sunni rivals in Baghdad where the Abbasid caliphate had been taken over by the Seljuk Turks. The Seljuks attacked the Byzantine empire and captured a large part of Anatolia where Christians were dispossessed by Muslim settlers or pastoralists. As a consequence there was much greater risk in overland travel by pilgrims headed for the holy places.

As his empire was in danger of collapse, the Byzantine ruler asked pope Urban II for military aid. The papal call to arms, in 1095, called for European capture of Palestine and its holy places. This whetted the interest of the feudal baronage of western Europe, who welcomed the prospect of acquiring new domains. The crusade was a military success, and four new buffer states were created in 1099–1109: (a) the kingdom of Jerusalem; (b) the principality of Antioch; and the counties of (c) Tripoli and (d) Edessa. The first three were on the coast of Palestine and Syria. Edessa stretched much further inland. Territorial control was vested in a variety of European aristocrats and royals, mainly French. The whole area was known as Outremer, but the four domains were autonomous.

In 1144, the Turks recaptured Edessa, and a second crusade was set up in 1147 by Pope Eugenius. It was led by Louis VII of France with his wife Eleanor of Aquitaine, and the German king Conrad III. St Bernard of Clairvaux was there to supply inspiration. Instead of trying to recapture Edessa, they attacked Damascus which seemed a richer target but was well defended. The attack was a fiasco. After four days, the crusader force ran away and the leaders went home. The only success went to a group of English, Flemish, and Frisians headed for Palestine by sea. Bad weather forced them to land in Portugal, where they helped the newly established kingdom to free Lisbon from Muslim rule (in 1147).

The third crusade was the largest. It was led by the German emperor Frederick I, king Philip Augustus of France, and the Angevin, Richard I, who had large domains in France and was also king of England. They left Europe separately in 1189. Their motive was to recapture Jerusalem and Acre. These towns had been taken by Saladin in 1187, in retaliation for a series of attacks by the kingdom of Jerusalem on Egypt. The crusade was a failure. In 1190, before he could seriously engage the enemy, the emperor Frederick fell off his horse into a river and was drowned by the weight of his armour. This effectively ended the participation of his troops in the campaign. Richard's forces were delayed in 1191 in Cyprus by shipwreck and the hostility of its Christian ruler. Richard took time out to conquer Cyprus before joining the French troops in the conquest of Acre. Richard broke the truce with Saladin by slaughtering the 2,700 Muslim troops who surrendered at Acre. The crusaders were unable to recapture Jerusalem. Philip Augustus went home sick in 1191. In 1192, Richard agreed to a truce with Saladin and left for home, but was held prisoner for more than a year by Leopold V of Austria whom he had insulted during the campaign in Palestine.

The fourth crusade, in 1204, was a fraud. In fact, it was an attack on Constantinople organized and financed by the Venetians, who gained tremendously from the venture. It was much more profitable for the so-called Crusaders than battle with Muslims. Baldwin, a Frank, was made Byzantine emperor, given a quarter of Constantinople, and control of most of the newly Latinized empire. A Venetian was installed as the new patriarch. The rest of Constantinople was divided between the Venetian traders and fiefs for crusading knights. Venice took the southern half of the Peloponnesus in Greece as well as Corfu, Crete, and bases in Dalmatia. It gained privileged trading rights in the Black Sea and Sea of Azov, which had previously been held by Genoa. In Constantinople, the main Crusader force concentrated on pillage and destruction. The Venetians were more careful in selecting treasures to embellish their native city. Once the spoils were distributed, the fight with the infidel was forgotten. The Latin kingdom lasted until 1261, when Byzantine rule was restored by Michael Paleologus.

The fifth (1218–21) and sixth (1248–50) crusades were both directed against Egypt. Their main purpose was to get European control of trade routes to India. Both were fiascos on an identical pattern, with initial capture of the port of Damietta and defeat by Egyptian forces at Mansura in the delta.

Apart from these six ventures there were others worth mention. In 1097, a People's crusade led by Peter the Hermit was massacred by Turkish forces. The Children's crusade of 1212 was equally ill-fated. Louis IX of France, who led the sixth crusade to disaster, led an attack on Tunis in 1270 where he died of dysentery. Pope Innocent III set up a 'crusade' to exterminate the Albigensian heretics of Provence in 1208–9.

The most astute of the European ventures in Palestine was that of Frederick II, in 1228–9. He had been brought up in the Arab-Norman court of Sicily, kept a harem, spoke Arabic, and knew how to negotiate. He was king of several domains in Italy and had managed to become emperor of Germany. He made a show of force in Palestine and, without a fight, cut a deal with the Muslims which made Jerusalem an open city, with free access for both Christians and Muslims. He cannot be considered a Crusader as he had been excommunicated at the time.

The Frankish domain on the coast of Syria and Palestine contained a variety of interest groups. The church was represented by the patriarchate of Jerusalem. A variety of European aristocrats and royals acquired dignity and income as rulers of petty kingdoms esconced with their retainers in fortified castles. The military orders: the Hospitallers of St John of Jerusalem (founded 1113), Templars (1119–1312), and Teutonic Knights (founded 1190) were able to act independently of both church and secular authorities. There were important trading interests, mainly Venetian and Genoese, protected by their home authorities. They formed a wealthy, highly sophisticated, and relatively independent urban bourgeosie who were frequently able to manipulate the other interest groups. There was a wide miscellany of local Christians— Greek orthodox, monophysites, maronites, etc.—who were part of the polity. In addition there were Muslims, some of them slaves. In spite of the frequency of conflict with their Muslim neighbours, the European presence created enormous scope for profitable European trade with the Middle East and indirectly with the rest of Asia. Equally important long term benefits accrued to Europe from transfer of Asian technology in cotton and silk textiles, sugar production and refining, glassware, and jewellery, paper manufacture, navigation tehniques and instruments. See Runciman (1954) for a brilliant survey of the crusading experience.

☐ ENDNOTES

1. See Bowman (1996: 18), for the 10/1 Egyptian seed yield ratio, and Hopkins (2000: 198) for the 4/1 Italian ratio.

2. See Johnson (1936) on Roman tax yields and Garnsey et al. (1983: 118–30) on the size of tribute grain shipments to Rome. Grain tribute was redirected to Constantinople after its foundation in 330AD. Bowman (1996: 46 and 237) quotes a sixth-century edict of the Emperor Justinian fixing the annual tribute at eight million artabs (240,000 metric tons). We know less about the burden of subsequent tribute to Arabia, Syria, and Baghdad.

3. See Bright (1992: vol. 1, pp. 174–5) for linguistic evidence on the Berbers.There are now more than 12 million people who speak 30 different, but closely related, Berber languages, which generally coexist with Arabic. Most speakers are in Morocco or Kabylie in Algeria, but there are people who use these languages further east, and as far south as Mali and Niger.

4. Labib (1970: 73) refers to a treaty, early in the Mamluk regime, between Sultan Baybars and the emperor Michael Palaeologus, conceding the right to load two slave ships each year and sail them through the Bosphorus to Egypt. 'Towards the middle of the fifteenth century, the numbers shipped annually to Alexandria from the Black Sea ports, above all Tana and Kaffa, were estimated at 2,000.' These Black Sea ports were the privileged sphere of the Genoese, whose trading links with Mamluk Egypt were strengthened.

5. For details of Mansa Musa's gold see Bovill (1995: 85–91). On the outward journey he was accompanied by 500 slaves, and took back Turkish and Ethiopian slave girls and eunuchs from Cairo (see Mauny 1961: 374 and 378). He also brought back a poet who was subsequently the architect of the mosques at Gao and Timbuktu (see Ibn Battuta 1929: 381).

6. Levtzion quotes Watson (1967: 30–1) as his source. Watson says almost two-thirds and refers to Africa as a whole. His source was B. Homan (1943), *Geschichte des ungarischen Mittelalters*.

7. The Kharijites (seceders) were the earliest renegade sect of Islam. They originated at the time of the fourth caliph, Ali (the prophet's son in law). Ali was assassinated by a Kharijite. They considered that the spiritual leader (whom they called *imam* rather than *caliph*) should be elected by universal suffrage, and not by family connections or military force. They regarded non-Kharijites as heretics. Many of the group left Iraq for the Maghreb when the Abbasid caliphate was established. Several variants of Kharijism developed in the Maghreb. Some were very militant, but the Ibadis, who were traders, were quiescent (see Ibn Khaldun, vol. 1, pp. 203–4, and Brett 1978: 518).

8. A rationale for the Dyula way of life and behaviour as intermediaries between Muslims and unbelievers was laid down in the fifteenth century by Salim Suwari. The Suwarian prescription for peaceful coexistence involved seven main precepts: (a) unbelievers are ignorant, not wicked; (b) it is God's design that some people remain ignorant longer than others; (c) their conversion will come in God's time, proseletizing is not necessary: (d) jihads should be undertaken only in self-defence; (e) Muslims may accept the authority of non-Muslim rulers, as long as they remain free to follow their own way of life in accordance with the *sunna* of the prophet; (f) Muslims must set an example to non-believers, so they will know how to behave when they are converted; (g) Muslims

must ensure that, by their commitment to education and learning, they keep their observance of the Law free from error (see Wilks in Levtzion and Pouwels 2000: 98).

9. See OECD (2005: Statistical Annex).

☐ REFERENCES

Abu-Lughod, J. L. (1989), *Before European Hegemony: The World System,* AD 1250–1350, Oxford University Press, New York.

Abun-Nasr, J. M. (1987), *A History of the Maghrib in the Islamic Period*, Cambridge University Press.

Acemoglu, D., S. Johnson and J. A. Robinson (2001), 'The Colonial Origins of Comparative Development: An Empirical Investigation,' *American Economic Review,* December.

Ajayi, J. F. A. and M. Crowder (1985), *Historical Atlas of Africa*, Cambridge University Press.

Amin, S. (1966), *L'Economie du Maghreb*, Editions de Minuit, Paris.

Ashtor, E. (1976), *A Social and Economic History of the Near East in the Middle Ages*, University of California Press, Berkeley.

Ashtor, E. (1978), *Studies on the Levantine Trade in the Middle Ages*, London.

Ashtor, E. (1983), *Levant Trade in the Later Middle Ages*, Princeton University Press.

Austen, R. A. (1979), 'The Trans-Saharan Slave Trade: A Tentative Census,' in Gemery and Hogendorn.

Austen, R. A. (1987), *African Economic History*, Heinemann, Portsmouth, NH.

Barrett, W. (1990), 'World Bullion Flows, 1450–1800,' in Tracy, pp. 224–54.

Birmingham, D. (1976), 'The Forest and Savannah of Central Africa,' in Page and Oliver, vol. 5.

Bloom, D. E. and J. D. Sachs (1998), 'Geography, Demography and Economic Growth in Africa,' *Brookings Papers in Economic Activity*, 2, pp. 207–73.

Bovill, E. W. (1995), *The Golden Trade of the Moors*, Wiener, Princeton.

Bowman, A. K. (1996), *Egypt after the Pharaohs, 332BC–AD642, from Alexander to the Arab Conquest*, British Museum Press.

Bowman, A. K., E. Champlin and A. Lintott (1996), *The Augustan Empire, 43BC–AD69, The Cambridge Ancient History*, vol. X, Cambridge University Press.

Bowman, A. K., P. Garnsey and D. Rathbone (eds) (2000), *The High Empire, AD70–192, The Cambridge Ancient History*, vol. XI, Cambridge University Press.

Bowman, A. K. and E. Rogan (eds) (1999), *Agriculture in Egypt from Pharaonic to Modern Times*, Oxford University Press.

Boxer, C. R. (1991), *The Portuguese Seaborne Empire, 1415–1825*, Cancarnet, Lisbon.

Brett, M. (1978), 'The Arab Conquest and the Rise of Islam in North Africa,' in Fage and Oliver, vol. 2.

Bright, W. (ed.) (1992), *International Encyclopedia of Linguistics*, Oxford University Press.

Bruijn, J. R. and F. S. Gaastra (1993), *Ships, Sailors and Spices*, NEHA, Amsterdam.

Casson, L. (1989), *The Periplus Maris Erythraei*, Princeton University Press.

Casson, L. (1995), *Ships and Seamanship in the Ancient World*, Johns Hopkins University Press, Baltimore.

Casson, L. (2001), *Libraries in the Ancient World*, Yale University Press, New Haven.

CHA, see Fage and Oliver *et al.* (1975–78).

Clark, C. and M. Haswell (1970), *The Economics of Subsistence Agriculture*, 4th edn, Macmillan, London.

Collins, R. O. (ed.) (1968), *Problems in African History*, Prentice Hall, New Jersey.

Commission for Africa (2005), *Our Common Interest: Report of the Commission for Africa*, London.

Cook, M. A. (ed.) (1970), *Studies in the Economic History of the Middle East*, Oxford University Press.

Crone, G. R. (1937), *The Voyages of Cadamosto and Other Documents on Western Africa in the Fifteenth Century*, Hakluyt Society, London.

Crosby, A. W. (1972), *The Columbian Exchange: Biological and Cultural Consequences of 1492*, Greenwood Press, Westport.

Crosby, A. W. (1986), *Ecological Imperialism: The Biological Expansion of Europe, 900–1900*, Cambridge University Press.

Curtin, P. D. (1969), *The Atlantic Slave Trade: A Census*, University of Wisconsin, Madison.

Curtin, P. D. (1984), *Cross Cultural Trade in World History*, Cambridge University Press.

Curtin, P. D. (1989), *Death by Migration: Europe's Encounter with the Tropical World*, Cambridge University Press.

Curtin, P., S. Feierman, L. Thompson and J. Vansina (1995), *African History: From Earliest Times to Independence*, Longman, London and New York.

Daly, M. W. (ed) (1998), *The Cambridge History of Egypt*, vol. 2, Cambridge University Press.

Day, C. (1921), *A History of Commerce*, Longmans Green, New York.

Deerr, N. (1949–50), *The History of Sugar*, 2 vols, Chapman & Hall, London.

Diagram Group (2000), *Encyclopedia of African Peoples*, Fitzroy Dearborn, Chicago and London.

Dols, M. (1977), *The Black Death in the Middle East*, Princeton University Press.

Duncan-Jones, R. (1994), *Money and Government in the Roman Empire*, Cambridge University Press.

Eltis, D., S. D. Behrendt and D. Richardson (forthcoming), *The Transatlantic Slave Trade: A Census*.

Engerman, S. L. (1995), 'The Atlantic Slave Economy of the Eigteenth Century: Some Speculations on Economic Development in Britain, America, Africa, and Elsewhere,' *Journal of European Economic History*, Spring, pp. 145–76.

Engerman, S. L. and R. E. Gallman (1996–2000), *The Cambridge History of the United States*, 3 vols, Cambridge University Press.

Fage, J. D. and R. Oliver et al. (1975–8), *The Cambridge History of Africa*, 8 vols, Cambridge University Press.

Feinstein, C. H. (2005), *An Economic History of South Africa*, Cambridge University Press.

Fourie, L. J. (1971), 'Contribution of Factors of Production to South African Econommic Growth', paper presented to conference of the International Assocociation for Research in Income and Wealth.

Frier, B. W. (2000), 'Demography,' in Bowman et al., pp. 787–816.

Garnsey, P. K. Hopkins and C. R. Whittaker, (eds) (1983), *Trade in the Ancient Economy*, University of California Press, Berkeley.

Garrard, T. F. (1980), *Akan Weights and the Gold Trade*, Longman, London.

Gellner, E. (1969), *Saints of the Atlas*, Weidenfeld & Nicolson, London.

Gellner, E. (1981), *Muslim Society*, Cambridge University Press.

Gellner, E. and C. Micaud (eds) (1973), *Arabs and Berbers*, Duckworth, London.

Gemery, H. A. and J. S. Hogendorn (1979), *The Uncommon Market: Essays in the Economic History of the Atlantic Slave Trade*, New York.

Godinho, V. M. (1978), 'L'emigration portugaise (xve–xx siecles),' *Revista de Historia Economica e Social*.

Goitein, S. D. F. (1967–93), *A Mediterranean Society: The Jewish Communities of the Arab World as Portrayed in the Documents of the Cairo Geniza*, 6 vols., Berkeley and Los Angeles.

Goldschmidt, A. (1979), *A Concise History of the Middle East*, Westview Press, Boulder, CO.

Goody, J. (1971), *Technology, Tradition and the State in Africa*, Oxford University Press.

Goody, J. (1996), *The East in the West*, Cambridge University Press.

Grassman, S. and E. Lundberg (eds) (1981), *The World Economic Order: Past and Prospects*, Macmillan, London.

Hansen, B. (1979), 'Income and Consumption in Egypt, 1886/1887 to 1937,' *International Journal of Middle Eastern Studies*, no. 10

Hansen, B. (1991), *The Political Economy of Poverty, Equity and Growth: Egypt and Turkey*, Oxford University Press, New York.

Hansen, B. and G. A. Marzouk (1965), *Development and Economic Policy in the UAR (Egypt)*, North Holland, Amsterdam.

Hibbert, C. (1982), *Africa Explored: Europeans in the Dark Continent, 1769–1889*, Allen Lane, London.

Hitti, P. K. (1970), *History of the Arabs*, 10th edn, St Martins Press, New York.

Hodgson, M. G. S. (1974), *The Venture of Islam*, 3 vols, Chicago University Press.

Holt, P. M. (1975), 'Egypt, the Funj and Darfur,' in Fage and Oliver, vol. 4.

Holt, P. M., A. K. S. Lambton, and B. Lewis (1970), *Cambridge History of Islam*, Cambridge University Press.

Hoodbhoy, P. A. (1991), *Islam and Science: Religious Orthodoxy and the Battle for Rationality*, Zed, London.

Hopkins, K. (1980), 'Taxes and Trade in the Roman Empire (200BC–400AD),' *Journal of Roman Studies*, vol. LXX, pp. 101–25.

Hopkins, K. (2002), 'Rome, Taxes, Rents and Rates,' in Scheidel and von Reden.

Hourani, A. (1983), *Arabic Thought in the Liberal Age, 1798–1939*, Cambridge University Press.

Hourani, G. F. (1951), *Arab Seafaring in the Indian Ocean in Ancient and Early Medieval Times*, Princeton University Press.

Hrbek, I. (1977), 'Egypt, Nubia and the Eastern Deserts,' in Fage and Oliver, vol. 3.

Huntingford, G. W. B. (ed) (1980), *The Periplus of the Erythraean Sea*, Hakluyt Society, London.

Ibn Battuta (1929), *Travels in Asia and Africa, 1335–1354* (translated and edited by H.A.R. Gibb), Routledge, London.

Ibn Khaldun (1958), *The Muqaddimah: An Introduction to History*, 3 vols (translated by Franz Rosenthal), Routledge & Kegan Paul, London.

Ibn Khaldun (1982) *Histoire des Berberes et des dynasties musulmans de l'Afrique septentrionale* 4 vols, (translated by M. G. de Slane, new edn. P. Casanova), Geuthner, Paris.

Iliffe, J. (1995), *Africans: The History of a Continent*, Cambridge University Press.

Issawi, C. (1966), *The Economic History of the Middle East*, University of Chicago Press.

Issawi, C. (1995), *The Middle East Economy*, Wiener, Princeton.

Johnson, A. C. (1936), *Roman Egypt to the Reign of Diocletian*, Johns Hopkins Press, Baltimore.

Johnson, A. C. and L. C. West (1949), *Byzantine Egypt: Economic Studies*, Princeton University Press.

Jones, W. O. (1959), *Manioc in Africa*, Stanford University Press.

Kiple, K. F. and K. C. Ornelas (2000), *The Cambridge World History of Food*, 2 vols, Cambridge University Press.

Klein, H. S. (1999), *The Atlantic Slave Trade*, Cambridge University Press.

Kuran, T. (2003), 'The Islamic Commercial Crisis: Institutional Roots of Economic Underdevelopment in the Middle East', *Journal of Economic History*, July, pp. 414–46.

Kuran, T. (2004), 'Why the Middle East is Economically Underdeveloped: Historical Mechanisms of Institutional Stagnation', *Journal of Economic Perspectives*, Summer, pp. 71–90.

Labib, S (1970), 'Egyptian Commercial Policy in the Middle Ages,' in Cook.

Laiou, A. E. (ed) (2002), *The Economic History of Byzantium from the Seventh to the Fifteenth Century*, 3 vols., Dumbarton Oaks, Washington.

Lambton, A. K. S. (1981), *State and Government in Medieval Islam*, Oxford University Press.

Landes, D. S. (1958), *Bankers and Pashas: International Finance and Economic Imperialism in Egypt*, Heineman, London.

Law, R. C. C. (1980), *The Horse in West African History*, Oxford University Press.

Leo Africanus (1981), *Description de l'Afrique* 2 vols, (translated by A. Epaulard, with notes by Monod, Lhote and Mauny), Maisonneuve, Paris.

Levtzion, N. (1973), *Ancient Ghana and Mali*, Methuen, London.

Levtzion, N. (1975), 'North-West Africa: From the Maghrib to the Fringes of the Forest,' in Page and Oliver, vol. 4.

Levtzion N. and J. F. P. Hopkins (eds) (2000), *Corpus of Early Arabic Sources for West African History*, Wiener, Princeton.

Levtzion N. and R. L. Pouwels (eds) (2000), *The History of Islam in Africa*, Currey, Oxford.

Lewis, B. (1982), *The Muslim Discovery of Europe*, Weidenfeld & Nicolson, London.

Lewis, B. (1995), *The Middle East: 2000 Years of History*, Phoenix Press, London.

Lewis, B. (2002), *What Went Wrong? Western Impact and Middle Eastern Response,* Phoenix, London.

Lewis, W. A. (ed) (1970), *Tropical Development, 1880–1913*, Northwestern University Press, Evanston.

Lovejoy, P. E. (2000), *Transformations in Slavery*, Cambridge University Press.

Maddison, A. (2001), *The World Economy: A Millennial Perspective*, OECD, Paris.

Maddison, A. (2003), *The World Economy: Historical Statistics*, OECD, Paris.

McEvedy, C. (1995), *The Penguin Atlas of African History*, Penguin Books, London.

McEvedy, C. and R. Jones (1978), *Atlas of World Population History*, Penguin, Middlesex.

McNeill, W. (1963), *The Rise of the West*, University of Chicago Press.

Mauny, R. (1961), *Tableau geographique de l'ouest africain au moyen âge*, Memoires de l'IFAN, No. 61, Dakar.

Mead, D. C. (1967), *Growth and Structural Change in the Egyptian Economy*, Irwin, Illinois.

Milton, G. (2004), *White Gold*, Hodder & Stoughton, London.

Mitchell, B. R. (1982), *International Historical Statistics: Africa and Asia*, Macmillan, London.

Montagne, R. (1930), *Les Berbères et le Makzhen dans le sud du Maroc*, Félix Alcan, Paris.

Montagne, R. (1973), *The Berbers, Their Social and Political Organisation*, London.

Mortimer, E. (1982), *Faith and Power: The Politics of Islam*, Faber & Faber, London.

Newman, J. L. (1995), *The Peopling of Africa: A Geographic Interpretation*, Yale University Press.

Nordenskjiold, A. E. (1897), *Periplus*, Norstedt, Stockholm.

O' Callaghan, J. F. (1975), *A History of Medieval Spain*, Cornell University Press.

OECD (2005), *African Economic Outlook, 2004/2005*, Development Centre, Paris.

OECD (2006), *African Economic Outlook, 2005/2006*, Development Centre, Paris.

Oliver, R. and J. D. Fage (1995), *A Short History of Africa*, Penguin Books, London.

Ostrogorsky, G. (1968), *History of the Byzantine State*, Blackwell, Oxford.

Parry, J. H. (1967) 'Transport and Trade Routes,' in Rich and Wilson, pp. 155–222.

Petry, C. F. (ed) (1998), *The Cambridge History of Egypt*, vol. 1, *Islamic Egypt' 640–1517*, Cambridge University Press.

Rich, E. E. and C. H. Wilson (1967), *Cambridge Economic History of Europe*, vol. IV, Cambridge University Press.

Richards, J. F. (ed) (1983), *Precious Metals in the Later Medieval and Early Modern Worlds*, Carolina Academic Press, Durham, North Carolina.

Ridgway, R. H. (1929), *Summarised Data of Gold Production*, Economic Paper No. 6, Bureau of Mines, US Dept. of Commerce, Washington, DC.

Rose, J. H. (1924), *The Life of Napoleon I*, Bell, London.

Ross, R. (1975), 'The 'White' Population of South Africa in the Eighteenth Century', *Population Studies*, 2, pp. 217–30.

Runciman, S. (1954), *A History of the Crusades*, Cambridge University Press.

Sachs, J. et al. (2004), 'Ending Africa's Poverty Trap,' *Brookings Papers on Economic Activity*, 1.

Said, E. W. (1995), *Orientalism*, Penguin Books, London.

Samuels, L. H. (ed) (1963), *African Studies in Income and Wealth*, Bowes & Bowes, London.

Schacht, J. (1964), *An Introduction to Islamic Law*, Clarendon Press, Oxford.

Scheidel, W. and S. von Reden (eds) (2002), *The Ancient Economy*, Edinburgh University Press.

Shepherd, V. and H. M. Beckles (eds) (2000), *Caribbean Slavery in the Atlantic World*, Wiener, Princeton.

Soetbeer, A. (1879), *Edelmetall-Produktion seit der Entdeckung Amerikas*, Perthes, Gotha.

Solow, B. L. (ed) (1991), *Slavery and the Rise of the Atlantic System*, Cambridge University Press.

South African Bureau of Census and Statistics (1960), *Union Statistics for Fifty Years*, Pretoria.

Steensgaard, N. (1974), *The Asian Trade Revolution of the Seventeenth Century, the East India Companies and the Decline of the Caravan Route*, University of Chicago Press.

Szereszewski, R. (1965), *Structural Changes in the Economy of Ghana*, Weidenfeld & Nicolson, London.

Temperley, H. (2000), *After Slavery: Emancipation and its Discontents*, Cass, London.

Thomas, R. P. (1965), 'A Quantitative Approach to the Study of the Effects of British Imperial Policy upon Colonial Welfare: Some Preliminary Findings,' *Journal of Economic History*, December.

Thornton, J. (1998), *Africa and the Africans in the Making of the Atlantic World, 1400–1800*, Cambridge University Press.

Tracy, J. D. (1990), *The Rise of Merchant Empires: Long Distance Trade in the Early Modern World, 1350–1750*, Cambridge University Press.

Udovitch, A. (ed.) (1981), *The Islamic Middle East, 700–1900: Studies in Economic and Social History*, Darwin Press, Princeton.

UNESCO (1981–99), *General History of Africa*, 9 vols, Paris.

Usher, A. P. (1932), 'Spanish Ships and Shipping in the Sixteenth and Seventeenth Century,' *Facts and Figures in Economic History, Festschrift for E.F. Gay*, Harvard University Press.

Vicens Vives, J. (1972), *Approaches to the History of Spain*, University of California Press, Berkeley.

Vilar, P. (1969), *A History of Gold and Money*, NLB, London.

Vries, J. de (forthcoming), 'Connecting Europe and Asia: A Quantitative Analysis of the Cape Trade Route, 1497–1795'.

Warmington, E. H. (1928), *The Commerce between the Roman Empire and India*, Cambridge University Press.

Watson, A. M. (1967), 'Back to Gold and Silver', *Economic History Review*, XX, pp. 1–34.

Watson, A. M. (1983), *Agricultural Innovation in the Early Islamic World: Diffusion of Crops and Farming Techniques, 700–1100*, Cambridge University Press.

Williams, E. (1944), *Capitalism and Slavery*, Russell & Russell, New York.

Part II

Advances in Macro-Measurement Since 1665

5 Political arithmeticians and historical demographers: the pioneers of macro-measurement

Macro-economic analysis began with William Petty's aggregate accounts of property and labour income, population, labour input, and capital stock for England and Wales in *Verbum Sapienti* (1665). Petty (1623–87) had an incredible range of activities—intellectual entrepreneur, physician, social engineer, inventor, confidante of kings, pioneer of macro-economic measurement—an exemplar of a new kind of cosmopolitan western intellectual, one of the finest examples of the English enlightenment. Like virtually all subsequent analysts in this field, his approach was inductive, trying to interpret the world by close study of the facts and systematic quantification. His adherence to the precepts of Francis Bacon (1561–1626) was quite overt. He was the founding father and ideas man of a group with several members. John Graunt (1620–74), the first demographer, who developed procedures that foreshadowed modern historical demography was a close friend of Petty. The third member of this school was Gregory King (1648–1712) who belonged to a younger generation. He systematized and extended Petty's macro-economic accounts and developed Graunt's demographic analysis. A fourth member was Charles Davenant (1656–1714), whose contributions (see Whitworth 1771) were more modest. He was an analyst of fiscal policy and war finance options, problems of colonies and foreign trade who interacted closely with King and used his estimates in assessing the costs and benefits of policy options.

The most striking thing about these political arithmeticians is the modernity of their macro-economic approach and anticipation of concepts and methods which now characterize national accounts and historical demography.

They were dealing with the policy problems and performance of a country (England and Wales) which had clearly emerged as a nation-state. The old feudal fragmentation of power and resources had been replaced by a much more centralized system. In 1540, Henry VIII seized a quarter of English landed property from the monastic orders and his daughter Elizabeth carried the confiscations further. The political power and intellectual influence of the church waned correspondingly.

The great bulk of ecclesiastical assets fell into the hands of a secular elite through royal sales and largesse. The nobility were demilitarized, no longer had private armies, and their country houses were no longer fortified. Most of them spent an increasing amount of time in London whose size had increased enormously. In the sixteenth and seventeenth century, the international standing of the country expanded considerably, with the establishment of colonies in North America, piratical inroads on the Spanish trade monopoly in Latin America, establishment of corporate monopoly enterprise for trade with Asia. In the 1650s there was a major change in property relationships in England's Irish colony, where more than two-thirds of land fit for agriculture was transferred from Irish to English landlords. The formal incorporation of Scotland into the kingdom did not take place until 1707, but the ground was prepared by the ascension of a Scottish king to the English crown in 1603. In the course of the seventeenth century there were major changes in the British mode of governance (which involved the temporary establishment of a republic and abolition of the House of Lords). It ended with a diminution of royal autocracy, and greater power for a secular elite of big landlords and merchants. It was a country with vigorous demographic and economic growth, and wealth accumulation processes which depended as much on political leverage and patronage as on market forces. Foreign economic relations were essentially based on beggar-your-neighbour mercantilist principles.

WILLIAM PETTY (1623–87)

Intellectual life was very vigorous and increasingly secular in the seventeenth century and there was close interaction between west European countries. Petty was a good example of this cosmopolitanism and promethean curiosity straddling many disciplines. He started work as a cabin boy on a boat trading between Southampton and Normandy. Stranded in France at age 14 with a broken leg, he made judicious use of his Latin verse to gain entry to the Jesuit College in Caen where he studied French and mathematics for more than a year. After a stint in the navy he returned to the continent in 1643–6, working his way through medical school in the Netherlands and Paris.

In Paris, Petty frequented the informal academy run by Marin Mersenne (1588–1648), a devotee of Bacon's experimental inductive approach. Mersenne brought together intellectuals interested in mathematics and measurement, maintained an active correspondence with a circle of scholars in other countries, and acted as an intellectual broker, e.g., in promoting an exchange of ideas between Descartes and Hobbes (see the 11 volumes of Mersenne's correspondence in de Waard, 1932–72). Mersenne's group was influential as a model for the French Academie Royale des Sciences created by Colbert in 1666. His circle included the mathematicians

Gassendi and Fermat, and the philosophers Descartes and Pascal. Thomas Hobbes (1588–1679) was an important member of the group during his 11-year exile in France, and Petty was his research assistant for a while. Hobbes' wide range of interests and contacts (he had known Bacon and Galileo) helped broaden and deepen the range of Petty's intellectual interests. Hobbes was also the tutor of the Prince of Wales (Charles II) in 1647, and may have facilitated Petty's later access to the Restoration court.

Petty returned to England in 1646, briefly took over the small family clothing business in Romsey after his father's death, patented a copying machine (a double-writing device) in 1647, allied himself with the Cromwellian interest, and found means to pursue his versatile intellectual activities in London. Between 1648 and 1652 he was in Oxford, one of the new wave of appointments when the university was purged of royalist scholars. In 1650 he created a great stir by reviving a young woman who had been pronounced dead. Nan Green was a servant girl who was hanged for the alleged murder of her bastard child. Her body was sent to the university for dissection, but she was in fact comatose and Petty was able to resuscitate her. She was subsequently pardoned and set free. In 1651, Petty became vice principal of Brasenose College, and professor of anatomy (at age 27). He was simultaneously a professor at Gresham College in London. This had been generously endowed in 1579 by Sir Thomas Gresham, an extremely wealthy banker and royal fiscal agent, to provide open access to higher education in the form of daily lectures on different topics. Gresham College was particularly active in applied mathematics and practical research into navigational instruments and shipbuilding. In the 1640s and 1650s it became a centre for intensive discussion of new results in experimental science, and was the precursor of the Royal Society, founded in 1662 on its premises. The leading activists for the creation of the Society were Christopher Wren (professor of astronomy at Gresham and at Oxford, and the architect who rebuilt London's churches after the great fire); John Wilkins, mathematician, warden of Wadham College and Oliver Cromwell's brother-in-law; Robert Boyle the chemist; and Petty. At that time Petty's interests were centred on natural science—astronomy, anatomy, microscopy, telescopy, and air-pumps. By the 1660s he had become rich and his interests shifted to economics.

In 1652, Petty moved to Ireland as physician general to the Cromwellian troops who put down the Irish rebellion which had festered for nearly a decade. The war had devastating effects. In his *Anatomy of Ireland* (1691), Petty suggested that the population fell by a quarter from 1641 to 1672 because of war deaths, famine, plague, and deportations. The war was followed by massive land confiscation and restructuring of Irish property relations in which Petty played a lead role as social engineer and a major beneficiary.

In 1654–6, he organized a cadastral survey of Ireland, which involved hiring and training hundreds of men to carry out detailed land measurement, and maintenance of security for his small army of surveyors working in what was generally hostile territory. In a separate exercise completed in 1673, he prepared detailed maps for the whole of Ireland. When this *Down Survey* was completed, Petty was the most active of the commissioners allocating land to soldiers whose pay was in arrears and to 'adventurers' who had financed the campaign. At the same time he was private secretary to Oliver Cromwell's son, Henry, who was Lord Deputy of Ireland. Before the ownership change, 69.3 per cent of the land belonged to Catholics and 30.7 per cent to Protestants. After the re-allocation these proportions were reversed.

Petty was paid mainly in cash and partly in land. He bought up land debentures at a discount from needy soldiers and bought some land directly. Most of his holdings were in Kerry in the southwest, he also had holdings in Limerick and his wife had landed property in Cork (see Barnard 1979). Petty's descendant, the Marquess of Lansdowne (1937) provided details of the accumulation process in Kerry. Petty was initially allocated 3,500 acres of good land there in partial lieu of salary, and bought another 2,000 acres of soldiers' claims. In 1661, having adroitly switched allegiance to the monarchy, Petty was knighted by Charles II, who granted him another 30,000 acres of contiguous 'woods, bogs and barren mountains'. In 1668–9 he secured another 60,000 acres of forfeited lands. Lansdowne (p. 8) estimated that 'he died possessed of something like 270,000 acres in South Kerry'.

Petty spent a good deal of time trying to exploit his grazing and crop land efficiently and established a port settlement at Kenmare with fisheries, mining, and timber activities. He spent even more time, over two decades, fighting lawsuits over his ownership rights. In terms of income, the returns were disappointing, but Petty loved his latifundia, and enjoyed being a landed grandee, able to found a dynasty.

Towards the end of his life (in 1686), Petty was in negotiation with his friend, William Penn, for a perpetual lease on a 50,000 acre tract of land in Pennsylvania for a ridiculously low down-payment. In return Petty would have had to clear the land and transport new settlers. This proposition was not implemented, but Petty's great-grandson, William, Earl of Shelburne (1737–1805), who was British prime minister in 1782–3 at the end of the American war of independence, did follow it up. Between 1777 and 1791, he tried, unsuccessfully, to press his right of succession to plots in and around Philadelphia (see Lansdowne 1927: section XVII on 'American Plantations').

Petty returned to London in 1659 as a member of the parliament convened by Oliver Cromwell's son and successor, Richard. When Richard Cromwell was forced to abdicate as Lord Protector, Petty lost his official posts and his Brasenose fellowship. Thereafter, he never held a significant public or academic appointment, and his career as an active social engineer was over. However, he was now a man of independent means, successfully defended his property rights in Ireland, and, in spite of his Cromwellian links, managed to capture the ear and interest of both Charles II and James II.

He resumed his activity as an intellectual entrepreneur and inventor, but diverted a significant part of his energy to problems of economic policy and administration, demography and macro-economic accounts (which he called political arithmetic).

He played a major role in founding the Royal Society in London in 1662 and the Dublin Philosophical Society in 1684, and he intensified his inventive activity. His biggest project was for a 'double-bottom' ship (a catamaran), designed to defy wind and tides, and make the journey between Ireland and England speedier. Four versions were built between 1662 and 1684. The third sank with all hands, and the fourth failed its initial trials (embarrassing Samuel Pepys, the diarist and secretary to the admiralty, who had helped secure official backing). Other inventions included a speedier form of land carriage, schemes for improving water pumps, de-salinating sea water, a heavily armed war chariot, and proposals for improving the postal service.

His main proposals for improving economic administration were the creation of a population census (covering births, deaths and marriages, age, sex, and occupational structure); a statistical office with regular reporting on trade, shipping, and prices; a registry for land and other forms of property in order to provide greater clarity in property rights and facilitate transfers; a unified administration for England, Wales, Ireland, and Scotland, and elimination of internal trade barriers.

Petty's role as the pioneer of macro-measurement had two main dimensions—national accounts and demography. In national accounts his concepts were startlingly original and brilliant. In demography, his contribution was subordinate to that of his friend, John Graunt. Many of Petty's writings were not published in his lifetime. This is true of his main work on national accounts and on the Irish economy (published in 1690 and 1691). His Irish land survey was published by Larcom in 1851, his collected economic papers by Hull (1895), other unpublished papers, and his correspondence by Lansdowne (1927 and 1928). Other remnants of the 53 chests of papers and manuscripts he left at his death were in the Lansdowne family archives at Bowood until 1975. They are now in the British Library in London.

Petty's outstanding contribution to national accounts was *Verbum Sapienti* written in 1665 and published posthumously in 1691. It presented estimates of population, income, expenditure, stock of land, other physical assets, and human capital in an integrated set of accounts for the whole economy of England and Wales. They were intended to provide a quantitative framework for effective implementation of fiscal policy and mobilization of resources in time of war (i.e., the second Anglo-Dutch war of 1664–7). The originality and ambition of these accounts is quite startling. He devised a method of making physical and human capital additive, foreshadowing techniques of growth accounting not fully developed until the twentieth century by Edward Denison. The derivation of capital expenditure and income flows was stated simply and clearly. There were three types of physical capital which he valued at market prices: (a) 24 million acres of land (excluding waste) with an average annual rental value of £8 million, which he capitalized at 18 years purchase for a total capital value of £144 million; (b) housing in urban and rural areas, whose annual and imputed rental value of £2.5 million he capitalized at 12 years purchase for a total of £30 million; (c) a third category of miscellaneous property he valued at £76 million, of which £36 for livestock and fisheries, £3 for shipping, £6 for gold and silver coinage (in a country without paper money) and £31 for business and farm inventories, furniture, jewelry, plate, clothing, mines, and forestry ('too troublesome to particularise'). Income from this third kind of property he assessed at £4.5 million. In 1665 he described it as the 'yield', but later, in *Political Arithmetic* (1676: 267), he called it 'profit'. Thus aggregate annual property income was £15 million, a 6 per cent return on a total capital stock of £250 million.

Labour income of £25 million was derived as follows: half of his six million population were assumed to be employed at different levels of remuneration, with average earnings of seven pence a day for each of 287 working days per year (deducting Sundays, holidays, absence for sickness and recreation). Thus three million people earned an average of £8.33 a year from employment. Petty believed that 'the most important consideration in political oeconomies' was 'how to make a par and equation between lands and labour' *Political Anatomy of Ireland* (1672: 181). 'Hands are the father and lands are the mother of wealth'. Hence he capitalized labour income at the same rate as property income, i.e., for 1665, at 16.7 years purchase. Labour income was assumed to be spent on consumption, with a small fraction for taxes in peace-time years. Saving (superlucration) was assumed to be confined to property owners. He assessed peace-time taxable capacity to be 2.5 per cent of national income rising to 7.5 per cent in war-time.

In spite of Petty's advocacy of an economic union of England, Ireland, and Scotland, he produced no integrated accounts for the kingdom as a whole. His brief note, *Doubling the People* (1687), estimated the population of the kingdom at 9.7 million in that year with a capital stock of £370 million in England, £20 million in Ireland, and £26 million in Scotland. In this work he did not quantify the income differential, and it cannot easily be inferred, as he assumed different rates of capitalization for each country and did not estimate the labour force in each. In the *Political Anatomy of Ireland* (1672: 188), he estimated Irish income at £4 per head, and in *Political Arithmetic* (1676), £7 per head for England and Wales at about the same period.

Table 5.1. Consolidated Income and Wealth Accounts for England and Wales: Petty (1665) and King (1688) (£ million in current values)

	Petty (1665)		King (1688)	
	Property Income	Capitalized Value of Physical Assets	Property Income	Capitalized Value of Physical Assets
Land	8.0	144.0 (18.0)	10.0	180.0 (18.0)
Housing	2.5	30.0 (12.0)	2.0	36.0 (18.0)
Other	4.5	76.0 (16.9)	1.0	86.0 (86.0)
Total Property	15.0	250.0 (16.7)	13.0	320.0 (24.6)
	Labour Income	Capitalized Value of Labour Force	Mixed Income	Capitalized Value of Population
Total Labour	25.0	417.0 (16.7)	30.5	330.0 (11.0)
Aggregate	**40.0**	**667.0 (16.7)**	**43.5**	**650.0 (14.9)**

Notes and Source: Petty, *Verbum Sapienti* (Hull 1899: vol. 1, pp. 104–10). Figures in brackets refer to number of years' purchase. Petty made a second estimate (for 1676) in *Political Arithmetic* (Hull 1899: vol.1, p. 267) in which property income was assessed at 16 million, labour income at 26 million, but physical assets and the labour force were capitalized at 20 years' purchase. King's consolidated account as stated above is from *Observations*, pp. 30–2.

Petty's *Political Arithmetic*, written in 1676 and published in 1690 was a comparative study of the economic performance of England, Holland, and France. It was a polemical, discursive, and disorganized piece, rather long by his standards, and mainly devoted to a bilateral comparison of Holland and France. It demonstrated that a 'small country and few people may be equivalent in wealth and strength to a far greater people and territory'. There was no attempt to present comparative macroeconomic accounts, but he used a series of key indicators to demonstrate Dutch superiority. The discussion is heavily biased against France, which is why Charles II, to whom it was dedicated, opposed publication.

Petty's discussion of the main issue is pithy, perceptive, and extremely interesting, providing a foretaste of the type of reasoning used later by Adam Smith and Douglass North. He estimated the population to be 13 million in France, one million in the two leading Dutch provinces (Holland and Zealand). However, the Dutch merchant fleet was nine times as big as the French, its foreign trade four times as big, its interest rate about half the French level, its foreign assets large, those of France negligible. The Dutch economy was highly specialized, importing a large part of its food, hiring mercenaries to fight its wars, and concentrating its labour force in high productivity sectors. Its flat terrain permitted substantial use of wind power. High density of urban settlement, good ports, and internal waterways reduced transport and infrastructure costs, cheapened government services, and reduced the need for inventories.

Dutch institutions favoured economic growth. Religious tolerance encouraged skilled immigration. Property rights were clear and transfers facilitated by maintenance of registers. An efficient legal system and sound banking favoured economic enterprise. Taxes were high but levied on expenditure rather than income. This encouraged savings, frugality, and hard work. Thus the Dutch were a model of economic efficiency with obvious policy lessons for Britain, where popular notions of French power were greatly exaggerated.

The initial purpose of the essay was to rebut the view that the English economy was in decline. There was no macro-quantification of growth performance, but citation of illustrative evidence on the expansion of cultivated area, recovery from the plague, growth of housing and shipping, the fall in interest rates, increasing splendour of 'coaches, equipage and household furniture'.

The *Treatise of Taxes and Contributions* (1662) was his most careful and best organized work. It provided an exhaustive survey of the structure of English public finance, proposed innovations to improve its efficiency, equity, and capacity to augment tax revnue. It reflected a clear macro-economic vision, clarifying the costs and benefits of alternative revenue sources. It was badly needed in an epoch when the fiscal system was just emerging from reliance on feudal levies and a mishmash of expedients designed to stem a fiscal crisis which had lasted for decades. Its long run impact in improving British fiscal analysis and policy was substantial.

His contribution to monetary policy and analysis (in a country with a metallic currency) was *Quantalumque Concerning Money*, written in 1682, and published in 1695, when a reform of the coinage was in process.

Petty's numerous papers on economics reveal his social engineering instincts very clearly. He assumed that there was a significant economic surplus above subsistence, which the ruler could readily reshuffle in the public interest, without undue concern for vested interests or individual property rights. In the 1662 *Treatise* he suggested cutting the number of clergy by at least half, with a large reduction in their stipends; a much bigger downsizing of the legal profession and its income; tight constraints on the number of doctors and university teachers. He advocated bigger income support for the poor, and creation of employment opportunities for them in public works and highways.

The *Political Anatomy of Ireland* (written in 1672, published in 1691) analysed the massive change in Irish property rights which he had helped to engineer. The *Treatise of Ireland* (written in 1687 for James II, and first published in 1895) suggested the transfer of a million Irish to England over a five-year period, leaving 300,000 behind as cattle herders and dairy women. He argued that the resultant increase in English prosperity and land values would be considerably bigger than the costs of transfer and the fall in Irish land values. He also suggested that a fall in the proportion of Catholics in Ireland, and a rise in the English proportion, would enhance political stability.

Petty wrote ten essays on demographic themes between 1683 and 1687. These made no methodological contribution, and his estimates were rather shaky. The most interesting was *Another Essay in Political Arithmetic* (1683) which dealt with the growth of the population of London, England and Wales, and the world. It carried forward Graunt's London analysis using data on burials for 1665–82, but was much cruder. He estimated London population to be around 670,000, derived by multiplying burials by 30. He used a multiplier of 11 (smaller than Graunt's 14) to estimate a total population of 7.4 million for England and Wales. He felt that this was confirmed by evidence on poll tax and hearth tax revenue, and episcopal estimates of the number of communicants. He made a retropolation to the Norman conquest, and extrapolated London's population to 1842. He suggested that world population was 320 million in 1682, but his method of estimation was not clear.

JOHN GRAUNT: THE FIRST DEMOGRAPHER (1620–74)

The first serious demographer was John Graunt, a close friend of Petty. His *Natural and Political Observations on the Bills of Mortality* was published at the beginning of 1662. It is a work of genius and masterpiece of statistical inference, which must have taken several years to prepare. It involved meticulous assemblage and adjustment of a very large database on burials and christenings in London, which was available on a weekly and annual basis for 1603 onwards, broken down by sex. For 20 years (1629–36 and 1647–58) he had data on causes of death (broken down into 81 categories). He had no direct information on age of death or on marriages. His information related to 97 parishes within the walls of London, 16 outside the walls and nine parishes included in his greater London area. In addition he had access to returns of a partial census for 1631 for 29 parishes, which provided a crosscheck on his growth estimates.

He started with a long section analysing causes of death, based on data for 229,250 burials. 'Ancient matrons' were paid a small fee to inspect corpses and report the presumed cause of death to the parish clerks. It seems clear that for this part of his book, Graunt, who was a haberdasher, had advice from Petty, who had much greater medical knowledge.

Graunt distinguished the regular pattern of chronic ailments from epidemic diseases which had an episodic impact. Plague was endemic but recurred at irregular intervals and tended to peter out after a few years. The worst year was 1603, when it caused 82 per cent of deaths. He noted that rickets was not recognized as a cause of death until 1634, and had been misclassified earlier. There was also substantial understatement of sexually transmitted diseases. The French pox (syphilis) appeared to cause only 0.2 per cent of deaths in the period he covered, but he noted that these cases were only reported in two parishes, and concluded that the reporting ladies were bribed to conceal 'infection of the spermatic parts'.

He had no direct information on age at death, but constructed a rough proxy by grouping illnesses which affected infants and young children, and those associated with old age. He constructed a crude survival table which showed 36 per cent mortality rate for those aged 0–6, with only 3 per cent surviving beyond age 66. This was the ancestor of life tables, and estimates of life expectation. This was a feature of the book which attracted wide interest in England, France, and Holland, where life annuities and tontines (a lottery on life expectation invented by Lorenzo Tonti in 1652) were part of the public debt. *Edmond Halley* (1656–1742) improved on Graunt's crude analysis of life expectation, and articulated the fundamental mathematical principles of life insurance in 'Degrees of Mortality of Mankind; with an Attempt to Ascertain the price of Annuities', *Philosophical Transactions of the Royal Society* (1693). As London's population was growing regularly, Halley based his estimates on data from Breslau, which had a much more stable population. The data were provided by Caspar Neumann, probably at the suggestion Leibniz (see Stone 1997: 240–51).

Graunt analysed the pattern of births by sex, and found a sex ratio of 14 males to 13 females, a much narrower gender differential than popular preconceptions before his time.

In confronting data on London burials and christenings, he found that burials were bigger. To some extent this was due to underreporting of christenings because of the growth of religious non-conformism, to zealous parsons who refused baptism when they had doubts about the worthiness of some parents, and to the disincentive effect of registration fees. The christening rate varied over time, but even after correcting for this, there was a substantial discrepancy. Although burials were rising substantially over time, it was clear that the population was growing, and the growth of the housing stock corroborated this. Graunt therefore concluded that there was substantial immigration to London from rural areas and smaller towns. By quantifying the average discrepancy between births and deaths, he concluded that there was net immigration of about 6,000 persons a year.

As a crosscheck, he analysed annual data for a 90-year period for Romsey, the town near Southampton where Petty was born and buried. It seems clear that Petty facilitated his access to the Romsey data, which covered marriages as well as births and deaths. For Romsey, therefore, Graunt could estimate fertility. He concluded that the average family had four children and adduced reasons for thinking that London fertility was lower. He found that Romsey christenings were bigger than burials. Over 90 years there was a net increase of 1,059 persons, of which 300 remained in Romsey, 400 emigrated to the Americas and 300–400 emigrated to London. In the third edition, in 1665, Graunt extended his analysis of country towns to cover Tiverton in Devon and Cranbrook in Kent, which confirmed the Romsey/London differentials he found earlier.

From his analysis of historical pattern of births, deaths, and assumed migration, Graunt concluded that the population of greater London was 460,000 around 1660. He assumed that the population of England was probably 14 times as big, i.e., 6,440,000. His 14-fold multiplier was derived from several indicators, i.e., London's share of the tax burden; cartographic analysis of the area of different parts of the country and likely density of settlement (four acres per head for the country as a whole); and his estimate that the average size of the 10,000 parishes in the country was 600 persons. Using inferences about age structure and likely fertility in conjunction with his other material, he suggested that London had grown 2.5-fold in the previous 56 years, i.e., a population of 184,000 for 1603, the initial year of his database.

Prior to Graunt, nobody had thought of using the mortality bills to reconstruct the demography of London. Indeed there is no indication that anyone had had the faintest idea of doing what he did. He clearly got encouragement and advice from Petty, but the meticulous inspection of data, adjustments for mismeasurement, the caution and modesty with which he explains his carefully structured inferences is totally different in spirit from anything one finds in Petty. Graunt's techniques of analysis were the foundation of modern historical demography, and he clearly belonged to the pantheon of seventeenth-century science.

GREGORY KING (1648–1712) AND CHARLES DAVENANT (1656–1714)

Gregory King's contribution to political arithmetic was much more comprehensive in scope than that of Petty, his style much closer to Graunt's. His research was scholarly and meticulous. He sifted and merged an incredible range of evidence from fiscal and other sources. He carried out supplementary enquiries to correct for shortcomings in his database to ensure that his inferences were based on representative samples. His main concern was to provide a quantitative underpinning to decision-making on economic policy. His accounts were comprehensive, systematic, and consistent, linking demography, national income and expenditure, wealth estimates, and a partial production account. He also made international comparisons of the economic performance of England, France, and Holland, and their capacity to finance the war of the League of Augsburg in which most of western Europe was engaged from 1689 to 1697.

King's work in this field was very intensive and concentrated in a relatively brief period from 1695 to 1700. Some of his findings were known through quotation in the writings of Davenant, but he published nothing. His *Natural and Political Observations and Conclusions on the State and Condition of England* (1696) appeared only in 1802. It presented his results in highly concentrated form, but to understand his methods and appreciate the wealth of sophisticated analysis behind it, one must turn to his manuscripts, in particular his *Notebook*, published in facsimile form by Laslett (1973).

It is worth looking at King's work in some detail, as it contains material that has not been fully exploited, which can yield new insights into the English economy of the seventeenth century. The quality of his demographic accounts stands up incredibly well in the light of the findings of the Cambridge Group on Population History (Wrigley et al. 1997) but his economic accounts need adjustment to bring their coverage into conformity with modern practice.

In the following, I have tried to explore King's professional background, the milieu and intellectual climate in which he worked, to explain his accounting system, and the revisions I have made.

After early experience helping his father who was a surveyor and mathematician, King left school at age 14 to work as a clerk for Sir William Dugdale. Dugdale was a distinguished antiquary and, as Norroy King of Arms, was responsible for genealogical matters, credentials of succession to aristocratic titles, authorization and design of coats of arms, and chief guardian of social protocol for England north of the river Trent. In 1662, Charles II directed him to make a 'visitation' of the northern provinces to establish the legitimacy of titles and status of the nobility and armigerous gentry. As the previous visitation had taken place 50 years earlier, this was a major assignment. In the course of five years, King saw a lot of the country, learned a great deal from Dugdale about genealogy, heraldry, and assessment of documentary records. He also acquired a knowledge of French, and learned to design and paint coats of arms. Thereafter, from 1667 to 1672 he had various jobs as an engraver, surveyor, cartographer, and antiquary. From 1672 to 1677, he returned to heraldry, performing a variety of tasks in the Earl Marshal's office. He also married his relatively prosperous first wife, 'a maiden gentlewoman', who had been his landlady.

In 1677, at age 29, he became one of the 13 members of the College of Arms as 'Dragon Rouge pursuivant'. Seven years later he became registrar of the College, and in 1689 was promoted to be Lancaster Herald. Except for the two top jobs of Garter and Clarenceux King of Arms, heraldic posts were poorly paid and he had to supplement his income by property speculation and outside activities (surveying, engraving, and cartography). Because of his expertise in the matter, he managed to get 11 'visitation' assignments in the south of England, an opportunity which disappeared when the procedure was discontinued in 1688. As his career progressed, his assignments became more elevated. He had a major role in arranging protocol for the coronations of James II in 1685, William and Mary in 1689, and Queen Mary's funeral in 1695. He also had some very lucrative assignments to present the Order of the Garter to the elector of Brandenburg in 1689, the Duke of Zell (George I's father-in-law) in 1691, the Elector of Saxony in 1692, and the Elector of Brunswick-Lunenburg (the future George I) in 1701. These visits were important for British foreign policy, reinforcing William III's ties with allies in the War of the League of Augsburg, and buttressing the Protestant succession. Each trip lasted for three months or more. King travelled in style with liveried footmen, hobnobbed with royalty, and received lavish expenses and presents. These trips reinforced his professional expectations. On three of these occasions he was acting Garter King of Arms. At the end of 1693, Sir John Dugdale (the son of King's first patron) offered to resign his post of Norroy King of Arms in favour of King. This arrangement was vetoed by the Earl Marshal, and was followed by other signs of disfavour, including loss of the office of registrar.

Although King's career in the herald's office was not over, he now needed to look elsewhere for further advancement. In 1703, King and his colleagues were infuriated by the appointment of a totally unqualified person to be Clarenceux King of Arms. Vanbrugh, a successful playwright and architect, got the appointment (at the age of 37) as a pay-off for building Castle Howard for the Earl of Carlisle, the acting Earl Marshal. Shortly thereafter, it was Vanbrugh, not King, who went to Germany to present the Garter to the future George II.

The College of Arms represented the old order of public service. The post of Earl Marshal was hereditary. Other appointments depended on patronage, purchase, or nepotism. Senior incumbents tended to be doddery, senile, or disposed to treat their job as a sinecure. Aspirants without family connections or money could occasionally succeed if they demonstrated talent, worked hard, and comported themselves with deference and discretion. The professionalism of William Dugdale and King was not a standard attribute. The old bureaucratic order is described in detail in Aylmer (1961). King's career environment was not too different from that of Samuel Pepys in the Admiralty (see Bryant 1943).

In the field of economic policy a major modernization of the administration had been under way for some years. Professional competence was increasingly relevant in public appointments, and improved statistics were becoming a significant guide to policy. Patronage was still important but political cronyism was replacing nepotism.

The farmers of the hearth tax were obliged to show full accounts from 1679. Tax farming of customs duties was abolished in 1671, and in 1696 an inspector general of exports and imports was appointed. Davenant was appointed commissioner of excise at £500 a year in 1678, his salary was doubled in 1683 when tax farming was abolished (Waddell 1958), and he became inspector general of exports and imports in 1703 at £1,000 a year (Clark 1938). The Board of Trade was created in 1696, with John Locke, the philosopher, as one of the commissioners at £1,000 a year (Laslett 1969). The Bank of England was created in 1694, and a major re-coignage took place in 1696. Monetary policy was modernized and a properly managed market for public debt was emerging.

Thanks to his work on political arithmetic and his political contacts, King was able to join this new bureaucratic elite. In 1702 he became commissioner for public accounts, in 1705–6 secretary to the commission on army accounts, in 1708 commissioner for King William's debts, and again for the army accounts.

King interacted closely with two important people in developing his demographic and macro-economic accounts. One was *Robert Harley* (1661–1724) who had time in 1697 to make a close scrutiny of King's *Observations*. Harley's comments and King's very full replies have survived and demonstrate the sophistication and seriousness of his political arithmetic. Harley later became speaker of the House of Commons, chancellor of the Exchequer, and Earl of Oxford. He founded the huge Harleian collection of manuscripts (including many by King) which was sold to the British Library in 1753.

The more important interaction was with *Charles Davenant* (1656–1714) who was a prolific and gifted analyst of economic policy. Davenant was the son of the poet laureate, and his grandfather was rumoured to be William Shakespeare. Davenant was a member of Parliament, and was at a loose end in the 1690s, when he did not hold public office.

Davenant published an *Essay Upon Ways and Means of Supplying the War* in 1694, which dealt with problems of war finance. The book had a galvanizing impact on King. It presented a quantified analysis of the English tax structure at the beginning of the war (when revenue consisted mainly of excises, the hearth tax, and local revenues to finance poor relief). He confronted these with new revenue from an array of taxes on property and income which had been levied to finance the war. His consolidated table with a breakdown showing ten different types of tax revenue for 39 counties and administrative units in England and Wales was a statistical *tour de force*. It also showed the number of households and the number of hearths at Lady Day 1690 (which was derived from analysis of the hearth tax returns).

Lady Day, the 25th march (the date of Christ's conception), was the first day of the year until 1752 when England and its American colonies moved from the Julian to the Gregorian calendar. The Julian calendar was introduced by Julius Caesar in 46BC. After a lapse of 18 centuries, it had fallen behind by several days. It was replaced in 1582 in the Catholic countries of Europe in line with a papal bull of pope Gregory XIII. The Protestant countries of northern Europe switched to the Gregorian calendar in 1700. The British parliament endorsed the change in 1751, stipulating that the year would end on 31 December, and subsequent years would start on 1 January. To complete the transition, 3 to 13 September were omitted from the 1752 calendar (Wednesday, 2 September being followed by Thursday, 14). The previous anachronistic system had meant that anything published between 1 January and 24 March was attributed to the preceding year (see Richards 1998: 252–3).

Davenant's table demonstrated to King that the new fiscal information could provide a much better basis for demographic and macro-economic analysis than was possible for Graunt and Petty. Not only had the tax structure changed, but tax receipts were much more transparent as tax farming had been replaced by governmental collection.

Davenant quoted Petty's exaggerated population estimates for England and Wales (7.4 million instead of 5.5), and referred to Petty 'as the best computer we ever had'. King had a different view. He regarded Petty as a sloppy and biased analyst, and felt he should rectify Davenant's judgement. It seems clear that King gave Davenant a detailed copy of his own demographic accounts, and impressed him with his skill as a political arithmetician.

When Davenant's *Discourses on the Public Revenue* was published in 1697–8, his views had changed. Political arithmetic: 'the art of reasoning by figures on things relating to government', was begun by Petty, but he was handicapped by lack of the information which the new tax structure had produced. More importantly he now regarded Petty as a politicized arithmetician, prone to exaggerate English population, to understate the numbers, strength, and wealth of other countries, and to advance propositions not quite right in themselves, 'but very grateful to those who governed'.

Davenant transferred his admiration to Gregory King who had 'a more distinct and regular scheme of the inhabitants in England, than peradventure was ever made concerning the people of any other country'. He acknowledged his obligation 'to that wonderful genius and master in the art of computing, for many lights and information'. He went on to quote a slightly amended version of King's income account, attributing 14 million sterling to property income, ten million to trade, and 20 million to arts and labour, and quoted King's comparative estimates of income and tax revenues of England, France, and Holland.

A further result of the interaction with King was Davenant's *Essay on the Probable Methods of Making a People Gainers in the Balance of Trade*, published in 1699. He started by acknowledging his debt to King, explaining how that 'skilful and laborious gentleman' developed his system of accounts and what sources he used. He quoted King's demographic findings, a slightly amended version of his detailed table on income and expenditure (see Whitworth 1771: vol. II, p. 184) and an amended version of his production accounts for agriculture (pp. 216–21).

It is clear that King and Davenant discussed these matters in detail, that King authorized Davenant to publish extensive quotations, and was content to forego publication himself. Publications on sensitive matters of public policy required an official licence, and exposed the author to sanctions in case of official disapproval. As a cautious public servant King preferred to avoid this risk. He was used to writing and circulating official memos, and did not have the freewheeling fluency of Davenant's pen.

The following are the main works of King that I consulted:

1. His autobiography. This ends in early 1695, and was designed in large part as a *curriculum vitae* to justify his aspiration of rising to the top in the heraldic profession. Though no mention of it is made, it seems likely that he had by this time scrutinized Graunt's work carefully, and had read Petty's published work on demography and political arithmetic. The autobiography was published by Dallaway (1793).

2. *Natural and Political Observations and Conclusions upon the State and Condition of England* (1696; Harleian manuscript 1898 in British Library) was published by Chalmers (1802) together with a note on the population of Gloucester and expenditures on hospitals. It was reprinted in Barnett (1936), which is the edition I cite below. It was also republished by Laslett (1973).

3. A second manuscript of *Observations*, with parallel columns containing comments by Harley in 1697, King's extensive replies, and a blank column for comments by a third party (probably Davenant) is manuscript 1458 in the National Library of Australia (available on microfilm).

4. King's *Notebook* contains 297 numbered pages, five unnumbered and 15 blank pages. Its content is more than five times as large as his *Observations*. It is extraordinarily neat and legible. It was indexed by King and seems designed to be read by people interested in further detail. Laslett (1973) contains a facsimile copy.

5. A bundle of papers in the Public Records Office at Kew (T 64/302) including his mini-census for Harfield (1699), and 16 other documents on fiscal matters, wealth distribution, and personal correspondence.

6. Harleian manuscripts in the British Library (see *Catalogue of the Harleian Manuscripts in the British Museum* (1808) for detailed contents). Many of these are papers and correspondence concerning King's heraldic work and are useful for details of his career after his autobiography stops, e.g., Harleian 6815 folio 288 shows his itinerary and expense account for his trip to Germany on 29 June to 7 October 1701; folio 226 is the 1703 petition of the heralds protesting Vanbrugh's appointment as Clarenceux King of Arms. There are a few documents on political arithmetic, e.g., Harleian 6832 contains a mini-census for Buckfastleigh in 1698 showing that his demographic interest had not flagged.

7. *Of the Naval Trade of England, 1688*, written in 1697, published in Barnett (1936). This was probably a background briefing for Davenant (1699). Its main interest for political arithmetic is that it estimated the growth of capital stock at current prices and with changing capitalization rates for 1600, 1630, 1660, and 1688.

In addition, the detailed analysis by Glass (1965) of the demographic accounts, and Stone's (1997b) exegesis of all King's work are extremely useful.

King's contributions are considered below under six heads: (a) demographic accounts; (b) consolidated wealth and income account; (c) expenditure account; (d) income account; (e) a partial production account. These were for England and Wales; (f) an international comparison of performance in France, Holland, and England and Wales.

King's Demographic Analysis

King's major demographic objective was to estimate the population of England and Wales. He made a significant improvement on Graunt's estimate. He was better equipped to do this because he had much more information on population outside London. He had the hearth tax returns on the number of houses and evidence from the chimney tax on house occupancy from Davenant (1694). He was able to exploit the first round (1695) of returns from the new tax on births, burials, and marriages. This tax was in operation for ten years and created a statistical reporting system without precedent in Britain. It imposed a progressive rate of tax on 20 categories of wealth and income, subdivided by marital status and family responsibility. The tax was not popular and was very costly to administer in relation to the rather low revenue it yielded, but it was tailor-made for political arithmetic. It is not clear what role King had in its creation, but the Act was passed in part because of a petition from the College of Arms in 1693. King published and may well have devised the schedule of tax incidence (see Glass 1966: ix–xvii). He certainly made very substantial use of the returns for both his demographic and economic accounts. As its administration was far from perfect, King had to make adjustments for coverage and errors in the database. As a crosscheck, he organized his own mini-censuses for Lichfield (his home town), Harfield, and Buckfastleigh. They identified persons and added information on household size, age, and sex structure.

King's demographic analysis was the most impressive part of his whole *oeuvre*, and he was very proud of it. In 1697, he wrote to Harley, 'I have that assuredness in my numbering that I make it the touchstone to all other calculations'. Table 5.2 shows his results for England and Wales. A surprising thing is the rather small size of households in an era when it was once believed that 'traditional' family size was bigger. In fact his households included 536,000 'servants', i.e., domestic servants, apprentices, and unmarried farm labourers who lived-in. Deducting the 'servants', average family size was 3.8, compared with 4.2 for households.

Table 5.3 compares King's results with those of Graunt and Petty and modern scholarship. King's population estimate was virtually identical with the sophisticated reconstitution of Wrigley et al. (1997).

Table 5.2. Gregory King's Estimates of English Population (1695) and their Derivation

	Inhabited Houses (000s)	Population (000s)	Persons Per Household
Greater London	105	530	5.05
Other Cities & Market Towns	195	870	4.46
Villages & Hamlets	1,000	4,100	4.10
Total	**1,300**	**5,500**	**4.23**

Notes and Sources: Observations, p.18. Estimates of inhabited houses were derived from hearth tax returns, adjusted for divided and empty houses. 'Souls' per home derived from assessments of the tax on marriages, births, and burials in 'several parts of the kingdom', adjusted to offset under-coverage and misreporting. King made a global adjustment for transients—seamen, soldiers, peddlers, gypsies, thieves and beggars (excluded from the foregoing)—and allocated them *pro rata* to those included in the estimates. Greater London refers to 135 parishes within and without the walls. King's households included 536 thousand live-in servants, see *Notebook*, p. 277. King's estimate of average household size was confirmed by the findings of Wall (1983) who estimated 4.18 as the average for 1650–1799, using mainly the evidence in the files of the Cambridge group on family history. Earlier Laslett (1973) had suggested that King's estimate was too low.

Table 5.4 shows King's estimates of gender and age structure, derived mainly from his own sample survey analysis. This shows clearly the gender differences in terms of birth coefficients, and longer female life expectation, which confirmed and extended the analysis of Graunt. Wrigley et al. (1997) show a lower proportion in the age group 0–4 for 1696 than King, but they do not explicitly discuss the difference, as was done in Wrigley and Schofield (1981).

King did not make a serious effort to produce population estimates for Ireland and Scotland. There is nothing in *Observations*. The *Notebook* has several rather casual references, p. 2 suggests one million each. Modern estimates for Ireland are substantially higher. Dickson et al. (1982: 156–62) estimate 1687 population at 1.97 million. Deane and Cole's (1964: 6) estimate suggests that he was right about

Table 5.3. Confrontation of King's Population Estimates for 1695 with Those of Other Demographers (000s)

Source	England & Wales	London	Reference Year
Graunt (1662)	6,440	460	(1660)
Petty (1683)	7,369	670	(1682)
King (1696)	5,500	530	(1695)
Glass (1950)	4,918	430	(1695)
Wrigley and Schofield (1981)	5,311	n.a.	(1695)
Wrigley et al. (1997)	5,486	n.a.	(1695)
Wrigley (1967)	n.a.	575	(1700)

Notes and Sources: Graunt, Petty, and King as above; Glass (1950) reprinted in Glass and Eversley (1965: 203); Wrigley and Schofield (1981: 533), 4,951,000 for England excluding Monmouth, adjusted by 1.0728 to include Monmouth and Wales (coefficient derived from Deane and Cole 1962: 203); Wrigley et al. (1997: 614), 5,113,000 for England adjusted to include Monmouth and Wales; Wrigley (1967: 44).

Table 5.4. King's Estimates of Population in England and Wales by Age and Gender in 1695 (000s)

Age	Male	Female	Total	M/F Ratio	Per cent in Age Group
0–1	90	80	170	1.125	3.09
1–4	325	325	650	1.000	11.82
5–9	349	351	700	0.994	12.93
10–15	358	362	720	0.989	13.09
16–59	1,308	1,352	2,660	0.968	48.36
60+	270	330	600	0.818	10.91
Total	2,700	2,800	5,500	0.964	100.00

Notes and Sources: Observations, p. 23. Derived from a 5,000 population sample constructed from responses to a special questionnaire of King. Wrigley *et al.* (1997: 615) estimate a lower proportion aged 0–4 (11.76%) compared with King's 14.91 per cent, but give no breakdown by gender.

Scotland. Modern estimates suggest a population of 8.47 million in the UK as a whole in 1688.

King had two estimates of world population for 1695, in *Observations* (p. 21) and *Notebook* (pp. 1, 2). The latter is better explained. Table 5.5 compares his estimates with those of the Jesuit, Riccioli, and with modern estimates. King was much closer to the latter than Riccioli in 1672 or Petty in 1682.

There are 11 pages of calculations in King's *Notebook* with variant estimates of world population from the creation or the flood (see Table 5.6). He assumed the

Table 5.5. Estimates of World Population by Region: Riccioli (1672), King (1695), and Modern Estimates for 1700 (million)

	Riccioli 1672	King 1695	Maddison 1700	McE. and J. 1700	Clark 1700
Europe	100	115	127	120	106
Asia	500	340	400	415	420
Africa	100	70	61	61	100
America	200	90	13	13	13
Oceania	100	11	2	2	2
Total	**1,000**	**626**	**603**	**611**	**641**

Notes and Sources: Riccioli (1672: 677–81); King, *Notebook*, pp. 1, 2. Maddison (2001: 232 and 241). McEvedy and Jones (1978); Colin Clark (1967: 64). The last region is called *terrae australi* by Riccioli. King stated in his reply to Harley that, 'By the unknown parts of the world, I mean only the *terra australis incognita*, and the North parts of Asia and America which have never yet been coasted about'. Modern estimates refer to Australia, New Zealand, Melanesia, and Polynesia. Riccioli and King used a similar method. For Europe they had detailed estimates, King for 17 countries, Riccioli for six countries and four groups of countries. For Asia more guesswork was involved, but there and in other continents they estimated land area and made assumptions about population density which were inferred to some extent from the range of variation in Europe.

Table 5.6. World Population: Confrontation of King's and Modern Chronology, and Futurology, 3935BC–2300AD (000s)

BC		King	McEvedy
3935	Creation (Adam & Eve)	0.002	7,811
3000		11,000	14,000
2279	Flood (Noah family)	0.008	23,077
1000		11,944	54,000
1		84,000	170,000
AD		**King**	**Maddison**
1		84,000	230,820
1000		315,000	267,573
1695		626,000	601,030
2000		834,000	6,071,144
		King	**UNPD**
2300		1,078,000	9,000,000
8100		9,334,000	

Notes and Sources: First column from King's *Notebook*, pp.1, 4, 5 (Laslett 1973). Second column interpolations for 3935 and 2279BC from McEvedy's estimates shown in Table 5.7, Maddison. (2003: 256) for 1–2000AD, projection for 2300 from UN Population Division, medium scenario (2003: 3). King's figure for 1695 was based on an estimate of the surface area of different countries and continents with population density assumed to vary with technological level. King's chronology before the year 1000BC is biblical—his date for the creation corresponds closely with that of Scaliger (1583) and Archbishop Usher (1650). He does not suggest that the world would end in 8100, as he experimented with alternative hypotheses which envisaged a much more distant horizon.

world to be 3,935 years old at the birth of Christ. In pre-Darwinian scholarship, such an assumption was not unusual.

Tables 5.3 and 5.5 show how close Gregory King's estimates for 1695 are to the results of modern scholarship. This is true for London, England, and the world. Perhaps King was able to make good spatial comparisons because Copernicus, Kepler, and Galileo had demolished the notion that the earth was flat and the centre of the universe. However, his backward temporal horizon came from the book of Genesis. Thus for 3935BC; his world population consisted of Adam and Eve. Noah and his family were assumed to be the only survivors of the Flood in 2279BC.

He assumed rapid recuperation after the Flood. For 1000–1695AD his estimate of the growth rate was not out of line with modern judgement. His projections for 2000 and 2300 assumed a growth rate similar to that for 1000–1695, and for the 5,800 years from 2300 to 8100 a slowdown by two-thirds. His futurology was not Malthusian or religious. He did not think the end of the world was near. Recent UN futurology has a shorter time horizon than King, but the UN medium scenario for 2300 also projects a big slowdown from the experience of the past three centuries. In fact, Biblical conceptions of time did not disappear until the first half of the nineteenth century, when they were demolished by the work of Lyell, Darwin, and the archaeologists.

Table 5.7. Colin McEvedy's World Population Estimates: 7500BC–1AD (000s)

	−7,500	5,000	4,000	3,000	2,000	1,000	1AD
Austria	2	4	10	20	40	120	500
Belgium	3	3	10	20	40	100	400
Denmark	2	2	5	10	20	50	200
Finland	1	2	3	4	5	7	10
France	50	100	200	400	1,000	2,000	5,000
Germany	20	40	80	150	300	600	3,000
Italy	30	75	150	300	1,000	2,000	7,000
Netherlands	2	2	5	10	20	50	200
Norway		1	1	2	5	10	100
Sweden		1	2	4	10	50	200
Switzerland	1	2	5	10	20	60	300
UK	6	6	6	27	81	212	780
12 country total	117	238	477	957	2,541	5,259	17,690
Portugal	5	10	20	40	100	200	450
Spain	50	100	200	400	1,000	2,000	4,600
Greece	4	25	50	100	300	1,000	2,000
Other	1	1	13	19	28	63	210
Total W. Europe	**177**	**374**	**760**	**1,516**	**3,969**	**8,522**	**24,950**
E. Europe	**27**	**66**	**160**	**355**	**770**	**1,600**	**4,750**
Former USSR	**80**	**200**	**335**	**680**	**1,100**	**2,070**	**5,100**
Total Americas	**200**	**250**	**300**	**600**	**1,250**	**2,500**	**4,700**
Japan	5	5	5	10	15	20	100
China	200	500	1,000	2,000	3,500	6,000	50,000
India	200	500	1,000	3,000	6,000	12,000	36,000
Other Asia	600	1,360	2,020	3,400	6,745	13,340	28,400
Total Asia	**1,000**	**2,365**	**4,020**	**8,400**	**16,260**	**31,360**	**114,400**
Oceania	**300**	**370**	**440**	**520**	**640**	**800**	**1,000**
Africa	**1,250**	**1,300**	**1,450**	**2,200**	**3,960**	**6,670**	**14,200**
World	**3,039**	**4,925**	**7,520**	**14,281**	**27,964**	**53,542**	**169,200**
World rounded	**3,000**	**4,900**	**7,500**	**14,000**	**28,000**	**54,000**	**170,000**

Notes and Sources: I am very grateful for these estimates supplied by Colin McEvedy, which will appear in the second edition of McEvedy and Jones (1978). His world aggregate remains virtually identical with that in the 1978 version (p. 344), where country and regional detail were not shown before 400BC. McEvedy's method of estimation for this period was explained on pp. 13–15. It was based on: (a) an assessment of habitable area, which increased substantially after 10,000BC as the ice-free area increased; and (b) the assumed density of population which could be sustained as technology advanced through three successive stages—stone age, bronze age, and iron age—and was diffused within each of these. The switch from hunter-gathering to food production started around 7500BC in Jericho (Kenyon 1958); the bronze age, shortly before 3000BC (when metal tools and weapons were introduced, and writing was invented); the iron age from 1200BC (when tools and weapons became much cheaper, writing began to be alphabetic, coinage was invented, scientific thought began, and inter-regional diffusion of technology accelerated).

Apart from the question of religious belief, King was wrestling with the problem of comparing growth performance over time, without knowing how to derive compound interest rates. He, Graunt, and Petty always compared growth rates in terms of the years needed to double an initial figure. Thus Petty felt that London was doubling every 40 years, and England every 360. In order to get their estimates right, they had to make these tedious exercises. In fact, logarithms were invented by Napier in 1614. Log tables were first produced by Briggs in 1631 and were widely used by navigators, but compound interest measures were introduced into economic growth analysis relatively recently. Colquhoun was still using the doubling concept for growth comparisons in 1815. Compound interest comparisons were not used by Mulhall in 1899 or by Colin Clark in 1940.

King's Consolidated Wealth and Income Accounts

This was the only macro-economic account developed by Petty, and the first of several by King. King's consolidated account was much more complex than Petty's.

Table 5.1 confronts Petty's accounts for 1665 and those of King for 1688 for England and Wales. Petty's estimate of the capitalized value of property and people was £667 million, King's £650 million. Petty estimated national income to be £40 million, King £43.5 million. Petty assumed a per capita income of £6.7, with a population of six million, King a per capita income of £7.9, and a population of 5.5 million.

The biggest capital asset was land which both valued at 18 years purchase. King disaggregated 39 million acres into 8 types of land, each of which produced different rates of rent. He estimated income from land to be £10 million. Petty presented a single aggregate of 24 million acres (excluding 'waste') He estimated income from land to be £8 million. In fact, the area of England and Wales is 37 million acres. Housing was the second type of asset. Petty's estimated income and imputed income from housing to be £2.5 million and its capital value at 12 years purchase. King estimated income and imputed income from housing to be £2 million and its capital value at 18 years purchase. Petty's third asset category included shipping, livestock, stocks of precious metals, household durables, and business inventories. He valued income from these at £4.5 million and capitalized them at somewhat less than 17 years purchase. King's third category was described as miscellaneous 'hereditaments', yielding an income of £1 million, and a capitalized value of £86 million. Thus his total property income was £13 million and its capital value £320 million.

In *Observations* (p. 35), King added another £1 million of income from 'personal estates', bringing his total property income to £14 million. This valuation was repeated in his essay on the *Naval Trade of England* (1697) where he reduced the capitalized value of all physical assets to £252 millions (i.e., an average of 18 years purchase). These second thoughts brought his estimate of total property income and capital value nearer to Petty, but left an inconsistency in his total income account which should have been raised to £ 44.5 million.

Petty estimated the earnings of labour by assuming half the population to be employed with a total income of to £25 million (three million people earning £8.33 a year). His average rate of capitalization for property and labour income was the same (16.7 years purchase). Thus the capital value of labour was £ 417 million.

King's approach was quite different. For him, non-property income was derived from 'trade' and the 'arts', as well as the earnings of labour.

His detailed procedure for estimating the value of human capital is shown in *Notebook* (p. 245) with variant versions on pp. 244 and 248. He assigned a capital value to everyone in the population as if they were slaves or horses. He attributed a positive value to the potential labour income of young children (in 'business'), though in their 'tender years' they were a charge rather than 'beneficial to the public'. 'Yet the prospect of future usefulness has an intrinsic value in like manner as an estate in reversion after a determinate term of years'. For males the capital value of those aged less than 9 years was £27 rising to £124 for the age group 15–20, declining thereafter to £9 for those aged 80–90, and to £1 for those 90 and over. Their average capital value (weighted by population in each age group) was £67.6. The valuation for 'business' was at ten years purchase, so the average annual income potential for males of all ages was £6.76. For females the average capital value was £36.5, and their average annual income potential £3.65, i.e., about 54 per cent of that for males. The age profile for female income peaked in the 15–20 age group, fell more slowly than for males to age 50–60, then dropped off more sharply. This grading system by gender and age was obviously related to some notion of potential labour earnings, but King did not discuss the derivation of his labour force/population ratio, earnings structure, or the gender differential in activity rates and earnings.

He gave a separate valuation for the procreative potential of males and females broken down by 11 age groups. Females aged 9–20 were rated higher than males; the same at age 20–30; and a lower rating thereafter. The average procreative value of males of all ages was, surprisingly, nearly one-fifth higher than that of females.

It is not possible to make an exact reconciliation of these detailed estimates with the very aggregative statement in *Observations*, which gave an average valuation of people of both sexes of £60 per head—'near 11 years purchase'—for their combined potential for business and procreation. One presumes that he valued 'business' potential at ten years purchase, and procreative value at less than one year.

It is interesting to compare King's human capital estimates with those of Fogel and Engerman (1974: 74–85 and 124–5) for US slaves in 1850. 1688 life expectation in England was identical (36 years) with that for US slaves in 1850, and the infant mortality rate was similar (189 compared with 183 in the US). The price schedule for US slaves by age group was similar to that of King, but the gender differential seems to have been smaller in the US. Their decomposition of female slave value for 'business and procreation' resembles that of King, but Fogel and Engerman discern no value for the procreative potential of males. The capitalization ratio of American slaves seems to have been equivalent to about eight years earnings in the Old South in 1850, i.e., a lower rate than King applied.

King's Expenditure Account

This is the best documented dimension of King's system of accounts, and has no counterpart in Petty's work. King's coverage of expenditure was incomplete, was restricted to personal consumption of commodities, and excluded services. It also excluded government consumption, and capital formation, though the latter could be inferred from the difference between his income and expenditure account—which he called the 'increase'.

Observations (hereafter abbreviated to *O*; pp. 54–5), provides a rather summary statement of consumer expenditure, starting with eight items of 'diet' (food and drink), a total for 'apparel' and for 'incidental charges', with no indication of source. With the help of the detail given in his *Notebook* (hereafter abbreviated to *N*), it is possible to provide much more detail for apparel and incidentals, and to augment coverage of the accounts to include services, government consumption, and gross fixed capital formation. Table 5.8 shows a breakdown for 43 categories of expenditure, and an adjusted aggregate approximating the modern concept of gross domestic expenditure, which is about 30 per cent higher than King's total. The items marked 'a' are my additions. Careful scrutiny reveals the derivation of the items he included. The degree of detail in the table demonstrates the astounding assiduity of his search for information and the sophistication of his consistency and reliability checks. For this reason and for the benefit of those who wish to push this study further, I describe the source of the estimates in some detail below.

Food

The first six entries are from *O* (pp. 54–5). King started from the production side, giving a detailed breakdown of land use, and showed estimates of value added for major cereals, vegetables, textile fibres, hay, livestock herds, production of meat, dairy products, wool, tallow, hides, transport animals, timber, and wood. He made no reference to potatoes which were a very marginal item at that time. He gives details of seed and feed which need to be deducted to get value added in the primary sector. For meat and dairy products his estimates of consumption are the same as for production, so it is not clear whether he valued them at farm prices without a retail mark-up, or whether he valued farm output at retail prices. In the case of cereal products he does seem to allow a margin for processing and marketing costs. Output of dairy products was derived by estimating the dairy herd, milk yield, and use of milk in liquid form, in cheese-making and butter production (*N*; p. 214). The derivation of the estimate of fruit and vegetable consumption is shown in *N* (p. 213). It involved a survey of fruits, flowers, and vegetables arriving four days a week at London's major market (Newgate) by water, porterage, horse, or cart transport. He inflated London per capita consumption proportionately to population of England and Wales as a whole, with allowance for lower prices in country areas, an imputation

Table 5.8. Gross Domestic Expenditure in England and Wales in 1688 (£000's at market prices)

Food	**13,900**	Sheet and table linen	1,500
Bread, biscuits, and pastry	4,300	Brass and pewterware	1000
Beef, mutton, and pork	3,300	Wood and glassware	1000
Fish, poultry, and eggs	1,700	**Education and health**	**1,150**
Dairy products	2,300	Schooling	250
Fruits and vegetables	1,200	Paper, books, and ink	500
Salt, spices, oil, and sweetmeats	1,100	Medical care	400a
Beverages and tobacco	**7,350**	**Personal and professional services**	**3,100**
Beer and Ale	5,800	Domestic servants	1,600a
Wine and brandy	1,300	Recreation	500
Tobacco, pipes, and snuff	250a	Legal, financial, hair-dressing, inns, and taverns	1,000a
Clothing	**10,393**	**Passenger transport**	**430**
Male outerwear	2,390	Passenger transport by road	280a
Shirts, cravats, and ruffles	1,300	Passenger transport by water	150a
Male underwear	100	**Government, religion, and defence**	**4,844**
Male accessories	85	Military pay	1,530a
Female outerwear	904	Ecclesiastical remuneration	514a
Female underwear	1,400	Civil government pay	1,800a
Nightgowns and aprons	500	Commodities	1,000a
Female accessories	335	**Gross capital formation**	**3,675**
Hats, caps and wigs	568	Structures	975a
Gloves, mittens' and muffs	410	Transport equipment	700a
Handkerchiefs	200	Other equipment	2,000
Stockings and socks	1,011	**Gross domestic expenditure**	**54,042**
Footwear	1,190	Gregory King's total	41,643b
Household operation	**9,200**	Additional items	12,399a
Rent and imputed rent	2,200a	**Population (thousands)**	**5,427**
Fire, candles, and soap	2,000	**Per capita GDP**	**£9.958**
Beds and bedding	1,500		

Notes: (a) indicates items added to King's account; (b) King's total. In addition, he indicated a £1.8 million 'increase', or saving, If treated as investment, this would raise his total to £43,443.

Sources: Gregory King's *Notebook* in Laslett (1973) and *Observations* in Barnett (1936: 54–6). The six food items and the two entries for beverages are taken from King's *Observations* and refer to 1695. For 1688, he showed a total £0.3 million higher for these eight items, but I have not added it because the detail is not shown. All the other items refer to 1688. In *Observations*, he showed a rounded total of £41.7 million for expenditure, £43.5 for income. Population in England, 5,059 thousand from Wrigley et al. (1997: 614), adjusted by 1.0728 to include Monmouth and Wales.

for direct consumption of non-marketed products by farmers and others, and adjustment for assumed differences in level of per capita consumption between town and country.

Beverages and Tobacco

The stages in the transformation of most of the barley crop into malt, home and commercially produced beer and ale are described in detail (*N*; p. 259), as is the incidence of excise duty. Expenditure on tobacco, pipes, and snuff is shown on *N* (p. 211). Expenditure on wine and brandy was derived from import statistics. There is no mention of coffee and tea consumption which began in the 1650s (see Brewer and Porter 1993: 140–1 and 184).

Clothing

N (p. 203) gives a very detailed picture of clothing consumption in 1688. For 40 items he gives quantities and price, for four items (ribbons and lace) he only gives values. Table 5.8 compresses King's detail and shows only 13 types of clothing expenditure. His estimates were based on knowledge of the inputs of different types of textile fibre and inquiries on prices and output addressed to textile traders. His own family budget is given in considerable detail (*N*; p. 250). He estimated patterns of clothing expenditure for 12 different income groups (*N*; p. 210). Consumption varied from £0.53 per person in the lowest income group, to £150 for the highest group (see Stone 1997: 79 for a convenient presentation of this extraordinary table, whose derivation is not clear from King's manuscripts). King (*N*; p. 203) estimated that more than half of clothing (£5.3 million) consisted of wool products. One of his tables in the Public Record Office (PRO 64/302) values hair and silk clothing at £1.25 million, leather at £1.25 million, linen £2 million and other materials £0.5 million. He does not mention cotton items; at that time most of these were calicoes imported by the East India Company (see Chaudhuri 1978).

Household Operation

The entries for fire, candles, and soap; beds and bedding; sheets and table linen; brass and pewterware; wood and glassware are from *N* (p. 211). For soap and candles he starts from his own household consumption, and makes adjustments for differences between households with different income levels (*N*, p. 257). Rent and imputed rent were derived from *O* (p. 35) where he imputes a rental value to residential buildings (£2 million) and to residential land (£0.45 million). These include a valuation for churches and churchyards, gardens and orchards, so I assumed a slightly lower figure for housing.

Education and Health

Schooling, paper, books, and ink are from *N* (p. 211). King derived his estimates for paper from a discussion with 'Mr. Carr, the stationer'. Judging from import duty assessments, annual imports were running at £200,000 a year, with domestic value added of £60,000 in 50 paper mills. King and Carr also discussed the relative share of material and labour costs, rents, and profit in the industry (see *N*; p. 205). There are three components for medical expenditure. King's estimates of sickness costs (£232,000) for six categories of people. Laslett (1973) show his estimate of the annual cost of 1,104 hospitals and almshouses catering to the sick and the poor. The sickness component was £115,000 I added £53,000 for midwife services (which King omits), to round out the total to £400,000.

Personal and Professional Services

Recreational expenses from N (p. 211). Expenditure on domestic servants as Deane (1955: 9) inferred from King's estimates. I assumed that professional services (legal and financial) were £300,000 (about a fifth of the income which King attributed to lawyers) and that expenditure on inns, taverns, barbers, and other personal services was £700,000. The latter is a guess as King provides no clues, but it seems fairly conservative. Massie estimated income of people running inns and alehouses to have been about £1.4 million in 1760, when the national income was about 50 per cent higher than King's estimate for 1688 (see Mathias 1957).

Passenger Transport

King did not include passenger transport in consumption, but his estimate of the total number of horses (N; p. 200) gives a breakdown of between final and intermediate uses (ploughing, draught animals, freight carriage, etc.) In total he estimated that 400,000 households kept 1.4 million horses. Of these 40,000 were saddle horses for noblemen, knights, esquires, and gentlemen or used for hackney carriages; 42,200 were used for 12,200 coaches. He provides estimates of consumption of oats, peas, and beans by horses, and an age distribution of the horse stock. O (p. 37) shows hay consumed by horses. I assume that feed for these 82,200 horses cost £100,000, coachmen, blacksmith services, and stabling another £100,000, replacement of dead or retired horses £30,000, maintenance of saddles, bridles and 12,200 coaches £50,000 (see N; p. 211). King provided estimates for the number of ships (N; p. 208), indicated the replacement rate and annual cost of replacement. Using his cost and quantity figures, I estimated new construction expenditure of £100,000 for passenger transport, ferry services, etc., and £50,000 for replacement (about 5 per cent of the total shipping depreciation shown in N, p. 211).

Government, Religion and Defence

Military pay, ecclesiastical remuneration, and civil government pay are from O (p. 32). Remuneration of 64,000 military personnel (naval and military officers, common soldiers, and 20,000 'common seamen') was £1.53 million. Ecclesiastical remuneration of £514,000 went to 'spiritual lords' (archbishops and bishops) and two levels of clergymen. Civil government pay is King's total for 10,000 persons in 'offices', i.e., public office. I assumed that expenditure on naval shipping, ship supplies, guns, ammunition, upkeep of 20,000 horses for troopers, upkeep of barracks and military buildings, as well as smaller supplies for civil servants and the clergy amounted to £1 million.

Capital Formation

King did not include capital formation in his expenditure accounts, but showed the difference between total income and expenditure as a measure of 'increase' which can be taken to represent savings or investment. The net amount in 1688 was £1.8 million, after social transfers. In addition, his expenditure total included £2 million for 'instruments of husbandry, trades and manufactures' which I have classified as investment. My total for capital formation (£3.7 million) is therefore similar to the £3.8 million in King's accounts.

King estimated an annual housing investment of £100,000 was needed to accommodate population growth, £1,450,000 for house repairs, £200,000 for repairs to 10,000 churches, and £100,000 for repairs to colleges, hospitals, and other public buildings (*N*; p. 246). I treated half the last three items as major repairs (i.e., final expenditure), and half as maintenance (intermediate expenditure), in line with modern national accounting practice.

King provided details of the stock of naval and merchant vessels, fire-ships, hospital ships, provision ships, yachts, sloops, and tenders, at original cost and 1688 values (broken down by hulks and rigging), for 15 categories of tonnage (*N*; p. 208). He estimated the annual cost of ship replacement as £400,000.

He allowed £300,000 for depreciation ('decay') of the stock of 100,000 carts and wagons, and 8,000 coaches (*N* p. 211)

King's Income Account

King's best known table for England and Wales is his 'Scheme of the income and expense of the several families of England calculated for the year 1688'. Unlike most of his work it did not disappear from view, as it was reproduced (with some modifications) in Davenant (1699). Its existence was known to King's contemporaries, e.g., Leibniz, the philosopher and Hanoverian librarian in Wolfenbüttel, and to the two French pioneers of national accounts, Boisguilbert and Vauban.

King delineated the social hierarchy in a dramatic way, showing the income and expenditure of 26 types of household from temporal lords to vagrants (see Table 5.9a). His top group had an average per capita income 35 times that of the lowest: 37.6 per cent of households earned 79.3 per cent of national income, and were responsible for all the savings of the economy (7 per cent of their income); the lower income group (the commoners and vagrants) had no savings but received income transfers (poor relief of various kinds), which added almost 7 per cent to their incomes. Total net saving ('superlucration') amounted to 4.2 per cent of national income. This quantitative depiction of the social panorama in 1688 had no precursors. There were estimates for 1600 by Thomas Wilson, and by King's contemporary, Edward Chamberlayne for 1692, but they were incomplete and not part of an articulate framework of accounts. As a result, subsequent authors with a taste for political arithmetic and an interest in changes in social structure over time,

Table 5.9a. King's Hierarchy of England's Income by Type of Household in 1688

	Households	Persons	Total income (000£)	Per capita income (£)
Temporal lords	160	6,400	448	70
Spiritual lords	26	520	33.8	65
Baronets	800	12,800	704	55
Knights	600	7,800	390	50
Esquires	3,000	30,000	1,200	*40*
Gentlemen	12,000	96,000	2,880	*30*
Persons in offices	5,000	40,000	1,200	30
Persons in lesser offices	5,000	30,000	600	20
Merchants and traders	2,000	16,000	800	50
Lesser merchants and traders	8,000	48,000	1,600	33
Persons in the law	10,000	70,000	1,400	20
Clergy men	2,000	12,000	120	10
Lesser clergy men	8,000	40,000	360	9
Freeholders	40,000	280,000	3,360	12
Lesser freeholders	140,000	700,000	7,000	10
Farmers	150,000	750,000	6,600	*8.8*
Persons science and liberal arts	16,000	80,000	960	12
Shopkeepers and tradesmen	40,000	180,000	1,800	10
Artisans and handicrafts	60,000	240,000	2,400	10
Naval officers	5,000	20,000	400	20
Military officers	4,000	16,000	240	15
Total above	**511,586**	**2,675,520**	**34,496**	**12.9**
Common seamen	50,000	150,000	1,000	*6.7*
Labourers and outservants	364,000	1,275,000	5,460	*4.3*
Cottagers and paupers	400,000	1,300,000	2,000	*1.3*
Common soldiers	35,000	70,000	490	7.0
Total commoners	**849,000**	**2,795,000**	**8,950**	**3.2**
Vagrants	30,000	30,000	60	2
Grand total	**1,390,586**	**5,500,520**	**43,506**	**7.9**

Notes and Sources: King's *Observations* (1696), in Barnett (1936: 31). Corrections are italicized in col. 4. This table is an abbreviated version of the original, which also shows expenditure, savings, and social transfers. I describe his basic unit as households rather than 'families' as he does, because it includes live-in servants and employees. 'Merchants and Traders' refers only to those trading by sea. The figures refer to England and Wales.

like Massie, Colquhoun, Lindert, and Williamson have taken King's income account as their starting point.

Over the past half century, many distinguished historians—Aylmer (1961), Mingay (1963), Stone (1965), Cooper (1967), and Holmes (1977)—have probed a variety of sources to throw new light on the fortune and careers of those in the upper reaches of British society. Most of them suggest that King understated the income of the upper groups. Until recently, the most vehement critic was Holmes, whose analysis is scholarly and illuminating, but I think quite wrong in suggesting that King deliberately distorted the picture for political reasons. Arkell (2006) a disciple of Holmes, thinks that King 'attempted the impossible', treats his work with disdain and suggests it be discarded: 'once shattered, his fragile Scheme, like Humpty Dumpty, cannot be reassembled'. This is a very odd conclusion. The approach of Lindert and Williamson (1982) was much more reasonable.

Lindert and Williamson reviewed the weaknesses and gaps in King's estimates in a spirit of constructive criticism, and made extensive repairs and revisions for reasons which are fully documented (see Table 5.9b). They raised King's income estimates for the upper crust of lords, baronets, knights, esquires, and gentlemen, and added estimates for income for categories of King omitted. Together these adjustments added £11 million. They made some reductions elsewhere, so their net addition to King's total was £10.8 million.

Lindert and Williamson are the only critics to attempt a detailed reformulation of King's income account by sector of activity. Their main interest was in comparisons of income distribution over time, confronting King's 1688 income-spread with Massie's one-page pamphlet for 1759, and Colquhoun (1806 and 1815). They drew on Lindert's (1980) attempt to derive by regression a representative picture of occupational structure from burial records of 26 parishes in the files of the Cambridge Group for Population History. They relied heavily on Holmes for revision of King's income estimates. They made four points: (a) they endorsed the critique of the historians and raised the income estimate for the wealthy elite; (b) they substantially augmented King's estimates of income originating in industry and service activities; (c) they reduced agricultural income and that of the poor; (d) the net result was to augment King's income estimate by a quarter. They accepted King's count of households.

Sectoral Distribution of Income

The Lindert and Williamson allocation of income by sector of economic activity is not comprehensive. Table 5.10 extends it by allocating the income of the wealthy elite and working poor by economic sector. This is a provisional revamping. Further research would be useful to check the Lindert and Williamson estimates. A major problem is that the source material on income in King's manuscripts is more exiguous than it is for expenditure. Nevertheless the Lindert and Williamson aggregate estimates and their judgement on points (a) and (b) seem perfectly respectable. Their income estimate is in fact very similar to my augmented version of King's expenditure estimate in Table 5.8.

In further exploration of the income account, it would be useful to break away from the household approach, and to try to flesh out a picture of labour force activity of individuals (see the three sector breakdown of labour force for 1700 in Table 2.5, Chapter 2 in this volume). Petty adopted this approach in very summary form, and it should be possible to go further, e.g., separating servants from households and assessing labour force potential by exploiting King's table on gender and age structure (Table 5.4).

Closer scrutiny of the activity rate and gender structure of earnings implicit in King's slave paradigm for capitalizing the value of labour would also be useful. Further material on occupational structure and activity rates such as that which was

Table 5.9b. Lindert and Williamson's Income Hierarchy by Type of Household in 1688

	Households	Average. Income (£)	Total Income (000 £)
Temporal lords	*200*	*6,060*	1,212
Spiritual lords	26	1,300	34
Baronets	800	*1,500*	1,056
Knights	600	800	480
Esquires	3,000	*563*	1,688
Gentlemen	*15,000*	280	4,200
Wealthy elite	**19,626**	**442**	**8,670**
Persons in offices	5,000	240	1,200
Persons in lesser offices	5,000	120	600
Persons in the law	*8,062*	*154*	1,242
Clergymen	2,000	72	144
Lesser clergymen	*10,000*	50	500
Persons science and liberal arts	*12,898*	60	774
Professions	**42,960**	**104**	**4,460**
Merchants and traders by sea	2,000	400	800
Lesser M. and Ts. by sea	8,000	200	1,600
Merchants and Ts. by land	*3,264*	400	1,306
Lesser M. and Ts. by land	*13,057*	200	2,611
Shopkeepers and tradesmen	*101,704*	45	4,577
Merchants	**128,025**	**85**	**10,894**
Artisans and handicrafts	*6,745*	*200*	1,349
Manufacturing trades	*162,863*	*38*	6,189
Building trades	*73,018*	*25*	1,825
Mining	*14,240*	*15*	214
Industry and building	**256,866**	**37**	**9,577**
Freeholders	*27,568*	91	2,509
Lesser freeholders	*96,490*	55	5,307
Farmers	*103,382*	42.5	4,394
Agriculture	**227.440**	**54**	**12,210**
Naval officers	5,000	80	400
Military officers	4,000	60	240
Common seamen	50,000	20	1,000
Common soldiers	35,000	14	490
Soldiers and seamen total	**94,000**	**23**	**2,130**
Labourers and outservants	*284,997*	15	4,275
Cottagers and paupers	*313,183*	6.5	2,036
Vagrants	*23,489*	2	47
Labourers and poor total	**621,669**	**10**	**6,358**
Grand total	**1,390,586**	**39**	**54,299**

Notes and Sources: Lindert and Williamson (1982: 393). They added five categories of household not shown by King, i.e., greater and lesser merchants by land, manufacturing trades, building trades, and miners. They raised the income estimates for temporal lords, baronets, knights, and artisans. In seven cases they used Davenant's (1699) revised version of King's table (see Whitworth 1771: vol. II, p.184). In 14 cases they used the per capita household incomes shown by King. In 13 cases they changed the number of households shown by King, but their total is the same as his. They corrected King's arithmetical errors by modifying household income. Their changes are shown in italics in the first two columns above. I derived the third column by multiplying the first two. My total of £54.3 million is slightly lower than their £54.4.

Table 5.10. Income by Economic Sector, in 1688: Lindert and Williamson Adjusted (£ 000)

Freeholders and farmers	12,210
Rental income of the wealthy elite	4,400
Agricultural income of 200,000 labouring households	3,000
Agricultural income of 200,000 cottager households	1,300
Total agriculture	**20,190** (39.2%)
Industry, mining, and construction	9,577
Industrial income of the wealthy elite	500
Industrial income of 50,000 labouring households	750
Industrial income of 50,000 cottager households	325
Total industry	**11,152** (20.9%)
Income from professions and commerce	15,354
Service income of the wealthy elite	3,770
Income of soldiers and seamen	2,130
Total services	**21,254** (39.9%)
Income of economically active households	**53,316** (100.0%)
Income of unemployed, pauper, and vagrant households	983
National income	**54,299**

Notes and Sources: This table makes a tentative allocation of the sectoral distribution of income of the wealthy elite and the working poor (in Table 5.9b). Wealthy elite: for this group King showed the distribution of rental income from land for England, excluding Wales in a document in the Public Record Office (T64/302). In a total of nearly £8 million, the share of peerage, knights, esquires, and gentlemen was about 44.3 per cent, freeholders 50 per cent, clergy 1.9 per cent, and crown about 3.8 per cent. If this percentage is applied to the £10 million total for landed property income in England and Wales shown in King's income and wealth account (Table 5.1), it implies a total agricultural income for the wealthy elite of £4.4 million. A large part of their other income was derived from service activities, such as income from public office, rental of housing properties, and returns on financial assets. The latter were limited in a country with no stock exchange, central bank, or funded national debt, but there was income from trading corporations, of which the largest was the East India Company. One must also remember that these accounts refer to households, and include income of live-in servants, tutors, secretaries, estate management personnel, etc. The average household size for the wealthy group was 9.2 persons compared with an average of 4.2 for the whole population. One can therefore infer that there were on average about four service personnel per wealthy household, i.e., around 66,000 servants, with a total income of nearly half a million. In total I assumed that £3.7 million of elite household income came from services, and half a million from industry. The above estimates exclude income of the royal household as do those of King, and Lindert and Williamson. Colquhoun (1815: 174–7 gives details of royal expenditure met from public funds. For 1688–9, the civil list amounted to £425,000 which could be considered a service sector activity. In addition there was £300,000 from rental of crown lands.

Lindert and Williamson left 621,699 poor households unallocated by sector. I assumed that 500,000 were employed, and allocated 80 per cent of them to agriculture and 20 per cent to industry, leaving a residual 121,669 without employment. This is a fairly arbitrary allocation but has some foundation in King's *Notebook* (p. 209).

found by Tawney and Tawney (1934) and Saito (1979) would be helpful. It should also be possible to develop a crosscheck by attempting to expand King's production account.

Absence of a Production Account

King provided no comprehensive production account, though he gave enough detail to estimate value-added in farming and forestry roughly compatible with the income account in Table 5.10. He showed £9.3 million of value-added in production of cereals, vegetables, hemp, flax, woad, saffron, and other dyestuffs in *Observations* (p. 36). Livestock products (including the higher of two estimates for the value of meat) amounted to another £9.3 million. He showed £1 million for hay consumed by cattle, but we can ignore this as it went to produce the livestock products already counted. Another £1.3 million of hay for horses should probably be included, as he shows no value of output from the existing stock of horses, but only the increment in the stock. He shows £1 million for the value of timber and firewood, but nothing for fishing. His total for farming and forestry value added is thus about £21 million. We should deduct the value of activities which would now be classified as manufacturing (e.g., butter and cheese-making) and add the net increase in the stock of farm animals other than horses (what he shows appears to refer to the gross stock). He suggested some minor modification to his agricultural accounts in response to queries by Harley. Davenant (1699) gave details of these revisions (see Whitworth 1771: vol. 2, pp. 216–20).

King quantifies some components of industrial production. His *Observations* (pp. 41 and 46) provides details of beer and ale production. The *Notebook* provides detailed quantification of the commodity flow in the textile sector, value added in the paper industry, a breakdown of material inputs and labour costs in construction and shipbuilding. Page 211 gives expenditure on furniture, ceramics, pottery, glass, tools, and transport equipment, which could be converted into production estimates, if one could make rough estimates to knock off transport and distributive margins and material inputs.

Table 5.10 attributes nearly 40 per cent of allocable income to services, whereas service items are less than 19 per cent of the expenditure account in Table 5.8. However, the end-use perspective in expenditure accounts means that the cost of many service activities (transport, storage, and marketing) is disguised because it is embedded in the retail price. The disparity in the service share between the expenditure and the income or production accounts is quite normal. Maddison (1983) showed a similar spread in the service share of GDP between the production and expenditure accounts for fourteen countries in 1975.

Estimates of the 1688 production structure are useful for analysis of the pace of economic growth since then. Deane and Cole (1964) and Crafts (1983) needed to make proxy estimates for this period to use as weights for their long-term estimates of GDP growth by industry of origin. Table 5.11 shows their respective assessments together with those of Lindert and Williamson.

King's International Comparisons of Income

Table 5.12 shows King's comparative estimates of aggregate income, population, and per capita income for England and Wales, France, and Holland. He included details

Table 5.11. Proxy Estimates of the Production Structure in 1688 (per cent of total)

	Deane and Cole	Crafts	Lindert and Williamson amended
Agriculture	40.2	37.0	39.2
Industry	20.6	20.0	20.9
Services	39.2	43.0	39.9
Total	100.0	100.0	100.0

Notes and Sources: Deane and Cole (1964: 156), showed a rough breakdown of GDP by sector, using King's production estimate for farming and forestry, and an augmented version of his income accounts for services. They derived industry (manufacturing, mining, and construction) as a residual, after augmenting his income total to £48 million. Crafts (1983: 188–9) used Lindert and Williamson (1982) to construct a sector breakdown of their total income estimate. The third column is derived from Table 5.10 and shows shares of a total allocable income.

of eight consumption items (food and drink) for 1695, and entries for 'apparel', 'incidental charges', and 'increase' (i.e., the gap between expenditure and income). For 1688, the account was given in more summary form. The major purpose was to compare capacity to mobilize resources for the war of the League of Augsburg. William III had organized a coalition of the UK, Netherlands, the German States, Spain, and Savoy against France which had challenged the legitimacy of his succession to the English throne, and annoyed its neighbours by trying to expand its frontiers. The war lasted nine years, and King's findings indicate that the cost was heavy. They

Table 5.12. Population and Income in England and Wales, France, and the Netherlands in 1688

	England & Wales	France	Netherlands
King's Estimate for 1688			
Aggregate income (million 1688 £)	43.5	84.0	17.8
Population (thousand)	5,500	14,000	2,200
Per capita income (1688 £)	7.9	6.0	8.07
England & Wales GDP. = 100	100	193	41
England & Wales population. = 100	100	255	40
England & Wales per cap. = 100	100	76	102
Maddison estimate for 1688			
GDP (million 1990 PPP $)	7,660	19,012	3,735
Population (thousand)	5,427	21,091	1,847
Per Capita Income (1990 PPP dollars).	1,411	901	2,022
England & Wales GDP. = 100	100	248	49
England & Wales population = 100	100	389	34
England & Wales per cap. = 100	100	64	143

Notes and Sources: King's estimates from *Observations* (1696) in Barnett (1936: 55. Maddison estimates of population and GDP for England and Wales in 1688 interpolated from Maddison (2001: 247). France and Netherlands interpolated from Maddison (2003: 34–5, 46–7, and 58–9). In 1688 per capita GDP was $702 in Ireland, $1,056 in Scotland; and $1,213 for the UK as a whole.

reinforce the more articulate critique of public policy objectives which Davenant (1694) advanced in his study on *Ways and Means of Supplying the War*.

King showed a rise in English public revenues and taxes from £2 million in 1688 (the last pre-war year) to £6.5 million in 1695; French from £10.5 to £17.5 million; and Dutch from £4.75 to £6.9 million. These figures were in current prices, but it was a period in which the general price level does not appear to have risen appreciably. King showed a very significant fall in French consumption between 1688 and 1695, and smaller falls in England and Holland. He showed large net disinvestment in England and France in 1695 compared with significant positive figures for 1688.

King converted all his estimates to sterling at exchange rates. He made no attempt to adjust for possible differences in the purchasing power of the three currencies.

There is supplementary information on these estimates in King's *Notebook*, but a good deal less than for his other accounts. He was probably able to make a reasonable assessment of per capita fiscal burdens, and degree of mobilization for war, but it is not clear how he estimated Dutch and French levels of consumption, GDP, or population.

King's estimates of population, GDP, and per capita GDP levels in 1688 are shown in Table 5.12 compared to my estimates in Maddison (2001, 2003). King understated French population by a third and overstated Dutch population by about a fifth. He understated the size of the French economy compared to England and Wales, and exaggerated the Dutch. He overstated the level of French per capita income relative to England and Wales, and understated the relative per capita performance of the Netherlands.

International comparisons were one of the weakest elements in King's accounts. I suggested that he substantially understated Dutch per capita income in Maddison (1982). De Vries (1984) took the same view. Le Roy Ladurie (1968) rejected King's estimates as they understated French population and showed no sources.

PATRICK COLQUHOUN (1745–1820)

King and Davenant added nothing to political arithmetic after 1699, and there was no further progress in the eighteenth century, except for Arthur Young's estimates of value-added in English agriculture (1770) and his comparison of agricultural conditions in France, northern Italy, and Spain (1794).

The last significant political arithmetician was Colquhoun, whose interest was probably sparked by Chalmers' publication of King's *Observations* in 1802, and by the availability of new statistical sources. He was able to use the first population censuses for 1801 and 1811 (for England, Wales, and Scotland). The income tax of 1798–1816 generated new information and new estimates of national income by Pitt, Beeke, and Bell. Eden (1797) produced a major historical study of poverty and its alleviation.

Government statistics were better organized, and more open to public scrutiny than in the days of Petty and King.

Colquhoun was an enterprising and successful businessman who left Scotland when he was 16 to try his fortune in Virginia. He returned to Glasgow, became Lord Provost in 1782–84, founded the Glasgow Chamber of Commerce, and acted as a lobbyist for cotton textile manufacturers. In 1789 he moved to London, and switched his interests to prevention of crime, improvement of policing, and alleviation of poverty. Thereafter he turned to questions of public finance and macro-economic issues.

His *Treatise on Indigence* (1806: 24) reproduced King's income table for 1688, and presented his own estimates of the situation in England and Wales in 1803. He assessed the 26 categories of income which King had covered, adding a breakdown between agricultural and other labourers. He also provided detail for 20 types of economic activity which King did not cover. These added 30 per cent to his income total. More than half were in manufacturing and services which had grown greatly in importance since 1688. The largest of these items was for capitalist entrepreneurs in manufacturing.

His *Treatise on the Wealth, Power and Resources of the British Empire in Every Quarter of the World* (1815) was a much more elaborate exercise, 540 pages with a full and reasonably transparent description of his accounts. It covered the whole British Empire as it emerged from the Napoleonic wars. He had four accounts: (a) For *Population*. Here he relied on census returns for England and Wales, and made rough estimates for the rest of the territories he covered. The latter were not particularly accurate. The first (1821) Irish census suggested a population a third higher than he estimated. (b) *Wealth* accounts for land, housing, shipping, business inventories, consumer durables, and governmental assets both civil and military. (c) An *income* account for 1812, with an integrated presentation of the 48 categories of activity he had shown earlier for 1803 (see pp. 124–5 of Colquhoun, 1815, and p. 198 of Stone, 1997). (d) A *value-added* account showing output in 91 different activities. This was a significant improvement on King's very partial production account, but Colquhoun, like King, omitted government services, house rental, professional and domestic services, from his expenditure account. We would now include these items. The omission was due to the influence of Colquhoun's Glasgow contemporary, Adam Smith, who regarded these activities as non-productive.

Although Colquhoun's accounts were rougher and less sophisticated than King's, they throw interesting light on the intervening changes that had occurred in the British economy. Cotton products and potatoes, which had not figured in King's accounts had become quite important. Cotton goods represented 20 per cent of manufacturing value-added and had overtaken woollens. Potatoes were equal in value to one-fifth of cereal output. Foreign transactions were much bigger proportionately. Books and printed matter had become much more important. Steam engines had become significant. The political entity had been expanded to incorporate Scotland

and Ireland. In spite of the loss of the American colonies, overseas possessions had a population 2.6 times as big as the UK.

FRENCH POLITICAL ARITHMETIC, 1695–1707

Between 1695 and 1707, two French authors ventured into political arithmetic. Both were much less sophisticated than Petty and King.

In 1695, *Pierre de Boisguilbert* (1646–1714), lieutenant-general (chief judge and president of the appeals court) in Rouen (capital of the province of Normandy), published anonymously *La France ruinée sous la règne de Louis XIV.* This was a very pessimistic assessment of the economic condition of France, the need to make its fiscal structure more effective and equitable, and to be less dirigiste in economic policy. In 1697 another version appeared, still anonymous but with a less provocative title *Le détail de la France.* Boisguilbert was impressed by the hunger crises and population decline which hit France in the early 1690s. He asserted that the national income had fallen by a third since 1660, but provided no detail.

Boisguilbert's books attracted little notice but stimulated the interest of *Sebastien le Prestre de Vauban* (1633–1707), a military engineer, who designed and supervised the construction of fortifications on the northern and eastern frontiers, successfully besieged many enemy cities, and constructed ports and forts on the Atlantic coast. Marshal Vauban had experience in galvanizing regional and local authorities and mobilizing resources for construction projects in many parts of France over a period of decades, so it is not surprising that he developed aspirations as a social engineer at the end of his career. Boisguilbert and Vauban were both convinced that the economy of their country was in a parlous state, whereas the English political arithmeticians were much more upbeat about England.

In 1707 Vauban published *Le dîme royal,* a proposal to transform the tax structure which provided a detailed assessment of potential revenue. He was encouraged in this endeavour by the success of an earlier proposal he made to Louis XIV in January 1695 for a temporary wartime capitation tax. This was adopted in 1695 and terminated in 1697 when the war ended. It was similar to the English poll tax of 1695–1705. Its incidence was graduated in descending order for 22 classes of taxpayer from the Dauphin down; social position being a proxy for income assessment. It was reintroduced in 1701 without the key feature of graduation by ability to pay (see Collins 2001: 133–4 and 165–7).

The French revenue system which Boisguilbert and Vauban wanted to transform was highly inefficient and inequitable. The main direct tax, the *taille,* involved large exemptions for the nobility and office holders. Some of these were for individuals (*personnelle*), others exempted specified properties (*réelle*). Tax rates varied regionally, between the *pays d'élection* and the *pays d'etat* (Brittany, Burgundy, Languedoc, and Provence, where tax rates were largely determined by the regional authorities). There were internal transit duties (*traites*) on merchandise crossing regional frontiers, inhibiting the development of a national market. Collection of direct and indirect taxes was done mainly by tax farmers and *traitants*, who made advance payments to the authorities and kept what they could collect. At the bottom level, in the 36,000 parishes, tax liability was fixed collectively. A large proportion of public officials obtained their posts by purchase or inherited them from relatives. Most of them paid an annual fee (*paulette*) to guarantee heritability of their office. In fact their salaries (*gages*) were equivalent to interest on the money they paid for their post. As a result the bureaucracy was swollen by officials who were only partially employed. The major indirect tax (*gabelle*), was on salt; the rate of tax varied between regions, virtually zero in producing regions like Brittany, and high in Burgundy, where wine taxes were low. As a consequence, there was large scale smuggling and expenditure on revenue police. In all these respects, England had a more efficient, transparent, and equitable fiscal system. In 1694 it had acquired a central bank and taken steps to create a market in long term government debt. In France the first attempt at a national budget was Necker's *Compte Rendu au Roi* in 1781, and the Banque de France was not created until 1800.

Vauban proposed to abolish all the existing taxes on property, income, and internal transit, and replace them with a single tax on income without exemptions or regional variation. He proposed to simplify the rate structure of the salt tax to reduce smuggling. He suggested new indirect taxes on luxuries and on liquor consumed in bars (*cabarets*).

In order to assess potential revenue from this new system he made estimates of national income, population, and area. For area, he used a rough average of five different cartographic sources for 38 regions of France. His estimated total was the equivalent of 60 million hectares. This was an exaggeration. The present area is 55 million and at that time (before Lorraine and Savoie were incorporated) was about 50 million (see Le Roy Ladurie 1992: 280). In fact, King's estimate of the area of France (51 million hectares) was much more exact. For population Vauban used estimates supplied by 28 provincial officials for years between 1694 and 1700. His total was 19.1 million, which tallies fairly well with modern estimates for the area he covered (see Bardet and Dupaquier 1997: 449). King's estimate for France (14 million) was much too low.

Vauban's estimates of national income were rough and hybrid. His measure for agriculture was gross output, with no deduction for feed, seed, and upkeep of buildings and equipment. He did not distinguish between different categories of agricultural income, and did not cover non-agricultural activity in rural areas. He specified ten types of non-agricultural income from property and labour. The sophistication of the analysis was greatly inferior to that of Gregory King, and he was dealing with a country where fiscal and other evidence for a coherent national analysis was much more exiguous than in England.

He estimated agricultural output on the basis of a sample study of Normandy. For this he had help from an anonymous friend (possibly Boisguilbert). He assumed that 80 per cent of the land yielded income from crops, livestock, vineyards, and forestry, with a third of cropland in fallow. He estimated the physical crop yield for wheat and its value per square league (20 square km). He assumed this value yield per league was also valid for pastoral activities, vineyards, and forestry. From this he estimated a potential tax yield about 24 per cent higher than the ecclesiastical tithe for Normandy. Nevertheless, he took the latter as representative and blew up it up by the ratio of the land area of France to that of Normandy. After a further conservative reduction of about 10 per cent, he concluded that the tax yield at the national level would be 60 million livres, assuming a 5 per cent levy (*vingtième*) on gross output. If we multiply his 5 per cent tax yield by 20, gross agricultural output for France would have been 1,200 million livres. His first estimate implied 1,667 million livres. If we deduct inputs into agriculture, adjust for his overstatement of the area of France and the fact that Normandy was more densely populated than the country as a whole, it seems likely that he was overstating national income from agriculture substantially.

Vauban's estimate of non-rural income was 352 million *livres*. Rent and imputed rent (net of repair and maintenance) from 320,000 urban houses he estimated to be 32 million *livres*. Interest on government debt 20 million, mixed income from commerce, banking, fishing, shipping, and grain milling 58 million, pensions and emoluments of government officials 40 million, income of lawyers 10 million. He assumed there were 1.5 million servants with emoluments of 30 million. Two million non-agricultural labourers and artisans were assumed to earn 162 million. He derived this from their average daily wage, and assumed a working year of 185 days (deducting 52 Sundays, 38 days for public holidays, 50 for intemperate weather, 20 days attending fairs and markets, and 25 for illness). Except for the last three groups, he gave no indication of the number of people involved in rural and non-rural activity. He proposed the introduction of a Chinese-style household registration system to remedy this defect, and appended a form showing the type of detail by age, sex, and occupation which should be garnered annually by local worthies. His estimate of the number of non-rural houses (320,000) is manifestly too low for a non-rural labour force of more than 3.5 million and their families.

Vauban insisted that costs of tax collection would be greatly reduced with his proposed system and that the transition from the existing order would be painless. He felt that one could dispense with the services of tax farmers and *traitants* whom he classified as bloodsuckers (*Sang-suës d'état*). He felt that there could be a smooth transition to collection of agricultural levies in kind to be stored in government warehouses. He did not explain how the government would dispose of these commodities. He was also insouciant about the protests of the elite who would lose their tax-exempt status. In chapter VIII he identified all the groups who might oppose his proposition and suggested that with 200,000 armed men at his disposal the king could easily quell any opposition. Politically his proposition was both naïve and provocative. In

February 1707, a month before his death, Vauban's book was officially condemned and the remaining copies were destroyed.

Studenski (1958) cited nine attempts to measure French national income later in the eighteenth century. Some of these were an improvement on Vauban, notably Lavoisier's *De la richesse territoriale du royaume de France* (1791), and Arthur Young's (1794: chap. 15) detailed estimates of French agricultural output for 1787–9. Young found that land productivity in Normandy was much higher than in the rest of France, which strengthens the impression that Vauban overstated agricultural output.

MACRO-MEASUREMENT IN THE NINETEENTH AND FIRST HALF OF THE TWENTIETH CENTURY

In the nineteenth century, the statistical basis for macro-economic measurement improved a good deal. Population censuses provided a much better basis for demographic analysis. Statistical offices collected data on trade, transport, fiscal, and monetary matters, employment, wages, and prices. There was an increasing array of information on commodity output in agriculture, mining, and manufacturing. Index number techniques were developed which made it possible to measure temporal changes or interspatial variance of complex aggregates.

Although there was a proliferation of national income estimates for individual countries, there was little improvement in their quality or comparability over those of the seventeenth century. They generally concentrated on the income dimension with no crosschecks on the expenditure and production side. They provided little help for serious analysis of economic growth. They were generally spot estimates for a given point in time, and there was significant inter-country variance in coverage and methodology. Except for Australia, none of the estimates were made by statistical offices.

Michael Mulhall (1836–1900) made a major contribution to international comparison by providing standardized estimates for 22 countries representing about 60 per cent of world product in 1894–5. He measured value added for each country He divided their economies into nine sectors, estimated gross output in each sector, and made an adjustment to deduct inputs to avoid double counting.

Colin Clark (1905–89) was a leading figure in the history of macro-economic measurement, the most innovative since the seventeenth century. His hero was Petty, the founder of the discipline. Like Petty, he began as a scientist, was self-taught in economics, had the same restless energy and creative imagination, self-confidence, and showmanship. He also had multiple ambitions as a scholar, politician, and public servant. In 1937 he produced the first integrated accounts for the UK which measured the growth of income, expenditure, and production at current and constant market prices. He linked his estimates for 1913 with those of Gregory King for 1688 to provide historical perspective. He interacted closely with Keynes in Cambridge, and demonstrated the importance of national accounts as a tool of economic policy. His work was the precursor of the first official British national accounts, created by Meade and Stone in 1941.

He was the first to present estimates of real income levels across countries adjusted for differences in the purchasing power of currencies. These were merged with inter-temporal measures of GNP in real terms of the type he had previously produced. This created a framework for comparative analysis of performance in space and time which was to revolutionizse the possibilities for comparative economic history, and analysis of problems of growth and development (see Maddison 2004).

☐ BIBLIOGRAPHY

Andrews, J. H. (1997), *Shapes of Ireland: Maps and their Makers, 1564–1839*, Dublin.

Arkell, T. (2006), 'Illuminations and Distortions: Gregory King's Scheme Calculated for the Year 1688 and the Social Structure of later Stuart England', *Economic History Review*, February, pp. 32–69.

Aylmer, G. E. (1961), *The King's Servants: The Civil Service of Charles I*, Routledge, London.

Bardet, J-P. and J. Dupaquier (1997), *Histoire des Populations de l'Europe*, 2 vols Fayard, Paris.

Barnard, T. C. (1979), 'Sir William Petty, his Irish Estates and Irish Population', *Irish Economic and Social History*, VI, pp. 64–9.

Barnard, T. C. (2000), *Cromwellian Ireland*, Oxford University Press.

Barnard, T. C. (2003), *A New Anatomy of Ireland*, Yale University Press.

Beeke, H. (1800), *Observations on the Produce of the Income Tax and its Proportion to the Whole Income of Britain*, London.

Bell, B. (1802), *Essays on Agriculture*, London.

Boisguilbert, P. de (1696), *La France ruinée sous la règne de Louis XIV par qui & comment*, Marteau, Cologne (anonymous, author's name not shown).

Boisguilbert, P. de (1697), *Le détail de la France* (author and publisher's name not shown).

Bottigheimer, K. S. (1971), *English Money and Irish Land*, Oxford University Press.

Braudel, F. (1985), *Civilisation and Capitalism, 15th–18th Century*, 3 vols, Fontana, London.

Braudel, F. and F. Spooner (1967), 'Prices in Europe from 1450 to 1750', in Rich and Wilson.

Braudel, F. and E. Larousse (eds) (1977), *Histoire economique et sociale de la France*, vol. 2, P.U.F., Paris.

Brewer, J. (1989), *The Sinews of Power: War, Money and the English State, 1688–1783*, Unwin Hyman, London.

Brewer, J. and R. Porter (eds) (1993), *Consumption and the World of Goods*, Routledge, London.

British Library, Petty Papers, Manuscripts Catalogue item 72850–76986; http://www.bl.uk/catalogues/manuscripts/DESC0010.ASP?CiRestriction=petty

Bryant, A. (1943), *Samuel Pepys: The Man in the Making*, Cambridge University Press.

Chalmers, G. (1802), *An Estimate of the Comparative Strength of Great Britain*, Stockdale, Piccadilly, London.

Clark, C. (1940), *The Conditions of Economic Progress*, Macmillan, London, 504 pp.

Cohen J. E. (1995), *How Many People Can the Earth Support ?* Norton, New York.

Collins, J. B. (1995), *The State in Early Modern France*, Cambridge University Press.

Colquhoun, P. (1806), *A Treatise on Indigence*, Hatchard, London.

Colquhoun, P. (1815), *A Treatise on the Wealth, Power, and Resources of the British Empire in Every Quarter of the World*, 2nd edn, Mawman, London.

Cooper, J. P. (1967), 'The Social Distribution of Land and Men in England, 1436–1700', *Economic History Review*, 20, pp. 419–40.

Crafts, N. F. R. (1983a), 'British Economic Growth, 1700–1831: A Review of the Evidence', *Economic History Review*, May, pp. 177–99.

Crafts, N. F. R. (1983b), 'Gross National Product in Europe, 1870–1910: Some New Estimates', *Explorations in Economic History*, 20, pp. 387–401.

Crafts, N. F. R. and C. K. Harley (1992), 'Output Growth and the British Industrial Revolution: A Restatement of the Crafts-Harley View', *Economic History Review*, November, pp. 703–30.

Dallaway, J. (1793*)*, *Inquiries into the Origin and Progress of the Science of Heraldry in England*, Gloucester and London.

Davenant, C. (1694), *An Essay on Ways and Means of Supplying the War*, in Whitworth (1771).

Davenant, C. (1699), *An Essay upon the Probable Methods of Making a People Gainers in the Balance of Trade*, in Whitworth (1771).

Deane, P. (1955), 'The Implications of Early National Income Estimates for the Measurement of Long-Term Economic Growth in the United Kingdom', *Economic Development and Cultural Change*, pp. 3–38.

Deane, P. (1955–56), 'Contemporary Estimates of National Income in the First Half of the Nineteenth Century', *Economic History Review*, VIII, 3, pp. 339–54.

Deane, P. (1956–57), 'Contemporary Estimates of National Income in the Second Half of the Nineteenth Century', *Economic History Review*, IX, 3, pp. 451–61.

Deane P. (1957), 'The Industrial Revolution and Economic Growth: The Evidence of Early British National Income Estimates', *Economic Development and Cultural Change*, pp. 159–74.

Deane, P. (1968), 'New Estimates of Gross National Product for the United Kingdom, 1830–1914', *Review of Income and Wealth*, June, pp. 95–112.

Deane, P. and W. A. Cole (1964), *British Economic Growth, 1688–1959*, Cambridge University Press.

Deevey, E. S. (1960), 'The Human Population', *Scientific American*, September, pp. 195–204.

Denison, E. F. (1993), 'The Growth Accounting Tradition and Proximate Sources of Economic Growth', in Szirmai, et al.

Dickson, D., C. O Grada and S. Daultrey (1982), 'Hearth Tax, Household Size and Irish Population Change, 1672–1981', *Proceedings of the Royal Irish Academy*, vol. 82 C, No. 6, Dublin.

Eden, F. M. (1797), *The State of the Poor*, 3 vols., Davis, London.

Feinstein, C. H. (1972), *National Income, Expenditure and Output of the United Kingdom, 1855–1965*, Cambridge University Press.

Feinstein, C. H. (1998), 'Pessimism Perpetuated: Real Wages and the Standard of Living in Britain during and after the Industrial Revolution', *Journal of Economic History*, September, pp. 625–58.

Fitzmaurice, E. (1895), *The Life of Sir William Petty*, J. Murray, London.

Fogel, R. W. (1964), *Railroads and American Economic Growth*, Johns Hopkins, Baltimore.

Fogel, R. W. and S. L. Engerman (1974), *Time on the Cross: The Economics of American Negro Slavery*, Little Brown, London.

Gille, H. (1949), 'The Demographic History of the Northern European Countries in the Eighteenth Century', *Population Studies*, III: 1, June, pp. 3–65.

Glass, D. V. (1965), 'Two Papers on Gregory King', in Glass and Eversley, pp. 159–221.

Glass, D. V. (1966), *London Inhabitants Within the Walls 1695*, London Record Society, London.

Glass, D. V. and D. E. C. Eversley (eds) (1965), *Population in History: Essays in Historical Demography*, Arnold, London.

Glass, D. V. and E. Grebenik (1966), 'World Population, 1800–1950', in H. J. Habakkuk and M. Postan, *Cambridge Economic History of Europe*, vol. VI:1, Cambridge University Press.

Glass, D. V. and R. Revelle (1972), *Population and Social Change*, Arnold, London.

Graunt, J. (1662), *Natural and Political Observations Made Upon the Bills of Mortality* (reprinted in Laslett).

Halley, E. (1693), 'An Estimate of the Degrees of Mortality of Mankind, Drawn from Curious Tables of the Births and Funerals at the City of Breslaw; With an Attempt to Ascertain the Price of Annuities Upon Lives', *Philosophical Transactions of the Royal Society*, vol. XVII, No. 198, pp. 596–610.

Holmes, G. S. (1977), 'Gregory King and the Social Structure of Pre-Industrial England', *Transactions of the Royal Historical Society*, 5th series, vol. 27, pp. 41–68.

Hull, C. H. (ed) (1899), *The Economic Writings of Sir William Petty*, 2 vols, Cambridge University Press.

Hunter, M. C. W. (ed) (forthcoming) *Archives of the Scientific Revolution: the Formation and Exchange of Ideas in Seventeenth Century Europe*.

Keynes, G. (1971), *A Bibliography of Sir William Petty*, Oxford University Press.

King, G. (1696), *Natural and Political Observations and Conclusions Upon the State and Condition of England*, in G. E. Barnett (ed) *Two Tracts by Gregory King*, Johns Hopkins (1936).

King, G. (1697), *Natural and Political Observations and Conclusions upon the State and Condition of England* (replica of 1696 manuscript with additional columns containing detailed comments and queries of Robert Harley on pp. 1–26, and 29 made between 26 April and 11 May 1697 and King's replies. Original manuscript MS 1458 in National Library of Australia, purchased from Museum Bookshop of Leon Kashnor in London in 1950s, downloadable from microfilm G20783. Manuscript bears bookplate and coat of arms of Reginald Marriott of Parsons Green in the County of Middlesex).

King, G. (1695–70), *Manuscript Notebook*, in Laslett (1973).

Kreager, P. (1988), 'New Light on Graunt', *Population Studies*, pp. 129–40.

Lansdowne, 6th Marquess (1927), *The Petty Papers*, 2 vols. Constable, London.

Lansdowne, 6th Marquess (1937), *Glanerought and the Petty-Fitzmaurices*, Oxford University Press.

Laslett, P. (1969), 'John Locke, the Great Recoinage, and the Origins of the Board of Trade', in Yolton.

Laslett, P. (ed) (1973), *The Earliest Classics: John Graunt and Gregory King*, Gregg International, London.

Lenihan, P. (1997), 'War and Population, 1649–52', *Irish Economic and Social History*, XXIV, pp. 1–21.

Le Roy Ladurie, E. (1978), 'Les comptes fantastiques de Gregory King', *Le territoire de l'historien*, 2 vols, Gallimard, Paris.

Le Roy Ladurie, E. (1992), in Vauban.

Lindert, P. H. (1980), 'English Occupations, 1670–1811', *Journal of Economic History*, XL, 4, pp. 685–713.

Lindert, P. H. and J. G. Williamson (1982), 'Revising England's Social Tables, 1688–1812', *Explorations in Economic History*, 19, pp. 385–408.

McEvedy, C. and R. Jones (1978), *Atlas of World Population History*, Penguin, Middlesex.

Maddison, A. (1982), *Dynamic Forces in Capitalist Development*, Oxford University Press.

Maddison, A. (1983), 'A Comparison of Levels of GDP per Capita in Developed and Developing Countries, 1700–1980', *Journal of Economic History*, March, pp. 27–41.

Maddison, A. (1998a), *Chinese Economic Performance in the Long Run*, OECD Development Centre, Paris.

Maddison, A. (1999a), 'Poor until 1820', *Wall Street Journal*, 11 January, p. 8.

Maddison, A. and H. van der Meulen (1987), *Economic Growth in Northwestern Europe: The Last 400 Years*, Research Memorandum 214, Institute of Economic Research, University of Groningen.

Maddison, A. and H. van der Wee (eds) (1994), 'Economic Growth and Structural Change: Comparative Approaches over the Long Run', proceedings of the Eleventh International Economic History Congress, Milan, September.

Maddison, A. (2004), 'Quantifying and Interpreting World Economic Development Before and After Colin Clark', *Australian Economic History Review*, March , pp. 1–34.

Marczewski, J. (1961), 'Some Aspects of the Economic Growth of France, 1660–1958', *Economic Development and Cultural Change*, April.

Mathias, P. (1957), 'The Social Structure in the Eighteenth Century: A Calculation by Joseph Massie', *Economic History Review*, pp. 30–45.

Meade, J. R. and R. Stone (1941), 'The Construction of Tables on National Income, Expenditure, Savings and Investment', *Economic Journal*, vol. 51, pp. 216–33.

Mersenne, in Waard (1932–72).

Mingay, G. E. (1963), *English Landed Society in the Eighteenth Century*, Routledge, London.

Mulhall, M. G. (1880), *The Progress of the World*, Stanford, London.

Mulhall, M. G. (1881), *Balance Sheet of the World for 10 Years, 1870–1880*, Stanford, London.

Mulhall, M. G. (1884), *The Dictionary of Statistics*, 4th edn 1899, Routledge, London.

Mulhall, M. G. (1896), *Industries and Wealth of Nations*, Longmans, London.

Ohlin, G. (1955), *The Positive and Preventive Check: A Study of the Rate of Growth of Pre-Industrial Populations*, Harvard PhD thesis, reprinted by Arno Press, New York (1981).

Overton, M. (1996), *Agricultural Revolution in England: The Transformation of the Agrarian Economy, 1500–1850*, Cambridge University Press.

Pebrer, P. (1833), *Taxation, Revenue, Expenditure and Debt of the Whole British Empire*, Baldwin & Cradock, London.

Petty manuscripts, see British Library.

Petty, W. (1997), *The Collected Works of Sir William Petty*, 8 volumes, Routledge/Thoemes Press, London (includes Hull's (1899) collection of Petty's economic writings; E.G. Fitzmaurice's (1895) biography of Petty; Lansdowne's (1927 and 1928) collection of Petty papers and the Southwell–Petty correspondence; Larcom's (1851) edition of Petty's Irish Land Survey, and critical appraisals by T.W. Hutchinson and others).

Riccioli, G. B. (1672), *Geographiae et Hydrographiae Reformatae, Libri Duodecim*, Venice.

Richards, E. G. (1998), *Mapping Time*, Oxford University Press.

Roncaglia, A. (1985), *Petty: The Origins of Political Economy*, Cardiff University Press.

Saito, O. (1979), 'Who Worked When: Life Time Profiles of Labour Force Participation in Cardington and Corfe Castle in the Late Eighteenth and Mid-Nineteenth Centuries', *Local Population Studies*, pp. 14–29.

Scaliger, J. J. (1583), *De Emendatione Temporum*.

Schultz, T. W. (1961), 'Investment in Human Capital', *American Economic Review*, March.

Slack, P. (2004), 'Measuring the National Wealth in Seventeenth-Century England', *Economic History Review*, November, pp. 607–35.

Slicher van Bath, B. H. (1963), *The Agrarian History of Western Europe, AD 500–1850*, Arnold, London.

Snooks, G. D. (1990), 'Economic Growth during the Last Millennium: A Quantitative Perspective for the British Economy', *Working Papers in Economic History*, no. 140, pp. 44, ANU, Canberra.

Snooks, G. D. (1993), *Economics Without Time*, Macmillan, London.

Spooner, F. C. (1972), *The International Economy and Monetary Movements in France, 1493–1725*, Harvard University Press, Cambridge: Mass.

Stone, L. (1964), 'The Educational Revolution in England, 1560-1640', *Past and Present*, No. 28, pp. 41–80.

Stone, L. (1965), *The Crisis of the Aristocracy*, Oxford University Press.

Stone, R. (1997b), *Some British Empiricists in the Social Sciences, 1650–1900*, Cambridge University Press.

Studenski P. (1958), *The Income of Nations: Theory, Measurement and Analysis: Past and Present*, New York University Press.

Szirmai, A., B. van Ark and D. Pilat (eds) (1993), *Explaining Economic Growth: Essays in Honour of Angus Maddison*, North Holland, Amsterdam.

Tawney, A. J. and R. H. (1934), 'An Occupational Census of the Seventeenth Century', *Economic History Review*, October.

Taylor, G. R. (1964), 'American Economic Growth Before 1840: An Exploratory Essay', *Journal of Economic History*, December, pp. 427–44.

Thorold Rogers, J. E. (1866–1902), *A History of Agriculture and Prices in England*, 7 vols. Clarendon Press, Oxford.

Thorold Rogers, J. E (1884), *Six Centuries of Work and Wages*, Swan Sonnenschein, London.

UN (2001), *World Population Prospects: The 2000 Revision*, vol. 1, *Comprehensive Tables*, Population Division, Dept. of Economic and Social Affairs, New York (Annual estimates on CD ROM Disk 2, Extensive Set).

UN (2003), *World Population in 2300*, Draft Report of Working Group on Long-Range Population Projections, Population Division, Dept. of Economic and Social Affairs, New York (ESA/P/WP.187, 9 December).

Usher, J. (1650), *The Annals of the Old and New Testament*, Armagh.

Vauban, S. (1707), *La dîme royale* (1992 edn, with introduction by E. LeRoy Ladurie), Imprimerie Nationale, Paris.

Waard, C. de (ed) (1932–72), *Correspondance du père Marin Mersenne*, eleven volumes and index, Beauchesne (1932–6); Presses Universitaires de Paris (1946–56); CNRS (1959–72), Paris.

Waddell, D. (1958), 'Charles Davenant (1656–1714): A Biographical Sketch', *Economic History Review*, pp. 179–88.

Westergaard, H. (1932), *Contributions to the History of Statistics*, King, London (Kelley reprint, 1969).

Whitworth, C. (ed) (1771), *The Political and Commercial Works of Charles Davenant*, 5 vols, London.

White, E. N. (2001), 'France and the Failure to Modernise Macro-economic Institutions' in Bordo and Cortès-Conde.

Willcox, W. F. (1931), 'Increase in the Population of the Earth and of the Continents since 1650', in W. F. Willcox, (ed) *International Migrations*, vol. II, National Bureau of Economic Research, New York, pp. 33–82.

Wrigley, E. A. (1967), 'A Simple Model of London's Importance in Changing English Society and Economy, 1650–1750', *Past and Present*, July, pp. 44–70.

Wrigley, E. A. (1987), *People, Cities and Wealth*, Blackwell, Oxford.

Wrigley, E. A. (1988), *Continuity, Chance and Change*, Cambridge University Press.

Wrigley, E. A. and R. S. Schofield (1981), *The Population History of England, 1541–1871*, Arnold, London.

Wrigley, E. A., R. S. Davies, J. E. Oeppen, and R. S. Schofield (1997), *English Population History from Family Reconstitution, 1580–1837,* Cambridge University Press.

Yolton, J. W. (ed) (1969), *John Locke: Problems and Perspectives*, Cambridge University Press.

Young A. (1770), *A Six Month's Tour through the North of England*, 4 vols, Strahan & Nicoll, London.

Young A. (1794), *Travels During the Years 1787–9 with a View to Ascertaining the Cultivation, Wealth, Resources and National Prosperity of the Kingdom of France*, 2nd edn, Richardson, London.

6 Modern macro-measurement: How far have we come?

Macro-measurement started in the seventeenth century, but did not emerge as a basic analytical tool for policy analysts and economic historians until the 1940s. In the past 60 years there has been an explosion in the sophistication of policy analysis and the interpretation of history. The explosion started in 1940 with two seminal works: Keynes' *How to Pay for the War*, which demonstrated its usefulness as a tool of macroeconomic management, and Colin Clark's *Conditions of Economic Progress*, which demonstrated its value in interpreting economic history. Dissemination and development of techniques of macro-measurement was a major objective of the founding fathers of the International Association for Research in Income and Wealth (IARIW). The initiative came from Simon Kuznets (1901–85), the pioneer of quantitative economic history. Milton Gilbert (1909–79) and Richard Stone (1913–91) were strategic partners with enormous international leverage in creating and diffusing standard procedures for construction of comparable national accounts by official statistical offices.

This chapter surveys the extent to which macro-economic measurement has developed and its impact in assessing economic performance in three epochs:

1. Since the 1940s its main purpose has been to illuminate policy options to improve growth performance at the national level, to analyse inter-country divergence in real income levels and to help devise policies for catch-up. We now have official estimates of growth and levels for the vast bulk of the world economy from 1950 onwards. Macro-measurement contributed to much more articulate and successful macro-management. From 1950 to 2003, world per capita GDP rose 2.1 per cent a year, nearly twice as fast as the 1.1 per cent in 1900–50.

2. For the epoch of capitalist economic growth back to 1820, quantitative historians have made great progress in measuring growth performance and interpreting its causes. There is still a need to fill gaps and crosscheck existing estimates, but the broad contours of world development in this period are not under serious challenge.

3. Until recently, serious quantitative investigation of the merchant capitalist epoch, 1500–1820, was neglected for three reasons: (a) growth was much slower than in the last two centuries; (b) the evidence is weaker and there is greater reliance on clues and conjecture; (c) many (under the influence of Malthus) thought and think that it was a period of stagnation interrupted by catastrophe. Like Adam Smith, I take a much more positive view of what happened.

Finally, I give my interpretation of the nature of the transition from merchant capitalism to modern economic growth. The roots of modernity were not a sudden 'take-off', but a long apprenticeship. The divergence in income levels between the west and the rest of the world started well before 1820.

DEVELOPMENT OF MACRO-MEASUREMENT AS A TOOL OF ECONOMIC POLICY SINCE 1950

Standardized Estimates of GDP Growth

Standardized national accounts provide a coherent macro-economic framework covering the whole economy, which can be crosschecked in three ways. National income is by definition equal in each of the three approaches. On the demand side, it is the sum of final expenditures by consumers, investors, and government. From the income side, it is the total of wages, rents, and profits. From the production side, it is the sum of value-added in different sectors (agriculture, industry, and services) net of duplication. In all three dimensions these measures need to be adjusted to eliminate changes in the price level in the period they cover, so that they show changes in volume.

Milton Gilbert was responsible for the official US accounts during the war and from 1950 to 1961 was head of statistics and national accounts in OEEC. The Marshall Plan required criteria for aid allocation, and NATO needed them for its burden-sharing exercises. Gilbert met these requirements by pushing official statistical offices of the 16 OEEC member countries to adopt the standardized system of national accounts (SNA) designed by Richard Stone.

Stone set up a programme in Cambridge to train official European statisticians to implement the standardized system. A set of handbooks was prepared to explain the problems of adjusting national estimates to conform to the standardized system. A first comparative set of accounts for the 16 OEEC member countries for 1938 and 1947–52 was published in 1954, with extensive notes explaining the adjustments which had been made to achieve comparability.

In 1953, Stone became chairman of a United Nations commission which established a standardized system of accounts for worldwide application. The UN could not exert as much leverage on its member countries to conform as was possible in OEEC. The communist countries used the Soviet MPS (material product system) which took a narrower view of the scope of economic activity than the SNA. MPS excluded many service activities which were considered 'non-productive' (passenger transport, housing, health, education, entertainment, banking, insurance, personal services, government and party administration, and the military). MPS involved double counting (measuring gross output without deducting inter-sector transfers of inputs) and exaggerated economic growth. The price system and tax-structures were different from those in capitalist countries, and measurement conventions gave incentives to exaggerate quality change when new products were introduced. Abram Bergson (1914–2003) pioneered procedures for re-estimation of Soviet GDP on a basis corresponding approximately to western conceptions in coverage, inclusion of the ignored activities, elimination of double-counting, and repricing on an 'adjusted factor cost' basis with imputation for capital costs which were not considered in Soviet-style accounting. These corrective procedures were applied to Soviet statistics by a team of CIA Sovietologists in Washington. In New York, Thad Alton and his colleagues did the same for Bulgaria, Czechoslovakia, East Germany, Poland, Romania, and Yugoslavia. This work was financed for intelligence purposes, but was publicly available in annual reports to the US Congress (see Maddison 1998b).

In the 1990s most of the former communist countries adopted the standardized SNA system in principle, but implementation was complicated by the massive change in ownership, in the level and structure of prices, allocation of resources between consumption and investment, and statistical reporting procedures. It will take some years before these problems can be fully resolved.

Another area of weakness is the national accounts for African countries, where there was and still is a great shortage of skills and money for such work. The gap in estimates of GDP growth was filled in substantial degree by the OECD Development Centre which compiled annual estimates of real GDP growth 1950–90 for 51 African countries. The Centre benefited from the expertise of Derek Blades, who had been chief statistician in Malawi for eight years, and by David Roberts who had similar experience in Gambia.

A third problem in the assessment of GDP growth performance in the higher income countries derives from recent changes in measurement conventions from 1995 onwards, involving adoption of hedonic indexes to adjust for assumed changes in quality of product, use of chain indices, and treatment of computer software as investment.

Hedonic indices are perfectly respectable in small doses, but one can be skeptical about the widespread assumption that quality changes have been so large and monotonically positive. In the US, where the switch to hedonics was most significant, their net impact was to raise the measured rate of growth to a somewhat greater degree than in western Europe and Japan. US official estimates go back to 1929, and the changes in measurement technique had their biggest impact for 1929–50, raising the GDP growth rate for that period from 2.6 per cent a year to 3.5. There was no counterpart to this long retrospective readjustment in other countries, and I have continued to use the earlier US official measure for 1929–50, for reasons explained in Maddison (2001: 138), and Maddison 2003a: 79–80). More than 40 years ago, Milton Gilbert warned that such adjustments could open Pandora's box: 'In the end, they would make it impossible to construct measures of output and price changes that are useful to the study of economic growth' (Gilbert 1961: 287). The danger which arises from an overdose of hedonics is discussed in Appendix 3, this chapter.

Ed Denison (1915–92) opposed changes in national accounting which treat accretions of knowledge as investment. He considered this a *'misclassification'* which made *'growth analysis chaotic'* (see Denison 1989: 10). A major justification for his complaint was that his growth accounts included, 'human capital', i.e., increments in the quality of the labour force due to increases in the level of education. In fact, the only form of knowledge which is now treated as investment is computer software. It is odd to treat this rapidly depreciating knowledge as investment whilst ignoring the more durable influence of books and education.

Purchasing Power Converters for Crosscountry Comparison of GDP Levels

Once standardized accounts of real GDP growth were available, the next step in inter-country comparison of economic performance and multi-country aggregation was the development of purchasing power parity converters (PPPs) to measure real GDP levels, rather than relying on exchange rate comparison. Measures of economic growth over time must be corrected to exclude the impact of inter-temporal price change. The purpose of PPP conversion is precisely analogous: the elimination of inter-country differences in price level, so that differences in the volume of economic activity can be compared across countries. By merging time series for economic growth with the crosscountry estimates of GDP levels now available we can make a coherent set of space–time comparisons.

OEEC initiated official estimates of purchasing parity and inter-country differences in the level of GDP. The first study was co-authored by Milton Gilbert and Irving Kravis (1954) and a second, by Gilbert and Associates (1958). They estimated 1950 and 1955 PPPs in order to compare real expenditure levels in seven west European countries and the US. Irving Kravis, Alan Heston, and Robert Summers (1975, 1978, and 1982) followed this up with more ambitious studies in their International Comparison Project (ICP) at the University of Pennsylvania from 1968 onwards. They involved collection of carefully specified price information by statistical offices for more than 2,000 representative items of consumption, investment and government services.[1]

The OEEC studies were binary comparisons of differences in price levels between pairs of countries. The three options were: (i) a Paasche PPP, with 'own-country' quantity weights; (ii) a Laspeyres PPP with the quantity weights of the numeraire country—the United States; (iii) a compromise geometric (Fisher) average of the first two measures. The corresponding measures of real expenditure were: (i) Laspeyres comparisons of GDP levels based on the prices (unit values) of the numeraire country; (ii) Paasche level comparisons based on 'own-country' prices (unit values); (iii) a Fisher geometric average of the two measures. Binary comparisons, e.g., for Germany/US and UK/US, could then be linked with the US as the star country. Such star comparisons could provide a proxy Germany/UK comparison, but it would not be 'transitive' (i.e., the result would not be identical to that derived from a direct Germany/UK comparison). This was not a great drawback for OEEC countries where the inter-country deviation in performance levels was not too wide. But Kravis, Heston, and Summers were engaged in comparisons over a much wider range of countries. They therefore adopted the Geary–Khamis (G–K) method, invented by Roy Geary (1896–1983) and Salem Khamis (1919–2005), which multi-lateralized the results, provided transitivity and other desirable properties. They used it in conjunction with the commodity product dummy method (CPD), invented by Robert Summers, for filling holes in the basic dataset. Their masterpiece was their third study, the 1982 volume *World Product and Income*, which contained estimates for 34 countries (in Africa, the Americas, Asia, and Europe) in 1975 prices and international Geary–Khamis dollars. These countries accounted for 64 per cent of world GDP in 2001.

The UN Statistical Office extended the ICP work and had covered 84 countries by 1985. UNSO then dropped this endeavour, though some of the regional UN bodies continued with it. The OECD recommended its comparisons on a regular basis in 1982. Its latest work covered the 28 OECD countries (see OECD 2002) and 20 others in eastern Europe, the 15 successor states of the USSR, and Mongolia (see OECD 2000).

Since 1978, Alan Heston and Robert Summers have produced short cut estimates of PPPs and real income levels for countries for which full scale ICP type measures are not available. The latest version of their Penn World Tables (PWT 6.1, October 2002) can be found on their website.[2] As a result, we now have reasonably acceptable PPP adjusted measures available for over 99 per cent of world GDP.

There were three Eurostat estimates (for 1980, 1985, and 1993) of PPPs for 22 African countries, but the results were erratic, and I preferred to use the more comprehensive and plausible results of the Penn World Tables. Table 6.1 summarizes the nature of the PPP estimates I used to create my 1990 benchmark estimates of world GDP.

Table 6.2 shows the difference between PPP and exchange rate conversion for ten large economies (which comprised 65 per cent of world GDP in 2003). The exchange rate conversions on the right hand side show much lower levels for the poorer countries (China, India, Russia, and Brazil) and somewhat higher levels for the west European countries and Japan relative to the US than the PPP converters.

Table 6.1. Nature of PPP Converters for Estimating GDP Levels in 1990 (billion 1990 Geary–Khamis dollars and number of countries)

	Europe and W. Offshoots	Latin America	Asia	Africa	World
ICP	15,273 (28)	2,131 (18)	8,017 (24)	0 (0)	25,421 (70)
PWT	59 (3)	71 (14)	524 (16)	891 (51)	1,516 (84)
Proxies	16 (10)	38 (15)	87 (17)	14 (6)	155 (48)
Total	15,349 (41)	2,240 (47)	8,628 (57)	905 (57)	27,122 (202)

Source: Maddison (2003a: 230).

In the case of China the deviation was very large. The PPP was more than five times higher than the exchange rate in 1990. In India the ratio was more than three times higher, in Russia twice as high, and in Brazil more than 50 per cent higher. In Japan and the west European countries, the exchange rate overvalued purchasing power relative to the US dollar. In fact the big differential for poorer countries is a fairly systematic outcome in such comparisons. For the west European countries and Japan the differential is smaller and has varied above and below parity in the past two decades. The implausibility of exchange rate conversion is clear when we look at the results for 1950 where exchange rate conversion implies a per capita GDP of $85 in

Table 6.2. Comparative Ranking of 10 Large Countries, 1950 and 2001 (constant 1990 prices, using 1990 Geary–Khamis PPP converters and 1990 exchange rates)

	1950	2001	1950	2001
GDP	**$billion, with 1990 PPP conversion**		**$billion, with 1990 exchange rate**	
US	1,456	8,080	1,456	8,080
China	240	4,613	47	886
Japan	161	2,672	206	3,358
India	222	2,009	62	558
Germany	265	1,579	337	1,951
France	221	1,289	261	1,491
UK	348	1,228	363	1,253
Italy	165	1,103	191	1,272
Brazil	89	988	58	638
Russia	315	814	154	388
GDP per capita	**$, with 1990 PPP conversion**		**$, with 1990 exchange rate**	
USA	9,561	28,347	9,561	28,347
China	439	3,627	85	695
Japan	1,921	21,062	2,458	26,466
India	619	1,963	172	545
Germany	3,881	19,196	4,928	23,717
France	5,271	21,613	6,244	24,985
UK	6,939	20,554	7,266	20,985
Italy	3,502	19,076	4,046	21,996
Brazil	1,672	5,559	1,077	3,588
Russia	3,086	5,573	1,515	2,669

Source: Maddison (2005a: 7, updated).

China and $172 in India (both in 1990 prices). These levels are much too far below subsistence to be credible.

There was reluctance on the part of many poorer countries to accept PPP conversion, because they felt it might weaken their case for foreign aid or favourable loan programmes of the IDA type (the cheap loan window of the World Bank). In fact, the World Bank has provided substantial financial support for the ICP programme, but generally avoids explicit use of PPP converters in its analytical work and loan decisions.

In spite of the creeping acceptance of PPP adjusted estimates, there continues to be significant error in comparative economic analysis because of ignorance of the pitfalls of exchange rate conversion. This is true in journalism, in political discourse, and also amongst some economists. Newspapers frequently refer to Japan as the world's second largest economy, though its GDP is now less than half the Chinese, and some British politicians continue to believe that their economy is bigger than China's.[3] In this situation, it is highly desirable that statistical offices be more vigorous in explaining the merits of PPP adjustment and in pushing for re-invigoration of this work on a worldwide basis.

Reasons for Worldwide Adoption of Macro-Measurement since 1950

The main reason for the massive increase in coverage and quality of official national accounts from 1950 onwards was the realization of their usefulness as a tool of macro-economic policy. Denison, Gilbert, Kaldor, Kuznets, Ruggles, Stone, and others in the UK and US, knew from personal experience that such accounts were also an extremely important tool for resource mobilization in wartime.[4]

In the 1950s, Keynesian analysis had a powerful influence on economic policy in many western countries and its fundamental concern was with macro-economic magnitudes (Keynes was the godfather of the first British accounts created by his pupils, Meade and Stone). Harold Macmillan discovered national accounts in 1956, when he became chancellor of the Exchequer. He compared them to a railway timetable, without which you wouldn't know when the trains were running.

This new macro-economic perspective was very different from that of Hayek and Schumpeter. The latter considered 'total output a figment which, unlike the price level, would not as such exist at all, were there no statisticians to create it. We seem indeed to be faced by a meaningless heap—for most purposes, a highly inconvenient composite' (Schumpeter 1939: 484, 561).

The operational significance of national accounts became obvious in OEEC, when Milton Gilbert became responsible for economic policy analysis from 1955 to 1961, and greatly improved its quality. National accounts became the bedrock on which analysis of comparative growth performance was based. It provided a yardstick for assessing the success of policy which had never existed before. We served as the secretariat for a new Group of Economic Experts which included Otmar Emminger from the Bundesbank, Etienne Hirsch, head of the French Plan, Jan Tinbergen from the Netherlands, Arthur Burns, chairman of the US Council of Economic Advisors, and Robert Hall, chief advisor to the UK Treasury. In 1955, Hall described the significance of this work as follows:

These meetings are really something quite exceptional for economists and I should think are quite new in the history of the world, in the sense that economic experts, if they existed at all as Government advisers, were not generally very important people until Keynes's ideas had been commonly accepted in the West. So that there were not the people to meet as we do: now we have 7 or 8 or 9 people who are by and large the chief professional advisers of the main Western Governments all have more or less the same professional training in that they understand how to maintain the level of activity and what forces operate on it.'

(Cairncross 1991: 35)

QUANTIFYING AND INTERPRETING WORLD ECONOMIC GROWTH FROM 1820 ONWARDS

Simon Kuznets (1901–85) did more than anyone else to push back the quantitative time horizon beyond 1950 by promoting the development of historical evidence on economic growth and interpreting its driving forces. He revolutionized the analytical scope of economic history by giving it a quantitative underpinning.

In the 1930s and 1940s, he made a massive scholarly contribution to the macroeconomic history of the US (growth and structure of GDP, capital stock, employment, immigration, distribution of income, and foreign trade), and made the first official US national accounts. In the 1950s and 1960s he played a major role in encouraging construction of similar accounts for other countries. He did this in IARIW sessions, was a driving force in creating the Yale Growth Center, whose graduate students produced growth studies on Argentina, Egypt, Korea, Sri Lanka, Taiwan, and the USSR, and he chaired a Social Science Research Council Committee which provided financial support for construction of basic historical accounts for China, France, Germany, and Italy, and a subsequent project on factors influencing economic growth in France, Germany, Italy, Sweden, and the USSR. He synthesized the international evidence on economic growth in four volumes containing 43 interpretive essays published between 1953 and 1989.

Kuznets spent more than four decades as a university teacher. He convinced many of his distinguished students, and an international network of scholars, that comparative research in quantitative economic history was feasible, exciting, and important. His persuasive power and influence stemmed mainly from his professional integrity

Table 6.3. Coverage of the Maddison GDP Sample of Regional and World GDP

	1500	1700	1820	1870	1913	1950
Western Europe	61.6	74.2	84.5	98.7	99.6	99.9
Western offshoots	0.0	84.9	94.2	99.2	99.0	100.0
Eastern Europe and former USSR	0.0	0.0	10.4	76.2	79.2	99.8
Latin America	49.2	49.4	54.5	63.6	85.0	99.9
Asia	80.6	85.5	92.9	91.8	94.8	98.5
Africa	0.0	0.0	0.0	0.0	37.9	99.5
World	64.8	70.2	78.6	88.5	93.1	99.6

Source: Maddison (2003a: 226).

and depth of scholarship. He was free from partisanship, avoided polemical confrontations, was open to new ideas, and willing to comment sympathetically in detail on the work of others. His influence was reinforced by his style of analysis—use of ideas and concepts that could be clearly expressed in literary form, implementable with relatively simple statistical techniques.

His technique of exposition virtually never made use of algebra or regressions. His approach was basically inductive. He was a cautious 'interpreter' of economic growth, very sensitive to the quality of the quantitative evidence, and the multi-layered complexity of causality. He did not try to 'explain' performance with the exactitude to which econometricians and growth accountants often aspire. He stuck to respectable macro-economic measures, whose scope and significance were clear and well defined. His estimating procedures were fully and transparently described. He had no time for proxy measures, metaphors, stylized facts, leading sector analysis, or real wage indicators, and was sometimes overly fastidious. However, he was not averse to what Paul David (1967) called controlled conjectures.

Thanks to the work of Kuznets and his successors, we now have fairly comprehensive coverage for the whole of the capitalist epoch from 1820 onwards (see Table 6.3). There is still scope for improvement, but the evidence available on world economic performance in the capitalist epoch is incomparably richer than it was 60 years ago.[5]

Characteristics of the Capitalist Epoch back to 1820: What Have We Learned?

1. Kuznets' evidence was fairly Eurocentric. He was not able to measure world performance. We now have a much broader range of country evidence on growth and levels. Table 2.1a in Chapter 2 shows the long term divergence in income levels between the advanced capitalist group and the rest. Average per capita income of the west rose 20-fold between 1820 and 2003, and seven-fold in the rest. The spread between the two groups rose from 2.1:1 to 5.7:1. The inter-regional gap increased much more from 3:1 to 18:1. Nevertheless, the

western share of world GDP peaked in the 1950s and will fall considerably more if India and China maintain their high growth momentum.

2. The evidence now available suggests that the transition to accelerated growth started around 1820, not 1760 as Kuznets thought. The work of Crafts and others (1983 and 1992) on British performance in the eighteenth century helped demolish the old notion of a sudden take-off in the second half of that century. The important point about Britain's exceptionalism was not an industrial revolution, but a much longer process of ascension, with per capita growth much faster from 1500 than anywhere else in Europe, except the Netherlands (see www.ggdc.net/Maddison).

3. The acceleration in western Europe was synchronous, not staggered as Gerschenkron and Rostow believed. Hansen's (1974–6) work on Denmark showed evidence of substantial advance in the early nineteenth century; Tilly (1978) found the same for Prussia; Levy-Leboyer and Bourguignon (1985) and Toutain (1987) for France; Hjerppe and Associates (1987) for Finland; Krantz (1988) for Sweden; Grytten (2004) for Norway; Smits, Horlings and van Zanden (2000) for the Netherlands. Their research strongly suggests that the acceleration of economic growth was quite general in western Europe after the Napoleonic wars. It was slower in 1820–70 than it became in 1870–1913. Nevertheless the pace of advance in western Europe in 1820–70 was clearly much faster than in the eighteenth century and earlier.

4. Kuznets (1930) demolished the Kondratieff notion of long cycles and Kuznets (1940) found Schumpeter's cyclical schema unacceptable: 'The failure to follow articulate methods of time series analysis reduces the statistical methods to a mere recording of impressions of charts, impressions with which it is often difficult to agree' (p. 269). Technical progress did not come in big Schumpeterian waves, but was a smoother more diffused process: 'flowing in a continuous stream, a stream magnified in a constant proportion by the efforts of imitators' (p. 263). This way of thinking he transmitted to his students, Fogel (1964) and Schmookler (1966), who gave it fuller articulation.

5. Kuznets concentrated on performance in the capitalist epoch as a whole, but we now have enough evidence to discern five phases from 1820 to 2003 in which the momentum of growth and fashions in economic policy differed substantially. The years 1950–73 were a golden age of unparalleled prosperity. World GDP rose at an annual rate of 5 per cent, per capita GDP near 3 per cent and world trade almost 8 per cent a year. There was a significant degree of convergence in per capita income, with most regions growing faster than the US (the lead economy). After 1973, there was a marked slowdown, with substantial divergence between different regions, and performance in many of them below potential. Nevertheless, on a world basis, this latest phase was the second-best since 1820. It is clear that what Kuznets called 'modern economic growth', has been much faster in all its phases than in the preceding centuries. From the year

1500 to 1820, world per capita income rose 0.05 per cent a year. From 1820 to 2003 it averaged 1.25 per cent—25 times as fast.

6. It is important to distinguish between lead and follower countries to understand the dynamics of technological diffusion, and analyse processes of catch-up and falling behind. 'Lead' countries are those whose economies operate nearest to the technical frontier; 'follower' countries have a lower level of labour productivity (or GDP per capita). Since 1500 there have been four lead countries, northern Italy in the sixteenth century, the Netherlands from the sixteenth century until the Napoleonic wars, when the UK took over. The British lead lasted until around 1890, and the US has been the leader since then.

Quantifying the Causes of Growth

As evidence on comparative GDP growth has accumulated, it has become feasible to quantify the reasons for inter-temporal and interspatial variance in performance.

The first step in growth accounting was to measure labour input and productivity. Labour input has grown unevenly over time and between countries. It has been very different from the movement of population. Since 1820, labour input has increased less than population; and labour productivity a good deal faster than GDP per capita.

Early post-war analysts laid great stress on the role of capital in economic growth, though for lack of accurate information, some assumed that the capital–output ratio was stable, some used incremental investment–output ratios, wealth surveys, insurance valuations, company book-values, or stock exchange values as a proxy. A major breakthrough came when Goldsmith (1951) pioneered the 'perpetual inventory' method in which stock estimates were derived by cumulating historical series on past investment at constant prices, and deducting assets scrapped, written off or destroyed by war. In the course of the 1970s and 1980s, several OECD countries developed official stock estimates of this type, when they had accumulated a long enough run of investment data to permit their construction. These official estimates are similar conceptually but need adjustment because of different assumptions about asset lives. Academic researchers such as Feinstein and Pollard (1988) and Gallmann (1986 and 1987) have pushed these capital stock estimates much further back in time.

I made standardized estimates of fixed non-residential capital for France, Germany, Japan, the Netherlands, UK, and the USA in Maddison (1995c) broken down into structures and machinery. This is a very pertinent distinction, as the rate of growth of the latter component has been much faster than the former, and technical progress is probably more rapidly embodied in machinery than in structures.

Schultz (1961) regarded 'human capital' as a factor of production. The main component he had in mind was formal education, but improvements in skill through working with sophisticated equipment, and improvements in health were also relevant. The idea proved attractive and measures of joint factor productivity were

Table 6.4. Determinants of Growth: UK, USA, and Japan, 1820–2003

	UK	USA	Japan		UK	USA	Japan
	Gross Stock of Machinery and Equipment Per Capita (1990$)				**Gross Stock of Non-Residential Structures Per Capita (1990 $)**		
1820	92	87	n. a.		1,074	1,094	n. a.
1870	334	489	94a		2,509	3,686	593a
1913	878	2,749	329		3,215	14,696	852
1950	2,122	6,110	1,381		3,412	17,211	1,929
1973	6,203	10,762	6,431		9,585	24,366	12,778
2003	14,291	32,240	31,232		22,957	35,687	52,589
	Primary Energy Consumption Per Capita (tons of oil equiv.)				**Average Years of Education Per Person Employed***		
1820	0.61	2.49	0.20		2.00	1.75	1.50
1870	2.21	2.45	0.20		4.44	3.92	1.50
1913	3.24	4.47	0.42		8.82	7.86	5.36
1950	3.14	5.68	0.54		10.60	11.27	9.11
1973	3.93	8.19	2.98		11.66	14.58	12.09
2003	3.86	7.86	4.06		15.79	20.77	16.78
	Land Area Per Capita (hectares)				**Exports Per Capita (1990 $)**		
1820	1.48	48.1	1.23		53	25	0
1870	1.00	23.4	1.11		390	62	2
1913	0.69	9.6	0.74		862	197	33
1950	0.48	6.2	0.44		781	283	42
1973	0.43	4.4	0.35		1,684	824	875
2003	0.41	3.2	0.30		5,342	2,762	3,152
	Hours Worked Per Head of Population				**GDP Per Hour Worked (1990 $)**		
1820	1,153	968	1,598		1.49	1.30	0.42
1870	1,251	1,084	1,598		2.55	2.25	0.46
1913	1,181	1,036	1,290		4.31	5.12	1.08
1950	904	756	925		7.93	12.65	2.08
1973	750	704	988		15.97	23.72	11.57
2003	694	746	853		30.69	38.92	24.86

Notes: (a)1890; *equivalent years of primary education.

Sources: Maddison (1995: 252–5), amended and updated. See Statistical Appendix B. Energy Consumption as for Table 7.11 in Chapter 7.

soon constructed in which education was treated as part of factor input. In growth accounts, the normal procedure is to treat increases in education as an improvement in labour quality, rather than as an independent factor of production analogous with physical capital.[6]

Edward Denison (1962) created expanded growth accounts to explain twentieth century American economic performance. In 1967 he applied the technique to explain differences in growth rates and levels of achievement in eight west European countries and the USA for 1950–64. Denison and Chung (1976) incorporated Japan into the sample.

Tables 6.4 and 6.5 present accounts for the two successive lead countries, the UK and the USA, back to 1820, and Japan, the most successful catch-up country, for the whole period of its 'modern economic growth'. The accounts show:

Table 6.5. Capital/Output Ratios, Labour, and Total Factor Productivity: UK, USA, and Japan, 1820–2003

	UK	USA	Japan	UK	USA	Japan
	Capital–Output Ratio Machinery & Equipment/GDP			**Capital–Output Ratio Non-Residential Structures/GDP**		
1820	0.05	0.07	n.a.	0.63	0.87	n.a.
1870	0.11	0.20	0.10a	0.79	1.51	0.59a
1913	0.18	0.52	0.24	0.65	2.77	0.61
1950	0.31	0.64	0.72	0.49	1.80	1.00
1973	0.52	0.64	0.93	0.80	1.46	1.12
2003	0.67	1.11	1.47	1.08	1.23	2.48
	(Annual Average Compound Growth Rates)					
	Labour Productivity			**Total Factor Productivity**		
1820–70	1.10	1.10	0.18	0.15	−0.15	n.a.
1870–1913	1.22	1.93	2.00	0.31	0.36	−0.21b
1913–50	1.66	2.47	1.79	0.81	1.62	0.20
1950–73	3.09	2.77	7.75	1.48	1.75	5.12
1973–2003	2.20	1.66	2.58	0.91	0.65	0.63

Notes: (a) 1890; (b) 1890–1913.

Source: See Table 6.4, labour productivity is the rate of growth of GDP per hour worked.

1. A huge increase in the stock of physical capital, significant for non-residential structures, but sensational for machinery and equipment. The ratio of the latter to GDP rose 13-fold in the UK and 16-fold in the USA between 1820 and 2003, and 15-fold in Japan from 1890 to 2003. These increases were linked to the acceleration of technical progress, much of which had to be embodied in machinery.

2. The education level rose eight-fold in the UK and more than eleven-fold in the US and Japan. This increase in human capital, measured by years of formal educational experience of those in employment (weighted by the earnings differential associated with years of primary, secondary, and tertiary) was also linked to technical progress. The increasing complexity of production processes required better educated people to make it operational, and the involvement of educated people in R&D helped institutionalize the process of innovation.

3. International specialization increased very significantly. The ratio of exports to GDP rose from 3 to 25 per cent in the UK and from 2 to nearly 10 per cent in the US between 1820 and 2003. Japan was an almost completely closed economy until the 1850s; between 1870 and 2003 its export ratio rose from 0.2 to 15 per cent of GDP.

4. Natural resource scarcities were not a constraint; land area per capita fell 15-fold in the US, about four-fold in Japan and the UK.

5. A significant part of the augmented production potential was taken in the form of leisure. Labour input per head of population dropped by 47 per cent in Japan, 40 per cent in the UK and 23 per cent in the US between 1820 and 2003.

6. The increase in energy inputs was relatively modest in the US (which made lavish use of its timber resources in the nineteenth century). Its per capita energy consumption rose only three-fold from 1820 to 2003. The UK made extensive use of coal in the nineteenth century and its per capita consumption rose only six-fold from 1820 to 2003. In Japan, there was a 20-fold increase in the same period.

ECONOMIC PERFORMANCE IN THE MERCHANT CAPITALIST EPOCH: 1500–1820

Divergent Interpretations of Merchant Capitalist Epoch

There were already two very different views on growth performance at the end of the eighteenth century. Adam Smith (1776) took a mildly euphoric position and Malthus (1798) was deeply pessimistic.

Positive

Adam Smith (1776), argued that the discovery of the Americas and southern route to Asia opened up new and significant opportunities for economies of scale and specialization through international trade. Though these possibilities were not fully exploited because of mutually hostile trade restrictions, Smith was mildly euphoric about progress achieved. He did not quantify growth performance explicitly, but arrayed countries in descending level of achievement: the Netherlands, England, France, North American colonies, Spanish America, China, Bengal, and Africa. For him, policy and institutions were a major reason for this inter-country variance.

Negative

Thomas Malthus' (1798) growth schema had only two factors of production-natural resources and labour, with no allowance for technical progress, capital formation or gains from international specialization. He portrayed the general situation of humanity as one where population pressure put such strains on the ability of natural resources to produce subsistence that equilibrium was attained only by various catastrophes—wars, famine, and disease—which brought premature death on a large scale and which he described as 'positive' checks. The only policy measures he envisaged to check catastrophe were 'preventive' checks to lower the birth rate. His influence has been strong and persistent, largely because his forceful rhetoric and primitive argument appeal to simple minds.

The dichotomy between positive and negative views persists. Kuznets (1965), Landes (1969), Cipolla (1976), Jones (1981), Jan de Vries (1993 and 1994) and Maddison (2001) took a view similar to Smith's, but there has been a raft of latter-day pessimists.

LeRoy Ladurie, a French Malthusian (1966 and 1978), thought the French economy was stagnant from 1300 to 1720. 'Real wage' pundits are more pessimistic. Phelps Brown and Hopkins (1956) suggested that English living standards in 1820 were 44 per cent lower than in 1500. Wilhelm Abel (1978) thought such a drop was characteristic for the whole of western Europe. These judgements were endorsed by Bairoch, Braudel, Wrigley and Schofield, but later all three switched sides. A new wave of real wage pessimism was launched by Robert Allen (2001) and Jan Luiten van Zanden (1999 and 2002). Allen found negative per capita growth for 1500–1820, van Zanden less than half the growth I find (see Appendix 1, this chapter). The problem with these real wage measures is that they are not macro-economic. They cover only a small fraction of economic activity, and their representativity is almost never examined.

Most of the pessimistic literature is Eurocentric, but Susan Hanley (1997) and Kenneth Pomeranz (2000) claimed, respectively, that Japan and China had living standards equal to those in the UK early in the nineteenth century. They imply or suggest that there was no significant European ascension in 1500–1820.[7]

Nature of the Quantitative Evidence on Economic Performance, 1500–1820

In 1965, Kuznets advanced an influential conjecture about the rate of population and per capita GDP growth in western Europe from the end of the fifteenth to the second half of the eighteenth century. Judging from the demographic evidence then available (Carr-Saunders, 1936, and Urlanis, 1941), the work of Deane and Cole (1962) on British per capita income growth in the eighteenth century, and adjusting for the likelihood of better than average performance in the UK, he 'set the possible (and perhaps maximum) long-term growth in per capita product for 1500–1750 in developed countries of Western Europe at about 0.2 per cent per year' (Kuznets 1973: 139). He felt that a higher rate was unlikely and that a lower growth rate was plausible. Kuznets did not advance a conjecture about growth rates in the rest of the world, but he clearly thought that they were lower than in western Europe, and that their 1750 level was lower than that in Europe.

Table 6.6. Per Capita GDP Levels: 1500 and 1820 (in 1990 G–K $)

	1500	1820	growth rate
Dynamic Countries & Regions			
Belgium	875	1,319	0.13
France	727	1,135	0.14
Germany	688	1,077	0.14
Italy	1,100	1,117	0.00
Netherlands	761	1,838	0.28
Portugal	606	923	0.13
Spain	661	1,008	0.13
Ireland	526	877	0.16
Britain (excl. Ireland)	762	2,122	0.32
Other western Europe	650	1,051	0.15
All western Europe	**772**	**1,202**	**0.14**
Brazil	400	646	0.15
Mexico	425	759	0.18
Caribbean	400	635	0.14
Total Latin America	416	691	0.16
US and Canada	400	1,231	0.35
All Americas	**415**	**871**	**0.23**
Less Dynamic Countries & Regions			
China	600	600	0.00
India	550	533	−0.01
Japan	500	669	0.09
All Asia	**568**	**581**	**0.01**
Russian empire	**499**	**688**	**0.10**
Eastern Europe	**496**	**683**	**0.10**
Egypt	475	475	0.00
Other north Africa	430	430	0.00
Black Africa	405	415	0.01
All Africa	**414**	**420**	0.004
Australia and NZ	**400**	**490**	**0.06**
World	**566**	**667**	**0.05**

Source: www.ggdc.net/Maddison.

Maddison (2001) was a major effort to test the Kuznets' conjecture and muster quantitative evidence on world economic performance before 1820. The nature of the evidence is summarized below. The quantitative results are shown in Table 6.6:

1. *For western Europe* I encouraged other researchers to extend their time horizon backward by interactive networking of the type which proved so fruitful in building up evidence for 1820 onwards. Between 1985 and 1994, I organized six workshops on quantitative economic history (two at the University of Groningen, two at IARIW conferences, and two at sessions of the International Economic History Association).

   Most of the papers involved exploration of pre-modern growth in western Europe and the evidence was mainly from production and expenditure side. As shown in Table 6.6, per capita growth averaged 0.14 per cent a year between

1500 and 1820, significantly slower than Kuznets hypothesized (see Maddison 2001: appendix B for details of the estimation procedure and the conjectures used to fill gaps in the GDP database).

Thanks to the work of modern demographic historians, the quality and coverage of estimates of population levels and movement have been greatly improved, and also yield useful corroborative evidence on changes in urbanization and life expectation, where European exceptionalism is clear.

Jan de Vries (1984, 1993, 1994, 2000) made a major contribution to analysis of this period in three dimensions: the comparative study of European urbanization; the changing structure of European expenditure patterns; and the demonstration that in this period per capita labour inputs rose, and productivity grew more slowly than per capita income. He called this latter phenomenon an 'industrious' revolution, in contrast to the long-term trend to reduced working hours in the course of the nineteenth and twentieth centuries.

2. For the *US and Canada; Australia and New Zealand; Brazil and Mexico*, I adopted what Noel Butlin (1986) called a 'multicultural' estimate, making separate estimates for the indigenous population, slaves, and white settlers. For the first two groups I used a stylized per capita income for 1500 of $400 intended to represent an income at near-subsistence level.

3. For the *Caribbean*, with its highly specialized export economies, I based the estimates on commodity production and exports. For the Americas as a whole, per capita GDP growth was faster than in western Europe.

4. For *China, India, and Japan*, there is evidence on production, expenditure patterns, and demography. Japanese per capita performance was better than Chinese or Indian, but for Asia as a whole, income levels were stagnant. It is clear however, that China had 'extensive' growth in this period. It sustained a large increase in population, without a fall in living standards, and its GDP growth rate was the same as that of western Europe.

   China had a strong physiocratic bureaucracy which kept printed records on population and agricultural performance back to the ninth century. There is also an impressive amount of scholarly work which I used in Maddison (1998). This includes Needham (1954–97 and 1970) on the development of Chinese technology, Ho (1959) on Chinese demography, the interpretative analysis of Balazs (1931–3) and Elvin (1973) on the economic history of the Tang and Sung dynasties, and Perkins (1969) on agricultural development from 1368. Grain output rose about five-fold from 1400 to 1820—in line with population. The cultivated area rose three-fold and yields about 80 per cent. Ester Boserup (1965) demonstrated that this was achieved by increased labour inputs per capita, and more intensive use of land by double-cropping, improved seeds, fastidious collection and application of manure, and the introduction of new crops from the Americas. Rozman's (1973) analysis of the demographic records shows no significant change in the relative size of the urban population over this period. Earlier, it is clear that that China did experience a growth in per capita agricultural output and GDP in the Sung dynasty (960–1280).

India: Maddison (1971) contained an analysis of the social structure and institutions of the Moghul empire and the British raj. For the Moghul period, I relied heavily on the economic survey made by Abul Fazl for the emperor Akbar in the sixteenth century (see Jarrett and Sarkar 1949). Between 1600 and the 1860s, the quantitative evidence is not so good, but the two leading historians of Moghul India, Irfan Habib and Shireen Moosvi (at Aligarh Muslim University), adduce evidence which led them to conclude, I think rightly, that there was some decline in per capita income after the collapse of the Moghul empire and the takeover by the East India Company.

Japan modelled its economy, society, literature, and institutions on China from the seventh century. The official commitment to catch up with the west started in 1867, but the Chinese model was abandoned in the eighteenth century, at about the time Japan had caught up with China. In 1720 the shogun lifted the ban on European books, and translations of Dutch learning (*rangaku*) had a significant impact in transmitting knowledge of European science and technology (see Maddison 2001: 204–6 and 252–60, and Chapter 2, this volume). The cadastral surveys of Hideyoshi contain a useful quantification of Tokugawa agriculture at the end of the sixteenth century. The work of Akira Hayami and Osamu Saito contains invaluable evidence on the historical demography of Japan.

5. For *Africa* there was a sharp division north and south of the Sahara. Egypt was specially favoured because the Nile provided abundant irrigation and an easily navigable transport route. The Maghreb had a higher degree of urbanization and literacy, more sophisticated economic and political institutions, and a greater participation in international trade than black Africa. In spite of losses due to the slave trade, demographic expansion was faster in black Africa, because agriculturalists were replacing hunter-gatherers, and had new crops—maize and manioc—from the Americas.

Proximate Causes of Growth in the Merchant Capitalist Epoch

In analysing the causes of growth in the merchant capitalist period, it is not possible to present the same kind of growth accounts as in Tables 6.4 and 6.5. However, Boserup (1965) and de Vries (1994) have shown that labour input per head of population increased in this period, instead of declining, as it did later. We also know that there was a big increase in capital formation in shipping, an improvement in human capital and knowledge. It is clear that the process of globalization was very important.

International Trade

Dramatic progress in western shipping and navigation permitted a 20-fold increase in world trade between 1500 and 1820 (see Table 2.6 in Chapter 2). It brought gains from specialization of the type stressed by Adam Smith. It provided European consumers with new products—tea, coffee, cacao, sugar, potatoes, tobacco, porcelain, silk, and cotton textiles. In relative terms this globalization process was a more important component of growth in these centuries than in the twentieth. European countries were also able to extract a colonial surplus: the Spanish and Portuguese from the Americas in the sixteenth century, the Dutch in Asia from 1600, the British and French in the eighteenth century. Spanish plunder was mainly in the form of precious metals. These were very important in financing European trade with Asians, who were not very interested in buying European products. Most of the European trading nations profited from the enslavement of Africans.

Ecological, Technical, and Demographic Transformation of the Americas

Agricultural potential in the Americas was increased by introduction of wheat, rice, sugar, coffee, vines, olives, onions, cabbages, lettuce, oranges, bananas, yams, cattle, pigs, chickens, sheep, and goats. Traction and transport was improved by the introduction of horses, oxen, asses, and mules. Production potential was increased by the introduction of iron weapons, tools and ploughs, wheeled vehicles, ships and shipbuilding, printing, literacy, education, political and economic institutions. European mining technology led to production and export of 1,700 tons of gold and 73,000 tons of silver in 1500–1820 which financed European trade with Asia.

The introduction of European diseases had a major adverse effect. They killed off two-thirds of the indigenous inhabitants. The continent was repopulated by African slaves and European migrants attracted to a continent with much greater land resources per capita. In 1820, 37 per cent of the population of the Americas were indigenous or mestizo; 41 per cent were white, and 22 per cent black or mulatto.

Ecological Gains Emanating from the Americas

The transfer of American crops: maize, manioc, potatoes, sweet potatoes, beans, peanuts, tomatoes, pineapples, and cacao enhanced production potential in Europe, Africa, and Asia. The availability of these new crops was a major factor in helping sustain accelerated population growth in all three areas, and their impact was particularly large in China and Africa.

Intellectual and Institutional Changes underlying Western Ascension

Looking beyond the proximate and measurable elements of causality, we can discern four intellectual and institutional changes which were important in western economic ascension and which had no counterpart elsewhere.

Development of Secular Knowledge and Science

From about 1500 there is evidence of a new awareness of human capacity to transform the forces of nature through rational investigation and experiment. The first European university was created in Bologna in 1080. By 1500 there were 70 such centres of secular learning in western Europe (see Goodman and Russell 1991: 25). Until the mid-fifteenth century, most of the instruction was oral, and the learning process was similar to that in ancient Greece. Things changed after Gutenberg printed his first book in Mainz in 1455. By 1500, 220 printing presses were in operation throughout western Europe and had produced eight million books (see Eisenstein 1993: 13–17). The productivity of universities and their openness to new ideas was greatly enlarged.

Venetian publishers regularly had a print-run of 1,000 copies or more. By the middle of the sixteenth century, they had produced some 20,000 titles, including music scores, maps, books on medical matters, and a flood of new secular learning. Before printing, books were cherished for their artistic or iconic value, and their content mainly reflected the wisdom and dogma of the past. Printing made books much cheaper. Publishers were much more willing to risk dissemination of new ideas and to provide an outlet for new authors. The proportion of the population with access to books was greatly increased, and there was a much greater incentive to acquire literacy. With the exception of China, the European printing revolution had no counterpart in most other parts of the world until the beginning of the nineteenth century. The major difference between Europe and China was the competitive character of European publishing, and the international trade in books.

Fundamental changes in intellectual horizons occurred between the sixteenth and seventeenth centuries, when medieval notions of an earth-centred universe were abandoned. Thanks to the Renaissance, the seventeenth-century scientific revolution and the eighteenth-century enlightenment, western elites gradually abandoned superstition, magic, and submission to religious authority. The scientific approach gradually impregnated the educational system. Circumscribed horizons were abandoned. A Promethean quest for progress was unleashed. The impact of science was reinforced by the creation of scientific academies and observatories which inaugurated empirical research and experiment. Systematic recording of experimental results and their diffusion in written form were a key element in their success.

Emergence of an Urban Bourgeoisie and Protection of Property Rights

In the eleventh and twelfth centuries, important urban trading centres emerged in Flanders and northern Italy with autonomous property rights. This fostered entrepreneurship and abrogated feudal constraints on the purchase and sale of property. Development of accountancy helped make contracts enforceable. New financial institutions and instruments provided access to credit and insurance, facilitated risk assessment and large-scale business organization.

Changes in the Nature of the Family, Marriage, and Inheritance

Adoption of Christianity as a state religion in 380AD led to basic changes in nature of European marriage, inheritance, and kinship. The papacy imposed a pattern which was dramatically different from that prevailing earlier in Greece, Rome, and Egypt, and later in the Islamic world. Marriage was to be strictly monogamous, with a ban on concubinage, adoption, divorce, remarriage of widows or widowers, consanguineous marriage with siblings, ascendants, descendants, including first, second, and third cousins, or relatives of siblings by marriage. A papal decision in AD385 imposed priestly celibacy. The primary intention of the new regime was to channel assets to the church which became a property owner on a huge scale, but it had much wider ramifications. Inheritance limited to close family members and widespread adoption of primogeniture broke down loyalties to clan, tribe, or caste, promoted individualism and accumulation, and reinforced the sense of belonging to a nation-state (see Goody 1983; Lal 2001).

Emergence of a System of Nation-States

A fourth distinctive feature was the emergence of a system of nation-states in close propinquity, with significant trading relations and relatively easy intellectual interchange in spite of linguistic differences. This benign fragmentation stimulated competition and innovation. Migration to or refuge in a different culture and environment were options open to adventurous and innovative minds. Mercantilist commercial policies of the leading European countries were mutually discriminatory and restrictive, and often led to wars. However, the balance of advantage lay with Europe, if one compares their regime with that of the Ottoman, Moghul, or Chinese empires.

THE ROOTS OF MODERNITY: 'TAKEOFF' OR LONG APPRENTICESHIP

Having considered the quantitative evidence on macro-economic performance in the epochs of modern economic growth and merchant capitalism, and the differences in the driving forces which determined their growth momentum, it is useful to consider the nature of the transition between the two epochs. There is in fact a sharp divergence of views on the 'roots of modernity', which echoes the divergence already noted between the Smithian and Malthusian interpretations of what happened in the merchant capitalist epoch.

Sudden 'Takeoff'

There is a school of thought which attributes modern economic growth to an 'industrial revolution' in Manchester, preceded by centuries of Malthusian stagnation. The metaphor was first popularized by Arnold Toynbee in 1884, and has had continuing resonance, e.g., in Rostow's (1960) 'take-off', and Mokyr's (2002) history of technology: 'most techniques before 1800 emerged as a result of chance discoveries ... Before the industrial revolution the economy was subject to negative feed back the best known of these negative feedback mechanisms are Malthusian traps.' (pp. 31–32). Nordhaus (1997) and DeLong (1998), overdosing on hedonics, have constructed fairytale scenarios which greatly exaggerate progress since 1800, before which they seem to believe that people lived like cavemen (see Appendix 3, this chapter). These views are fundamentally flawed.

Or Long Apprenticeship?

In 1500, western Europe already had 70 universities. Education and diffusion of knowledge were revolutionized by printing.

By the end of the eighteenth century, great progress had been made in the design of ships and rigging, in gunnery, in meteorological and astronomical knowledge, and in the precision of navigational instruments. Mariners acquired logarithmic tables, sextants, naval almanacs, and accurate watches. Maps were enormously improved and supplemented by detailed coastal surveys, knowledge of winds and currents. Sailing had become safer, the duration of voyages more predictable, the incidence of shipwreck had fallen, disease mortality was greatly reduced on long voyages.

These changes were the result of scientific endeavour. In 1543 Copernicus rejected the notion that the earth was the centre of the universe. Kepler and Galileo made detailed observation of celestial bodies, the nature and mutability of their orbits. Newton in 1687 showed that the whole universe was subject to the laws of motion and gravitation. Progress in astronomy and physics was accompanied by major advances in mathematics and design of telescopes, microscopes, micrometers, thermometers, barometers, air pumps, clocks and watches, and the steam engine.

These developments in Europe were an essential prelude to the much faster economic development that occurred in the nineteenth and twentieth centuries. They had no counterpart elsewhere.

☐ APPENDICES

Appendix 1: Real Wage Revivalists—Robert Allen and Jan Luiten van Zanden

In an extensive review of Maddison (2001), Giovanni Federico (2002) suggested that I may have exaggerated west European performance in the merchant capitalist epoch, citing alternative estimates of Robert Allen which imply that aggregate west European per capita income actually fell in this period, and those of Jan Luiten van Zanden which imply a growth rate of only 0.06 per cent a year. I do not regard their gloomier conclusions as an effective challenge to my estimates for the reasons explained below.

Allen (2001) presented real wage estimates for Europe, 1500–1913. He showed nominal wages (in grams of silver per day) for building craftsmen and labourers in 18 European towns, and consumer price indices based on 12 items, two-thirds of which were bread, beer, and meat. The results were presented for 50-year time segments. His basic data were for daily wages, which he converted to an annual basis by assuming a working year of 250 days (this multiplier was apparently applied uniformly to his inter-temporal and cross-country data). For the 14 towns where he had results for craftsmen for both 1500–49 and 1750–99, the average real wage in the latter period was 66 per cent of that in 1500–49, London was the only case where the real wage was higher, with a rise of less than 1 per cent. In the 12 towns for which he had results for building labourers for the two periods, there was a rise of about 3 per cent in Amsterdam and a fall everywhere else. The average real wage for labourers was 76 per cent of the 1500–49 level in the end period (p. 428). This is less gloomy than Phelps Brown, but the clear implication is that living standards in western Europe declined substantially from 1500 to 1800. Allen (2000) was 'an exercise in historical reconstruction based on simple economic theory' which presented estimates of the movement in agricultural output per capita for nine countries for 1500–1800. He shows a fall in all nine countries between these two points of time, and in most cases they are very substantial. For England, he shows a 32 per cent drop (see p. 19). This is very different from Wrigley's estimate that English agricultural output per

Table 6.7. Confrontation of Maddison and van Zanden Per Capita GDP Estimates for Five European Countries, 1500–1820

	Maddison		Van Zanden	
	1500	*1820*	*1500*	*1820*
Belgium	875	1,319	989	1,319
Italy	1,100	1,117	1,353	1,117
Netherlands	761	1,838	1,252	1,838
UK	714	1,706	792	1,706
Spain	661	1,008	946	1,008
Average	882	1,345	1,116	1,345

Notes and Sources: Cols. 1, 2, and 4 from Maddison (2003a: 262). Col. 3 derived from growth rates implicit in the index numbers of Van Zanden (2002: 76). Van Zanden presented his estimates as ratios to the UK per capita GDP level in 1820 as estimated by Maddison. For Spain I assumed van Zanden's 1580–1820 growth rate also applied for 1500–1820. The bottom row is a weighted average for the five countries. For 1500–1820, my average grew by 0.132 per cent per annum, van Zanden's by 0.058 per cent.

capita doubled in the shorter period 1600–1800. It also differs substantially from the estimates presented by van Zanden and Horlings (1999: 28). Allen does not measure agricultural output directly. He derives it econometrically from his estimates of occupational structure and the assumption that his real wage measures are a valid proxy for total output per capita.

Van Zanden (2002) presents estimates of real GDP for five countries which imply that, from 1500 to 1820, average west European per capita income grew less than half as fast as I estimated in Maddison (2003a). Table 6.7 compares his estimates with mine.

For the UK, he shows slightly slower growth, because he uses a different source for agriculture. We both agree that growth was most rapid in the UK, and I see no reason to modify my estimate. For the Netherlands, our estimates are quite similar for 1570 onwards. The main difference is that he assumes Dutch per capita income have been stagnant from 1500 to 1570, whereas I assume a substantial increase. Between 1470 and 1570 the Dutch merchant fleet increased nearly four-fold—a growth rate of 1.4 per cent a year (see Maddison 2001: 77), and urbanization was increasing substantially.

Van Zanden agrees with me that Dutch per capita income in 1500 was lower than in what is now Belgium. Nevertheless his estimates show the opposite situation in 1500. To mitigate this he adjusted the Blomme-van der Wee (1994) growth rate for Belgium downward, whereas I accepted it. Van Zanden and I agree that Italy was the highest income country in 1500, but he assumes an 18 fall in per capita GDP from 1500 to 1820, whereas I assumed stagnation. He quotes Malanima's (1994) estimate for northern Italy as his source. In fact, Malanima (1994 and 1995) suggested a fall of 7 per cent, but van Zanden's estimate is near that of Malanima (2003), and shows a fall of about a fifth. The evidence for Italy as a whole is not very good and there are two schools of thought on performance in this period. Malanima's judgement resembles that of Cipolla (1976), whereas Rapp (1976) and Sella (1979) argued that per capita income was stagnant from 1500 to 1820. I lean towards their judgement, but as the urbanization rate was slightly higher in 1800 than in 1500, I assumed a very slight rise. For Spain, van Zanden shows a growth rate of 0.02 per cent a year for 1570–1820, which he derives by modifying the estimate of Yun (1994) for Castile, 1580–1800. In fact, Yun's estimate (p. 105) shows growth twice as fast as this. In Maddison (2001, p. 249), I explained my reasons for modifying Yun's estimate, which omits the years 1500–80 when Spain's economy received a major boost from the conquest of the Americas.

Van Zanden (1999) presented real wage estimates for unskilled building labourers in 14 European cities/regions, using cereal prices (rye or wheat) as a deflator. He shows a fall in all the ten cases where he had estimates for 1500–20 and 1780–1800, the average for the latter period was 60 per cent of that in 1500–20, an annual average change of −0.17 per cent a year. This is more pessimistic than the Allen (2001) results for labourers, but is similar to the findings of Phelps Brown and Hopkins (1956: 29–30) for English building craftsmen for the same period. Van Zanden feels that real wage estimates are 'an important source of information on living standards' (p. 178), even though they are in sharp conflict with a large body of other evidence. He suggests that a reconciliation may be possible. His estimates are for daily wages, and he suggests that there may have been a substantial increase in average annual working time of labourers over the period covered and that their family income may have been supplemented by increased labour force activity of women and children. It seems likely that there were changes in this direction as indicated in de Vries (1993), but van Zanden does not attempt to quantify them, and it is highly doubtful that their effect would be big enough to achieve a reconciliation. Van Zanden's desire for reconciliation may have introduced a downward bias in his (2002) estimates of real per capita GDP for 1500–1820.

The founder of real wage analysis, Thorold Rogers (1823–90), was professor of economics in Oxford and a liberal member of parliament who argued that the condition of English wage earners could be improved by extending the franchise and encouraging trade union activity. For him, low wages were the result of exploitation of the labourer by the ruling elite. He made a sharp distinction between wage income and national income, as is clear from his citation of Gregory King's estimates of inequality in 1688 (Rogers 1884: 463–5). He summarized his position, saying (p. 355): 'society may make noticeable progress in wealth, and wages remain low...relatively speaking, the working man of today is not so well off as he was in the fifteenth century'.

Some of the real wage revivalists have forgotten this and use real wages for a small group of workers as a proxy for GDP per head, without considering their representativity in macroeconomic analysis. Lindert and Williamson (1982: 393) show that only 5.3 per cent of families derived their livelihood from the building trades in 1688.

In the Phelps Brown-Hopkins study, whose sources were meticulously documented, there were about three wage quotations a year for building labourers, and for 1500 to 1800 there were 82 years without an estimate. The real wage enthusiasts do not discuss changes in the nature of building work. Over such a long period there were big changes for those whose wages are recorded, with a shift from decorative ecclesiastical stonework to bricklaying.

Appendix 2: Joel Mokyr and the 'Industrial Revolution'

The most recent and distinguished devotee of the 'industrial revolution' metaphor is Joel Mokyr (2002) who considers that modern economic growth derived from a sudden leap in industrial technology. He provides a detailed, erudite, illuminating but complex history of the interaction of 'propositional' and 'prescriptive' (useful) knowledge since the mid-eighteenth century, with a more cursory acknowledgement of what happened earlier. He suggests (pp. 31–2) that 'most techniques before 1800 emerged as a result of chance discoveries, trial and error'. He makes a grudging acknowledgement of the importance of printing (p. 8), and only a fleeting reference to advances in shipping and navigation technology but is dismissive about their impact:

those earlier mini-industrial revolutions had always petered out before their effects could launch the economies into sustainable growth. Before the Industrial Revolution, the economy was subject to negative feedback; each episode of growth ran into some obstruction or resistance that put an end to it . . . The best known of these negative feedback mechanisms are Malthusian traps, in which rising income creates population growth and pressure on fixed natural resources (p. 31).

He is very insistent on the narrowness of the 'epistemic base' before 1800, and argues that positive feedbacks between the two types of knowledge have increased hugely in the course of three 'industrial revolutions' since the eighteenth century. There has been a cascading interaction (p. 100) and we have now arrived at a point where modern information technology has produced 'an immensely powerful positive feedback effect from prescriptive to propositional knowledge' (p. 115). His analysis of the economic impact of this new knowledge is based on assertions rather than quantitative evidence. They are presented with characteristic fervour, e.g., his assessment of the impact of his second 'industrial revolution': 'The pivotal breakthrough in the propositional knowledge set was the identification of the structure of the benzene molecule by the German chemist August von Kekulé in 1865...the discovery of the chemical structure is a paradigmatic example of a broadening of the epistemic base of an existing technique' (p. 85). My problem with Mokyr's analysis is with his judgement on the impact of science and not with his model which can be useful in explaining why the scientific revolution of the seventeenth century had a delayed payoff, and why the innovative impact of science and technology accelerated in the past two centuries. The problem is that he assumes no net improvement in living standards before 1800, and a constantly accelerating cornucopia since then. This contradicts the quantitative findings of historical national accounts in the Kuznetsian tradition for the period before and after 1800. Mokyr is of course aware of this. In his defence (pp. 116–17) he suggests that 'aggregate output figures and their analysis in terms of productivity growth may be of limited use in understanding economic growth over long periods. The full economic impact of some of the most significant inventions over the past two centuries would be entirely missed in that way'. Instead he opts for the Silicon-valley serendipity of DeLong (see Appendix 3, this chapter).

Appendix 3: Hallucigenic History (Nordhaus and DeLong)

Nordhaus (1997) was an ambitious attempt to measure long term changes in the price of light using the hedonic approach. He estimated that the 'true', i.e., hedonic price of artificial light *fell* by 4.2 per cent a year (about 3,450-fold) between 1800 and 1992 in the US, whereas the annual *rise*, using the conventional consumer price approach, was 1.2 per cent a year. He neglects the fact that the supply of daylight did not change between 1800 and 1992. If we take this into account, the impact of artificial light would seem a good deal more modest than he claims. At the beginning of his analysis, he says that 'unobstructed daylight provides about 10,000 lux, while the level of illuminance of an ordinary home is about one hundred lux. In the candle age, a room lit by two candles would enjoy about 5 lux' (p. 31). Thus there was a 20-fold increase in artificial light per house, but total daylight appears to have been augmented only 1 per cent since 1800! The main impact of artificial light was to augment moonlight, brighten up the evenings, and lengthen the time that could be spent working or reading. The invention of spectacles was obviously very important in the latter respect, but is not mentioned by Nordhaus.

He illustrates the implications of his approach in measuring real wages. The conventional measure showed a 13-fold increase between 1800 and 1992. The 'true' rise, he suggests, was between 40- and 190-fold. He derived this result by converting conventional price indices into hedonics for three economic sectors. For 'run-of-the-mill' activities, where the characteristics of goods and services have changed relatively little, he adjusted conventional price indices downward to eliminate 'bias'-assumed to be 0.5 per cent a year. For 'seismic' sectors where the goods and services of 1800 have changed, but are still recognizable, conventional price indices received a downward adjustment equal to half of his measure of bias for light. For 'tectonic' sectors, where the nature of the good or service has changed drastically, or did not exist in 1800, he applied his bias adjustment for light. He assumed that 75 per cent of goods and services were in the first category in 1800, and that this proportion fell to 28 per cent in 1992, when 36 per cent were seismic and 37 per cent tectonic. I estimate that US per capita GDP rose 21-fold from $1,087 in 1800 to $23,169 in 1992. An increase of 190-fold would mean an 1800 level of $122 which would be well below subsistence.

Taking his cue from Nordhaus, DeLong (1998) rather cavalierly suggested that my estimate of the rise in world GDP per capita involved massive understatement because of uncaptured quality improvements (which he does not specify). To correct the alleged mismeasurement he assigned 'somewhat arbitrarily… an additional fourfold multiplication to output per capita since 1800'. He shows a 35-fold increase in world GDP per capita from 1800 to 2000, against my nine-fold increase.

⬜ ENDNOTES

1. OEEC experimented with an alternative technique, measuring comparative performance levels from the production side (see Paige and Bombach 1959). This approach is particularly useful in comparisons of productivity. It has been neglected by international agencies, but I made and promoted estimates of this kind for a large number of countries. Maddison (1970) was a comparative survey of growth experience in the six biggest OECD countries, the USSR, and 22 developing countries for 1870–1968 representing about 75 per cent of world GDP. The biggest statistical challenge was the absence of comparative measures of GDP levels at that time. I constructed benchmark estimates for 1965, measuring real value added by sector at US prices. Output of farm, fishery, and forestry products was derived from detailed FAO data, with deduction of feed, seed, and non-farm inputs. For mining, manufacturing, and utilities, I used Shinohara (1966). He had a sample of 70 commodities, weighted by value-added derived from the US Census of Manufactures. For services, direct measurement was not possible, so I used estimates of employment and a conjectural level of labour productivity, assumed to be related systematically to that in the commodity sector (i.e., agriculture plus industry). In Maddison (1998a), I used the industry of origin approach to make a much more elaborate comparison of the Chinese GDP level in 1990 compared with that of the USA. Maddison (1983) was a confrontation of the Maddison (1970) results, by the product method, with the expenditure estimates of Kravis, Heston and Summers (1982). For the advanced countries, my results were on average about 4 per cent lower. For developing countries the divergence was much bigger. The expenditure approach yielded per capita GDPs averaging 16.7 per cent of the USA, the product method 11.3 per cent. The difference arose primarily from the treatment of comparison-resistant services. For teachers and civil servants, they assumed average labour productivity in developing countries to be about the same as in the USA, whereas my average was one-third of the US level. When I returned to academic life, I set up the ICOP programme (International Comparisons of Output and Productivity) at the University of Groningen in 1983. It has since produced more than 80 research papers, a dozen PhD theses, and established a worldwide network of researchers in this field. The overall results of the ICOP project are surveyed in Maddison and van Ark (2002). The only whole-economy results as yet available on an ICOP basis are for Brazil, Mexico, Korea, Japan, and the USA for 1975. The average per capita GDP for these four countries relative to the USA was 34.8 per cent with the ICOP approach against 36.9 for the ICP, a much smaller discrepancy than I found in my 1983 confrontation. However, confrontation/reconciliation of the two methods needs to be done more rigorously and for a larger number of countries.

2. See http://www.pwt.econ.upenn.edu/

3. Christopher Patten, the last British governor of Hong Kong, stated in an article in *The Economist* newspaper of 4 January 1997 that, 'Britain's GDP today is almost twice the size of China's'. If he had been briefed on PPP converters, he might have said that Britain's GDP was one-third the size of the Chinese.

4. Kaldor (1946) concluded that 'Germany made no serious attempt to exploit her own war potential fully, except for a brief period in August and September 1944, when it was too late to be of any consequence'. Galbraith (1971) made the same point. Kaldor's analysis was drawn from material gathered as a staff member of the US Strategic Bombing Survey (1945), and interrogation of Karl Otto Saur, Albert Speer's deputy in the Armaments Ministry. The survey team was directed by Galbraith, and included Paul Baran, Ed Denison, Burton Klein, and Tibor Scitovsky (under the nom de guerre 'Thomas Dennis'). Kaldor and Scitovsky interrogated Saur in Austria, the day the war ended (see Scitovsky 1999). He indicated where they could find the war-time production records, and they whisked them away just before the Russians arrived. Denison and Haraldson made a detailed estimate of German GNP, 1936–44, to put military mobilization in perspective. Richard Ruggles served with the US Office of Strategic Services in London, inferred German production of tanks, trucks, and planes by decoding information on serial numbers of captured equipment (see Tobin 2001). Stone worked with British intelligence and predicted the date of Italian entry in the war, by tracking movement of ships in the Mediterranean. Kuznets used national accounting to help organize the massive expansion of US military output in the Planning Committee of the War Production Board (see Kapuria-Foreman and Perlman 1995), with help from Moe Abramovitz. The moral of this digression is that the initial stage in construction of national and historical accounts is not a boring bureaucratic business. It requires detective work and imagination, and can be as exciting as the adventures of Sherlock Holmes.

5. Colin Clark (1940) had estimates (some of them very rough) of GDP growth for 16 countries, with an average coverage of 19 years for the period since 1820. We now have historical accounts for a much wider range of countries and for these 16 countries we have better quality accounts for an average of 151 years. At that time there were only ten countries with some kind of official national accounts. In 2001 there were 179 countries producing official estimates, using standardized SNA guidelines.

6. Estimation of the stock of human capital is analogous to the procedure for physical capital. A useful starting point is scrutiny of successive population censuses where respondents report the age at which their formal education ended (see estimates for 19 countries by gender and age cohort in OECD 1975: vol. 1, pp. 31–108). These can be updated by annual cumulation of increments to the stock (see annual school enrolment in OECD, *Education at a Glance*, and its predecessor volumes), and deduction for people who retire from the labour force. The value of the stock can be derived from estimates of earnings of people with primary, secondary, and higher education (see Psacharopoulos 1975). This is the procedure I used in growth accounts for advanced OECD countries (see Maddison 1987) and for 22 developing counties (Maddison 1970: 45–50).

7. Kenneth Pomeranz (2000) asserted that China was ahead of Europe until 1800. He suggests that western Europe was 'a non-too-unusual economy: it became a fortunate freak only when unexpected and significant discontinuities in the late eighteenth and especially nineteenth centuries enabled it to break through the fundamental constraints of energy and resource availability that had previously limited everyone's horizons'. I explained my disagreement at length in Maddison (2003: 248–51). Hanley had a similar view about Japan, see my comment in Maddison (1999).

☐ REFERENCES

Abel, W. (1978), *Agrarkrisen und Agrarkonjunktur*, Parey, Hamburg.

Abrams, P. and E. A. Wrigley (eds) (1978), *Towns in Societies: Essays in Economic History and Historical Sociology*, Cambridge University Press.

Abramovitz, M. (1956), 'Resource and Output Trends in the United States since 1870', *American Economic Review*, May, pp. 5–23.

Abramovitz, M. (1986), 'Simon Kuznets, 1901–1985', *Journal of Economic History*, March, pp. 241–6.

Abramovitz, M. (1989), *Thinking About Growth*, Cambridge University Press.

Abramovitz, M. (2000), 'Days Gone by: a Memoir for my Family', Stanford University Press.

Abu-Lughod, J. L. (1989), *Before European Hegemony: The World System,* AD*1250–1350*, Oxford University Press, New York.

Aldcroft, D. H. and A. Sutcliffe (eds) (1999), *Europe in the International Economy, 1500–2000*, Elgar, Cheltenham.

Allen, R. C. (2000), 'Economic Structure and Agricultural Productivity in Europe, 1300–1800', *European Review of Economic History*, 3, pp. 1–26.

Allen, R. C. (2001), 'The Great Divergence in European Wages and Prices from the Middle Ages to the First World War', *Explorations in Economic History*, 38, pp. 411–47.

Allen, R. C, T. Bengtsson and T. Dribe (2005) (eds) *Living Standards in the Past*, Oxford University Press.

Balazs, S. (1931–33), 'Beiträge zur Wirtschaftsgeschichte der T'ang-Zeit (618–906)', *Mitteilungen des Seminars für Orientalische Sprachen*, pp. 34, 35, 36.

Beckerman, W. (1966), *International Comparison of Real Incomes*, OECD, Paris.

Blomme, J. and H. van der Wee (1994), 'The Belgian Economy in a Long-Term Historical Perspective: Economic Development in Flanders and Brabant, 1500–1812', in Maddison and van der Wee.

Boomgaard, P. (1993), 'Economic Growth in Indonesia, 500–1990', in Szirmai et al.

Booth, A. W. J. O'Malley and A. Weideman (eds) (1990) *Indonesian Economic History in the Dutch Colonial Era*, Yale University Southeast Asia Studies.

Boserup, E. (1965), *The Conditions of Agricultural Growth*, Allen & Unwin, London.

Boserup, E. (1981), *Population and Technology*, Blackwell, Oxford.

Braudel, F. (1985), *Civilisation and Capitalism, 15th–18th Century*, vol. 3, Fontana, London.

Braudel, F. P. and F. Spooner (1967), 'Prices in Europe from 1450 to 1750' in Rich and Wilson.

Brewer, J. and R. Porter (eds) (1993), Consumption and the World of Goods, Routledge, London.

Butlin, N. G. (1983), *Our Original Aggression*, Allen & Unwin, Sydney.

Butlin, N. G. (1993), *The Economics of the Dreamtime: A Hypothetical History*, Cambridge University Press.

Cairncross, A. (ed) (1991), *The Robert Hall Diaries, 1954–61*, Unwin Hyman, London.

Carr-Saunders, A. M. (1936), *World Population, Past Growth and Present Trends*, Oxford University Press.

Cipolla, C. M. (1974), *The Economic History of World Population*, Penguin, London.

Cipolla, C. M. (1976), *Before the Industrial Revolution: European Society and Economy, 1000–1700*, Norton, New York.

Clark, C. (1940), *The Conditions of Economic Progress*, 1st edn, Macmillan, London.

Clark, G. (2005) 'The Condition of the Working Class in England, 1209–2004', *Journal of Political Economy*, vol. 113, no. 61, pp. 1307–40.

Cole, A. H. and R. Crandall (1964), 'The International Scientific Committee on Price History', *Journal of Economic History*, September, pp. 381–8.

Crafts, N. F. R. (1983), 'British Economic Growth, 1700–1831: A Review of the Evidence', *Economic History Review*, May, pp. 177–99.

Crafts N. F. R. and C. K. Harley (1992), 'Output Growth and the British Industrial Revolution: A Restatement of the Crafts–Harley View', *Economic History Review*, November, pp. 703–30.

Crosby, A. W. (1972), *The Columbian Exchange: Biological and Cultural Consequences of 1492*, Greenwood Press, Westport.

David, P. (1967), 'The Growth of Real Product in the United states Before 1840: New Evidence, Controlled Conjectures', *Journal of Economic History*, June.

Deane, P. and W. A. Cole (1962), *British Economic Growth, 1688–1959*, Cambridge University Press.

Delbeke, J. and H. van der Wee (1983), 'Quantitative Research in Economic History in Europe after 1945', in Fremdling and O' Brien.

DeLong, J. B. (1998), 'Estimating World GDP, One Million BC-Present', http://www.j-bradford-delong.net

DeLong, J. B. (2000), 'Cornucopia: Increasing Wealth in the Twentieth Century', http://www. j-bradford-delong.net

Denevan, W. M. (ed.) (1976), *The Native Population of the Americas in 1492*, University of Wisconsin.

Denison, E. F. (1947), 'Report on Tripartite Discussions of National Income Measurement', *Studies in Income and Wealth*, Vol.10, NBER, New York.

Denison, E. F. (1962), *The Sources of Economic Growth in the United States*, Supplementary Paper No. 13, Committee for Economic Development, Washington, DC.

Denison, E. F. (1967), *Why Growth Rates Differ*, Brookings, Washington, DC.

Denison, E. F. (1969), 'Some Major Issues in Productivity Analysis: An Examination of Estimates by Jorgenson and Griliches', *Survey of Current Business*, May, pp. 1–27.

Denison, E. F. (1989), *Estimates of Productivity Change by Industry*, Brookings, Washington, DC.

Denison, E. F. (1993), 'The Growth Accounting Tradition and Proximate Sources of Growth', in Szirmai, van Ark and Pilat, pp. 37–64.

Denison, E. F. and W. K. Chung (1976), *How Japan's Economy Grew So Fast*, Brookings, Washington, DC.

Eisenstein, E. L. (1993), *The Printing Revolution in Early Modern Europe*, Cambridge University Press.

Elvin, M. (1973), *The Pattern of the Chinese Past*, Methuen, London.

Federico, G. (2002), 'The World Economy 0–2000: A Review Article', *European Review of Economic History*, 6, pp. 111–21.

Feinstein, C. H. and S. Pollard (1988), *Studies in Capital Formation in the United Kingdom, 1750–1920*, Oxford University Press.

Fogel, R. W. (1964), *Railroads and American Economic Growth*, Johns Hopkins University Press, Baltimore.

Fremdling, R. and P. K. O'Brien (eds) (1983), *Productivity in the Economies of Europe*, Klett-Cotta, Speyer.

Galbraith, J. K. et al. (1945), *The Effects of Strategic Bombing on the German War Economy*, US Strategic Bombing Survey, Washington, DC.

Galbraith, J. K. (1971), 'A Retrospect on Albert Speer', *Economics, Peace and Laughter*, Deutsch, London.

Gallman, R. E. (1986), 'The United States Capital Stock in the Nineteenth Century', in Engerman, S. L. and R. E. Gallman (eds), *Long Term Factors in American Economic Growth*, University of Chicago Press.

Gallman, R. E. (1987), 'Investment Flows and Capital Stocks: US Experience in the Nineteenth Century', in P. Kilby (ed) *Quantity and Quiddity: Essays in US Economic History*, Wesleyan University Press, Middletown.

Gerschenkron, A. (1965), *Economic Backwardness in Historical Perspective*, Praeger, New York.

Gilbert, M. (1961), 'Quality Changes and Index Numbers', in Hoselitz, pp. 287–94.

Gilbert, M. and I. B. Kravis (1954), *An International Comparison of National Products and Purchasing Power of Currencies*, OEEC, Paris.

Gilbert, M. and Associates (1958), *Comparative National Products and Price Levels*, OEEC, Paris.

Glass, D. V. and D. E. C. Eversley (eds) (1965), *Population in History: Essays in Historical Demography*, Arnold, London.

Goldsmith, R. W. (1951), 'A Perpetual Inventory of National Wealth' in M. R. Gainsburgh (ed) *Studies in Income and Wealth*, vol. 14, Princeton University Press.

Goldsmith, R. W. (1961), 'The Economic Growth of Tsarist Russia, 1860–1913', *Economic Development and Cultural Change*, April.

Goodman, D. and C. A. Russell (eds) (1991), *The Rise of Scientific Europe, 1500–1800*, Hodder & Stoughton, London.

Goody, J. (1983), *The Development of the Family and Marriage in Europe*, Cambridge University Press.

Grytten, O. (2004), 'The Gross Domestic Product for Norway, 1830–2003' in Eitrheim et al. (eds), *Historical Monetary Statistics for Norway, 1819–2003*, Norges Bank, Oslo.

Habib, I. (1978–9), 'The Technology and Economy of Moghul India', *Indian Economic and Social History Review*, vol. XVII, No. 1, pp. 1–34.

Habib, I. (1995), *Essays in Indian History*, Tulika, New Delhi.

Hanley, S. (1997), *Everyday Things in Premodern Japan*, University of California, Berkeley.

Hansen, S. A. (1974–76), *Økonomisk vaekst i Danmark*, 2 vols, Institute of Economic History, Copenhagen.

Heikkinen, S. and J. L. van Zanden (2004), *Explorations in Economic Growth*, Aksant, Amsterdam.

Heston, A. (1983), 'National Income', in Kumar and Desai (eds) Cambridge Economic History of India, vol. 2, pp. 376–462.

Heston, A., R. Summers, and B. Aten (2002), *PWT Version 6.1 (CICUP)*, http://www.pwt.econ. upenn.edu

Hjerppe, R. and Associates (1987), 'Förändringar I levnadsstandarden I Finland, 1750–1913', in G. Karlsson (ed), *Levestandarden i Norden 1750–1914*, Reykjavik.

Hoselitz, B. F. (ed) (1961), 'Essays in the Quantitative Study of Economic Growth presented to Simon Kuznets on his Sixtieth Birthday', *Economic Development and Cultural Change*, April.

Hulten, C. R. (2003), 'Price Hedonics: A Critical Review', *Federal Reserve Bank of New York Policy Review*, September, pp. 5–15.

Jarrett, H. S. and J. N. Sarkar (1949), *'Ain-I-Akbari of Abul Fazl-I-'Allami*, Royal Asiatic Society of Bengal, Calcutta.

Jones, E. L. (1981), *The European Miracle*, Cambridge University Press.

Jones, E. L. (1988), *Growth Recurring: Economic Change in World History*, Clarendon Press, Oxford.

Jones, E. L. (2001), *The Record of Global Economic Development*, Elgar, Cheltenham.

Jorgenson, D. W. and Z. Griliches (1969), 'The Explanation of Productivity Change', *Survey of Current Business*, May, pp. 249–82.

Jorgenson, D. W. and Z. Griliches (1972), 'Issues in Growth Accounting: A Reply to Edward F. Denison', *Survey of Current Business*, May, pp. 65–94.

Kaldor, N. (1945–46), 'The German War Economy', *Review of Economics and Statistics*, vol. XIII, (1).

Kapuria-Forman, V. and M. Perlman (1995), 'An Economic Historian's Economist: Remembering Simon Kuznets', *Economic Journal*, November, pp. 1524–47.

Kendrick, J. W. (1961), *Productivity Trends in the United States*, Princeton University Press.

Keynes. J. M. (1940), *How to Pay for the War*, Macmillan, London.

Kim, K. S. and S. D. Hong (1997), *Accounting for Rapid Economic Growth in Korea, 1963–1995*, Korea Development Institute, Seoul.

Krantz, O. (1988), 'New estimates of Swedish Historical GDP Since the Beginning of the Nineteenth Century', *Review of Income and Wealth*, June.

Kravis, I., A. Heston and R. Summers (1975), *A System of International Comparisons of Gross Product and Purchasing Power*, Johns Hopkins University Press, Baltimore and London.

Kravis, I., A. Heston and R. Summers (1978), *International Comparisons of Real Product and Purchasing Power*, Johns Hopkins University Press, Baltimore and London.

Kravis, I., A. Heston and R. Summers (1982), *World Product and Income: International Comparisons of Real Gross Product*, Johns Hopkins University Press, Baltimore and London.

Kremer, M. (1993), 'Population Growth and Technological Change, One Million BC to 1990', *Quarterly Journal of Economics*, August, pp. 681–716.

Kuznets, S. (1930), *Secular Movements in Production and Prices*, Houghton Mifflin, Boston.

Kuznets, S. (1940), 'Schumpeter's Business Cycles', *American Economic Review*, XXX, June, pp. 250–71.

Kuznets, S. (1956–67), 'Quantitative Aspects of the Economic Growth of Nations', ten articles in *Economic Growth and Cultural Change*.

Kuznets, S. (1961), *Capital in the American Economy*, NBER, Princeton.

Kuznets, S. (1965), 'Capital formation in Modern Economic Growth', paper presented to third International Conference of Economic History (reprinted in Kuznets (1973: 121–64).

Kuznets, S. (1971), *Economic Growth of Nations: Total Output and Production Structure*, Harvard University Press.

Kuznets, S. (1973), *Population, Capital and Growth: Selected Essays*, Norton, New York.

Kuznets, S. (1989), *Economic Development, the Family and Income Distribution: Selected Essays*, Cambridge University Press.

Lal, D. (1988), *The Hindu Equilibrium*, Oxford University Press.

Lal, D. (2001), *Unintended Consequences*, MIT Press, Cambridge, MA.

Landes, D. S. (1969), *The Unbound Prometheus*, Cambridge University Press.

Landes, D. S. (1998), *The Wealth and Poverty of Nations*, Little, Brown and Company, London.

LeRoy Ladurie, E. (1966), *Les paysans de Languedoc*, Mouton, Paris,

LeRoy Ladurie, E. (1978), 'L'histoire immobile', *Le territoire de l'historien*, vol. II, Gallimard, Paris.

Levy-Leboyer, M. and F. Bourguignon (1985), *L'economie française au XIX siècle*, Economica, Paris.

Lindert, P. H. and J. G. Williamson (1982), 'Revising England's Social Tables, 1688–1812', *Explorations in Economic History*, 19, pp. 385–408.

McDonald, J. and G. D. Snooks (1986), *Domesday Economy: A New Approach to Anglo-Norman History*, Clarendon Press, Oxford.

McEvedy, C. (2002), *The New Penguin Atlas of Ancient History*, Penguin. London.

McEvedy, C. (1995), *The Penguin Atlas of African History*, 2nd edn, Penguin, London.

McEvedy, C. and R. Jones (1978), *Atlas of World Population History*, Penguin, London.

Macfarlane, A. (1997), *The Savage Wars of Peace: England, Japan and the Malthusian Trap*, Blackwell, Oxford.

Maddison, A. (1952), 'Productivity in an Expanding Economy', *Economic Journal*, September.

Maddison, A. (1964), *Economic Growth in the West*, Allen & Unwin, London, and Norton, New York.

Maddison, A. (1969), *Economic Growth in Japan and the USSR*, Allen & Unwin, London, and Norton, New York.

Maddison, A. (1970), *Economic Progress and Policy in Developing Countries*, Allen & Unwin, London and Norton, New York.

Maddison, A. (1971), *Class Structure and Economic Growth: India and Pakistan Since the Moghuls*, Allen & Unwin, London.

Maddison, A. (1972), 'Explaining Economic Growth', *Banca Nazionale del Lavoro Quarterly Review*, September, pp. 211–62.

Maddison, A. (1983), 'A Comparison of Levels of GDP Per Capita in Developed and Developing Countries, 1700–1980', *Journal of Economic History*, March, pp. 27–41.

Maddison, A. (1985), 'Alternative Estimates of the Real Product of India, 1900–46', *Indian Economic History Review*, April–June.

Maddison, A. (1987a), 'Growth and Slowdown in Advanced Capitalist Countries: Techniques of Quantitative Assessment', *Journal of Economic Literature,* June, pp. 649–98.

Maddison, A. (1987b), 'Recent Revisions to British and Dutch Growth, 1700–1870 and their Implications for Comparative Levels of Performance', in Maddison and van der Meulen.

Maddison, A. (1988), 'Ultimate and Proximate Growth Causality: A Critique of Mancur Olson on the Rise and Decline of Nations', *Scandinavian Economic History Review*, no. 2, pp. 25–9 (reproduced in Maddison 1995b).

Maddison, A. (1989a), *The World Economy in the Twentieth Century*, OECD, Paris.

Maddison, A. (1989b), 'Dutch Income in and from Indonesia, 1700–1938', *Modern Asian Studies*, pp. 645–70.

Maddison, A. (1991a), *Dynamic Forces in Capitalist Development*, Oxford University Press.

Maddison, A. (1991b), 'A Revised Estimate of Italian Economic Growth, 1861–1989', *Banca Nazionale del Lavoro Quarterly Review*, June, pp. 225–41.

Maddison, A. (1992), 'Brazilian Development Experience, 1500 to 1929', see website http://www.ggdc. net/Maddison/

Maddison, A. (1995a), *Monitoring the World Economy, 1820–1992*, OECD, Paris.

Maddison, A. (1995b), *Explaining the Economic Performance of Nations: Essays in Time and Space*, Elgar, Aldershot.

Maddison, A. (1995c), 'Standardized Estimates of Fixed Capital Stock: A Six Country Comparison', in Maddison (1995b).

Maddison, A. (1995d), 'The Historical Roots of Modern Mexico: 1500–1940', in Maddison (1995b).

Maddison, A. (1998a), *Chinese Economic Performance in the Long Run*, Development Centre Studies, OECD, Paris.

Maddison, A. (1998b), 'Measuring the Performance of A Communist Command Economy: An Assessment of the CIA Estimates for the USSR', *Review of Income and Wealth*, September.

Maddison, A. (1999), Review of Hanley (1997), *Journal of Japanese and International Economies*.

Maddison, A. (2001), *The World Economy: A Millennial Perspective*, Development Centre Studies, OECD, Paris.

Maddison, A. (2003a), *The World Economy: Historical Statistics*, Development Centre Studies, OECD, Paris.

Maddison, A. (2003b), 'Growth Accounts, Technological Change, and the Role of Energy in Western Growth', *Economia e Energia Secc. XIII–XVIII*, Instituto Internazionale di Storia Economica 'E. Datini', Prato.

Maddison, A. (2004a), 'Quantifying and Interpreting World Development: Macro-Measurement before and after Colin Clark', *Australian Economic History Review*, March.

Maddison, A. (2004b), 'When and Why did the West get Richer than the Rest', in Heikkinen and van Zanden (2004).

Maddison, A (2004c), http://www.ggdc.net/Maddison

Maddison, A. (2005), *Growth and Interaction in the World Economy: The Roots of Modernity*, Wendt Lecture, American Enterprise Institute, Washington, DC.

Maddison, A. (2005a), 'Measuring and Interpreting World Economic Performance, 1500–2001', *Review of Income and Wealth*, March, pp. 1–36.

Maddison, A. and B. van Ark (1988), 'Comparisons of Real Output in Manufacturing', *World Bank Working Paper WPS5*, Washington, DC, pp. 1–132.

Maddison, A. and B. van Ark (1989), 'International Comparison of Purchasing Power, Real Output and Labour Productivity: A Case Study of Brazilian, Mexican and US Manufacturing, 1975', *Review of Income and Wealth*, 35, pp. 31–55.

Maddison, A. and B. van Ark (2002), 'The International Comparison of Real Product and Productivity', in Maddison et al.

Maddison, A. and Associates (1992), *The Political Economy of Poverty Equity and Growth: Brazil and Mexico*, Oxford University Press, New York.

Maddison, A. and H. van Ooststroom (1995), 'The International Comparison of Value Added, Productivity and Purchasing Power Parities in Agriculture', in Maddison (1995b).

Maddison, A. and G. Prince (eds) (1989), *Economic Growth in Indonesia, 1820–1940*, Foris, Dordrecht.

Maddison, A., D. S. Prasada Rao and W. Shepherd (eds) (2002), *The Asian Economies in the Twentieth Century*, Elgar, Cheltenham.

Maddison, A. and H. van der Meulen (eds) (1987), *Economic Growth in Northwestern Europe: The Last 400 Years*, Research Memorandum 214, Institute of Economic Research, University of Groningen.

Maddison, A. and H. van der Wee (eds) (1994), *Economic Growth and Structural Change: Comparative Approaches over the Long Run*, Proceedings of the Eleventh International Economic History Congress, Milan, Università Bocconi, September.

Malanima, P. (1994), 'Italian Economic Performance, 1600–1800', in Maddison and van der Wee.

Malanima, P. (1995), *Economia Preindustriale*, Mondadori, Milan.

Malanima, P. (1998), 'Italian Cities 1300–1800: A Quantitative Approach', *Revista di Storia Economica* XVI, August, pp. 91–126.

Malanima, P. (2002), *L'economia Italiana*, il Mulino, Milan.

Malanima, P. (2003), 'Measuring the Italian Economy, *1300–1861*', *Rivista di Storia Economica* XIX, December, pp. 265–95.

Malthus, T. R. (1798), *Essay on the Principle of Population as it Affects the Future Improvement of Society*, Johnson, London.

Manarungsan, S. (1989), *Economic Development of Thailand, 1850–1950*, PhD thesis, University of Groningen.

Mathias, P. and M. M. Postan (eds) (1978), *Cambridge Economic History of Europe*, Vol VII, I, Cambridge University Press.

Mitchell, B. R. (1975), *European Historical Statistics*, Macmillan, London.

Mokyr, J. (2002), *The Gifts of Athena: Historical Origins of the Knowledge Economy*, Princeton University Press.

Moosvi, S. (1987), *The Economy of the Moghul Empire c.1595: A Statistical Study*, Oxford University Press, New Delhi.

Mulder, N. (2002), *Economic Performance in the Americas: the Role of the Service Sector in Brazil, Mexico and the USA*, Elgar, Cheltenham.

Needham, J. (1954–97), *Science and Civilisation in China*, Cambridge University Press.

Needham, J. (1970), *Clerks and Craftsmen in China and the West*, Cambridge University Press.

Nordhaus, W. D. (1997), 'Do Real-Wage Measures Capture Reality? The Evidence of Lighting Suggests Not', in Bresnahan, T. F. and R. J. Gordon (eds) *The Economics of New Goods*, NBER and University of Chicago Press.

North, D. C. (1990), *Institutions, Institutional Change and Economic Performance*, Cambridge University Press.

North, D. C. and R. P. Thomas (1973), *The Rise of the Western World*, Cambridge University Press.

OECD (1964), *The Residual Factor and Economic Growth*, Conference papers by Ed. Denison, Ingvar Svennilson, Jan Tinbergen, John Vaizey, John Kendrick and Tibor Scitovsky (discussants included Erik Lundberg, Edmond Malinvaud, Trygve Haavelmo, Nicholas Kaldor, Thomas Balogh, Amartya Sen, John Kendrick, and Harry Johnson), Paris.

OECD (1975) *Education, Inequality and Life Chances*, 2 vols. Paris.

OECD (2000), *A PPP Comparison for the NIS*, Centre for Cooperation with Non-Members document CCNM/STD, 2, Paris

OECD (2002), *Purchasing Power Parities and Real Expenditures, 1999 Benchmark Year*, Paris.

Olson, M. (1982), *The Rise and Decline of Nations*, Yale University Press.

Özmucur, S. and S. Pamuk (2002), 'Real Wages and Standards of Living in the Ottoman Empire, 1489–1914', *Journal of Economic History*, June, pp. 293–321.

Paige, D. and G. Bombach (1959), *A Comparison of the National Output and Productivity of the UK and USA*, OEEC, Paris.

Perkins, D. H. (1969), *Agricultural Development in China, 1368–1968*, Aldine, Chicago.

Persson, K. G. (1988), *Preindustrial Economic Growth*, Blackwell, Oxford

Phelps Brown, H. and S. V. Hopkins (1956), 'Seven Centuries of the Price of Consumables, Compared with Builders' Wage Rates', *Economica*, November (reprinted in their (1981) *Perspective on Wages and Prices*, Methuen, London).

Pilat, D. (1994), *The Economics of Rapid Growth: The Experience of Japan and Korea*, Elgar, Aldershot.

Pomeranz, K. (2000), *The Great Divergence: China, Europe and the Making of the Modern World Economy*, Princeton University Press, New Jersey.

Psacharopoulos, G. (1975), *Earnings and Education in OECD Countries*, OECD, Paris.

Rapp, R. T.(1976), *Industry and Economic Decline in Seventeenth Century Venice*, Harvard University Press, Cambridge, MA.

Raychaudhuri, T. and I. Habib (1982), *The Cambridge Economic History of India, c.1200–1750*, vol. I, Cambridge University Press.

Rich, E. E. and C. H. Wilson (eds) (1967), *Cambridge Economic History of Europe*, Vol. IV, Cambridge University Press.

Rostas, L. (1948), *Comparative Productivity in British and American Industry*, Cambridge University Press.

Rostow, W. W. (1960), *The Stages of Economic Growth: A Non-Communist Manifesto*, Cambridge University Press.

Rostow, W. W. (ed) (1963), *The Economics of Take-Off into Sustained Growth*, Macmillan, London

Rozman, G. (1973), *Urban Networks in Ch'ing China and Tokugawa Japan*, Princeton University Press.

Schmookler, J. (1966), *Invention and Economic Growth*, Harvard University Press.

Schultz, T. W. (1961), 'Investment in Human Capital', *American Economic Review*, March.

Schumpeter, J. A. (1939), *Business Cycles: A Theoretical, Historical, and Statistical Analysis of the Capitalist Process*, McGraw-Hill, New York.

Scitovsky, T. (1999), 'A Proud Hungarian, Excerpts from a Memoir', Part 2, *The Hungarian Quarterly*, 156, Winter, pp. 24–43 (excerpt from 'Egy büszke magyar emlékiratai', Közgazdasági Szemle Alapítvány, Budapest, 1997).

Sella, D. (1979), *Crisis and Continuity, The Economy of Spanish Lombardy in the Seventeenth Century*, Harvard University Press, Cambridge, MA.

Shinohara, M. (1966), *Japan's Industrial Level in International Perspective*, Ministry of Foreign Affairs, Tokyo.

Singer, C., E. J. Holmyard, A. R. Hall and T. I. Williams (eds) (1954–8), *A History of Technology*, 5 vols, Clarendon Press, Oxford.

Sivasubramonian, S. (2000), *The National Income of India in the Twentieth Century*, Oxford University Press, New Delhi.

Sivasubramonian, S. (2004), *The Sources of Economic Growth in India, 1950–1 to 1999–2000*, Oxford University Press, New Delhi.

Smil, V. (1994), *Energy in World History*, Westview Press, BO, and Oxford.

Smith, A. (1776), *An Inquiry into the Nature and Causes of the Wealth of Nations*, University of Chicago (Reprint 1976).

Smits, J-P., E. Horlings and J. L. van Zanden (2000), *Dutch GDP and its Components, 1800–1913*, University of Groningen.

Snooks, G. D. (1990), 'Economic Growth During the Last Millennium: A Quantitative Perspective', *Working Papers in Economic History*, No. 140, Australian National University, Canberra.

Snooks, G. D. (1993), *Economics Without Time*, Macmillan, London.

Snooks, G. D. (1996), *The Dynamic Society: Exploring the Sources of Global Change*, Routledge, London.

Snooks, G. D. (1997), *The Ephemeral Civilisation*, Routledge, London.

Solow, R. M. (1956), 'A Contribution to the Theory of Economic Growth', *Quarterly Journal of Economics*, February.

Stone, R. (1997), *Some British Empiricists in the Social Sciences, 1650–1900*, Cambridge University Press.

Studenski, P. (1958), *The Income of Nations: Theory, Measurement and Analysis: Past and Present*, New York University Press.

Szirmai, A., B. van Ark and D. Pilat (eds) (1993), *Explaining Economic Growth: Essays in Honour of Angus Maddison*, North Holland, Amsterdam.

Thorold Rogers, J. E. (1862–92), *A History of Agriculture and Prices in England*, 7 vols, Clarendon Press, Oxford.

Thorold Rogers, J. E (1884), *Six Centuries of Work and Wages*, Swan Sonnenschein, London.

Tilly, R. H. (1978), 'Capital Formation in Germany in the Nineteenth Century', in Mathias and Postan.

Tinbergen, J. (1942), 'Zur Theorie der langfristigen Wirtschaftsentwicklung', *Weltwirtschaftliches Archiv*, 55.

Tobin, J. (2001), 'In Memoriam: Richard Ruggles (1916–2001)', *Review of Income and Wealth*, September, pp. 405–8.

Toynbee, A, (1884), *Lectures on the Industrial Revolution in England*, Rivingtons, London.

Toutain, J-C. (1987), *Le produit intérieur de la France de 1789 a 1982*, PUG, Grenoble.

Urlanis, B. Ts (1941), *Rost Naselenie v Evrope*, Ogiz, Moscow.

Van Ark, B. and N. Crafts (eds) (1996), *Quantitative Aspects of Post-war European Economic Growth*, Cambridge University Press.

Van der Eng, P. (1993), *Agricultural Growth in Indonesia since 1880*, Groningen University Press.

Van Zanden, J. L. (1993), 'The Dutch Economy in the Very Long Run, 1500–1805', in Szirmai et al.

Van Zanden, J. L. (1999), 'Wages and the Standard of Living in Europe, 1500–1800', *European Review of Economic History*, August, pp. 175–98.

Van Zanden, J. L. (2002a), 'Early Modern Economic Growth: A Survey of the European Economy, 1500–1800', in M. Prak (ed), *Early Modern Capitalism*, Routledge, London.

Van Zanden, J. L. (2002b), 'Taking the Measure of the Early Modern Economy: Historical National Accounts for Holland in 1510/14', *European Review of Economic History*, 6, pp. 131–63.

Van Zanden, J. L. (2003), 'Rich and Poor Before the Industrial Revolution: Java and the Netherlands at the Beginning of the 19th Century', *Explorations in Economic History* 40, pp. 1–23.

Van Zanden, J. L. (forthcoming), 'Economic Growth in Java, 1815–1939: Reconstruction of the Historical National Accounts' (http://iisg.nl/research/jvz-reconstruction.pdf).

Van Zanden, J. L. and E. Horlings (1999), 'The Rise of the European Economy 1500–1800', in Aldcroft and Sutcliffe.

Vries, J. de (1974), *The Dutch Rural Economy in the Golden Age, 1500–1700*, Yale.

Vries, J. de (1984), *European Urbanization, 1500–1800*, Methuen, London.

Vries, J. de (1985), 'The Population and Economy of the Preindustrial Netherlands', *Journal of Interdisciplinary History*, XV: 4, pp. 661–82.

Vries, J. de (1993), 'Between Purchasing Power and the World of Goods: Understanding the Household Economy in Early Modern Europe', in Brewer and Porter.

Vries, J. de (1994), 'The Industrial Revolution and the Industrious Revolution', *Journal of Economic History*, June, pp. 249–70.

Vries, J. de and A. van der Woude (1997), *The First Modern Economy; Success, Failure and Perseverance of the Dutch Economy, 1500–1815*, Cambridge University Press.

Vries, J. de (2000), 'Dutch Economic Growth in Comparative-Historical Perspective, 1500–2000', *De Economist*, 148, no. 4, pp. 443–67.

Williamson, J. G. (1995), 'The Evolution of Global Labor Markets since 1830: Background Evidence and Hypotheses', *Explorations in Economic History*, 32, pp. 141–96.

Woytinsky, W. S. and E. S. (1953), *World Population and Production: Trends and Outlook*, 20th Century Fund, New York.

Wrigley, E. A. (1987), *People, Cities and Wealth*, Blackwell, Oxford.

Wrigley, E. A. (1988), *Continuity, Chance and Change*, Cambridge, University Press.

Wrigley, E. A. (2004), *Poverty, Progress and Population*, Cambridge University Press.

Wrigley, E. A. (2006), 'The Transition to an Advanced Organic Economy: Half a Millennium of English Agriculture', *Economic History Review*, August. pp. 435–80.

Wrigley, E. A. and R. S. Schofield (1981), *The Population History of England, 1541–1871*, Arnold, London.

Wrigley, E. A., R. S. Davies, J. E. Oeppen, and R. S. Schofield (1997), *English Population History from Family Reconstitution, 1580–1837,* Cambridge University Press.

Yun, B. (1994), 'Proposals to Quantify Long-Term Performance in the Kingdom of Castile, 1580–1800', in Maddison and van der Wee.

Part III
The Shape of Things to Come

7 The world economy in 2030

Futurology is a more speculative business than history. Hard evidence is lacking and we have to project trends from the past which seem plausible but may well be reversed by unforeseeable events. However, there has been such a striking divergence in the pace and pattern of growth in different regions of the world in the past 30 years, that it is worth considering the changes which seem likely in the next quarter century. I have therefore constructed a scenario showing the likely structure of the world economy in 2030.

The projections have two components: growth of population and per capita GDP. The GDP projection is derivative. I assumed that world development will not be interrupted by major military conflicts in addition to those already under way.

PROJECTIONS OF POPULATION AND CHANGES IN DEMOGRAPHIC CHARACTERISTICS

Table 7.1 shows the population projections to 2030 in historical perspective. They were made by the International Programs Department, US Bureau of the Census (www.census.gov/ipc).

The major assumptions of the USBC about changes in life expectation and birth rates are shown in Table 7.2, together with the consequential changes in age structure which are likely to affect labour input.

Life expectancy is projected to increase in all regions, with the biggest proportionate increase (20 per cent) in sub-Saharan Africa. Overall this implies closer inter-regional convergence, but still leaves a large gap between the high income countries and Africa. Birth rates are projected to fall in all regions, with milder convergence. The sub-Saharan birth rate is still expected to be a multiple of that in the high income countries. In the high income countries, eastern Europe, the countries of the former USSR, and China, the proportion of working age is expected to fall; in India, Latin America, and Africa it will increase.

The USBC population projections also incorporate the impact of migration. The most significant cases were as follows. In 2003, the US had a net *immigration* ratio of 3.5 persons per 1,000 inhabitants, projected to be 3.4 in 2030; Australia, Canada, and New Zealand have higher ratios. For western Europe, the net immigration ratio was

Table 7.1. Population of the World and Major Regions, 1950–2030

	Population Levels (million)					Average annual rate of change	
	1950	1973	1990	2003	2030	1990–2003	2003–2030
W. Europe	305	359	378	395	400	0.33	0.05
USA	152	212	250	290	364	1.15	0.84
*Other W.O.	24	39	48	56	67	1.15	0.70
Japan	84	109	124	127	116	0.23	−0.33
'Rich'	**565**	**718**	**800**	**868**	**947**	**0.63**	**0.32**
E. Europe	88	110	122	121	115	−0.02	−0.21
Russia	102	133	148	145	126	−0.18	−0.49
Other f. USSR	78	117	141	143	161	0.13	0.43
Lat. America	166	308	442	541	702	1.58	0.97
China	547	882	1,135	1,288	1,458	0.98	0.46
India	359	580	839	1,050	1,421	1.74	1.13
Other Asia	393	678	1,007	1,269	1,795	1.79	1.29
Africa	228	390	625	853	1,449	2.43	1.98
'Rest'	**1,960**	**3,198**	**4,458**	**5,411**	**7,227**	**1.50**	**1.08**
World	**2,526**	**3,916**	**5,257**	**6,279**	**8,175**	**1.37**	**0.98**

Notes: 'Other Western Offshoots' refers to Australia, Canada, & New Zealand; 'Latin America' includes Caribbean countries.

Sources: Maddison website www.ggdc.net/Maddison shows detail for all 224 component countries annually from 1950 to 2008 and for 2030. The alternative projections of the United Nations Population Division are not significantly different, see the 'medium variant' of the UN Population Division, *World Population Prospects, 2004 Revision*, New York, 2005. The UN projection for world population in 2030 was 8,199 million, 961 million for the 'Rich' and 7,237 million for the 'Rest'.

Table 7.2. Assumptions Underlying the Demographic Projections

	Life Expectancy at birth in 2030	Birthrate Per 100 in 2030	%Population aged 15–64 in 2030	Life Expectancy in 2030	Birthrate per 100 in 2030	%Population aged 15–64 in 2030
W. Europe	81.9	0.90	61.1	78.8	1.03	66.7
USA	81.2	1.36	60.7	77.1	1.41	66.7
Japan	83.1	0.78	59.2	80.9	0.96	67.0
E. Europe	78.9	0.82	64.4	73.7	1.01	69.1
Russia	71.7	0.81	64.3	66.4	0.94	71.0
CIS	73.0	1.12	64.9	65.8	1.26	68.3
Baltics	78.0	0.75	63.3	71.8	0.87	68.1
China	78.0	0.99	66.9	71.6	1.30	69.6
India	72.3	1.57	67.7	63.6	2.33	63.1
Total Asia	73.9	1.42	66.8	66.5	1.95	65.3
Latin America	77.4	1.41	66.7	71.9	2.04	63.9
North Africa	77.4	1.48	68.1	71.1	2.25	62.8
Africa sub-Sahara	57.4	2.95	59.1	48.0	3.93	53.7
Total Africa	59.1	2.73	60.5	50.6	3.63	55.3
World	**70.2**	**1.36**	**65.0**	**64.0**	**2.05**	**64.3**

Notes and Source: www.census.gov/ipc 'Baltics' refers to Estonia, Latvia and Lithuania; 'CIS' refers to the Commonwealth of Independent States, which includes the Russian federation and the other 11 successor states of the former USSR; 'Latin America' includes all Caribbean countries.

Table 7.3. Per Capita GDP: The World and Major Regions, 1950–2030

	Level in 1990 international PPP $					Average annual rate of change	
	1950	1973	1990	2003	2030	1990–2003	2003–30
W. Europe	4,578	11,417	15,965	19,912	31,389	1.71	1.7
USA	9,561	16,689	23,201	29,037	45,774	1.74	1.7
Other W.O.	7,424	13,399	17,902	22,853	36,025	1.90	1.7
Japan	1,921	11,434	18,789	21,218	30,072	0.94	1.3
'Rich'	**5,648**	**13,082**	**18,781**	**23,345**	**37,086**	**1.69**	**1.73**
E. Europe	2,111	4,988	5,440	6,476	11,054	1.35	2.0
Russia	3,086	6,582	7,779	6,323	16,007	−1.58	3.5
Other f. USSR	2,520	5,468	5,954	4,461	7,614	−2.20	2.0
Latin America	2,503	4,513	5,072	5,786	8,648	1.02	1.5
China	448	838	1,871	4,803	15,763	7.52	4.5
India	619	853	1,309	2,160	7,089	3.93	4.5
Other Asia	924	2,046	3,078	4,257	8,292	2.53	2.5
Africa	890	1,410	1,449	1,549	2,027	0.52	1.0
'Rest'	**1,094**	**2,072**	**2,718**	**3,816**	**8,504**	**2.64**	**3.01**
World	**2,113**	**4,091**	**5,162**	**6,516**	**11,814**	**1.81**	**2.23**

1.9 in 2003, projected to be 1.7 in 2030. The biggest net *emigration* ratios were 1.6 in Latin America and the Caribbean in 2003, falling to 0.6 in 2030. In the Baltics, the ratio was also 1.6 in 2003, expected to be 1.9 in 2030. In north Africa the ratio was 0.4 in 2003, projected to be 0.3 in 2030. In China the ratios were 0.4 for 2003 and 0.2 for 2030.

Table 7.4. Growth of GDP: The World and Major Regions, 1950–2030

	Levels in billion 1990 PPP dollars					Average annual rate of change	
	1950	1973	1990	2003	2030	1990–2003	2003–30
W. Europe	1,396	4,097	6,033	7,857	12,556	2.05	1.75
USA	1,456	3,537	5,803	8,431	16,662	2.91	2.56
Other W.O.	180	522	862	1,277	2,414	3.07	2.39
Japan	161	1,243	2,321	2,699	3,488	1.17	0.95
'Rich'	**3,193**	**9,398**	**15,020**	**20,265**	**35,120**	**2.33**	**2.06**
E. Europe	185	551	663	786	1,269	1.33	1.79
Russia	315	872	1,151	914	2,017	−1.76	2.98
Other f. USSR	199	641	837	638	1,222	−2.17	2.43
Latin America	416	1,389	2,240	3,132	6,074	2.61	2.48
China	245	739	2,124	6,188	22,983	8.56	4.98
India	222	495	1,098	2,267	10,074	5.73	5.68
Other Asia	363	1,387	3,099	5,401	14,884	4.36	3.83
Africa	203	550	905	1,322	2,937	2.96	3.00
'Rest'	**2,144**	**6,625**	**12,117**	**20,649**	**61,460**	**4.19**	**4.12**
World	**5,337**	**16,022**	**27,136**	**40,913**	**96,580**	**3.21**	**3.23**

ASSUMPTIONS UNDERLYING THE PROJECTIONS OF PER CAPITA GDP

For population the USBC made individual projections for 224 countries, see www.ggdc.net/Maddison. My projections of per capita GDP are much more aggregative. They cover seven major regions, the four countries with the biggest shares of world GDP and Russia. They are not the result of an econometric exercise, but are based on an analysis of changes in the momentum of growth in different parts of the world economy, and my asessment of the likelihood of their continuation or change. They were conceived as likely continuation or deviation from the momentum of growth in 1990–2003.

Rich Country Group

For the advanced capitalist group, i.e., western Europe, the US, the other western offshoots, and Japan, I assume their aggregate per capita GDP will grow at about the same rate as in 1990–2003. This does not mean that all component countries will advance at the same pace. The rapid and widespread catch-up on US per capita income levels in the golden age (1950–73) had ended for most countries by the 1990s. France, Germany, Italy, and Japan advanced more slowly than the US in 1990–2003, but Ireland made a remarkable bound forward, while Australia, Spain, and the UK had a respectable degree of catch-up. Labour input per head of population is generally lower in western Europe than in the USA, so the gap in performance is substantially smaller in terms of productivity than in per capita GDP (see Table 7.5). This is due in part to shorter working hours and longer holidays, but in France, Germany, and Italy unemployment rates were much higher than in the US and UK from 1990 to 2003. This contrasts with the situation in the golden age, when European unemployment rates were much lower than in the USA. With more flexible labour market policies there would be some scope for better European performance (see van Ark 2006, and Gordon 2006).

Asia

In the past three decades, the biggest change in the structure of the world economy was the increased share of Asia. I expect a continuance of high momentum and a significant degree of catch-up on the USA. China has been the most dynamic of the Asian economies, but growth will probably decelarate over the period 2003–30 for several reasons. In the reform period, the emphasis on population control and changes in age structure made it possible to raise the activity rate to a degree that cannot be repeated. Because of the low starting point, the average educational level of the labour force was multiplied by a factor of 6 from 1952 to 2003. China has

Table 7.5. Comparative Performance of Advanced Capitalist Countries, 1990–2003

	1990	2003	1990–2003 annual % growth	2003 level USA = 100
Per Capita GDP (1990 GK dollars)				
USA	23,201	29,037	1.74	100
France	18,093	21,861	1.47	75
Germany	15,929	19,144	1.42	66
Ireland*	11,818	24,739	5.85	85
Netherlands	17,262	21,479	1.70	74
Spain	12,055	17,021	2.69	59
UK	16,430	21,310	2.02	73
Japan	18,789	21,218	0.94	73
GDP per hour worked (1990 GK dollars)				
USA	30.10	38.92	2.00	100
France	29.12	38.19	2.09	98
Germany	23.12	30.43	2.14	78
Ireland	18.60	33.87	4.30	87
Netherlands	28.72	32.36	0.92	83
Spain	19.73	22.79	1.12	42
UK	21.42	30.69	2.80	79
Japan	19.14	24.86	2.03	64
Percent of Population Employed				
USA	48.4	48.0	−0.10	100.0
France	39.9	40.9	0.20	85.2
Germany	47.7	43.5	−0.70	90.6
Ireland	33.1	45.3	2.44	94.4
Netherlands	42.5	49.6	1.20	103.3
Spain	33.5	41.5	1.66	86.4
UK	46.9	47.8	0.15	99.6
Japan	50.6	49.6	−0.15	103.3
Annual Hours worked per Person Employed				
USA	1,594	1,556	−0.19	100
France	1,558	1,398	−0.83	90
Germany	1,541	1,446	−0.49	93
Ireland	1,922	1,612	−1.34	104
Netherlands	1,414	1,338	−0.42	86
UK	1,627	1,453	−0.92	93
Spain	1,824	1,799	−0.11	116
Japan	1,941	1,719	−0.93	110

Notes: In Ireland, there is a big difference between GDP (gross domestic product) and GNP (gross national product); in 1990 GNP was only 92 per cent of GDP. By 2003, it had fallen to 85 per cent, due to large transfers of profits on foreign investment. Thus GNP per capita rose from $10,877 in 1990 to $20,929 in 2003.

Sources: Statistical Appendix B for USA, UK, and Japan. Other countries from Groningen Growth & Development Centre

suffered environmental deterioration in its push for rapid growth. In future it will have to devote greater resources to mitigate this damage.

Income growth has lagged in rural areas and there has been a neglect of rural educational and health facilities. Bigger resources will be needed to compensate for this. Some slowdown can also be expected as Chinese wages rise and the average technological level gets closer to the frontier in the advanced countries. By 2030,

Table 7.6. Shares of World GDP, 1820–2030

	1820	1870	1950	1973	2003	2030
Western Europe	23.0	33.1	26.2	25.6	19.2	13.0
Western offshoots*	1.9	10.0	30.7	25.3	23.7	19.8
Asia (incl. Japan)	59.4	38.3	18.6	24.1	40.5	53.3
Eastern Europe	3.6	4.5	3.5	3.4	1.9	1.3
Former USSR	5.4	7.5	9.6	9.4	3.8	3.4
Latin America	2.1	2.5	7.8	8.7	7.7	6.3
Africa	4.5	4.1	3.8	3.4	3.2	3.0

Notes: *Includes USA.

Source: Table 7.4.

according to my projection, China will have a per capita income level near that in western Europe in 1990. As it approaches this level, technical advance will be more costly as imitation is replaced by innovation. Even on my rather conservative assumptions, China would again become the world's biggest economy by 2018, the US would be number two, and India number three. The average per capita income level in China would still be a good deal lower than in the US, western Europe, and Japan, but it would be well above the world average.

I have assumed that India will have the same 4.5 per cent a year per capita growth as China up to 2030. Indian growth is accelerating. It has dropped the Nehruvian policies which stressed high levels of public investment in heavy industry and detailed controls on the private sector and abandoned the Gandhian emphasis on self sufficiency. The investment rate and exports of goods and services are rising and its catch-up potential is very promising as its level of per capita income is less than half of that in China.

For the rest of Asia (excluding Japan) I assume per capita growth a little higher than the world average. By 2030, Asia is likely to produce 53 per cent of world GDP, compared with 33 percent for western Europe and western offshoots. It should therefore become the major driving force in world trade and development.

Table 7.7. Per Capita GDP Levels relative to the USA, 1820–2030 (per cent of US level)

	1820	1870	1950	1973	2003	2030
Western Europe	95.6	80.2	47.9	68.4	68.6	68.6
Other w. offshoots	60.5	91.8	77.7	80.3	78.7	78.7
Asia (incl. Japan)	46.2	24.8	7.5	10.3	15.3	23.5
Eastern Europe	56.8	28.3	22.0	29.9	22.3	24.1
Former USSR	54.7	38.6	29.7	36.3	18.5	24.7
Latin America	55.0	27.9	26.2	27.0	19.9	18.9
Africa	33.4	20.4	6.6	8.4	5.3	4.4

Source: Table 7.3.

Countries Transiting from Communism to Capitalism

The second big change change in the world economic picture in the past quarter century was the collapse of the communist command economies. They have since attempted to move towards capitalist modes of resource allocation and property ownership and to shift from virtual autarchy to participation in international trade and capital markets. The most sudden change was the collapse of the Soviet sytem in 1990–91, which led to the breakup of the USSR into 15 successor states (each with its own currency and central bank). Soviet hegemony in eastern Europe ended and the Comecom trading bloc was dissolved. Eleven of the Soviet successor states still have loose political links with the Russian federation, but are fairly independent in economic policy. The three Baltic states, the Czech Republic, Hungary, and Poland have joined the EU and Nato. In China the transition started in 1978, has been much more gradual in political terms, and incomparably more successful economically.

Table 7.8 shows the comparative growth performance of the three groups of transition economies. The record of the 15 successor states of the USSR has been far worse than any other region of the world economy since 1990. Per capita income in 11 of them was well below the 1990 level in 2003 and the only one with significant positive growth was Estonia.

The east European countries which were formerly part of the Soviet bloc have done much better, but their average performance in per capita terms lagged behind western Europe except for Poland and Slovenia. They have been able to build new trade links with capitalist countries and attract foreign investment, which most of the Soviet successor states were not able to do. The west European countries could have been more helpful if they had spent less effort on their own integration and had given earlier attention to integrating eastern Europe. They could also have done more to prevent the violent conflicts involved in the breakup of Yugoslavia.

Russia

The economy which the Russian reformers inherited was very inefficient. Capital–output ratios were higher than in capitalist countries. Materials and energy were used wastefully as they were supplied below cost. Shortages created a chronic tendency to hoard inventories. The ratio of energy consumption to GDP was much higher than in western Europe. The steel consumption/GDP ratio was four times as high as in the United States. Transfer of technology from the west was hindered by trade restrictions, lack of foreign direct investment, and restricted access to foreign investors, technicians and scholars. Work incentives were poor, malingering on the job was commonplace. The quality of consumer goods was poor. Retail outlets and service industries were few. Prices bore little relation to cost. Bread, butter, and housing were heavily subsidized. Consumers wasted time

Table 7.8. Per Capita GDP Performance and GDP Levels in the Successor States of the USSR, Eastern Europe, China, and Vietnam 1973–2003

	GDP per capita(1990 PPP $)			Growth rate		GDP million 1990 PPP$
	1973	1990	2003	1973–90	1990–2003	2003
Armenia	6,152	6,066	6,648	−0.80	0.71	19,957
Azerbaijan	4,434	4,639	3,394	0.27	−2.38	26,851
Belarus	5,233	7,184	7,387	1.88	0.21	76,250
Estonia	8,657	10,820	14,340	1.32	2.19	19,370
Georgia	5,932	7,616	4,040	1.48	−4.76	19,034
Kazakhstan	7,625	7,458	7,566	−0.13	0.20	115,647
Kyrgyzstan	3,727	3,602	2,354	−0.20	−3.22	11,814
Latvia	7,846	9,916	9,722	1.39	−0.15	22,583
Lithuania	7,593	8,663	7,986	0.78	−0.62	28,911
Moldova	5,365	6,165	2,581	0.82	−6.48	11,459
Russian Fed.	6,582	7,779	6,323*	0.99	−1.58	914,181
Tajikistan	4,095	2,979	1,102	−1.85	−7.36	7,564
Turkmenistan	4,826	3,626	2,489	−1.77	−2.85	11,887
Ukraine	4,924	6,027	3,547	1.20	−4.00	169,088
Uzbekistan	5,097	4,241	3,768	−1.18	−0.81	97,905
Former USSR	**6,059**	**6,890**	**5,397**	**0.76**	**−1.86**	**1,552,231**
Albania	2,273	2,499	3,173	0.56	1.85	11,189
Bulgaria	5,284	5,597	6,278	0.34	0.89	47,641
Czechoslovakia	7,401	8,512	9,728	0.83	1.03	152,411
Czech Rep.	n.a.	8,895	9,905	n.a.	0.83	101,537
Slovakia	n.a.	7,763	9,392	n.a.	1.48	50,873
Hungary	5,596	6,459	7,947	0.85	1.60	79,927
Poland	5,340	5,113	7,674	−0.26	3.17	296,237
Romania	3,477	3,511	3,510	0.06	0.00	78,563
Yugoslavia	4,361	5,720	5,101	1.61	−0.88	120,440
Slovenia	n.a.	10,160	13,995	n.a.	2.49	28,152
Other f. Yugos.	n.a.	5,226	4,273	0.51	−1.54	92,288
Eastern Europe	**4,988**	**5,440**	**6,476**	**0.51**	**1.35**	**786,408**
China	**838**	**1,871**	**4,803**	**4.84**	**7.52**	**6,187,983**
Vietnam	**836**	**1,025**	**2,147**	**0.12**	**5.85**	**175,569**

Notes: *On the basis of Goskomstat's real GDP estimates, and allowing for population decline, GDP per capita in the Russian federation in 2005 was $7,270.

Source: www.ggdc.net/Maddison

queueing, bartering, or sometimes bribing their way to the goods and services they wanted. There was an active black market, and special shops for the *nomen-klatura*. There was increasing cynicism, frustration, alcoholism, and a decline in life expectation.

Spending on the military and space effort was around 15 per cent of GDP in the 1980s, nearly three times the US ratio and five times higher than in western Europe.

The disintegration of the USSR had substantial costs for an economy where decisions had hitherto been highly centralized. It was dissolved at a clandestine meeting of Yeltsin as president of Russia, Kravchuk from the Ukraine, and Shuskevich of Belarus early in December 1991. The Baltic states were left free to pursue the capitalist path. The old party bosses of the Asian republics had no prior warning, or ideas for

Table 7.9. Ranking of the 20 Biggest Countries in 2003 and 2030

	2030			2003		
	GDP billion 1990 PPP $	Population million	Per capita GDP 1990 PPP $	GDP billion 1990 PPP $	Population million	Per capita GDP 1990 PPP $
China	22,983	1,458	15,763	6,188	1,288	4,803
US	16,662	364	45,774	8,431	290	29,037
India	10,074	1,421	7,089	2,267	1,050	2,160
Japan	3,488	116	30,072	2,699	127	21,218
Germany	2,406	80	30,179	1,577	82	19,144
France	2,171	63	34,462	1,316	60	21,861
UK	2,150	64	33,593	1,281	60	21,310
Russia	2,017	126	16,007	914	145	6,323
Indonesia	1,973	285	6,924	763	214	3,555
Brazil	1,853	223	8,316	1,013	182	5,563
Italy	1,686	55	30,661	1,111	58	19,450
S. Korea	1,532	50	30,643	758	48	15,732
Mexico	1,442	135	10,668	740	104	7,137
Canada	1,429	39	36,629	748	32	23,236
Turkey	1,101	84	13,111	458	68	6,731
Spain	1,046	39	26,832	685	40	17,021
Thailand	995	71	14,014	455	63	7,195
Iran	928	86	10,789	372	67	5,539
Australia	844	23	36,710	460	20	23,287
Taiwan	842	25	33,666	391	23	17,284
Total 20	**77,722**	**4,806**	**16,172**	**29,577**	**4,003**	**7,394**
World	**96,580**	**8,175**	**11,814**	**40,913**	**6,279**	**6,516**

change, but acquiesced, became presidents, and entered into a loose federation (the Commonwealth of Independent States). The Soviet Communist party was dissolved and its assets seized.

In the Russian republic, the first government of radical economic reformers had two aims—destruction of the old economic order and rapid creation of a market economy through shock—therapy. It jettisoned the old command structure, freed most domestic prices, removed obstacles to foreign trade, cut the military budget to a fraction of its earlier level, abolished state trading, legalized all forms of private trading, and began a process of privatization which eventually sold off most state enterprises at knockdown prices to the 'oligarchs'. Between 1990 and 1998, proceeds from Russian privatization totalled $7.5 billion compared with Brazilian privatization receipts of $66.7 billion in the same period. The average GDP of the two economies was similar over these years, but Brazilian sales were a very much smaller fraction of its capital stock.

Between 1990 and 1998, shock therapy had disappointing results. Russian GDP fell by 46 per cent. Fixed investment fell precipitously and there was a big drop in government military spending, so the fall in real private consumption per capita was much milder (about 10 per cent). However, the reform process increased the instability of economic life with major short term fluctuations in consumer purchasing power, big increases in inequality between persons and regions, and a large increase in poverty at the bottom of the income scale.

One reason why shock therapy failed and the transition to capitalism was so painful was the weakness of monetary and fiscal policy which led to hyperinflation. Consumer prices rose at an annual rate of 387 per cent from 1990 to 1998. It was also difficult to devise and implement a new tax structure in an economy where the legal system was so murky. Enterprises had rapidly become adept at tax avoidance, tax evasion, concealment of profits at home, and large scale capital flight to foreign tax havens.

After the re-election of Yeltsin in July 1996, there was a large inflow of foreign investment. The stock market rose three-fold from mid-1996 to the end of 1997 without much change in the exchange rate. Most foreign investors hedged their exchange risk by buying forward dollar contracts from Russian banks. The banks did not cover these commitments and borrowed dollars to buy high interest government paper. The dismissal of prime minister Chernomyrdin caused large withdrawals of foreign funds. The Russian government propped up the overvalued exchange rate for a couple of weeks with nearly $5 billion from the IMF, but in August 1998 devalued, defaulted on much of domestic debt, and declared a moratorium on debt repayments to foreigners by Russian companies and banks.

After the devaluation, Russia experienced rapid growth. Between 1998 and 2005, GDP rose nearly 7 per cent a year. The 2005 GDP level was still below that of 1990, but personal consumption and export earnings had risen rapidly. The major driving force was the increase in world demand for energy and the big rise in oil prices on the world market (from $13 a barrel in 1998 to $70 in 2006) which greatly improved Russia's terms of trade. Eighty-four per cent of exports consist of oil, gas, and metals. The growth in energy exports was not derived from development of new oil and gas fields but mainly from the drop in domestic consumption. Within Russia, use of energy is still very wasteful, and the ratio of carbon emissions to GDP is not much lower than in 1990. There is large scale flaring of gas by producers without access to Gazprom pipelines. Domestic prices for energy are still a fraction of those in the world market. Subsidies for natural gas and electricity consumption amount to $40 billion a year (see IEA 2006a: 279). There is still a significant, but declining element of subsidy in Russia's gas sales to some of the successor states of the USSR.

Gas production and pipelines are largely a state monopoly of Gazprom, and its position was strengthened in 2006, when it took a majority shareholding in the Sakhalin 2 project from three foreign companies. Most oil production has now been taken over by the state. In 2004–5, the assets of biggest oil company, Yukos, were seized for alleged tax evasion. The government clearly does not welcome foreign investment in the energy sector, even though the potential for discovering and developing new sources of oil and gas seems more promising than in the Middle East.

As a result of the export boom, Russia has a positive trade and budgetary balance, has repaid almost all of its foreign debt and the rouble has appreciated significantly. By mid-2006, it had accumulated $265 billion of foreign currency reserves and another \$59 billion in the federal Stabilisation Fund. In addition, private Russian capital invested abroad was about \$200 billion. The outstanding feature of this kind of growth is that financial resources are far in excess of actual domestic investment. Were these funds used for investment inside the country, economic growth could be substantially accelerated. (see Menshikov 2006).

Table 7.10. Growth of Per Capita GDP in the 20 Biggest Countries, 1950–2030 (annual average compound growth rates)

	1950–73	1973–90	1990–2003	2003–2030
China	2.76	4.84	7.52	4.5
USA	2.45	1.96	1.74	1.7
India	1.40	2.55	3.93	4.5
Japan	8.06	2.96	0.94	1.3
Germany	5.02	1.70	1.42	1.7
France	4.04	1.91	1.47	1.7
UK	2.42	1.85	2.02	1.7
Russia	3.35	0.99	−1.59	3.5
Indonesia	2.56	3.10	2.66	2.5
Brazil	3.73	1.41	0.94	1.5
Italy	4.95	2.55	1.24	1.7
S. Korea	5.34	6.85	4.66	2.5
Mexico	3.17	0.99	1.23	1.5
Canada	2.82	1.84	1.61	1.7
Turkey	3.37	2.67	1.67	2.5
Spain	5.60	2.70	2.69	1.7
Thailand	3.68	5.47	3.44	2.5
Iran	5.06	−2.54	3.53	2.5
Australia	2.43	1.68	2.40	1.7
Taiwan	6.68	5.33	4.39	2.5
World	2.92	1.38	1.81	2.23

Source: Growth rates 1950–2003 derived from www.ggdc.net/Maddison and 2003–30 from Table 7.3.

Though Russian policy has shortcomings, its comparative advantage in the energy sector gives it a potential for faster growth than eastern Europe and the other successor states of the USSR, I assumed that Russia had a potential per capita growth to 2030 of 3.5 per cent a year. For the other former communist economies, I assumed a per capita growth potential of 2 per cent a year.

Latin America

In Latin America per capita income in 2003 was one-third higher than that of Asia, but only a fifth of that in the US. In the golden age, performance was respectable, with slightly faster growth than the US. At that time, economic policy was populist and very different from that in the advanced capitalist group. Most countries never seriously tried to observe the fixed rate discipline of Bretton Woods. National currencies were repeatedly devalued, IMF advocacy of fiscal and monetary rectitude was frequently rebuffed, high rates of inflation became endemic.

The basic parameters changed in the early 1980s. By then, the OECD countries were pushing anti-inflationary policy very vigorously and interest rates rose suddenly and sharply. The credit-worthiness of Latin America as a whole was grievously damaged by Mexico's debt delinquency in 1982. The inflow of foreign investment stopped abruptly, and created a massive need for retrenchment in economies teetering on the edge of hyper-inflation and fiscal crisis.

Attempts to resolve these problems brought major changes in economic policy. But in most countries, the changes were made reluctantly. After experiments with heterodox policy options in Argentina and Brazil, most countries eventually tried some elements of the neo-liberal mix pioneered by Chile. They moved towards greater openness to international markets, reduced government intervention and trade barriers, less distorted exchange rates, better fiscal equilibrium and establishment of more democratic political systems. However, there was stagnation in the 1980s and only modest advance in per capita income in 1990–2003. The star performer was Chile where per capita income rose 4.2 per cent a year, but this was more than four times faster than the average for the other countries. In Argentina, Colombia, Mexico, Uruguay, and Venezuela per capita income in 2003 was below peaks achieved several years earlier. There are varying degrees of disillusion with neo-liberal policy, from outright rejection to half-hearted implementation.

I assumed that there will be some modest improvement in Latin American per capita performance in 2003–30.

Africa

Africa has nearly 13 per cent of world population, but only 3 per cent of world GDP. It is the world's poorest region, with a per capita income 5 per cent of that in the US. Its population is growing nine times as fast as in western Europe. Average per capita income in 2003 was less than 1 per cent above its 1980 level. African economies are more volatile than most others because export earnings are concentrated on a few primary commodities. Extremes of weather (droughts and floods) are more severe and have a heavy impact.

As a result of rapid population growth, age structure is very different from that in western Europe. In Europe two-thirds are of working age. In Africa little more than half. Forty per cent of the adult population are illiterate. There is a high incidence of infectious and parasitic disease (malaria, sleeping sickness, hookworm, river blindness, yellow fever). Over two-thirds of HIV infected people live in Africa. As a result the quantity and quality of labour input per head of population is much lower than in other parts of the world.

Many African countries have been or are plagued by armed conflict. In Algeria, Angola, Mozambique, Sudan, Zaire, and Zimbabwe, the struggle for independence involved war with the colonial power or the white settler population. Burundi, Eritrea, Ethiopia, Liberia, Nigeria, Rwanda, Sierra Leone, Somalia, Sudan, Uganda, and Zaire have all suffered from civil wars and bloody dictators.

In many African states, rulers have kept their positions for life, relying for support on a narrow group who share the spoils of office. Corruption is widespread, property rights insecure, capital flight substantial.

A major factor in the slowdown after 1980 was the burden of external debt service. As the cold war faded, foreign aid leveled off, and net lending to Africa fell. Although foreign direct investment has risen in the past few years, it is low compared with that to Asia, Latin America, and eastern Europe. The official aid flow rose, but was low compared to the debt overhang. In 2003, net official development assistance flows (grants and loans, bilateral and multilateral) totalled $26 billion.

There has been increasing recognition of Africa's need for help. The most significant move was the decision by the July 2005 G-8 summit to double development assistance to a total of $50 billion in 2010, and to make a start with debt cancellation for 18 countries. This should improve growth performance, but would be more effective if western countries fulfilled their promise to phase out agricultural trade barriers and subsidies. However, the outlook for this looks bleak and indigenous obstacles to improved performance are still very significant. There is also very little recognition by African governments of the role which birth control and family planning could play in accelerating the growth of per capita income. I have assumed that African countries will have a modest growth in per capita income of 1 per cent a year to 2030.

THE RELATIONSHIP BETWEEN ECONOMIC GROWTH, ENERGY CONSUMPTION, CARBON EMISSIONS, AND GLOBAL WARMING

In some quarters there will be doubts about the feasibility of a scenario which projects a 2.25-fold increase in world GDP by 2030. One fear is that development may be interrupted by energy shortages or political developments which block normal channels of supply. Another is that carbon emissions may be on a scale which will create significant global climate change. It is therefore useful to review the historical relation between world GDP, energy consumption, and carbon emissions.

In 1820, fossil fuels were less than 6 per cent of world energy consumption. Before that, energy was derived from organic sources—wood, biomass, wind, peat, animal, and human muscle power. Since then the greater part of energy has been supplied by

Table 7.11. World Consumption of Primary Energy, 1820–2030 (metric tons of oil equivalent)

	Fossil fuels (million tons)	Other sources (million tons)	Total (million tons)	Tons per $1,000 of GDP	Tons per capita
1820	12.9	208.2	221.1	0.32	0.21
1870	133.0	255.5	388.5	0.35	0.31
1900	499.0	326.1	815.1	0.41	0.52
1913	737.7	369.1	1,106.8	0.40	0.62
1940	1,229.6	495.6	1,725.2	0.38	0.75
1950	1,567.9	561.7	2,129.6	0.40	0.84
1973	5,405.4	842.6	6,248.0	0.39	1.60
1990	7,126.0	1,684.7	8,810.7	0.32	1.68
2003	8,612.0	2,111.0	10,723.0	0.26	1.71
2030	11,215.1	3,368.9	14,584.0	0.15	1.78

Notes and Sources: Fossil fuels include coal, oil, and natural gas. Other sources include hydro, wind, and nuclear power as well as biomass (wood, peat, dung, straw, and other crop residues). No allowance is made here for animal and human muscle power. Conversion coefficients are one ton of wood = 0.323 ton of oil; one ton of coal = 0.6458 of oil. Fossil fuels, hydro, wind, and nuclear power 1820 from Mitchell (1975), 1870–1950 derived from Woytinsky and Woytinsky (1953: 930). Biomass 1820–50 assumed to be 0.20 tons per head of population, see Smil (1994: 185–7) for rough estimates back to 1700. My estimate of biomass 1820–1950 is somewhat lower than Smil suggests. In 1973 world per capita supply of biomass was 0.17 and in 2003 0.18 of a ton. 1973 and 2003 from International Energy Agency, *Energy Balances of OECD Countries, 2002–2003*, Paris; 2005; *Energy Balances of Non-OECD Countries 2002–2003*, Paris 2005: II, 223–6 and *Key World Energy Statistics*, Paris 2005: 49ff. Energy figures for 2030 are from the Maddison projection in Table 7.15.

fossil fuels which have been cheaper and more efficient. By 2003, fossil fuels provided 80 per cent of energy needs. Energy consumption rose 48-fold from 1820 to 2003, but fossil fuel consumption rose more than 650-fold. (see Tables 7.11 and 7.12). In the nineteenth century, energy consumption rose faster than GDP. From 1900 to 1973, it advanced more or less at the same pace, but the energy intensity of world GDP declined significantly after the oil shocks of the 1970s. The rise in energy prices

Table 7.12. Structure of World Energy Demand, 1900, 2003, and 2030

	(Million tons of oil equivalent)			% share	% share	% share
	1900	2003	2030	1900	2003	2030
Coal	474.5	2,582	3,512	58.24	24.1	22.8
Oil	18.0	3,785	4,955	2.20	35.3	32.2
Gas	6.5	2,244	3,370	0.80	20.9	21.9
Nuclear	0.0	687	1,070	0.00	6.4	6.9
Hydro	3.0	227	422	0.36	2.1	2.7
Biomass and waste	312.7	1,143	1,703	38.40	10.7	11.1
Other renewables	*	54	373	*	0.5	2.4
Total	814.7	10,723	15,405	100.00	100.0	100.0

Note: *included with biomass.

Source: 1900 as in Table 7.11. 2003 from IEA (2005), *World Energy Outlook, 2005*; 270. 2030 (alternative scenario estimate) from IEA, *World Energy Outlook, 2006*: 528.

Table 7.13. Incidence of World Carbon Emissions, 1820–2030 (emissions in million metric tons)

	Fossil fuel emissions	Fossil fuel as % of total energy	Emissions: tons per $1,000 of GDP	Emissions: tons per head of population	Weight of carbon emitted as % of energy consumed
1820	14	6.0	0.020	0.01	6
1870	147	34.2	0.132	0.12	38
1900	534	61.2	0.271	0.34	66
1913	943	66.6	0.345	0.53	86
1940	1,299	71.3	0.289	0.57	75
1950	1,630	73.6	0.306	0.65	77
1973	4,271	86.5	0.267	1.09	68
1990	5,655	80.9	0.209	1.08	64
2003	6,705	80.4	0.166	1.07	63
2030	8,794	76.9	0.091	1.08	60

Notes and Sources: Column 1, 1820–1950 from Marland, Boden and Andres (2005), US Dept. of Energy. 1973, 1990 and 2003 from the International Energy Agency (2005: 93). 2030 emissions from Maddison estimate in Table 7.15. The estimates are confined to carbon emissions from fossil fuels. Emissions from burning biomass are assumed to be offset by subsequent sequestration of carbon. Other sources of energy (hydro, solar, wind, and nuclear) are carbon free.

created incentives to use energy more efficiently, and recent rises may well have a similar effect. The IEA expects that, by 2030, energy intensity will fall to less than half the 1990 ratio. Nevertheless per capita consumption has risen eight-fold since 1820 and continues to increase, though at a much slower pace than it did before 1973.

Carbon emissions rose dramatically from 1820 to 1913 in relation to GDP and population as fossil fuel replaced biomass (see Table 7.13). They fell somewhat in relation to GDP from 1913 to 1973 and sharply from 1973 to 2003. IEA forecasts a further fall by 2030. The ratio of emissions to energy consumption peaked in 1913 and has fallen significantly since then (see last column of Table 7.13). Some of the fall in the emission ratio is due to increases in energy efficiency and legislation to reduce air pollution. However, the declining share of coal and the rising share of gas in energy consumption (see Table 7.12) also had a major impact. 'The carbon intensity of natural gas is twenty-five per cent less than that of oil and forty per cent less than that of coal' (Houghton 2004: 272).

In spite of this, total carbon emissions will continue to rise. As world population and GDP grow, the atmospheric concentration of carbon dioxide and most other greenhouse gases will increase (methane and CFCs excepted).

Table 7.14 shows the level of carbon emissions in 1990 and 2003 and the incidence of emissions in relation to population, GDP, and energy use in 2003. The top ten countries were responsible for 66 per cent of world emissions and the top 20 nearly 80 per cent. The two big countries with the lowest ratio of emissions relative to GDP are France and Brazil, due to large scale production of energy by atomic power and by

Table 7.14. Top Twenty Carbon Emitters in 2003

	2003 Emissions million tons	Emissions per capita tons	Emissions per $1000 of GDP	Primary Energy Use m. toe	Energy Use per capita toe	1990 Emissions million tons
USA	1,562.3	5.38	0.19	2,280.79	7.86	1,320.5
China	1,042.9	0.81	0.17	1,409.38	1.09	615.3
Russia	416.4	2.88	0.46	639.72	4.42	551.5
Japan	327.7	2.57	0.12	517.10	4.05	276.2
India	286.3	0.27	0.13	553.39	0.53	163.0
Germany	233.0	2.83	0.15	347.12	4.21	263.5
Canada	150.9	4.69	0.20	260.64	8.09	114.6
UK	147.3	2.45	0.11	231.95	3.86	152.8
Italy	123.7	2.13	0.11	181.03	3.12	109.1
S. Korea	122.3	2.54	0.16	205.30	4.26	61.7
France	106.3	1.76	0.08	271.29	4.51	96.9
Mexico	102.1	0.98	0.14	159.94	1.55	80.0
Iran	95.2	1.42	0.18	136.44	2.03	47.8
Australia	94.7	4.80	0.20	112.65	5.71	70.8
Indonesia	86.8	0.40	0.11	161.55	0.75	39.9
S. Africa	86.7	1.95	0.45	118.57	2.67	69.4
Spain	85.4	2.12	0.13	136.10	3.38	56.4
S. Arabia	83.6	3.32	0.44	130.78	5.20	48.1
Brazil	82.6	0.45	0.08	193.24	1.06	52.5
Ukraine	80.9	1.70	0.63	132.56	2.78	162.4
Top 20	**5,316.9**	**1.33**	**0.19**	**8,179.54**	**2.05**	**4,352.4**
Others	**1,388.6**	**0.62**	**0.11**	**2,543.60**	**1.11**	**1,302.7**
World	**6,705.5**	**1.07**	**0.164**	**10,723.14**	**1.71**	**5,655.1**

Notes and Sources: N.B. First five columns refer to 2003. Emissions for top 20 countries from International Energy Agency, *CO2 Emissions from Fuel Combustion, 1971–2003*, Paris 2005: II, 4–5. This source reports CO2 emissions, where tons of carbon dioxide emitted are estimated by multipying tons of carbon emissions by 3.667 (i.e., 44/12—the molecular weight ratio of carbon dioxide to carbon). Total 2003 carbon emissions from IEA, *World Energy Outlook* (2005: 93). Primary energy supply (use) (in million tons of oil equivalent) from IEA, *Energy Balances of OECD Countries, 2002–2003*, Paris, 2005, and *Energy Balances of Non-OECD Countries, 2002–2003*, Paris, 2005.

ethanol (Norway has the same low coefficient). If all countries had the same success in producing carbon-free energy, world emissions would be cut by half.

The IEA (International Energy Agency), projects energy consumption and emissions to the year 2030 based on two fully articulated scenarios. The 'Reference' scenario provides a 'baseline vision' of how energy markets would evolve if governments do nothing beyond their present commitments, without considering 'posssible, potential or even likely future policy action'. The 'Alternative' scenario analyses the impact of policies that countries in all regions are considering adopting or might reasonably be expected to adopt at some point over the projected period (see IEA 2006: 54). There is also a short analysis (pp. 256–65) of the technologies required to keep carbon emissions in 2030 at their 2004 level.

Given the fact that oil prices rose sharply from $13 a barrel in 1998 to an average above $60 in 2006, that many countries are worried about the security of energy

Table 7.15. Projections of World Energy Demand and Emissions, 2003–30: IEA and Maddison

	IEA 2004 Projection		IEA 2006 Projection		Maddison Projection	
	2003	2030	2003	2030	2003	2030
World GDP, billion 1990 PPP dollars						
	40,664	94,322	40,664	101,900	40,913	96,580
World energy demand, million metric tons of oil equivalent						
	10,709	14,654	10,709	15,405	10,760	14,584
Energy intensity, tons per $1000 GDP						
	0.263	0.155	0.263	0.151	0.263	0.151
Carbon emissions, million metric tons						
	6,705	8,640	6,705	9,294	6,736	8,794
Emissions tons per ton of energy consumed						
	0.626	0.590	0.626	0.603	0.626	0.603

Notes and Source: IEA 2004 alternative projection from *World Energy Outlook*, Paris, 2004: 44 and 416; IEA 2006 alternative projection from *World Energy Outlook*, Paris, 2006: 59 and 528–9; Maddison GDP projection from Table 7.4, Maddison 2030 energy demand derived by using IEA 2006 energy intensity coefficient, Maddison 2030 emissions derived by using the IEA 2006 emissions coefficient. Here emissions are shown in carbon units (3.667 tons of carbon dioxide=1 ton of carbon). The IEA 2004 GDP projections were in 2000 prices and PPPs, their world GDP being $49,434 billion in 2003; the IEA 2006 GDP projections were in 2005 prices and PPPs, with a world GDP of $55,851 billion in 2003. I rebased both of them on my numeraire (1990 prices and PPPs), and used their 2003–2030 volume movement for world GDP. I am grateful to IEA for providing a detailed breakdown of its GDP projections.

supply and the prospect of global warming, the alternative projection seems the most plausible and I used it in Table 7.15.

The IEA 'World Energy Model' is fairly complex as it involves projections broken down for seven categories of energy, by sector of use in ten countries and 11 regions. However, the broad outline is fairly simple. The expected growth of population and GDP are the basic driving forces in energy demand. The second element is the changing intensity of energy demand in relation to GDP, and the third is the changing ratio of carbon emissions to growth in energy use. The IEA world aggregate for GDP is constructed using estimates of purchasing power parity rather than exchange rates, and their population projection is from the UN Population Division. The population and GDP projections are the same in both the Reference and the Alternative scenarios.

Table 7.15 shows the major components of the projections made by IEA in 2004 and 2006. It raised its projection of 2003–30 world GDP growth from 3.16 per cent a year in the 2004 exercise to 3.46 in the 2006 version. The intensity of energy use falls substantially in both versions, but somewhat more in the 2006 version. However, the ratio of carbon emissions to energy consumption is somewhat higher in the 2006 version as the increased price of oil was assumed to lead to a bigger proportionate use of coal than in the 2004 projection.

My projection of world GDP growth for 2003–30 (3.23 per cent a year) is faster than IEA 2004, but significantly slower than the IEA 2006 projection, which seems on the high side for non-OECD countries. I used the same energy to GDP growth ratio as IEA 2006, and the same ratio of emissions to energy use. My estimate of population growth is virtually identical to that of IEA (see source note for Table 7.1).

A major reason for the rise in energy prices from 2000 to 2006 was the inelastic supply of oil. Most of the major exporters are members of the OPEC cartel, and their government owned companies are not eager to expand production to a degree which might lead to or reinforce a price collapse. They underinvested because of the fall in oil prices from 1980 to 1998. In the Middle East, oil production in 2003 was only 4 per cent higher than in 1973, in Venezuela it had fallen by a quarter. In Nigeria it increased by a sixth, but supply has been interrupted by sabotage in the producing regions. In Iraq and Iran, production fell because of wars. In the countries of the former USSR, oil output was 10 per cent lower in 2003 than in 1990. In 2003, world oil output was 29 per cent higher than in 1973, but natural gas production had risen 2.25-fold, and coal by three-quarters (see Tables 7.19 and 7.20). IEA expects this differential in the supply situation to continue; 'proven reserves of natural gas and coal are much larger' than than the cumulative consumption it projects up to 2030. For gas they are equal to 64 years of current consumption, for coal 164 years and barely 42 years for crude oil and natural gas liquids (IEA 2006a: 72–3).

Limits to Growth?

From 1820 to 2003, world population rose six-fold and per capita income nearly ten-fold. There have been repeated warnings that this is too good to last and that natural resources will bring the process to a halt or dramatic slowdown. The most prominent pessimist was Malthus. Other ecodoomsters such as Ehrlich, Meadows, and the Club of Rome have echoed his message more recently with varying degrees of emphasis and stridency.

Thomas Malthus (1766–1834) had a growth schema with only two factors of production—natural resources and labour—with no allowance for technical progress, capital formation, or gains from international specialization. In 1798, he portrayed the general situation of humanity as one where population pressure put such strains on the ability of natural resources to produce subsistence that equilibrium would be attained only by various catastrophes. His influence has been strong and persistent, largely because of his forceful rhetoric and primitive scaremongering.

Sickly seasons, epidemics, pestilence, and plague will advance in terrific array, and sweep off their thousands and ten thousands. Gigantic inevitable famine stalks in the rear, and with one mighty blow levels the population with the food of the world.

He would have been very surprised to discover that Britain in 2003 would have only 1.2 per cent of its working population in agriculture and a life expectation of 78 years.

Other analysts have stressed the possibility of energy constraints rather than food shortage as threats to economic growth. William Stanley Jevons (1835–82), was much more interested in empirical evidence than the young Malthus. In *The Coal Problem* (1865) he saw coal production as the essential element in the dynamism of the British economy. In 1865, the UK was the world leader. Its per capita GDP ($3,000) was bigger than in any of the other advanced capitalist countries (Australia, France, Germany, the Netherlands, and the US) and so was its total GDP. Its coal output was over 80 million tons out of a world total of 136 million, and it was the major coal exporter. Coal was the only significant fossil fuel and represented about a third of the world energy supply.

Jevons estimated that British coal output was 83.6 million tons in 1861, and projected a need for 2,607 million tons in 1961, if 'the present' annual rate of growth of 3.5 per cent persisted (in fact production grew from 1820 to 1860 at about 3.8 per cent a year). Such growth 'would exhaust our mines to a depth of 4,000 feet, or 1,500 feet deeper than our present deepest mines' (p. 274), and bring a prohibitive rise in prices. He rejected the feasibility of substitutes—timber, wind, water, tidal energy, hydrogen, or petroleum. He thought that supply of the latter 'more limited and uncertain than that of coal' (p. 185). He also rejected the feasibility of large scale imports, because of heavy transport costs. Hence he concluded that 'our present happy progressive condition is a thing of limited duration', eventually, 'the larger part of the rising generation will find themselves superfluous, and must either leave the country in a vast body, or remain here to create painful pressure and poverty' (p. 422). He recommended 'wholesale emigration' to countries like Australia or the US which had much larger coal reserves. In fact British coal production peaked at 292 million tons in 1913, fell to 118 million in 1973 and 26 million in 2003. In 2003, British energy consumption was equivalent to 370 million tons of coal, about a seventh of what he projected for 1961, and British coal provided only 7 per cent of it. Thus Jevons failed to see the possibilities for reducing energy intensity, was wrong about the substitution possibilities and the pace of technological advance. He also demonstrated the fragility of centennial forecasts.

In the 1870s, Jevons argued without much success that decennial variation in the intensity of solar radiation had a major impact on harvests and the duration of the business cycle. Although his evidence was weak he provided an interesting foretaste of the recent debate on global warming.

Global Warming

The major thrust of the modern debate on energy is assessment of the impact of human economic activity in raising the global temperature by causing a change in the net impact of solar radiation.

The earth's surface is warmed by incoming radiation from the sun. Most is absorbed by the earth and oceans. A third is bounced back from clouds, and reflective areas of the earth's surface such as deserts. Some is re-radiated back into space as infra-red energy; part of this is trapped in the atmosphere by water vapour and 'greenhouse gases' (such as carbon dioxide and methane) which bounce the heat back to earth again. Without this blanketing effect the earth's average surface temperature would be 33 °C colder, and night-time temperatures much lower than they are. A growing concentration of carbon dioxide in the atmosphere due to increased use of fossil fuels and, to some extent, to changes in land use, is the reason why more heat is bouncing back and the world has been getting warmer.

Quantifying the Causes and Extent of Global Warming

The Intergovernmental Panel on Climate Change (IPCC) produced a detailed examination of the driving forces likely to induce global warming in its *Special Report on Emissions Scenarios* (SRES 2000). It was prepared to provide guidance to the 164 countries which have ratified the Kyoto Protocol which aims to mitigate the warming process by reduction of greenhouse gases. It examined the prospects over successive decades to the year 2100. It was benchmarked on the situation in 1990, which is the baseline for the Kyoto policy target for its Annex 1 member countries (i.e., a reduction in their carbon emissions to 95 per cent of their 1990 level by 2012).

SRES presented 40 assessments for the 110-year period, which it called 'storylines and scenarios', rather than projections. The main influences considered were population growth, per capita GDP and GDP growth, changes in the intensity of energy consumption per head of population and GDP, changes in the composition of energy used, emissions of ten types of greenhouse gas, and the cumulative increase of carbon dioxide (by far the most important). The increased concentration of these gases in the atmosphere is the final cause of climate change. The IPCC's causal elements are anthropogenic There is no consideration of possible variations in solar radiation or differences in the earth's exposure to them in the course of its orbit. The scenarios were developed by six different forecasting groups—two in Japan, two in the US, one in Austria, and another in the Netherlands.

IPCC projection techniques differ from those of the IEA. Its futurology deals with more distant horizons and, like the Meadows report of the 1970s, it uses the analyical tools of 'systems analysis' rather than economics.

The scenarios show a four-fold division of the world: (i) *OECD*—western Europe, North America, Australia, New Zealand, Japan, and Turkey—with the highest per capita incomes and emissions, and three regional groups which currently have much lower per capita incomes; (ii) *REF*—former communist countries of eastern Europe and the successor states of the USSR; (iii) *Asia* excluding Japan and some west Asian countries; (iv) *ALM*—an amalgam of Latin American, African, and some 'Middle

Table 7.16. Dynamic Forces Driving Global Warming in and within the IPCC Storylines

	Annual compound growth rates 1990–2100				Carbon emissions	1990–2100 Cumulative emissions billion tons	2100 Per cap. GDP 1990 $
	Population	Per capita GDP	GDP	Energy consumption			
A1 world	0.26	2.70	2.98	1.63	0.59	1,499	74,900
A2 world	0.96	1.30	2.28	1.55	1.45	1,938	15,888
B1 world	0.26	2.29	2.55	0.78	−0.13	1,060	47,880
B2 world	0.62	1.60	2.23	1.12	0.62	1,388	22,767
A1 OECD	0.23	1.60	1.83	0.79	−0.18	344	109,099
A1 other	0.27	3.89	4.18	1.99	0.88	1,155	68,517
A2 OECD	0.51	1.08	1.59	0.91	0.86	507	57,888
A2 other	1.03	2.15	3.20	1.86	1.70	1,431	11,258
B1 OECD	0.23	1.30	1.53	0.02	−0.78	278	84,734
B1 other	0.27	3.42	3.71	1.13	0.14	782	41,466
B2 OECD	0.07	1.06	1.13	0.25	−0.36	317	61,099
B2 other	0.70	2.69	3.41	1.49	0.93	1,071	19,017

Notes and Sources: SRES, pp. 381–5 for A; pp. 466–70 for A2; pp. 496–500 for B1; pp. 541–5 for B2. Carbon emissions include those from fossil fuels and other sources. All the scenarios understate GDP growth, because 1990 exchange rates are used instead of purchasing power parities (see Tables 7.17 and 7.18).

Eastern' countries. All their scenarios project significant convergence between per capita income levels in the Rich and the Rest, This assumption is a major driving force in projected energy use and carbon emissions.

The top panel of Table 7.16 summarizes the four basic 'storylines' for the world as a whole. It shows the main driving forces which explain aggregate growth of carbon emissions and their cumulation in the atmosphere (i.e., the troposphere to about 10km above the earth, and the stratosphere above reaching 50km from the earth). The bottom panel shows the big differences between growth momentum expected in the advanced OECD countries and the rest of the world between 1990 and 2100. Growth is not expected to be monotonic. It is faster to 2050 and slows down thereafter.

All the scenarios project a fall in the energy intensity of GDP and assume that emissions rise more slowly than energy consumption. In 1990, the OECD group was responsible for 40 per cent of world emissions. By 2100, this is expected to fall to 17 per cent in scenario A1, to 21 per cent in A2, 19 per cent in in B1, and 14 per cent in B2.

A1 assumes the most rapid growth of world GDP per capita, the highest degree of convergence between the four groups, and a rapid introduction of new and more efficient technologies. Coal is assumed to be only 4 per cent of world energy consumption in 2100. Carbon emissions grow only a third as fast as energy consumption. There are 17 variants of this scenario. They project cumulative carbon emissions from 1990 to 2100 ranging from 1,094 to 2,532 billion tons.

A2 assumes the fastest growth of population (nearly four times as fast as A1). Population in 2100 is projected to be bigger than the high estimate of the UN (2003).

It assumes the slowest growth and convergence of per capita income. Coal is assumed to be half of world energy consumption in 2100 and emissions grow almost as fast as energy consumption. The six variants of this storyline project cumulative carbon emissions ranging from 1,352 to 1,938 billion tons in 2100.

B1 shows the same population growth as A1, somewhat slower per capita income growth, and less convergence. Coal is assumed to be 8 per cent of energy use in 2100. Energy consumption is expected to increase about one-third as fast as GDP, with carbon emissions lower in 2100 than in 1990. The nine variants of this storyline project cumulative emissions ranging from 773 to 1,390 billion tons.

B2 assumes population growth more than twice as fast as A1 and B1, with slower per capita growth, less convergence, and slower technical progress. Coal is assumed to be 19 per cent of energy consumption in 2100. Energy consumption is expected to grow half as fast as GDP and emissions half as fast as energy consumption. The eight variations of this storyline project cumulative emissions ranging from 1,164 to 1,686 billion tons in 2100.

Thus, between all 40 scenarios, cumulative emissions from 1990 to 2100 range from 733 to 2,532 billion tons—a ratio of 3.5:1. This gives a preliminary notion of the possible range in degree of global warming envisioned by IPCC for 2100.

Problems with IPCC's Quantification of Energy Demand and Emissions

Curiously the IPCC makes no assessment of the plausibility of the different options advanced. My hunch is that B1 is the most plausible, but there are several problems with all the scenarios:

1. There is inadequate attention to history. No attempt is made to quantify the driving forces which explain why global average temperatures rose by 0.65 °C from 1860 to 2000. As the warming process was uneven in this period and historical indicators of the driving forces are available (see Tables 7.11, 7.12 and 7.13), it is strange that IPCC embarked on such detailed futurology before testing its basic models against the firmer historical evidence. There was a wobbly pattern of global temperature change from 1860 to 1910, with no net increase between the terminal points, a rise in average temperature of about 0.4 °C from 1910 to 1945 when world GDP rose about 1.7 per cent a year, an interval of global cooling from 1945 to 1976 when world GDP rose more than 4 per cent a year, and a rise from then to 2000, which raised the temperature 0.25 °C above the 1945 level (IPCC, Synthesis Report, 2001: 171). It is odd that the cooling happened when the pace of world economic growth was a good deal faster than in 1910–45 and 1976–2000 (see www.ggdc.net/Maddison for the

pattern of world GDP growth). The cooling occurred when aerosol emissions were reaching their peak but it is not clear whether this explains all of it.

2. IPCC assumed that the global climate in the northern hemisphere was stable for 1,000 years before 1860. This view has been challenged by a number of critics including Lindzen, McKitrick, Robinson, Reiter, Ruddiman, and the Wegman report to the US Congress. These critics draw attention to the warm medieval period and the little ice age in the northern hemisphere. Ruddiman also suggests that there was a very slow upward movement in global temperature over 8,000 years prior to 1820 due to anthropogenic causes—the development and spread of agriculture. He suggests that the long run climatic impact was comparable in magnitude to that from 1860 to 2000 and that it helped prevent the onset of an ice age. He also stresses the importance of 'thermal inertia', i.e., the impact of the oceans in dampening and delaying the impact of the forces driving global warming. The oceans cover 70 per cent of the earth's surface to an average depth of 4 km, and provide an important sink for carbon dioxide. 'The total amount of carbon in the ocean is about 50 times greater than the amount in the atmosphere, and is exchanged with the atmosphere on a time scale of several hundred years' (see *Climate Change: The Scientific Basis,* chapter 3.2.3).

3. The SRES report did not estimate the change in total carbon concentration in the atmosphere, but only the likely cumulative emissions over the 110 year period 1990–2100. To estimate the net change in concentration we need to know the degree of concentration in 1990 and the rate of decay of greenhouse gases which existed in 1990. The House of Lords report on the *Economics of Climate Change* (2005: 11, 14, 21, and 32) made several references to this depreciation process but it is not mentioned in the SRES (2000) report. The IPCC *Synthesis Report* (2001: 182) estimated the 'atmospheric lifetime' of carbon dioxide to be 5 to 200 years and adds that 'no single lifetime has been defined for CO_2 because of different rates of uptake by different removal processes'.

4. The final results of the SRES exercise were shown in the IPCC *Synthesis Report*. Atmospheric concentration of carbon dioxide rose from 280 ppm in 1750 to 350 in 1990 and 368 ppm in the year 2000 (ppm 'parts per million' is the number of CO_2 molecules per million molecules of dry air, i.e., 0.0368 per cent of the atmosphere). IPCC 'carbon cycle models' from the 'illustrative SRES scenarios' predicted a range of 540–970 ppm in 2100. Allowance for uncertainties widened the range by 10 to 30 per cent, giving a total range of '490 to 1,260 ppm' (p. 159). On page 244, a range of 478 to 1,099 is given. Thus the reported range was adjusted from 1:1.8 to 1:2.6 or 1:2.3. However, the global mean temperature in 2100 was estimated to be 1.4°–5.8 °C above the average for 1990, i.e., a range of 1:4.1 (see *Synthesis Report*, pp. 1, 69, 156, 159, and 244). There is no clear explanation of the process by which this final range was estimated.

5. The International Energy Agency (2006) projected carbon emissions in 2030 smaller than most of the IPCC Scenarios. The IEA reference scenario shows emissions of 11 billion in 2030, and the more plausible alternative scenario 9.3 billion (see Table 7.15). Thirty-eight of the IPCC scenarios show emissions higher than the IEA's alternative scenario and 27 are higher than its reference scenario. Hence most of the IPCC scenarios seem to overstate emissions and climate change up to 2030.

6. The SRES scenarios are very aggregative, and divide the world into only four regions. It is odd that Latin America, Africa, and Middle Eastern oil producers are conjoined when their levels of income and historical momentum have been so different. It is also odd that the experience of no individual country is examined. In 2003, 69 per cent of world carbon emissions came from 12 countries (see Table 7.14). Their comparative prospects and problems in reducing emissions would certainly have been worth scrutiny. In China, for instance 60 per cent of energy is derived from coal, the most polluting source of energy. In France the proportion is 5 per cent, in the UK, 16, Russia, 17, and the US 23 per cent.

7. It is legitimate to assume some degree of economic convergence in the future between the rich group of OECD countries and some other regions such as Asia, but the degree of convergence assumed in the IPCC scenarios seems implausible and differs sharply from historical experience. In fact, the convergence they assume is much bigger than it appears, because exchange rates rather than purchasing power converters were used to measure the relative income levels of different regions in the benchmark year. The top panel of Table 7.17 shows the IPCC A1 scenario for the world and its four component groups in 2100 using 1990 exchange rates of the benchmark year. The last column shows the per capita multipliers used by IPCC to produce its 2100 scenario. Average per capita income reaches $109,000 in OECD countries, about $101,000 in the former communist group, $72,000 in Asia, and $61,000 in Africa.

The bottom panel shows what happens if we use PPP converters and the same per capita multipliers. There is a much narrower initial divergence in per capita income between the groups and a higher total for world GDP in 1990. All three of the poorer groups become richer than OECD countries in 2100, and world GDP increases 49-rather than 25-fold, i.e., a growth rate of 3.6 a year instead of 3.0 per cent in the top panel. In the IPCC scenario, 77 per cent of 2100 GDP is generated by non-OECD countries, in the PPP scenario, 91 per cent.

Table 7.18 makes a similar confrontation for the shorter period 2000–30. The top panel shows world GDP growing by 4.1 per cent a year using 1990 exchange rates. The bottom panel using 1990 PPPs shows greater convergence and a growth rate of 5.6 per cent. Both show much faster GDP growth than the IEA and Maddison projections for 2030 (see Table 7.15 above). The A1 scenario projects world energy consumption rising by 2.5 per cent a year in

Table 7.17. IPCC A1 Scenario with Exchange Rate and PPP Converters, 1990–2100

	1990 Population million	1990 Per capita GDP 1990 ER $	1990 With IPCC GDP billion 1990 ER $	2100 Population million	2100 Per capita GDP 1990 ER $	2100 GDP billion 1990 ER $	1990–2100 Per capita multipliers
OECD	859	19,092	16,400	1,110	109,099	121,100	5.71
REF	413	2,421	1,100	339	100,885	34,200	41.67
Asia	2,798	536	1,500	2,882	71,929	207,300	134.20
ALM	1,192	1,594	1,900	2,727	60,836	165,900	38.17
World	5,262	3,972	20,900	7,056	74,901	528,500	18.86

	Population million	With Per capita GDP 1990 PPP $	MADDISON GDP billion 1990 PPP $	Population million	Per capita GDP 1990 PPP $	GDP billion 1990 PPP $	Per capita multipliers
OECD	800	18,781	15,020	1,110	107,240	119,036	5.71
REF	411	6,450	2,651	339	268,772	91,114	41.67
Asia	2,980	2,121	6,321	2,882	284,638	820,327	134.20
ALM	1,066	2,948	3,145	2,727	112,525	306,856	38.17
World	5,257	5,162	27,136	7,056	189,531	1,337,333	36.72

Notes and Sources: Top panel 1990 and 2100 population (million) and GDP (billion 1990 dollars with 1990 exchange rate conversion) from IPCC (2000: 381–5); per capita GDPs and 1990/2100 per capita multipliers derived from the same source. Bottom left panel 1990 population from Table 7.1 and GDP estimates (in billion 1990 dollars with Geary-Khamis PPP conversion) from Table 7.4 and www.ggdc.net/Maddison. Bottom right panel 2100 population and regional per capita GDP multipliers as for IPCC. Because of the difference in the 1990 benchmark weights, the 2100 aggregate per capita multiplier is twice as big as that of the IPCC. The IPCC includes Turkey in the OECD group, and 13 other west Asian countries (including the major oil producers—Iraq, Iran, Kuwait, Qatar, Saudi Arabia, and the United Arab Emirates) in the ALM group; I have included all 14 west Asian countries in Asia.

Table 7.18. IPCC A1 Scenario with Exchange Rate and PPP Converters, 2000–2030

	2000 Population million	2000 With Per capita GDP 1990 ER $	2000 IPCC GDP billion 1990 ER$	2030 Population million	2030 Per capita GDP 1990 ERs$	2030 GDP billion 1990 ER$	2000–30 Per capita multipliers
OECD	919	22,307	20,500	1,043	36,433	38,000	*1.63*
REF	419	1,909	800	435	12,184	5,300	*6.38*
Asia	3,261	827	2,700	4,147	6,318	26,200	*7.64*
ALM	1,519	1,777	2,700	2,557	7,626	19,500	*4.29*
World	**6,117**	**4,365**	**26,700**	**8,182**	**10,890**	**89,100**	2.49

	Population million	With Per capita GDP 1990 PPP$	MADDISON GDP million 1990 PP$	Population million	Per capita GDP 1990 PPP$	GDP billion 1990 PPP$	Per capita multipliers
OECD	855	21,929	19,400	947	35,816	33,918	*1.63*
REF	411	4,882	2,005	402	31,159	12,526	*6.38*
Asia	3,478	3,179	11,059	4,674	24,286	113,515	*7.64*
ALM	1,318	3,217	4,240	2,151	13,806	29,697	*4.29*
World	**6,062**	**6,054**	**36,704**	**8,175**	**23,200**	**189,656**	3.83

this period, IEA (2006a) 1.36 per cent. A1 projects carbon emissions from fossil fuels growing by 2.4 per cent a year, IEA only 1.2 per cent. IPCC made global temperature projections for 2025 and 2050 (see *Synthesis Report*, p. 69); interpolating between these, their implied projection for 2030 is an increase over the 1990 level ranging from 0.5 to 1.3 °C. In view of my scepticism about the higher IPCC projections of GDP, energy consumption and emissions, the lower end of their temperature projections seems the more plausible.

8. Unlike the IEA, IPCC uses exchange rates rather than PPPs in its GDP scenarios. The problems which arise from this were pointed out on a number of occasions by Ian Castles, David Henderson, Alan Heston, William Nordhaus, and myself.[1] IPCC had two kinds of response to this point: (a) they did use 'calibrated' PPPs for nine scenarios in addition to the 40 scenarios using exchange rates (see pp. 401, 416, 431, 446, 481, 516, 526, 531, and 561 in SRES 2000); (b) their energy and emissions projections were not affected by using exchange rates rather than PPPs.

IPCC's nine calibrated PPP estimates were constructed by IIASA (the International Institute for Applied Systems Analysis) for their 'Message' scenarios. Their derivation is not described and they depart from normal practice by assuming that the ratio of the PPP to the exchange rate changes (converges) between 1990 and 2100. By 2100 the differential disappears. The real GDP growth rates using these IIASA PPPs are all slower than the counterpart using exchange rate weights, but the estimate of the growth of primary energy consumption and emissions associated with the alternative measures are identical in all nine Message scenarios. Understandably, the IPCC did not include these phantom scenarios in the 40 they used for analytical purposes.

THE IMPACT OF CLIMATE CHANGE

The IPCC foresees two types of impact from global warming: changes which are considered more or less certain and predictable within their 110-year time frame; and potential impacts over a longer period which are less certain and could trigger irreversible disruptions in the world climate system.

The Main First Category Consequences

1. An increasing frequency of extreme weather events-floods, droughts, heat-waves, and hurricanes.

2. A rise in sea level ranging from 9 to 88 cm by 2100, with widespread damage to coastal areas and countries operating near to sea-level such as Bangladesh and the Maldives.

3. Thawing of permafrost, shrinking of snow cover and glaciers.

4. Threats to human health in hot climates, offset by reductions in cold-related disease and mortality in presently cold climates.

5. Extinction of some vulnerable species and loss of biodiversity by land and by sea.

6. A differentiated impact on agriculture, with declining crop yields in some regions and increases in others.

The possible impact of these changes is analysed in some detail for eight major regions (Africa, Asia, Europe, North America, Latin America, Australasia, polar regions, and small island states). In Europe the positive features would seem to predominate, and richer countries have a greater capacity to cushion negative impacts by adaptive policy action. The adverse impacts are expected to be strongest in Africa.

The IPCC surveyed possibilities for mitigating global warming by reducing or eliminating carbon emissions. Options for taxation, subsidy, and regulation, and their costs and benefits were explored for different sectors. It examined the prospects for joint research on solar energy, improvements in photovoltaic cells, development of nuclear fusion, clean coal technology combined with carbon sinks, ethanol and other biofuels, wind and wave power, hybrid engine cars, etc.

The Second Category of Long-Term Irreversible Catastrophic Risks

1. Melting of the Greenland and west Antarctic ice-sheets, each of which could raise the sea level by 3 metres over a thousand years.

2. Collapse of thermohaline circulation would eliminate the warming effect of the Gulf Stream, reducing west European temperatures by 8 °C.

3. Collapse of the Amazon rainforest which would be replaced by savannah.

4. Melting of the Himalayan ice and snowcaps, so that rainfall would come in floods and change the Indian river systems and monsoons.

5. Melting of Siberian permafrost would release methane on a large scale and accelerate global warming.

6. Increased desertification in Africa.

This set of problems is expected to emerge if the greenhouse gas concentration passes a critical tipping point. Beyond this, IPCC argues that there would be no effective possibility of corrective action.

All these potential longer run threats would have global implications and would require coordinated global action to prevent them happening. There would be major problems in deciding now on expenditure to benefit future generations and in dividing costs between countries at widely differing levels of income (see Nordhaus 2006).

THE KYOTO PROTOCOL

Joint action of a limited kind was initiated in 2005 when the Kyoto protocol came into force. It has been ratified by more than 160 countries. It consists of two groups. The advanced capitalist countries of the OECD (except Australia and the US) and the former communist countries of the Soviet bloc (Annex 1 countries) made a collective commitment to cut their emissions of six key greenhouse gases by 5 per cent of their 1990 level by 2008–12 (individual gases being converted into equivalent CO2 on the basis of their relative radiative potency). The percentage commitment varies between Annex 1 countries. Lower income countries, which include China and India have no commitment of this kind. The intention is to renew the Kyoto commitments at unspecified intervals in the future. An 'emissions trading' scheme established by EU countries permits participants to buy and sell emission reduction credits; a Clean Development Mechanism enables the advanced countries to finance emissions reduction projects in developing countries and receive credit for doing so. All countries agreed to share information on national programmes and research on technologies of carbon reduction.

As one can see from Table 7.14, it seems very unlikely that the 2012 Kyoto goal will be met. There is little real scope for imposing penalties on countries which fail to observe their commitments, or on 'free rider' countries which have not commited themselves. However, it is conceivable that a renewal of the Kyoto Protocol after 2012 could be more effective. The 1987 Montreal Protocol has been successful in bringing a substantial reduction in fluorocarbons which depleted the ozone layer in the stratosphere (see D. I. Stern 2006), and tax incentives to reduce use of leaded gasoline have also had a large degree of successs internationally.

THE REPORT OF THE HOUSE OF LORDS ON CLIMATE CHANGE

In July 2005 the House of Lords Select Committee on Economic Affairs issued an authoritative report on *The Economics of Climate Change*. It was based on oral evidence from 18 invited experts and written submissions from 25 others to the 15 lords who constituted the committee. The experts were a cosmopolitan bunch, drawn from 20 different countries. The evidence was published in full in volume II of the report. The main concerns were to evaluate the IPCC reports SRES (2000) and Climate Change (2001), to consider the costs and benefits of policy options, and to scrutinize the UK government's commitment to reduce Britain's carbon emissions 60 per cent by 2050. There was a wide-ranging and even-handed discussion of these issues by sceptics and believers.[2]

The committee's own conclusions were presented in volume I of the report: (a) 'we have some concerns about the objectivity of the IPCC process, with some of its emissions scenarios and summary documentation apparently influenced by political considerations'; (b) 'there are significant doubts about some aspects of the emissions scenario exercise, in particular, the high emissions scenarios'; (c) there are some positive aspects to global warming and these appear to have been played down in the IPCC reports'. It concluded that 'the scientific context is one of uncertainty' and 'encouraged a dispassionate evidence-based approach to debate and decision making'.

THE STERN REVIEW OF THE ECONOMICS OF CLIMATE CHANGE

This is a British government document, published in November 2006 by HM Treasury, but its perspective is global and its content and presentational technique more like a double-size World Bank report. It is a plan of action requested by the 2005 Gleneagles summit of the G8. It is intended to raise public awareness of the policy implications of climate change and influence government policies worldwide. It is a clarion call for action, and disregards the sceptics who participated in the House of Lords review of the same problem a year earlier.

It was prepared by a 23 person team headed by Sir Nicholas Stern, backed by 36 specially commissioned reports, and visits to 13 countries to explore their policy initiatives in this field. There is also a special IEA volume *Energy Technology Perspectives* (2006), requested by the G-8, which provides a comprehensive survey of technological advances which seem likely to facilitate 'strategies aimed at a clean, clever and competitive energy future'.

Unlike the IPCC which presented 40 different scenarios of the impact of climate change, Stern bases its argument on a single mainstream scenario of future prospects with and without effective policy action.

The first 200 pages analyse the causes and impact of global warming, which is presented as a serious and urgent threat to the world economy and environment. The Review endorses the first order risks predicted by IPCC as inevitable within a twenty-first century timeframe, and the second category of longer term catastrophic risks which may emerge if the atmospheric concentration of greenhouse gases passes a critical tipping point. Given the assumption that 'global stocks of carbon fuel that are profitable to extract' are more than enough to last through the twenty-first century, inaction would virtually commit 'us to a global average temperature rise of over 2 °C. In the longer term there would be more than a 50% chance that the temperature rise would exceed 5 °C'. Unlike the IPCC whose main emphasis was on CO2, the basic numeraire is CO_{2e}, 'carbon dioxide equivalent', a composite measure of six categories of greenhouse gas. This reached 430 ppm in 2006 and the tipping point would be 550 ppm. As CO_{2e} emissions are expected to rise 3 ppm a year, the tipping point is likely to be reached in 40 years time. There is therefore a window of opportunity for policy action to discourage use of carbon fuels within this period. The trade-off is stated thus: either we start now to spend 1 per cent of world GDP to mitigate this accumulation process, or

if we don't act, the overall costs and risks of climate change will be equivalent to losing at least 5 per cent of global GDP each year, now and forever. If a wider range of risks and impacts is taken into account, the estimates of damage could rise to 20% of GDP or more (p. vi).

On page 285, the trade-off is restated as follows: 'In broad brush terms, spending somewhere in the region of 1% of gross world product on average forever could prevent the world from losing the equivalent of 10% of gross world product forever'. These 'broad brush' estimates are derived from a probabilistic integrated assessment model (Page 2002 IAM) which produces 'estimates based on Monte Carlo simulation'. 'It chooses a set of uncertain parameters randomly from pre-determined ranges of possible results' and estimates damage stochastically (see p. 153).

Unlike the IPCC scenarios, there is no quantification of what global per capita income is likely to be in 2050. There is a passing suggestion (p. 239) that 'economic output in the OECD countries is likely to rise by over 200% by then, and in developing regions as a whole by 400% or more', but this seems to be derived rather casually by interpolating Holtsmark's version of an IPCC B1 scenario (p. 180).

The Review's use of the phrase 'now and forever' is not explained. It seems to imply that carbon emissions cumulate to infinity and makes no clear distinction between the cumulation process and the atmospheric concentration. However, its table 8.1 shows the life expectation of different greenhouse gases, e.g., 5–200 years for carbon dioxide, 10 years for methane and 115 years for nitrous oxide, and the Review states that 'It is the stock of carbon in the atmosphere that drives climate change, rather than the annual flow of emissions. Once released, carbon dioxide remains in the atmosphere for up to 100 years' (p. 310). Given these finite magnitudes, it seems clear that the phrase 'now and forever' is rhetorical.

In his critique of the Stern Review, William Nordhaus, the leading US analyst of global warming issues, argues that it exaggerates the urgency and scale of remedial action, given the fact that future generations are expected to have much higher income levels than presently prevails (see Nordhaus 2006b).

In spite of these reservations about the urgency of the Stern review's political message, it is an impressive document, and a useful counterweight to the dismissive official US position.[3] Most of it is a pragmatic, prescriptive and persuasive analysis of policy options for mitigation of global warming by international action. The main options explored are carbon taxes, emissions trading, regulation, cooperative research and diffusion of its results, and aid to promote carbon reduction in developing countries.

There is major emphasis on the potential effectiveness of carbon taxes such as those in force in Scandinavia and tested with success in China. These can be a powerful lever in discouraging use of fossil fuels. It favours harmonization of the incidence of such taxes, and termination of fossil fuel subsidies which amounted to $57 billion a year in OECD countries in 1995–8, and $162 billion in developing countries.

It advocates an extension of the emissions trading schemes which emerged from the Kyoto process.

It points to the success of regulatory action on building codes, and standards for electrical appliances in increasing efficiency in energy use.

It recommends increased governmental support for research and development on non-fossil fuel options. Expenditure has fallen to about half of what it was in the 1980s. It indicates areas where the payoff seems promising, and advocates temporary government subsidies as an initial boost to their uptake 'policy should aim at bringing a portfolio of low-carbon technology options to commercial viability and introduce incentives to redirect consumption to non-carbon sources'.

As the process of reducing use of carbon fuels will be fairly slow, it stresses the need to develop and subsidize facilities for carbon capture and storage, particularly in countries which use a high proportion of coal.

The Review's major concern is with fossil fuels, but 18 per cent of carbon emissions come from land use and 14 per cent from agriculture (p. 171). 'Eight thousand years ago, 50 per cent of the global land surface was covered by forest, compared with only 30 per cent now.' Nevertheless,

the earth's vegetation and soils currently contain the equivalent of almost 7,500 Gt CO_2 ... more than double the amount of carbon accumulated in the atmosphere. The carbon presently locked up in forest ecosystems alone is greater than the amount of carbon in the atmosphere. (pp. 536 and 544).

For this reason, the Review stresses the importance of reforestation as a major and relatively cheap way to reduce carbon emissions. It lists net gains in forest area in 2000–5 as a result of government action in different countries. In China the total was over four million hectares, Spain nearly 300,000, Vietnam quarter of a million, and 159,000 in the US. For agriculture, the main recommendation is to encourage a move from deep ploughing to conservation tillage.

The Review indicates the scope for reducing wastage which is currently 3 per cent of global energy use. It cites Russian gas losses from leaky pipelines and compressors—70 billion cubic metres—and another 60 billion from gas flaring. In India, low investment and maintenance leads to losses in transmission of electricity, reinforced by widespread incidence of theft and uncollected bills (see pp. 275 and 279).

In fact, there clearly is scope for substantial reduction in the emissions intensity of GDP. France and Norway have achieved an intensity half the world average by using policies which were not too expensive and could be replicated elsewhere. The motivation for action is not only the risk of global warming, but the desire for energy security and reduction of air pollution. However, the experience with the Kyoto process, where the US and Australia are dropouts, and the agreed cuts are quite modest makes it clear that international cooperation on the scale the Stern review postulates will be difficult to achieve.

The review recognizes this. It investigates the possibility of improving the mechanisms for international cooperation which already exist between developed countries and it recommends a substantial increase in funds and technical assistance to promote projects to reduce carbon emissions in developing countries

It assesses the policy experience of the '10 largest economies' (p. 456), which jointly produce 64 per cent of global emissions. This is a useful advance on the IPCC reports which were concerned with regions, not countries. As China may fairly soon surpass the US as the biggest carbon emitter, it is very useful that the Review analyses Chinese efforts to mitigate carbon emissions in some detail. This should be useful in undermining the official US view that China is a free rider in this field.

CONCLUSIONS ON GLOBAL WARMING

In spite of scepticism about the higher IPCC scenarios for the twenty-first century, and the doomsday outlook beyond that point, it would be a mistake to dismiss the likelihood and implications of a milder degree of global warming. Proven reserves of fossil fuels are in any case likely to be inadequate to sustain the growth potential of the world economy to the end of the present century, so it would seem sensible to reduce dependence on them and encourage research on and development of alternative sources of energy.

As the IPCC seems unable (as a UN body) to make a detailed critical assessment of policy options for the major countries responsible for the bulk of carbon emissions, the wisest course would be to create another forum for analysis of the issues raised by the IPCC.

It seems appropriate for the International Energy Agency assume this function. It is already well equipped to monitor the world energy situation, its members already include most of the biggest carbon emitters, and it is closely associated with OECD which has decades of experience in country analysis of economic policy. If China, India, and Russia were to become associate members of IEA, this forum would cover about 80 per cent of world energy users.

☐ APPENDIX

Table 7.19. Production of Crude Oil, NLG, and Natural Gas, 1973–2003

	Crude oil and NLG			Natural gas		
	1973	1990	2003	1973	1990	2003
USA	553.8	432.6	350.8	490.8	419.2	446.6
Canada	96.3	94.4	144.2	61.4	88.6	150.6
Mexico	27.5	154.1	185.8	10.5	22.8	33.9
Venezuela	191.5	122.8	146.8	10.8	20.8	22.1
Other	67.9	115.3	191.3	11.5	33.3	78.5
All Americas	**973.0**	**919.2**	**1,018.9**	**585.0**	**584.6**	**731.9**
Norway	1.5	84.5	154.4	0.0	24.1	66.3
UK	0.5	95.2	110.7	24.4	40.9	92.6
Other OECD Europe	21.3	32.3	40.2	100.7	98.8	97.1
Non-OECD Europe	19.6	12.1	9.3	26.0	25.3	12.6
All Europe	**42.9**	**224.1**	**314.6**	**151.1**	**189.1**	**268.6**
Kazakhstan	n. a.	n. a.	51.7	n. a.	n. a.	13.9
Russia	n. a.	n. a.	420.8	n. a.	n. a.	499.7
Former USSR	**431.2**	**573.5**	**512.4**	**195.4**	**656.3**	**629.0**
China	**54.6**	**138.3**	**169.8**	**5.0**	**15.8**	**36.2**
India	7.4	35.3	38.6	0.6	9.8	23.1
Indonesia	67.4	74.6	60.5	0.3	42.7	68.9
Other Asia	18.4	54.6	89.0	10.9	50.7	113.8
Saudi Arabia	387.0	349.0	484.6	1.5	27.4	49.1
Iran	298.7	158.9	197.5	10.1	19.1	65.6
UAE	75.1	93.3	123.3	1.1	16.1	35.9
Kuwait	153.7	47.1	112.9	5.0	3.3	7.8
Iraq	101.8	101.4	67.1	1.0	3.3	1.3
Other Middle East	64.7	96.8	142.9	2.7	13.1	67.5
All Middle East	**1081.0**	**846.5**	**1128.3**	**21.4**	**82.3**	**227.2**
Algeria	52.6	61.3	83.8	4.0	43.2	79.4
Nigeria	103.5	90.2	120.1	0.4	3.3	16.1
Other Africa	139.9	174.6	214.8	4.1	14.2	34.4
World	**2,935.8**	**3,222.9**	**3,782.9**	**999.5**	**1,706.8**	**2,250.3**

Sources: IEA (2005), *Energy Balances of OECD Countries*, pp. II 159 and II 161 and *Energy Balances of Non-OECD Countries*, pp. II, 208–9, and 213–14.

Table 7.20. Production of Coal, 1973–2003 (million tons of oil equivalent)

	1973	1990	2003
USA	333.4	539.2	526.1
Canada	11.7	37.9	30.2
All Latin America	5.6	20.5	42.8
Germany	141.4	121.8	57.9
Poland	100.7	94.5	70.8
UK	75.9	53.6	16.8
Other Europe	106.2	116.3	85.2
Former USSR	329.3	300.5	203.8
Australia	40.3	106.3	185.0
China	206.8	537.3	920.1
India	37.7	108.0	171.0
Indonesia	0.1	6.5	70.9
Other Asia	46.2	40.1	137.0
South Africa	35.1	100.2	135.5
World	**1,476.1**	**2,199.3**	**2,562.1**

Source: As for Table 7.19.

Table 7.21. Biggest Net Exporters and Importers of Energy, 2003 (million tons of oil equivalent)

Exporters		Importers	
Russia	456	US	661
S. Arabia	401	Japan	437
Norway	208	Germany	214
Australia	139	Korea	177
Algeria	130	Italy	149
Iran	129	France	137
Canada	129	Spain	110
Venezuela	125	India	100
Nigeria	116	Taiwan	88
UAE	113	Ukraine	57
Kuwait	97	Belgium	52
Indonesia	85	Thailand	42
Mexico	83	China	40
Libya	59	Singapore	39
Oman	49	Netherlands	36
Qatar	48	Brazil	26
Colombia	45	Hong Kong	22
Iraq	43	Belarus	22
Angola	42	Israel	20
Argentina	24	Philippines	20

Source: As for Table 7.19.

⬚ END NOTES

1. Within most countries, official statisticians provide regular estimates of the growth of aggregate output in real terms, after correcting for price change over time. The purpose of PPP (purchasing power parity) conversion is precisely analogous: to correct for intercountry price differences to permit meaningful comparisons of levels of real output. This is true of binary comparisons at a point of time, it is true when one constructs aggregate estimates for a region or the world economy, and for historical or futurological comparisons of world economic performance. For instance, if one compares the 2003 GDP level of the US and China in US dollars, using the yuan/dollar exchange rate, the US economy appears to be more than four times as big as the Chinese. Comparison using a PPP converter shows Chinese GDP to be about 70 per cent of the American level. Similarly, if one wants to compare the efficiency with which the two countries use energy, China appears much more inefficient when exchange rates are used. It is true that it is harder to get PPP converters than exchange rates, but for 1990, the IPCC benchmark year, reasonably reliable estimates are available for more than 99 per cent of the world economy (see Table 6.1 in Chapter 6). IPCC uses MEX or MER as acronyms to describe exchange rates. It hallows their status by persistently calling them 'market' rates In fact, the yuan/dollar exchange rate is not a market phenomenon, but the result of official pegging.

2. The witnesses who endorsed and defended the IPCC reports were were Nebojsa Nakicenovic, the editor of the SRES report, Rajendra Pachauri, the president of IPCC, John Houghton the leading scientific expert on climate change, David King the chief scientific advisor to the UK government, the UK department of the Environment, and the Royal Society. Michael Grubb and Adair Turner took the IPCC analysis seriously but concentrated on policy options for promoting technological change and improving the Kyoto process. There were several brands of scepticism. Richard Lindzen, a leading meteorologist, considered the IPCC projections alarmist and challenged their scientific basis. He argued that: (a) they exaggerated the climatic impact of increased CO2 emissions, as warming over the past century was less than anticipated by their models; (b) that they were wrong to assume that water vapour and clouds amplify the impact of increases in greenhouse gases; (c) they were wrong to assume that the frequency of extreme weather events would be augmented by global warming; (d) there have always been wobbles in climate whose causes are difficult to diagnose and the evidence for stability over the past 1,000 years is very weak. Ross McKitrick and David Holland also challenged the IPCC interpretation of climate history. Nils-Axel Mörner, a leading expert on paleogeophysics, rejected the IPCC projection of a rise in sea level, which in the past 600 years has had 'an almost linear relationship with solar variability, not CO2'. Paul Reiter, a leading epidemiologist, rejected the IPCC suggestion that global warming would increase the incidence of malaria and mosquito borne disease. He considered it 'ill-informed, biased and scientifically unacceptable'. Colin Robinson pointed out that climate change had beneficial as well as harmful effects, and Rosemary Righter denounced the longer run catastrophic IPCC predictions as scare-mongering. There were several critics of the IPCC scenarios; Ian Castles and David Henderson concentrated on their use of exchange rates rather than PPPs; Martin Agerup argued that the high emissions scenarios were implausible, and that their methodology could be improved in ways he specified. Dieter Helm's contribution was mainly a critique of the UK government's ambitious emissions reduction programme. He argued that it understated the costs and put too much emphasis on renewables rather than basic research on new technologies.

3. Nordhaus (2006b), quotes a pithy letter of President Bush in March 2001 addressed to four senators: 'I oppose the Kyoto Protoccol because it exempts 80 per cent of the world, including major population centers such as China and India, from compliance, and would cause serious

harm to the U.S. economy'. Nordhaus notes that there is no record of a fact sheet or other economic analysis accompanying the letter.

☐ BIBLIOGRAPHY

Ehrlich, P. (1968), *The Population Bomb*, Hutchinson, London.

Garnaut, R. (2006), 'Driving Forces in Chinese Growth since 1978 and the Outlook to 2030', paper presented to Seminar on World Economic Performance; Past, Present and Future, Queensland University, Brisbane, 5–6 December.

Gordon, R. J. (2006), 'Future US Productivity Growth: Looking Ahead by Looking Back', paper presented to workshop on World Economic Performance; Past, Prent and Future' University of Groningen, 27 October.

House of Lords, Select Committee on Economic Affairs (2005), *The Economics of Climate Change*, vol. I: Report, vol. II: Evidence.

House of Representatives, US Congress, Committee on Energy and Commerce (2006), *Wegman Report: The 'Hockey Stick' Global Climate Reconstruction'* http://energycommerce.house.gov/108/home/07142006

Henderson, D. (2005), 'SRES, IPCC and the Treatment of Economic Issues: What has Emerged?', *Energy & Environment*, vol. 16, nos. 3 & 4, pp. 549–78.

IEA (2004) , *World Energy Outlook*, Paris.

IEA (2005), *CO2 Emissions from Fuel Combustion, 1971–2003*, Paris.

IEA (2005), *Energy Balances of OECD Countries, 2002–2003*, Paris.

IEA (2005), *Energy Balances of Non-OECD Countries, 2002–2003*, Paris.

IEA (2006) *Energy Technology Perspectives: Scenarios and Strategies to 2050*, Paris.

IEA (2006a) , *World Energy Outlook*, Paris

IPCC (Intergovernmental Panel on Climate Change) (2000), *Special Report on Emissions Scenarios*, Cambridge University Press.

IPCC (Intergovernmental Panel on Climate Change) (2001), *Climate Change 2001: The Scientific Basis*, Cambridge University Press.

IPCC (Intergovernmental Panel on Climate Change) (2001), *Climate Change 2001: Synthesis Report*, Cambridge University Press.

International Programs Department, US Bureau of the Census (www.census.gov/ipc).

Jevons, W. S. (1865), *The Coal Question*, reprint of 3rd edn, Kelley, New York (1965).

Jevons, W. S. (1909) *Investigations in Currency and Finance*, Macmillan, London (contains 'The Solar Period and the Price of Corn', 1875, and 'Commercial Crises and Sunspots', 1878–9).

Heston, A. (2004), *'The Flaw of One Price: Some Implications for MER-PPP Discussions'*, paper presented to MERvsPPP Workshop, Stanford University.

Houghton, J. (2004), *Global Warming: the Complete Briefing*, Cambridge University Press.

Kander, A. (2002), *Economic Growth, Energy Consumption and CO_2 Emissions in Sweden, 1800–2000*, Almquist & Wiksell, Stockholm.

Lal, D. (2006), 'Driving Forces Behind the Acceleration of Indian Growth and the Outlook to 2030', paper presented to Seminar on World Economic Performance; Past, Present and Future, Queensland University, Brisbane, 5–6 December.

Lin, J. Y. (2006), 'Needham Puzzle, Weber Question and China's Miracle: Long Term Performance since the Sung Dynasty', paper presented to Seminar on World Economic Performance; Past, Present and Future, Queensland University, Brisbane, 5–6 December.

Lomborg, B. (1998), *The Sceptical Environmentalist*, Cambridge University Press.

Lomborg, B. (ed) (2004), *Global Crises, Global Solutions*, Cambridge University Press.

Maddison, A. (2005) *Memorandum of Evidence*, House of Lords, vol. II, pp. 249–56.

Maddison, A. (2007), www.ggdc.net/Maddison/

Malanima, P. (2006), *Energy Consumption in Italy in the Nineteenth and Twentieth Centuries: A Statistical Outline*, Consiglio Nazionale delle Ricerche, Naples.

Marland, G. T., A. Boden and R. J. Andres (2005), 'Global, Regional and National Fossil Fuel CO_2 Emissions, 1751–2002', in *Trends: A Compendium of Data on Global Change*, Carbon Dioxide Infornation Analysis Center, Oak Ridge National Laboratory, US Dept. of Energy.

McIntyre S. and R. McKitrick (2003), 'Corrections to the Manne et al. (1998) proxy data base and Northern Hemisphere average temperature series', *Energy and Environment*, 14, 6, pp. 775–7.

Meadows, D. H. (ed) (1972), *Limits to Growth, A Report to the Club of Rome on the Predicament of Mankind*, Potomac, London.

Menshikov, S. (2006), 'Analysis of Russian Performance since 1990 and Future Outlook', paper presented to workshop on World Economic Performance; Past, Prent and Future' University of Groningen, 27 October.

Mitchell, B. R. (1975), *European Historical Statistics*, Macmillan, London.

Nordhaus, W. (2005), '*Alternative Measures of Output in Global Economic–Environmental Models: Purchasing Power Parity or Market Exchange Rates*', IPCC Expert Meeting, Washington, DC.

Nordhaus, W. (2006a), 'After Kyoto: Alternative Mechanisms to Control Global Warming', *American Economic Review*, May, pp. 31–4.

Nordhaus, W. (2006b), 'The Stern Review on the Economics of Climate Change', http://nordhaus.econ.yale.edu/Stern ReviewD2.pdf

Reiter, P. (2000), 'From Shakespeare to Defoe: Malaria in England in the Little Ice Age', *Perspectives*, vol. 6, no. 1, January–February, pp. 1–11.

Ruddiman, W. F. (2006), *Plows, Plagues and Petroleum: How Humans Took Control of Climate*, Princeton University Press.

Smil, V. (1994), *Energy in World History*, Westview Press, Boulder CO, and Oxford.

Stern, D. I. (2006), 'Reversal of the Trend in Global Anthropogenic Suphur Emissions', *Global Environmental Change*, 16, 2, pp. 207–20.

Stern, N. (2006), '*What is the Economics of Climate Change?*', Oxford Institute of Economic Policy.

Stern, N. (2006), *Stern Review of the Economics of Climate Change*, HM Treasury.

Unger, R. (2006), '*Changing Energy Regimes and Early Modern Economic Growth*', paper presented at International Economic History Congress, Helsinki.

Watson, R. M. C. Zinyowera, and R. Moss (1995), Climate Change, Cambridge University Press.

Woytinsky, W. S. and E. S. (1953), *World Population and Production: Trends and Outlook*, Twentieth Century Fund, New York.

UN Population Division (2003), *World Population in 2300, Highlights*, New York.

UN Population Division (2005), *World Population Prospects, 2004 Revision*, New York.

van Ark, B. (2006), 'Europe's Productivity Gap: Catching Up or Getting Stuck', paper presented to workshop on World Economic Performance; Past, Present and Future, University of Groningen, 27 October.

Appendices

☐ STATISTICAL APPENDIX A

This is an amended version of the Appendices presented in Maddison (2001: 229–65) and Maddison (2003: 241–63), which contain extensive source notes. The most significant revisions are the new estimates for the Roman Empire.

For Asia, amendments were made to the GDP estimates for South and North Korea, 1911–74, to correct an error in Maddison (2003). Estimates for the Philippines, 1902–40 are amended in line with Richard Hooley (2005), 'American Economic Policy in the Philippines, 1902–40', *Journal of Asian Economics*, 16. My 1820 estimates were amended for Hong Kong, the Philippines, Singapore, Sri Lanka, Taiwan, and Thailand. For most Asian countries GDP was revised and updated for 1998–2003 from Asian Development Bank, *Key Indicators 2005*, for South Korea and Japan OECD sources were used. estimates Chinese GDP for 1950–2003 have been revised with help from Professor Harry X. Wu.

For Chile, GDP 1820–1990 is from Rolf Lüders (1998), 'The Comparative Economic Performance of Chile 1810–1995', *Estudios de Economia*, vol. 25, no. 2, with revised population estimates in Diaz J., R. Lüders, and G. Wagner (2005) *Chile, 1810–2000: la Republica en Cifras*, mimeo, Instituto de Economia, Universidad Católica de Chile. For Peru, GDP 1896–1990 and population 1896–1949 from Bruno Seminario and Arlette Beltran, *Crecimiento Economico en el Peru, 1896–1995*, Universidad del Pacifico, 1998.

For OECD countries GDP was revised and updated 1991–2003 from *National Accounts for OECD Countries*, vol. I, 2006. Norway 1820–1990 GDP from Ola Grytten (2004), 'The Gross Domestic Product for Norway, 1830–2003' in Eitrheim, Klovland, and Qvigstad (eds), *Historical Monetary Statistics for Norway, 1819–2003*, Norges Bank, Oslo.

GDP for African countries updated 2000–3 from IMF, *World Economic Outlook*, April 2005. Latin American GDP 2000–3 revised and updated from ECLAC, *Statistical Yearbook 2004* and preliminary version of the 2005 *Yearbook* supplied by Andre Hofman.

Population estimates for all countries except China and India revised and updated 1950–2003 from *International Data Base*, International Programs Center, Population Division, US Bureau of the Census, April 2005. China's population 1990–2003 from *China Statistical Yearbook 2005*, China Statistics Press, Beijing.

Table A.1. World Population: 20 Countries and Regional Totals, 1–2003AD (000s)

	1	1000	1500	1600	1700	1820	1870	1913	1950	1973	2003
Austria	500	700	2,000	2,500	2,500	3,369	4,520	6,767	6,935	7,586	8,163
Belgium	300	400	1,400	1,600	2,000	3,434	5,096	7,666	8,639	9,738	10,331
Denmark	180	360	600	650	700	1,155	1,888	2,983	4,271	5,022	5,394
Finland	20	40	300	400	400	1,169	1,754	3,027	4,009	4,666	5,204
France	5,000	6,500	15,000	18,500	21,471	31,250	38,440	41,463	41,829	52,157	60,181
Germany	3,000	3,500	12,000	16,000	15,000	24,905	39,231	65,058	68,375	78,950	82,398
Italy	8,000	5,000	10,500	13,100	13,300	20,176	27,888	37,248	47,105	54,797	57,998
Netherlands	200	300	950	1,500	1,900	2,333	3,610	6,164	10,114	13,438	16,223
Norway	100	200	300	400	500	970	1,735	2,447	3,265	3,961	4,555
Sweden	200	400	550	760	1,260	2,585	4,169	5,621	7,014	8,137	8,970
Switzerland	300	300	650	1,000	1,200	1,986	2,655	3,864	4,694	6,441	7,408
UK	800	2,000	3,942	6,170	8,565	21,239	31,400	45,649	50,127	56,210	60,095
12 country total	**18,600**	**19,700**	**48,192**	**62,580**	**68,796**	**114,571**	**162,386**	**227,957**	**256,377**	**301,103**	**326,920**
Portugal	400	600	1,000	1,100	2,000	3,297	4,327	5,972	8,443	8,976	10,480
Spain	3,750	4,000	6,800	8,240	8,770	12,203	16,201	20,263	28,063	34,837	40,217
Other	2,300	1,260	1,340	1,858	1,894	2,969	4,590	6,783	12,058	13,909	16,987
Total western Europe	**25,050**	**25,560**	**57,332**	**73,778**	**81,460**	**133,040**	**187,504**	**260,975**	**304,941**	**358,825**	**394,604**
Eastern Europe	**4,750**	**6,500**	**13,500**	**16,950**	**18,800**	**36,457**	**53,557**	**79,530**	**87,637**	**110,418**	**121,434**
Former USSR	**3,900**	**7,100**	**16,950**	**20,700**	**26,550**	**54,765**	**88,672**	**156,192**	**179,571**	**249,712**	**287,601**
US	680	1,300	2,000	1,500	1,000	9,981	40,241	97,606	152,271	211,909	290,343
Other western offshoots	440	570	800	800	750	1,250	5,847	13,795	24,186	38,932	55,890
Total western offshoots	**1,120**	**1,870**	**2,800**	**2,300**	**1,750**	**11,231**	**46,088**	**111,401**	**176,457**	**250,841**	**346,233**
Mexico	2,200	4,500	7,500	2,500	4,500	6,587	9,219	14,970	28,485	57,557	103,718
Other Latin America	3,400	6,900	10,000	6,100	7,550	15,004	31,180	65,965	137,453	250,316	437,641
Total Latin America	**5,600**	**11,400**	**17,500**	**8,600**	**12,050**	**21,591**	**40,399**	**80,935**	**165,938**	**307,873**	**541,359**
Japan	**3,000**	**7,500**	**15,400**	**18,500**	**27,000**	**31,000**	**34,437**	**51,672**	**83,805**	**108,707**	**127,214**
China	59,600	59,000	103,000	160,000	138,000	381,000	358,000	437,140	546,815	881,940	1,288,400
India	75,000	75,000	110,000	135,000	165,000	209,000	253,000	303,700	359,000	580,000	1,049,700
Other east Asia	11,400	21,100	37,600	43,600	50,700	64,228	89,506	145,893	333,310	565,057	1,018,844
West Asia	19,400	20,000	17,800	21,400	20,800	25,147	30,290	38,956	59,847	112,918	249,809
Total Asia (excl. Japan)	**165,400**	**175,100**	**268,400**	**360,000**	**374,500**	**679,375**	**730,796**	**925,689**	**1,298,972**	**2,139,915**	**3,606,753**
Africa	**17,000**	**32,300**	**46,610**	**55,320**	**61,080**	**74,236**	**90,466**	**124,697**	**228,181**	**390,202**	**853,422**
World	**225,820**	**267,330**	**438,492**	**556,148**	**603,190**	**1,041,695**	**1,271,919**	**1,791,091**	**2,525,502**	**3,916,493**	**6,278,620**

Table A.2. Rate of Growth of World Population: 20 Countries and Regional Totals, 1–2003AD (annual average coumpound growth rates)

	1–1000	1000–1500	1500–1820	1820–70	1870–1913	1913–50	1950–73	1973–2003
Austria	0.03	0.21	0.16	0.59	0.94	0.07	0.39	0.24
Belgium	0.03	0.25	0.28	0.79	0.95	0.32	0.52	0.20
Denmark	0.07	0.10	0.20	0.99	1.07	0.97	0.71	0.24
Finland	0.07	0.40	0.43	0.81	1.28	0.76	0.66	0.36
France	0.03	0.17	0.23	0.42	0.18	0.02	0.96	0.48
Germany	0.02	0.25	0.23	0.91	1.18	0.13	0.63	0.14
Italy	−0.05	0.15	0.20	0.65	0.68	0.64	0.66	0.19
Netherlands	0.04	0.23	0.28	0.88	1.25	1.35	1.24	0.63
Norway	0.07	0.08	0.37	1.17	0.80	0.78	0.84	0.47
Sweden	0.07	0.06	0.48	0.96	0.70	0.60	0.65	0.33
Switzerland	0.00	0.15	0.35	0.58	0.88	0.53	1.39	0.47
UK	0.09	0.14	0.53	0.79	0.87	0.25	0.50	0.22
12 country average	**0.01**	**0.18**	**0.27**	**0.70**	**0.79**	**0.32**	**0.70**	**0.27**
Portugal	0.04	0.10	0.37	0.55	0.75	0.94	0.27	0.52
Spain	0.01	0.11	0.18	0.57	0.52	0.88	0.94	0.48
Other	−0.06	0.01	0.25	0.88	0.91	1.57	0.62	0.67
Total western Europe	**0.00**	**0.16**	**0.26**	**0.69**	**0.77**	**0.42**	**0.71**	**0.32**
Eastern Europe	**0.03**	**0.15**	**0.31**	**0.77**	**0.92**	**0.26**	**1.01**	**0.32**
Former USSR	**0.06**	**0.17**	**0.37**	**0.97**	**1.33**	**0.38**	**1.44**	**0.47**
USA	0.06	0.09	0.50	2.83	2.08	1.21	1.45	1.06
Other western offshoots	0.03	0.07	0.14	3.13	2.02	1.53	2.09	1.21
Total western offshoots	**0.05**	**0.08**	**0.44**	**2.86**	**2.07**	**1.25**	**1.54**	**1.08**
Mexico	0.07	0.10	−0.04	0.67	1.13	1.75	3.11	1.98
Other Latin America	0.07	0.07	0.13	1.47	1.76	2.00	2.64	1.88
Total Latin America	**0.07**	**0.09**	**0.07**	**1.26**	**1.63**	**1.96**	**2.72**	**1.90**
Japan	**0.09**	**0.14**	**0.22**	**0.21**	**0.95**	**1.32**	**1.14**	**0.53**
China	0.00	0.11	0.41	−0.12	0.47	0.61	2.10	1.27
India	0.00	0.08	0.20	0.38	0.43	0.45	2.11	2.00
Other east Asia	0.06	0.12	0.17	0.67	1.14	2.26	2.32	1.98
West Asia	0.00	−0.02	0.11	0.37	0.59	1.17	2.80	2.68
Total Asia (excl. Japan)	**0.01**	**0.09**	**0.29**	**0.15**	**0.55**	**0.92**	**2.19**	**1.76**
Africa	**0.06**	**0.07**	**0.15**	**0.40**	**0.75**	**1.65**	**2.36**	**2.64**
World	**0.02**	**0.10**	**0.27**	**0.40**	**0.80**	**0.93**	**1.93**	**1.59**

Table A.3. Share of World Population: 20 Countries and Regional Totals, 1–2003AD (per cent of world total)

	1	1000	1500	1600	1700	1820	1870	1913	1950	1973	2003
Austria	0.2	0.3	0.5	0.4	0.4	0.3	0.4	0.4	0.3	0.2	0.1
Belgium	0.1	0.1	0.3	0.3	0.3	0.3	0.4	0.4	0.3	0.2	0.2
Denmark	0.1	0.1	0.1	0.1	0.1	0.1	0.1	0.2	0.2	0.1	0.1
Finland	0.0	0.0	0.1	0.1	0.1	0.1	0.1	0.2	0.2	0.1	0.1
France	2.2	2.4	3.4	3.3	3.6	3.0	3.0	2.3	1.7	1.3	1.0
Germany	1.3	1.3	2.7	2.9	2.5	2.4	3.1	3.6	2.7	2.0	1.3
Italy	3.5	1.9	2.4	2.4	2.2	1.9	2.2	2.1	1.9	1.4	0.9
Netherlands	0.1	0.1	0.2	0.3	0.3	0.2	0.3	0.3	0.4	0.3	0.3
Norway	0.0	0.1	0.1	0.1	0.1	0.1	0.1	0.1	0.1	0.1	0.1
Sweden	0.1	0.1	0.1	0.1	0.2	0.2	0.3	0.3	0.3	0.2	0.1
Switzerland	0.1	0.1	0.1	0.2	0.2	0.2	0.2	0.2	0.2	0.2	0.1
UK	0.4	0.7	0.9	1.1	1.4	2.0	2.5	2.5	2.0	1.4	1.0
12 country total	**8.2**	**7.4**	**11.0**	**11.3**	**11.4**	**11.0**	**12.8**	**12.7**	**10.2**	**7.7**	**5.2**
Portugal	0.2	0.2	0.2	0.2	0.3	0.3	0.3	0.3	0.3	0.2	0.2
Spain	1.7	1.5	1.6	1.5	1.5	1.2	1.3	1.1	1.1	0.9	0.6
Other	1.0	0.5	0.3	0.3	0.3	0.3	0.4	0.4	0.5	0.4	0.3
Total western Europe	**11.1**	**9.6**	**13.1**	**13.3**	**13.5**	**12.8**	**14.7**	**14.6**	**12.1**	**9.2**	**6.3**
Eastern Europe	**2.1**	**2.4**	**3.1**	**3.0**	**3.1**	**3.5**	**4.2**	**4.4**	**3.5**	**2.8**	**1.9**
Former USSR	**1.7**	**2.7**	**3.9**	**3.7**	**4.4**	**5.3**	**7.0**	**8.7**	**7.1**	**6.4**	**4.6**
USA	0.3	0.5	0.5	0.3	0.2	1.0	3.2	5.4	6.0	5.4	4.6
Other western offshoots	0.2	0.2	0.2	0.1	0.1	0.1	0.5	0.8	1.0	1.0	0.9
Total western offshoots	**0.5**	**0.7**	**0.6**	**0.4**	**0.3**	**1.1**	**3.6**	**6.2**	**7.0**	**6.4**	**5.5**
Mexico	1.0	1.7	1.7	0.4	0.7	0.6	0.7	0.8	1.1	1.5	1.7
Other Latin America	1.5	2.6	2.3	1.1	1.3	1.4	2.5	3.7	5.4	6.4	7.0
Total Latin America	**2.5**	**4.3**	**4.0**	**1.5**	**2.0**	**2.1**	**3.2**	**4.5**	**6.6**	**7.9**	**8.6**
Japan	**1.3**	**2.8**	**3.5**	**3.3**	**4.5**	**3.0**	**2.7**	**2.9**	**3.3**	**2.8**	**2.0**
China	26.4	22.1	23.5	28.8	22.9	36.6	28.1	24.4	21.7	22.5	20.5
India	33.2	28.1	25.1	24.3	27.4	20.1	19.9	17.0	14.2	14.8	16.7
Other east Asia	5.0	7.9	8.6	7.8	8.4	6.2	7.0	8.1	13.2	14.4	16.2
West Asia	8.6	7.5	4.1	3.8	3.4	2.4	2.4	2.2	2.4	2.9	4.0
Total Asia (excl. Japan)	**73.2**	**65.5**	**61.2**	**64.7**	**62.1**	**65.2**	**57.5**	**51.7**	**51.4**	**54.6**	**57.4**
Africa	**7.5**	**12.1**	**10.6**	**9.9**	**10.1**	**7.1**	**7.1**	**7.0**	**9.0**	**10.0**	**13.6**
World	**100.0**	**100.0**	**100.0**	**100.0**	**100.0**	**100.0**	**100.0**	**100.0**	**100.0**	**100.0**	**100.0**

Table A.4. World GDP, 20 Countries and Regional Totals, 1–2003AD (million 1990 international $)

	1	1000	1500	1600	1700	1820	1870	1913	1950	1973	2003
Austria	213	298	1,414	2,093	2,483	4,104	8,419	23,451	25,702	85,227	173,311
Belgium	135	170	1,225	1,561	2,288	4,529	13,716	32,347	47,190	118,516	219,069
Denmark	72	144	443	569	727	1,471	3,782	11,670	29,654	70,032	124,781
Finland	8	16	136	215	255	913	1,999	6,389	17,051	51,724	106,749
France	2,366	2,763	10,912	15,559	19,539	35,468	72,100	144,489	220,492	683,965	1,315,601
Germany	1,225	1,435	8,256	12,656	13,650	26,819	72,149	237,332	265,354	944,755	1,577,423
Italy	6,475	2,250	11,550	14,410	14,630	22,535	41,814	95,487	164,957	582,713	1,110,691
Netherlands	85	128	723	2,072	4,047	4,288	9,952	24,955	60,642	175,791	348,464
Norway	40	80	183	266	361	777	2,360	5,988	17,728	44,852	118,591
Sweden	80	160	382	626	1,231	3,098	6,927	17,403	47,269	109,794	193,352
Switzerland	128	123	411	750	1,068	2,165	5,581	16,483	42,545	117,251	164,773
UK	320	800	2,815	6,007	10,709	36,232	100,180	224,618	347,850	675,941	1,280,625
12 country total	**11,146**	**8,366**	**38,450**	**56,784**	**70,988**	**142,399**	**338,979**	**840,612**	**1,286,434**	**3,660,561**	**6,733,430**
Portugal	180	255	606	814	1,638	3,043	4,219	7,467	17,615	63,397	144,694
Spain	1,867	1,800	4,495	7,029	7,481	12,299	19,556	41,653	61,429	266,896	684,537
Other	1,240	504	632	975	1,106	2,110	4,712	12,478	30,600	105,910	294,733
Total western Europe	**14,433**	**10,925**	**44,183**	**65,602**	**81,213**	**159,851**	**367,466**	**902,210**	**1,396,078**	**4,096,764**	**7,857,394**
Eastern Europe	**1,956**	**2,600**	**6,696**	**9,289**	**11,393**	**24,906**	**50,163**	**134,793**	**185,023**	**550,756**	**786,408**
Former USSR	**1,560**	**2,840**	**8,458**	**11,426**	**16,196**	**37,678**	**83,646**	**232,351**	**510,243**	**1,513,070**	**1,552,231**
USA	272	520	800	600	527	12,548	98,374	517,383	1,455,916	3,536,622	8,430,762
Other western offshoots	176	228	320	320	306	951	13,119	65,558	179,574	521,667	1,277,267
Total western offshoots	**448**	**748**	**1,120**	**920**	**833**	**13,499**	**111,493**	**582,941**	**1,635,490**	**4,058,289**	**9,708,029**
Mexico	880	1,800	3,188	1,134	2,558	5,000	6,214	25,921	67,368	279,302	740,226
Other Latin America	1,360	2,760	4,100	2,629	3,788	9,921	21,097	94,875	347,960	1,110,158	2,391,919
Total Latin America	**2,240**	**4,560**	**7,288**	**3,763**	**6,346**	**14,921**	**27,311**	**120,796**	**415,328**	**1,389,460**	**3,132,145**
Japan	**1,200**	**3,188**	**7,700**	**9,620**	**15,390**	**20,739**	**25,393**	**71,653**	**160,966**	**1,242,932**	**2,699,261**
China	26,820	26,550	51,800	96,000	82,800	228,600	189,740	241,431	244,985	739,414	6,187,984
India	33,750	33,750	60,500	74,250	90,750	111,417	134,882	204,242	222,222	494,832	2,267,136
Other east Asia	4,845	8,968	20,822	24,582	28,440	36,451	53,155	122,874	256,922	839,258	3,926,975
West Asia	10,120	12,415	10,495	12,637	12,291	15,270	22,468	40,588	106,283	548,120	1,473,739
Total Asia (excl. Japan)	**75,535**	**81,683**	**153,617**	**207,469**	**214,281**	**391,738**	**400,245**	**609,135**	**830,428**	**2,621,624**	**13,855,834**
Africa	**8,030**	**13,835**	**19,383**	**23,473**	**25,776**	**31,266**	**45,234**	**79,486**	**203,131**	**549,993**	**1,322,087**
World	**105,402**	**120,379**	**248,445**	**331,562**	**371,428**	**694,598**	**1,110,951**	**2,733,365**	**5,331,689**	**16,022,888**	**40,913,389**

Table A.5. Rate of Growth of World GDP: 20 Countries and Regional Totals, 1–2003AD (annual average compound growth rates)

	1–1000	1000–1500	1500–1820	1820–70	1870–1913	1913–50	1950–73	1973–2003
Austria	0.03	0.31	0.33	1.45	2.41	0.25	5.35	2.39
Belgium	0.02	0.40	0.41	2.24	2.02	1.03	4.08	2.07
Denmark	0.07	0.23	0.38	1.91	2.66	2.55	3.81	1.94
Finland	0.07	0.43	0.60	1.58	2.74	2.69	4.94	2.44
France	0.02	0.28	0.37	1.43	1.63	1.15	5.05	2.20
Germany	0.02	0.35	0.37	2.00	2.81	0.30	5.68	1.72
Italy	−0.11	0.33	0.21	1.24	1.94	1.49	5.64	2.17
Netherlands	0.04	0.35	0.56	1.70	2.16	2.43	4.74	2.31
Norway	0.07	0.17	0.45	2.25	2.19	2.98	4.12	3.29
Sweden	0.07	0.17	0.66	1.62	2.17	2.74	3.73	1.90
Switzerland	0.00	0.24	0.52	1.91	2.55	2.60	4.51	1.14
UK	0.09	0.25	0.80	2.05	1.90	1.19	2.93	2.15
12 country average	**−0.03**	**0.31**	**0.41**	**1.75**	**2.13**	**1.16**	**4.65**	**2.05**
Portugal	0.03	0.17	0.51	0.66	1.34	2.35	5.73	2.79
Spain	0.00	0.18	0.32	0.93	1.77	1.06	6.60	3.19
Other	−0.09	0.05	0.38	1.62	2.29	2.45	5.55	3.47
Total western Europe	**−0.03**	**0.28**	**0.40**	**1.68**	**2.11**	**1.19**	**4.79**	**2.19**
Eastern Europe	**0.03**	**0.19**	**0.41**	**1.41**	**2.33**	**0.86**	**4.86**	**1.19**
Former USSR	**0.06**	**0.22**	**0.47**	**1.61**	**2.40**	**2.15**	**4.84**	**0.09**
USA	0.06	0.09	0.86	4.20	3.94	2.84	3.93	2.94
Other western offshoots	0.03	0.07	0.34	5.39	3.81	2.76	4.75	3.03
Total western offshoots	**0.05**	**0.08**	**0.78**	**4.31**	**3.92**	**2.83**	**4.03**	**2.95**
Mexico	0.07	0.11	0.14	0.44	3.38	2.62	6.38	3.30
Other Latin America	0.07	0.08	0.28	1.52	3.56	3.57	5.17	2.59
Total Latin America	**0.07**	**0.09**	**0.22**	**1.22**	**3.52**	**3.39**	**5.39**	**2.75**
Japan	**0.10**	**0.18**	**0.31**	**0.41**	**2.44**	**2.21**	**9.29**	**2.62**
China	0.00	0.17	0.41	−0.37	0.56	−0.02	4.92	7.34
India	0.00	0.12	0.19	0.38	0.97	0.23	3.54	5.20
Other east Asia	0.06	0.17	0.18	0.76	1.97	2.01	5.28	5.28
West Asia	0.02	−0.03	0.12	0.78	1.38	2.64	7.39	3.35
Total Asia (excl. Japan)	**0.01**	**0.13**	**0.29**	**0.04**	**0.98**	**0.82**	**5.13**	**5.71**
Africa	**0.05**	**0.07**	**0.15**	**0.75**	**1.32**	**2.57**	**4.43**	**2.97**
World	**0.01**	**0.15**	**0.32**	**0.94**	**2.12**	**1.82**	**4.90**	**3.17**

Table A.6. Share of World GDP: 20 Countries and Regional Totals, 1–2003AD (percent of world total)

	1	1000	1500	1600	1700	1820	1870	1913	1950	1973	2003
Austria	0.2	0.2	0.6	0.6	0.7	0.6	0.8	0.9	0.5	0.5	0.4
Belgium	0.1	0.1	0.5	0.5	0.6	0.7	1.2	1.2	0.9	0.7	0.5
Denmark	0.1	0.1	0.2	0.2	0.2	0.2	0.3	0.4	0.6	0.4	0.3
Finland	0.0	0.0	0.1	0.1	0.1	0.1	0.2	0.2	0.3	0.3	0.3
France	2.2	2.3	4.4	4.7	5.3	5.1	6.5	5.3	4.1	4.3	3.2
Germany	1.2	1.2	3.3	3.8	3.7	3.9	6.5	8.7	5.0	5.9	3.9
Italy	6.1	1.9	4.7	4.3	3.9	3.2	3.8	3.5	3.1	3.6	2.7
Netherlands	0.1	0.1	0.3	0.6	1.1	0.6	0.9	0.9	1.1	1.1	0.9
Norway	0.0	0.1	0.1	0.1	0.1	0.1	0.2	0.2	0.3	0.3	0.3
Sweden	0.1	0.1	0.2	0.2	0.3	0.4	0.6	0.6	0.9	0.7	0.5
Switzerland	0.1	0.1	0.2	0.2	0.3	0.3	0.5	0.6	0.8	0.7	0.4
UK	0.3	0.7	1.1	1.8	2.9	5.2	9.0	8.2	6.5	4.2	3.1
12 country total	**10.6**	**7.0**	**15.5**	**17.1**	**19.1**	**20.5**	**30.5**	**30.8**	**24.1**	**22.8**	**16.5**
Portugal	0.2	0.2	0.2	0.2	0.4	0.4	0.4	0.3	0.3	0.4	0.4
Spain	1.8	1.5	1.8	2.1	2.0	1.8	1.8	1.5	1.2	1.7	1.7
Other	1.2	0.4	0.3	0.3	0.3	0.3	0.4	0.5	0.6	0.7	0.7
Total western Europe	**13.7**	**9.1**	**17.8**	**19.8**	**21.9**	**23.0**	**33.1**	**33.0**	**26.2**	**25.6**	**19.2**
Eastern Europe	**1.9**	**2.2**	**2.7**	**2.8**	**3.1**	**3.6**	**4.5**	**4.9**	**3.5**	**3.4**	**1.9**
Former USSR	**1.5**	**2.4**	**3.4**	**3.4**	**4.4**	**5.4**	**7.5**	**8.5**	**9.6**	**9.4**	**3.8**
USA	0.3	0.4	0.3	0.2	0.1	1.8	8.9	18.9	27.3	22.1	20.6
Other western offshoots	0.2	0.2	0.1	0.1	0.1	0.1	1.2	2.4	3.4	3.3	3.1
Total western offshoots	**0.4**	**0.6**	**0.5**	**0.3**	**0.2**	**1.9**	**10.0**	**21.3**	**30.6**	**25.3**	**23.7**
Mexico	0.8	1.5	1.3	0.3	0.7	0.7	0.6	0.9	1.3	1.7	1.8
Other Latin America	1.3	2.3	1.7	0.8	1.0	1.4	1.9	3.5	6.5	6.9	5.8
Total Latin America	**2.1**	**3.8**	**2.9**	**1.1**	**1.7**	**2.1**	**2.5**	**4.4**	**7.8**	**8.7**	**7.7**
Japan	**1.1**	**2.7**	**3.1**	**2.9**	**4.1**	**3.0**	**2.3**	**2.6**	**3.0**	**7.8**	**6.6**
China	25.4	22.1	24.9	29.0	22.3	32.9	17.1	8.8	4.6	4.6	15.1
India	32.0	28.1	24.4	22.4	24.4	16.0	12.1	7.5	4.2	3.1	5.5
Other east Asia	4.6	7.5	8.4	7.4	7.7	5.2	4.8	4.5	4.8	5.2	9.6
West Asia	9.6	10.3	4.2	3.8	3.3	2.2	2.0	1.5	2.0	3.4	3.6
Total Asia (excl. Japan)	**71.7**	**67.9**	**61.8**	**62.6**	**57.7**	**56.4**	**36.0**	**22.3**	**15.6**	**16.4**	**33.9**
Africa	**7.6**	**11.4**	**7.8**	**7.0**	**6.9**	**4.5**	**4.1**	**2.9**	**3.8**	**3.4**	**3.2**
World	**100.0**	**100.0**	**100.0**	**100.0**	**100.0**	**100.0**	**100.0**	**100.0**	**100.0**	**100.0**	**100.0**

Table A.7. World per Capita GDP: 20 Countries and Regional Averages, 1–2003AD (1990 international $)

	1	1000	1500	1600	1700	1820	1870	1913	1950	1973	2003
Austria	425	425	707	837	993	1,218	1,863	3,465	3,706	11,235	21,231
Belgium	450	425	875	976	1,144	1,319	2,692	4,220	5,462	12,170	21,205
Denmark	400	400	738	875	1,039	1,274	2,003	3,912	6,943	13,945	23,133
Finland	400	400	453	538	638	781	1,140	2,111	4,253	11,085	20,513
France	473	425	727	841	910	1,135	1,876	3,485	5,271	13,114	21,861
Germany	408	410	688	791	910	1,077	1,839	3,648	3,881	11,966	19,144
Italy	809	450	1,100	1,100	1,100	1,117	1,499	2,564	3,502	10,634	19,151
Netherlands	425	425	761	1,381	2,130	1,838	2,757	4,049	5,996	13,082	21,480
Norway	400	400	610	664	723	801	1,360	2,447	5,430	11,323	26,035
Sweden	400	400	695	824	977	1,198	1,662	3,096	6,739	13,493	21,555
Switzerland	425	410	632	750	890	1,090	2,102	4,266	9,064	18,204	22,243
UK	400	400	714	974	1,250	1,706	3,190	4,921	6,939	12,025	21,310
12 country average	**599**	**425**	**798**	**907**	**1,032**	**1,243**	**2,087**	**3,688**	**5,018**	**12,157**	**20,597**
Portugal	450	425	606	740	819	923	975	1,250	2,086	7,063	13,807
Spain	498	450	661	853	853	1,008	1,207	2,056	2,189	7,661	17,021
Other	539	400	472	525	584	711	1,027	1,840	2,538	7,614	17,351
West european average	**576**	**427**	**771**	**889**	**997**	**1,202**	**1,960**	**3,457**	**4,578**	**11,417**	**19,912**
Eastern Europe	**412**	**400**	**496**	**548**	**606**	**683**	**937**	**1,695**	**2,111**	**4,988**	**6,476**
Former USSR	**400**	**400**	**499**	**552**	**610**	**688**	**943**	**1,488**	**2,841**	**6,059**	**5,397**
USA	400	400	400	400	527	1,257	2,445	5,301	9,561	16,689	29,037
Other western offshoots	400	400	400	400	408	761	2,244	4,752	7,425	13,399	22,853
Average western offshoots	**400**	**400**	**400**	**400**	**476**	**1,202**	**2,419**	**5,233**	**9,268**	**16,179**	**28,039**
Mexico	400	400	425	454	568	759	674	1,732	2,365	4,853	7,137
Other Latin America	400	400	410	431	502	661	677	1,438	2,531	4,435	5,465
Latin American average	**400**	**400**	**416**	**438**	**527**	**691**	**676**	**1,493**	**2,503**	**4,513**	**5,786**
Japan	**400**	**425**	**500**	**520**	**570**	**669**	**737**	**1,387**	**1,921**	**11,434**	**21,218**
China	450	450	600	600	600	600	530	552	448	838	4,803
India	450	450	550	550	550	533	533	673	619	853	2,160
Other east Asia	425	425	554	564	561	568	594	842	771	1,485	3,854
West Asia	522	621	590	591	591	607	742	1,042	1,776	4,854	5,899
Asian average (excl. Japan)	**457**	**466**	**572**	**576**	**572**	**577**	**548**	**658**	**639**	**1,225**	**3,842**
Africa	**472**	**425**	**414**	**422**	**421**	**420**	**500**	**637**	**890**	**1,410**	**1,549**
World	**467**	**450**	**566**	**596**	**616**	**667**	**873**	**1,526**	**2,113**	**4,091**	**6,516**

Table A.8. Rate of Growth of World per Capita GDP: 20 Countries and Regional Averages, 1–2003AD (annual average compound growth rates)

	1–1000	1000–1500	1500–1820	1820–70	1870–1913	1913–50	1950–73	1973–2003
Austria	0.00	0.10	0.17	0.85	1.45	0.18	4.94	2.14
Belgium	−0.01	0.14	0.13	1.44	1.05	0.70	3.54	1.87
Denmark	0.00	0.12	0.17	0.91	1.57	1.56	3.08	1.70
Finland	0.00	0.03	0.17	0.76	1.44	1.91	4.25	2.07
France	−0.01	0.11	0.14	1.01	1.45	1.12	4.04	1.72
Germany	0.00	0.10	0.14	1.08	1.61	0.17	5.02	1.58
Italy	−0.06	0.18	0.00	0.59	1.26	0.85	4.95	1.98
Netherlands	0.00	0.12	0.28	0.81	0.90	1.07	3.45	1.67
Norway	0.00	0.08	0.09	1.06	1.38	2.18	3.25	2.81
Sweden	0.00	0.11	0.17	0.66	1.46	2.12	3.06	1.57
Switzerland	0.00	0.09	0.17	1.32	1.66	2.06	3.08	0.67
UK	0.00	0.12	0.27	1.26	1.01	0.93	2.42	1.93
12 country average	**−0.03**	**0.13**	**0.14**	**1.04**	**1.33**	**0.84**	**3.92**	**1.77**
Portugal	−0.01	0.07	0.13	0.11	0.58	1.39	5.45	2.26
Spain	−0.01	0.08	0.13	0.36	1.25	0.17	5.60	2.70
Other	−0.03	0.03	0.13	0.74	1.37	0.87	4.89	2.78
Total western Europe	**−0.03**	**0.12**	**0.14**	**0.98**	**1.33**	**0.76**	**4.05**	**1.87**
Eastern Europe	**0.00**	**0.04**	**0.10**	**0.63**	**1.39**	**0.60**	**3.81**	**0.87**
Former USSR	**0.00**	**0.04**	**0.10**	**0.63**	**1.06**	**1.76**	**3.35**	**−0.38**
USA	0.00	0.00	0.36	1.34	1.82	1.61	2.45	1.86
Other western offshoots	0.00	0.00	0.20	2.19	1.76	1.21	2.60	1.80
Total western offshoots	**0.00**	**0.00**	**0.34**	**1.41**	**1.81**	**1.56**	**2.45**	**1.85**
Mexico	0.00	0.01	0.18	−0.24	2.22	0.85	3.17	1.29
Other Latin America	0.00	0.00	0.15	0.05	1.77	1.54	2.47	0.70
Total Latin America	**0.00**	**0.01**	**0.16**	**−0.04**	**1.86**	**1.41**	**2.60**	**0.83**
Japan	**0.01**	**0.03**	**0.09**	**0.19**	**1.48**	**0.88**	**8.06**	**2.08**
China	0.00	0.06	0.00	−0.25	0.10	−0.56	2.76	5.99
India	0.00	0.04	−0.01	0.00	0.54	−0.22	1.40	3.14
Other east Asia	0.00	0.05	0.01	0.09	0.82	−0.24	2.89	3.23
West Asia	0.02	−0.01	0.01	0.40	0.79	1.45	4.47	0.65
Total Asia (excl. Japan)	**0.00**	**0.04**	**0.00**	**−0.10**	**0.43**	**−0.08**	**2.87**	**3.88**
Africa	**−0.01**	**−0.01**	**0.00**	**0.35**	**0.57**	**0.91**	**2.02**	**0.32**
World	**0.00**	**0.05**	**0.05**	**0.54**	**1.31**	**0.88**	**2.91**	**1.56**

STATISTICAL APPENDIX B: INGREDIENTS OF GROWTH ACCOUNTS IN JAPAN, UK, AND US, 1820–2003

Table B.1. Basic Components of Growth Accounts I: US, UK, and Japan, 1820–2003

	Total population (000s)	Employment (000s)	Total hours worked (million)	Average years of education per person employed	Land area (000 ha.)	Per cent of employment in		
						Agriculture forestry and fishery	Industry	Services
USA								
1820	9,981	3,222	9,666	1.75	463,061	70.0	15.0	15.0
1870	40,241	14,720	43,630	3.92	934,646	50.0	24.4	25.6
1890	63,302	23,937	66,760	5.43	934,646	38.3	23.9	37.8
1913	97,606	38,821	101,129	7.86	937,289	27.5	29.7	42.8
1929	122,245	47,904	112,191	9.11	937,323	21.1	29.4	49.5
1938	130,476	44,906	92,597	9.93	937,323	17.9	31.2	50.9
1950	152,271	61,651	115,102	11.27	939,669	12.9	33.6	53.5
1973	211,909	86,838	149,101	14.58	939,669	4.1	31.2	64.7
1990	250,132	120,960	192,810	17.64	939,669	2.8	25.7	71.5
2003	290,343	139,236	216,638	20.77	939,669	2.0	20.0	78.0
UK								
1820	21,226	8,160	24,480	2.00	31,427	37.6	32.9	29.5
1870	31,393	13,157	39,260	4.44	31,427	22.7	42.3	35.0
1890	37,485	15,361	43,118	6.11	31,427	16.1	43.2	40.7
1913	45,649	19,884	52,176	8.82	31,427	11.7	44.1	44.2
1929	45,672	18,936	43,288	9.55	24,410	7.7	45.2	47.1
1938	47,494	20,818	47,194	9.99	24,410	5.9	44.0	50.1
1950	50,363	22,400	43,859	10.60	24,410	5.1	44.9	50.0
1973	56,223	25,076	42,328	11.66	24,410	2.9	40.3	56.8
1990	57,493	26,942	44,104	13.81	24,410	2.1	32.2	65.7
2003	60,095	28,716	41,724	15.99	24,410	1.2	23.5	75.3
Japan								
1820	31,000	16,819	49,532	1.50	38,256	n.a.	n.a.	n.a.
1870	34,437	18,684	55,024	1.50	38,256	70.1	n.a.	n.a.
1890	40,077	20,305	56,245	2.71	38,256	69.0	n.a.	n.a.
1913	51,672	25,751	66,644	5.36	38,256	60.1	17.5	22.4
1929	63,244	29,332	69,341	6.74	38,256	50.3	20.9	28.8
1938	71,879	32,290	77,205	7.67	38,256	45.2	24.1	30.7
1950	83,805	35,683	77,289	9.11	36,848	48.3	22.6	29.1
1973	108,707	52,590	107,389	12.09	37,780	13.4	37.2	49.4
1990	123,537	62,490	121,293	14.31	37,780	7.2	34.1	58.7
2003	127,214	63,160	108,572	16.78	37,780	4.6	28.8	66.6

Table B.2. Basic Components of Growth Accounts II: USA, UK, and Japan, 1820–2003

	GDP (1990 $ million)	Gross stock of machinery and equipment (1990 $ million)	Gross stock of non-residential structures (1990 $ million)	Total stock of gross non-residential fixed capital (1990 $ million)	Commodity exports (1990 $ million)	GDP per capita (1990 $)	GDP per hour worked (1990 $)
USA							
1820	12,548	873	10,876	11,749	251	1,257	1.29
1870	98,374	19,695	148,343	168,038	2,495	2,445	2.25
1890	214,714	98,120	554,811	652,930	7,755	3,392	3.22
1913	517,383	268,359	1,434,437	1,702,796	19,196	5,301	5.12
1929	843,334	485,301	2,174,926	2,660,227	30,368	6,899	7.52
1938	799,357	444,826	2,432,557	2,877,382	24,129	6,126	8.63
1950	1,455,916	930,386	2,620,695	3,551,081	43,114	9,561	12.65
1973	3,536,622	2,280,288	5,163,463	7,443,690	174,548	16,689	23.72
1990	5,803,200	4,786,703	8,327,741	13,114,444	393,592	23,201	30.10
2003	8,430,762	9,360,800	10,361,587	19,722,387	801,784	29,037	38.92
UK							
1820	36,232	1,943	22,793	24,736	1,125	1,707	1.49
1870	100,179	10,786	78,756	89,542	12,237	3,191	2.55
1890	150,269	17,118	107,740	124,858	21,681	4,009	3.49
1913	224,618	40,071	146,775	186,846	39,348	4,921	4.31
1929	242,068	64,678	152,594	217,272	31,990	5,300	5.59
1938	286,631	86,853	170,945	257,797	22,546	6,035	6.06
1950	347,850	106,884	171,863	278,747	39,348	6,907	7.93
1973	675,941	348,786	538,886	887,672	94,670	12,002	15.97
1990	944,610	555,739	990,488	1,546,227	185,326	16,430	21.42
2003	1,280,625	858,796	1,379,595	2,238,391	321,021	21,310	30.69
Japan							
1820	20,739	n.a.	n.a.	n.a.	n.a.	669	0.42
1870	25,393	n.a.	n.a.	n.a.	51	737	0.46
1890	40,556	3,946	23,767	27,712	222	1,012	0.72
1913	71,653	16,979	44,010	60,989	1,684	1,385	1.08
1929	128,115	55,344	88,416	143,760	4,343	2,026	1.85
1938	176,050	64,967	133,085	198,052	9,907	2,449	2.28
1950	160,966	115,409	161,223	276,632	3,538	1,926	2.08
1973	1,242,932	698,778	1,388,481	2,087,259	95,105	11,439	11.57
1990	2,321,153	2,148,610	4,260,763	6,409,373	287,648	18,789	19.14
2003	2,699,261	3,973,086	6,690,088	10,663,174	402,861	21,218	24.86

Table B.3. Comparative Growth Performance of the US, UK, and Japan, 1820–2003 (annual average compound growth rates)

	1820–70	1870–1913	1913–50	1950–73	1973–2003	1820–2003
GDP						
USA	4.20	3.94	2.84	3.93	2.93	3.62
UK	2.05	1.90	1.19	2.93	2.15	1.97
Japan	0.41	2.44	2.21	9.29	2.62	2.70
Population						
USA	2.83	2.08	1.21	1.45	1.06	1.86
UK	0.79	0.87	0.27	0.48	0.22	0.57
Japan	0.21	0.95	1.31	1.15	0.53	0.77
GDP per capita						
USA	1.34	1.82	1.61	2.45	1.99	1.73
UK	1.26	1.01	0.92	2.43	1.93	1.39
Japan	0.19	1.48	0.90	8.05	2.08	1.91
GDP per hour worked						
USA	1.12	1.93	2.47	2.77	1.66	1.88
UK	1.08	1.22	1.66	3.09	2.20	1.67
Japan	0.18	2.00	1.79	7.75	2.58	2.25
Total factor productivity						
USA	−0.15	0.36	1.62	1.75	0.91	0.70
UK	0.15	0.31	0.81	1.48	0.65	0.61
Japan	n.a.	0.21a	0.20	5.12	0.63	1.23b
Land area						
USA	1.41	0.01	0.01	0.00	0.00	0.39
UK	0.00	0.00	−0.68	0.00	0.00	−0.14
Japan	0.00	0.00	−0.03	0.11	0.00	−0.01
Total hours						
USA	3.06	1.97	0.30	1.13	1.25	1.71
UK	0.95	0.66	−0.47	0.15	−0.05	0.29
Japan	0.21	0.45	0.40	1.44	0.04	0.43
Non-residential capital stock						
USA	5.46	5.53	2.01	3.27	3.30	4.14
UK	2.61	1.73	1.09	5.17	3.31	2.49
Japan	n.a.	3.49a	4.17	9.18	5.59	5.41b
Export volume						
USA	4.64	4.86	2.21	6.27	5.21	4.51
UK	4.90	2.80	0.00	3.90	4.15	3.14
Japan	n.a.	8.50	2.00	15.40	4.93	6.98c

Notes and Source: (a) 1890–1913; (b) 1890–2003; (c) 1870–2003. Maddison (1995: 252–5), updated from 1990. In calculating total factor productivity, crude labour input (hours) was given a weight of 0.7, education 0.42, non-residential capital 0.27, and land area 0.03. Surface area was taken as a proxy for natural resources.

☐ INDEX

Note: page numbers in *italics* refer to Figures and Tables.